History of Multicultural Education, Volume I

Conceptual Frameworks and Curricular Issues

T0347658

History of Multicultural Education

Edited by Carl A. Grant and Thandeka K. Chapman

History of Multicultural Education, Volume I

Conceptual Frameworks and Curricular Issues

Edited by

Carl A. Grant
University of Wisconsin, Madison

Thandeka K. Chapman
University of Wisconsin, Milwaukee

Routledge
Taylor & Francis Group

NEW YORK AND LONDON

First published 2008
by Routledge
711 Third Avenue, New York, NY 10017

Simultaneously published in the UK
by Routledge
2 Park Square, Milton Park, Abingdon, Oxon OX14 4RN

Routledge is an imprint of the Taylor & Francis Group, an informa business

First issued in paperback 2011

© 2008 Taylor & Francis

Typeset in Sabon by
RefineCatch Limited, Bungay, Suffolk

Library of Congress Cataloging in Publication Data
History of multicultural education / edited by Carl A. Grant and Thandeka K. Chapman.
    p.cm.
Includes bibliographical references and index.

ISBN 978-0-8058-5439-8 (hardback, volume i : alk. paper) – ISBN 978-0-8058-5441-1
(hardback, volume ii : alk. paper) – ISBN 978-0-8058-5443-5 (hardback, volume iii :
alk. paper) – ISBN 978-0-8058-5445-9 (hardback, volume iv : alk. paper) – ISBN
978-0-8058-5447-3 (hardback, volume v : alk. paper) – ISBN 978-0-8058-5449-7
(hardback, volume vi : alk. paper)

1. Multicultural education–United States.   I. Grant, Carl A.   II. Chapman, Thandeka K.
LC1099.3.H57 2008
370.1170973–dc22   2008016735

ISBN13: 978-0-415-50483-6 (pbk)
ISBN13: 978-0-8058-5439-8 (hbk)
ISBN13: 978-0-415-98889-6 (set)

CONTENTS

PREFACE TO THE SIX-VOLUME SET

How we came to this work

We were invited by a large publishing house to create a multi-volume set on what we are calling the history of multicultural education. A change within the organizational structure of the publishing house resulted in the discontinuation of the initial project. However, over the course of the last seven years, the project was embraced by a second publishing house that later merged with our first publishing home. Our 360 degree turn has been both a professional challenge and an amazing opportunity. The project has grown and expanded with these changes, and given us the opportunity to work with many different people in the publishing industry.

We relate this series of events for multiple reasons. First we want to encourage new scholars to maintain their course of publication, even when manuscripts are not accepted on the first or second attempt to publish. Second, we would like to publicly thank Naomi Silverman and Lawrence Erlbaum Associates for throwing us a necessary lifeline for the project and for their vision concerning this project. Lastly, we would also like to thank Routledge Press for warmly welcoming us back to their publishing house and providing ample resources to support the publication of the six-volume set.

What we got out of it and what we saw

Over the course of six years, we have worked to complete these volumes. These volumes, separately or as a set, were marketed for libraries and resources rooms that maintain historical collections. For Thandeka it was an opportunity to explore the field of multicultural education in deep and multifaceted ways. For Carl, it was a bittersweet exploration of things past and an opportunity to reflect on and re-conceptualize those events and movements that have shaped multicultural education. Collectively, the time we spent viewing the articles, conceptualizing the volumes, and writing the introductions was also a meaningful chance to discuss, critique, lament, and celebrate the work of past and present scholars who have devoted time to building and expanding the literature on equity and social justice in schools.

Looking across journals and articles we noticed patterns of school reform that are related to political and social ideas that constantly influence and are influenced by the public's perceptions of the state of education and by professionals working in the field of education. We would also like to recognize authors who have made consistent contributions in journals to multicultural education. These authors have cultivated lines of inquiry concerning multicultural education with regard to teachers, students, parents, and classroom events for decades. Although we would like to list these scholars, the fear of missing even one significant name keeps us from making this list.

Moreover, we recognize that a good deal of the significant work in the field was not published in journal articles or that articles were greatly altered (titles, tone, examples, word choice) to suit the editors and perceived constituents of the journal. There are many stories that are told between the lines of these articles that may go unnoticed by readers who are less familiar with the field, such as the difficulty authors had with finding publication outlets, and questions and criticism from colleagues about conducting research and scholarship in the areas of multicultural education. Although these pressures cannot be compared across groups, scholars of color, white scholars, men and women all felt marginalized because they chose to plant their careers in the rich but treacherous soil of multicultural education.

Just as we can see career patterns, we also saw patterns of journals that were willing to publish articles that focused on multicultural education. While many journals have created an *occasional* special issue around topics of equity, social justice, and students of color, there are journals that have consistently provided outlets for the work of multicultural scholars over the past three decades.

Our hopes for the use of the volumes

We began this project with the desire to preserve and recount the work conducted in multicultural education over the past three decades. As scholars rely more heavily on electronic resources, and funding for ERIC and other national databases is decreased, we are concerned that older articles (articles from the late 60s thru the early 80s) that may never be placed in this medium would eventually be lost. The volume set is one attempt to provide students, teacher educators, and researchers with a historical memory of debates, conceptualizations, and program accounts that formed and expanded the knowledge-base of multicultural education.

GENERAL INTRODUCTION TO THE VOLUMES

Multicultural education's rich and contested history is more than thirty years old; and is presently having an impact on the field of education, in particular, and society in general. It is time to provide a record of its history in order that the multiple accounts and interpretations which have contributed to the knowledge base, are maintained and documented. Whereas this account is not comprehensive, it nevertheless serves as a historically contextualized view of the development of the field and the people who have contributed to the field of multicultural education.

The paradigm of multicultural education as social reconstruction asserts the need to reform the institutional structures and schooling practices that maintain the societal status quo. These reforms are fashioned by socially reconstructing the ways that educators and politicians approach issues of equity and equality in our public schools. Multicultural education has become the umbrella under which various theoretical frameworks, pedagogical approaches, and policy applications are created, shared, critiqued, and implemented through on-going struggles for social justice in education. These campaigns for educational reform influence and benefit all citizens in the United States.

As a movement, multicultural education has brought forth an awareness of and sensitivity to cultural differences and similarities that continues to permeate the highest institutional infrastructures of our nation. Although the movement is rooted in struggles for racial equality, multicultural education readily includes physical disabilities, sexual orientation, issues of class and power, and other forms of bias affecting students' opportunities for academic and social success. The inclusion of other forms of difference beyond skin color is one way that multicultural education acknowledges diversity in a myriad of forms and dismantles the assumptions of homogeneity within racial groups.

The purpose of this set of volumes on the history of multicultural education is to locate, document, and give voice to the body of research and scholarship in the field. Through published articles spanning the past thirty years, this set of books provides readers with a means for knowing, understanding, and envisioning the ways in which multicultural education has developed; been implemented and resisted; and been interpreted in educational settings. By no means consistent in definition, purpose, or philosophy, multicultural education has influenced policy, pedagogy, and content in schools around the United States and the world. In addition, it has stimulated rigorous debates around the nature and purpose of schooling and how students and teachers should be educated to satisfy those purposes.

This set of volumes draws attention to how scholars, administrators, teachers, students, and parents have interpreted and reacted to various political and social events that have informed school policy and practices. Each volume in the set documents and tells a story of educators' attempts to explicate and advocate for the social and academic needs of heterogeneous and homogeneous communities. Through their struggles to achieve access and equity for all children, different scholars have conceptualized the goals, roles, and participants of multicultural education in numerous ways. Through the academic arena of scholarly publications, and using diverse voices from the past thirty years, the *History of Multicultural Education* acknowledges the challenges and successes distinguished through struggles for equity in education.

Methods for collecting articles and composing the volumes

It is because of the multifaceted nature of multicultural education that we have taken multiple steps in researching and collecting articles for this volume set. Keeping in mind the many ways in which this set of volumes will enrich the study and teaching of education, we have approached the task of creating the texts using various methods. These methods reflect the spirit of inclusion intrinsic to scholarship in multicultural education and respect for diversity in the academic communities that promote and critique multicultural education. This was a multiple step process that included the following stages of data collection.

In the Spring of 2000, we began collecting articles using an electronic data bank called the *Web of Science*. This program allows the Editors to discover the number of times articles have been referenced in a significant number of refereed journals. We submitted proper names, article titles, and subject headings to create lists of articles that have been cited numerous times. The number of citations gave us an initial idea of how frequently the article had been cited in refereed journals. Using the *Web of Science* we established a list of articles, which because of their extensive referencing, have become seminal and historical works in the field of multicultural education. The authors cited in these pieces generated the names of over forty scholars who are both highly recognized or not immediately recognized for their scholarship in the area of multicultural education.

To extend the breadth and depth of these volumes, we returned to the *Web of Science* and used various subject headings to uncover other articles. The articles found in our second round of searching were also highly referenced by various scholars. The two searches were then cross-referenced for articles and authors. Through this process we attempted to reveal as many significant articles that dealt with multicultural education as possible. Some articles are foundational pieces of literature that have been copiously cited since their publication, while other articles represent a specific area of scholarship that has received less attention. For example, articles specific to early childhood and middle school education were not as easily identified as conceptual pieces that articulated various aspects of multicultural education.

The *Web of Science* program has some limitations. Articles that were published in less mainstream or more radical journals may not appear. The creation of a list of articles based solely on this program begs the questions of "What knowledge is of most worth?" and "How do we validate and acknowledge those significant contributions that have been marginalized in educational discourses?"

As multicultural educators, we were cautious not to re-instantiate those very discourses and practices that marginalize academic conversations. Therefore we used other educational and social science databases and traditional library-stack searches to present a more comprehensive set of texts that represent the field of multicultural education. For example, the reference sections in the first two searches were cross-referenced for articles that may not have appeared on-line. These articles were manually located, assessed, and used for their reference pages as well.

The main program limitation that haunted us was the lack of articles from the late 1960s and early 1970s that appeared in the electronic searches. We realized that educational research is lacking a comprehensive knowledge of its history because many scholars only cite articles written in the last ten to fifteen years when reporting their findings in academic journals. The lack of citations from the early years of multicultural education scholarship forced us to take a third approach to researching articles.

Using the ERIC files from 1966–1981 and manually sifting through bounded journals from the 1960s and 1970s, we were able to uncover other significant articles to include in the volumes. The decision to include or exclude certain articles rested primarily on the editors and other scholars who reviewed earlier drafts of the introductions to each volume and the references cited for that volume. We used the feedback from these scholars to complete our search for articles.

The volumes are a reflection of the field of research in multicultural education as well as a reflection of the community of scholars who contribute to the discourse(s) concerning issues of equity and equality in public schools. Our concern with shouldering such an awesome responsibility and our desire to include the voices from the many communities of multicultural education scholarship lead us to the final approach to finding quality articles. We solicited the opinions of over twenty multiculturalists. We asked them to choose the articles they believed belong in the volumes and suggest articles or areas that were not represented. Several scholars such as Sonia Nieto, Carlos Ovando, and Christine Sleeter answered our request and provided us with valuable feedback.

Polling various academic communities made the project a more inclusive effort, but also served as a tool to communicate the work of multicultural scholars. We appreciated the opportunity to engage with other scholars during the creation of these volumes. The multi-step research methodology for this project strengthens and enhances the finished product, making the volumes a valuable contribution to the field of education. This set of volumes, because it represents the voices of many scholars, is a spirited set of articles that reflects the tenets of multicultural education, its history, its present, its ideas for the future, and the people who believe in equity and social justice for all citizenry.

Features of the volumes

Each volume in the set includes a diverse group of authors that have written in the field of multicultural education. The array of work is based on the article's contribution to educational scholarship; they represent well-known and lesser-known points of view and areas of scholarship. The volumes do not promote one scholar's vision of multicultural education, but include conflicting ideals that inform multiple interpretations of the field.

Many of the articles from the early 1970s and 1980s are difficult for students to obtain because technology limits the number of years that volumes can be accessed through web databases. Volumes in the set provide students with access to the foundational articles that remain solely in print. Students and veteran scholars doing historical research may be especially interested in the volumes because of the rich primary sources.

The volumes are delineated by six subject groupings: *Conceptual Frameworks and Curricular Content, Foundations and Stratifications, Instruction and Assessment, Policy and Governance, Students and Student Learning,* and *Teachers and Teacher Education.* These six, broadly defined areas reflect the diversity of scholarship dealing with issues of equity and social justice in schooling. The articles illustrate the progression of research and theory and provide a means for readers to reflect upon the changes in language and thought processes concerning educational scholarship. Readers also will see how language, pedagogical issues, policy reforms, and a variety of proposed solutions for equity attainment have been constructed, assimilated, and mutated over the thirty year time period.

Volume I: Conceptual Frameworks and Curricular Issues

The articles in this volume illustrate the initial and continued debates over the concepts, definitions, meanings, and practices that constitute multicultural education. The authors articulate how best to represent the history and citizens of the United States, what types of content should be covered in public schools, and the types of learning environments that best serve the needs of all students. For example, this volume shows how multicultural education challenged the representations of people of color that are presented or ignored in textbooks. Conversely, articles that challenge conceptions of multicultural education are also included. Content wars over the infusion of authors of color, the inclusion of multiple historical perspectives, and an appreciation for various scientific and social contributions from people of color that reflect challenges to Eurocentric knowledge and perspectives are presented in this volume.

Volume II: Foundations and Stratifications

This volume presents theoretical and empirical articles that discuss the institutional factors that influence schooling. Issues such as the historical configurations of schools, ideologies of reproduction and resistance, and administrative structures that often maintain imbalances of power and equity in schools are discussed. In addition, articles explicating the various ways that students and educational opportunities are racially and socio-economically stratified are present in this volume.

Volume III: Instruction and Assessment

The articles in this volume elucidate general pedagogical approaches and specific instructional approaches with consideration given to content areas and grade level. Diverse instructional practices and the relationships between students and their teachers are discussed. Although content and pedagogy are difficult to separate, the work in this volume addresses the dispositions of the teacher and his/her awareness of learning styles, and his/her ability to incorporate aspects of students' culture and community affiliations into pedagogy. Also included in this volume are theories and models of multicultural assessment tools that reflect the needs of diverse learning communities.

Volume IV: Policy and Policy Initiatives

This volume on policy and governance explores the effects of federal and state mandates on school reforms dealing with equity in education. The articles in this volume show how educational organizations and associations have attempted to influence and guide school policy, instructional practices, and teacher-education programs. In addition, the volume presents articles that discuss how interest groups (e.g., parents and concerned teachers) influence enactments of education policy in schools.

Volume V: Students and Student Learning

This volume on "Students and Student Learning" focuses on students as individuals, scholars, and members of various social and cultural groups. The articles highlight different aspects of students' lives and how they influence their academic behaviors and includes students' affective responses to their schooling and their beliefs about the value of education. The articles also address how schools socially construct student learning through the lenses of race, class, and gender. In addition, the articles show how students act as political agents to structure, direct, and often derail their academic progress. Arguing that multicultural education is necessary for everyone, the articles highlight specific racial and cultural groups as well as offer generalizations about the academic needs of all students.

Volume VI: Teachers and Teacher Education

The teacher education volume addresses issues of multicultural education for preservice and experienced teachers. The articles cover the racial and social demographics of the past and current teaching force in the United States and the impact of these demographics on the structure of multicultural teacher education programs. Several articles speak to the role(s) of the university concerning multicultural preservice and in-service education classes, field placements, and institutional support for veteran teachers. These articles explore the nature of teaching for social justice in higher education, the desire to attract teachers of color, and the juncture between theory and practice for newly licensed teachers.

ACKNOWLEDGEMENTS

There are many who deserve a public thank you for their support of and participation in this project. We would like to thank the many colleagues and graduate students who offered constructive criticism, suggested articles, read drafts of the introductions, and helped to conceptualize the placement of articles in the different volumes. These people include: Barbara Bales, Anthony Brown, Keffrelyn Brown, Nikola Hobbel, Etta Hollins, Gloria Ladson-Billings, Sonia Nieto, Carlos Ovando, Christine Sleeter, and Michael Zambon.

We would like to offer a special thank you to the journals that, because of the nature of the project, reduced or forgave their fees for re-printing.

Thanks to Director JoAnn Carr and the staff in the Center for Instructional Materials and Computing (CIMC) for putting up with our large piles of bound and unbound journals that we pulled from the shelves and made unavailable for others for days at a time. Thank you for re-shelving all the publications (sometimes over and over again) and never reprimanding us for the amount of work we created.

A super big thank you to Jennifer Austin for compiling, organizing, and maintaining our files of publishers' permission requests. Jennifer also contacted and reasonably harassed folks for us until they gave her the answers we needed. Brava!

Thank you to our families for their support and only occasionally asking "Aren't you finished yet?"

STATEMENT CONCERNING ARTICLE AVAILABILITY AND THE CONFLICT WITH REPRINT COST

During this insightful, extensive process, the goal was to share re-printings of all the articles with our readers. However, as we moved to the end of our journey, we discovered that it was financially unfeasible to secure permissions from the publishers of all the articles. We found most publishers more than willing to either donate articles or grant us significant breaks on their re-printing prices. Other publishers were more intractable with their fees. Even if the budget allowed for the purchasing of the 200-plus articles, the price of the books would have become prohibitive for most readers. Therefore, the printed articles found in the volumes do not represent all the articles that met the criteria outlined in the Preface and are discussed in each of the volumes' introductions.

At first we decided not to summarize these articles and use them solely as support for the rest of the volume(s). As we refined our introductions and re-read (and read again) the articles, we could not discount how these pieces continued to provide significant knowledge and historical reflections of the field that are unique and timely. Therefore, if the volumes are to represent the most often referenced examples and keenly situated representations of multicultural education and paint a historically conceptualized picture of the field, we had no choice but to include the works of these scholars in our introductions. Unfortunately, for the reasons explained here, some of these articles are not included in these volumes. In Appendix 2, we have provided a list of all the publishers and publishing houses so that individuals and organizations may access these articles from their local or university libraries or web services free of charge.

LIST OF JOURNALS REPRESENTED IN THE SIX-VOLUME SET

Action in Teacher Education
American Association of Colleges for Teacher Education
American Educational Research Association
American Journal of Education
American Sociological Association
Anthropology and Education
Association for Supervision and Curriculum Development
Comparative Education Review
Curriculum and Teaching
Education
Education and Urban Society
Educational Horizons
Educational Leadership
Educational Research Quarterly
Educators for Urban Minorities
English Journal
Exceptional Children
FOCUS
Harvard Educational Review
Interchange
Journal of Curriculum Studies
Journal of Curriculum and Supervision
Journal of Teacher Education
Journal of Research and Development in Education
Journal of Negro Education
Journal of Literacy Research (formerly *Journal of Reading Behavior*)
Journal of Educational Thought
Journal of Teacher Education
Language Arts
Momentum
Multicultural Education
National Catholic Educational Association
National Council for the Social Studies
National Educational Service
Negro Educational Review
Peabody Journal of Education

Phi Delta Kappan
Race, Class, and Gender in Education
Radical Teacher
Researching Today's Youth: The Community Circle of Caring Journal
Review of Educational Research
Southeastern Association of Educational Opportunity Program Personnel
   (SAEOPP)
Teacher Education and Special Education
Teachers College Record
The American Scholar
The Educational Forum
The High School Journal
The Journal of Educational Research
The New Advocate
The Social Studies
The Teacher Educator
The Urban Review
Theory into Practice
Viewpoints in Teaching and Learning
Young Children

INTRODUCTION TO VOLUME I

This volume presents articles that when read as a text will place the reader on the front line of the discussions about the conceptualization of multicultural education and the debates over curricular issues during the early days of the multicultural education movement. The articles help to explain the "confusion" which exists even today—more than thirty years after the movement began—over the meaning(s) of multicultural education. Collectively they capture the range of the theoretical conceptualizations and practical definitions of multicultural education and the ideologies that underpin these writings. When reading this volume the reader sees how the notions of power and privilege become prevalent in the multicultural education discourse.

In 1859 Herbert Spencer argued, "Before there can be a rationale *curriculum*, we must settle which things it most concerns us to know; we must determine the relative values of knowledge" (p. 11). For Spencer and many others throughout the ages the "question of questions" about curriculum was "What knowledge is of most worth?" In an essay where he analyzed human affairs from a naturalistic-evolutionary perspective, Spencer concluded that "Science" was the most important knowledge to know. During the multicultural education movement, Spencer's question of "What knowledge is of most worth?" was redefined to "Whose knowledge is of most worth?"

The articles in this volume are the voices of multicultural advocates who argued that the "What" in "What knowledge is of most worth?" was a taken-for-granted assumption. That is the "What" was defined by a person who was "white and male." Multicultural advocates recognized that imbedded within the theories that undergird all academic subjects was a "What" that was limited by generalizability requirements, and biased by the particular interests and experiences of the person(s) who developed the theory. Multicultural advocates argued that all ideas that are conveyed to others as "knowledge" should be interrogated and questioned in terms of "Whose knowledge is this?" In addition, they argued that a great deal of the knowledge in schools and colleges is partial and biased. Therefore, a series of questions were asked of public school curricula: whose theory/knowledge is this, whose interest is being served by using it, and who is being marginalized by these theories and knowledge?

In the 1960s and 1970s advocates of multicultural education faced challenges from within their own ranks to locate multicultural education conceptually and practically from a human relations "Can't we all get along" perspective to a social justice and critical education agenda. Foes of multicultural education argued that it would bring on intergroup tension, and sabotage the efforts of public schools that were the major instrument of assimilation and "e pluribus unum" (Ravitch, 1990). In part because of both of these struggles, it was difficult for advocates to agree upon a conceptual meaning and define the goals of multicultural education. The articles show how the dispute over curriculum, which was the major site of controversy and debate in the early years of the multicultural movement, moved from the mistreatment of minorities in textbooks (e.g., omission, stereotypes, lack of fair representation) to ways to make the curriculum culturally relevant to all students.

The articles are presented in three separate sections: conceptual frameworks, curriculum content, and critiques. These three areas are thematically intertwined and individuated through the various foci on multicultural education debates. Within each area, the articles are discussed in chronological order. This sequencing is used for two reasons.

First, and primarily, the articles demonstrate how multiculturalists from the beginning of the movement advocated issues of fairness and equity. The focus on these issues was eroded in the 1980s and replaced with a more politically correct tolerance and human relations perspective. In the 1990s, there was a return to discourses concerned with equity, social justice, and the interrogation of power and privilege. In the article titles there is a change in language from strong words like "justice" (Taxel, 1978) and "sex-role stereotypes" (Saario, Jacklin & Tittle, 1973) that were used in the 1970s, to multiple authors using words like "understand and accept" (Sears, 1991) and "pluralize" in the 1980s and early 1990s. The late 1990s and early millennium gave us phrases such as "democratic education" (Gay, 1997) and "empowering multicultural curriculum" (Sleeter, 2000).

Second, the articles show the ebb and flow of curricular debates. Debates over the curriculum continue to surround and impact multicultural education, but do not explicitly call upon issues of race, gender, and class. In the 1970s multicultural education disrupted notions of privilege and power that governed whose stories were told in the curriculum, how groups of people were being represented, and access to a more equitable education beyond integrated classrooms. Political shifts in the 1980s, specifically 1983 and the *A Nation At Risk Report*, spun curriculum debates in a different direction that overpowered debates on equity and excellence from race and cultural standpoints. The Back to Basics Movement moved the focus on education to international competition and the United States ability to maintain dominance in a global business arena. Borrowing from discourses of the 1970s and the 1980s, the 1990 curriculum debates were re-envisioned through high stakes testing that strove to elevate curricular rigor for all children, but failed to encapsulate understandings of culture, power, and privilege that continued to maintain the status quo of underachieving students of color and poor children.

Conceptual Frameworks

When thinking about the conceptual frameworks in most early multicultural education writings, it should be remembered that much of the early work was published during the time, or shortly after the time when U.S. society was in the preliminary stages of a major social movement toward racial integration/equality. Lunch counters were integrated; signs that read, "Colored Only" and "White Only" over toilets and water fountains were removed. The statement "Black Power" was striking fear and confusion in some whites, and the autobiography of Malcolm X was increasingly becoming expected reading. In other words, multicultural education comes out of a time when the ideology driving the Civil Rights Movement was clearly *equality and social justice*; and the practice expressed through the action of (most of) the people was clearly to achieve equality and social justice through nonviolence. Dr. Martin Luther King Jr's words at the end of the Selma to Montgomery march on March 25, 1965 expressed both implicitly and explicitly the early conceptual frame for multicultural scholars. Dr. Martin Luther King Jr said to the 25,000 people at the end of their Selma to Montgomery march:

They told us we wouldn't get there. There were those who said we would get here only over their dead bodies, but all the world today knows that we are here and that we are standing before the forces of power in the state of Alabama saying "We ain't goin' let nobody turn us around."

When one reads this volume as a text, it become clear that multicultural education is not static. Whereas the ideology and conceptual lenses—equality, equity, social justice—which guide multicultural education remain firmly in place, the framing of multicultural education has been modified to welcome concepts other than race, socioeconomic status and gender. Disability, sexual orientation, and religion have joined race, socioeconomic status, and gender at the ideological and conceptual center of multicultural education; and discussions of power and privilege have increased. Reading this volume as a text also shows when and how multicultural scholars increased their attention to different populations, broadened and strengthened the ideologies which guided their efforts, and increased the number of academic disciplines that informed their work. In addition, this volume shows that the welcoming of concepts other than race has caused critics of multicultural education to claim that the conceptual framework for multicultural education has been disseminated across racial/ethnic and other cultural groups (e.g., disabled, LDGB, religious) to the point of almost total dilution.

In contrast, the articles in this volume also demonstrate that the tenets espoused by multicultural theorists and researchers—equity, equality, social justice—have remained steadfast. The articles show substantial agreement among multicultural advocates concerning the building blocks significant to creating a multicultural environment. By noting the chronology of the articles, one can discover that debates—sometime often heated—over whether a cultural group should be included under the multicultural umbrella usually takes place at the point when the group is vying for entry. Once the group has been *accepted* the rhetoric against the group to a great extent subsists. This point will be illustrated primarily through the articles that address gender and sexual orientation.

Moreover, the authors in this section make clear distinctions between various approaches to multicultural education. Gibson (1976), Gollnick (1980), and McCarthy (1990) offer typologies for situating teacher and school practices within the framework of multicultural education. These typologies depict a hierarchical status in the approaches to multicultural education. The approaches at the highest stage speak of personal transformation that will lead to social justice and equity in education, as well as an understanding of the function of power and privilege to control those who are not in the mainstream. The article by Gibson, for example, was one of the earliest typologies and gives the reader a ringside seat at the discussions of the various assumptions imbedded in the stages of multicultural education. In addition, Gibson critiques the lower stages as being limited in scope and action as a means of reaching all students and changing school cultures.

It is interesting to look across the articles in this volume and examine the extent to which multicultural scholars conveyed the critical need for a conception of multicultural education that would reach all students: white and students of color. MCE has roots planted in the inter-group education movement, women's movement, and the ethnic studies movement. These complimentary and competing discourses have distinct histories in progressive education that are often conflated with MCE. Multicultural education brought elements of each of these movements together to create something new and unique.

Political conversations around the "culture of poverty" and "deficit v. different" debates influenced the emergence of multicultural education. Challenges to terminology that described groups encouraged multiculturalists to interrogate the connotation and denotation of words used to advocate for equity and equality among all stratifications of students.

Given these various frames of reference, we note how terminology has changed (e.g., culturally deprived students, culturally disadvantaged children, culturally different students, diverse students). This volume shows how advocates of multicultural education used different terminology and language to make the case for equity and social justice. Grant's (1978) article is an excellent case in point. He manipulates the language of multicultural education to "education that is multicultural" to defy more conservative notions of MCE as merely a change in content or a highly specific means of teaching different groups of children.

It should be noted that during the early years of the movement, authors were not always able to publish articles with "Multicultural Education" in the title. Titles of articles were changed. There was some censoring of "multicultural education" to so called more acceptable terms (e.g., diversity, culturally different). As one reads across this volume, he/she may note when "multicultural education" as a term became accepted by journal editors.

Literature reviews in the articles tell the story of how multicultural education has grown and changed. Today, it is expected that scholars of multicultural education will support their question(s) under study with a review of the literature that gives both a historical and current overview of the topic. During the early days of the multicultural movement many authors used historical antecedents and polemic arguments, much like authors today use a literature review, to support their rationale and purpose for multicultural education. The article in this volume by Gollnick (1980) is such an example. Gollnick uses historical antecedents (e.g., intercultural and intergroup movements as precursors to multicultural education) to make the case that multicultural education should be conceptualized as a reform effort for multiple groups including: race, gender, religion, age, socioeconomic status, and physical, mental, and emotional exceptionalities.

With the availability of multicultural scholarship, Hollins (1982) and Foerster (1982) built upon the growing field to defy race-based definitions of multicultural education and call for a shared understanding of the paradigm. Foerster categorizes and critiques ethnic studies to advocate for multicultural education as a means to push schools to be more inclusive of diversity. Hollins proposes that a new theory on learning needs to value students' cultural backgrounds that are connected to but not solely identified by race or ethnicity. Bennett's (2001) review of the literature in multicultural education demonstrates the growth of the field and sheds light on the challenges of implementing and sustaining a curriculum such as the one Sleeter (2000) envisions for schools. Her review of literature explores the gap between the conceptualization of the field, the practice, and the research conducted on successful programs and schools. Her comprehensive look at multicultural research speaks to the expansive nature of multicultural education theory and research and its continued growth which allows present scholars to build on the works of the past thirty years.

By the late 1980s and early 1990s, critics of multicultural education knew that despite their efforts to shut the movement down, it continued to flourish. Opponents of MCE changed their strategy to weaken it by inundating multicultural education with myths. Consequently, advocates of multicultural education often spent much of their writing, conference presentation time, and workshop time in schools debunking myths and clarifying what they meant by multicultural education, instead of moving the idea along (e.g., from theory to practice).

In addition to addressing myths and critiques of multicultural education, multiculturalists have continuously fought for multicultural education to remain as an actively debated and growing field of study. While several trends in the field of education have at times overshadowed multicultural education, these new conceptualizations of public schooling continue to echo the idea of education as equity, equality, and social justice that stem from the tenets of multicultural education. Gay's (1997) article is an example of reclamation. By paralleling the tenets of MCE with the goals of a democratic society in which all citizens/students receive equal access and opportunities for success, she articulates how democratic education is actually multicultural education. In a democratic society, distributions of power are said to be more equal than in other political configurations. All people are meant to hold the same rights and opportunities for success.

Multicultural education was born out of political struggles to hold the U.S. accountable to its democratic principles. Therefore, multicultural scholars have, for the most part, continuously addressed the concept of power in their writing. These discussions have evolved from a limited focus on the power of the elite and privileged to impose certain norms and values on the curriculum to the nuances of power that are complicated, not only by race, gender, and class, but also by situated contexts and individual choices. For example, early works paid attention to the power that white teachers had in relation to the success of all students and their curriculum choices regarding content and pedagogy. Increasingly, discussions of power (and privilege) extend to the intersectionality of race, class, and gender, the various stakeholders and unlikely allies in the events, and contexts inside/outside the school that impact student learning. More recently, Sleeter (2000) moves the discussion of shared power to include all actors in the school: the students, their teachers, administrators, and staff. She asserts that each group has specific elements of power that must be recognized and respected in a multicultural environment.

Curriculum Content

School textbooks are considered the "guardians of traditions." They are "privileged as the 'real' account of the past and from which the intent, will, and purpose of historical actors can be obtained" (Baker, 1977, p. 71). In the 1960s, as the Civil Rights Movement advocated for the inclusion of people of color into society's mainstream, multicultural scholars similarly advocated for the inclusion of the histories and contributions of people of color in textbooks and other school material. They argued that the images and written texts stereotype and marginalize different racial groups and women: making their contributions to the United States appear peripheral and diminished. In other words, they were excluded from the "real" account of the past. Advocates for multicultural education were able to prove this through quantitative measures that enumerated the numbers of images depicting different groups, and qualitative methods that deconstructed text and images. Banks's (1962) article in this volume, where he uses a combination of both qualitative and quantitative methods to quantify the different ways that African Americans were shown in 5–8 grade history textbooks, will inform some multicultural scholars that years ago, both quantitative and qualitative research methods were used to counter injustice in the curriculum. Therefore as the research pendulum hovers around mix-method research techniques, Banks's article has much to say to multicultural scholars.

At the same moment that scholars were critiquing representations of race in the curriculum, others were highlighting gender discrimination issues that hailed from a powerful history of social justice. In what was considered the first feminist movement, women like Elizabeth Cady Stanton, Lucretia Mott, Susan B. Anthony, and Sojourner Truth challenged the legal and social inequalities between men and women. In 1848, under the leadership of Stanton and Mott, the first women's rights conference was convened in Seneca Falls, New York. It was here that Stanton demanded women's suffrage, along with reform in the marriage contract. One hundred years and a bit more than a decade later, and riding the way of the Patsy T. Mink Equal Opportunity Education Act 1972 (Title IX), the second feminist movement got underway. Feminist advocates raised social consciousness by pointing out the sexism in public policies and practices that explicitly discriminated on the basis of sex. They argued that assumptions about sex and gender remain embedded in cultural and social discourses that invisibly and systemically reproduce male power generation after generation.

In this volume, several scholars bring the feminist discourse into the school and classroom. They point out the negative influence of sex-role stereotyping and the lack of positive consciousness raising toward women. Saario, Jacklin, and Tittle (1973) for example, investigated the sex-role stereotyping that occurred in early grade level assessments. They noted that students were socialized into distinct, narrowly constructed gender roles through the language and pictures used in these assessments. Sadker and Sadker (1980), who spent the bulk of their careers pushing for changes in curriculum content at all levels of instruction, analyzed the textbooks used by teacher candidates in teacher education programs. In doing so, the authors placed teacher education programs on notice, that they too were sites for conducting multicultural–sex equity research. In their study Sadker and Sadker targeted the most widely used preservice textbooks for a study of sexism in teacher education texts. The study drew on the ideology of the first and second feminist movement in that it sought to investigate the textbook as conscious raising technology for teachers and students. In particular the study sought to determine if teacher education texts discussed how teachers should combat sexism in their classrooms, how boys and girls may differ in motivation and learning, and the number and types of images provided of both sexes.

Although many advocates supported the inclusion of different groups under the multicultural umbrella, MCE scholarship primarily focused on race, class, or gender. Taxel's (1978) article exemplifies this early trend and provides a greater explication of how racism and sexism are intertwined within curriculum materials, the underlying ideology of white middle-class schooling that shapes this relationship, and the interplay of power and resources in society. Situating his argument between what he calls two compelling values or causes—intellectual freedom and the elimination of racism, sexism, and other forms of prejudice—Taxel addresses the moral, ethical, and legal issues at stake when intellectual freedom clashes with the rights of all children to utilize materials which respect those qualities which defines them as distinctive human beings. Similarly, Grant and Grant (1981) utilized empirical evidence to argue that although the representation of people of color in textbooks was greater than twenty years ago when Banks (1962) conducted his study, the majority of textbooks were still homogeneously white, and those with people of color still promoted white characters as the primary protagonists.

As racial groups struggled for positive and accurate representations of people of color, other groups also fought to be made present in the curriculum. The movement to provide students with handicaps a quality education reached a milestone with the passage of PL 94-142, the Education for All Handicapped Children Act, in 1975. Since the passage of PL 94-142, educators have been teaching students identified as having disabilities in the same classroom with students not labeled with disabilities. The terminology and practice within this strand of multicultural education, like other strands has undergone several changes. In the beginning, students were identified and defined by their disability, often in derogatory terms. Today they are acknowledged as whole people with identifiable constraints. The article by Britton, Lumpkin, and Britton (1984) further expands the borders of multicultural education to include the physically handicapped, the elderly, and one-parent families. The authors use an analysis of basal reading texts as their case to argue that handicapped, elderly, and single-parent families should be portrayed in textbooks as fully functioning members of society. In the last sentence of their article they declare, "Tomorrow's attitudes are formed today—from textbooks." They assert that the curriculum is responsible for creating the ways that people are perceived and understood by their fellow citizens.

Re-envisioning the Curriculum

Whereas the predominate argument of the 1970s was to expand the curriculum through the inclusion of authors of color, the 1980s began the shift from multicultural education curriculum as additive to a re-envisioning of the entire curriculum in the 1990s. The articles in this volume represent six different approaches to overhauling the curriculum to re-distribute power and equally privilege the experiences of all students.

Sears (1991) contended that educators need to help students accept sexual diversity; and argued that the curriculum is biased because of its un-interrogated heterosexual orientation. His article is one of a few articles that discusses heteronormativity and homophobia as a function of the curriculum. He suggested that a re-vamping of the curriculum is necessary to eradicate the inherent cultural curricular bias against homosexuals.

Hilliard's (1992) notion of re-invisioning the curriculum moves past ethnic studies and group studies programs, to include multiple facets of identity that are experienced simultaneously. Hilliard argued that the re-envisioned curriculum would not make students choose certain elements of their experiences or identities over others. He claimed that only the lives of people of color are carved into sections by race, or gender, or class in the curriculum; that white males are taken as whole people.

Greene (1993) moved the discussion from one of understanding and acceptance to include multiple, critical perspectives of society. She asserts that an "oppositional world view" must be a part of the curriculum so that students may become agents of change and fight oppressive systems. Greene uses the words of poets, alludes to the works of artists, and recounts the lives of great men and women activists to share a vision for education that thrives on the diversity of race and gender. She calls on poetry and art to challenge curriculum changes of the 1980s that deleted artistic aesthetics and expression from the curriculum in order to privilege the sciences and math subject areas. Although couched in the human relations rhetoric of the 1980s and early 1990s, her re-envisioning of the curriculum is one of the early moves in the 1990s to return to a critical agenda in multicultural education.

In order to significantly alter the curriculum to support a more critical agenda, Cornbleth (1998) stated that textbooks must be re-written as democratic texts that share power and privilege in the choices of stories, dates, and historical actors. She argued that current textbooks reinstantiated power and did not allow teachers or students to critically explore the past and present of the United States. Because teachers rely on the text and veer very little from its content, Cornbleth maintained that textbooks must be re-articulated to value the ideals of democracy and shared power.

Critique

Critiques of multicultural education have greatly helped the movement. As opponents and advocates have critiqued the conceptual frameworks of multicultural education, multicultural advocates have used these same discussions to improve upon the theoretical framing and articulations of the paradigm. In some cases, opponents of multicultural education criticized the value and contributions to the field. In other cases they criticized the more transformative approaches to MCE. Advocates used these attacks to develop more meaningful and appropriate ways to helps teachers and students in public classrooms. These criticisms of MCE have further advanced discussions of equity, equality, and social justice in ways that would not be possible if the disapprovals had remained silent. In critiquing multicultural education, critics demonstrate the serious threat that multicultural education has posed to traditional answers to the question, "What knowledge is of most worth?"

In this volume articles that generated some of the strongest criticism of multicultural education are included. Critics of multicultural education flourished and felt empowered in the 1980s. Conservative politicians were in the white house, and A Nation At Risk advocates were marketing a Back to Basics curriculum that posed students as homogeneously "American" in social culture and academic needs. Arthur Schlesinger Jr., E. D. Hirsch, and several conservative scholars, including Denish D'Souza and Lynn Chaney demanded that school districts maintain the Eurocentric curriculum as an essential tie to the "founding fathers" of the United States. Hirsch (1983) argued that the curriculum should remain focused on a canonized literature that gives Americans a sense of a cohesive culture and history. Tesconi (1984) warned readers that group affiliations could lead to more division between groups and "unthinking and unimaginative" (p. 92) education. He warned that multiculturalism had not become a concrete well-conceived enterprise for educators to facilitate with meaningful results. Ravitch (1990) argued for a pluralistic curriculum that heals and connects communities by concealing the more painful and less appealing incidents and experiences in the collective American historical memory, as opposed to more critical multicultural scholars who wished to expose oppressions and confront injustice. She straddled the fence in the debate by accepting the need for diverse voices in the American school curriculum, but negated the need for painful conversations concerning issues of race, class, gender, and othering that accompany the experiences of people of color. Her compromise is a prime example of how the differing ideological camps of the conservative scholars and critical scholars who advocate for multiculturalism helped to keep the debate active, while at the same time making it a challenge to gain consensus on issues of curriculum and the societal roles of the school.

Glazer (1994) questioned the radical nature of multicultural education given other U.S. movements towards educational equity. He demonstrated how arguments over language instruction and content changes in public education have occurred repeatedly over the twentieth century. Mattai (1992) also used history to highlight the evolving definitions of multicultural education from the 1970s and 1980s. He suggested that there has not been a strong enough focus on issues of race to sustain and meld the movement into a more cohesive, political education reform movement. He cautioned multicultural educators to slowly work towards their goals for diversity so that the process will maintain a focus on issues of race, class, and gender, and so that different groups may form political coalitions that can utilize group agency for systemic change.

Conclusion

Using the strength of political movements of the 1960s and 1970s, many multicultural scholars strove to apply the same societal gains to education. The articles show how these trials and tribulations, and struggles to conceptualize a generalizable view of multicultural education have shaped the paradigm. This volume's contributors represent the racial, cultural, and ideological diversity that remains indicative of scholarship in multicultural education. These articles pushed the boundaries of curricular possibilities and encouraged others to question the very formations of certain policies, practices, and traditions. What remains clear throughout the progression of these articles is that multiculturalists continue to grapple with the same two questions concerning "Whose knowledge should be privileged?" and "What knowledge should be taught?"

References

Baker, G. (1977). Multicultural imperatives for curriculum development in teacher education. *Journal of Research and Development in Education, 11*(1), 70–83.

Banks, J. A. (1962). A content analysis of the Black American in textbooks. *Social Education*, 954–958.

Bennett, C. (2001). Genres of research in multicultural education. *Review of Educational Research, 71*(2), 171–217.

Britton, G., Lumpkin, M., & Britton, E. (1984). The battle to imprint citizens for the 21st century. *The Reading Teacher, 37*(8), 724–732.

Cornbleth, C. (1998). An American curriculum? *Teachers College Record, 99*(4), 622–646.

Foerster, L. (1982). Moving from ethnic studies to multicultural education. *The Urban Review, 14*(2), 121–126.

Gay, G. (1997). The relationship between multicultural and democratic education. *The Social Studies*, 5–11.

Gibson, M. A. (1976). Approaches to multi-cultural education in the United States: Some concepts and assumptions. *Anthropology and Education Quarterly, 7*(4), 7–18.

Glazer, N. (1994). A new word for an old problem. *Multicultural Education, 1*(5), 6–9.

Gollnick, D. (1980). Multicultural education. *Viewpoints in Teaching and Learning, 56*(1), 1–17.

Grant, C. (1978). Education that is multicultural—Isn't that what we mean? *Journal of Teacher Education, 29*(5), 45–48.

Grant, C. A., & Grant, G. (1981). The multicultural evaluation of some second and third grade textbook readers: A survey analysis. *Journal of Negro Education, 50*(1), 63–74.

Greene, M. (1993). Diversity and inclusion—Toward a curriculum for human beings. *Teachers College Record, 95*(2), 211–221.

Hilliard, A. (1992). Why we must pluralize the curriculum. *Educational Leadership, 49*(4), 12–14.

Hirsch, E. D. (1983). Cultural literacy + school curriculum and the decline in reading and writing skills. *American Scholar, 52*(2), 159–169.

Hollins, E. (1982). Beyond multicultural education. *Negro Educational Review, 33*(3–4), 140–145.

Mattai, P. R. (1992). Rethinking the nature of multicultural education: Has it lost its focus or is it being misused? *Journal of Negro Education, 61*(1), 65–77.

McCarthy, C. (1990). Multicultural approaches to racial inequality in the United States. *Curriculum and Teaching, 5*(1/2), 25–34.

Ravitch, D. (1990). Multiculturalism. *American Scholar*, 337–354.

Saario, T., Jacklin, C. N., & Tittle, C. K. (1973). Sex role stereotypes in the public schools. *Harvard Educational Review, 43*(3), 386–416.

Sadker, M., & Sadker, D. (1980). Sexism in Teacher Education Texts. *Harvard Educational Review, 50*(1), 36–46.

Sears, J. T. (1991). Helping students understand and accept sexual diversity. *Educational Leadership, 49*, 54–56.

Sleeter, C. (2000). Creating an empowering multicultural curriculum. *Race, Class, and Gender, 7*(3), 178–196.

Spencer, H. (1859). What Knowledge is of Most Worth? *Westminster Review*, 11.

Suzuki, B. H. (1979). Multicultural education: What's it all about? *Integrateducation, 17*(97), 43–50.

Takaki, R. (1989). An educated, culturally literate person must understand America's cultural diversity. *Chronicle of Higher Education*.

Taxel, J. (1978). Justice and cultural conflict: Racism, sexism, and instructional materials. *Interchange, 9*(1), 56–83.

Tesconi, C. A. (1984). Multicultural education: A valued but problematic idea. *Theory into Practice, 23*(2), 87–92.

PART 1

CONCEPTUAL FRAMEWORKS

CHAPTER 1

APPROACHES TO MULTICULTURAL EDUCATION IN THE UNITED STATES (1976)

Some concepts and assumptions

Margaret Alison Gibson

Introduction

The purpose of this paper is to analyze several existing approaches to the conceptualization of multicultural education within the United States in an effort to increase conceptual clarity and to make explicit a number of assumptions which underlie each conceptualization. Specifically, I shall present five approaches to multicultural education. For each of the first four, all programmatic, I shall delineate basic assumptions regarding underlying values, change strategies, intended outcomes, and target populations. The fifth conceptualization stems from an anthropological perspective on both education and culture and, unlike the others, does not equate education with schooling or view multicultural education as a type of formal educational program.

To systematize the alternative approaches to conceptualizing multicultural education, I have reviewed the educational literature pertaining to bilingual/bicultural education, education for pluralism, ethnic studies, and multicultural education, and have delineated the assumptions of those agencies and individuals who are advocating support for such programs. The literature is drawn largely from the publications of the American Association of Colleges for Teacher Education and the articles found in the Educational Resources Information Center (ERIC) of the U.S. Office of Education. My analysis of the several approaches and the assumptions underlying them stems primarily from the anthropological literature on cultural pluralism, ethnicity, and acculturation.

The five approaches I have distinguished overlap and interrelate, but for purposes of analysis I discuss each separately. Contrasts among the first four can most readily be seen in terms of their differing objectives. For this reason, I begin the discussion of each with a statement of purpose. I then present the conditions which gave rise to the approach, the major proponents of the approach, and the underlying assumptions regarding values, strategies, outcomes, and target populations. I conclude each section with a discussion of the assumptions. The following summary briefly gives the statements of purpose for approaches one through four and provides a title for each approach. (1) *Education of the Culturally Different or Benevolent Multiculturalism*—The purpose of multicultural education is to equalize educational opportunities for culturally different students. (2) *Education about Cultural Differences or Cultural Understanding*—The purpose of multicultural education is to teach students to value cultural differences, to understand the meaning of the culture concept, and to accept others' right to be different. (3) *Education for Cultural Pluralism*—The purpose of multicultural education is to preserve and to extend cultural pluralism in American society. (4) *Bicultural Education*—The purpose of multicultural (or bicultural) education is to produce learners who have competencies in and can operate successfully in two different cultures.

Approach One: Education of the culturally different or benevolent multiculturalism[1]

The purpose of the first approach to multicultural education is to equalize educational opportunity for culturally different students. The conditions giving rise to this approach are, first, the continuing academic failure of students from a certain minority ethnic group whose school performance continues to lag behind national norms, and second, the rejection of cultural and genetic deficit hypotheses regarding students' school failure. The most frequent proponents of this approach are concerned members of the educational establishment who reject the compensatory remedies, such as Head Start, which grew out of the deficit hypotheses, and who view multicultural education as a more viable strategy for decreasing the disparity in school achievement between mainstream and minority youth.

The key assumptions underlying the first approach are that culturally different children face unique learning handicaps in schools dominated by mainstream values; that to remedy this situation multicultural education programs must be devised which will increase home/school cultural compatability; and that these new programs will, in turn, increase students' academic success. The target populations for this approach are the children from certain minority ethnic groups who lag furthest behind national norms on school performance. These children are labelled culturally different because they share only peripherally in the mainstream culture. The assumptions that either individual or organizational proponents have regarding the values, strategies, outcomes, and target populations of Approach One are detailed below.

Assumptions regarding values: (1) There are fundamental and important differences between mainstream (i.e., middle-class Anglo-American) culture and minority ethnic groups' cultures. (2) Public schooling in the United States is dominated by mainstream culture (Forbes, 1969; Johnson, 1971; Zintz, 1971). (3) Given one and two, there exists a discordance between home and school culture for children from minority ethnic groups. Hence these children are called "culturally different" because their home culture differs markedly from mainstream culture. (4) This discordance causes special learning handicaps for the culturally different student (Cordasco et al., 1970; Greenberg, 1968). (5) American public education should provide equal educational opportunities to all children. Advocates of the first approach are generally interpreting equal to mean equal benefit from as well as equal access to educational opportunity (Mazon and Arcineago, 1974). (6) It is the school, not the child or the child's home culture, which must be altered to promote equal opportunity.

Assumptions regarding strategies: (1) Educational programs must be devised and implemented which will decrease home and school discordance or, put positively, will increase the compatability between home and school environments. (2) Multicultural education is one strategy for increasing home and school compatability.

Assumption regarding outcomes: The increased home and school compatability brought about by multicultural education will result in increased learning and greater academic success for the culturally different student.

Assumptions regarding target population: (1) It is the children from certain minority ethnic groups who lag furthest behind national norms on school performance. (2) Therefore, it is these groups of children, e.g., Puerto Rican, Native American, or Black American, who are most in need of and can benefit most from multicultural education.

Discussion

This approach, which I have titled "benevolent multiculturalism," differs fundamentally from those which equate "cultural difference" with "cultural deficit." Like the cultural deficit approach, it recognizes the poor performance of certain minority group students (Jencks, 1972; Coleman, 1966), but it is an attempt to go beyond the faulty assumptions which formed the basis for early childhood intervention programs such as Head Start (Baratz and Baratz, 1969, 1970; Valentine, 1971). Multicultural education in this view avoids the assumptions of those compensatory programs which deny cultural differences, assume a pathology of the home environment, and attempt to change children, their language, and even their parents' patterns of childrearing. It rejects the assumptions of those programs that presume the difficulties children encounter in school result from their disadvantaged upbringing, and instead recognizes that the school represents for these children an alien culture. Proponents of this first approach to multicultural education view the American public school system as having been built on a homogeneous model of society which all too often has demanded that students conform to this model to benefit from school programs (Johnson, 1971). Instead of demanding school conformity, the proponents of benevolent multiculturalism propose, as an alternative, educational programs which will address the special needs of the culturally different, i.e., those who are peripheral members of the mainstream culture and whose primary social performance is in some other cultural unit (Sanday, 1970). The strength of this approach, labelled the Cultural Difference Model by Lee and Groper (1974), is that it

> helps to identify functional cultural differences and to place them in meaningful context. Thus, variations in customs are defined as ecologically coherent rather than exotic phenomena. This would presumably modulate one culture's effort to change key aspects of another culture. The Cultural Difference Model assumes no hierarchy of cultures; on the contrary, it assumes parity among cultures.

While the first approach to multicultural education appears to have overcome some of the weaknesses of the cultural deficit approach, it, too, contains major short-comings. First, it accepts without question that cultural differences are the cause of minority groups' failure in mainstream schools, and it assumes that multicultural education is a viable solution to the problem of past failure. Yet, as Pettigrew (1974) noted at a recent American Association of Colleges for Teacher Education (AACTE) conference on multicultural education, "There is no empirical evidence that the development of a multicultural school system has any direct relationship to minority pupils' achievements." To support their claims for multicultural education, proponents of the first approach will need to establish a clear relationship between school success and multicultural education programs.

The second major shortcoming relates to the assumed parity resulting from multicultural education. Unfortunately, parity among cultural groups is unlikely to result. The Cultural Difference Model can all too easily be collapsed into a deficit model if one cultural group is dominant and also seeks to impose its "own norms of cultural practice as standards for both cultures" (Lee and Groper, 1974). Although the Cultural Difference Model is not viewed by its proponents as compensatory, it in fact runs the danger of becoming yet another addition to the list of unsuccessful compensatory strategies. For it is still conceived of as a special program for special groups of students (the culturally different) to compensate for past learning deficits. The collapsing of cultural differences into cultural deficits is often unintentional. For example, while stating that multicultural education was not be viewed as a special program for minority children, the recent AACTE conference on multicultural education was structured to focus on the "educational problems and situations of Black Americans, Spanish-speaking Americans, and Native Americans" (Hunter, 1974). The conference included as one of its chief purposes the identification of "competencies needed by teachers to teach culturally different youth," and stated as one basic assumption that "there are certain unique competencies needed by teachers who teach culturally different children" (Hunter, 1974). That some members of the conference strongly reject a benevolent approach to multicultural education is highlighted by the following comments:

> There is no substantial difference between the competencies needed to teach Black Americans and those needed to teach everyone. To say that there are unique competencies needed by teachers of Black Americans . . . is antithetical to the concept of multicultural education. The notion that the CBTE [competency-based teacher education] process is particularly beneficial to Black Americans and other minority groups represents a perpetuation of the patronizing and condescending attitudes that characterize minority education. Such a notion implies that minority-group children are different with respect to their ability to attain the desired competencies and are, as implied before, inferior to their fellow students (James et al., 1974).

The sentiments of those who find this first approach "patronizing and condescending" may be summed up in one further comment:

> "Benevolent multiculturalism" says that oppressed groups are being given help and have little to offer a helper. Nothing could be further from the truth. As Freire suggests, it is vital to both the helper and the person being helped that a "dialog" be established (Hilliard, 1974).

In using benevolent multiculturalism as the title for approach one, I wish to emphasize the paternalistic aspects of this approach. For, as Freire (1970) notes, "Pedagogy which begins with the egoistic interests of the oppressors (an egoism cloaked in the false generosity of paternalism) and makes of the oppressed the objects of its humanitarianism, itself maintains and embodies oppression."

Approach Two: Education about cultural differences or cultural understanding

The second approach differs from benevolent multiculturalism in that its target population is all students; all need to learn about cultural differences. Further, its focus is education about cultural differences rather than education for the so-called culturally different. In this case, the purpose of multicultural education is to teach students to value cultural differences, to understand the meaning of the culture concept, and to accept others' right to be different. Such an approach is an outgrowth of the struggles of various ethnic groups in the United States to confirm their ethnic identities and the insistent demands by these groups that schools become more sensitive to cultural differences and modify school curricula to reflect more accurately their concerns (Seifer, 1973; Wynn, 1974).

The demands for education about cultural differences came first from those groups most oppressed by and least assimilated into the American mainstream (what Ogbu calls subordinate minorities).[2] More recently, however, the movement has been taken up by white Americans of southern and central European descent (Ogbu calls these immigrant minorities) to counter-balance demands for black and other minority studies (Laubenfels, 1971; Driscoll, 1972; Seifer, 1973). And, in response to these demands, federal, state, and local educational agencies, as well as colleges of teacher education, have fostered the development of ethnic studies programs (Congressional Record, 1972: James, 1971).

The key assumptions underlying this approach are that schools should be oriented toward the cultural enrichment of all students, that multicultural education programs will provide such enrichment by fostering understanding and acceptance of cultural differences, and that these programs will in turn decrease racism and prejudice and increase social justice. The assumptions underlying Approach Two are given below.

Assumptions regarding values (See AACTE, 1973; James et al., 1974; Banks, 1974; Seifer, 1973): (1) America is a culturally diverse nation. (2) Cultural diversity is a positive force in the development of the American society and a valuable resource to be preserved. (3) Cultural diversity is so basic to the life of our nation that it must become an integral part of our educational process at all levels. (4) Educational institutions to date have not reflected the nation's cultural diversity in school programs. (5) Schools in the future should be oriented toward the cultural enrichment of all students through programs which positively endorse cultural differences and foster an appreciation and acceptance of the differences.

Assumptions regarding strategies: (1) Formal educational programs can be developed which preserve cultural diversity. (2) "Multicultural education values differences" (James et al., 1974). (3) Multicultural education is a "dramatic response to the debilitating effects" of monoculturalism and ethnocentrism (James et al., 1974). (4) Multicultural education means "learning about various cultural groups" (Hilliard, 1974). (5) Although there is a large intersection between ethnic studies and multicultural education, "multicultural education differs from ethnic studies because its methods or teaching strategies can be employed in all disciplines rather than being limited to social studies" (James et al., 1974).

Assumptions regarding outcomes: (1) Educational institutions play a major role in shaping the attitudes and beliefs of the nation's youth (AACTE, 1973). (2) Multicultural education will result in increased teacher and student understanding of cultural differences, respect for these differences, and acceptance of others' right to be different (AACTE, 1973). (3) Multicultural education will produce students who feel pride in their heritage and value a multicultural society (Title VII, 1973). (4) Multicultural education will decrease racism and prejudice. (5) Multicultural education will increase social justice by giving a fairer share to minority groups through increasing their participation in the academic process (Banks, 1974; Smalley, 1973). (6) Multicultural education will increase students' ability to live and work in a culturally diverse society (Wynn, 1974).

Assumptions regarding target population: (1) All students need to learn about cultural differences and deserve the opportunity to benefit from multicultural education (Baty, 1972; Zintz, 1971). (2) Therefore, multicultural education programs should be provided to all students, mainstream and majority alike.

Discussion

Most people find little argument with the intended outcomes of Approach Two, i.e., cultural sensitivity, respect for cultural differences, fuller and more accurate understanding of our nation's heritage, increased social justice, a reduction of prejudice and discrimination, preparation for life in a heterogeneous society. The major shortcomings of this approach stem from its unintended outcomes and from the expectation that the goals can be achieved from within the traditional educational system. In connection with the first inadequacy, Pettigrew (1974) notes that

> multiculturalism focuses its concepts on behavioral differences exclusively rather than on both similarities between and among all segments of the society. To continue to focus on differences is perhaps to continue subtly to support the inferiority-superiority hypotheses while at the same time postulating an acceptance on a level of parity of differential behavior manifestations from all cultures. There is an inherent conflict in this approach since it tends to reinforce the seldom verbalized, but currently accepted, belief that ethnic minority pupils cannot manifest an achievement level equal to that of majority of white pupils. At the same time, it proposes that all cultural values and their resultant behaviors are equal. At worst, such a conflict will inevitably promote the continuation of teacher training practices which behaviorally reinforce negative attitudes about ethnic minority children. At best, it will increase the patriarchial condescending view of ethnic minority persons that exists in America today.

Similarly, Garcia (1974) signals the danger of categorizing the Chicanos or any ethnic group as a "monolithic entity possessing uniform, discernable traits." Garcia goes on to observe that multicultural education appeals to our urge to "categorize and classify, to sort and pigeonhole." The literature of multicultural education alludes to

> Chicano culture as if it were a set of values and customs possessed by all who are categorized as Chicanos or Mexican Americans. . . . This fallacy serves to create the new stereotype which is found in the completion of the statement, "Mexican American children are . . ."

Both Pettigrew and Garcia point to potential unintended outcomes of multicultural education, on the one hand ignoring similarities among all groups and on the other hand neglecting differences within any one group. In her recent article on positive stereotyping in the classroom, Kleinfeld (1975) examines the effects of teacher stereotyping on Indian students and points to their bases in teachers' misinterpretation of anthropological theory. Kleinfeld notes that the "ethnocentric teacher" is becoming a rare specimen and that the new type of teacher could be named the "cultural relativist." This teacher admires "Indian culture, at least in its aboriginal form." This teacher's "emphasis on differences between Indians and Whites often creates unease among Indian students and reinforces their fears of being peculiar and strange." This teacher, while overtly praising a romanticized version of Indian culture, conveys messages which too frequently are patronizing and demeaning. Further,

> the cultural relativist teachers tend to view any deviant behavior of an Indian or Eskimo student as an expression of his culture which they should be very hesitant about trying to change.
>
> These teachers' concern about cultural differences results in a pervasive anxiety and uncertainty in dealing with students. . . . [T]he cultural relativist teachers cannot transmit to Indian students an underlying sense of meaning or of purpose in what they are teaching. . . . It is as if the teachers had decided that "You are Indian and I am White, and there is nothing about us that is alike."
>
> In short, the new breed of teacher emerging in the cross-cultural classroom is as "racist" (in the dictionary definition of the word) as the older type. Both . . . assume that social traits and capacities are determined by race, that races differ radically from one another, and that one race is superior. But, while the ethnocentric teacher views such racial differences as deficiencies to be corrected, the cultural relativist views them as assets to be cultivated.

The dangers to which Kleinfeld and others point have import for multicultural education programs in general and do not apply exclusively to approach two. As noted earlier, the several approaches are interrelated and overlapping. So, too, are their shortcomings and the issues they generate.

The second weakness of this approach is that it presumes to change the existing social order from within the established educational system. There is no particular reason to assume that courses directed toward "ethnic literacy" (Banks, 1974) and cultural appreciation will halt prejudice and discrimination or solve the fundamental problem of inequity. Yet, as indicated already, these are indeed part of the agenda of those who advocate approach two.

> For some educators, multicultural education is simply a matter of infusing regular school content with material which deals with . . . cultural appreciation. This is a very limited perspective and will contribute little to the solution of the fundamental problem of inequity. The main reason is that it leaves out consideration of individual and institutional racism or other prejudice as part of the foundation for victimization (Hilliard, 1974).

Newman (1973) draws a distinction between social and sociological problems and points out that prejudice and discrimination are problems of both types:

> Social problems are situations in which dislocations, pain, and suffering exist for society at large or for groups and individuals in society. . . . Sociological problems are those that concern the structures, processes, and conditions under which events occur in society.
>
> Prejudice and discrimination represent both social and sociological problems. They are the source of immense human pain and suffering. They have also been the focus of much social scientific research, theorizing, controversy, and puzzlement.

Employing Newman's distinction, we see that the cultural understanding approach to multicultural education attempts to treat a social problem without attending also to the sociological problems. It is concerned with social ills but fails to analyze the structures which cause them. Newman analyzes the variables of prejudice and discrimination in relationship to two other sets of variables, reward parity/deprivation and social integration/segregation. His typology indicates the interrelationships between the latter two sets of variables and both prejudice and discrimination. While it is beyond the scope of this paper to discuss Newman's sociological analysis in detail, his conclusions speak to the weaknesses of multicultural understanding as a strategy for increasing social justice:

> If prejudice and discrimination are to be understood and combatted, the sociology of majority-minority relationships must pay greater attention to the majority side of the coin. For while it is useful to know the consequences of prejudice and discrimination for minority groups, changing the situation requires an equally clear understanding of how majority groups maintain their taken-for-granted view of social structure.

The next approach to multicultural education can be viewed as one attempt to change this taken-for-granted social order.

Approach Three: Education for cultural pluralism

From the perspective of those who advocate the third approach, the purpose of multicultural education is to preserve and extend cultural pluralism in American society. Multicultural education for cultural pluralism is the hardest approach to depict, even as an abstract, ideal-type construct. Cultural pluralism, like multicultural education, is a term that "everybody understands in a general sort of way but few people care to define precisely" (R. Smith, 1961). For some, it is an ideal toward which social action should be directed. Itzkoff (1970) describes a philosophy of "equalitarian pluralism" as "an approach to social organization . . . and as a possible guide to the future." Others use cultural pluralism simply as a synonym for cultural diversity. For still others, it is a concept with an analytical function. Anthropologists have used the term as a tool to differentiate among various types of multi-ethnic societies. In anthropology, the concept has been used most frequently in connection with social stratification theory to analyze relationships among ethnic groups in former colonial countries and to distinguish a plural society from the homogeneous or heterogeneous society (M. Smith, 1965; Rubin, 1960; Despres, 1968; Benedict, 1962). And, finally, cultural pluralism has entered the literature of inter-group relations in the United States as a theory to explain aspects of ethnic group relations and the assimilation process (Glazer and Moynihan, 1963; Gordan, 1964; Schermerhorn, 1970; Newman, 1973).

It might be possible, though not necessarily profitable, to typologize all the varying approaches to cultural pluralism and their implications for or applications to the educational process. As this is a paper addressed to multicultural education, I shall attempt no such exercise and, instead, will focus my discussion of cultural pluralism on the current usage of the term in the educational literature on multicultural education.

Most generally, as Sanday (1972) indicates, educators equate pluralism with heterogeneity. In this case, cultural pluralism can hardly be viewed as a third approach to multicultural education. Rather, it is incorporated in either or both of the first two approaches to multicultural education (benevolent multiculturalism and cultural understanding). However, some proponents of the cultural pluralism approach see pluralism as a particular type of structural arrangement which multicultural education should attempt to foster, preserve, and even extend. It is this latter sense of pluralism which the following discussion addresses.

Education for cultural pluralism stems from the rejection by ethnic minorities of majority-enforced acculturation and assimilation and from their rejection of an American "melting pot," both in theory and in practice. Proponents of this approach assume that neither cultural assimilation nor cultural fusion (the melting pot notion) are acceptable as ultimate societal goals because they have led in practice to Anglo-American domination and, in some cases, oppression. Proponents further assume (1) that the maintenance of cultural diversity is critical to the survival of particular groups, (2) that schools should seek to preserve and extend cultural pluralism through school programs (AACTE, 1973), and (3) that such programs will increase the power of minority groups, thereby promoting the necessary climate for academic success and alleviating the critical problems of racism and oppression.

The programs are intended to serve the needs of the children from the specific ethnic groups proposing them. There is, however, another more long-range target population for this approach, that is, the majority or mainstream group which has promoted the coercive assimilation ideal and caused the ideal of the melting pot to become little more than another form of majority conformity. Education for cultural pluralism seeks to increase reward parity among groups by decreasing the power of the majority. The proponents of the third approach are the subordinate minority groups who feel most oppressed by the mainstream majority. The assumptions upon which the cultural pluralism approach is based are listed below.

Assumptions regarding values: (1) Neither assimilation nor separatism are acceptable as ultimate societal goals (Laosa, 1974; AACTE, 1973). (2) Fusion (the melting pot notion) is not an attainable nor necessarily desirable goal. Melting pot ideals have in practice fostered Anglo-American domination leading to neglect—and in some cases, oppression—of certain culturally different groups (Laosa, 1974). (3) Cultural pluralism is an antidote to racism in the American society (Seda-Bonilla, 1973). (4) The maintenance of cultural diversity is critical to the survival of particular groups and the basic tenets of a democratic society (James et al., 1974). (5) Schools should not seek to melt away cultural differences (AACTE, 1973). (6) Schools should seek to preserve and extend cultural pluralism through school programs (AACTE, 1973).

Assumptions regarding strategies: (1) Multicultural education programs will arrest the processes of assimilation and fusion. (2) Multicultural education programs will preserve and extend cultural pluralism. (3) Multicultural education programs will increase minority group power, including decision-making power, over the educational forces which impinge upon the lives of minority group students (Davies, 1974; Hilliard, 1974).

Assumptions regarding outcomes: (1) Motivation for learning and academic success are related to decision-making and other types of power over the educational process. (2) As education for cultural pluralism increases the power of minority groups, it will provide minority students with the necessary climate for learning and academic success (Hilliard, 1974). (3) Racism and oppression in schools are related to the locus of power in American education. (4) As education for cultural pluralism increases the power of minority groups, it will alleviate the critical problems of racism and oppression (James et al., 1974).

Assumptions regarding target population: (1) It is the majority or mainstream group which has promoted the coercive assimilation ideal and caused the ideal of the melting pot to become little more than another form of majority conformity. (2) It is the majority which has denied parity to various minority groups. (3) The majority, therefore, is the ultimate target of the cultural pluralism approach. Education for cultural pluralism seeks to increase reward parity among groups by decreasing the power of the majority.

Discussion

The difficulties underlying the cultural pluralism approach stem from a confusion of ideology and theory. As noted above, the impetus for cultural pluralism was the rejection of both assimilation and fusion. To support education for cultural pluralism is to support an ideal, and to reject assimilation and fusion is to reject them as ideals. This, unfortunately, has little to do with whether the propositions that utilize these concepts are valid or have implications for understanding or changing formal schooling. Assimilation, fusion, and pluralism may all be viewed as results of the acculturation process (Hackenberg, 1962). "Acculturation is a broad process defined as change in formerly autonomous cultures that come into contact.' 'Assimilation, a more specific process, consists of structural and organizational absorption of formerly autonomous institutions or members of one society by another.' Fusion is 'the combination of distinctive culture traits into new complexes" (Walker, 1972). When two cultures maintain some degree of autonomy, usually developing parallel institutions, a situation of "stabilized pluralism" will occur. Some have viewed this to result from acculturation, when fusion is arrested or assimilation incomplete (Barnet et al., 1954).

Newman (1973) expresses the meaning of these concepts in simple formulas: (1) assimilation: A + B + C = A, where A, B, and C represent different social groups and A represents the dominant group. (2) fusion: A + B + C = D, where A, B, and C represent different social groups and D represents a distinct new group. (3) pluralism: A + B + C = A + B + C, where A, B, and C represent different social groups that over time maintain their own unique identities. Cultural pluralism is frequently seen as a "peaceful coexistence between groups" (Newman, 1973).

The difficulty with this presentation is that assimilation, fusion, and pluralism should not be viewed as the only consequences of culture contact. Each of the formulas assumes a linear approach to the acculturation process which is inadequate on a number of counts (Lebra, 1972; Newman, 1973), for certain cultural elements may be replaced, others fused, and still others maintained. Further, culture contact may result in "biculturation," Polgar's (1960) label for concurrent socialization in two or more cultures. Approach four deals with this possibility.

Even if we accept cultural pluralism as an adequate description of the arrangement of various groups in American society, I believe that education for cultural pluralism is fundamentally different from multicultural education and needs to be distinguished from it. Education for cultural pluralism is actually a strategy for the extension of ethnic groups' sociopolitical interests. For cultural pluralism to exist in a complex society such as ours, structural pluralism must also exist. At least some levels of primary group relationships must remain separated, such as clubs, churches, or schools (Gordon, 1964; Newman, 1973). Only in this way can the group preserve its identity. As Barth (1969) has indicated, boundary maintenance, not cultural similarities and differences, is the key to the continuity of an ethnic group. Like Barth, Cohen (1969) points to the importance of boundary maintenance and sees ethnic groups as essentially social and political rather than cultural. Traditional customs are used as idioms and as mechanisms for group alignment. They serve to form the boundary and to maintain the group's exclusiveness. Ethnic groups call upon their cultural distinctiveness, not out of conservatism or traditionalism but rather as a tool for maximizing group interests. The degree to which a group emphasizes or de-emphasizes cultural differences is determined by the degree of profit to be gained.

While any full treatment of ethnicity and education lies well beyond the purpose of this paper, at a minimum it would require the application of social theory regarding majority-minority relations (Schermerhorn, 1970; Newman, 1973) to the educational process. One such application is R. G. Paulston's (1975) examination of "the changing ethnic context of educational programs for Swedish *Same*, or Lapps." Paulston concludes that

> the Lappish movement's efforts to institutionalize their ideology in edu-
> cational programs ... presents a noteworthy example of the conditions under
> which education can contribute to cultural and social-change efforts. The
> *Same* case, along with the occurrence of closely comparable ethnic-revival
> movements and consequent attempts to innovate new educational programs
> as resistance to acculturation among indigenous people in Canada and the
> United States present rich opportunities for comparative studies on the
> little-examined but increasingly important phenomena of education in
> ethnic-revival movements. ... Although such educational innovations may
> have only limited potential to advance manifest movement goals, they are
> nevertheless often highly valued by movement adherents as alternatives to
> schooling dominated by the superordinate ideology.

Along these same lines, but in connection with bilingual education, C. B. Paulston (1974) points out that

> In societies when ethnic groups—who have sufficient power to enforce it—
> want to maintain their language in a situation of rapid language shift toward
> another language, they typically take measures to protect their language by
> legal measures. This is what happened in Belgium where bilingual education
> was outlawed, and it is what is happening in Canada. At present there are
> pressure groups which are urging the Quebec provincial government not only
> to preserve but to strengthen the position of the French language.

Bilingual education tends to promote assimilation into the mainstream, because it demands education in the national language as well as in the native language. This occurs in spite of bilingual education's stated goals of language maintenance (Kjolseth, 1972). Ethnic groups wishing to preserve ethnic distinctions and to prevent cultural assimilation are thus rejecting bilingual education and pushing for education in their native language and culture alone.

In the face of mainstream domination, an ethnic group may use education for cultural pluralism as a political strategy to preserve the life of the group and to promote group interests. The strategy is discussed under the rhetoric of cultural tradition and, indeed, cultural tradition and cultural symbols are critical to group cohesion and boundary maintenance. Here in the United States we see Black Muslims or certain groups of Native Americans resisting the goals of multi-cultural education because they believe that separate schools are at this time a better strategy for increasing group power. While accepting that education for cultural pluralism may be an effective strategy for furthering ethnic interests, it needs, I believe, to be distinguished separately from the other approaches to multicultural education. Education for cultural pluralism seeks to create and preserve boundaries between groups, while multicultural education, by every other definition, seeks to promote at least some sort of competence in operating across cultural and ethnic boundaries.

As mentioned above, the fourth approach focuses on biculturation, or bi-culturalism. Like Approach Three, it can be analyzed in terms of acculturation theory. But, unlike the third approach, its focus is the individual rather than the ethnic group.

Approach Four: Bicultural education

In this case, the purpose of multicultural (or bicultural) education is to produce learners who have competencies in and can operate successfully in two different cultures. The term bicultural education is used most frequently in conjunction with bilingual education programs. Many, if not all, of these programs contain elements of the three approaches presented thus far. They seek to foster or main-tain pride in the native culture, to develop a fuller understanding of one's heritage and traditions, to strengthen identity, to increase motivation and academic suc-cess, to reduce prejudice and discrimination, to increase educational opportunities and social justice, and so forth. When attached to bilingual programs, bicultural or multicultural education programs are obviously also aimed at developing language competence. My purpose here is not to review the field of bilingual bicultural education (for an overall discussion, see Anderssen and Boyer, 1970; Saville and Troike, 1971; U.S. Commission on Civil Rights, 1975), nor is it to repeat the discussion pertaining to the first three approaches. Rather, I shall focus on the key aspect of bicultural education which distinguishes it from the other approaches; that is, its concern with fostering biculturalism. Even with this limita-tion, the variation in approaches is too great to address adequately. For example, some programs are transitional in purpose, others seek to maintain home lan-guage and culture, and still others may be viewed as restorationist (Gonzalez, 1975). Indeed, one can draw parallels between benevolent multiculturalism and the transitional approach, and similarly between cultural pluralism and either the maintenance or restorationist approaches. The presentation which follows addresses biculturalism only as a general educational goal and does not attend to the varying reasons bicultural education programs are supported.

Like education for cultural pluralism, bicultural education is an outgrowth of minority groups' rejection of both majority enforced assimilation and of the melting pot ideal. Proponents assume that one's "native" culture (including language) ought to be maintained and preserved and that the "mainstream" culture (if different than the native culture) ought to be acquired as an alternative or "second" culture. Further, supporters believe that students whose native culture is the mainstream culture will also profit from the acquisition of competencies in a second culture. Bicultural education programs are seen as the avenue for providing instruction in two cultures. Unlike the benevolent multiculturalism approach, proponents of Approach Four view multicultural education as a reciprocal process, advocating bicultural education programs, at least ideally, for all students.

Since it is difficult to practice, if not in theory, to divorce bicultural education from bilingual education, the most frequent proponents of this approach are also the proponents of bilingual education, that is, minority groups whose mother tongue is not English. The bicultural approach has also been advocated in connection with the need to teach Standard English as a second dialect to speakers of other dialects. A more detailed list of the assumptions underlying Approach Four is presented below.

Assumptions regarding values: (1) One's "native" culture (including language) ought to be maintained and preserved. (2) The "mainstream" culture (if different than the native culture) ought to be acquired as an alternative or "second" culture. (3) Students whose native culture is the mainstream culture will also profit from the acquisition of competencies in a second culture.

Assumptions regarding strategies: (1) Just as it is possible to provide instruction in two languages, so, too, is it possible to provide instruction in two cultures. (2) Bicultural education is a strategy for providing instruction in two cultures. (3) Bicultural education, as an approach to formal instruction, parallels and is adapted from the methods and techniques of bilingual education.

Assumptions regarding outcomes: (1) Bicultural education will enhance a student's ability to function in both the native culture and the mainstream culture (or mainstream and a second culture for the mainstream child). (2) Competencies in a second culture will be acquired without rejection of the student's native culture. (3) Bicultural education will lead ultimately to full participation for non-mainstream and mainstream youth alike in the socioeconomic opportunities which this nation offers (Trueba, 1974).

Assumptions regarding target population: (1) Bicultural education is a reciprocal process. (2) If bicultural education were recommended only for those students whose mother tongue is other than English (i.e., the national language), it would collapse into a compensatory program for the culturally different. (3) Therefore, bicultural education is aimed, at least ideally, at all students; all students will benefit from competencies in two cultures.

Discussion

Like the cultural pluralism approach, the bicultural education approach rejects both assimilation and fusion. But it overcomes the weakness of viewing acculturation as a linear process resulting in complete assimilation or fusion, or in stabilized pluralism (Polgar, 1960; Newman, 1973). Rather, it sees that acculturation can (and program proponents say should) result in biculturalism, thereby permitting dual participation in cultural systems (Spicer, 1961). Unlike assimilation, fusion, and pluralism, biculturation need not involve change in the cultural systems themselves. The focus is on the individual, not on the group, and as bicultural research has demonstrated, competence in a new culture need not require rejection of the old culture (Polgar, 1960; McFee, 1968). Thus a "multi-lineal" model is used to describe "concurrent socialization in two or more cultures" (Polgar, 1960).

The shortcomings of the bicultural education approach to multicultural education result from its application of biculturalism theory to educational practice. First, in actual practice it runs the danger of equating culture with a language or ethnic group, for example, Chicanos, Chicano culture. I have already addressed this danger in connection with the cultural understanding approach. Second, it tends to over-emphasize ethnic identity, running the risk of preventing students from choosing to emphasize other identities. Third, it tends to see bilingual bicultural education as a panacea for all social and educational ills. For a discussion of the ambiguities and contradictions among bilingual education findings alone and the questions they raise, see C. B. Paulston (1974, 1975). There have been no comparable efforts to assess on a comparative basis the results of bicultural education, and indeed it will not be possible to do so until terms are operationalized and relationships specified. Even individual case studies of bilingual bicultural programs have generally neglected the bicultural component and focused solely on language outcomes. One exception is Erickson's (1969) evaluation of the Navajo community school at Rough Rock and the BIA school at Rock Point. And, finally, a fourth weakness with the bicultural education approach—and also with the other three approaches—is that it tends to equate education with formal school instruction and to presume that the school is responsible or should take responsibility for the child's "socialization in two or more cultures." This is not to say that the school has no responsibility for socialization. Rather, teachers and other educational personnel must recognize that formal schooling is but one part of education and, thus, but one avenue to the acquisition of multicultural competencies.

Preliminary summary

To summarize the discussion thus far, I have suggested that the literature on multicultural education lacks clarity with regard to key concepts and abounds with untested and sometimes unsupportable assumptions regarding goals, strategies, and outcomes. As a method for organizing the range of approaches, I have provided four admittedly interrelated and overlapping ideal-type program conceptualizations. The first is basically compensatory and views students' cultural differences as best attended to through special programs for the culturally different within mainstream dominated schools. The second approach is aimed at cultural understanding for all students and is a response to ethnic groups' pressure for a fairer representation in school curricula and programs of their heritage and place in American history and society. The third approach may be similar in content to the first but differs in one basic regard—instead of being a majority-group program for minorities, it is a minority strategy for minority students and seeks a more equitable distribution of power over formal educational programs and processes. Like the third, the fourth approach rejects enforced assimilation, but rather than tending toward separation as a strategy for group preservation, it seeks to produce a student who is able to operate successfully across group boundaries.

All four approaches tend to equate education with schooling and to overlook the educational processes occurring outside of school. All of the approaches include among their goals increased social justice yet, with the exception of education for cultural pluralism, they tend to overlook the larger socio-political context of formal education. For each of these approaches I have suggested several major shortcomings. In doing so, I do not intend to negate the value of ongoing multicultural education programs, but wish to emphasize the need for greater conceptual clarity, which in turn will enhance our ability to test underlying assumptions and to evaluate program success. The following is a summary of the analysis of approaches one through four with regard to (1) major proponents, (2) conditions giving rise to each approach, (3) underlying values, (4) target populations, and (5) intended outcomes.

Benevolent Multiculturalism: *Proponents:* Mainstream educators. *Precondition:* Rejection of cultural and genetic deficit models. *Underlying Value:* Compatability of home and school cultures. *Target Population:* Culturally different students. *Intended Outcomes:* Equity in educational benefits.

Cultural Understanding: *Proponents:* (1) Subordinate minorities, (2) Immigrant minorities, (3) Mainstream educators. *Precondition:* Immigrant minorities' demands for ethnic studies (to counter-balance subordinate minorities' demands). *Underlying Value:* Cultural understanding and cultural relativity. *Target Population:* All students. *Intended Outcomes:* Respect and acceptance of others' right to be different.

Cultural Pluralism: *Proponents:* Subordinate minorities. *Precondition:* Rejection of majority enforced cultural assimilation. *Underlying Value:* Preservation and extension of ethnic groups. *Target Population:* Subordinate minority-group students. *Intended Outcomes:* Increased power for minority groups.

Bicultural Education: *Proponents:* Non-English mother tongue minorities. *Precondition:* Rejection of majority enforced cultural assimilation. *Underlying Value:* Reciprocal learning. *Target Population:* All students. *Intended Outcomes:* Bicultural competencies.

Approach Five: Multicultural education as the normal human experience[3]

As stated at the paper's outset, the fifth concept differs in several basic regards from the other four. The first four approaches are derived from the educational literature on bicultural and multicultural education. The fifth approach begins instead with the key concepts of education and culture, drawing upon anthropological definitions of them. A conceptualization of multicultural education is thus developed from the concepts themselves, rather than from existing or proposed school programs which the programs' proponents purport to be multicultural in quality or content.

Education can be variously defined, but the anthropological view of education as a cultural process is basic to the fifth conceptualization:

> [Anthropologists] see education as part of the general human process of socialization whereby young people are prepared to fit successfully into the internal environment of the community of their upbringing and into the external environment within which exists the total community of human beings of which they are a part (Thomas and Wahrhaftig, 1971).

Or, following Spindler (1974), we may simply view education as cultural transmission. And, following Goodenough (1971), culture consists of

> the various standards for perceiving, evaluating, believing, and doing that . . . (a person) attributes to other persons as a result of his experience of their actions and admonitions. . . . By our definition of culture, the standards that a person thus attributes to a particular set of others are for him the culture of that set. . . . Insofar as a person finds he must attribute different standards to different sets of others, he perceives these sets as having different cultures. . . . A person may not only attribute different systems of standards to different sets of others, he may also be competent in more than one of them—be competent, that is, in more than one culture.

We may now define multicultural education as the process whereby a person develops competencies in multiple systems of standards for perceiving, evaluating, believing, and doing. Such a definition has important implication for our analysis of the meaning of multicultural education and allows us to overcome a number of the conceptual weaknesses of the four approaches previously presented.

First, we no longer are restricted to the view which equates education with schooling or multicultural education with formal school programs. The broader view of education as cultural transmission relieves educators from assuming the primary responsibility for students' acquisition of cultural competencies and suggests the need for multicultural education proponents to consider more carefully the relationship of school programs to informal school and out-of-school learning.

Second, we no longer are restricted to the view that tends to equate culture and ethnic group. Following Goodenough (1971), we need not associate culture solely or even principally with ethnic groups. Traditionally, anthropologists—and hence educators—have associated culture only with relatively self-sufficient social groups, rather than with sets of people who "repeatedly participate with one another in one or more activities." But just as individuals have varying degrees of competence in varying numbers of dialects or languages, and varying understandings of the situations in which each is appropriate, so, too, individuals have varying degrees of competence in varying numbers of cultures (Goodenough, 1971). While an ethnic group may indeed share a particular set of standards, its members can also be sorted into other sets which participate in common activities, related, for example, to work or religion or recreation. Some of these sets will cut across ethnic boundaries, others will lie within the boundaries. In this way, we can see that the members of any given ethnic group will represent a range of cultures. Such a perspective, if adopted by proponents of multicultural education programs, would alleviate the tendency to stereotype students according to ethnic identities and would promote a fuller exploration of the similarities as well as the differences between students of different ethnic groups.

Third, since the development of competence in a new culture usually requires intensive interaction with people who already are competent, we can see even more clearly that efforts to support ethnically separate schools are antithetical to the purposes of multicultural education.

> Because competence in the standards one associates with a set of others can be developed only through intensive interaction with at least some of those others, the sets of persons who are competent in what they perceive as the

same culture overlap very largely the sets of persons who repeatedly participate with one another in one or more activities. The greater the variety of
activities in which they repeatedly have dealings with one another, the wider
the range of subject matter for which the people will preceive themselves as
competent in the same standards (Goodenough, 1971).

To preserve and extend group solidarity, ethnic groups may choose to resist
concurrent socialization in new cultures. Ethnic schools may serve purposes
equally valid to those of multicultural education, but they are different and need
to be distinguished. Education for cultural pluralism and multicultural education
cannot logically be equated.

Fourth, the concerns that multicultural education proponents have with fostering students' cultural identity, or their fears that mainstream schools will cause
students to reject such identities, result from a confusion of social identification
with cultural competence. For

> just as individuals can be multi-lingual they can also be multicultural, the
> particular culture that is to be regarded as *theirs*—as when we talk of a
> person's culture—being determined by considerations of social identification
> rather than simply of competence (although obviously the culture of the
> group with which a person identifies himself is inevitably one in which he is
> highly competent) (Goodenough, 1971).

Multicultural education promotes competence in multiple cultures. Which
culture an individual will draw upon on any given occasion will be determined by
the particular situation. Though clearly interrelated, we must distinguish conceptually between the multiple identities individuals have available to them and
their primary social identities in a particular ethnic group.

And finally, the possibility, and indeed likelihood, that education (both in and
out of school) promotes awareness of and competence in multiple cultures leads
us away from the notion of bicultural education and dichotomies between native
and mainstream culture. Such dichotomies are restrictive and deny individuals the
freedom for full expression of cultural diversity. The fifth conceptualization
brings instead an increased awareness of "multiculturalism as the normal human
experience" (Goodenough).[3] Such an awareness, I believe, has the potential for
leading multicultural education away from divisive dichotomies and toward a
fuller appreciation of the range of cultural competencies available to all students,
minority and mainstream alike.

Conclusions

Spurred initially by minority-group pressure for equity in educational opportunities and greatly accelerated by federal legislation for bilingual and ethnic
studies programs, multicultural education has become in a few short years one of
this decade's fastest growing educational slogans. In reviewing the literature on
multicultural education, we find that program proponents have provided no
systematic delineation of their views, and that all too frequently program statements are riddled with vague and emotional rhetoric. To promote conceptual
clarity and to bring some order to the field's broad scope, we have suggested that
extant programs can be organized into four separate approaches: (1) Benevolent
Multiculturalism, (2) Cultural Understanding, (3) Cultural Pluralism, and (4)

Bicultural Education. As a basis for analyzing the implications of each for school reform, program proponents need to define key concepts and to explicate their assumed relationships. Secondly, they need to consider more carefully both informal and out-of-school education and their relationships to formal school programs. Thirdly, proponents must be more realistic about the ability of multicultural education programs to solve social problems. If proponents are seriously concerned with changing the existing social structure through school programs, they must investigate more fully the economic, political, and social forces which impinge upon the formal educational processes.

As an alternative to the four existing approaches to multicultural education, a fifth conceptualization is offered which builds upon anthropological definitions of both education and culture and provides one basis for the evaluation of the other four approaches. Each of the first four approaches tends to restrict its view of culture to the culture of an ethnic group. This leads to unintentional pigeonholing and stereotyping of students. The fifth approach recognizes that there may be a culture shared by members of an ethnic group. Indeed, it is this shared competence which provides members with a common sense of ethnic identity. But members of the ethnic group will also acquire competence in the cultures of other sets and clusters of people. Such a perspective leads to an exploration of the differences among members of any given ethnic group and of the similarities of persons across ethnic lines. Given that individuals can and normally do develop competencies in multiple cultures, the question for educators is how best to create learning environments which promote rather than inhibit the acquisition of multicultural competencies. Social scientists can help to answer this question by studying the relation between the maintenance of group boundaries and the development of cultural competence across such boundaries. By focusing on school situations, such an avenue for research may yield important insights for promoting multicultural education as part of the formal education process.

Notes

1   The term "benevolent multiculturalism" is Hilliard's (1974). The ideas underlying the term come from Freire (1972), who discusses the "paternalism" and "false generosity" of the oppressor toward the oppressed.
2   The distinction between "subordinate minorities" and "immigrant minorities" comes from Ogbu (1974):

> By subordinate minorities I mean those minority groups who were incorporated into the United States more or less against their will. Subordinate minorities include the American Indians who were already here before the dominant whites arrived and conquered them, the Mexican-Americans of the Southwest and Texas who were similarly incorporated by conquest, and blacks who were brought here as slaves. Immigrant minorities include Arabs, Chinese, Filipinos, Japanese, among others. These groups came to the United States for the same reasons as the dominant whites—for political or religious asylum, but especially for economic betterment. Subordinate and immigrant minorities appear to differ in the way they perceive American society and how they respond to the educational system.

3   The notion of multicultural education "as the normal human experience" comes from Goodenough's paper in this issue.

References

American Association of Colleges for Teacher Education (AACTE) "No One Model American." 24 *Journal of Teacher Education* 264, 1974.

Anderson, T. and M. Boyer. "Bilingual Schooling in the United States." Austin: AEDL (GPO, Washington DC) 1970.

Banks, J. A. "Multi-cultural Education: In Search of Definitions and Goals." Paper presented at the Association for Supervision and Curriculum Development Institute on Cultural Pluralism, Chicago. ERIC No. ED 100 792, 1974.

Baratz, J. C. and S. S. Baratz. "The Social Pathology Model: Historical Bases for Psychology's Denial of the Existence of Negro Culture." Paper presented at APA, Washington DC, 1969.

Baratz, S. S. and J. C. Baratz. "Early Childhood Intervention: The Social Science Base of Institutional Racism." 40 *Harvard Educational Review* 29, 1970.

Barnett, H. G. et al. "Acculturation: An Exploratory Formulation." 56 *American Anthropologist* 973, 1954.

Barth, F. (ed.) *Ethnic Groups and Boundaries.* Boston: Little, Brown, 1969.

Baty, R. M. *Reeducating Teachers for Cultural Awareness.* New York: Praeger, 1972.

Benedict, B. "Stratification in Plural Societies." 64 *American Anthropologist* 1235, 1962.

Cohen, A. *Custom and Politics in Urban Africa.* Berkeley: Univ. of Calif. Press, 1969.

Coleman, J. S. et al. *Equality of Educational Opportunity.* Washington DC: U.S. Government Printing Office, 1966.

Congressional Record, Vol. 118, No. 96, Washington DC, 1972.

Cordasco, F., M. Hillson and H. A. Bullock. *The School in the Social Order.* Scranton PA: International Textbook Co., 1970.

Despres, L. A. "Anthropological Theory, Cultural Pluralism, and the Study of Complex Societies." 9 *Current Anthropology* 3, 1968.

Driscoll, J. Concept paper calling for policy center analysis of ethnic studies. Washington DC: U.S. Office of Education, Office for Special Concerns, 1972 (mss.)

Erickson, D. A. et al. Community school at Rough Rock: an evaluation for the Office of Economic Opportunity. U.S. Department of Commerce. Springfield VA: Clearinghouse for Federal Scientific and Technical Information, 1969.

Forbes, J. D. *The Education of the Culturally Different: A Multi-cultural Approach.* Berkeley: Far West Laboratory for Educational Research and Development, 1969.

Freire, P. *Pedagogy of the Oppressed.* New York: Herder and Herder, 1972.

Garcia, E. "Chicano Cultural Diversity: Implications for Competency-Based Teacher Education." In Hunter (ed.), 1974.

Glazer, N. and D. P. Moynihan. *Beyond the Melting Pot.* Rev. ed., 1970. Cambridge MA: MIT Press, 1963.

Gonzalez, J. M. "Coming of Age in Bilingual/Bicultural Education: A Historical Perspective. 19 *Inequality in Education* 5, 1975.

Goodenough, W. *Culture, Language and Society.* Reading MA: Addison-Wesley (a McCaleb Module in Anthropology), 1971.

——. "Multi-culturalism as the Normal Human Experience." VII:4 *CAE Quarterly,* 1976.

Gordon, M. M. *Assimilation in American Life.* New York: Oxford Univ. Press, 1964.

Greenberg, N. C. "Cross-cultural Implications for Teachers." In Chilcott et al. (eds.). *Readings in Socio-Cultural Foundations of Education.* Belmont CA: Wadsworth, 1968.

Hackenberg, R. A. "Process Formation in Applied Anthropology." 21:4 *Human Organization* 235, 1962.

Hilliard, A. G. "Restructuring Teacher Education for Multi-cultural Imperatives." In Hunter (ed.), 1974.

Hunter, W. A. (ed.). *Multi-cultural Educational Through Competency-Based Teacher Education.* Washington DC: American Association of Colleges for Teacher Education, 1974.

Itzkoff, S. W. *Cultural Pluralism and American Education.* Scranton PA: International Textbook Co., 1970.

James, R. L. (comp.). *Directory of Multi-cultural Programs in Teacher Education.* Washington DC: American Association of Colleges for Teacher Education and ERIC Clearinghouse on Teacher Education. ED 055 964, 1971.

James, R. et al. "Multi-cultural Education From a Black Educator's Perspective." In Hunter (ed.), 1974.

Jencks, C. et al. *Inequality*. New York: Harper and Row, 1972.

Johnson, N. J. "America, A Pluralistic Community: Myth or Fact." Paper presented at the International Reading Association Annual Convention, Atlantic City NJ. ED 051349, 1971.

Kjolseth, R. "Bilingual Education Programs in the United States: For Assimilation or Pluralism." In B. Spolsky (ed.) *The Language Education of Minority Children*. Rowley MA: Newbury House Publishers, 1972.

Kleinfeld, J. "Positive Stereotyping: The Cultural Relativist in the Classroom. 34 *Human Organization* 269, 1975.

Laosa, L. M. "Toward a Research Model of Multi-cultural Competency-Based Teacher Education." In Hunter (ed.), 1974.

Laubenfels, J. (comp.) *Ethnic Studies*. Columbus OH: Association Referral Information Service (ARIS) of the Ohio Educational Association, 1971.

Lebra, T. S. "Acculturation Dilemma: The Function of Japanese Moral Values for Americanization." I *Council on Anthropology and Education Newsletter III* 6, 1972.

Lee, P. C. and N. B. Gropper. "Sex-role Culture and Educational Practice." 44 *Harvard Educational Review* 369, 1974.

Mazon, M. R., T. Arciniega. "Competency-based Education and the Culturally Different: A Ray of Hope or More of the Same?" In Hunter (ed.), 1974.

McFee, M. "The 150% Man, A Product of Blackfeet Acculturation." 70:6 *American Anthropologist* 1096, 1968.

Newman, W. M. *American Pluralism*. New York: Harper and Row, 1973.

Ogbu, J. U. *The Next Generation*. New York: Academic Press, 1974.

Paulston, C. B. "Questions Concerning Bilingual Education." Paper presented at the American Anthropological Association Annual Meeting, Mexico City DF, 1974.

——. *Implications of Language Learning Theory for Language Planning*. Washington DC: Center for Applied Linguistics, 1975.

Paulston, R. G. "Ethnic Revival and Educational Conflict in Swedish Lapland." Paper presented at the Comparative and International Education Society Annual Meeting, San Francisco CA, 1975.

Pettigrew, L. E. "Competency-based Teacher Education: Teacher Training for Multicultural Education." In Hunter (ed.), 1974.

Polgar, S. "Biculturation of Mesquakie Teenage Boys." 62 *American Anthropologist* 217, 1960.

Rubin, V. (ed.) "Social and Cultural Pluralism in the Caribbean." 83 *Annals of the New York Academy of Sciences* 5, 1960.

Sanday, P. R. "The Relevance of Anthropology to U.S. Social Policy." 3 *Council on Anthropology and Education Newsletter III* 1, 1972.

Saville, M. R. and R. C. Troike. *A Handbook of Bilingual Education* (rev. ed.). Washington DC: TESOL, 1971.

Schermerhorn, R. A. *Comparative Ethnic Relations: A Framework for Theory and Research*. New York: Random House.

Seda Bonilla, E. "Ethnic and Bilingual Education for Cultural Pluralism." In Stent et al. (eds.), 1973.

Seifer, N. "Education and the New Pluralism: A Preliminary Survey of Recent Progress in the 50 States." Paper presented at the Annual Meeting of the National Coordinating Assembly on Ethnic Studies, Detroit MI. ED 081 885, 1973.

Smalley, M. J. "Pluralism and Cultural Pluralism in the Training the Teacher Trainers Program." In Stent et al. (eds.), 1973.

Smith, M. G. *The Plural Society in the British West Indies*. Berkeley: Univ. of Calif. Press, 1965.

Smith, R. T. "Book Review: Social and Cultural Pluralism in the Caribbean." 63 *American Anthropologist* 155, 1961.

Spicer, E. H. "Types of Contact and Processes of Change." In Spicer (ed.). *Perspectives in American Indian Cultural Change*. Chicago: Univ. of Chicago Press, 1961. Reprinted in Walker (ed.), 1972.

Spindler, G. D. *Education and Cultural Process: Toward an Anthropology of Education.* New York: Holt, Rinehart & Winston, 1974.

Stent, M. D., W. R. Hazard and H. N. Rivlin (eds.) *Cultural Pluralism in Education.* New York: Appleton-Century-Crofts, 1973.

Thomas, R. K. and A. L. Wahrhaftig. "Indians, Hillbillies, and the 'Education Problem.' " In Murray Wax, et al. (eds.). *Anthropological Perspectives on Education.* New York: Basic Books, Inc., 1971.

Title VII, ESEA. Manual for project applicants and grantees. Washington DC: U.S. Office of Education, 1971.

Trueba, H. T. "Bilingual-Bicultural Education for Chicanos in the Southwest." 3 *Council on Anthropology and Education Quarterly* V 8, 1974.

United States Commission on Civil Rights. *A Better Chance to Learn: Bilingual-Bicultural Education.* Washington DC: U.S. Commission on Civil Rights, Clearinghouse Publication No. 51, 1975.

Valentine, C. A. "Deficit, Difference, and Bicultural Models of Afro-American Behavior." 41 *Harvard Education Review* 136, 1971.

Walker, D. E., Jr. (ed.). *The Emergent Native Americans, A Reader in Culture Contact.* Boston: Little, Brown & Co., 1972.

Wynn, C. "Teacher Competencies for Cultural Diversity." In Hunter (ed.), 1974.

Zintz, M. V., M. L. Ulibarri and D. Gonzales. *The Implications of Bilingual Education for Developing Multi-cultural Sensitivity Through Teacher Education.* Washington DC: ERIC Clearinghouse on Teacher Education, 1971.

CHAPTER 2

MULTICULTURAL EDUCATION (1980)
Donna M. Gollnick

With the advent of new accreditation standards (NCATE, 1977), the focus of attention by educators on multicultural education has increased dramatically in the past two years. Multicultural education accreditation standards have been further reinforced by state certification requirements for a multicultural education component (e.g., Texas and Ohio). However, multicultural education is not a new concept in education, instead it is a new name for some concepts that have existed for more than 30 years. In the 1940's some educators and organizations were writing about and providing training in intergroup or human relations and in intercultural education. Kilpatrick and VanTil wrote in 1947 about the need and expectations for intercultural education:

> It is a denial of the values of equal participation with, mutual acceptance of, and full respect for persons of all groups which has brought intercultural education into existence. Whole groups ... are still in some measure excluded from full participation in the life of the community. Intercultural education aims at the best possible achievement of the values of participation with, acceptance of, and respect for others. It is an effort to bring education to bear as constructively as possible on actual and possible intercultural tensions and on the evils of any and all bias, prejudice and discrimination against minority groups. In short, the effect of intercultural education is to ensure to all the adequate realization of these social values and to remove and cure the bias and prejudice leading to such discriminations. This is the fundamental meaning of intercultural education, and it explains the presence of inter-cultural education as an integral part and aspect of modern democratic education. (p. 4)[1]

During this period, several national organizations supported intercultural and intergroup education activities (Cole & Cole, 1954). Especially active in the con-vening of investigative groups, preparation of materials, and providing training to educators were the National Conference of Christians and Jews, the American Council on Education (ACE), the Anti-Defamation League, the American Jewish Committee, and the National Education Association.

The American Council on Education (ACE) established a Committee on the Study of Teaching Materials in Intergroup Relations in 1948. In one of their publications the need for teachers to understand stereotypes and cultural diversity was outlined:

Firsthand contacts with ethnic, economic, social, and religious backgrounds are, of course, the best possible means of learning to think about and interact with individuals as individuals and to accept casually the differences which mark them as group members. . . . Books may supplement these firsthand experiences. (ACE. 1948, pp. 25-26)

Based on the assumption that schools have part of the responsibility for improvement of intergroup relations, this ACE Committee later stated that

An alert school will approach the task of intergroup education through improvement of administrative practices, student club and organization arrangements, methods of teaching, techniques of guidance, as well as through the formal course of study and the provision of pertinent teaching materials. (ACE, 1949, p. 11)

Members of this committee also felt that what is directly, or by implication, taught to students in courses affects the attitudes of students toward persons of different ethnic and cultural backgrounds.

In the ACE Committee's review of 266 elementary and secondary textbooks, 60 courses of study, and 49 college textbooks, constant examples of ethnocentrism were found (many of these same characteristics are still being identified by critics). The most common errors found in this 1949 study included the omission of pertinent, basic information, undue simplification, distortion, and unwarranted generalizations concerning groups and individuals from different backgrounds. Cole and Cole (1954) outlined major issues that should be included in intercultural education:

1   Study of physical anthropology that includes concepts such as race, creed, class, and sex;
2   Study of cultural anthropology;
3   Study and correcting of authoritarian and ethnocentric assumptions in American culture that breed prejudice, divisiveness and kindred diseases; and
4   Development of respect for the individual and intergroup understanding (pp. 219–222).

During the remainder of that decade and into the sixties, the organizational support for intercultural education and intergroup relations waned. However, a new emphasis on racial and ethnic pride emerged during this decade. Demands for programs in black studies led to the establishment of this and other ethnic studies programs in colleges and universities across the country; later, similar programs were established in secondary schools. Students and participants in these early ethnic studies programs were primarily members of the group being studied. The focus was the study of the history and culture of various ethnic groups. The main objective was to provide students with insight and to instill pride in their own racial/ethnic background. These programs were ethnic specific—one ethnic group was studied. Sometimes the objectives included an understanding of the relationship and conflict between the ethnic group and the dominant or majority group, but seldom was the scope multiethnic.

Although ethnic studies programs are no longer as prevalent as in the 1960's and early 1970's, they still flourish. In fact, much of the historical and contemporary information about U.S. ethnic groups has been developed as a result of these programs.

Concurrent with the Civil Rights movement and growth of ethnic studies, emphasis on intergroup or human relations again emerged. Often these programs accompanied ethnic studies content for teachers. The objective was again to promote intergroup, especially interracial, understanding.

With the growth and development of ethnic studies came the realization that those programs alone would not guarantee support for the promotion of cultural diversity in this country. Majority students also needed to learn about the history, culture, and contributions of minority groups: American Indian students needed to study Hispanic Americans and Polish Americans, etc. Thus, ethnic studies expanded to multiethnic studies.

Although intergroup and intercultural education was being promoted as early as 1943, today the curriculum continues to emphasize assimilation and still does not effectively address intercultural education. In what way is multicultural education similar to intercultural education of the 1940's and ethnic studies and human relations of the 1960's and 1970's? To describe multicultural education the writings of proponents of multicultural education will be examined. The major tenets, approaches, components, and trends of this concept will be examined in the remainder of this paper.

What is multicultural education?

Early proponents of multicultural education believed that the recognition and preservation of cultural pluralism should be a goal of education. Their concern focused on the role of schooling in transmitting the culture of a nation. Anthropologists generally agree that education (not always synonomous with schooling) serves as the transmittor of culture (Spindler, 1974). Moreover, schools are the institutionalized mechanisms for enculturating groups into a national culture (Cohen, 1970).

Cultural pluralism and ethnicity

Three theories describe the role of ethnicity in the assimilation strategies predominant in various spans of U.S. history. These three ideologies—Anglo-conformity, melting pot, and cultural pluralism—were described by Gordon (1964):

> "Anglo-conformity" theory demanded the complete renunciation of the immigrant's ancestral culture in favor of the behavior and values of the Anglo-Saxon core group; the "melting pot" idea envisaged a biological merger of the Anglo-Saxon peoples with other immigrant groups and a blending of their respective cultures into a new indigenous American type; and "cultural pluralism" postulated the preservation of the communal life and significant portions of the culture of the later immigrant groups within the context of American citizenship and political and economic integration into American society. (p. 85)[2]

Cultural pluralism represented a rejection of the Anglo-conformity and melting pot ideologies. Supporters of cultural pluralism felt that schooling encouraged Anglo-conformity—that students were expected to deny their ancestral culture in order to be accepted as "American."

As early as 1915, a few educators and philosophers were questioning the validity of either a melting pot or Anglo-conformity model to describe group life in the United States. These writers described a nation in which the various ethnic groups would preserve their identity and cultures within an American culture (Gordon, 1964). The term "cultural pluralism" was first used by Horace Kallen in his volume of papers published in 1924. In his first essay describing what was later to be called "cultural pluralism," Kallen described this model:

> Its form would be that of the federal republic; its substance a democracy of nationalities, cooperating voluntarily and autonomously through common institutions in the enterprise of self-realization through the perfection of men according to their kind. The common language of the commonwealth, the language of its great tradition, would be English, but each nationality would have for its emotional and involuntary life its own peculiar dialect or speech, its own individual and inevitable esthetic and intellectual forms. The political and economic life of the commonwealth is a single unit and serves as the foundation and background for the realization of the distinctive individuality of each nation that composes it and of the pooling of these in a harmony above them all. (p. 124)

Today, Banks (1977) discusses cultural pluralism in terms of ideologies related to ethnicity and pluralism in the United States. In his paradigm, the cultural pluralist ideology is characterized by separation, where common ancestry and heritage unity the members of the group with its own economic and political interests. At the opposite end of the continuum, Banks identifies an assimilationist ideology characterized by a common, shared culture in which cultural differences do not exist. Somewhere in the middle of this continuum, Banks describes a pluralist-assimilationist ideology in which ethnic attachments exist while recognizing that all groups in America share many cultural traits. Banks' pluralist-assimilationist ideology describes best the "cultural pluralism" to which most proponents of multicultural education refer.

Most writers today use cultural pluralism to describe the existence of cultural diversity in the nation. They emphasize the right of individuals to maintain their ethnic identity while sharing a common culture with Americans from many different national origins. In its statement, "No One Model American," the American Association of Colleges for Teacher Education's (AACTE) Commission on Multicultural Education describes cultural pluralism in terms of its common usage:

> To endorse cultural pluralism is to endorse the principle that there is no one model American. To endorse cultural pluralism is to understand and appreciate the differences that exist among the nation's citizens. It is to see these differences as a positive force in the continuing development of a society which professes a wholesome respect for the intrinsic worth of every individual ... Cultural pluralism rejects both assimilation and separatism as ultimate goals. (Commission, 1973)

Beginning as early as 1920, some writers referred to the desirability of promoting the preservation of ethnic groups. At the same time, they argued for greater flexibility and alternatives of choice for individuals. They felt that "individuals should have the right *either* to 'preserve their group's corporate identity,' or, if they so desired, to reject their ethnic heritage and 'lose themselves in the population as a whole' " (Gordon, 1964, p. 157). Vickery and Cole (1943) reiterated this theme for intercultural education programs. In 1978 Banks and Gay further elaborated on individual ethnic identity:

> Our analysis suggests that every American is a member of an ethnic group, that ethnicity exists on a continuum in contemporary American life, and that some individuals and groups are much more "ethnic" than others. Thus, it is more useful to attempt to describe the degree to which an individual or group is ethnic, rather than to try to determine whether a particular individual or group is ethnic. The lower-class Black individual who lives in an all-Black community, speaks Black English, and who is active in Black political and economic activities is clearly more "ethnic" than the highly acculturated Black who tries desperately to avoid any contact with other Blacks. (pp. 245–246)[3]

While Banks and Gay may be correct in their suggestion that every American is a member of an ethnic group, it is possible that many Americans function as non-ethnics. These individuals have become so acculturated and so assimilated into the dominant societal group that only their family names suggest their national origins. Even among the more visible ethnic groups such as Blacks, Hispanics, Asians, and Native Americans, there are individuals who think, speak, eat, and maintain values identified with the dominant society.

Cultural pluralism within the context of multicultural education refers to the right of individuals to choose how ethnic they wish to be. Within a multicultural society individuals are neither forced to conform to the dominant Anglo culture nor to maintain ethnic identity separate from the common culture. The nature and contributions of the many ethnic groups that compose our nation are recognized as a fundamental part of all education. Cultural diversity is accepted as a national strength rather than an obstacle to be overcome.

Cultural pluralism beyond ethnicity

Cultural pluralism has been identified primarily with ethnicity and translated into ethnic studies programs as an educational concept. However, if defined narrowly as ethnic studies, its focus is limited. It is based on an understanding and acceptance of ethnicity in American life. An ethnic group is generally defined by race, religion, or national origin (Gordon, 1964). This neglects the recognition of other cultural differences based on sex, age, socioeconomic status, and physical and mental exceptionalities. Thus, within the context of multicultural education, cultural pluralism is defined broadly. Cultural pluralism extends far beyond the parameters of ethnic studies. While ethnic studies is an integral and critical component of multicultural education, other equally critical cultural components include sex, age, socioeconomic status, and physical, mental, and emotional exceptionalities.

The objective of multicultural education is to help all students reach their potential. To provide this help, the educator must understand that students are different from one another not only in intellectual ability, but in the way in which they learn. Learning patterns may be based on the student's ethnic or religious background, language, sex, socioeconomic level, as well as physical or mental exceptionalities. The ability of educators to facilitate students in reaching their potential is diminished if there is a lack of understanding of cultural factors which affect a student's learning and behavior patterns in school.

Banks believes that any cultural group which experiences prejudice and discrimination should be the primary focus of multicultural education. In multi-ethnic education, ethnic groups as defined within the framework of cultural pluralism are the focus of courses or programs. According to Banks, the major objective of both educational strategies is "to help reduce discrimination against stigmatized cultural (ethnic) groups and to provide them equal educational opportunities." A second objective of multicultural education is "to present all students with cultural alternatives" (Banks, 1977, p. 6).

The emphasis in this expanded definition of multicultural education is an extension of cultural pluralism. It rejects assimilation theories because many cultural groups were not allowed to "melt" into the proposed "one model American" of the melting pot model. Even those individuals who rejected their ethnic identity to become American within the Anglo-conformity model were often not allowed the same rewards as those individuals who composed the core culture initially. Although cultural pluralism rejects the notion that groups must give up their ethnic identity to be "American," subordinate groups have had to adjust and adapt to an Anglo-conformity system throughout this century to reap societal benefits. These subordinate groups are classified by sociologists as minority groups "whose members experience a wide range of discriminatory treatment and frequently are relegated to positions relatively low in the status structure of a society" (Gittler, 1956). In this country minority groups include Blacks, Hispanic Americans, Asian Americans, Pacific Islanders, American Indians, and Eskimos. Other ethnic groups have also suffered discrimination at various periods of our history. Today, individuals who have immigrated from southern and eastern Europe and Arabic nations may be discriminated against. Some religious groups may suffer similar discrimination. Both women and older persons also face discrimination today. All of these groups are now addressed in this expanded definition of multicultural education.

Moreover, the existence of cultural diversity causes intergroup conflict. Most minority groups are easily distinguishable from the majority group because of racial and/or language differences. Because "all groups tend to be ethnocentric concerning their own values, norms, attitudes, and ways of defining and interpreting reality" (Yetman & Steele, 1975, p. 371), cultural conflict between groups occurs. Although cultural diversity can easily be identified in this country, the ethnocentric pattern of the dominant group is transformed into cultural discrimination within the sociopolitical structure of the country. Yetman and Steele (1975) maintain that this problem is caused by the "differential power of the majority group to define their cultural attributes—their values, beliefs, and definitions of reality—as the standards and criteria for evaluation for the entire society and to exclude alternative perceptions or inter-pretations" (p. 371). Weinberg (1977) describes this phenomena as institutional racism:

> By incorporating the allocation of differential rewards into institutions such as the economy, education, and government, dominant white society created an impersonal system that served racist purposes very effectively. (p. 29)

One of the major goals of multicultural education is to recognize and accept the right of different cultural groups to exist and share equally in the differential rewards of our institutions. Johnson (1977) believes that "only with the sterilization of racism and cultural imperialism will a true multicultural society emerge". (p. 12)

Schools are one of the major institutions accused of perpetuating racism and cultural imperalism. If an assimilationist ideology is accepted as a national goal, then educators are encouraged, or expected, to transmit such a model. However, such a model is an inaccurate reflection of U.S. society. Education should accurately reflect the culturally diverse nature of our multicultural society. This would recognize cultural differences as positive forces in society and not as deficit models to be eliminated. Weinberg (1977) states,

> Today one-seventh of all children attend an interracial or interethnic public school. Yet the heritage with the past still weighs heavily upon the American classroom. Practices originally created to serve racist purposes linger as thoughtless monuments to the past. . . . The goal of multicultural training is congruent with a human rights approach to education. Essentially groups have the absolute right to define their own ethnic, cultural, or language status. (p. 30)

The incongruence that results when students from a distinct cultural group enter school is described by Cross, Happel, Doston, and Stiles (1977):

> The school, next to the home, is the major socializing agency. The individual child learns those behaviors, values, and norms espoused by the home and school; when such are congruent, there is no conflict. But when the cultural traditions and priorities of the home differ from those of the dominant culture, the school's goals—those of the majority—become imposed in a resocializing process. (p. 7)

The question becomes whether it is possible for schools to adequately reflect cultural diversity. It is much easier to continue in the past mode where students were expected to become "one model Americans." To meet the goals of multicultural education, it is necessary for educators to utilize a strategy for change or for re-education (Grant, 1977a).

Continued low achievement scores, high dropout rates, and an ever-widening education and income gap between minority poor and white middle class populations (Pacheco, 1977) would seem to indicate that schools are not currently serving minority populations well. The development of a school environment and curricula that recognizes that cultural differences exist may lead to the narrowing of the gap that now exists between minority and majority students. Desired cultural attributions expected at home and at school often differ, causing incongruence for the student. The school must learn to accept the child's existing cultural attributes as having as much validity as those usually espoused by the school. Perhaps then, the school can progress to the creative development of an environment and curriculum for multicultural education.

It is easy for educators to proclaim the need for multicultural education, and to make some superficial changes toward implementation, but that is not enough. This fear was described by Cross, et al. (1977):

> Goals of pluralism are severely threatened by values that encourage divisiveness. They are equally threatened by the failure of educators to recognize their tendency to avoid issues by cosmetic educational planning—planning that creates new titles, positions, and satellite programs in the name of "good education," but that does little or nothing to diminish racism or to stimulate

the kind of humaneness needed to support the integrity of diverse perspectives. (p. 6)

Cross, et al. (1977) also identified two considerations that they consider paramount in designing, implementing, and evaluating strategies for multicultural education:

1   [T]hat we in the United States are socialized to ignore the close connection between racial myths, stereotypes, and racism—perpetuated in the past and present through nonproductive conflicts on local, national, and international levels; and
2   [T]hat we are socialized to ignore the fact that it is the reaction to cultural differences, not cultural differences in themselves, that creates social conflicts. (pp. 3–4)

In the past, schools have promoted and rewarded those who come from or are able to adapt to the dominant culture. Students from minority groups have typically been unable to compete equally with majority students for rewards following school. Likewise, females are often discouraged from competing equally with males. This suggests that schools are not serving students in the same way. These facts support the need for a change in the schools—a change toward the accurate reflection of a multicultural society. Although multicultural education can not in itself overcome the long history of racism, sexism, and cultural imperialism in this country, it is a necessary step toward combating those factors in one of the major institutions of our society.

Thus, multicultural education includes more than the recognition and promotion of cultural diversity in the curriculum and school environment. It supports and extends the concepts of cultural pluralism and equity into the formal school setting. According to the writers in this field, multicultural education is predicated upon the following fundamental beliefs:

1   Strength and value of cultural diversity (Grant, 1977b; Baptiste, 1977; Banks, 1977; Commission, 1973);
2   Human rights and respect for human dignity (Grant, 1977b; Cross, et al., 1977; Weinberg, 1977; Hazard & Stent, 1973; Commission, 1973);
3   Alternative life choices for people (Grant, 1977b; Banks, 1977; Johnson, 1977; Commission, 1973);
4   Social justice and equal opportunity for all people (Hazard & Stent, 1973; Cross, et al., 1977; Banks, 1977; Grant, 1977b); and
5   Equity distribution of power among members of all ethnic groups (Hazard & Stent, 1973; Hilliard, 1974; Commission, 1973).

The responsibility of education is summarized in this statement to secondary school administrators:

Education for a society based on racial and cultural pluralism is now an inescapable task being imposed on all schools, no matter what their student mix may be. The segregated school, be it all black, all brown, all yellow, all white, has a responsibility equal to that of the integrated school in preparing its students for a self-fulfilling existence in the world they are to inherit. (Evaluation Guidelines, 1973, p. 5)

Approaches to multicultural education

Over the past decade there has been much rhetoric about the need for multicultural education, but little assistance in how to implement such programs. A major obstacle to the development of strategies may have been a lack of understanding of multicultural education. In the South, educators were concerned about black and white conflict as schools were desegregated; often this was also a major concern in northern urban schools. In the Southwest, the emphasis was on developing educational programs to cope with language differences. Multicultural education seemed not to be needed in middle class schools where students were white, middle class, and from similar religious backgrounds.

Until recently, teaching about our multicultural society was unnecessary unless there were minority or low socioeconomic students attending the school. Handicapped students attended special classes, special schools, or were excluded from the educational process. Few educators seemed concerned that girls did not achieve as well as boys in mathematics or science after a certain grade level. Few educators felt that it was necessary to teach about blacks, Hispanics, American Indians, Asian Americans, or Jews if there were none attending the school (and often these groups were still not included in curriculum when they did attend the school).

The definition proposed in this article suggests that multicultural education is necessary for all students. Not only must educators teach accurately about cultural diversity in this country and the world, they must also be aware of cultural differences among students to build an educational environment that will help all students reach their potential.

In analyzing the publications on multicultural education, Gibson (1976) was able to identify five major approaches. She classified these approaches according to their assumptions for the values, strategies, target groups, and outcomes. An examination of these approaches may help the reader understand how multicultural education might be implemented. What follows are five approaches and purposes of each (summarized from Gibson, 1976, pp. 8–13):

1   Benevolent multiculturalism (Hilliard, 1974)—to equalize educational opportunity for students from different cultural backgrounds;
2   Education about cultural differences or cultural understanding—to teach students to value cultural differences, to understand the meaning of the culture concept, and to accept others' right to be different;
3   Education for cultural pluralism—to preserve and extend cultural pluralism in American society;
4   Bicultural education—to produce learners who have competencies in and can operate successfully in two different cultures; and
5   Multicultural education as the normal human experience (Goodenough, 1976)—to promote competence in multiple societies.

The literature on multicultural education emphasizes one or more of Gibson's approaches. The achievement for her fifth approach, "multicultural education as the normal human experience," might be the ultimate goal of multicultural education.

The first, benevolent multiculturalism, suggests that education programs must be devised and implemented that will decrease home and school discordance or will positively increase the compatibility between home and school environments

(Gibson, 1976). The need to provide quality education and equal educational opportunity for all of America's youth (Banks, 1977; Gay, 1977) would be included here. Compensatory education programs have been the major strategy for implementing this approach. Because many of these programs have not been successful in providing minority students with the equal educational opportunity should not suggest that this approach be eliminated. It suggests only that more appropriate means for accomplishing it need to be designed. Riessman (1976), for instance, suggests that there haven't been any significant improvements in the learning of inner city youngsters as a result of the compensatory programs because:

1   Educators continue to use, whether implicitly or explicitly a basic compensatory model that assumes that inner city youngsters are inadequate and need all kinds of special help to make them like middle class children.
2   While the great emphasis on teaching has led in some ways to the improvement of the teacher's ability to contact youngsters, most teachers do not know how to move beyond the contact stage to higher stages of learning and development.
3   The improvement of teachers has not led to the improvement of the management of the educational system.
4   We have not developed sound organizational and management strategies, so that good programs and strength-based approaches that have emerged in various demonstrations can be carried over and institutionalized in the system as a whole.

Riessman implies that cultural differences were not used as strengths in the compensatory programs of the past.

The second approach, cultural understanding, assumes that formal education programs that preserve cultural diversity can be developed. Banks (1977), Gay (1977), Baptiste (1977), Hilliard (1974), and Grant (1977b) support this notion through the encouragement of multiethnic studies. They feel that students can be taught to recognize, understand, and prize cultural diversity. This approach allows a response to the debilitating effects of monoculturalism and ethnocentrism that exists in our society (Hunter, 1974). Gay (1977) views it as a means "to avoid perpetuating a monolithic view of society and set of values and behavioral patterns that are Anglo-centric as the only acceptable ones."

The third approach, cultural pluralism, could serve as a means for arresting the processes of assimilation in an effort of preserve and extend cultural pluralism (Gibson, 1976). Hilliard (1974) and Grant (1977b) view this approach as necessary for increasing minority group power. This would include minorities' decision-making power over the educational forces that impinge upon the lives of minority group students.

Bicultural education, Gibson's fourth approach, assumes that it is possible to provide instruction in two cultures. She believes that such an approach leads to a dichotomy between the majority and minority group on many issues (1976). However, biculturalism is the natural existence for most minorities in this country because they practice their ethnic culture at home, but must adapt to the dominant culture at work.

"Multicultural education as the normal human experience" is an anthropological approach. Education in this approach is viewed much broader than formal schooling; it is the relationship between informal school and out-of-school learning and school programs. Through this process a person develops competencies in multiple systems of standards for perceiving, evaluating, believing, and doing. Such an approach would alleviate the tendency of educators to stereotype students according to ethnic identities. It should promote a fuller exploration of the similarities as well as differences between students of different ethnic groups. It supports multiple identities that individuals have available to them as well as their primary social identities in a particular ethnic group. Finally, it decreases the dichotomies that exist between minority and majority cultures (Gibson, 1976). Banks (1977), Grant (1977b), Gay (1977), and Johnson (1977) are supportive of this position as a goal for multicultural education.

Components of multicultural education programs

If multicultural education is to become a reality in the formal school situation, the total environment must reflect a commitment to multicultural education. This environment would include, but not be limited to the following:

1   Staffing composition and patterns throughout the organizational hierarchy that reflects the pluralistic nature of the U.S. (Grant, 1977a; Banks, 1977; Commission, 1973; Evaluation Guidelines, 1973; Herman, 1974);
2   Curricula that are appropriate, flexible, unbiased and that incorporate the contributions of all cultural groups (Grant, 1977a; Evaluation Guidelines, 1973; Herman, 1974);
3   Instructional materials free of bias, omissions and stereotypes that are inclusive rather than supplementary (Grant, 1977a; Banks, 1977; Gay, 1977);
4   Affirmation of the existence of various cultural, especially racial and language, groups as different rather than deficient (Grant, 1977a; Riessman, 1976);
5   Educational evaluation procedures, which assess not only content of the curricula and instructional materials, but also how successful the experiences and materials are in accomplishing a better understanding of the respect for humankind (Grant, 1977a);
6   Educators that see themselves as learners enhanced and changed by understanding, appreciating and reflecting cultural diversity (Cross, et al., 1977); and
7   Educators who can deal with questions of race and intergroup relations on an objective, frank, professional basis (Deutsch, 1967; Herman, 1974; Gay, 1977).

Several organizations have developed guidelines for educators to use in the implementation of multicultural curricula. One example is the *Curriculum Guidelines for Multiethnic Education* developed by a Task Force of the National Council for the Social Studies (Banks, et al., 1976). These 23 guidelines provide direction to the nation's schools for designing and implementing ethnic studies programs and for integrating their curricula with ethnic content. The guidelines address the school environment with heavy emphasis on the curriculum.

Although the total school environment must be examined and changed in the implementation of multicultural education, most writers focus on what the curriculum should include. McDonald (1977), Grant (1977a), Wright (1965), and

Glock and Siegelman (1969) believe that it is important that students have experiences in multicultural settings to increase intergroup contact. Various authors consider the following specific learning outcomes desirable for multicultural education programs:

1   Communication skills to enable cross-cultural and interethnic group interaction; this is sometimes referred to as intergroup or human relation (ASCD, 1977; Gay, 1977; Walsh, 1973; Evaluation Guidelines, 1973);
2   Perceptual, analytical, and application skills to be applied in personal and institutional settings (ASCD, 1977; Walsh, 1973);
3   Abilities to make dependable, responsible decisions and to gain, maintain, and exercise political power (ASCD, 1977);
4   Knowledge of cultural experiences, value systems, and historical traditions of different ethnic groups (Gay, 1977; Hilliard, 1974; Baptiste, 1977; Banks, 1977);
5   Positive attitudes, respect and empathy toward other groups (Gay, 1977);
6   Understanding of the social dilemma of minority groups within the context of the American experience; this would include an understanding of powerlessness, isolation and anomaly, immigration and migration, discrimination, racism, sexism, classism, prejudice, stereotyping, and acculturation, and assimilation (Gay, 1977; Grant, 1977a; ASCD, 1977; Cross, et al., 1977).

It is the responsibility of preservice and inservice programs for educators to prepare school personnel to develop and implement multicultural education programs. If educators do not understand and practice multicultural education, it will fail. Teachers, like the children they teach, have been reared in a national climate that places significance on racial, ethnic, language, religious, sex, and socioeconomic differences. They bring these feelings to class, despite any disclaimer offered to the contrary. Walsh (1973), in his book on intercultural education, stated that

> . . . most teachers are one-culture persons; that is, they do not as a group have an intercultural or transcultural outlook themselves, and they do not show genuine concern with developing intercultural understanding among their students. (p. 171)

The following eight experiences are recommended by authors for inclusion in preservice and inservice programs:

1   Study of the concept and philosophies of ethnic diversity and cultural pluralism (Gay, 1977; Baptiste, 1977; Banks, 1977; Herman, 1974);
2   Study of psychological and sociocultural process of early childhood growth and development (Gay, 1977);
3   Examination of own attitudes and feelings toward ethnic, racial, and cultural differences (Gay, 1977; Grant, 1977a, 1977b; Banks, 1977; Banks, et al., 1976; Herman, 1974);
4   Designing and experimenting with nontraditional teaching techniques during the training program (Gay, 1977);
5   Living for one year in a cultural setting different from one's own background (Johnson, 1977);

6   Increasing skills in creating, selecting, evaluating, and revising instructional materials with a multicultural perspective (Banks, et al., 1976);
7   Training experiences and interactions with people of diverse cultures (Grant 1977a; Banks, 1977); and
8   Techniques for handling problems of interpersonal relations that arise from cultural conflicts between groups (Grant, 1977a; Herman, 1974).

As a minimum, Banks (1977) believes that teachers should be able to relate positively to students from diverse ethnic groups and be able to function effectively within educational environments that reflect ethnic pluralism. The 1973 conclusions of the U.S. Commission on Civil Rights' study of educational opportunity of Mexican American students in the Southwest (1973) indicate the importance of the teacher in the total educational process:

The heart of the educational process is in the interaction between teacher and student. It is through this action that the school system makes its major impact upon the child. The way the teacher interacts with the student is a major determinant of the quality of education the child receives.

It is imperative that teachers learn both to teach multiculturally and to more effectively teach students from various cultural backgrounds.

Both the inner city and suburban child have one thing in common—they are deprived of a larger view of life (Grambs, 1968). The intent of multicultural education is to expose these students to that larger view. Such education is, therefore, for both the minority and majority group student (Evaluation Guidelines, 1973). Research has shown that the minority child can gain a great deal of personal ego-strength by being aided in an examination of his/her own place and history in American life and culture (Kvarceus, 1965). Multicultural education is equally as important for the children who are isolated in the affluent cocoon of suburbia who know nothing except what they may hear or read about the problems that face minority group children and children of poverty (Miel & Kiester, 1967).

Thus, no matter what the level of formal schooling, multicultural education should permeate the total environment. It is directed at all students, both those of the majority and minority groups. It is as important that students in a monocultural situation learn from a multicultural perspective as for students in a multicultural situation. The development of competencies to function comfortably in multiple cultural settings should lead to a greater respect for cultural groups different from one's own, the extension of cultural pluralism and equity in the United States, and fewer intergroup conflicts caused by ignorance and misunderstanding.

Notes

1   From *Intercultural Attitudes in the Making* by W. H. Kilpatrick and W. VanTil, 1947. Copyright 1947 by Harper. Reprinted by permission.
2   From *Assimilation in American Life: The Role of Race, Religion, and National Origins* by M. M. Gordon, 1964. Copyright 1964 by Oxford University Press. Reprinted by permission.
3   From "Ethnicity in Contemporary American Society: Toward the Development of a

Typology" by J. A. Banks and G. Gay, *Ethnicity*, 1978, 5, 238–251. Copyright 1978 by
Academic Press. Reprinted by permission.

References

American Council on Education. *Intergroup relations in teaching materials: A survey and appraisal.* Washington, D.C.: Author, 1949.
American Council on Education. *Literature for human understanding.* Washington, D.C.: Author, 1948.
ASCD Multicultural Education Commission. Encouraging multicultural education. In C. A. Grant, (Ed.). *Multicultural education: Commitments, issues, and applications.* Washington, D.C.: Association for Supervision and Curriculum Development, 1977.
Banks, J. A. The implications of multicultural education for teacher education. In F. H. Klassen, & D. M. Gollnick (Eds.). *Pluralism and the American teacher: Issues and case studies.* Washington, D.C.: American Association of Colleges for Teacher Education, 1977.
Banks, J. A., Cortés, C. E., Gay, G., Garcia, R. L., & Ochoa, A. S. *Curriculum guidelines for multiethnic education.* Arlington, Va.: National Council for the Social Studies, 1976.
Banks, J. A. and Gay, G. Ethnicity in contemporary American society: Toward the development of a typology. *Ethnicity*, 1978, 5, 238–251.
Baptiste, H. P., Jr. Multicultural education evolvement at the University of Houston: A case study. In F. H. Klassen & D. M. Gollnick (Eds.). *Pluralism and the American teacher: Issues and case studies.* Washington, D.C.: AACTE, 1977.
Cohen, Y. Schools and civilizational states. In J. Fischer (Ed.). *The social sciences and the comparative study of educational systems.* Scranton: International Textbook Co., 1970.
Cole, S. G., & Cole, M. W. *Minorities and the American promise: The conflict of principle and practice.* New York: Harper, 1954.
Commission on Multicultural Education. No one model American. *Journal of Teacher Education*, Winter 1973, 24(4), 264–265.
Cross, D. E., Happel, M., Doston, G. A., & Stiles, L. J. Responding to cultural diversity. In D. E. Cross, G. C. Baker, & L. J. Stiles (Eds.). *Teaching in a multicultural society: Perspectives and professional strategies.* New York: Free Press, 1977.
Deutsch, M. *The disadvantaged child.* New York: Basic Books, 1967.
Evaluation guidelines for multicultural/multiracial education. Reston, Va.: National Study of School Evaluation, 1973.
Gay, G. Curriculum for multicultural teacher education. In F. H. Klassen & D. M. Gollnick (Eds.). *Pluralism and the American teacher: Issues and case studies.* Washington, D.C.: AACTE, 1977.
Gibson, M. A. Approaches to multicultural education in the United States: Some concepts and assumptions. *Anthropology and Education Quarterly*, 1976, 7, 7–18.
Gittler, J. B. *Understanding minority groups.* New York: John Wiley & Sons, 1956.
Glock, C. Y., & Siegelman, E. *Prejudice U.S.A.* New York: Praeger, 1969.
Goodenough, W. Multiculturalism as the normal human experience. *Anthropology and Education Quarterly*, 1976, 7.
Gordon, M. M. Assimilation in America: Theory and reality. In N. R. Yetman, & C. H. Steele (Eds.). *Majority and minority: The dynamics of racial and ethnic relations* (2nd ed.). Boston: Allyn & Bacon, 1975.
Gordon, M. M. *Assimilation in American life: The role of race, religion, and national origins.* New York: Oxford University Press, 1964.
Grambs, J. D. *Intergroup education: Methods and materials.* Englewood Cliffs, N.J.: Prentice-Hall, 1968.
Grant, C. A. Education that is multicultural and P/CBTE: Discussion and recommendations for teacher education. In F. H. Klassen, & D. M. Gollnick (Eds.). *Pluralism and the American teacher: Issues and case studies.* Washington, D.C.: AACTE, 1977. (a)
Grant, C. A. The teacher and multicultural education: Some personal reflections. In M. J. Gold, C. A. Grant, & H. N. Rivlin (Eds.). *In praise of diversity: A resource book for*

multicultural education. Washington, D.C.: Teacher Corps and Association for Teacher Educators, 1977. (b)

Hazard, W. R., & Stent, M. D. Cultural pluralism and schooling: Some preliminary observations. In M. D. Stent, W. R. Hazard, & H. N. Rivlin (Eds.). *Cultural pluralism in education: A mandate for change.* New York: Appleton Century-Crofts, 1973.

Herman, J. (Ed.). *The schools and group identity: Educating for a new pluralism.* New York: Institute on Pluralism and Group Identity and American Jewish Committee, 1974.

Hilliard, A. G. Restructuring teacher education for multicultural imperatives. In W. A. Hunter (Ed.). *Multicultural education through competency-based teacher education.* Washington, D.C.: AACTE, 1974.

Hunter, W. A. (Ed.). *Multicultural education through competency-based teacher education.* Washington, D.C.: AACTE, 1974.

Johnson, N. B. On the relationship of anthropology to multicultural teaching and learning. *Journal of Teacher Education*, 1977, 28, 10–15.

Kallen, H. M. *Culture and democracy in the United States.* New York: Boni & Liveright, 1924.

Kilpatrick, W. H. and VanTil, W. *Intercultural attitudes in the making.* New York: Harper, 1947.

Kvarceus, W. C., et al. *Negro self-concept: Implications for school and citizenship.* New York: McGraw-Hill, 1965.

McDonald, J. B. Living democratically in schools: Cultural pluralism. In C. A. Grant (Ed.). *Multicultural education: Commitments, issues, and applications.* Washington, D.C.: ASCD, 1977.

Miel, A. and Kiester, E. *The short-changed children of suburbia.* New York: Institute of Human Relations Press of the American Jewish Committee, 1967.

National Council for Accreditation of Teacher Education. *Standards for the accreditation of teacher education.* Washington, D.C.: NCATE, 1977.

Pacheco, A. Cultural pluralism: A philosophical analysis. *Journal of Teacher Education*, 1977, 28, 16–20.

Porter, J. D. R. *Black child, White child: The development of racial attitudes.* Cambridge, Mass.: Harvard University Press, 1971.

Riessman, F. *The inner-city child.* New York: Harper & Row, 1976.

Spindler, G. D. *Education and cultural process: Toward an anthropology of education.* New York: Holt, Rinehart & Winston, 1974.

U. S. Commission on Civil Rights. *Teachers and students. Report 5. Mexican American education study: Differences in teacher interaction with Mexican American and Anglo students.* Washington, D.C.: U.S. Government Printing Office, 1973.

Vickery, W. E. and Cole, S. G. *Intercultural education in American schools.* New York: Harper & Brothers, 1943.

Walsh, J. E. *Intercultural education in the community of man.* Honolulu: University Press of Hawaii, 1973.

Weinberg, M. A historical framework for multicultural education. In D. E. Cross, G. C. Baker, & L. J. Stiles (Eds.). *Teaching in a multicultural society: Perspectives and professional strategies.* New York: Free Press, 1977.

Wright, B. A. *Educating for diversity.* New York: John Day Co., 1965.

Yetman, N. R. & Steele, C. H. *Majority and minority: The dynamics of racial and ethnic relations* (2nd ed.). Boston: Allyn & Bacon, 1975.

CHAPTER 3

MULTICULTURAL APPROACHES TO RACIAL INEQUALITY IN THE UNITED STATES (1990)

Cameron McCarthy

Historical background

For over one hundred years and up until two decades ago, a basic assimilationist model formed the centerpiece of education and state policies towards ethnic differences in the United States. Schooling was looked upon as the institution par excellence through which American educational policy-makers and ruling elites consciously attempted to cultivate norms of citizenship, to fashion a conformist American identity, and to bind together a population of diverse national origins (Kaestle, 1983; Olneck & Lazerson, 1980). This assimilationist ideology was rooted in the nativisite response of dominant Anglo-Americans to the waves of immigrants from southern Europe who came to work in urban factories at the turn of the century. These southern European immigrants were seen as a threat to a social order that was based on the values of earlier settled Euro-American citizenry. The latter traced their ancestry to England, the Netherlands, and other northern European countries.

In 1909, Ellwood P. Cubberley, a proponent of "social efficiency" (Kliebard. 1986, p. 223), clearly stated the case for using civil institutions such as schools as vehicles for cultivating dominant Anglo-Saxon values among the new immigrants and their offspring:

> Everywhere these people (immigrants) tend to settle in groups or settlements, and to set up here their national manners, customs, and observances. Our task is to break up these groups or settlements, to assimilate and amalgamate these people as part of our American race, and to implant in their children, as far as can be done, the Anglo-Saxon conception of righteousness, law and order, and popular government, and to awaken in them a reverence for our democratic institutions and for those things in our national life which we as a people hold to be of abiding truth. (Cubberley, 1909, pp. 15–16).

In addition to promoting highly conformist practices and values in schools, policy-makers turned to the coercive apparatuses of the state to control the flow of non-Anglo immigrants into the United States. Highly exclusionary clauses were written into the United States Immigration Acts of 1917 and 1924 which drastically limited the number of immigrants that came from southern and eastern Europe, Asia, and Latin America (Banks, 1981).

For American minority groups, institutional assimilationist practices were even more stringent and definitively conformist. Efforts were made in educational institutions serving Hispanic, Native American, and black youth, to rid these groups of "ethnic traits" (Banks, 1981, p. 4) that were considered inimical to the dominant American culture. Consequently, early-twentieth-century institutions such as the Hampton Institute were designed to equip black and Native American youth with "the skills that would bring them to the level of the white middle class" (Kliebard, 1986, p. 126). The courses in economics at Hampton, for example, "attempted to get blacks and American Indians to abandon certain undesirable practices in specific areas of practical concern such as the purchase of clothing and the consumption of food" (Kliebard, 1986, p. 126).

For most of the first half of the century, this assimilationist model of education was not seriously challenged, even though black protest groups such as the United Negro Improvement Association, led by Marcus Garvey, championed separatism and pluralism. Indeed, many prominent black as well as white middle-class intellectuals regarded assimilation and cultural incorporation of American ethnic groups as a highly desirable social goal. In the 1920s and '30s, the so-called Chicago School of sociologists, led by Robert E. Park (a former secretary to Booker T. Washington), outlined the basic assimilation model that was so influential in shaping research and social policy on race relations during the period. Park postulated that all immigrant and ethnic minority group members went through a "race relations cycle" or trajectory on their way to eventual incorporation into the mainstream of American life. This cycle consisted of four stages: *contact, conflict, accommodation, and assimilation* (Omi & Winant, 1986, p. 15).

But for minorities such as blacks, and Native Americans, assimilation meant a special kind of cultural incorporation into a racial order in which they were accorded merely a secondary status. The ideology of assimilation clearly benefited white Americans. White "ethnics," over time, were able to share in the rewards of the society from which black Americans were systematically excluded (Banks, 1981). Blacks, Native Americans, and Hispanics continued to experience severe discrimination and racial exclusion in housing, employment, and education during the first half of this century. During this same period, European immigrants—Irish, Italian, and Greek—came, settled, and consolidated their status in American society.

By the '50s and '60s, policies of assimilation lost credibility among many groups of racial minorities and were subjected to unprecedented challenges by oppositional black groups and the civil rights movement. These challenges were particularly strong in the area of education. Black and other minority groups contended that schools as they were organized in America were fundamentally racist and did not address the needs and aspirations of minority peoples. Minority groups demanded more control of institutions in their communities. They demanded greater representation in the administration and staffing of schools. Even more significantly, black youth and their political leaders demanded a radical redefinition of the school curriculum to include Black Studies. The latter demand constituted a strategic challenge to the taken-for-granted Eurocentric foundations of the American school curriculum (McCarthy & Apple, 1988).

Essentially then, the assimilationist approach to race relations and to the education of minorities had become unstuck. Blacks and other oppositional racial minorities had begun to champion a radical pluralism (Berlowitz, 1984). It is in this context of radical black discontent with American schooling that educational policy-makers and liberal intellectuals began to forge a "new" discourse of multiculturalism. Educators and social researchers such as Baker (1973), Banks (1973), and Glazer and Moynihan (1963) attempted to replace the assimilationist model that undergirded the American school curriculum with a pluralist model that embraced the notion of cultural diversity. Multicultural education as a "new" curricular form disarticulated elements of black radical demands for the restructuring of school knowledge and rearticulated these elements into more reformist professional discourses around issues of minority failure, cultural characteristics, and language proficiency.

Multicultural policy discourses

Over the years, policy discourses on multicultural education have consistently identified the variable of culture as the vehicle for the resolution of racial inequality and racial antagonism in schooling (Troyna & Williams, 1986). This central motif does represent a certain continuity with an earlier emphasis on minority culture identifiable in the proposals of liberal scholars for compensatory education. However, unlike the earlier liberal preoccupation with cultural deprivation, multicultural proponents tend to emphasize the positive qualities of minority cultural heritage. Proponents of multicultural education have therefore promoted curriculum models that emphasize the following: (a) *cultural understanding*—the idea central to many ethnic studies and human relations programs that students and teachers should be more sensitive to ethnic differences in the classroom; (b) *cultural competence*—the insistence in bilingual and bicultural education programs that students and teachers should be able to demonstrate competence in the language and culture of groups outside their own cultural heritage; and (c) *cultural emancipation*—the somewhat more possibilitarian and social reconstructionist thesis that the incorporation/inclusion of minority culture in the school curriculum has the potential to positively influence minority academic achievement and consequently life chances beyond the school (Grant & Sleeter, 1989; Rushton, 1981).

In this section of my essay I will discuss in some detail the contradictions and nuances that are embodied in these three multicultural approaches to racial inequality in education. First, I examine the policy discourse of cultural understanding.

Models of cultural understanding

Models of cultural understanding in multicultural education exist in the form of various state—and university—supported ethnic studies and human relations programs which place a premium on "improving communication" among different ethnic groups (Montalto, 1981). The fundamental stance of this approach to ethnic differences in schooling is that of cultural relativism. Within this framework, all social and ethnic groups are presumed to have a formal parity with each other. The matter of ethnic identity is understood in terms of individual choice and preference—the language of the shopping mall.

This stance of cultural relativism is translated in curriculum guides for ethnic studies in terms of a discourse of reciprocity and consensus: "We are different but we are all the same." The idea that racial differences are only "human" and "natural" is, for example, promoted in the teaching kit, "The Wonderful World of Difference: A Human Relations Program for Grades K-8," in which the authors "explore the diversity and richness of the human family" (Anti-Defamation

League of B'nai B'rith, 1986). In their *Multicultural Teaching: A Handbook of Activities. Information, and Resources* (1979), Tiedt and Tiedt tell teachers and students that there are many different ways of grouping individuals in "our society." Income, religious beliefs, and so on are some of the criteria "we use" in the United States. One of the handbook's many activities requires students to make up a list of cultural traits that would be characteristic of "Sue Wong" (p. 144). Students are also asked to supply the appropriate cultural information that would help to complete the sentence, "Sue Wong is . . ." (p. 144). This tendency to focus on the acceptance and recognition of cultural differences has led in recent years to a movement for the recognition of the cultural "uniqueness" of "white ethnic" groups (for example, Poles, Italians, Norwegians, and Swedes) to counterbalance demands for the study of black. Hispanic, and Native American cultures (Gibson, 1984).

But the emphasis on cultural understanding goes beyond the development of communication skills and respect for ethnic differences. Various preservice teacher education programs and state human relations guides emphasize the elimination of racial and sexual stereotypes and the development of positive attitudes towards minority and disadvantaged groups (Wisconsin Department of Public Instruction, 1986). This emphasis on attitudinal change is, for example, reflected in the Ann Arbor, Michigan, Board of Education's regulations of the '70s:

> Beginning in the 1972–73 school year, no student-teacher shall be accepted by the Ann Arbor schools unless he (she) can demonstrate attitudes necessary to support and create the multiethnic curriculum. Each student-teacher must provide a document or transcript which reflects training in or evidence of substantive understanding of multicultural or minority experience. (Baker, 1977, p. 80).

In a similar manner, the University of Wisconsin's Steering Committee on Minority Affairs, in its 1987 report, strongly emphasizes the need for course work that would promote racial tolerance:

> The University must implement a mandatory six-credit course requirement: and create and develop various Ethnic Studies Programs. These measures will recognize the contributions of ethnic minorities to American society and promote cross-cultural understanding and respect among the entire student body. (p. 4).

Cultural understanding models of multicultural education such as the one promoted in the University of Wisconsin's Steering Committee on Minority Affairs report, generally take a "benign" stance (Troyna & Williams, 1986) towards racial inequality in schooling and consequently place an enormous emphasis on promoting racial harmony among students and teachers from different cultural backgrounds. The following are some of the ideological assumptions that centurally inform this approach to racial differences in education.

Core Ideological Assumptions—(a) The United States is a culturally and ethnically diverse nation. (b) This cultural diversity has had a positive effect on the overall growth and development of America as a powerful country (King, 1980; Tiedt & Tiedt, 1986). (c) All of America's ethnic groups have in their different ways contributed to the growth and development of America (Wisconsin Department of Instruction, 1986). (d) The educational system in the past has not sufficiently fostered this multicultural view of American society, and this has contributed to prejudice and discrimination against certain ethnic groups. (e) Schools and teachers must therefore positively endorse cultural diversity and foster an appreciation and respect for "human differences" in order to reduce racial tension and estrangement of minority groups in the school and in society (Tiedt & Tiedt, 1986).

Desired Outcomes—The principal expectation of those who promote the cultural understanding model of multicultural education is that American schools will be oriented towards the "cultural enrichment of all students" (Gibson, 1984, p. 99). It is assumed that teachers will provide such enrichment in their classrooms. By fostering understanding and acceptance of cultural differences in the classroom and in the school curriculum, it is expected that educational programs based on the cultural understanding approach will contribute toward the elimination of prejudice (Baker, 1977).

Commentary—Proponents of cultural understanding models of multicultural education attach enormous significance to the role of attitudes in the reproduction of racism. Human relations and ethnic studies programs based on this approach pursue what Banks (1981) called the "prejudiceless goal." The strong version of these program directly targets white students and teachers. White students and teachers are portrayed as the flawed protagonists in their racial relations with blacks and Native Americans. It is expected that negative white attitudes towards minorities will change if these prejudiced individuals are exposed to sensitivity training in human relations programs. The weak version of the cultural understanding approach emphasizes the promotion of racial harmony and tolerance of social and ethnic differences.

Various pre-test/post-test evaluations of multicultural education and human relations programs that emphasize attitudinal change and cultural understanding suggest that these programs have not been very successful in achieving their espoused goal of eliminating majority/minority prejudice. For instance, though in her evaluation of the University of Michigan's human relations program Baker (1973) claims modest changes in white "pro-irrational attitudes" (p. 307), these changes are not reported in the critical area of black/white relations. Thus, according to Baker, the Michigan students' perceptions of blacks remained at the "pretest level" and were not significantly changed by their participation in the university's human relations program: "No statistically significant differences obtained on the black anti-irrational or pro-irrational subscales. Therefore it can be concluded that the change in the perception of blacks held by the (white) students remained fairly constant" (p. 307).

Like Baker, Fish (1981) reports findings of "no significant effects" in his study of the impact of the field experience component of Wisconsin's human relations program on white students' perceptions of blacks and other disadvantaged groups. According to Fish:

> Students who completed a fieldwork experience did not over a semester's time show significantly greater positive attitudes towards the population worked with than students who did not complete a fieldwork experience. (p. xi).

Indeed, Fish indicates a worsening of attitudes towards blacks during the course of the Wisconsin program:

> One semester after completion of a fieldwork experience, subjects' attitudes towards the mentally retarded and the physically disabled persisted at the pre-test level, whereas subjects' attitudes towards black significantly worsened from the pre-test level. (p. xii).

But Fish is not alone in his findings of unanticipated negative effects of attitudinal change programs. Buckingham (1984) draws similar conclusions in his case study of responses to "The Whites of Their Eyes"—a Thames Television educational program on "Racism in the British media." In his study of the responses of "a number of groups of London school pupils to the program," Buckingham drew the following conclusions:

> In general, for instance, pupils failed to perceive that the programme was concerned with racism in the media, and this led many to assume that the programme was suggesting that all white people are racist. Likewise few pupils picked up on the programme's arguments about the causes of racism, and fewer still seem to have noticed its implicit suggestions about how racism might be eradicated. While the programme provides a fairly clear historical context for the discussion of racism, pupils generally failed to make connections between this and the examples of racism in the media today. (Buckingham, 1984, p. 139).

American school critics have raised other concerns about attitudinal change and cultural understanding programs. Writers such as Pettigrew (1974) and Garcia (1974) have argued that the content and methods of these programs are significantly flawed. Pettigrew (1974), Garcia (1974), and Kleinfield (1974) point to the tendency of proponents of cultural understanding models to over-emphasize the difference among ethnic groups, neglecting the differences within any one group. They also draw attention to the unintended effect of stereotyping which results from multicultural approaches that treat ethnic groups as "monolithic entities possessing uniform, discernible traits" (Gibson, 1984, p. 100). For instance, Garcia contends that advocates of cultural understanding models tend to discuss: "Chicano culture as if it were a set of values and customs possessed by all who are categorized as Chicanos or Mexican Americans . . . This fallacy serves to create the new stereotype which is found in the completion of the statement, Mexican American children are . . ." (quoted in Gibson, 1984, p. 100).

The rather disturbing and contradictory findings of Baker (1974), Fish (1981), and Buckingham (1984), and the complaints about methods and content raised by minority educators such as Garcia (1974) have cast doubt on the educational and practical value of cultural understanding approaches to racial differences in schooling. Some proponents of multicultural education have therefore suggested different curriculum and instructional approaches to race relations in school. These curriculum theorists, led by educators such as Banks (1981, 1988) assert that all students should be able to demonstrate cultural competence in the language and cultural practices of ethnic groups other than their own.

Models of cultural competence

Underpinning the cultural competence approach to multicultural education is a fundamental assumption that values of cultural pluralism should have a central place in the school curriculum. This concept of social institutions as representing a plurality of ethnic interests was first formulated by liberal social scientists such as Riesman, Glazer, and Denny (1969) and Glazer and Moynihan (1963). Some educators such as Banks (1973, 1981), Cortes (1973), Pettigrew (1974), and Gollnick (1980), contend that there is a general lack of cross-cultural competencies, especially in the area of language, among minority and majority groups in the American populace. These educators argue for various forms of bilingual, bicultural, and ethnic studies programs based on pluralist values. These programs aim at preserving cultural diversity in the United States, particularly the language and identity of minority groups such as blacks. Hispanics, and Native Americans. Banks summarizes this pluralist approach to ethnic differences in the following terms:

> The pluralist argues that ethnicity and ethnic identities are very important in American society. The United States, according to the pluralist, is made up of competing ethnic groups, each of which champions its economic and political interests. It is extremely important, argues the pluralist, for the individual to develop a commitment to his or her ethnic group, especially if that ethnic group is "oppressed" by more powerful ethnic groups within American society. (p. 62).

The American Association of Colleges for Teacher Education (AACTE) in its often-cited "No One American Model" also makes a particularly strong case for cultural pluralism in education. AACTE maintains that:

> Multicultural education is education which values cultural pluralism. Multicultural education rejects the view that schools should merely tolerate cultural pluralism. Instead, multicultural education affirms that schools should be oriented toward the cultural enrichment of all children and youth through programs rooted to the preservation and extension of cultural alternatives. Multicultural education recognizes cultural diversity as a fact of life in American society, and it affirms that this cultural diversity is a valuable resource that should be preserved and extended. It affirms that major education institutions should strive to preserve and enhance cultural pluralism. (AACTE, 1973, p. 264).

Proponents of multicultural education as cultural competence such as the AACTE's Commission on Multicultural Education (1973) argue that multicultural in education should mean more than the fostering of cultural understanding and awareness about America's ethnic groups. They argue that "teachers (should) help students develop ethnic identities, knowledge about different cultural groups ... and competence in more than one cultural system" (Gram & Sleeter, 1985, p. 101). By integrating the language and culture of a plurality of ethnic groups into the curriculum, proponents argue that teachers can help to "build bridges" between America's different ethnic groups (Sleeter & Grant, 1986, p. 4). The target population of this cultural competence approach to multicultural education is mainly minority students. It is expected that minority students will develop competence in the "public culture" and the skills and the attitudes of the dominant white society (Lewis, 1976, p. 35). This familiarity with mainstream culture must not take place at the expense of the minority student's own ethnic heritage—a difficult balancing act indeed.

Core Ideological Assumption—The cultural competence approach to multicultural education is underpinned by some basic assumptions about race relations in education and society in the United States. The following are some of the principal ideological assumptions and values of the cultural competence approach: (a) Previous assimilationist approaches to education, which characterized the United States as a melting pot of ethnic groups, actually helped to foster the hegemony of Anglo values. This has led to the virtual subordination or exclusion of minority culture from the American mainstream (Banks, 1981; Commission on Multicultural Education, 1973). (b) Cross-cultural interaction through bilingual/bicultural education programs will help to guarantee the survival of minority language and minority culture (Banks, 1981: Cortes, 1973; Ramirez and Castenada, 1974). (c) Cross-cultural interaction between America's ethnic groups is regarded as a powerful antidote to the racial prejudice that continues to limit the presence of blacks, Hispanies, and Native Americans in America's mainstream (Grant & Sleeter, 1989).

Desired Outcomes—Proponents of the cultural competence approach to multicultural education champion a pluralism which has as its principal objective the preservation of minority language and culture. Bicultural and bilingual programs associated with this cultural competence approach aim to prepare minority students for their social and cultural negotiation with dominant white mainstream society. At the same time, it is expected that white students will also acquire knowledge and familiarity with the language and culture of minority groups. It is felt that such cross-cultural interaction will contribute to reduce antagonism between majority and minority ethnic groups.

Commentary—Proponents of the cultural competence approach to multicultural education have attempted to develop programs that go beyond cultural awareness and attitudinal change. This approach to multiculturalism is particularly critical of earlier compensatory education programs, such as Headstart, which worked centrally on the assumption that minority students were "culturally deficient." Instead, proponents of models of cross-cultural competence valorize minority cultural heritage and language and argue for the meaningful inclusion in the curriculum of "aspects of minority culture that a teacher could build on" (Sleeter & Grant, p. 4).

But the emphasis on cultural competence as a set of curricular strategies for enhancing minority negotiation with mainstream society precipitates a central contradiction. On the one hand, the affirmation of minority culture in various bilingual, bicultural, and ethnic studies programs represents a direct challenge to the centrality of Anglo values in the school curriculum and the notion that minority culture and language are "naturally" deficient (McCarthy, 1988, Banks, 1988). On the other, the closely related objective of "building bridges" (Sleeter & Grant, 1986, p. 4) from minority groups to mainstream society privileges individual mobility over a collective identity politics oriented toward change in the current structure of race relations in schools and society. As such the cultural competence approach to multiculturalism has a significant unintended consequence. Attempts to have minority students learn how to cross over to the language and culture of the Anglo mainstream also commit these students to a trajectory that leads towards incorporation and assimilation—an educational and social result that is antithetical to one of the principal concerns of biculturalism—the valorization and preservation of minority cultural identity.

In sum then, despite the emphasis on diversity within the cultural competence model, the minority child is just like anybody else's, free to make his or her choices in the marketplace of culture, ethnicity, and heritage. As Banks (1987) argues, "[Minority and majority] students need to learn that there are cultural and ethnic alternatives within our society that they can freely embrace" (1987, p. 12). Presumably, the responsibility that the enterprising minority youth undertakes in exchange for his participation in the cultural market is that of respecting the society's institutions and the rules that make them "work" for those in the American mainstream.

Within recent years, challenges to the cultural understanding and cultural competence approaches to multiculturalism have led to the reformulation and reconceptualization of multicultural perspectives on racial inequality in education. Proponents of multicultural education such as Suzuki (1984) and Swartz (1988) link the current demands for multiculturalism to a more reformist policy discourse of cultural emancipation and social reconstruction. It is this policy discourse that I would now like to discuss.

Models of cultural emancipation and social reconstruction

Like proponents of curriculum and educational policies of cultural understanding and cultural competence, educators who promote the idea of cultural emancipation within the framework of multiculturalism attach a positive value to minority culture (Grant & Sleeter, 1989; Suzuki, 1984; Swartz, 1989). These educators argue that multiculturalism in education can promote the cultural emancipation and social amelioration of minority youth in two vital ways. First, proponents of emancipatory multiculturalism argue that the fostering of universal respect for the individual ethnic history, culture, and language of the plurality of students to be found in American schools would have a positive effect on individual minority self-concepts. Positive self-concepts should in turn help to boost achievement among minority youth (Bullivant, 1981). This first set of claims therefore retraces some of the ground of the cultural deprivation theorists in that it is suggested that minority students do poorly in school because of their lack of self-esteem, among other things. But proponents of emancipatory multiculturalism add a new twist. They link the issue of minority underachievement in the classroom to the attitudinal prejudice of teachers and the suppression of minority culture in the school curriculum. These reformist educators then argue that a reversal in teacher attitudes and curriculum and instructional policies that suppress minority cultural identities would have a positive effect on minority school achievement. Individual minority school performance would improve since such students would be motivated by a multicultural curriculum and classroom environment in which teachers and students treated minority culture and experiences with respect (Olneck, 1989). For example, Swartz (1988) insists that students who come from family backgrounds in which ethnic pride and identity are emphasized are likely to do well in school, or at least better than those who do not:

A curriculum which values diverse cultures in an equitable way is self-affirming . . . It makes a statement to students about the importance of their present and future roles as participants and contributors to society. Research findings by Cummins (1984) and Ogbu (1978) point out that significant school failure does not occur in cultural groups that are positively oriented toward both their own and others' cultures. These students demonstrate a higher educational success rate. (p. 6).

The second conceptual strand of this emancipatory agenda is related to the first, but more directly links race relations in the classroom to the economy. Proponents of multicultural education as an emancipatory program suggest that improved academic achievement would help minority youth break the cycle of missed opportunity created by a previous biography of cultural deprivation. The labor market is expected to verify emancipatory multicultural programs by absorbing large numbers of qualified minority youth. This thesis of a "tightening bond" between multicultural education and the economy is summarized in the following claim by James Rushton (1981).

The curriculum in the multicultural school should encourage each pupil to succeed wherever he or she can and strive for competence in what he or she tries. Cultural taboos should be lessened by mutual experience and under-standings. The curriculum in the multicultural school should allow these things to happen. If it does, it need have no fear about the future career of its pupils. (Rushton, 1981, p. 169).

This emancipatory or "benevolent" type of approach to multicultural education (Gibson 1984: Troyna & Williams, 1986) rests, in part, on an earlier curriculum philosophy of "social resconstructionism." Like earlier curriculum theorists such as Rugg (1932) and Counts (1932), proponents of the emancipatory approach to multiculturalism offer the powerful ideology of the "quiet revolution." They suggest that cultural and social changes in minority fortunes are possible if the school curriculum is redefined in response to the needs of minority youth (Grant & Sleeter, 1989; Troyna & Williams, 1986).

Ideological Core Assumptions—Proponents of emancipatory multiculturalism operate on some basic assumptions about the role of education in the reproduction and transformation of race relations. These assumptions can be summarized as follows: (a) There is a fundamental mismatch between the school curriculum and the life experiences and cultural backgrounds of American minority youth (Swartz, 1988). (b) This mismatch exists because schools privilege white middle-class values while simultaneously suppressing the culture of minority youth (Williams, 1982). (c) Thus, schools play a critical role in the production of differential educational opportunities and life chances for minority and majority youth. (d) Educators should help to redress this pattern of inequality by embarking upon multicultural curricular reform that would provide equality of opportunity for academic success for minority students.

Desired Outcomes—A genuine multicultural curriculum which includes knowledge about minority history and cultural achievements would reduce the dissonance and alienation from academic success that centrally characterizes minority experiences in schooling in the United States. Such a reformed school curriculum is expected to enhance minority opportunities for academic success and better futures in the labor market. And, in keeping with this thesis, employers are expected to allocate jobs on the basis of market-rational criteria, namely, the credentials and academic qualifications of prospective employees (Bullivant, 1981; Rushton, 1981).

Commentary—Proponents of an emancipatory approach to multicultural education offer a "language of possibility" (Giroux, 1985) with respect to the school curriculum—a language that is not present within earlier assimilationist frameworks. In an ideological sense, such a multicultural program allows for the possibility that the scope of current school knowledge would be "enlarged" to include the radical diversity of knowledge, histories, and experiences of marginalized ethnic groups. It is possible, for example, that radical ideas associated with minority quests for social change would also find their way into the discourse of the classroom (Olneck, 1983).

In addition, the powerfully attractive "social reconstructionist" theme running throughout the thesis of emancipatory multiculturalism raises the issue of inequality in the job market itself. Models of cultural understanding or cultural competence tend not to venture so far beyond the textbook, the classroom, and the school.

However, radical school theorists have, with good reason, criticized the tendency of these multicultural proponents to lean toward an unwarranted optimism about the impact of the multicultural curriculum on the social and economic futures of minority students (McLaren & Dantley, in press; Mullard, 1985; Troyna & Williams, 1986). Indeed, the linear connection asserted by multicultural education proponents between educational credentials and the economy is problematic. The assumption that higher educational attainment and achievement via a more sensitive curriculum would lead to a necessary conversion into jobs for black and minority youth is frustrated by the existence of racial practices in the job market itself. Troyna (1984) and Blackburn and Mann (1979), in their incisive analyses of the British job market, explode the myth that there is a necessary "tightening bond" between education and the economy. In his investigation of the fortunes of "educated" black and white youth in the job market. Troyna (1984) concludes that racial and social connections, rather than educational qualifications per se, "determined" the phenomenon of better job chances for white youth even when black youth had higher qualifications than their white counterparts. The tendency of employers to rely on informal channels or "word of mouth" networks, and the greater likelihood that white youth would be in a position to exploit such networks, constitute one of the principal ways in which the potential for success of qualified black youth in the labor market is systematically undermined. Of course, Carmichael and Hamilton (1967) and Marable (1983) have made similar arguments about the racial disqualification of black youth in the job market in the United States. Expanding this argument, Crichlow (1985) makes the following claim:

> In combination with subtle forms of discrimination, job relocation, and increasing competition among workers for smaller numbers of "good" jobs, rising entry level job requirements clearly underscore the present employment difficulties experienced by young black workers. Whether they possess a high school diploma or not blacks, in this instance, continue to experience high rates of unemployment despite possessing sound educational backgrounds and potential (capital) to be productive workers.

Besides the issues of naivete about the racial character of the job market, further criticism can be made of the multicultural thesis. Proponents of multicultural education as an emancipatory formula tend to ignore the complex social and political relations that are constituted in the internal order of the schools. Issues of policy formation, decision-making, trade-offs, and the building of alliances for specific reformist initiatives have not really been addressed within multicultural frameworks. For these reformist educators educational change hinges almost exclusively upon the reorganization of the content of the school curriculum. But as Troyna and Williams (1986) have pointed out, attempts at the reorganization of the school curriculum to include more historically and culturally sensitive materials on minorities have not significantly affected the unequal relations that exist between blacks and whites in schools.

It is criticisms such as those advanced by Troyna and Williams that have seriously called into question the validity of liberal reformist claims about the emancipatory potential of multicultural education and its ability to positively influence minority futures in schools and society in the United States.

Conclusion

Spurred forward by minority group pressure for equality of opportunity in education and society, and by the efforts of liberal scholars to provide practical solutions to racial inequality, multicultural education became one of the most powerful educational slogans in the '70s and '80s. Federal legislation for ethnic studies and bilingual programs reinforced the state's ideological commitment to multicultural approaches to racial differences in schooling (Grant & Sleeter, 1989). A growing number of school districts and university-based teacher education preservice programs have also espoused various forms of multicultural education (Baker, 1977). In this essay, I explored the conceptual and practical claims of three approaches or discourses of multicultural education. I described these approaches as "models" of cultural understanding, cultural competence, and cultural emancipation. As we saw, each of these approaches represents a subtly different inflection on the issue of what is to be done about racial inequality in schooling. Thus, proponents of cultural understanding advocate sensitivity and appreciation of cultural differences—a model for racial harmony. Cultural competence proponents insist on the preservation of minority ethnic identity and language and "the building of bridges" between minority and mainstream culture. Finally, models of cultural emancipation go somewhat further than the previous two approaches in suggesting that a reformist multicultural curriculum can boost the school success and economic futures of minority youth.

But, as I have tried to show, these multicultural approaches to curriculum reform really do not offer viable explanations or "solutions" to the problem of racial inequality in schooling. School reform and reform in race relations within these frameworks depend almost exclusively on the reversal of values, attitudes, and the human nature of social actors understood as "individuals." Schools, for example, are not conceptualized as sites of power or contestation in which differential interests, resources, and capacities determine maneuverability of competing racial groups and the possibility of pace of change. In significant ways, too, proponents of multiculturalism fail to take into account the differential structure of opportunities that help to define minority relations to dominant white groups and social institutions in the United States. In abandoning the crucial issues of structural inequality and differential power relations, multicultural proponents end up placing an enormous responsibility on the shoulders of the classroom teacher in the struggle to transform race relations in American schools and society.

References

American Association of Colleges for Teacher Education (1974). No one model American. *Journal of Teacher, Education*, 24, 264–265.

Anti-Defamation League of B'nai B'rith (1986). *The wonderful world of difference. A human relations program for grades K-8*. New York: Anti-Defamation League of B'nai B'rith.

Baker, G. (1973, Winter). Multicultural training for student teachers. *The Journal of Teacher Education*, 24, 306–307.

Baker, G. (1977) Development of the multicultural program: School of Education. University of Michigan. In F. Klassen and D. Gollnick (Eds.), *Pluralism and the American teacher. Issues and case studies* (pp. 163–169). Washington, D.C.: Ethnic Heritage Center for Teacher Education.

Banks, J. (1972, January). Imperatives in ethnic minority education. *Phi Delta Kappan, 53*, 266–269.

Banks, J. (Ed.) (1973). *Teaching ethnic studies: Concepts and strategies*. Washington, D.C.: National Council for the Social Studies.

Banks, J. (1981). *Multiethnic education: Theory and practice*. Boston: Allyn & Bacon.

Banks, J. (1987). *Teaching strategies for ethnic studies*. Boston: Allyn & Bacon, 1988.

Banks, J. (1988). *Multiethnic education: Theory and practice*. Boston: Allyn & Bacon, 1988.

Berlowitz, M. (1984). Multicultural education: Fallacies and alternatives. In M. Berlowitz & R. Edari (Eds.), *Racism and the denial of human rights: Beyond Ethnicity* (pp. 129–136). Minneapolis: Marxism Educational Press.

Blackburn, R. & Mann, M. (1979). *The working class in the labor market*. London, MacMillan.

Buckingham. D. (1984). The whites of their eyes: A case study of responses to educational television. In M. Straker-Welds (Ed.), *Education for a multicultural society* (pp. 137–143). London: Bell & Hyman, 1984.

Bullivant, B. (1981). The pluralist dilemma in education: *Six case studies* Sydney: Allen & Unwin.

Bullivant, B. (1984). *Pluralism: Cultural maintenance and evolution*. Clevedon, England: Multilingual Matters Limited.

Carmichael, S. & Hamilton, C. (1967). *Black power*. New York: Vintage Books.

Cones, C. (1973). In J. Banks (Ed.), Teaching ethnic studies concepts and strategies. Washington, D.C.: National Council for Social Studies.

Counts, G. (1932). *Dare the school build a new social order?* New York: John Day.

Cubberley, E.P. (1909). *Changing conceptions of education*, Boston: Houghton Mifflin.

Fish, J. (1981). *The psychological impact of fieldwork experiences and cognitive dissonance upon attitude change in a human relations program. Ph.D. Dissertation. University of Wisconsin-Madison.*

Fiske, J. & Hartley, J. (1978). *Reading television*. London: Methuen.

Garcia, E. (1974). Chicano cultural diversity: Implications for competency-based teacher education. In W. Hunter (Ed.), *Multicultural education through competency-based teacher education*. Washington, D.C.: American Association of Colleges for Teacher Education.

Gibson, M. (1984). Approaches to multicultural education in the United States: Some concepts and assumptions. *Anthropology and Education Quarterly, 15*, 94–119.

Giroux, H. (1985). Introduction to P. Freire's *The politics of education*. South Hadley, Massachusetts: Harvard University Press.

Glazer, N. & Moynihan, D.P. (1963). *Ethnicity: Theory and experience*. Cambridge, Massachusetts: Harvard University Press.

Gollnick, D. (1980). Multicultural education. *Viewpoints in Teaching and Learning, 56*.

Grant, C. & Sleeter, C. (1985). The literature on multicultural education: Review and analysis. *Educational Review, 37*, 2, 97–118.

Grant, C. & Sleeter, C. (1989). *Turning on learning: Five approaches for multicultural teaching plans for race, class, gender, and disability.* Columbus: Merrill Publishing Company.

Kaestle, C. (1983). *Pillars of the republic: Common schools and American society, 1780–1860.* New York: Hill and Wang.

King, E. (1980). *Teaching ethnic awareness.* Santa Monica: Good Year.

Kleinfeld, J. (1975). Positive stereotyping: the cultural relativist in the classroom. *Human Organization, 34,* 269–274.

Kliebard. H. (1986). *The struggle for the American curriculum 1983–1958.* Boston: Routledge and Kegan Paul.

Lewis, D. (1976). The multicultural education model and minorities: Some reservations. *Anthropology and Education Quarterly, 7.*

McCarthy, C. (1988). Reconsidering liberal and radical perspectives on racial inequality in schooling. Making the case for nonsynchrony. *Harvard Educational Review 58, 2,* 265–279.

McCarthy, C. & Apple, M. (1988). Race, class and gender in American educational research: toward a non-synchronous parallelist position, in: L. Weis (Ed.), *Class, Race, and Gender in American Education* (Albany, NY, State University of New York Press).

McLaren, P. & Dantley, M. (1990). Leadership and a critical pedagogy of race: Cornel West, Stuart Hall, and the prophetic tradition, *The Journal of Negro Education,* 59(1), pp. 29–44.

Marable, M. (1983). *How Capitalism Underdeveloped Black America: Problems in Race, Political Economy, and Society* (Boston, South End Press).

Montalto, N. (1981). Multicultural education in the New York City public schools, 1919–1941, in: D. Ravitch & R. Goodenow (Eds), *Educating an Urban People: The New York City Experience* (New York, Teachers College Press).

Mullard, C. (1985). Racism in society and school: History, policy and practice, in: F. Rizvi (Ed.), *Multiculturalism and Educational Policy* (Geelong, Victoria, Deakin University Press).

Ogbu, J. (1978). *Minority Education and Caste* (New York, Academic Press).

Olneck, M. (1983). Ethnicity, Pluralism, and American schooling, Unpublished paper.

Olneck, M. (1989, March). The Recurring Dream: Symbolism and Ideology in Intercultural and Multicultural Education. Unpublished paper.

Olneck, M. & Lazerson, M. (1980). Education in: S. Thernstrom, A. Orlov & O. Hanlin (Eds), *Harvard Encyclopedia of American Ethnic Groups* (Cambridge, MA, Harvard University Press).

Omi, M. & Winant, H. (1986). *Racial Formation in the United States* (New York, Routledge and Kegan Paul).

Pettigrew, L. (1974). Competency-based teacher education: teacher training for multicultural education, in: W. Hunter (Ed.), *Multicultural Education through Competency-based Teacher Education* (Washington, DC, AACTE).

Ramirez, M. & Castenada, A. (1974). *Cultural Democracy, Bicognitive Development, and Education* (New York, Academic Press).

Riesman, D., Glazer, N. & Denney, R. (1969). *The Lonely Crowd* (New Haven, Yale University Press).

Rugg, H. (1932). Social reconstruction through education, *Progressive Education,* 9, 11–18.

Rushton, J. (1981). Careers and the multicultural curriculum, in: J. Lynch (Ed.), *Teaching in the Multicultural School* (London, Ward Lock).

Sleeter, C. & Grant, C. (1986). The literature on Multicultural Education in the USA. Paper presented at the American Educational Research Association Conference, San Francisco, April 1986.

Suzuki, B. (1984). Curriculum transformation for multicultural education. *Education and Urban Society,* 16, 294–322.

Swartz, E. (1989). *Multicultural Curriculum Development* (Rochester, New York, Rochester City School District).

Terman, L. (1916). *The Measurement of Intelligence* (Boston, Houghton Mifflin).

Tiedt, I. & Tiedt, P. (1986). *Multicultural Teaching: A Handbook of Activities, Information, and Resources* (Boston: Allyn and Bacon).

Troyna, B. (1984) Multicultural education: emancipation or containment, in: L. Barton & S. Walker (Eds), *Social Crisis and Educational Research* (pp. 75–97) (London, Croom Helm).

Troyna, B. & Williams, J. (1986). *Racism, Education and the State* (London, Croom Helm).

University of Wisconsin-Madison Steering Committee on Minority Affairs Report, 1987.

Williams, M. (1982). Multicultural/pluralistic education: Public education in America "The way it's 'spoze to be", *Clearing House*, 3, 131–135.

Wisconsin Department of Public Instruction (1986). *A Guide to Curriculum Planning in Social Studies* (Madison, WI, Wisconsin Department of Public Instruction).

CHAPTER 4

BEYOND MULTICULTURAL EDUCATION (1982)

Etta Ruth Hollins

For the past two decades a great deal of emphasis has been placed on multicultural education. During the 1960s curriculum specialists were busy developing units and course outlines for ethnic studies. By the end of the decade James Banks, at the University of Washington in Seattle, had emerged as the nation's authority. Because of the tenor of the times and the absence or misrepresentation of ethnic minorities in the curriculum ethnic studies was implemented as an appendage to the regular curriculum. During the 1970s the concept of "education that is multicultural" was popularized by Carl Grant, at the University of Wisconsin at Madison. This concept facilitated the move toward a culturally integrated curriculum. The intent of both Banks and Grant was to facilitate the development of an integrated curriculum at the elementary and secondary levels and to maintain departments of ethnic study at the college and university level. Ideally, departments of ethnic study were to promote indepth study and research related to ethnic history and culture. Regular courses at the college and university level were to reflect the total society in content.

With the introduction of multicultural education the concept of cultural pluralism replaced the "melting pot" theory. According to William L. Smith, cultural pluralism means that, "all people would retain a healthy ethnic pride, an abiding sense of their own culture, and a respect for and appreciation of people and individuals from ethnically and culturally different heritages."[1] The "melting pot" theory had held as ideal the development of a single American culture. Thus, both concepts aim at defining the direction of social change. Both concepts aim at promoting more positive intergroup relationships and ultimately increased national unity.

In a narrower sense, multicultural education had as one of its goals the improvement of the atmosphere in schools and classrooms. Teachers and pupils were expected to become more understanding and accepting of individual and group differences. It was thought that ultimately these good feelings about self and others would lead to an improvement in the classroom atmosphere that would result in the improvement of academic performance among minority pupils. The public school curriculum and curriculum materials do, indeed, more positively reflect the culture and achievements of American minorities. Classroom teachers seem to demonstrate greater understanding and acceptance of pupils from diverse cultural backgrounds. The pupils appear more accepting of each other. Although multicultural education seems to have had a positive effect on the nation's schools, however, the academic performance of some ethnic minority groups lags far behind that of others.

The failure of public schools

That public schools have failed to impart basic skills to the majority of Black, Mexican American, and poor Anglo children is a well documented fact. The reasons proposed for this failure can be categorized as: (1) the deprivation thesis: blaming the client; (2) the institutional racism thesis: blaming the professionals; (3) the cultural conflict thesis: blaming ethnic cultural differences; (4) the caste structure thesis: blaming the social structure of society; and (5) the class conflict thesis: blaming the capitalist economic system. Although each of these theses has some elements of validity and each proposes specific solutions to the problem of poor academic performance among minority and poor pupils, the condition prevails. The purpose of this paper is to examine the need for a theory of learning that is multicultural. A new theory of learning would serve to organize and clarify existing knowledge relative to the nature of learning as it relates to culture. This would provide a framework for the development and testing of culture-free and/ or culture-specific curriculum programs.

Although multicultural education has brought about many very significant curriculum improvements, it is quite apparent that the experiences, perceptions, and values are still too much that of an idealized Anglo American middle class culture. The objectives, content, and activities have been disproportionately carved out of the Anglo American experience. The images contained in the materials used in the classroom too much symbolize the Anglo American experience, and too little the experiences of other Americans.[2] Given this situation, the assumption that existing curricula are suitable for all children in the American society, and that the rate and degree of acquisition and mastery of what is presenting in school is primarily dependent on the pupils' intellectual ability and maturation, is a disregard for difference in experience, preception, and values. This assumption seems to be predicated on the belief that what is good for the majority is good for the minority, even if it fails to produce the desired outcomes. Contained in this notion is a basic disregard for culture.

How one learns how to learn

According to Edward T. Hall, "How one learns is culturally determined, as is what one learns."[3] Culture teaches one how to intake, output, store, retrieve, and attend to information, as well as how to interact with other human beings. These behaviors are learned through participation in the customs, rituals, folkways, and mores of a culture. Because of different practices within cultures, groups develop different perceptual and performance strengths.[4] A careful analysis of schools and classrooms where Black pupils experience high levels of academic achievement shows that these schools reflect the participation models found in the culture outside the school.[5]

Cultural bias in theories of learning

Theories of learning are basic to curriculum development. The cultural bias found in theories of learning serves to impede progress in multicultural education. Because culture is such a dominant theme, it generally cannot be ignored. The concept of culture is generally addressed in learning theory at some point and the theorist takes either an implict or explicit position relative to the direction of social change. Unfortunately, most learning theory is consistent with the "melting pot" theory, thus, antithetical to the concept of cultural pluralism.

B. F. Skinner asserts that "the culture constructs special contingencies to promote thinking. It teaches a person to make fine discriminations by making differential reinforcement more precise. It teaches techniques to use in solving problems. It provides rules that make it unnecessary to expose a person to the contingencies from which the rules derive, and it provides rules for finding rules."[6] Although Skinner perceives that culture does, in fact, determine how and what an individual learns, his view is consistent with the "melting pot" theory. Skinner believes that man can be engineered toward a single perfect culture. Skinner has attempted to develop a master plan for such a utopian society.

According to James Mangan, Piaget is "the strongest current proponent of the existence of universal processes of thought . . .," yet, he "discusses two of the 'main' cultural factors of educational transmission: educational activities of adults (as they affect children) and language itself. He has further remarked that cultural differences in classification are due to language differences . . ."[7] It seems probable that cultural differences in classification systems, regardless of derivation, have serious implications for teaching and learning. All that a child learns prior to entering school is contained in this culture-specific classification system. If this is true, it seems imperative that a multicultural curriculum include activities designed to build on the system already familiar to the pupils, rather than attempt to teach a new classification system.

Although the existence of cultural differences is recognized, according to H. G. Furth, Piaget's theory "does not take account of differences but rather focuses on what is common and biologically characteristic of human intelligence."[8] As Furth suggests, Piaget's focus on commonalities in the characteristics of human learning may be a process to expedite study and understanding; however, the consequence is that, when applied to curriculum development, it translates into the "melting pot" theory. It is often incorrectly concluded that the age ranges in Piaget's stages of development are fixed and are not altered by cultural experiences had by the pupils. Mangan points out that "fundamental values and beliefs which vary culturally can also affect cognitive testing. Far from remaining free from cultural bias, tests for conservation and formal operations reflect notions of validity conveyed by modern scientific paradigms, themselves cultural conventions."[9]

It has already been established that a child enters school with an existing knowledge classification system or structure. David P. Ausubel states, ". . . the structure of a student's existing knowledge is regarded as the crucial factor influencing new learning, retention, and problem solving. Only in so far as it is possible to enhance the organizational strength of this structure is it possible to increase the functional retention of new subject-matter knowledge, both as end in itself and for purposes of problem solving."[10] Ausubel further points out, ". . . the various individual meanings possessed by members of a given culture are ordinarily sufficiently similar to permit communication and interpersonal understanding. This intracultural homogeneity of shared meanings reflects both the same logical meaning inherent in potentially meaningful propositions and the interindividual commonality of ideational background."[11] Ausubel fails to explain further that much of the "intracultural homogeneity of shared meanings" is frequently lost in cross-cultural interactions. It is the lack of shared meanings that in part explains the failure of public schools to educate minorities and the poor. The curriculum must be constructed so as to develop a system of shared meanings by provided representations of culture-specific or cultural-free meanings upon which to build these shared meanings. This would allow each cultural group to maintain its specific system of meaning, yet, participate in expressing ideas through the use of meanings shared across cultures.

Although learning theorists seem to generally recognize the significance of culture in how learning takes place, it is not certain that any of the theories actually embrace the cultural pluralism concept. Ausubel probably comes closer to explaining the culture-specific nature of learning than do the others. This points out the need to develop a theory of learning that is pluralistic in nature and can be applied in a multicultural setting and not conflict with the established learning set of the children from different cultural backgrounds.

Directing the development of multicultural education

Even before the concept of cultural pluralism was introduced, there was an abundance of research on the schooling of various ethnic groups. There is especially a tremendous volume of research on teaching Black and Mexican American pupils. The next step in the process of multicultural education appears to be the development of a theory of learning that would order, clarify, and give meaning to the presently isolated findings.

Those who propose new multicultural theories of learning must be able to identify the cultural bias that exists in the research, to explain its existence and its impact on the development and practices of multicultural education. The theorists must be able to order and clarify the existing research to provide provisional explanations for observed events and relationships in the education of people of diverse cultural backgrounds. A good theory of multicultural education will organize existing knowledge and present a framework for the prediction of what is not yet known about learning and culture.

A new multicultural theory of learning must explain whether learning can be culture-free and/or culture-specific. The learning theory needs to establish a culture-free or culture-specific framework for predicting the potential effectiveness of specific curriculum and instructional strategies for specific groups of pupils. The theorists must provide general principles concerning the relationship between culture and learning that are testable.

In conclusion, because theories of learning direct curriculum development, instruction, and teacher education, the life and permanence of multicultural education is contingent upon the development of a viable and testable learning theory that is multicultural. As important as it is to the survival of the nation and its schools, without a theory of learning multicultural education is certain to disappear in the archives of education along with numerous other fads.

Notes

1 Carl A. Grant, Editor, *Multicultural Education: Commitments, Issues, and Applications* (Washington, D.C.: Association for Supervision and Curriculum Development, 1977), p. 40.
2 Gary D. Borich, Marilynn M. Kash, and Fred D. Kemp, *What the Teacher Effectiveness Research Has to Say About Teaching Practices and Student Performance* (Austin, Texas: Southwest Educational Development Laboratory, 1979).
3 Edward T. Hall, *Beyond Culture* (Garden City, New York: Anchor Books, 1977), p. 190.
4 G. S. Lesser, G. Fifer, and D. H. Clark, "Mental Abilities of Children from Different Social-Class and Cultural Groups," *Monographs of the Society for Research in Child Development*, vol. 30, no. 4 (1965).

5   Etta Ruth Hollins, "The Marva Collins Story Revisited: Implications for Regular Classroom Instruction," *The Journal of Teacher Education*, vol. 33, no. 1 (January-February 1982).

6   B. F. Skinner, "All the World's a Box," *Psychology Today*, vol. 5, no. 3 (August 1971), p. 171.

7   James Mangan, "Piaget's Theory and Cultural Difference," *Human Development*, vol. 21, no. 3 (1978), p. 171.

8   H. G. Furth, "Piaget, IQ and the Nature-Nurture Controversy," *Human Development*, vol. 16, no. 1–2 (1973), p. 65.

9   James Mangan, "Piaget's Theory and Cultural Differences," *Human Development*, vol. 1. no. 3 (1978), p. 171.

10 David P. Ausubel, *The Psychology of Meaningful Verbal Learning* (New York: Grune & Stratton, 1963), p. 76.

11 David P. Ausubel, *The Psychology of Meaningful Verbal Learning* (New York: Grune & Stratton, 1963), p. 41.

CHAPTER 5

CONTINUING DILEMMAS, DEBATES, AND DELIGHTS IN MULTICULTURAL LITERATURE (1996)

Violet J. Harris

Several months ago, I was in Washington, D.C. for a presentation to the local reading council. As I prepared my overheads, books, and handouts for the speech, the waitress, who had served my breakfast earlier, passed the table where I was working. She stopped in her tracks and inquired if the books were for sale. *Cool Salsa* (Carlson, 1994), a collection of bilingual, Latina/o poetry, captured her attention. She was disappointed when I told her that it wasn't for sale. We talked and she told me that she was from South America, had two sons, and enjoyed reading books in English to them. She also wanted bilingual or Spanish-language books for her sons so they would remain bilingual.

Our conversation continued. She inquired about places to purchase books like *Cool Salsa, Family Pictures* (Garza, 1990). I gave her a short list of books and bookstores and told her that many booksellers would be willing to order the books if they were not in stock. She was quite happy with this information and returned to her work.

I thought about her curiosity, joy, and desire to purchase the books. I had with me some poetry books that were excerpted from *A Chorus of Cultures* (1993), edited by Alma Flor Ada, Lee Bennett Hopkins, and me. I went back to the restaurant and gave her one of the mini-anthologies, *I'll Tell You Something*. She was quite happy because I highlighted poems available in Spanish and English.

This kind of exchange happens frequently and symbolizes one delight in working with multicultural literature. When individuals find literature that captures and sustains their attention, they have the opportunity to experience the world through the written word. Examples such as the aforementioned inspire those who advocate using multicultural literature when it seems as if the opposition, backlash, and debates about multicultural literature garner the majority of attention and its continued existence is questionable. In the following pages, I identify and evaluate some of those dilemmas, debates, and delights.

DILEMMAS AND DEBATES

In 1986, author Walter Dean Myers wrote an article entitled, "I Actually Thought We Would Revolutionize the Industry," which appeared in the *New York Times* (1986). Myers explained that his stories stemmed from a particular cultural milieu, Harlem, and argued that Harlem's children have a right to read stories depicting their lives and experiences:

I write books for children, filled with the images I've accumulated over the years, with stories I've heard from my father and my grandfather. Many take place in the Harlem of my youth. The names of boyhood friends, Binky, Light Billy, Clyde, creep into the stories, and memories of them and of summer days playing endless games of stoopball next to the Church of the Master on Morningside Avenue keep the stories ever alive for me. I'm drawn to the eternal promise of childhood, and the flair of the young for capturing the essence of life. (Myers, 1986, p. 50)

Myers assumed that revolutionary effects would occur because he and other authors with corresponding views created stories for children:

I understood, and I know the others did too, that it was not only for black children that we wrote. We were writing for the white child and the Asian child too. My books did well and so did the books of other black writers. Tom Feelings was being published, and so were John Steptoe, Moneta Barnett and Carole Byard. Things were looking up. I believed that my children and their contemporaries would have strong, positive images as well. And, though I was not happy with all the titles being published, the quality of the books written by blacks in the 70's was so outstanding that I actually thought we would revolutionize the industry, bring to it a quality and dimension that would raise the standard for all children's books. Wrong. Wrong. Wrong. (Myers, 1986, p. 50)

The limited number of books published in the early 1980s was not enough to sustain the "revolutionary" intentions of Myers, Steptoe, and others. Sims (1985) documented the meager output; less than two percent of children's books featured African Americans by the mid-eighties. Comparable numbers existed for other racial groups. This ebb and flow continues today. Publishers did respond to the entreaties for more multicultural books in the late 1980s and early 1990s so that currently the percentage is greater than the two percent reported by Sims for the late 1980s.

Myers (1995) continues to assert the right of the author to draw upon personal memories and experiences as the wellsprings for creativity. Harlem, Chicago's "Bronzeville," East Los Angeles, El Paso, San Francisco's Chinatown, and other segregated residential areas inspire and nurture creativity in individuals that leads to exceptional literature, art, music, and dance. Recognizing and appreciating the artistry and cultural products emanating from these enclaves requires a leap of faith or cognition that is nearly impossible for some. Further, arguing that the artists and their work will appeal to European American children is viewed as ludicrous by some. Instead, rap music becomes "black noise" rather than a legitimate art form; bilingual poetry requires too much effort to read; and picture books about the internment of Japanese Americans seem too impolite a topic to share in a social studies class.

Myers tackled the opposition of some teachers and librarians to his insistence that Black literature deserves placement in classrooms and libraries. These professionals are not ogres, but are probably the teacher or librarians in the room next door. According to Myers, they simply do not believe the stories, cannot find any literary merit within them, or perceive that there is no connection to the lives of their European American students. Why and how do they "get away" with such actions? Quite simply, so many others share their views.

The literary and artistic standards about which Myers wrote have been raised. Many more authors and illustrators have joined the ranks of those listed by Myers, and a recognizable demand for the books exists. Yet, a revolution has not occurred. We still muddle along and wrestle with several dilemmas.

Definitions

First, confusion exists about how to refer to members of a group: Black or African American, Chicano/a or Mexican American, gals or women, deaf or hearing impaired and so forth. That the groups are not monolithic should be obvious, but many deny that reality and resort to stereotypes or sweeping generalities. Not so long ago, "nigra," "jap," "injun," and "gimp" were common terms in print and electronic media. Some individuals slip occasionally and use the epithets and feign ignorance about the negative reactions generated by their use. Naming is clearly political and indicative of the power (or lack of it) wielded by a group. Hyphenating "American" may symbolize the double (or multiple for a few) consciousness, the "warring" of souls articulated by W. E. B. Du Bois. Perhaps it is best to allow individuals or groups to self-identify in the manner they wish.

The terms "minority" and "non-white" engender similar considerations. I tend not to use these terms; several factors account for this decision. Minority always seemed to imply inferiority. Non-white acquires an absurdity that could become comical if the same method were used to make other distinctions—non-males, for example. Virginia Hamilton offered the term "parallel cultures" as a replacement for minority cultures. This seemed less hierarchical and more accurate. I adopted this term rather than minority cultures.

Other terms—for example, race and ethnicity—evoke similar linguistic conundrums. Race and ethnicity are not synonymous. However, the historic development of academic studies that focused on race issues resulted in their being tagged with the label "ethnic." The conflating of race and ethnicity is evident also in the terms multiethnic and multicultural. Here, multiethnic refers to groups such as those of African, Asian/Pacific Islander, Latino/a, or Native American ancestry. In contrast, multicultural can include race, ethnicity, gender, class, and other elements that denote difference.

Culture, too, embodies a multitude of meanings. Culture as used in this article refers to beliefs, attitudes, values, world-views, institutions, artifacts, processes, interactions, and ways of behaving. It is not static but occasionally fluid and flexible; other times, it seems unyielding and stifling.

Second, no consensus exists about definitions and conceptions of multiculturalism. Should the focus remain on race, gender, and class? Is a more expansive conception required that includes disability, linguistic variation, sexual orientation, religion, and other categories of difference?

Consider the comments of one of my undergraduates last semester. As a Jewish person, she wanted to understand why Judaism was included in multicultural listings and other religions were excluded or mentioned briefly. She argued that Judaism was not a culture but a religion. I agreed that Judaism was a religion and noted that Judaism's adherents were not monolithic: Eshkenazy/Sephardic; conservative/reformed/orthodox; Ethiopian/Russian/Brooklynite, for example. I also argued that one could consider Judaism a culture. Individuals in these groups share a common religion, but other cultural markers—language, world views, geographic location, gender—differ and influence the practice of Judaism.

I was not born a multiculturalist. My support for the ideology emerged gradually and remains in a state of flux. I came to support some of the tenets of multiculturalism because I strongly valued and argued for the inclusion of African American literature and history in curricula. When individuals from other groups tacitly or overtly inquired about arguing for their group's inclusion, I was pushed towards multiculturalism. My struggles with conceptions of multiculturalism are evident in my past and emerging attitudes about literature featuring gays and lesbians.

Some years ago, a colleague inquired if I included books about gays and lesbians in my multicultural literature course. Mainly, my students read multiethnic literature with some attention to Appalachian Whites and Jewish people. I wanted to focus more on ethnic literature because racism, in all its manifestations, remains one of the most significant issues facing the country. If the multiethnic literature incorporated characters or themes unique to gays and lesbians, then it was included, for example, Jacqueline Woodson's *The Dear One* (1993). However, the presence of gay and lesbian characters was not the main consideration.

Other reasons, such as discomfort and my perception that many gays and lesbians did not agitate for the equality of other groups in a public manner, shaped my decision. I was somewhat angered by gays and lesbians who adopted the symbols and rhetoric of the modern civil rights movement. I had parallel concerns for other groups listed under the multicultural umbrella. Was I being homophobic and bigoted? Self-reflection and self-criticism suggested that I was. Still, the battle for including literature featuring gays and lesbians was one I did not wish to shoulder. I wanted to see and read about more gay and lesbian authors, poets, and illustrators "coming out of the closet" and enduring the opposition that those agitating for ethnic literature have borne.

I reasoned that sociocultural conditions existed that allowed gays and lesbians to highlight other identities they possessed without having to reveal their orientation. They could assume identities based in gender, occupation, region of birth, and so forth. Basically, they could "pass" as straights. Many people of color cannot shed their racial identities and exist as writer, poet, artist, editor, or reviewer. In time, my dogmatism about the issue lessened as self-criticism suggested that if I wanted others to share multiethnic literature, then I should also practice what I preached. The struggle to come to terms with the matter has not been easy. Over the years, I read essays written by bell hooks, Cornell West, Angela Davis, and Audre Lourde in which they argued for inclusiveness in human rights struggles. Gradually, my attitudes began to change. Their writings urged analysis of the ways in which an individual embodies many identities that are fluid and which exert influence in everchanging ways. Because of these changes, I now include books such as *Deliver Us From Evie* (Kerr, 1994), and discuss the historic development of gay and lesbian literature, including the appearance of the ground-breaking anthology, *Am I Blue?* (Bauer, 1994).

Authorial strictures

Another related and major dilemma is our demand that authors of literature we label multicultural create characters who are "role models." The stories must either uplift and inspire or correct and usurp stereotypic works. Positive images are preferred and deemed crucial. Novels that include lessons that inform readers of the group's history and on-going struggles are a preferred type of didacticism. Many factors account for the emphasis that many readers, critics, parents, and others place on sociopolitical concerns. Books with stereotypes, inaccuracies, and hurtful sections remain in publication and available for distribution. Textbook authors may only include cursory examinations of crucial events in a group's history. Consider the treatment of Rosa Parks' involvement in the Montgomery Bus Boycott in elementary and secondary social studies with the treatment included in her children's autobiography (Parks, 1992). Textbooks tend to depict her as an apolitical individual who acted on the spur of the moment. In contrast, her autobiography documents her family's liberatory stance, her long-term involvement with the NAACP, and her participation in the Highlander Center, a training site for those engaged in nonviolent political action.

We cannot compel an author to assume the mantle of defender of the race, gender, class, or other elements of difference. Most want an outlet for their creativity. A few accept the mantle willingly without compromising standards of excellence. Eloise Greenfield (1975) presented an eloquent statement of her responsibilities as a writer. Among the responsibilities she listed were the provision of entertainment as well as the desire to inspire pride in one's race. Milton Meltzer (Saul, 1994) aptly demonstrated that the author's social responsibilities need not sacrifice artistic truth or beauty.

Virginia Hamilton (1993) created the category "liberation literature" for her attempts to imbue the reader with a literary experience that entertained and transformed:

> Books of mine such as *Many Thousand Gone, Anthony Burns*, and *The People Could Fly*, I term Liberation Literature. In this literature, the reader travels with the character in the imagined world of the book and bears witness to the characters' trials and suffering and triumphs. To the extent that the protagonist finds liberty, so too does the witness, the reader, recognize the struggle as a personal one and perceive a spiritual sense of freedom. (p. 375)

Greenfield, Meltzer, and Hamilton create many works that appeal to children while maintaining fidelity to their personal philosophies and refusing to compromise literary excellence.

Bemusement and a measure of anger characterize the response of a few authors placed in the multicultural category. Allen Say (1991), for instance, has written about his discomfort with "identity" issues:

> I was 35 when my first children's book was published. *Dr. Smith's Safari* (1972) had a cast of wild animals; a gang of faceless teenagers; and an obese, middle-aged white hunter with an enormous nose and gun—not an Oriental in sight. My reasoning was that I wanted to shine as a nondenominational artist and be recognized for my abilities, not for my heritage. A commendable sense of fair play and sportsmanship. And what hogwash! (p. 45)

Say discussed further how he reconciled his heritage with his artistic sensibilities and the expectations of others. Artistic and literary excellence are the primary concerns of Say, not his or his readers' race or ethnicity.

Authenticity

One of the more divisive questions relates to authenticity and authorial freedom. Can a person write about another culture? And how authentic are the resulting portrayals? A sampling of opinions from the *Horn Book Magazine* of March/ April 1995 capture conflicting perspectives. Writer Thelma Seto declared:

> I feel very strongly that it is morally wrong for Euro-American writers to "steal" from other cultures in order to jump on the multicultural bandwagon, unless they have direct, personal experience in the country where that culture originates—more than simply being a tourist doing research in the library. ... I find it personally terrifying to live in a society where racist misrepresentations of non-Europeans are considered cute or funny or even poetic, either at the front door on Halloween or between book covers on our children's bookshelves ... what better way to control the image of "otherness" than to define the cultural discourse by representing everyone yourself and silencing those who demand the right to represent themselves? (pp. 169–170)

In contrast, Marc Aronson (1995) urged for "intellectual honesty" that recognized the complexity of culture along with an elimination of what he termed "ethnic essentialism." He pondered the issue this way: "Why can we allow this cultural crossing in music and not in books for children? Why can't our authors, after sufficient preparation, do what they like?" (p. 167). Aronson argued that extensive preparation, immersion in the culture, and practice worked for musicians and that a comparable strategy would benefit writers.

As expected, some *Horn Book* readers were angered by Seto's comments. Marjorie Allen's (1995) remarks captured the sentiments of many who wrote letters to the editor:

> I can only hope that Thelma Seto will try to understand my Euro-American ethnicity as I am trying to understand Asian-American ethnicity. We are involved in such a chaotic effort to include all Americans in our literature that no one knows anymore how we should refer to each other. Are we really so different? Can't we just be Americans? (p. 390)

Well, yes and no. We share certain experiences because we are humans or Americans. Other experiences stem from differences that offer innumerable privileges for some and oppressive strictures for others. How many European Americans were lynched well into the 1960s on dubious charges without benefit of trial by jury? How does it feel to pay taxes for public schooling from which your children will not benefit? Imagine your government confiscating your property and interning you in camps because of your ancestry. Close an artistic eye to the anger that results when any immigrant from Europe can attain citizenship and voting privileges while you, a lifelong citizen, needed numerous constitutional amendments, Supreme Court decisions, federal laws, and human sacrifices, including the deaths of children, in order to exercise your rights.

These historical truths require artistic excellence and not artistic dilettantism if propaganda, stereotypes, and mediocrity are to be avoided. It is the exceptional writer or illustrator who successfully depicts this anguish, hurt, and hope. Consider that Tom Feelings needed twenty years and lengthy sojourns in Caribbean and African countries in order to create paintings conveying the unspeakable horrors and degradation of the Middle Passage. His book, *The Middle Passage: White Ships/Black Cargo* (1995) should give pause to any writer or artist who blithely takes on another's culture.

The anger underlying Seto's comments is recognizable, understandable, and

shared by some. These realities are not pleasant and they can engender complicated responses. Historical truths, however, cannot be sugar-coated. Nor should
collective amnesia about history prevent children from knowing the truth.

Very few individuals argue for their right to depict people with disabilities,
bilingual proficiencies, the elderly, or religious minorities. Debates about race
create primordial responses that indicate a racial chasm that appears permanent.
A more important question is not the authorial freedom of European American
authors to write about any group or culture they wish. Rather, it is the authorial
arrogance of some European American authors who demand freedom to write
about whatever they wish without subjecting their work to critical scrutiny. They
seem guilty of what Toni Morrison (1992) labels as "willful critical blindness."
Further, these authors ignore or refuse to acknowledge literary and critical history, including the fact that for years members of parallel cultures were denied
access to publishing.

For hundreds of years, European Americans have written about African Americans; with few exceptions, the works were one-note variations of the same
refrain. Notably, the authors produced Sambo, Epaminondas, Little Brown
Koko, contented slaves such as Amos Fortune, unnamed sharecroppers as in
Sounder (1969), and fathers who willingly sacrifice their lives so that a "white"
character can recognize the error of his racism. It is the rare "white" author—for
example, Mary White Ovington, Milton Meltzer, Arnold Adoff, Robert D.
San Souci, Juanita Havill, or Katherine Paterson—who creates an artistic,
multifaceted, and plausible depiction of African Americans.

Author Kathryn Lasky (1995) illustrates the complexities and contradictions
of these issues. She warns against "a kind of literary version of ethnic cleansing,
with an underlying premise that posits that there is only one story and only one
way to tell it" (p. 4). She recounts a discussion with an editor about her desire to
write a biography of Sarah Breedlove Walker or Madame C. J. Walker. The editor
informed Lasky that the "book would be panned by critics and wouldn't sell" (p.
5). Why? According to the editor, her "whiteness" was the central factor. Lasky
labeled this as censorship.

Any author, including Lasky, who creates a biography of Walker, should be
held to standards of biographical and literary excellence that include accuracy,
authenticity, and style. Such a biography must meet the standards set by Virginia
Hamilton's biographies of Paul Robeson and W. E. B. Du Bois, or Russell Freed-
man's biographies of Eleanor and Franklin Roosevelt. The author must recreate
the social, political, and cultural milieu in which Madame C. J. Walker lived. The
complex status, roles, and feelings of and about African American hair and Madame Walker's almost mythical role in the creation of African American beauty
rituals must be understood. This culture is explored in *Saturday At The New You*
(Barber, 1994), a picture book, about the social interactions in a beauty shop and
in the revolutionary subtext of Alexis Deveaux's *Enchanted Hair Tale* (1987) with
its emphasis on braids and "locks." The process and terminology of "straighten-
ing" hair—the "hot comb," oiling the scalp, "nappy edges," sectioning of the hair,
and the problem of "reversion" when the "pressed" hair is wet—must be
described in a convincing manner.

Further, the author must convey Walker's role in and importance to several
socio-political and cultural movements in the 1920s. Walker's home served as a
cultural salon for prominent individuals. Her business acumen enabled hundreds
of African American women to become economically liberated from the kitchens
of "white" women who typically did not pay them a fair wage. These women felt

exhilaration when they did not have to answer to "gal" or "auntie" or leave their families and work for subsistence wages. Unless Lasky immerses herself in research, discussions with others, and contact with artifacts, the rhythm of text is likely to be Revlon not Ultra Sheen, *Life* magazine rather than *Ebony* magazine, the milquetoast sounds of Pat Boone rather than the whoops and hollers of Little Richard. It might be far more interesting, artistic, and insightful if Lasky created a picture book or novel depicting a "white" girl's appropriation of an African American woman as a hero.

Lasky's description of William Styron's *Sophie's Choice* (1979) is a valid example of a powerful book written outside the author's own culture. However, Styron faltered badly when he created a "hagiography" of Nat Turner, the leader of a slave insurrection in the 1800s. His "literary" crucifixion of Turner engendered a firestorm of criticism and a book of essays (Clarke, 1968) that attempted to correct his historical inaccuracy and artistic misrepresentation.

Lasky also argues that this "new insistence on certain rules for authorship and provenance of a story (or who writes what and where) is indeed threatening the very fabric of literature and literary criticism" (p. 6). This statement is without foundation. The major journals devoted to literary criticism of children's literature—*Horn Book Magazine, The Lion and the Unicorn, Children's Literature Association Quarterly*, or *Children's Literature in Education*—do not have editors *Association Quarterly*, or *Children's Literature in Education*—do not have editors who are people of color. The majority of articles published in these journals do not relate to multiculturalism or any of its attendant controversies. Further, book publishing in its various aspects—editorial, marketing, and sales— remains overwhelmingly the province of "whites." How have proponents of multiculturalism managed to "take control" of the production, dissemination, and evaluation of this cultural product without even knowing it?

I view the near impossibility of authors of color being able to write about "non-racial" issues as far more important than the competition and critical heat that European American authors feel. Moreover, the authors who protest the most are not in the vanguard arguing for the same freedom for writers of color. W. D. Myers attributes this situation to the inability of editors to envision the possibility of writers assuming multiple perspectives:

> The publishing world touts itself as very liberal, but I keep challenging people to name books written over the last 20 years by Blacks that are on non-black subjects. So when you have a black writer who says, "I've got this great idea about space monkeys that talk," he or she is turned down. And what they are allowed to write about very often reflects the editor's opinion. (Sutton, 1994, p. 26)

Virginia Hamilton, despite being one of the most honored writers in the world, faces some barriers as well. When Rochman (1992) asked Hamilton, "Do you consider yourself a black writer?" she responded:

> And an American writer. And a woman. I'm all those things. It doesn't matter to me. *The People Could Fly* is a collection of American black folktales. I always put American first. But I say black or African American, what is politically correct, like everybody else. I'm sure that the categories people use for me depend on their own consciousness. It all depends on how you see things. My themes are universal. (p. 1021)

How many times has a European American author been asked, "Do you consider yourself a White writer?" Not often enough. We ignore the construction and historical development of Whiteness as equivalent to "American." Everyone else is the exotic, the different, the "Other" stripped of any symbolic designation of "American."

Some editors ignore Hamilton's assertions that she is an American writer and capable of creating stories outside a predetermined black experience:

> . . . But it's very difficult when you're a black writer to write outside of the black experience. People don't allow it; critics won't allow it. If I would do a book that didn't have blacks, people would say, "Oh, what is Virginia Hamilton doing? Yet a white writer can write about anything . . . I feel the limitation. I'm always running up against it and knocking it down in different ways, whichever way I can. But I know that it's there and will always be there. I mean there were people who said in the middle of my career, "Now Virginia Hamilton has finally faced who she is." Well, how dare they? (Rochman, 1992, p. 1021)

Hamilton's artistic abilities and literary philosophy suggest that any stories she would create about European Americans would have multifaceted characters, intriguing plots, and creative narrative forms. No shortcuts in the form of stereotypes or formulaic plots are likely to litter her work, as they do with some others who write cross-racially or, in the jargon of the day, cross borders.

I do not want to suggest that a European American author, one without disabilities, or a man, for example, cannot create an artistic, culturally-authentic literary work. Linda Crew's *Child of the River* (1991) demonstrates the good results of research, cross-cultural friendships, writing excellence, and how the adherence to truth can combine to create an exciting and well-received novel.

When an author writes that she only wants to write a story about people who "happen to be" African American, Asian/Pacific Islander, Latino/a, or Native American (Cameron, 1992), I question the need to eliminate the essence of feelings, experiences, and aspects of culture that shape who a people are. How many authors are likely to have an understanding of the "Other" that does not stem from media stereotypes, pseudo-science, or well-intentioned, paternalistic writers? Still, questions about authenticity, insider/outsider views, and authorial freedom remain unresolved.

Related to the questions about authenticity is the problem of stereotypic texts. Some retain appeal for teachers, parents, and children. A case in point is the immensely popular *Ten Little Rabbits* (1991), written by Virginia Grossman and illustrated by Sylvia Long. It is a best-seller that appears in day care centers, kindergartens, and primary classrooms. Many do not understand why some consider the book offensive. In the Spring 1995 issue of *The New Advocate*, Teresa McCarty detailed reasons for the opposition: 1) the objectification of whole groups of people as "cute," diminutive animals; 2) the trivialization of important and/or sacred ceremonial aspects of indigenous social and cultural life; 3) the monocultural stereotype that all Indian people are alike; 4) the fact that it is perverse and racist to think that children learn to count by diminutive-ethnic-group characters; 5) the depiction of people as animals; and 6) the symbolism of Indian "rabbits" multiplying (p. 98). Stereotypic texts such as *Ten Little Rabbits* become entrenched when they are elements of popular culture—for example, movies, toys, and other products.

Commercial considerations

Business trends affect the availability of multicultural issues. Reasoned arguments failed to dislodge venerated, stereotypic texts from earlier generations and it is unlikely that publishers will voluntarily relinquish the profits from best-sellers. *The Indian in the Cupboard* (Banks, 1985) is instructive. Despite convincing arguments from individuals such as Beverly Slapin and Doris Seale (1992) about the pervasive stereotypes in the book, you can view the film version of the book, purchase one of four best-selling sequels, or collect miniature figurines based on the film's characters with your purchase of Baskin-Robbins ice cream. Some progress is apparent; at least the Baskin-Robbins' Indian figurine was predominantly blue and not red.

More publishing companies are becoming components of multinational corporations. For example, Simon & Schuster purchased Macmillan. Some industry insiders bemoaned the acquisition of the Macmillan book group; others viewed it as an opportunity to create a publishing group that would survive into the future (Dunleavey, 1994). Dunleavey reported that Simon & Schuster publisher Willa Perlman instituted significant changes. For instance, 16 imprints were reduced to six. Most telling, the number of books published prior to the merger by both companies was approximately 700 titles (Dunleavey, 1994, p. 27). Perlman hopes to reduce that total to 400 by 1997 or 1998 (Dunleavey, 1994, p. 27).

One implication that can be drawn from the mergers and downsizing is that fewer books labeled multicultural will be published. Sims (1985) demonstrated as much when she analyzed the status of African American children's literature in the 1980s. I hope this prediction is erroneous. More than likely, major authors such as Laurence Yep, Virginia Hamilton, and Walter Dean Myers will not have to worry about finding publishers receptive to their work. Unknown talents may remain unpublished. Some evidence exists to support this conclusion (Maughn, 1992). After decades of struggle by individuals such as Augusta Baker, Charlemae Rollins, and Virginia Lacey and help from Nancy Larrick's (1965) pivotal article, "The All-White World of Children's Books," publishers made available many more books about African Americans. Similar increases were noted for other groups in the 1970s.

The goodwill efforts in publishing did not last. Sims Bishop (1985) reported that the percentage of children's books about African Americans dropped precipitously, to nearly two percent, in the early 1980s. Bookseller surveys appearing in *Publishers Weekly* are also informative. Some indicated that they did not see a need for multicultural literature (Roback, 1990) only to reverse this view a few years later.

Another implication is that publishers may focus on reproducing books that sell, such as classics and horror and romance series, rather than taking chances on books that lack blockbuster appeal or those written by unknown authors. Granted, publishing is a profit-making venture. However, some books require more than a year to find an audience. Further, some children simply do not want to read horror and romance series, classics, or endless folk tale variations.

Significant numbers of multicultural books are published but their marketing needs adjustment. More of the larger companies need to duplicate the policies followed by Pleasant Company as they publicized the Addy Series. Company executives hired African American consulting and advertising firms. They created an advisory board comprised of African Americans with expertise in history, literature, film, and library science. Most importantly, ads were placed in the major African American periodicals such as *Ebony, Jet, Essence, Emerge*, and *Black Enterprise*. The author, Connie Porter, embarked on an extensive tour with stops at African American bookstores, sorority events, and political meetings. The fact that the first three Addy books were best-sellers and among the top 30 books sold in 1993 should not surprise anyone. Pleasant Company's core audience was supplemented with new members because of the marketing strategy. Recently, the company ran an ad in the October 1995 issue of *Essence* magazine offering a free video, "The World of Addy Walker." Radio ads trumpeted the free video, too.

Golden Books™ embarked upon a similar collaboration with Essence™. The advertisement in *Publishers Weekly* (July 17, 1995) read: "The publisher of Golden Books™ is proud to present a publishing program created in cooperation with the publisher of Essence™. Each books is written and illustrated by an African American author and artist." Eight books (mostly board books) were published. Their availability in a variety of outlets—for example, grocery and drug stores—will likely ensure success.

Additionally, publishers should consider coordinating author tours that do not focus solely on traditional sites such as children's bookstores in upper-income neighborhoods. Instead, the booking agents should try to interest the hosts of talk shows on Black Entertainment Television (BET), Univision, or any of the ethnic language television and radio stations located across the country in programs on multicultural children's literature. It would help, too, if publishers sent some authors to urban and rural school districts where pupils rarely have visits from authors.

More independent publishing companies exist such as Just US Books, Arté Publico and its Piñata children's division, Polychrome, Children's Book Press, Lee and Low, and others. These companies are dedicated to the production of quality multiethnic literature. Some of them have made substantial inroads. For example, Just Us Books has agreements with Scott Foresman and Scholastic. Unfortunately, it is not easy to find some of the books published by these companies in traditional venues; special orders are typical. This year students enrolled in a multicultural literature course I teach could not find *Ziggy and the Black Dinosaurs* (Draper, 1994) at local libraries or bookstores located throughout the community even though I had placed the orders in advance.

Political correctness?

Finally, one last area of contention revolves around mistaken notions of "political correctness." Few who use the phrase choose to make explicit their conceptions of the term. One of the assignments in my undergraduate course is the reading and analysis of trends in Caldecott books published from 1960 through the current year. Each semester, several students label the appearance of literature from parallel cultures as award winners in the 1970s–1990s as political correctness. They question whether members of the committee bowed to outside political pressure. Although I explain how Caldecott winners and honor books are selected, some persist in this belief. They cling to the explanation of political correctness even though I critique the exclusionary policies of many publishing companies and booksellers in earlier historic periods. Rarely will a student who adopts this stance characterize the periods of exclusion as indicative of white supremacist ideology. Thankfully, many more students focus on the artistic value of the works.

Comments about the current winners, Sharon Creech's *Walk Two Moons* (1994) and Eve Bunting's *Smoky Night* (1994), echo these sentiments. For instance, Hal Piper (1995), an editor of *The Baltimore Sun's* op-ed page, criticized these books. His editorial appeared in the *Chicago Tribune*:

> Giving awards for books about hellish childhood nightmares instead of blissful childhood idyll is an ironic trend. . . . Now the award given in his name [John Newbery] honors books about adult fears and concerns. Sophisticated New York editors and jaded librarians bored with Doctor Doolittle, Rabbit Hill, and Johnny Tremain (past Newbery laureates) look for something a little more cutting-edge. But children don't live on the cutting edge. They need stories to help them become readers and to broaden their interests. But a steady diet of books about children forced to leave childhood and take on adult roles is no healthier to read about than to experience. A surfeit of anguish is no better than a surfiet of sunshine. (p. 13)

Mr Piper presents some compelling concerns. I suppose he has not seen some of the current crop of horror books that are immensely popular with readers and which, according to Campbell (1994), depict sexualized violence. In an ideal world, Piper's indignation and moral correctness would not apply selectively. Some children lead anguished lives and denying publication of stories about their world will not make them invisible.

DELIGHTS

Efforts by several major publishing companies in publishing multicultural books are laudable and create positive notes or delights. For example, HarperCollins houses the Multicultural Mentoring Program. Other companies and organizations, Little Brown and Company and the Multicultural Publishing Exchange, sponsor contests to discover new talent and publish examples of their work. However, only three books have resulted from the contests thus far and, to my knowledge, no new author or illustrator has emerged from the mentoring program.

The children's books now being published are more expansive in terms of genre, themes, narrative structure, and illustrations. The following books highlight some of these aspects. Ellis Island is an icon dedicated to primarily European immigration. Two other islands are equally important, Angel and Goree. Angel Island was the processing center for Asian immigrants. The Island of Goree was a major port in the African slave trade. Steve Barboza's *Door of No Return* (1994) chronicles this neglected historical point. Barboza documents the development of Goree as a major trading center and its current status as a shrine and tourist attraction through drawings, photographs, and historical research.

The Glory Field (Myers, 1994) depicts several generations of a family beginning with the enslavement of the patriarch in Africa. Each chapter focuses on a different branch of the family tree. Myers creates drama with cliffhangers for each chapter. In much the way that Alex Haley's *Roots* (1976) became a prototypic story of African American experiences, so might *Glory Field* perform the same function for youth.

Poetry deserves special attention. One of the few books of poetry focusing on Asian American experiences, Janet Wong's *Good Luck Gold*, debuted in 1994. African American poetry was bolstered with the publication of Wade Hudson's *Pass It On* (1993), Tom Feelings' *Soul Looks Back in Wonder* (1994), and

Langston Hughes' (1994) *Sweet and Sour Animal Book*, along with the biography of Hughes, *Coming Home* (Cooper, 1994). Other volumes featuring Native Americans—such as *The Trees Stand Shining* (Carlson, 1993) and *Many Waters* (Wood, 1995)—and Latinos—such as *Cool Salsa* (Carlson, 1994)—illustrate a certain amount of vibrancy in poetry that heralds a mini-renaissance.

One complaint heard periodically is the need for easy-to-read books and series fiction that are light or humorous reading fare. Several publishers heeded the call, especially Just Us Books with its N.E.A.T.E. and Ziggy series. Another wish fulfilled by publishers is multiracial board books. Angela Johnson had four "Joshua" books published by Orchard Books; Eloise and Monica Greenfield contributed at least seven, most published by HarperCollins or Black Butterfly Books. HarperCollins published five board books by Dessie and Chevelle Moore.

Finally, more multicultural books are appearing in book clubs at reasonable prices for children and teachers. In previous years, greater quantities of books appeared in conjunction with particular celebratory months such as Black History Month in February. Now, Trumpet and Scholastic book clubs typically include at least one or more offerings in each order booklet. These clubs are invaluable. Many children, especially urban and rural ones, do not have access to bookstores or cannot afford to pay $5.95 for a softcover or $15.95 for a hardcover. Book clubs provide a valuable alternative. Parents, teachers, and librarians can purchase the books and share them with children; integrate the books in literature, social studies, and science curricula; and place them on recommended reading lists.

Supporting multiculturalism forces an individual to engage in a great deal of critical self-reflection. What constitutes multicultural literature? What does it mean to be an "American"? Why are some groups classified as "them" or the "Other"? Who has access to publication and what are the effects of differential access to publishing? How do popular culture, books, and textbooks create images that are reinforced by societal institutions? What accounts for the appeal of stereotypic texts? Will children enjoy reading the texts we label multicultural? Yet, the ultimate purpose of literature is to engage the reader in an aesthetic experience. While the issues discussed in this article are crucial, our debates and efforts are worthless if children do not have an opportunity to read the literature.

References

Allen, M. (1995, July/August). Letters to the editor. *Horn Book Magazine, 61*, 390.

Aronson, M. (1995, March/April). A mess of stories. *Horn Book Magazine, 61*, 163–168.

Cameron, A. (1992, January). Untitled article. *School Library Journal, 38*, 29–30.

Campbell, P. (1994, March/April). The sand in the oyster. *Horn Book Magazine, 70*, 234–238.

Clarke, J. H., ed. (1968). *William Styron's Nat Turner: Ten black writers respond*. Boston: Beacon Press.

Dunleavey, M. P. (1994, June 13). Anatomy of a merger. *Publishers Weekly, 241*, 26.

Greenfield, E. (1975). Something to shout about. *Horn Book Magazine, 51*, 624–626.

Haley, A. (1976). *Roots*. New York: Doubleday.

Hamilton, V. (1993). Everything of value: Moral realism in the literature for children. *Journal of Youth Services in Libraries, 6*, 363–377.

Larrick, N. (1965). The all-white world of children's books. *Saturday Review, 48*, 63–65, 84–85.

Lasky, K. (1995). To Stingo with love: An author's perspective on writing outside one's culture. *The New Advocate, 9*(1), 1–7.

Maughn, S. (1992, January 20). Shortchanging the children. *Publishers Weekly, 239*, 39–40.

McCarty, T. (1995). What's wrong with *Ten Little Rabbits? The New Advocate, 8*(2), 97–98.

Morrison, T. (1992). *Playing in the dark*. Cambridge, MA: Harvard University Press.

Myers, W. D. (1986, November 9). I actually thought we would revolutionize the industry. *New York Times Book Review, 91*, 50.

Myers, W. D. (1995). 1994 Margaret A. Edwards Award Acceptance Speech. *Journal of Youth Services in Libraries, 8*, 129–133.

Piper, H. (1995, April 21). *Chicago Tribune* (National Edition). April 21, 1995, Section 1, p. 13.

Roback, D. (1990, November 30). Bookstore survey: Zeroing in. *Publishers Weekly, 237*, 36–38, 42–44.

Rochman, H. (1992, February 1). The Booklist interview: Virginia Hamilton. *Booklist, 88*, 1020–1021.

Saul, W. E. (Ed.). (1994). *Nonfiction for the classroom: Milton Meltzer on writing, history, and social responsibility*. New York: Teachers College Press.

Say, A. (1991, December). Musings of a walking stereotype. *School Library Journal, 37*, 45–46.

Seto, T. (1995, March/April). Multiculturalism is not Halloween. *Horn Book Magazine, 71*(2), 169–174.

Sims, R. (1983). What has happened to the all-white world of children's books? *Phi Delta Kappan, 64*, 650–653.

Sims, R. (1985). Children's books about Blacks: A mid-eighties status report. *Children's Literature Review, 8*, 9–13.

Slapin, B. & Seale, D. (1992). *Through Indian eyes: The native experience in books for children*. 3rd ed. Philadelphia: New Society Publishers.

Styron, W. (1979). *Sophie's Choice*. New York: Random House.

Sutton, R. (1994, June). Threads in our cultural fabric: A conversation with Walter Dean Myers. *School Library Journal, 40*, 24–28.

Children's books cited

Ada, A., Harris, V., & Bennett, L. (Eds.). (1993). *A chorus of cultures*. Carmel, CA: Hampton Brown.

Ada, A., Harris, V., & Bennet, L. (Eds.). (1994). *I'll tell you something*. Carmel, CA: Hampton Brown.

Armstrong, W. H. (1969). *Sounder*. New York: Harper & Row.

Banks, L. (1985). *The Indian in the cupboard*. New York: Doubleday.

Barbara, B. (1994). *Saturday at the new you*. New York: Lee & Low.

Barboza, S. (1994). *Door of no return*. New York: Cobble Hill/Dutton.

Bauer, M. (Ed.). (1994). *Am I blue?* New York: HarperCollins.

Bunting, E. (1994). *Smoky night*. New York: Harcourt Brace.

Carlson, L. (Ed.). (1994). *Cool salsa*. New York: Holt.

Cooper, F. (1994). *Coming home: From the life of Langston Hughes*. New York: Putnam.

Creech, S. (1994). *Walk two moons*. New York: HarperCollins.

Crew, L. (1991). *Child of the river*. New York: Dell.

Deveaux, A. (1987). *An enchanted hair tale*. New York: Harper & Row.

Draper, S. (1994). *Ziggy and the black dinosaurs*. Orange, NJ: Just Us Books.

Feelings, T. (1994). *Soul looks back in wonder*. New York: Dial.

Feelings, T. (1995). *The middle passage: White ships/black cargo*. New York: Dial.

Garza, C. (1990). *Family pictures*. San Francisco: Children's Book Press.

Grossman, V. (1991). *Ten little rabbits*. New York: Chronicle Books.

Hudson, W. (1993). *Pass it on*. New York: Scholastic.

Hughes, L. (1994). *Sweet and sour animal book*. New York: Oxford.

Jones, H. (1993). *The trees stand shining: Poetry of North American Indians*. New York: Dial.

Kerr, M. (1994). *Deliver us from Evie*. New York: HarperCollins.

Myers, W. D. (1994). *The glory field*. New York: Scholastic.

Parks, R. (1992). *Rosa Parks: Mother to a movement*. New York: Dial.

Wong, J. (1994). *Good luck gold*. New York: Margaret McElderry Books.

Wood, N. (1995). *Many waters: Prose and poetry of the pueblos*. New York: Scholastic.

Woodson, J. (1993). *The dear one*. New York: Dell.

CHAPTER 6

MOVING FROM ETHNIC STUDIES TO MULTICULTURAL EDUCATION (1982)

Leona Foerster

Ethnic studies programs, which were so popular in the 1970s, appear to have come and gone with little fanfare in many quarters. Some educators taking a conservative posture may have viewed these programs as curriculum fads which, like other fads, were destined from their inception to reach their apogee and then slowly descend into oblivion. To a certain extent, these foretellers of doom have been correct. The thrust to incorporate ethnic studies into curricula at all levels, which was characteristic of the late 1960s and early 1970s, appears to have come to a standstill in the 1980s. However, despite their limitations, ethnic studies programs have made a significant impact on American education and their influence is continuing to be felt in many quarters. These programs represented a move toward providing for students a more realistic and relevant curriculum that takes into account the cultural diversity within our society and the need for a cognitive base which will foster among young people an understanding of the ethnic/racial minorities which comprise America.

Several explanations are possible for the waning of ethnic studies programs in schools. First, the success of any program is highly dependent upon the commitment of the teacher who will implement it. The rapidity with which many ethnic studies were incorporated into curricula may have precluded the careful and thorough design and implementation of in-service training experiences. Obviously, the in-service component can be the key to the future success of any new program or strategy with which teachers may be unfamiliar or about which they are skeptical.

Many ethnic studies programs were accompanied by excellent teachers' guides. However, such guides were often minimally effective. They may have provided the teacher with some background knowledge needed for successful implementation of the program, but these guides often stopped at that point. Certainly, the teacher needs a strong knowledge base in order to be an effective leader and resource for student learning. But unless there is a concomitant affective base, implementation likely will be ineffective.

Teachers, after all, are human beings first—a fact sometimes ignored by some curriculum planners, administrators and even the general public. As humans, they bring to the learning arena a complexity of feelings, emotions, attitudes, values, biases, and even prejudices as a result of their interfacing with the world around them. If teachers remain unconvinced that a program is "worth the effort," if their feelings and attitudes toward this dimension of the curriculum are negative, if inherent clashes of values exist which remain concealed, obviously no amount of cognitive input will overcome these obstacles. Teacher biases and prejudices cannot be overlooked or ameliorated merely by prescribing a reading list or a course in ethnic studies at a nearby university.

The bridge between the cognitive and affective dimensions of the individual tends to be elusive, undefined, and ethereal. Knowledge does not always lead to understanding and appreciation. An in-service program that either ignores or fails to deal adequately with teacher feelings is incomplete. If committment to a program is what is needed for its success, then teachers need to have experiences which will enable them to examine their own attitudes, develop positive feelings about the program's worth, and cause them to set priorities in their classrooms that include implementing the components of the target program. Until a strong, positive affective base undergirds a program, effectiveness will be minimal at best.

Programs which have little teacher input may find implementation a thorny process. Many ethnic studies programs were developed by consultants outside of the school system in which they were to be used. Often these consultants represented particular minority groups. Certainly such contributions are valuable. Black studies programs *should* have the input of black educators; Native American studies should reflect the thoughts and concerns of Native Americans, and so on. Unfortunately, however, many programs may have smacked of certain biases and prejudices and, whether accurately or not, may have been viewed as the result of pressure tactics employed by certain factions within the community. Under these circumstances, teacher negativism is likely to set in. In many cases, this is what happened to ethnic studies programs. When teachers perceive programs as imposed from without, resistance may run rampant and may not be tempered even by the best efforts of the supervisory and administrative personnel of the district.

Time pressures work against the implementation of any "extras" that tend to be tacked on to the existing curriculum. In order to avoid this pitfall, career education programs, for example, have been filtered into the curriculum via supplementary readers, aspects of the language arts program, or as part of existing social studies curricula. Similarly, ethnic studies may appear in almost any component of the curriculum, but most often in the social studies. Even in the latter case, however, articulation with the rest of the social studies program may result in fragmented and compartmentalized learning. They may appear as a two-week unit that is disposed of as quickly as possible and forgotten during the remainder of the year.

Perhaps an example will clarify the statement above. It is popular to study "Indians" in schools around Thanksgiving time. (Pupils may learn that Squanto helped the Pilgrims grow corn!) It is better to omit the study of "Indians" (or any other group) if pupils are to be left only with partial knowledge that leads to distortions and misconceptions. There is much more to Native American studies than isolated and unrelated facts. Unfortunately, teachers still teach that Columbus *discovered* America and frequently pupils are amazed to learn that Indians are alive and well today. If you ask students if Indians can be cowboys (actually many are these days), you will have some notion of the confusion which clouds the study of America's first inhabitants. Similarly, it is an injustice to "study" black people only around Martin Luther King's birthday and neglect during the remainder of the school year the history, heritage, and significant contributions to our nation made by black people.

Another stumbling block to the success of ethnic studies has revolved around the controversy over *what* should be included in these programs, for *whom*, and *when*. Let's consider each of these questions separately.

What should be included in ethnic studies programs has been of continuing debate. It is apparent that America's population is exceedingly diverse and that the content of ethnic studies must be delineated in some way. Within Texas alone, for example, there are Chicanos, blacks, Germans, Czechs, and several Indian tribes, to name the major groups. Programs that attempt to include too many groups often lack effectiveness and fail to promote a depth of understanding of any of the groups.

Unfortunately, in the minds of the public and educators alike, ethnic studies programs have been linked with the particular group or groups studied in that program. Black studies have been considered appropriate only for black students, Chicano studies for Chicanos, and so on. Some insightful individuals have perceived that the white middle class student may need ethnic studies most of all. But by and large there was (and still is) a tendency to place ethnic studies programs only in schools serving minority populations.

When to implement these programs also has been a problem. Ethnic studies are far more prevalent at the secondary level than in the elementary school. When found in the elementary grades, ethnic studies are often part of the intermediate social studies program. Seemingly little attention has been given to implementing ethnic studies in kindergarten and the early primary grades. Again, this is unfortunate and unrealistic. Pupils live in a pluralistic society and are well aware of differences in skin color, facial features, etc., at an early age. There is a real need for building an understanding of and appreciation for diversity at the earliest educational levels.

Lack of community support may have scuttled some ethnic studies programs. For the many reasons cited in this article, as well as resistance to anything new and general apathy, the necessary community commitment may have been withheld. Perhaps the fault has rested with public relations programs in our schools. It is also possible that the blame lies with the orientation of the school staff. Or maybe society is not "ready" for school programs which may elicit discomforting questions from students. For whatever reason, ethnic studies programs by and large have failed to rally the support needed for their successful implementation and continuance.

Perhaps what is needed is not a new program but a new orientation. Such an orientation has surfaced and is labeled "multicultural education." The remainder of this article will attempt to build a rationale for making multicultural education a reality for all students.

It would seem imperative at this point to describe what is meant by the concept of multicultural education as it is used here. Multicultural education compares and contrasts all people across racial and ethnic lines in an open atmosphere that is uncritical and free from value judgments. It studies diversity across cultures, examines the strengths and contributions of each, and promotes cultural pluralism as the ideal posture for society. It differs from ethnic studies in that generally the latter program offers an in-depth study of a racial or cultural group (black American, Mexican American, Native American, etc.). Even the term "multiethnic" would seem to be a less desirable label, because it may carry the notion of the compartmentalization that frequently has been characteristic of ethnic studies programs in general, rather than the desired diffusion throughout the curiculum. Multicultural education is the broader term, and it encompasses ethnic studies, which may provide much of the cognitive input for the program. But multicultural education goes beyond a content base. It is an orientation which has its inception in the teacher's mind and permeates the entire curriculum. The implementation is accomplished by a sensitive and perceptive teacher who is alert to possibilities for "multiculturalizing" the existing curriculum on a day-to-day basis. This should answer the question concerned with the *what* of multicultural education.

Now it is pertinent to consider questions surrounding the problems of *for whom* and *when*. It is the position of this writer that multicultural education can and should be for *all* students at *every* grade level. Educators must move from the orientation that multicultural education is relevant only for minority students or for students in certain schools and at particular grade levels. Most students in schools now eventually will live and work in our culturally pluralistic society. Therefore, it would appear imperative that educators provide many varied opportunities for students to acquire strong cognitive and affective bases which will enable them to function successfully in a world of diversity. Obviously, this is a challenge which cannot be met in a six-week social studies unit at one or more grade levels. Rather, the spiral curriculum approach in which basic concepts and generalizations are introduced in the early grades and understandings are deepened and broadened as students move through the grades utilizing different content and experiences would appear to offer a more promising approach to implementation.

If a school district or individual school is truly interested in multiculturalizing the curriculum, then these guidelines may be useful in order to accomplish this goal. The beginning point is a strong commitment on the part of the community, the school administration, and the teachers. It is apparent that this is a difficult but surmountable obstacle. However, if it is not hurdled successfully, the project may be doomed to failure from the outset. Regardless of where the thrust for multicultural education originates, with a group of teachers, school administrators, an enlightened school board, a parents' group, etc., a good "selling job" will need to be done so that support is forthcoming from all levels.

Given that this is accomplished to a sufficient degree, then resource guides will need to be written to enable teachers to capitalize on opportunities to provide a multicultural emphasis at all levels. Local teachers *must* be involved so that the program is not *imposed upon* them but rather *developed by* them. Outside consultants, of course, can and should enhance the process considerably.

Teachers within the district, however, understand the nature of the local situation best—including the orientation of the community, the existing curriculum, and the needs of students. Ethnic studies guides can be helpful as resources and can be obtained from districts having such programs. Librarians may be able to suggest multiethnic books and other media which might be germaine to the program. The state department of education, colleges and universities, and community agencies may be tapped for assistance in the project. Perhaps most important to note is that the product of these efforts should *not* be a curriculum guide for a new curriculum component. Instead, it should contain suggestions for adapting the existing curriculum, and it should include a myriad of resources which may help students build understanding of and appreciation for diverse peoples, for implementing activities which will strengthen the bond between the community and school, and for evaluating all materials in the classroom. To be avoided, of course, are materials which tend to perpetuate biases and stereotypes or otherwise show or imply that diversity is negative. When completed, the multicultural education resource guide should include background information for the teacher, which will enable him/her to serve as a resource for students and to guide student learning effectively. Further, the guide should contain a variety of suggestions for activities to promote affective learning. Dramatic activities, such as role-playing, are useful in values exploration. Experiences in the community—for example, high school students working in an after school recreation program—can be important in enabling students to interact successfully in a multicultural setting.

In addition to the preparation of a guide in which local teachers have had a part, an in-service education program is an important consideration. Such a program should deepen teachers' understanding of cultural and linguistic differences and alert them to a greater variety of possibilities for promoting cultural pluralism in their classrooms. Outside speakers can enhance the curriculum and make excellent use of community resources. Ways to bring the community into the schools and to bring the school to the community are numerous and should be included in the in-service component. Teachers who lack interest in, knowledge of, and commitment to multicultural education simply will be ineffective in multiculturalizing the school curriculum. It is important to strengthen this commitment before the inception of the program.

The thrust that multicultural education will take can and should differ according to the local setting. Certainly minority students should be helped to maintain and extend their pride in and identification with their own heritage. Thus, the knowledge base for the program must take into account the minority groups present in any given community and radiate from there. However, just as ethnic studies have been too restrictive, attempts at multicultural education which stop short of including a major portion of the great diversity found within American society similarly may lack effectiveness. Within the K-12 curriculum, opportunities abound for including the study of diversity in a variety of contexts. It is critical to keep in mind that multicultural education is more than an add-on to the social studies program. For maximum effectiveness, it should permeate everything that is included in the curriculum.

If multicultural education is to succeed and endure as a national thrust, it must be demonstrated that it adds a valuable dimension to the education of all students. Those of us who believe in it, of course, feel that it will. Present-day society is culturally pluralistic. Persons who are members of minority groups are becoming better educated, better trained, and socially mobile. Students in schools presently will live among and work with people of vastly differing racial and ethnic backgrounds, from different family organlzations, employing various methods of childrearing, and utilizing a variety of linguistic codes. Rather than a fad or a frill, it may well be that multicultural education will emerge as an important key to the very survival of the American way of life and the realization of the great American dream.

CHAPTER 7

GENRES OF RESEARCH IN MULTICULTURAL EDUCATION (2001)

Christine Bennett

On several recent occasions I have been invited to explain the field of multi-cultural education in a session or two to educators from abroad—in the past year to Russians and South Africans. Often I am asked to give a speech to students or teachers who are new to the field. I also encounter graduate students who have taken one or two courses in multicultural education, or who developed literature reviews for dissertations, and who perceive lack of definition, conceptual clarity and purpose in the field other than broad affirmations of diversity. The idea of mapping genres of research and practice in multicultural education originally came to mind as a means of introducing newcomers, as well as more experienced students, to the complexity and richness of the field.[1] At the same time, the map invites critical dialogue with veteran scholars who would parse the field differently.

To offer a prelude to the map, I often give a brief overview of the origins of multicultural education and the foundational ideas, to provide cohesiveness to the map's conceptual framework. I describe the field of multicultural education as a hopeful and idealistic response to the Civil Rights Movement of the 1950s and 1960s that developed into a Black Power movement and spread to include many other minority groups, including women. The Brown decision in 1954 reversed the legality of "separate but equal schools" and triggered rising expectations and aspirations for equal opportunity and social justice, especially in public educa-tion. Instead, disproportionately high numbers of the nation's African-American, Native-American, and Latino children and youth were placed in special education for the handicapped or culturally disadvantaged. Others were suspended or expelled for reasons of teacher discretion or attended schools where teachers and the curriculum reflected primarily Anglo-European American perspectives. In reaction, the field of multicultural education emerged quickly and passionately, drawing on a long history of multidisciplinary inquiry, artistic and literary achievement, social action, and scholarly writing (e.g., C. Banks, 1996). The earliest expressions were disparate, taking numerous shapes such as ethnic studies curriculum projects, human relations workshops for teachers, community action programs, and studies of school desegregation (Gay, 1983; Gollnick, 1995). By the early 1970s, however, the field had embraced a set of core values and ideals that provide conceptual clarity and power to its contemporary research and practice. Yet, since its beginnings and continuing into the present, multicultural education has been perceived as lacking definition and purpose (e.g., Gibson, 1976, 1984; Hoffman, 1996; Sleeter & Grant, 1987), posing a threat to continued vision and accomplishment. The complexity seems invisible to critics who ask for research studies to show that multicultural education works. As a possible antidote, this article provides a conceptual framework of research genres that illustrate the multidisciplinary nature of multicultural education (see Table 7.1).

Principles of multicultural education and the genres

This conceptual framework stands in contrast to the culturally disadvantaged and assimilationist Anglo-Eurocentric perspectives that underlie much of the educational research in the past century (Grant & Tate, 1995; Padilla & Lindholm, 1995). It rests on four broad principles of multicultural education: (a) the theory of cultural pluralism; (b) ideals of social justice and the end of racism, sexism, and other forms of prejudice and discrimination; (c) affirmations of culture in the teaching and learning process; and (d) visions of educational equity and excellence leading to high levels of academic learning for all children and youth.

Table 7.1 Genres of research in multicultural education

Cluster One: Curriculum reform	Cluster Two: Equity pedagogy	Cluster Three: Multicultural competence	Cluster Four: Societal equity
Assumptions Knowledge is contested and constructed. A Eurocentric curriculum in the United States is a tool of cultural racism.	**Assumptions** All children have special talents and the capacity to learn. The major goal of public education is to enable all children to reach their fullest potential. Cultural socialization and sense of ethnic identity influence the teaching and learning process	**Assumptions** The reduction of racial and cultural prejudice is possible and desirable. Individuals can become multicultural; they need not reject their familial worldview and identity to function comfortably in another cultural milieu.	**Assumptions** Societal change is a necessary condition to bring about equitable education access, participation and achievement. Societal equity (change) is possible and consistent with basic democratic values and the American creed.
Genre 1 Historical inquiry **Genre 2** Detecting bias in texts and instructional materials **Genre 3** Curriculum theory	**Genre 4** School and classroom climate **Genre 5** Student achievement **Genre 6** Cultural styles in teaching and learning	**Genre 7** Ethnic identity development **Genre 8** Prejudice reduction **Genre 9** Ethnic group culture	**Genre 10** Demographics **Genre 11** Culture and race in popular culture **Genre 12** Social action

In particular, the ideal of cultural pluralism is a foundational principle of multicultural education in the United States (although it is insufficient as noted below). The concept of cultural pluralism was developed early in the 20th century by democratic philosopher Horace Kallen (Kallen, 1924; Konvitz, 1974) and has been transformed by scholars of color such as Carter G. Woodson (1933/1969), W. E. B. DuBois (1961), Jack Forbes (1973), Ronald Takaki (1989), and Richard Ruiz (1991). This ideal vision of society affirms the democratic right of each ethnic group to retain its own heritage. It envisions a society based on core values of equity and social justice, respect for human dignity and universal human rights, and freedom to maintain one's language and culture, provided the human dignity and rights of others are not violated. It stands as a compromise between cultural assimilation on the one hand, whereby ethnic minority groups are expected to give up their language and culture to blend into mainstream Anglo-European culture, and segregation or suppression of ethnic minorities on the other hand (Feagin & Feagin, 1993; Sills, 1968). Although ethnic minorities may be expected to compromise in some areas to maintain societal harmony and national identity, implicit are the assumptions that every child's home culture must be affirmed and respected and opportunities must be provided for all children to reach their fullest potential.

The transformation of Kallen's (1924) ethnicity paradigm to embrace multiple diversities (such as race, racial or ethnic identities, class, and gender) and eliminate structural inequities related to these groups constitutes the second foundational principle. In particular, the redress of *racial* inequities in a society built on and maintained by White privilege is a primary focus of foundational multicultural education scholars (e.g., Baker, 1983; J. A. Banks, 1970, 1973; Cortés, 1973; Forbes, 1973; Gay, 1973; Grant, 1978; Suzuki, 1979, 1984). They concentrated on deep-seated structural injustices and systematic patterns of dominance and suppression that denied people of color material and political equality. Therefore, they moved beyond efforts to end prejudice and discrimination by individuals, and included societal structures. Institutional and cultural racism are at the heart of their writings, even when conceptions of diversity are expanded to include gender, class, disabilities, and sexual preference.

A third foundational principle is the importance of culture in teaching and learning (e.g., Bennett, 1979; Pai, 1990; Shinn, 1972). The concept of culture has been described as anthropology's "seminal contribution" and a "welcome palliative to existing notions of inherited, and therefore immutable, racial differences" (Gonzalez, 1995, p. 234). Culture refers to a society's shared beliefs, social values, world-views, and preferred standards of behaving. In a culturally diverse society such as that of the United States, it is not possible to individualize or personalize instruction, an idea most teachers embrace, without considering culture. Geneva Gay reaffirmed this principle in her new book, *Culturally Responsive Teaching* (2000). Gay argues that "culture counts" and "is at the heart of all we do in the name of education, whether that is curriculum, instruction, administration, or performance assessment" (2000, p. 8). She writes that

> race, culture, ethnicity, individuality, and intellectuality of students are not discrete attributes that can be neatly assigned to separate categories, some to be ignored while others are tended to. Instead, they are inseparably interrelated; all must be carefully understood, and the insights gleaned from this understanding should be the driving force for the redesign of education for cultural diversity. (p. 14)

Finally, the need for academic excellence and equity is a foundational principle of multicultural education (e.g., Bennett, 1986–1999; Gay, 1979, 1994; Irvine, 2000). Equity in education means equal opportunities for all students to reach their fullest potential. It must not be confused with equality or sameness of result, or even identical experiences. Student potentials may be diverse, and at times equity requires different treatment according to relevant differences, such as instruction in a language the child can understand. Achieving educational excellence requires an impartial, just education system whereby all students are perceived to be capable of learning at high levels and are provided opportunities to be academically successful.

These principles of cultural pluralism, social equity for racial and ethnic minorities, the importance of culture in teaching and learning, and high equitable expectations for student learning provide the basic premises and philosophy that underlie multicultural education and the genres of research. They provide a unifying ideology for the four genre clusters that constitute the conceptual framework proposed in Figure 7.1: Curriculum reform, equity pedagogy, multicultural competence, and societal equity. By way of this map, the field of multicultural education commands more conceptual integrity and complexity than critics and advocates may realize.

A conceptual framework of research genres

The map in Figure 7.1 provides a way to view research in the complex and rich field of multicultural education. The framework is an adaptation of the dimension of multicultural education developed in *Comprehensive Multicultural Education: Theory and Practice* (Bennett, 1990). In their totality, the genre clusters reflect the canonical core of the field evident in curriculum revision and reform, equity pedagogy, multicultural competence, and societal equity.[2] Several compatible fields that are sometimes equated with multicultural education, such as ethnic studies, social studies, gender studies, bilingual education, and special education are excluded from my conceptual framework. These fields have their own extensive bodies of theory and research and are beyond the scope of this article.

Twelve genres of research have been identified and categorized into one of the four clusters; these clusters are interactive categories of studies within the larger body of educational research that reflect the principles of multicultural education previously described. Each genre cluster represents a different dimension of multicultural education and each genre, or category of studies, focuses on a particular way of thinking about making a difference in the intellectual, social, and personal development of all children and youth in our society. I call them *genres* because studies within each genre share a similar primary emphasis in content and purpose that differ substantially from studies in the other categories. Each contains several lines of research that span a decade or more, and researchers within each genre tend to use similar theoretical frameworks and build on other research within the genre. Research is defined broadly and methodology is not a distinguishing factor in the suggested genres; thus, for example, it would be possible to find survey, experimental, and ethnographic studies within a single genre.

In the discussion that follows, a definition and brief overview of theory and research within each cluster is provided, followed by an explanation of the related genres. One or two research studies are used to illustrate each genre, for a total of 22 examples. Neither meta-analysis, nor a comprehensive review of the research within these genres, nor a critical review of the research methodology in the

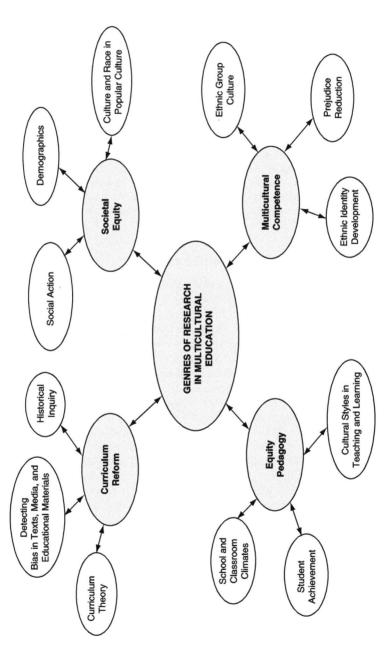

Figure 7.1 A conceptual framework of research genres.

selected research illustrations, is possible within this article. Therefore, the selected research illustrations are all taken from publications in scholarly journals known for rigorous review of methodology or from books published by an academic press. Other considerations I used in the selection process include (a) a diversity of disciplines, primarily in the social sciences; (b) a diversity of ethnic perspectives; (c) a diversity of authors; (d) saliency of the study or series of studies; and (e) a sampling of studies that range over several decades. These factors behind my selection process limit the pool of possible illustrations and leave out some important scholarship in the field that appears in other books, book chapters, and journals with less emphasis on research methodology. The illustrations, like the genres and sources they represent, differ in terms of the methodological detail and description I include. A brief summary of the state of research to date is provided for each cluster of research genres.

Cluster one: curriculum reform

Research genres in this cluster focus on subject matter inquiry aimed at rethinking and transforming the traditional curriculum that is primarily Anglo Eurocentric in scope. Curriculum reform requires active inquiry to discover and include knowledge and perspectives that have previously been ignored or suppressed. Two assumptions that underlie research in curriculum reform are that (a) knowledge is contested and constructed and (b) a Eurocentric curriculum in a multicultural society such as that of the United States is a tool for cultural hegemony.

The idea of centricity, or using students' own culture and history as a context for learning and helping them relate socially and psychologically to other cultural perspectives, is at the heart of the three genres in this cluster. As defined by Asante (1991),

> Centricity is a concept that can be applied to any culture. The centrist paradigm is supported by research showing that the most productive method of teaching any student is to place his or her group within the center of the context of knowledge. For White students this is easy because almost all the experiences discussed in American classrooms are approached from the standpoint of White perspectives and history. American education, however, is not centric; it is Eurocentric. Consequently, non-White students are also made to see themselves and their groups as "acted upon." Only rarely do they read or hear of non-White people as active participants in history. [For example] most classroom discussions of the European slave trade concentrate on the activities of Whites rather than on the resistance efforts of Africans. A person educated in a truly centric fashion comes to view all groups' contributions as significant and useful. Even a White person educated in such a system does not assume superiority based upon racist notions. (p. 171)

Asante argues that Eurocentricity is "based on White supermacist notions whose purposes are to protect White privilege and advantage in education, economics, politics, and so forth" (p. 171). A truly centric education is different from Eurocentrism in that it is nonhierarchical and recognizes and respects diverse cultural perspectives on world phenomena. The subject matter research found in the three genres within this cluster is necessary to create the multicentric curriculum advocated by proponents of multicultural education. It is required for rethinking and transforming the curriculum in most U.S. schools. This category is rich and highly complex, and it can be analyzed in terms of historical inquiry in the content areas; studies of bias in textbooks, trade books, and other instructional media; and curriculum theory.

Genre 1: historical inquiry in the content areas

Research and teaching in this genre involves rethinking history and the history of any discipline (e.g., physics, mathematics, American literature, music, or art) through a lens of race, ethnicity, culture, class, and gender. Major events, persons, themes, and societal, cultural, or political developments are studied from multiple perspectives and experiences to create an inclusive curriculum. Gay (2000) writes that

> Students should learn how to conduct ideological and content analysis of various sources of curriculum content about ethnic and cultural diversity. These learning experiences involve revealing implicit values and biases, modifying attitudes and perceptions, developing different evaluation criteria, and acting deliberately to first deconstruct and then reconstruct common ethnic and gender typecasting. . . . [Students] might learn how to search for evidence of how ... "positionality factors" affect the presentations writers and typecasters make about ethnic issues and groups. (p. 143)

J. A. Banks (1993) describes the knowledge generated within this research genre as transformative academic knowledge:

> [This] knowledge consists of concepts, paradigms, themes, and explanations that challenge mainstream academic knowledge and that expand the historical and literary canon. [It] challenges some of the key assumptions that mainstream scholars make about the nature of knowledge. . . . Transformative academic scholars assume that knowledge is not neutral but is influenced by human interests, that all knowledge reflects the power and social relationships within society, and that an important purpose of knowledge is to help people improve society. (p. 9)

Examples of this genre include revisions of U.S. history by Ronald Takaki (1993), Eric Foner (1990), and Howard Zinn (1995); ethnic studies by Lawrence Levine (1977), Rudolf Acuña (1988), and Sonia Nieto (1998); social science research such as the work of Joe and Clarice Feagin in sociology (1993) and Roger Abrahams in folklore (1992), as well as Afrocentric research by scholars such as Appiah and Gates (1999), Asante (1987, 1990, 1991), and Diop (1974). Examples of revised theory and scholarship literature include *Criticisms in the Borderlands: Studies in Chicano Literature, Culture, and Ideology* (1991) edited by Calderón and Saldívar; "Victorians and Africans: The Genealogy of the Myth of the Dark Continent" (1985) by Brantlinger; and *The Sacred Hoop* (1986) by Paula Gunn Allen. Retheorizing is also occurring in the fields of mathematics (e.g., Zavslasky, 1993), science (e.g., Gill & Levidow, 1987), and art (e.g., Cahan & Kocur, 1996).

An illustration of the historical and subject matter research genre is found in two books written by Jack Weatherford, *Indian Givers: How the Indians of the Americas Transformed the World* (1988) and *Native Roots: How the Indians of the Americas Enriched America* (1991). Weatherford draws on primary and secondary historical, anthropological, and archeological sources to make the case that Indian achievements in mining, architecture, agriculture, medicine, commerce, and government contributed to the development of human societies throughout the world in ways that remain largely unrecognized. His research spanned over a decade and engaged a team of family and professional colleagues, several of them Native-American scholars with connections in indigenous communities across several continents. He argues that Indian skill and hard labor in gold and silver mining in the Americas led to the industrial revolution in Europe and the rise of capitalism; that Indian agricultural technology contributed 60% of the world's food products (including the potato that transformed European agriculture and social structures); that sophisticated Indian pharmacology produced healing substances that contribute to modern medicine; and that Northeast Indian confederacies such as the Iroquois League influenced political ideas that are at the core of the U.S. federal system of government.

Another illustration is the study of Chinese-, Japanese-, Korean-, Indian-, Filipino-, Vietnamese-, Cambodian-, and Laotian-American stories and perspectives by Ronald Takaki (1989). In *Strangers From a Different Shore: A History of Asian Americans*, Takaki corrects the misconception that the United States is a nation of immigrants from Europe who were the only pioneers in a westward expansion movement. In this narrative study of Asian immigrants, Takaki shows that

> the term "shore" has multiple meanings. These men and women came from Asia across the Pacific rather than from Europe across the Atlantic. They brought Asian cultures rather than the traditions and ideas originating in the Greco-Roman world. Moreover, they had qualities they could not change or hide—the shape of their eyes, the color of their hair, the complexion of their skin. They were subjected not only to cultural prejudice, or ethnocentrism, but also racism. . . . Unlike the Irish and other groups from Europe, Asian immigrants could not become "mere individuals, indistinguishable in the cosmopolitan mass of population." (p. 13)

Asians migrated east, through Oahu, Hawaii, or Angel Island in San Francisco Bay, not through Ellis Island. They contributed to such national undertakings as the transcontinental railroads and development of agriculture in Hawaii and California. Takaki (1989) documents the diversities and similarities in their experiences and perspectives, the history of racism such as the anti-Asian immigration laws and the internment of Japanese-American citizens during World War II, as well as the resurgence of racism directed at the "model minority" today. Despite the privileging of Anglo-European peoples and cultures, Takaki argues that America also has a counter tradition and vision, springing from the reality of racial and cultural diversity. The country has been, "as Walt Whitman celebrated so lyrically, 'a teeming Nation of nations' composed of a 'vast, surging, hopeful army of workers,' a new society where all should be welcomed." (p. 16)

Genre 2: detecting bias in texts, trade books, and instructional materials

The study of bias in curriculum and text materials is one of the earliest and most prolific areas of inquiry in multicultural education. Much of this research builds on the foundational research by the Council on Interracial Books for Children (CIBC) that used evaluation criteria in five main categories: characterization, language, historical authenticity, cultural accuracy, and illustrations. Textbook studies in the 1970s revealed "some improvement from the blunt racism of previous decades," although the portrayal of African Americans, Native Americans and other people of color was still marginalized, omitted, or presented inaccurately or negatively (Grant & Tate, 1995, p. 148). More recent studies provide evidence that ethnic and gender stereotypes in trade books and the curriculum are still a problem (e.g., J. Garcia, 1993; Pewewardy, 1998).

"An Analysis of Stereotypes and Biases in Recent Asian American Fiction for Adolescents" by Violet Harada (1994) provides the first illustration of this genre. Harada's study draws upon research that documents a century and a half of stereotypical depictions of Asian-Americans in fiction through images that "ranged from Asians portrayed as sinister, inscrutable heathens and sexually alluring China dolls to Asians depicted as super-achieving success models" (p. 43). The purpose of her study was to determine how many titles published between 1988 and 1993 included Asian-American characters, to identify the nature of Asian American stereotypes found in previous trade-book research, and to determine the degree to which these biased images still exist in recent fiction for adolescents or children ages 11 to 17. In the study, Asian-American characters included those from the following countries of origin: China, Japan, Korea, Vietnam, Cambodia, Thailand, Philippines, Laos, Burma, Taiwan, and India (p. 45).

An extensive search for appropriate titles identified 24 books published between 1988 and 1993, out of approximately 5,000 works of children's fiction published annually. Only 6 of the 11 Asian-American groups were represented, including Chinese, Cambodian, Japanese, Korean, Taiwanese, and Vietnamese (Harada, 1994, p. 47). A three-page checklist was created by adapting and expanding on CIBC guidelines, and three raters independently analyzed and documented their findings for all 24 titles. A variety of biases and stereotypes were discovered in all but 1 of the 24 titles. More than half of the books presented an image of Asians as a superachieving model minority. Other images included "mysterious but alluring Orientals" and "yellow bananas," a reference to "those who are Asian in appearance but who are striving to be white on the inside" (p. 55). In one third of the books, Asian-Americans were portrayed as passive characters who required assistance from White characters to resolve problems (p. 52). Derogatory language, token references to history, and the absence of cultural references about customs and lifestyles was also noted in these books.

A content analysis of California textbooks and follow-up case study by Joyce King (1992) provides the second illustration of this research genre. King had served on the California Curriculum Development and Supplemental Materials Commission (the advisory body of the State Board of Education in California) during the 1986–1990 history textbook adoption period. Her work expands traditional textbook studies based on CIBC guidelines by adding a Black studies, or Afrocentric, lens to the analysis. King grounded her textbook inquiry in "Diaspora literacy," defined as "the ability to comprehend the literature of Africa, Afro-America, and the Caribbean from an informed, indigenous perspective" (Clark, 1991, p. 42, cited in King, 1992, p. 318). Her analyses focused on "ideological representation of the Middle Passage and how slavery began, as depicted in classroom textbooks utilized by public schools in the state of California" (p. 318). King challenged the "immigrant perspective" that "distorts the historical continuity of African Americans, Native Americans, and the indigenous peoples now known as Chicanos, Hispanics, or Latinos, who did not come to America in search of material gain or freedom but were conquered by European American settlers" (p. 326). She argued that the "reified immigrant experience" affirms visions of *individual* opportunity for upward mobility and economic advancement, more so than collective struggle for justice. For the descendents of indigenous peoples forced off and forced to give up their lands, one political consequence of accepting this ideology is the forfeiture of any basis of collective claims for redress and justice. On the other hand, to identify with one's collective interests is not "excessive veneration of one's ancestors," but a logical antidote to domination and alienation. . . .

Black students' ancestral origins are doubly tainted within the cultural model framework that naturalized the immigrant experience. Not only did their ancestors "come" to this land as slaves, but the masses of black folk still live in poverty. The reality of the African presence, then, as now, contradicts the myth of America as a land of freedom, justice, and equality of opportunity. . . . [The immigrant experience] inherently implies that Black people's failure is a failure to assimilate and acculturate. The immigrant bias in the textbooks obscures the contradictions occasioned by racial injustice and misequates the Middle Passage [the trans-Atlantic slave trade] with Ellis Island, thus distorting the African experience and making it an anomaly rather than a paradox of the American reality. (p. 327)

King (1992) followed up this analysis with an exploratory case study based on parent and educator responses to her critical analysis of the textbooks. Study participants, African American parents and multicultural education specialists, were presented a Black studies scholarly critique of ideology in California's adopted textbooks. King convened two meetings, one with the parents and another with Black multicultural education specialists, to view a videotape and experience a presentation of her textbook critique. Before the presentation of this critique, King gathered data on the parents' and consultants' images of the Middle Passage. Follow-up focus group discussions encouraged participants to reflect on their own educational and social experiences (including racism) and the needs of Black children and youth. Participants expressed ideas about individual and collective social action strategies, power structures in schools and society, and areas of disagreement with the videotape. King concluded that although a Black studies ideology critique does provide a lens to understand the textbook controversy, it also illuminates "a deeper crisis of legitimacy within the disciplines and in the nature of schooling itself" (p. 334) and "the role of textbooks under conditions of racism" (p. 336).

Genre 3: curriculum theory

Research in this genre focuses on the nature of multicultural education in terms of concepts and principles, as well as curriculum goals, rationales, models, and designs. These theoretical studies may be descriptive analyses, critical explanations, or prescriptive recommendations. Writings of the scholars and theoreticians in the field who emphasize multicultural curriculum goals, concepts, and development are included in this genre (e.g., Baker, 1983; J. A. Banks, 1993, 1994; Bennett, 1986–1999; Gay, 1995; Sleeter & Grant, 1987).

One selection from James Banks's extensive writings within this genre provides a classic example: "The Canon Debate, Knowledge Construction, and Multicultural Education" (1993). In the "Canon Debate," Banks identifies and describes five types of knowledge that have implications for both formal and informal multicultural curriculum development and design: (a) personal or cultural knowledge, (b) popular knowledge, (c) mainstream academic knowledge, (d) transformative academic knowledge, and (e) school knowledge. He argues that

> an important goal of multicultural education is to help students to understand how knowledge is constructed. Students should be given the opportunity to investigate and determine how cultural assumptions, frames of references, perspectives, and the biases within a discipline influence the ways the knowledge is constructed. Students should also be given opportunities to create knowledge themselves and identify ways in which the knowledge they construct is influenced and limited by their personal assumptions, positions, and experiences. (p. 11)

Personal or cultural knowledge refers to "the concepts, explanations, and interpretations that students derive from personal experiences in their homes, families, and community cultures" (J. A. Banks, 1993, p. 7) and is central to this view of multicultural teaching. It provides a lens through which knowledge in the other domains is viewed and interpreted. Personal or cultural knowledge may help to explain why many low income students develop an oppositional culture to school culture, why many students of color are unfamiliar with school cultural knowledge regarding power relationships, and why resegregation often occurs when students from ethnically encapsulated neighborhoods meet in desegregated schools. Furthermore, when the personal or cultural knowledge of students and teachers differs, uninformed teachers may lower their expectations for student success. On the other hand, informed teachers can use this knowledge as a vehicle to motivate students and as a foundation to teach school knowledge. *Transformative Academic Knowledge*, as noted previously in the historical inquiry genre, challenges the basic assumptions of *Mainstream Academic Knowledge* and its offshoot, *School Knowledge*.

Iroquois Corn in a Culture-Based Curriculum: A Framework for Respectfully Teaching About Cultures by Carol Cornelius (1999) provides a second illustration of this genre. That author develops a case study of the Haudenosaunee, "The People of the Longhouse" (Iroquois or Six Nations of New York State, including the Mohawk, Oneida, Onondaga, Cayuga, Seneca, and Tuscarora). A culture-based curriculum rests on four assumptions—that all cultures (a) have value, (b) have a worldview that structures their values and society, (c) have an indigenous knowledge base, and (d) are dynamic (p. 37). In a culture-based curriculum, teachers and students conduct cultural research about the worldview of a particular people and how it influences their thinking and way of life; about cross-cultural interactions; and about change and continuity in culture and worldviews, including contemporary times. Cornelius demonstrated the curriculum inquiry process in her own case study of the complexity and continuity of Haudenosaunee culture. She reviewed historical documents beginning in the 1500s, studied 240 paintings by Ernest Smith, Tonawanda Seneca (1907–1975), and interviewed the elders during 1991 to 1992 to develop her case study of the Haudenosaunee worldview and the role of white flint corn, from the people's creation story to the present day.

The state of research in curriculum reform

Curriculum reform is the most visible dimension of multicultural education, and it is sometimes misconceived as the totality of multicultural education. Research in the historical inquiry genre spans several decades, has contributed dramatically to revisionist U.S. and world histories, and has led to the discovery of contributions of women and ethnic minorities in numerous fields. The impact of this research is most significant at the university-level curriculum, resulting in new courses, programs, and departments in ethnic studies and women's studies on campuses across the country, as well as revision of courses in Western civilization, art history, and American and world literature. However, with some exceptions, the core curriculum on most campuses does not require students to take these courses, or any course in multicultural studies. For example, a survey of a random sample of 270 colleges and universities stratified to be representative of American higher education showed that only about 30% have a multicultural general education requirement and offer coursework in ethnic and gender studies, and 54% have introduced multicultural studies into some of their departmental offerings, particularly English, history, and the social sciences (Levine & Cureton, 1992). Still, the vibrant research in African and African-American studies, Latino studies, Asian studies. Women's studies, and (increasingly) American-Indian studies over the past three decades, has inspired the curriculum transformations that are now occurring.

However, the work of scholars such as Takaki (1989, 1993) and Weatherford (1988, 1991), not to mention the impressive line of historical research by African, African-American and Latino scholars, is charged with controversy. It has led to conflicts regarding "political correctness" as well as academic and political opposition that perceives such work as divisive and a threat to national unity, or based on biased or even shoddy scholarship. Critics of multicultural historical inquiry and curriculum reform identify a set of problems: the narrow set of issues, tendentious definitions and heightened politicization, a focus on "special problems" of minorities and women, and an emphasis on differences (at the expense of sameness) that brings divisiveness into the academy (Butler & Schmitz, 1992). Advocates assert that under conditions of democratic pluralism where society is free of social inequalities based on race, culture, or gender, the affirmation of differences need not lead to divisiveness.

To date there exists little evidence to show any K-12 classroom impact from the years of curriculum reform research. Scholarly research into the impact of a multicultural curriculum on the knowledge, dispositions, and school success of young children and adolescents is extremely limited. Thus, the field is often perceived as having failed to fulfill its early promise to achieve equity and excellence in education through curriculum transformation. Furthermore, there is a small but growing body of research, primarily dissertations, that points to a gap between multicultural curriculum theory and classroom practice (e.g., Dilworth, 2000; Titus, in press). For example, studies of teachers who do use multicultural content in their classroom focus on multiple perspectives in history and the reduction of prejudice and stereotypes, but not the curriculum transformation and social action advocated by multicultural curriculum experts (e.g., Dilworth, 2000; Titus, in press). The textbook stands as a centerpiece of their instruction, a phenomenon that underscores the importance of research such as Joyce King's that found evidence of "egregious racial stereotyping and inhumane social practices, including racial slavery" (King, 1992, p. 322). Early research in detecting bias in texts and educational materials has resulted in cosmetic changes in textbooks and some inclusion of contributions by members of underrepresented ethnic groups and women. Also, both genres have contributed to greater ethnic and gender diversity and authenticity in children's literature, as well as an increase in multicultural trade books for children and adolescents. However, given the standardization of K-12 curricula through state and national content standards, the commercialization of textbooks, and the prevalence of mandated statewide testing, the minimal level of curriculum transformation at this level is understandable as well as disturbing.

Cluster two: equity pedagogy

A second dimension of multicultural education is the movement toward equity (Bennett, 1990, p. 11) that addresses the disproportionately high rates of school dropouts, suspensions, and expulsions among students of color and students from low-income backgrounds. This movement aims at achieving fair and equal educational opportunities for all of the nation's children and youth, particularly ethnic minorities and the economically disadvantaged. It attempts to transform the total school environment, especially the hidden curriculum that is expressed in teacher attitudes and expectations for student learning, grouping of students and instructional strategies, school disciplinary policies and practices, school and community relations, and classroom climates. Greater equity would thus help reverse the problems that many ethnic minorities and low-income students face in school and ensure that they attain the highest standards of academic excellence.

Three genres of research fall within equity pedagogy: studies of school and classroom climate (genre 4), student achievement (genre 5), and cultural styles in teaching and learning (genre 6). Three important assumptions underlie these genres: (a) all children have special talents and the capacity to learn, (b) the major goal of public education is to enable all children to reach their fullest potential, and (c) teachers' and students' cultural socialization influence the teaching and learning process. Theory and research in this cluster argue that low-income and ethnic minority students often experience mismatches between home and school cultural expectations that may impair school success. Furthermore, teachers are likely to lower their academic expectations for low-income and ethnic minority students if they are uninformed about cultural styles and differences such as communication patterns, social values, learning styles, time and space orientations, and discussion and participation modes.

Genre 4: school and classroom climates

Research within this genre focuses on school and classroom conditions and the positive (or negative) influences on children and youth. Positive climates refer to school and classroom structures and practices, as well as the attitudes, values and beliefs of teachers and administrators, which contribute to high and equitable levels of student achievement and positive intergroup relations. The main point is that positive teacher–student (as well as student–student) relationships based on caring, respect, and trust, facilitate learning. A number of scholars within this genre use social contact theory as a conceptual framework to study positive school and classroom climates (e.g., Allport, 1954; Schofield, 1995). According to contact theorists, at least four basic conditions are necessary if social contact between groups (e.g., racially diverse students who have had little previous contact) is to be positive: (a) opportunities to become acquainted and develop friendships; (b) equal status among students from the different groups; (c) experiences that require intergroup cooperation to achieve a common goal; and (d) authority figures who encourage, model, and support comfortable intergroup contact and relationships. Included are studies of schools and the degree to which they are integrated (e.g., Forehand & Ragosta, 1976; Sager & Schofield, 1984), school tracking and grouping for instruction (e.g., Cohen, 1994; Oakes, 1985), teacher expectations (Rist, 1970; Steele, 1997), and equitable school discipline practices (e.g., Bennett & Harris, 1982). An important line of research spanning more than two decades is the study of student interaction in heterogeneous classrooms aimed at solving problems of unequal status among students (Cohen & Lotan, 1997). These researchers have developed an instructional strategy, Complex Instruction, to enable teachers to teach at high intellectual levels with ethnically and linguistically diverse groups of students. Cooperative team learning is another line of research in this genre to strengthen academic achievement and positive intergroup relations among racially and culturally diverse students (e.g., Slavin, 1995).

The first illustration of research in this genre is Stacey Lee's ethnography (1996), *Unraveling the "Model Minority" Stereotype: Listening to Asian American Youth.* Lee spent an entire semester immersed in campus life at "Academic High School" (AHS), interviewing Asian and non-Asian students, faculty and staff, observing classes and extracurricular activities, making careful field notes, and analyzing documents. She had regular contact with 82 of the 356 Asian students on campus and taped semistructured interviews with 47 of them. Her research shows how high-status extracurricular activities at AHS, such as the school newspaper and instrumental music program, contributed to the negative school climate. It also reveals how a highly competitive school climate can hinder equity pedagogy by undermining student achievement. All students who were admitted to AHS had scored at the 85th percentile or higher on standardized placement tests and were strongly recommended by their junior high schools. (Asians who scored below the cutoff score on the English language test but significantly higher on the mathematics test were provided special English-as-a-second-language [ESL] coursework throughout their freshmen year.) Despite the previous academic success of all students who were accepted, AHS tracking policies divided them into Advance Placement (AP) classes, Star (honors) classes, regular classes, and the remedial classes (ESL for Asian ninth graders). There were also "mentally gifted" classes for some of the AP and Star students who received special tutors and mentors. Few African-American students were placed in the AP or Star classes, which contained a disproportionately high number of Asian students. In 1990, among the 93 distinguished graduates, 44% were White, 38% were Asian, and 16% were African American. African-American students were perceived by most teachers to be lazy or lacking in interest and talent, whereas the success of Asian students was seen as proof that anyone, regardless of race, could succeed if he or she puts in the proper effort.

The second illustration of this genre is a study of Latino immigrant youth by Susan Katz (1999), which examined "how teachers' attitudes and practices that the Latino students perceived as racist were linked to structural conditions within the school that went beyond the responsibility of the individual teachers" (p. 811). Findings are based on data gathered through interviews and observations during a year-long ethnographic study focused on the school experiences of eight Latino students at a desegregated middle school in Northern California. Five teachers were also interviewed regarding their perceptions of the ESL students.

Coolidge Middle School, rated as one of the city's best in terms of standardized test scores, was located in a quiet middle-class Asian and European-American neighborhood. As a result of a federal court order to desegregate in 1984, 270 of the school's 1,400 students were bused in from the barrio of Las Palmas (historically one of the city's most vibrant neighborhoods but known for intense poverty and the highest level of gang activity) or from Oakdale, an African-American community. However, through tracking or ability grouping, segregation was maintained. One third of the student population was enrolled in the gifted and talented program (GATE), in which 43% were Asian and 49% were European American, with only 1% Latino, 2% African American, and 5% other. On the other hand, among the Latino students, 31% were in ESL classes (located in dingy "cottages" outside the school building) and another 6.5% were in special education (located in the school basement); 21% of the African-American students were in special education. Latino and African-American students rarely participated in after school activities (due largely to the busing schedule) and none were in school government; on the other hand, 75% of the students on the dean's list of discipline problems were African American or Latino.

Students selected for the study included four females and four males, six of whom were first-generation immigrants (two were second generation) from Central America and Mexico. Spanish was spoken at home and all had experienced bilingual education in elementary school, where most were perceived to be bright and promising. At the time of the study, all were enrolled in the Grade 7 intermediate-level ESL class (where Spanish was actively discouraged), had developed "well-defined friendship groups within the class," had older siblings or close friends involved in gangs, and were viewed to be at risk because of poor grades (D average or below), standardized test scores below 26%, and perhaps for poor attendance (S. Katz, 1999, p. 823).

Despite their good or excellent elementary school records, all eight students became increasingly alienated from school during Grades 6 through 8. The Latino students and their teachers both felt tensions in their relationships. Students perceived that their teachers discriminated against them as a group and preferred the Asian students; they felt the teachers regarded them as criminals, prostitutes, and students unable to learn. As a result of feeling uncared for and disrespected at school, many of them developed a reshaped Latino identity through "their own styles of language, literacy, and representation" (S. Katz, 1991, p. 828) and formed social groups to create a space of their own at school. Teachers, on the other hand, stated that they assessed Latino students as individuals and singled out those that were worth investing in. They also saw the peer group pressure among Latino students (manifested in dress and hair styles, graffiti-style writing, and nicknames) as a negative force and tried to single out the higher-achieving students for encouragement and support.

S. Katz (1999) concluded that social structures at the school shaped teacher attitudes and practices, which led to the students' perceptions of racism against them as Latinos. "The structural factors of tracking, resegregation, English-only curriculum, and reliance on standardized test scores along with high teacher turnover in all but the GATE programs together contributed to an environment that greatly limited the Latino students' opportunities for success. They also discouraged the establishment of productive teacher-student relationships" (p. 837). Although all eight students completed the seventh grade, three dropped out in eighth grade, and only two made it to their senior year.

Genre 5: student achievement

Research in this genre focuses primarily on successful teachers of children who historically have been poorly served by the school. Researchers within this genre describe the characteristics of successful teaching as "culturally appropriate," "culturally congruent," "culturally compatible," or "culturally responsive" (e.g.,

Au, 1980, 1993; Escalante & Dirmann, 1990; E. Garcia, 1999; Gay, 2000; Irvine, 1990; Ladson-Billings, 1994, 1995a, 1995b; Locust, 1988). In contrast to the previous genre that focuses on school and classroom climate, this genre focuses on teaching and learning. Culturally relevant pedagogy focuses on "reversing the underachievement of students of color" (Gay, 2000, p. 1) and can be defined as

> using the cultural knowledge, prior experiences, frames of reference, and performance styles of ethnically diverse students to make learning encounters more relevant to and effective for them. It teaches *to and through* the strengths of these students. It is culturally *validating and affirming*. (Gay, 2000, p. 29)

Through culturally relevant pedagogy, students maintain or develop cultural competence, as their culture becomes a vehicle for learning, and they experience genuine academic success and a strong sense of self-esteem. Furthermore, students are encouraged to develop a "critical consciousness" through which they learn to challenge social injustices. Some of the research also focuses on communication processes whereby teachers interact with their culturally and linguistically diverse students and families (e.g., Delpit, 1995; Garcia, 1999).

A classic illustration of research in this genre is *The Dream Keepers: Successful Teachers of African American Children* (1994, 1995a, 1995b), by Gloria Ladson-Billings. This is a two-year ethnography in schools serving a predomin-antly African-American community in northern California. Parents and principals in four schools were asked to nominate excellent teachers, and eight of the nine teachers who were on both lists became the primary participants. The study included in-depth interviews with each teacher, unannounced classroom visit-ations, extensive videotaping of classroom instruction, and collaborative reflec-tion and inquiry with the eight teachers. These teachers differed from each other in classroom organization, teaching style, and personality. Nevertheless, they were quite similar in how they viewed themselves as teachers; how they viewed their students, students' parents, and others in the community; and how they structured social relations inside and outside their classroom; and how they viewed knowledge. First, they were proud of teaching as a profession and had chosen to teach in this low-income, primarily African-American community. Each of these teachers felt a strong sense of purpose and believed it was his or her responsibility to ensure the success of each student. Second, whether African American or not, they were aware of the societal conditions of discrimination and injustice for African Americans and understood how this influenced the school's academic expectations for students of color. Third, they avoided "assimilationist" approaches to teaching and wanted to prepare their students to become change agents, not just fit into mainstream society. Finally, they capitalized on their stu-dents' home and community culture by creating a flexible, fluid, and collaborative learning climate where everyone (including the teacher) learned from everyone else.

From these similarities and points of convergence, the principles of culturally relevant pedagogy emerged. First, students must experience high levels of aca-demic success, including literacy, numeracy, and the technological, social, and political skills they need to be active participants in a democratic society. Second, students must develop and maintain cultural consciousness and competence, and the students' home culture becomes a knowledge source for teaching and learning. Finally, students must develop a critical consciousness through which they may challenge social injustice.

The second illustration of research within the culturally relevant pedagogy genre is Carol D. Lee's investigation of the implications of signifying (a prevalent form of social discourse and verbal play within African-American communities that uses metaphoric language to inform, persuade or criticize), as a scaffold for teaching literary interpretation skills to African-American high school students (C. D. Lee, 1991, 1995).

> Signifying as ritual insult [the popular view of what signifying means] may involve what has traditionally been called "the Dozens": "Yo mama so dumb she thought a quarterback was a refund." . . . Signifying (in its many forms) almost always includes double entendre and a play on meanings. Language is to be interpreted figuratively, not literally. . . . Because the ability to participate in such verbal display is often highly prized in adolescence, it was expected that the high school students in this study would be highly proficient in this arena. This proved to be the case. (C. D. Lee, 1995, p. 614)

The study included six world literature classes in two high schools located in a large urban school district in the Midwest. The graduation rates in both schools were low (39.8% and 50.9%), approximately one third of the students came from low-income families, and 85% of the students scored below the 50th percentile on national standardized test scores. Six classes, taught by five teacher, participated in the study; all students were African American and all but 8.25% of the study participants scored below the 50th percentile rank nationally on standardized tests in reading.

An experimental curriculum based on the cognitive apprenticeship model using principles of culturally responsive pedagogy and contemporary African-American works of literature was implemented in four of the classrooms; the two remaining classes experienced the usual curriculum. In a cognitive apprenticeship, the teacher models and explains to the students the thinking processes that he or she uses to solve a problem; students then engage in practice and the teacher serves as a coach. C. D. Lee (1995) hypothesized that African-American adolescents who are skilled in signifying use strategies to interpret signifying dialogue that are comparable to strategies used by expert readers who interpret figurative language in narrative texts. She developed an experimental unit that included teacher coaching to help students become aware of and transfer the strategies they use to process signifying in their everyday social discourse to their reading of selected African-American literary works.

Both quantitative and qualitative data were collected in a pretest and posttest design to analyze student achievement gains, classroom discourse within the whole class and small groups, and the correlation between tests of prior knowledge of signifying with pretest to posttest change scores by treatment. The results showed statistically significant achievement gains for the experimental group only, and significant correlations between prior knowledge and signifying and posttest gains among students in both the experimental and contrast groups. Analysis of the classroom discourse transcripts showed qualitative transformations of knowledge about signifying from "an intuited informal social usage to a formal concept with psychological, structural, and symbolic functions within a literary context" (C. D. Lee, 1995, p. 617). Although it was "not possible to disentangle the effect of specific variables in the experimental treatment that account for the change from pre- to posttest," Lee argued that an understanding of the language capabilities of ethnically and linguistically diverse students may serve as a platform for equitable pedagogy.

Genre 6: cultural styles in teaching and learning

Research within this genre is highly interactive with the previous research genre, student achievement. Whereas genre 5 emphasizes teacher skills and practices that foster student learning, this genre explores aspects of ethnicity that teachers must understand. There are studies of verbal and nonverbal communication, participation modes, time and space orientations, social values, types of knowledge most valued, and preferred modes of learning that may be prevalent within certain ethnic groups (e.g., Boykin, 1978, 1994; Boykin & Allen, 1988; Kochman, 1972, 1981; Smitherman, 1977, 1998). Within this genre there is a long line of research focused on learning styles among African-American (Hale-Benson, 1986; Hilliard, 1992; Shade, 1982, 1989, 1994); Native-American and Pacific-Islander (e.g., Au, 1980; Deyhle & Swisher, 1997; Vogt, Jordan, & Tharp, 1987); Latino (e.g., Ramirez & Castañeda, 1974); and Asian (Pang, 1995) children and youth. Researchers argue that pedagogy in U.S. public schools is founded on European-American cultural values, language, time and space orientations, and epistemology. This Eurocentric orientation creates inequitable learning conditions for many low-income and language minority children, and children of color who are less familiar with mainstream culture than their middle-income European-American classmates.

The first illustration of research within this genre is the work of Wade Boykin and his associates at Howard University (Allen & Boykin, 1991, 1992; Boykin, 1978, 1982, 1994; Boykin & Allen, 1988). Boykin (1983) has developed a conceptual framework for the study of African-American child socialization that reflects the bicultural nature of the African-American community and captures the "uniformity, diversity, complexity and richness of Black family life" (Boykin & Toms, 1985, p. 38). This framework is based on the premise that African-American culture encompasses three different realms of experience: mainstream, minority, and Black cultural or Afro-cultural.

> [M]ainstream experience entails beliefs, values, and behavioral styles common to most people living in the United States, whereas minority experience refers to certain coping strategies and defense mechanisms developed by many minority groups to face life in an oppressive environment. Afro-cultural experience is essentially the link between contemporary African descendants throughout the Diaspora and traditional West African worldviews. (Allen & Boykin, 1992, p. 588)

On the basis of a distillation of scholarly writing on linkages between West African cultural ethos and the core character of African-American culture, Boykin identified nine "interrelated but distinct dimensions" that are manifested, mostly in terms of stylistic behaviors, in the lives of African Americans (Boykin & Toms, 1985, p. 41). The nine dimensions are as follows:

> (a) spirituality, a vitalistic rather than mechanistic approach to life; (b) harmony, the belief that humans and nature are harmoniously conjoined; (c) movement expressiveness, an emphasis on the interweaving of movement, rhythm, percussiveness, music, and dance; (d) verve, the special receptiveness

to relatively high levels of sensate stimulation; (e) affect, an emphasis on emotions and feelings; (f) communalism, a commitment to social connected-ness where social bonds transcend individual privileges; (g) expressive indi-vidualism, the cultivation of a distinctive personality and a proclivity for spontaneity in behavior; (h) orality, a preference for oral/aural modalities of communication; and (i) social time perspective, an orientation in which time is treated as passing through a social space rather than a material one.

Inspired by studies of the relationship between cultural contexts and cognitive performance among Native Hawaiian children conducted by Tharp and his associates (Tharp, 1989; Tharp et al., 1984), Allen and Boykin (1992) conducted a series of basic research studies guided by Boykin's conceptual framework of African-American culture. One set of studies focused on verve, a second focused on movement expressiveness, and a third set focused on communalism. Overall, the results of this research supported the conclusion that aspects of African-American culture can be incorporated into classroom pedagogy to facilitate learning among African-American children. These studies lend support to the view that cultural discontinuity between home and school settings contribute to the academic difficulties that many children of color experience in mainstream schools.

The second illustration of research in this genre is a decade-long ethnographic study of Navajo youth by Donna Deyhle (1995). Her research focused on the lives of Navajo youth in a border reservation community and compared their experi-ences both in and out of school. The students attended one of two high schools: Border High School (BHS), which is located 20 miles from the Navajo reservation and serves a student population that is approximately half Navajo, and Navajo High School (NHS), which is located on the reservation and serves a student body that is 99% Navajo. Deyhle developed a main database that tracked by name all Navajo students who attended the two schools from 1980–81 through 1988–89. Her information included attendance records, GPA, standardized test scores, dropout and graduation rates, current employment, and post-high school educa-tion for 1,489 youth. She conducted formal interviews with 168 students who left school before graduating and another 100 who graduated or were still in school.

NHS was more successful than BHS in retaining and graduating Navajo stu-dents, even though the curriculum was identical (a 28% dropout rate compared to 41% at BHS). NHS students come from the most traditional parts of the reserva-tion, and there are four Navajo teachers. Navajo is the dominant language in most of the homes, and 90% of the students are eligible for subsidized school meals (Deyhle, 1995, p. 420). The greater success of students at NHS may be due to a stronger sense of cultural identity and the

> sympathetic connection between the community and its school. Where there are fewer Anglo students and more Navajo teachers, racial conflict is minimal and youth move through their school careers in a more secure and supportive community context. (Deyhle, 1995, p. 420)

Furthermore, Navajo students from the reservation who attended BHS were more likely to stay in school and felt more positive about their education experi-ences than did Navajo students who lived in the town. Deyhle (1995) concluded that Navajo students who identify with and maintain connections with their trad-itional culture are more academically successful in schools that implement an assimilationist curriculum and are vocationally centered than students who are not secure in their traditional culture:

> The Anglo community views assimilation as a necessary path to school success. In this view, the less "Indian" one is, the more academically "successful" one will become. Anglos perceive living in town, off the reservation, to be a socially progressive, economically advantageous move for Navajos. In fact, the opposite is true. The more academically successful Navajo students are more likely to be those who are firmly rooted in their Navajo community . . . are not alienated from their cultural values and who do not perceive themselves as inferior to the dominant group. . . . In contrast, those who are not academically successful are both estranged from the reservation community, and bitterly resent the racially polarized school context they face daily. (Deyhle, 1995, pp. 419–420)

The state of research in equity pedagogy

In contrast to curriculum reform, the dimension of equity pedagogy is often overlooked as an essential component of multicultural education. It has been invisible in the political and academic attacks against multicultural education. Yet, there exists decades of research on school and classroom climate that affirms conditions of integrated pluralism and classroom conditions of acceptance due to its positive influence on student learning and peer relations in desegregated classrooms. Research related to student achievement also spans several decades. There exists a strong body of research composed primarily of small-scale studies focused on a single ethnic group, mainly African-American, or Native-American, and Pacific-Islander children. These studies provide consistent evidence of positive impact on student learning when teaching is based on principles of culturally relevant pedagogy. However, to date there are fewer studies of culturally relevant pedagogy with Latinos or Asians, and none in multiethnic classroom settings. Given that many children of color attend predominantly White schools and that Asian and Latino children may be uncomfortable with teaching that includes confrontation and controversy (aspects of culturally relevant pedagogy that are affirmed with African-American youth), more research on culturally relevant teaching in these settings is important. On the other hand, when one considers bilingual education research (which is beyond the scope of this article), there is considerable evidence that language, a central aspect of culture, can serve as a foundation to facilitate student learning. Furthermore, in *Lessons from High-Performing Hispanic Schools* by Pedro Reyes, Jay D. Scribner, and Alicia Paredes Scribner (1999), several case studies show that culturally and linguistically responsive pedagogy were related to strong student performance in schools that serve a high percentage of Latino students.

The research on cultural styles associated with ethnic groups is both promising and risky. We see promise in Boykin's work (Boykin & Toms, 1985), for example, with increased student learning when pedagogy is compatible with the cultural styles of African-American children whose socialization is strongly influenced by an African-American ethos. On the other hand, the research has also contributed to ethnic stereotyping. There is the danger that researchers and practitioners will apply these cultural characteristics uniformly to all members of an ethnic group; they may attempt to teach to a particular style without realizing that individuals within any group vary in the strength of their ethnic identities. Furthermore, this research can create misconceptions that culture is reified and static. Used properly, however, knowledge about cultural styles provides teachers with a means for accurately interpreting students' thoughts, feelings and actions that are indeed fundamentally different from their own, while raising their expectations for student success.

Cluster three: multicultural competence

Some time ago, I suggested, "Multicultural competence may soon become one of the basic skills that schools are required to teach. Just as some states have recently added decision-making or thinking skills to the traditional basics of reading, writing, and computation, so they might require competence in multiple ways of perceiving, evaluating, and doing" (Bennett, 1986, p. xv). More recently, Gay (1995) identified "Multicultural Social Competence" as one of the major goals of multicultural education. She wrote,

> It is imperative that students learn how to interact with and understand people who are ethnically, racially, and culturally different from themselves. The United States and the world are becoming increasingly more diverse, compact, and interdependent. Yet, for most students, the formative years of their lives are spent in ethnically and culturally isolated or encapsulated enclaves. This existence does not adequately prepare them to function effectively in ethnically different and multicultural settings. Attempts at cross-cultural interactions are often stymied by negative attitudes; cultural blunders; and by trying to impose rules of social etiquette from one cultural system onto another. The results are often heightened interracial and interethnic group frustrations, anxiety, fears, failures, and hostilities. (p. 18)

Research genres in this cluster emphasize the nature or development, or both, of individual competence in a multicultural society. Implicit in the idea of multicultural competence are dispositions of open-mindedness and the absence of racial or cultural prejudice, and knowledge about the worldviews and funds of knowledge associated with various culture groups, as well as the diversity within and across ethnic groups. Also implicit is a sense of cultural consciousness, or the recognition on the part of an individual that he or she has a view of the world that is not universally shared and that differs profoundly from that held by many members of different nations and ethnic groups. It includes an awareness of the diversity of ideas and practices found in human societies around the world and some recognition of how one's own thoughts and behaviours might be perceived by members of differing nations and ethnic groups (Bennett, 1995, p. 343).

Multicultural competence includes the ability to interpret intentional communications (language, signs, gestures), unconscious cues (such as body language), and customs in cultural styles different from one's home culture. It varies along a continuum of high to low, and the interculturally competent person can communicate and empathize to some degree with culturally different others and is well aware of his or her own culturally conditioned assumptions. Since an individual's knowledge, attitudes and beliefs are limited by opportunities to experience and learn about the cultural heritage of his or her primary heritage group, there is a great deal of diversity within any one group. Individuals also differ in their access to multiple cultures and therefore differ in their multicultural competence. Some studies focus on ethnic identity development (genre 7); other studies focus on prejudice reduction (genre 8) or ethnic group cultures (genre 9).

The genres in this cluster differ from equity pedagogy genres in that research focuses on cognitive and social psychological variables of individuals (e.g., the knowledge, attitudes, and beliefs of teachers or students, or both, associated with their primary cultural group) that indirectly influence or interact with school and classroom climates, teaching strategies, and student learning. In contrast, research in the equity pedagogy genres focus primarily on social structures, teacher skills and pedagogical practices, or broad-based cultural norms and worldviews associated with groups (often based on ethnicity, gender, or social class) that have a direct impact on student learning.

Research in multicultural teacher education is evident in all three genres within the multicultural competence cluster, and it is particularly prevalent in the prejudice reduction genre. There exists a long line of research on the impact of teacher preparation programs on the knowledge, attitudes and beliefs of preservice and in-service teachers (e.g., Zeichner, 1996). The broader view of multicultural education to include attitudes and intergroup competence focused on race, class, culture, gender, disability, and sexual preference is not an updated approach. It has long been the preferred view of some multicultural theoreticians; others have argued that the expanded view of diversity detracted from efforts to address racial prejudice and discrimination that they believe (in the United States) trumps all other forms. Most of the research within these genres focuses primarily on interethnic competence (race, culture, or both) and the intersections with class and gender. A major assumption is that the reduction of racial and cultural prejudice is possible and desirable. A second assumption is that individuals can in fact become multicultural; they need not reject their familial worldview and identity to function comfortably in another cultural milieu.

Genre 7: ethnic identity development

Ethnic identity refers to the degree to which a person feels connected with a "racial" or cultural group, one's familial ethnic group while growing up. It is a complex cluster of factors such as self-labeling, feelings of belonging or feeling set apart, and a desire to participate in activities associated with the group. The genre focuses on stages of ethnic identity development and themes of preexposure and precontact, encounter or conflict, retreat into one's own culture or (for Whites) overidentification (that is, trying to be like and to gain acceptance) with minorities, developing a healthy sense of one's own ethnicity, and becoming multicultural and committed to social justice. Ethnic identity research has important implications for teaching and learning in racially and culturally diverse classrooms. Students' readiness and comfort with intergroup contact is influenced by their sense of ethnic identity; students in stages of immersion or retreat are less able to interact comfortably in a diverse setting. Most scholars in the field argue that teachers who work with racially and culturally diverse students need a strong sense of their own ethnic identity. Teachers must be at a stage of ethnic identity clarification or higher to be effective in helping all students in their classroom be academically successful (J. A. Banks, 1984; Ford, 1979).

Most of the research has focused on ethnic identity development among African Americans (e.g., Cross, 1979, 1991; Cross, Strauss, & Fhagen-Smith, 1999). Several theories of White identity development also exist, notably Hardiman's White Identity Development Model (WID), Helm's Model of White Racial Identity Development, and Ponterotto's White Racial Consciousness Development Model. These models share common themes and have been integrated into an all-inclusive model of White identity development consisting of five stages:

Pre-Exposure/Pre-Contact, Conflict, Pro-Minority/Antiracism, Retreat into White Culture, and Redefinition and Integration (Ponterotto & Pedersen, 1993).

Racial identity research by William Cross provides the first illustration of research within this genre. Cross developed his original typology of Black racial identity several decades ago through a quantitative analysis of the responses of large samples of African-American and White participants on a pencil-and-paper questionnaire that was published first in an article entitled "The Negro-to-Black Conversion Experience" (Cross, 1979). Cross has continued to develop and refine his work over the years and has strongly influenced other research within this genre (Cross, 1991; Cross & Fhagen-Smith, 1999). Cross (1979, 1991) focused on the identity transformation process that began as African Americans lived through the civil rights movement of the 1950s and 1960s. Although his theory focuses on Nigrescence, the "process of becoming Black," it may be applicable to any group that has experienced oppression and is moving toward liberation, for example, other ethnic minority groups and women. Cross identified five developmental stages: Pre-Encounter, Encounter, Immersion-Emersion, Internalization, and Internalization-Commitment.

African Americans in stage one, or pre-encounter, accept the dominant Anglo-European worldview. They seek to be assimilated into White mainstream society and could be described as anti-Black and anti-African. The second stage, encounter, is triggered by a shattering experience that destroys the person's previous ethnic self-image and changes his or her interpretation of the conditions of African Americans in the United States. Individuals in stage three, immersion-emersion, want to live totally within the Black world. Cross (1979) described the stage-three person as having a pseudo-Black identity because it is based on hatred and negation of Whites rather than on the affirmation of a pro-Black perspective. Stage-three Blacks often engage in "Blacker than thou" antics and view those Blacks who are accepting of Whites as Uncle Toms. In stage four, internalization, the individual internalizes his or her ethnic identity and achieves greater inner security and self-satisfaction. There is a healthy sense of Black identity and pride and less hostility toward Whites. Individuals who move into stage five, internalization-commitment, differ from those in stage four by becoming actively involved in plans to bring about social changes.

The second illustration of research within this genre is Beverly Tatum's decade-long applied research on ethnic identity development among college undergraduates enrolled in a class about the psychology of racism (Tatum, 1992). She taught the course 18 times, at three different institutions: a large public university, a small state college, and a private, elite women's college. In all cases, student enrollment was limited to 30, with 24 as an average. The class makeup has been predominantly White and female, but it has always been mixed in terms of gender and race; the students of color include Latino and Asian, but most frequently have been Black. Over the years, Tatum has noted a profound change in many of her students' ethnic identity development, "although movement through all the stages of racial identity development will not necessarily occur for each student within the course of a semester, or even four years of college" (p. 18).

Tatum (1992) has identified four strategies for reducing student resistance and promoting student development. First, a safe classroom environment must be created. Through years of inquiry and reflection, she identified a number of factors that contribute to a climate of safety: small class size; clear guidelines for discussion, such as confidentiality, mutual respect, and speaking from one's own experience; and interracial dialogue. Second, opportunities for self-generated knowledge must also be created; they are an important way to reduce "the initial stage of denial many students experience." Tatum learned that outside of class, hands-on assignments that accompany course readings—such as interviews, community visits to grocery stores and shopping malls in neighborhoods of diverse racial groups—were highly effective. For example, a powerful assignment for White students was to go apartment hunting with an African-American student and experience the discrimination first hand (p. 19). Third, an appropriate model that helps students understand their own process of ethnic identity development must be provided. She argues that students need to know that their feelings after learning about and discussing racism are "quite predictable and related to their own racial identity development" (p. 19). Feelings of "guilt, shame, embarrassment, or anger" must be understood as normal and natural, however painful they may be. Finally, the exploration of strategies to empower students as change agents must be included over the semester. Tatum argues that to heighten students' awareness of racism without also developing an awareness of possibilities for change creates feelings of despair and is unethical (p. 20). She recommends reading news media, biographies, and autobiographies about individuals who serve as models of effective change agents. Tatum found that meta-comment papers help students analyze and reflect on course journal entries and enable them to reflect on their own process of racial identity development.

Genre 8: prejudice reduction

Clearly, research in this genre is closely connected with ethnic identity research previously described. Stages of ethnic identity are marked by one's relative degree of prejudice or openness toward other racial and cultural groups. The prejudice reduction genre differs from the foregoing genres in that it includes all types of prejudice, not only race and culture, and moves beyond description and identification of a stage of ethnic identity. It seeks an understanding of prejudice reduction, as well as reduction of discrimination that is typically expressed as a result of these prejudices.

The *Nature of Prejudice* by Gordon Allport, published originally in 1954, provides a theoretical framework for much of this research. Allport's theory of positive intergroup contact is also a foundation for research in genre 4, school and classroom climate, which falls within the equity pedagogy cluster. Research studies in these two genres can be distinguished by their primary focus; studies in the climate genre examine how structures and aspects of the hidden curriculum influence student academic achievement, whereas studies in prejudice reduction examine how structures and teaching practices influence attitudes and interpersonal relations. The long line of promising research in cooperative learning illustrates these interactions; both climate and prejudice reduction research build on social contact theory as a foundation for cooperative learning. However, one genre is primarily concerned with the impact of structured intergroup relations on student achievement and the other emphasizes prejudice reduction (e.g., Slavin, 1990). Thus, although studies of cooperative learning (e.g., Slavin, 1995) and complex instruction (e.g., Cohen & Lotan, 1997) show promise for prejudice reduction, they are aimed primarily at student achievement in ethnically diverse classrooms and therefore fall into cluster 2, equity pedagogy.

Prejudice is an attitude based on preconceived judgments or beliefs that are based on unsubstantiated or faulty information. These attitudes are learned from significant others, such as parents and peers, experiences in school, and societal messages in films, television, and the news media. Prejudice becomes discrimination when the individual actively excludes the group, or denies them participation in some desired activity. Research in this genre includes sociological studies in housing projects, the workplace, and schools; socio-psychological studies; curriculum intervention studies; and studies of anti-racist teaching. Although no single theory adequately explains the development of prejudice, Allport (1954) argued that less prejudiced people feel less aggression toward others, hold a generally favorable view of their parents, and perceive their environment as friendly and nonthreatening. No child is born prejudiced; prejudices are learned within a context influenced by personal needs and social influence.

The first illustration of this research genre is a study of teacher efficacy among preservice teachers and in-service teachers in Southern California, with a particular focus on teacher beliefs about their ability to teach students of color (Pang & Sablan, 1995). On the basis of the realization that "stereotypical notions about specific ethnic groups exist in the minds of many teachers," and studies of underachievement among students of color have not focused on "issues of teacher-student relationships," Pang and Sablan investigated "how confident preservice and in-service teachers feel about their skills to teach African American students" (p. 2). An underlying assumption of the research was a relationship between ethnic prejudice and a sense of teacher efficacy with students of color. Presumably, the more prejudice that teachers hold regarding African-American students (or other students of color), the lower their sense of teaching efficacy, and the less efficacious they will be in the classroom.

Participants in the study were 100 preservice and 75 in-service teachers enrolled in multicultural education courses at a large Southern California university; three fourths were female, three fourths were Caucasian American, 13% were Latino or Latina, 6% were Asian American, about 3% were Native American, and less than 3% were African American. At the beginning of the course, participants completed a paper-and-pencil questionnaire that included sections on teaching experience, previous multicultural study and experience, and beliefs about personal and teaching efficacy with African-American students. The results showed that preservice teachers expressed higher levels of personal efficacy than did in-service teachers, and that the predominantly Caucasian sample had limited knowledge of African-American students and culture (less than half had African-American friends and 69% had not taken any multicultural coursework). Furthermore, 41% did not disagree that they had little or no influence on African-American students; they perceived that a negative home environment was to blame for poor academic achievement. The authors concluded that teacher efficacy is an important construct in student achievement; unfortunately teachers' stereotypes about students of color influence their ability to teach children from underrepresented groups. They cautioned that the more hopeful view of preservice teachers (higher personal efficacy) might erode over time. The study did not explore connections between teacher prejudice or teacher efficacy and student achievement in the classroom.

The second illustration of this genre is a study that describes the development of two empirical measures of educators' beliefs and diversity in personal and professional contexts (Pohan & Aguilar, 2001). The researchers took a broad view of multicultural education, inclusive of many socio-cultural variables, to match their interest in measuring beliefs about a range of diversity issues. Their two-dimensional approach to assessing beliefs was based on the idea that an individual's personal beliefs about issues of diversity might differ from his or her beliefs in a professional context. After reviewing the multicultural beliefs literature, the researchers concluded that few studies reported instrument reliability and validity data, and most focused on only one or two aspects of diversity, such as race, gender, ethnicity, and social class. On the basis of the results of this review, their approach included historically marginalized groups of gender, social class, religion, languages (other than English), and sexual orientation rather than what previously existed. They addressed both personal and professional beliefs about diversity (i.e., educational contexts) and set out to develop an attitude assessment tool that was rigorous and psychometrically sound (p. 163). During an extensive process of pilot and field-testing, reliability scores ranged from 0.71 to 0.81 on the personal beliefs scale, and from 0.78 to 0.90 on the professional beliefs scale (p. 173). Construct validity was established through a number of analyses (e.g., relationships with variables such as courses in multicultural education, cross-cultural experience, and scores on the Rokeach dogmatism scale (p. 175).

The researchers concluded, "the developmental process of the measures has been rigorous, leading to psychometrically promising measures" (Pohan & Aguilar, 2001, p. 175) and included copies of both scales in the appendix. However, they cautioned that their interpretations are limited by a number of factors, such as the fact that most respondents to date have been White, and most have been enrolled in multicultural or diversity related courses. Nevertheless, studies like this one can contribute to prejudice reduction research in teacher education where there is a long line of pretest and posttest studies designed to assess the impact of multicultural education interventions.

Genre 9: ethnic group cultures

Studies of ethnic group culture (including European-American "mainstream" culture in the United States) focus on the changing systems of beliefs, social values, worldviews, standards of behaving, and artifacts of other cultures, and can help develop consciousness of one's own culture (including basic assumptions, prejudices, and stereotypes). This genre originates from a line of anthropological studies of non-Western societies and cultures, as well as indigenous people and traditional societies in the Americas conducted early in the 20th century. Early ethnographies are sometimes criticized as ethnocentric and voyeuristic, but they have laid a foundation for contemporary research.

Research in this genre is distinguished from genre 6, cultural styles in teaching and learning, in that the primary purpose is to uncover knowledge about culture that will enhance an individual's intercultural competence. When the individual is a teacher, it is assumed that new cultural knowledge will enable the teacher to facilitate learning among culturally diverse students. Simply learning about cultural styles and socialization patterns (genre 6) may not be sufficient; dispositions of caring and respect, rooted in new cultural knowledge, are also required for multiculturally competent teaching.

Studies by Edward T. Hall, which began in the 1950s, provide a theoretical foundation for much of the research in this genre, although some contemporary critics argue that his work fosters a reified and essentialist view of culture. Hall's writings, such as *The Silent Language* (1959), *The Hidden Dimension* (1966), *Beyond Culture* (1976), and *The Dance of Life* (1983) are classics in the area of intercultural study and vividly describe how humans can be unknowingly influenced by their culture. People from different cultures may perceive the world differently, often unaware that there are alternative ways of perceiving, believing, behaving, and judging. Hall argues that most humans hold unconscious assumptions about what is appropriate in terms of personal space, time, interpersonal relations, and ways of seeking truth (e.g., scientific inquiry, meditation, revelation, etc.). He argues that these cultural differences exist to varying degrees among Anglo-Europeans and ethnic minorities within our society (for example, Native-American nations such as the Hopi and Navajo, African Americans, Mexican Americans, Puerto Ricans, Jews, Chinese Americans, and rural Appalachians), as well as among the peoples of different nations.

The first illustration of this genre is the cultural funds of knowledge research by Luis Moll and a team of educators and anthropologists working with schools and communities in Southern Arizona (Moll, Amanti, Neff, & Gonzalez, 1992). It focuses on teachers learning about the "household knowledge" of Mexican origin and Yaqui families living in the borderlands near Tucson, Arizona. In the original study, 10 teachers each conducted research in three households of children in their classroom. In partnership with an anthropologist skilled in ethnographic inquiry, the teachers entered these households as learners or ethnographers who wanted to know and understand their students and their students' households' "funds of knowledge." This term refers to "historically accumulated and culturally developed bodies of knowledge and skills essential for household or individual functioning and well-being." To discover these funds of knowledge, the teachers interviewed family members and served as participant observers, keenly listening and watching, and learning about the lived practices of their students' households.

> As they approached the households, they noted gardens, recreational areas, tools, equipment, physical and spatial layouts of the homes, books, toys, and any other material clues that might lead to the discovery of household strategies and resources. They engaged in a series of open-ended interviews with parents that focused on family histories and social networks, labor histories of households, and language and child-rearing ideologies. In this way, teacher-researchers came to appreciate the repertoire from which households draw in order to subsist and validated household knowledge as worthy of pedagogical notice. (Gonzalez, 1995, p. 238)

The household funds of knowledge that the teachers initially gathered are based on a sample of about 100 families and include areas such as ranching and farming, including horse and riding skills, animal management, soil and irrigation systems; mining and timbering, including minerals and blasting; business, such as market values, appraising, renting and selling, loans, labor laws, building codes, accounting and sales; household management such as budgeting, child care, cooking, and appliance repairs; home construction, design, and maintenance; repair of airplanes, automobiles, and heavy equipment; contemporary and folk medicine; and religion such as catechism, Baptism, Bible stories, moral knowledge, and ethics.

While they were engaged in this research, the teachers worked together in after-school study groups to develop innovative teaching practices that made strategic connections between homes and classrooms. The authors of this research emphasize that their approach avoids ill-founded attempts at teaching a "culture-sensitive curriculum" that is based on "folkloric displays, such as storytelling, arts, crafts, and dance performance." Instead, the students' funds of knowledge are drawn on to enhance student learning in all the content areas, such as mathematics, language arts, science, social studies, and physical education.

The second example of research within the ethnic group culture genre is grounded in the theory of cultural therapy, a philosophy and process created by George and Louise Spindler through decades of ethnographic research with Ojibwe communities and villages in Western Germany (Spindler & Spindler, 1994). Conceived as a means to help teachers and students cope with cultural diversity, cultural therapy is also a vehicle for school reform in culturally diverse schools (e.g., Phelan & Davidson, 1993). Cultural therapy is a process of bringing one's own culture—assumptions, goals, values, beliefs, and communicative modes—to a level of awareness that permits one to perceive it as a potential bias in social interaction and in the acquisition or transmission of skills and knowledge. One's own culture is perceived in relation to other cultures, so that potential conflicts, misunderstandings, and blind spots in the perception and interpretation of behavior may be anticipated. Culture becomes a third presence, removed somewhat from the person, so that one's actions can be taken as caused by one's culture and not by one's personality.

Spindler and Spindler (1993) argue that when teachers become conscious of their own culture and understand how it shapes their attitudes, values, beliefs, and behaviors, they will become more effective teachers. Likewise, when students understand themselves better and become more aware of the culture of their school and how it interacts with their own personal cultures, they will become more empowered as learners. All members of the school community, including parents, can participate in cultural therapy exercises and become involved in changing the school toward mutually agreed-on goals. Cultural therapy can provide guidelines and a process to help teachers, students, and parents become more effective decision makers as they work toward high academic standards in multicultural classrooms.

For teachers, cultural therapy can be used to increase awareness of the cultural assumptions they bring to the classroom that affect their behavior and their inter-actions with students—particularly students of color. It can be used as a first step to affect and change behaviors, attitudes, and assumptions that are biased (and often discriminatory) and thus detrimental to the academic success of students whose cultural backgrounds are different from their own. For students, cultural therapy is essentially a means of consciousness-raising to make explicit unequal power relationships in the classroom, the school, and the larger society. It can be used to help students clarify the steps necessary to obtain the instrumental competencies they need to gain access to opportunities within the school system and the larger society.

The state of research in multicultural competence

As previously noted, much of the research about multicultural competence focuses on in-service and preservice teachers' knowledge and dispositions related to cultural and racial diversity. Although implications for teaching and learning are important, pedagogy is not the primary focus. It is assumed that teachers must have a strong sense of ethnic identity, to work effectively in schools that serve ethnic minority children and youth, especially those from low-income areas who are ill served by the school. However, the research evidence to support this assumption is thin. Scholars express concern that more than 90% of the nation's teaching force is composed of White middle-income teachers, a majority of whom are uninformed about the life experiences of children and youth who are not part of the racial and linguistic mainstream (e.g., Gomez, 1996). Moreover, as many scholars have written, ethnic prejudice among teachers and students is still alive and hurtful. Thus, an active line of research in the prejudice reduction genre has focused on the racial attitudes of preservice teachers as well as on the efficacy of teacher education to reduce prejudice while preparing teachers for a culturally diverse society (Zeichner, 1996). The study by Pang and Sablan (1995) illustrates the complexity of inquiry within this genre, with research that goes beyond more typical studies of a single multicultural course designed to reduce teacher prejudice (e.g., Bennett, Niggle, & Stage, 1990). However, like most of the research in this genre, it does not provide evidence that a strong sense of ethnic identity and low levels of ethnic prejudice have a positive impact on student achievement.

Prejudice reduction has been an important goal of multicultural education from the beginning; it remains a pillar of purpose in the discipline today. Yet, there is a paucity of substantive research evidence about appropriate interventions to bring it about. The major exception is cooperative learning group research (e.g., Aronson & Patnoe, 1997; Aronson & Thibodeau, 1992; Johnson & Johnson, 1992a, 1992b); much of the cooperative learning research uses sociometric and semiprojective data collection techniques to document attitude change, making it less vulnerable to the weak attitudinal measures available. Ethnic identity development, on the other hand, is a hot topic in current research on college students and adults. The two genres are highly interactive, as seen in research such as Tatum's, but not conflated. The stage of ethnic identity research provides research questions or variables for research into prejudice reduction interventions, a topic in need of methodologically sound research.

Studies in the ethnic group culture genre illuminate school and home discontinuities that undermine teaching and learning, and the evidence related to student learning is stronger. The illustration of funds of knowledge research, as a "processual" (that is, dynamic process) approach to multicultural education helps avoid cultural mosaic approaches often found in teacher education. In the latter approaches, practitioners rely on a decontextualized knowledge transmission model for learning about their students, which tends to create new stereotypes (Gonzalez, 1995). Through this study of household and classroom practices within working-class, Mexican-origin communities in Tucson, Arizona, educators are developing innovations in teaching that draw on the knowledge and skills found in local households. A basic assumption of this research is that students will learn more in classrooms where teachers know and understand these funds of knowledge. In contrast to research in the ethnic identity and prejudice reduction genres, there is evidence that student learning is positively influenced. Other community-based projects in teacher education include similar approaches to cultural studies that enhance multicultural competence (e.g., Aguilar & Pohan, 1998; Mahan, 1982, 1993; Zeichner & Melnick, 1996). There also exists a great deal of research on ways to improve intercultural competence in nonschool settings, which has implications for research and practice aimed at strengthening the multicultural competence of teachers and their students. For example, effective cross-cultural training programs to prepare people for work or study abroad use techniques such as the cultural sensitizer (e.g., Cushner & Landis, 1996; Triandis, 1972), role-playing simulations, and international fieldtrips and cultural immersions to increase intercultural knowledge, understanding and respect (e.g., Brislin & Yoshida, 1994; Brislin, Cushner, Cherrie, & Yong, 1986; Gudykunst & Hammer, 1983).

Cluster four: societal equity

In contrast to the first three genre clusters that address curriculum, pedagogy, and the individual, respectively, research in this cluster focuses on society—especially aspects of equitable access, participation, and achievement in social institutions. Multicultural ideals of cultural pluralism, anti-racism, and multicultural competence place the field at odds with social structures and cultural norms in societies such as that of the United States. Hence the research genres in this companion cluster envision social action and reform to create societal conditions of freedom, equality, and justice for all. Christine Sleeter provides a context for these genres in her writings about multicultural education as a means of empowerment and social change (Sleeter, 1991). She argues that *"empowerment* and *multicultural education* are interwoven, and together suggest powerful and far-reaching school reform" (p. 2). Students must be taught how to advocate for themselves individually as well as collectively, and must develop "the insights and skills to work collectively for social justice" (p. 6). She argues for education that is multicultural and social reconstructionist, and that "forges a coalition among various oppressed groups as well as members of dominant groups, teaching directly about political and economic oppression and discrimination, and preparing young people directly in social action skills" (p. 12).

Research explores inequitable economic policies, such as school funding; inequitable social structure, such as access to health care and post-secondary education; inequitable representations in popular culture, such as stereotypes and omissions in film and the news media; and interventions to prepare students to become social change agents. An important assumption is that broad societal change is a necessary ingredient for equity in educational access, participation, and achievement. A second assumption is that such change is possible and consistent with basic democratic values and the American creed. The overall purpose is working for societal justice along a continuum from developing knowledge and awareness of social inequities at one end to active engagement in reform at the other end. The genres focus on studies of population stratification patterns (genre 10); popular culture, particularly its problematic images of culture and race (genre 11); and civic education to prepare students for social action (genre 12).

Genre 10: demographics

Demographics refers to population trends, particularly statistical profiles and trends of educational and socioeconomic attainment that are stratified by gender, ethnic group and socioeconomic status. The studies emphasize high school graduation and dropout rates; course enrollments and school achievements in the content areas; college enrollment, participation, and completion rates; and school desegregation trends. Also included are population trends in occupational attainment; income levels; languages spoken in the home; health care access; welfare enrollments; and marriage, divorce, and birth rates. The demographics genre often draws on documents published by the National Center for Education Statistics, such as *The Digest of Education Statistics* and *The Condition of Education*. U.S. Statistical Profiles by the U.S. Bureau of the Census also are published as research studies. These studies provide guidelines for educational policies and further research.

The demographics genre is illustrated in a case study of minority and non-minority access to higher education, conducted by Gary Orfield (1988). That study investigated declining college access and public policy in Los Angeles since the early 1970s. It showed that nearly a fifth of the nation's Latinos live in the greater Los Angeles area, as well as many African Americans and Asians. Orfield found that African-American and Latino students attend schools that are inferior to those serving European Americans and Asian Americans. Furthermore, the college-going pool is shrinking for African-American and Latino youth due to high rates of school dropout (43% for African Americans and Latinos compared to 25% for Whites and 15% for Asians) and inability to obtain admission into 4-year colleges. Only the top 7% of high school graduates are eligible for the University of California system. Thus, most African Americans and Latinos "are entitled to nothing but a community college system from which few earn degrees or certificates and few transfer successfully and eventually win a B.A. degree" (p. 152). Orfield concluded that

> The educational policies needing close examination include those that increase high school dropouts, that increase the burdens on low-income families desiring a college education, that increase standards for admission to public four-year colleges and universities, that increase reliance on community colleges to prepare successful transfer students, that reduce and deemphasize minority recruitment and retention programs, and that curtail civil rights enforcement. (p. 157)

He was particularly critical of California's 1960 Master Plan that established "a huge system of public higher education on the basis of a highly selective system of access to the four-year college" (Orfield, 1988, p. 157), and relies on two-year community colleges for everyone else. He argued that since "high school education is unequal, and [since] there are tremendous racial differences in eligibility for public education . . . low-income minority families are paying state taxes that very heavily subsidize the universities which few of their children may attend" (p. 157), especially since the state funding of community colleges is declining. Orfield's more recent research indicates that nationwide school desegregation is declining, and more Latino, African-American, and Native-American youth are attending poorly funded schools in segregated urban areas than in the past decade (Orfield, 1999).

A second example of this genre is Guadalupe Valdés's (1996) ethnographic study of Mexican origin families in South Texas, *Con Respeto: Bridging the Distance Between Culturally Diverse Families and Schools* (1996). Her research spanned three years (1983–1986), during which time she developed portraits of 10 families that provide insights and human faces behind the raw statistics that highlight important immigration trends along the U.S.-Mexican border. The original design of the study was "to follow ten children as they started school in a community close to the Mexican border (Las Fuentes) over a 3-year period" (p. 6). The goal was to "understand how schools could best build on the experiences children had in communities in which two languages were used by most adult individuals" (p. 6). However, the initial focus on children's acquisition of language and literacy in a bilingual environment soon shifted toward understanding and explanation of "how multiple factors, including culture and class, contribute to the academic 'failure' of Mexican-origin children" (p. 7). No answers or solutions were presented in the conclusions. However, important questions are raised that educational policy makers need to consider. The 10 family portraits and mother's perspectives shed new light on immigrant experiences of entering the

United States and deciding to stay; surviving and mediating a new environment through "the family's collective wisdom" (p. 94); raising children; and parental involvement and interactions within the school context. They cause one to question many of the interventions intended to foster school success for immigrant children because they ignore or disrespect the immigrant parents' familistic values, as well as the social and linguistic competence—the cultural capital that immigrant families bring with them from Mexico.

Genre 11: culture and race in popular culture

This research genre is similar to the detecting bias genre in cluster 1 that emphasizes content analysis studies to detect stereotypes, omissions, and inaccuracies in textbooks and other educational materials developed for classroom use. The difference lies in its societal focus, with studies of popular culture and "societal curriculum." In a scholarly review of multicultural education inquiry related to mass media, Carlos Cortés (1995) wrote,

> The mass media—through such avenues as newspapers, magazines, motion pictures, television, and radio—disseminate information, images, and ideas concerning race, ethnicity, culture, and foreignness. Media educate both for better *and* for worse. This media multicultural curriculum functions whether or not individual media makers actually view themselves as educators, whether or not they are aware that they are spreading ideas about diversity, and whether they operate in the realm of fact or fiction. (p. 169)

Most of the research focuses on motion pictures, and to a much lesser degree television (see Cortés, 1995, for examples). Content analysis typifies this genre, such as "The Distorted Image: Stereotype and Caricature in Popular American Graphics, 1850–1922" (filmstrip [ND] produced and sold by the Anti-Defamation League); *The Kaleidoscopic Lens: How Hollywood Views Ethnic Groups* (Miller; 1978); media research and "ideological manipulation" (Spring, 1992); and studies of children's literature published by *Multicultural Review*. Writing about portrayals of Native Americans in popular culture, Pewewardy (1998) discussed the problem of stereotypical images that

> homogenize hundreds of indigenous cultures, robbing them of their distinctive identities and distorting their roles in U.S. history. . . . Today I see silent genocide in the way indigenous people are integrated and reinvented by non-Indians. Appropriation of indigenous ceremonies, religions, and identities has been the most threatening practice. [Examples include] using Indians as mascots and logos in sports culture; new age shamanism; and eugenics research. (p. 73)

A book by Carlos Cortés, *The Children Are Watching: How the Media Teach About Diversity* (2000) provides an illustration of scholarship within this genre. Drawing on decades of personal interest and scholarly inquiry about popular film, most recently films for children as well as television, Cortés provides a framework for continual research on mass media. Cortés finds that the mass media provide a "powerful, pervasive multicultural curriculum." He argues that, "over time, the mass media have provided five distinct but interrelated *types* of multicultural content" by (a) presenting information, (b) organizing information and ideas, (c) disseminating values, (d) addressing audience expectations; and (e) providing models for behavior (p. 55). Research, as well as the media itself, tends to focus on one ethnic group or issue rather than including multiple perspectives or cross-group comparisons. He describes popular media as "ongoing, recurring, transitory, and [focused on] one-shot themes, whose presentation is influenced by media structural patterns." When multiple perspectives on diversity are presented in the media, they are muted by "severe imbalances in the power to disseminate ideas [according to] ideological battlegrounds" presented as multiculturalist, desegregationist, and Americanist (p. 130). Although popular media have the potential to be highly influential in shaping views about race, culture, and other aspects of diversity, there are mediating factors. They include coincidence, or the extent to which a new message is in agreement with one's beliefs; conflict, when a message challenges or disagrees with one's beliefs; marginalism, a message that neither conflicts nor agrees with one's beliefs; and novelty, a message about which one knows little or nothing. In the final chapters of his book, Cortés (2000) develops implications of his research for the school curriculum, including how teachers can help students become critical viewers of the mass media by looking for patterns as well as stereotypes, and becoming aware of the difference.

Scholarly writings by critical theorists such as Henry Giroux in *Channel Surfing: Racetalk and the Destruction of Today's Youth* (1997a) also contribute to scholarship within this genre. In "Rewriting the Discourse of Racial Identity: Towards a Pedagogy and Politics of Whiteness" (1997b), Giroux's analysis of two films with "contrasting narratives of race," "Dangerous Minds" and "Suture," illustrates how a critical analysis of "the representation of race and ethnicity in the media" can illuminate racial politics. Multicultural educators can use such films as a tool to deconstruct Whiteness and to critically examine White privilege in popular culture and the media more broadly. The study of racial and cultural images in popular film become a liberating experience for people of color as well as for Whites, and it can become a step toward anti-racism and social action in the next genre.

Genre 12: social action

Social action refers to individual and group efforts to bring about changes to redress inequities and injustices in home, school, community, state, national, or global contexts. Anti-racist teaching, fair-minded critical thinking, and an ethic of caring are aspects of these efforts (Ayres et al., 1998; J. A. Banks, 1995; Bennett, 1986/1999; M. Katz, Noddings, & Strike, 1999; Sleeter, 1996). The genre is rooted in political socialization research focused on the political attitudes, values, and beliefs of minority and nonminority children and adolescents, such as cynicism and political efficacy, and the implications for political action (e.g., Abramson, 1972; Easton & Dennis, 1967; Greenberg, 1972; Greenstein, 1960; Hess, 1968). Other examples include research guided by a Freirean conceptual framework (e.g., Diaz-Greenberg, 1998; Freire, 1997), and curriculum interventions (e.g., Button, 1974; Ramos-Zayas, 1998).

A study of the impact of a social action high school government curriculum on Anglo, African-American, and Latino 12th graders in Texas illustrates this genre (Button, 1974). The study population consisted of 262 students in two newly desegregated high schools, with even distributions of African-American, Anglo, and Latino students. Two experimental and two contrast classrooms were selected in each school; these were comparable classrooms in terms of student characteristics, including an equivalent tri-ethnic student group. Identical data were collected in the four experimental and four contrast classrooms throughout two months of the intervention. Data included pretests and posttests of students' political attitudes and knowledge, and coding of student initiated interaction two hours a week in all eight classrooms. In addition, follow-up interviews were conducted with a random sample of students, half from the experimental and half from the contrast classrooms, three to four months after the curriculum intervention had ended.

The overriding goal of the experimental curriculum was to "teach for political efficacy" (Button, 1974). It concentrated on getting students to think about the development and use of political strategy to bring about social and political change and to become involved in community action related to their studies. Curriculum units focused on the following: (a) critical self analysis of one's political socialization, particularly key agents and influences; (b) elitist theories of the American political system, power structures, and institutionalized racism; (c) historical and current case studies of political action by dissatisfied minority groups to bring about change through nonviolent and violent means; and (d) student action research in the community. The action research focused on concerns selected by the students who then worked individually or in small groups for about four months to study and attempt to bring a resolution to the problem.

Even though this study was clearly exploratory, findings showed that African-American, Anglo, and Latino students in the experimental classrooms (and not in the contrast classrooms) developed increased feelings of political efficacy, interest, and knowledge. The impact was strongest among African-American males and females, and Anglo females. African-American and Latino and Latina adolescents were strongly influenced by the case studies of political change and viewed them as models of political action; the actual fieldwork, along with the studies of racism, seemed to be most salient for Anglo students.

Another example of this genre is O'Connor's (1997) case analysis of six high-achieving African-American high school students who held high aspirations for their future, even though they were well aware of the barriers they faced based on race, class, and (for two) gender. O'Connor described these students as resilient because they were optimistic and high achieving, even though they were aware of societal inequities and expressed "dominant theories of making it which have been shown to make others give up and lose hope" (p. 597). The students were selected from a larger study that examined how 46 low-income, African-American adolescents in two Chicago high schools conceived of the American opportunity structure and their chances of reaching their aspirations for the future. Participants in the larger study were sophomores who attended two nonselective public schools that drew its students primarily from public housing developments and low-income tenement housing.

> Both schools were situated in areas of concentrated poverty where unemployment, low-wage work, and reliance on public assistance were the day-to-day realities of the residents. The communities were racially segregated, high school attrition was common, gang violence was prevalent, and drug dealing was evident. . . . The achievement levels for most of the student body were low, and attendance and high school completion rates were dismal. The student body was overwhelmingly poor and wholly African American. (p. 603)

The primary method of data collection was the structured open-ended interview; forty-six students were interviewed in private comfortable settings and lasted 1 hour to 1.9 hours. Interview questions focused on students' conceptions of the opportunity structure, as well as their aspiration and expectations for the future. There were 12 high-achieving females, 12 low-achieving females, 11 high-achieving males, and 11 low-achieving males in the broader study.

The six case study students were similar to other high-achieving students in terms of strong academic achievement and optimism for the future. However, they differed in terms of their recognition of institutionalized discrimination experienced by African Americans, their references to collective struggle as a means of bringing about social change, and the existence of sponsors or role models of social mobility and change. Their knowledge of racism and struggle did not hinder their academic success, as some scholars have argued, and may have contributed to their academic motivation and sense of personal efficacy. Thus, the researcher's findings question research spanning over two decades that has shown that marginalized youths' awareness of limited opportunities for job and school success leads to disengagement from school. O'Connor (1997) argues that

> [T]he resilient youths seemed to have received distinct messages (via the actions and ideologies of their significant others) which conveyed that oppression and injustice can be actively resisted and need not be interpreted as a given. ... [T]hese messages, especially those which emphasized the potential for collective action, conveyed the agency that resides (even when dormant) within marginalized communities. In short, resilient youths, unlike other optimistic respondents, appeared to have not only insight into human agency at the personal and individual level but also a basis for interpreting Black individuals and collectives as agents of change. (p. 621)

State of research in societal equity

Research in the demographics genre consists primarily of statistical surveys, although case studies are becoming more important (e.g., Morris & Morris, 2000; Price, 2000; Valenzuela, 1999). Demographic analyses provide helpful benchmarks within trends of success or failure of policies and programs aimed at equitable societal access, especially school attainment. For example, we find significant attainment gains among African-American students, yet their college enrollments (participation percentage rates) are declining; moreover, college enrollments are declining for all students of color except Asians (Bennett, 1995). The poor academic preparation provided to many Alaskan Natives, other Native Americans, African Americans, Mexican Americans, and Puerto Ricans in our nation's schools is well documented by extensive research within this genre (College Board, 1985; Kozol, 1991; Oakes, 1985; Orfield, 1999). These groups are overrepresented in general and vocational tracks, in classes for the mentally retarded, and in schools that have outdated books and inadequate facilities. In many schools across the nation, racial and language minority students constitute a majority of minorities. Children of color usually attend schools with large concentrations of students who are economically disadvantaged or lower achieving, or both. These are schools where teachers often deemphasize higher-order thinking skills and higher levels of teacher questions because of misconceptions that low-achieving students must master basic skills before they can develop higher-level skills (Foster, 1989). Studies suggest that there is differential treatment and lower teacher expectations of racial and language minority students, compared with teacher behavior toward their nonminority peers.

However, these demographic studies are limited by several factors (Bennett,

"Research on racial issues in American higher education," 1995). Researchers lack a national database that is representative of Native Americans, Asian Americans, and Hispanics. Reports ignore diversity such as various socio-economic backgrounds and regions within the various ethnic groups. Also, find-ings lead to contradictory conclusions when trends are reported in terms of college enrollments, the actual head counts provided by colleges and universities each fall, rather than college participation rates, the percentage of a given age group that is currently enrolled in college or has attended for one year or more (Carter & Wilson, 1991). A major problem in research on Hispanics is the failure to distinguish among groups of differing national origin within the Hispanic population; and research on Native Americans is inadequate because for most national educational data Indians have been ignored or categorized as "other."

Scholarly writing is abundant in the remaining genres, culture and race in popular culture and social action. That is reflected in multicultural theoretical writings (e.g., J. A. Banks, 1993, 1994/1999, 1995; Sleeter, 1996). However, the connections with multicultural education research and practice are less extensive than in the other genres. Despite decades of research in the popular culture genre, it is a relatively recent focus of interest for multicultural education researchers and teachers. The work in this genre by Cortés (1995, 2000) provides a rich founda-tion for new inquiry. In contrast, social action has been an important focus in multicultural education since the early 1970s. Nevertheless, the classroom inter-vention research remains thin. One reason may be difficulty in mounting "change agent" studies, such as the Button study (1974), in schools as the political climate has changed. Another may pertain to human subjects approval, owing to possible invasions of student privacy. Moreover, social action research has developed a new thrust with studies of student qualities of resilience and empowerment, and the importance of role models such as found in the O'Connor (1997) study.

Implications for practice

The very idea of mapping the field of multicultural education may raise questions or be disturbing to some readers. Perhaps it conjures up images of reification of structures and knowledge bases in multicultural education. My intent is very different. I view the framework as one conceptual map out of many possibilities, a tool that expands and explores multiple areas of knowledge, perspectives, and understandings of research and practice in multicultural education. It can help identify areas of omission and commission in one's multicultural research, writ-ing, and teaching, and it is immutable and restrictive only if the user so chooses. What then is the use of such a map, if it has no definite shape and definition?

The genres were piloted in the summer of 1999 with two groups of teacher educators from South Africa and the United States. From this experience come several benefits. First, the genres provide a tool for comprehension. Last summer's pilot tests indicate that the 12 genres helped relative newcomers to understand, in a relatively quick way, the complex, comprehensive, and potentially powerful nature of multicultural education in a diverse society. Scholars from a wide var-iety of fields, and who included administrators, teacher educators, and classroom teachers, participated in three half-day seminars focused on the genres. They believed that the genres moved them beyond awareness of multicultural issues. Many participants used the framework to design proposals for research or practice, or both, that focused on their personal and professional interests and concerns in multicultural education.

Second, the genres provide a tool for thinking critically about multicultural education research and practice. The interactive nature of the genre clusters, and the overlap among the genres within and across clusters, provides a springboard to identify primary and secondary genres reflected in a selected study or line of research. For example, studies of cooperative team learning (e.g., Slavin, 1990; Cohen, 1994; Cohen & Lotan, 1997) might fit into genre 4, school and classroom climate, or genre 8, prejudice and prejudice reduction. But when cooperative team learning is defined as an instructional strategy, genre 4 is primary because it is part of cluster two, equity pedagogy. Likewise, funds of knowledge research could fit into genre 6, cultural styles in teaching and learning, because it does have implications for pedagogy. However, because that research focuses on strengthening teachers' intercultural competence, one can argue that the primary genre is genre 9, ethnic group culture. Such an analysis of the genres can stimulate careful thought about the goals, perspectives, and implications of any specific research project in multicultural education.

Third, the genres could be used as tools for more comprehensive decision making and thinking about multicultural educational policies and practices. For example, plans for tracking and instructional grouping might be viewed from the perspective of the three genres in cluster two—equity pedagogy (school and classroom climate, student achievement, and cultural styles in teaching and learning)—as well as from the perspective of genre 10, demographics. Textbook adoption committees could benefit from a review of research in genre 1: historical and subject matter inquiry; genre 2, detecting bias in textbooks and educational materials; and genre 7, ethnic identity development. The framework itself could provide an impetus for considering diverse research perspectives on practices of concern.

Fourth, the genres could be used for new inquiry as well as meta-analyses of existing research in the field of multicultural education. Mapping the field in a comprehensive manner provides an immediate means to discern areas of research activity that invite further inquiry as well as inform practice. Use of the genres could provide new researchers with reference points to get started and, it is hoped, would stimulate experienced researchers to think about possibilities for making new connections for theory and practice. For example, studies of popular culture (genre 11) might influence or connect with studies of ethnic identity development (genre 7). Also, researchers interested in school and classroom climate (genre 4) might find inspiration in cultural styles in teaching and learning (genre 6) such as the Spindlers' (1993, 1994) theory of cultural therapy.

Finally, and perhaps most importantly, the genres could be used by teacher educators as a means toward rethinking programs and research for multicultural teacher preparation, or for designing new ones. Each of the genres offers a way to focus on thinking about teaching and learning in a multicultural society. The genre clusters of curriculum reform, equity pedagogy, and multicultural competence are compatible with major content areas in most professional teacher preparation programs. Those programs typically include studies in general academic knowledge and knowledge in the major and supporting content areas; general and content specific pedagogy and curriculum development; and theories of child and adolescent development and learning within social and cultural contexts. The individual genres of research and practice within each cluster could provide a content focus to strengthen teachers' multicultural knowledge and dispositions, which could be developed into thematic teacher education programs to restructure and rethink these programs at the transformative level (J. A. Banks,

1994/1999). For example, a thematic program could center on reflective teaching guided by practices of inquiry and principles of social justice. The fourth cluster of societal equity provides a multicultural perspective that could be incorporated into foundational studies in teacher education (e.g., historical, philosophical, social, economic, legal, and ethical dimensions of teacher preparation programs). An inclusion of genres 10 to 12—demographics, popular culture, and social action—could move a program from Banks's (1994/1999) third level of curriculum transformation to the higher level of social action. Overall, these genres of research and the implications for practice could be used to evaluate and strengthen school policies and practices, as well as teachers' knowledge and dispositions, in terms of principles of multicultural education. They provide a framework for creating agendas in teacher education research and practice based on principles of multicultural education, such as the ideals of freedom, equality, and social justice in a culturally and racially diverse society.

Acknowledgments

Two colleagues contributed valuable insights to this article, and I am grateful for their assistance. Thomas Schwandt provided thoughtful comments on an early draft of the conceptual framework and research genres presented, and Geneva Gay provided extensive written and oral feedback on the first revision of my original paper presented on April 25, 2000, during the annual meeting of the American Educational Research Association in New Orleans. I am also grateful to the anonymous *Review of Educational Research* reviewers who offered helpful criticism and suggestions for the revisions.

Notes

1 The conceptual framework presented in this article is influenced by my own knowledge of the multicultural education field and related scholarship. It reflects my understanding of what multicultural education means, its evolution over the past three decades, and its visions for the future. My knowledge of the field is influenced by early studies in sociology, intercultural and ethnic studies, and social studies; by teaching experiences in multicultural classrooms; and by years of teacher education work aimed at preparing teachers (primarily White and from middle-income backgrounds) for work with diverse student populations. I am also deeply engaged in work with preservice teachers of color at a predominantly White institution in pursuit of teaching for social justice. This conceptual framework is influenced by my research as well, an agenda that has emphasized action research in a variety of multicultural contexts. For example, I have studied the impact of a social studies curriculum on tri-ethnic classrooms; classroom climates in desegregated middle schools; causes of racial inequities in school suspensions and expulsions in desegregated high schools; explanations of minority student attrition in predominantly White universities; the impact of multicultural education on teacher knowledge, attitudes, and sense of ethnic identity; and teacher perspectives as a tool for reflection and professional development.

2 Originally I described the four dimensions as the movement toward equity; curriculum reform; the process of becoming multicultural; and the commitment to combat racism, sexism, and all forms of prejudice and discrimination. See pages 11–13 in the second edition published in 1990. These dimensions are also discussed in chapter 1 in later editions published in 1994 and 1999.

References

Abrahams, R. D. (1992). *Singing the master: The emergence of African American culture in the plantation South.* New York: Pantheon.

Abramson, P. (1972). Political efficacy and political trust among Black schoolchildren: Two explanations. *Journal of Politics, 34,* 1243–1275.

Acuña, R. (1988). *Occupied America: A history of Chicanos.* New York: Harper & Row.

Aguilar, T. E., & Pohan, C. A. (1998). A cultural immersion experience to enhance cross-cultural competence. *Sociotam 8*(1), 30–49.

Allen, B., & Boykin, W. (1991). The influence of contextual factors on Afro-American and Euro-American children's performance: Effects of movement opportunity and music. *International Journal of Psychology, 26*(3), 373–387.

Allen, B., & Boykin, W. (1992). African-American children and the educational process: Alleviating cultural discontinuity through prescriptive pedagogy. *School Psychology Review, 21*(4), 586–596.

Allen, P. G. (1986). *The sacred hoop.* Boston: Beacon Press.

Allport, G. (1954). *The nature of prejudice.* Reading, MA: Addison Wesley.

Appiah, K. A., & Gates, H. L. (Eds.). (1999). *Africana: The encyclopedia of the African and African American experience.* New York: Basic Books.

Aronson, E., & Patnoe, S. (1997). *The jigsaw classroom.* New York: Longman.

Aronson, E., & Thibodeau, R. (1992). The jigsaw classroom: A cooperative strategy for reducing prejudice. In J. Lynch, C. Modil, & S. Modil (Eds.), *Cultural diversity in the schools* (Vol. II, pp. 231–256). London: Falmer Press.

Asante, M. (1987). *The Afrocentric idea.* Philadelphia: Temple University Press.

Asante, M. (1990). *Kemet, Afrocentricity and knowledge.* Trenton, NJ: Africa World Press, Inc.

Asante, M. (1991). The Afrocentric idea in education. *The Journal of Negro Education, 60*(2), 170–180.

Au, K. H. (1980). Participation structures in a reading lesson with Hawaiian children: Analysis of a culturally appropriate instructional event. *Anthropology and Education Quarterly, 11*(2), 91–115.

Au, K. H. (1993). *Literacy in multicultural settings.* New York: Harcourt Brace.

Ayers, W., Hunt, J., & Quinn, T. (Eds.). (1998). *Teaching for social justice.* New York: Teachers College Press.

Baker, G. (1983). *Planning and organizing for multicultural instruction.* Menlo Park, CA: Addison-Wesley.

Banks, C. (1996). The Intergroup Education Movement. In J. Banks (Ed.), *Multicultural education, transformative knowledge, and action* (pp. 251–277). New York: Teachers College Press.

Banks, J. A. (1970). *Teaching the Black experience: Methods and materials.* Belmont, CA: Fearon.

Banks, J. A. (1984/1999). *Teaching strategies for ethnic studies.* Boston: Allyn & Bacon.

Banks, J. A. (1993). The canon debate, knowledge construction, and multicultural education, *Educational Researcher, 22*(5), 4–14.

Banks, J. A. (1994/1999). *An introduction to multicultural education.* Needham Heights, MA: Allyn & Bacon.

Banks, J. A. (1995). Historical reconstruction of knowledge about race: Implication for transformative teaching. *Educational Researcher, 24*(2), 15–25.

Bennett, C. I. (1979). Individual and cultural differences: A necessary interaction. *Educational Leadership, 37,* 259–268.

Bennett, C. I. (1986/1990/1995/1999). Comprehensive multicultural education: Theory and practice. (Editions 1–4). Needham Heights, MA: Allyn & Bacon.

Bennett, C. I. (1995). Research on racial issues in American higher education. In J. A. Banks & C. M. Banks (Eds.), *Handbook of research on multicultural education* (pp. 663–682). New York: Macmillan.

Bennett, C. I., & Harris, J. J., III. (1982). Suspensions and expulsions of male and Black students: A study of the causes of disproportionality. *Urban Education, 16*(4), 399–423.

Bennett, C., Niggle, T., & Stage, F. (1990). Preservice multicultural teacher education: Predictors of student readiness. *Teaching and teacher education, 8*(1), 243–254.

Boykin, A. W. (1978). Psychological/behavioral verve in academic task performance: Pretheoretical considerations. *Journal of Negro Education, 47*(8), 343–354.

Boykin, A. W. (1982). Task variability and the performance of Black and White school children: Vervistic explorations. *Journal of Black Studies, 12*(4), 469–485.

Boykin, A. W. (1983). The academic performance of Afro-American children. In J. Spence (Ed.), *Achievement and achievement motives* (pp. 221–271). San Francisco: W. Freeman.

Boykin, A. W. (1994). Afrocultural expression and its implications for schooling. In E. R. Hollins, J. E. King, & W. C. Hayman (Eds.), *Teaching diverse populations: Formulating a knowledge base* (pp. 243–256). Albany, NY: SUNY Press.

Boykin, A. W., & Allen, B. A. (1988). Rhythmic movement facilitated learning in working-class Afro-American children. *Journal of Genetic Psychology, 149*(3), 335–347.

Boykin, A. W., & Toms, F. D. (1985). Black child socialization: A conceptual framework. In H. P. McAdoo & J. L. McAdoo (Eds.), *Black children: Social, educational, and parental Environments* (pp. 33–51), New York: Sage.

Brantlinger, P. (1985). Victorians and Africans: The genealogy of the myth of the dark continent. In H. L. Gates, Jr. (Ed.), *"Race" writing and difference* (pp. 185–222). Chicago: The University of Chicago Press.

Brislin, R. W., Cushner, K., Cherrie, C., & Yong, M. (1986). *Intercultural interactions: A Practical guide.* Beverly Hills, CA: Sage.

Brislin, R. W., & Yoshida, T. (Eds.). (1994). *Improving intercultural interaction.* Thousand Oaks, CA: Sage.

Butler, J., & Schmitz, B. (1992). Ethnic studies, women's studies, and multiculturalism. *Change, 24*(1), 37–41.

Button, C. I. (1974). Political education for minority groups. In R. G. Neimi (Ed.), *The politics of future citizens* (pp. 167–198). San Francisco: Jossey-Bass.

Cahan, S., & Kocur, Z. (Eds.). (1996). *Contemporary art and multicultural education.* New York: Routledge and The New Museum of Modern Art.

Calderón, H., & Saldívar, J. D. (Eds.). (1991). *Criticism in the borderlands: Studies in Chicano literature, culture, and ideology.* Durham, NC: Duke University Press.

Carter, D. J., & Wilson, R. (Eds.). (1991). *Ninth annual status report: Minorities in higher education.* Washington, DC: American Council on Education.

Clark, V. (1991). Developing Diaspora literacy and *marasa* consciousness. In H. Spillers (Ed.), *Comparative American identities* (pp. 41–61), New York: Routledge.

Cohen, E. G. (1994). Restructuring the classroom: Conditions for productive small groups, *Review of Educational Research, 64*(1), 1–35.

Cohen, E. G., & Lotan, R. A. (1997). *Working for equity in heterogeneous classrooms: Sociological theory in practice.* New York: Teachers College Press.

College Board. (1985). Equality and excellence: The educational status of Black Americans. New York: Author.

Cornelius, C. (1999). *Iroquois corn in a culture-based curriculum: A framework for respectfully teaching about cultures.* Albany, NY: SUNY Press.

Cortés, C. E. (1973). Teaching the Chicano experience. In J. A. Banks (Ed.), *Teaching ethnic studies: Concepts and strategies* (pp. 181–199). Washington, DC: National Council for the Social Studies.

Cortés, C. E. (1995). Knowledge construction and popular culture: The media as multicultural educator. In J. A. Banks (Ed.), *Handbook of research on multicultural education* (pp. 169–183). New York: Macmillan.

Cortés, C. (2000). *The children are watching: How the media teach about diversity.* New York: Teachers College Press.

Cross, W. E., Jr. (1979, July). The Negro to Black conversion experience: Toward a psychology of Black liberation. *Black World, 20*(9), 17–27.

Cross, W. (1991). *Shades of Black: Diversity in African-American identity.* Philadelphia: Temple University Press.

Cross, W., Strauss, L., & Fhagen-Smith, P. (1999). African American identity development across the life span: Educational implications. In R. Sheets & E. Hollins (Eds.), *Racial & ethnic identity in school practices* (pp. 29–45). Mawah, NJ: Lawrence Erlbaum Associates.

Cushner, K., & Landis, D. (1996). The intercultural sensitizer. In D. Landis & R. S. Bahgat

(Eds.), *Handbook of intercultural training* (92nd ed., pp. 185–202). Thousand Oaks, CA: Sage.

Delpit, L. (1995). *Other people's children: Cultural conflict in the classroom.* New York: The New Press.

Deyhle, D. (1995). Navajo youth and Anglo racism: Cultural integrity and resistance. *Harvard Educational Review, 65*(3), 403–444.

Deyhle, D., & Swisher, K. (1997). Research in American Indian and Alaska native education: From assimilation to self-determination. In M. W. Apple (Ed.), *Review of research in education* (Vol. 22, pp. 113–194). Washington, DC: American Educational Research Association.

Diaz-Greenberg, R. (1998, April). *Latino voices of high school students: Overcoming the culture of silence.* Paper presented at the annual meeting of the American Educational Research Association, San Diego, CA.

Dilworth, P. P. (2000). *Multicultural content integration in the social studies.* Unpublished doctoral dissertation, Emory University, Atlanta, Georgia.

Diop, C. A. (1974). *The African origin of civilization: Myth or reality.* Chicago: Lawrence Books.

DuBois, W. E. B. (1961). *The souls of Black folk.* New York: New American Library.

Easton, D., & Dennis, J. (1967). The child's acquisition of regime norms: Political efficacy. *American Political Science Review, 61*(6), 229–246.

Escalante, J., & Dirmann, J. (1990). The Jamie Escalante math program. *Journal of Negro Education, 59*(30), 407–423.

Feagin, J., & Feagin, C. (1993). *Racial and ethnic relations* (4th ed.). Englewood Cliffs, NJ: Prentice-Hall.

Foner, E. (Ed.). (1990). *The new American history.* Philadelphia, PA: Temple University Press.

Forbes, J. D. (1973). Teaching Native American values and cultures. In J. A. Banks (Ed.), *Teaching ethnic studies: Concepts and strategies* (pp. 201–225), Washington, DC: National Council for the Social Studies.

Forehand, G. A., & Ragosta, M. (1976). *A handbook for integrated schooling.* Princeton, NJ: Educational Testing Service.

Foster, M. (1989). It's cooking now: A performance analysis of the speech events of a Black teacher in an urban community. *Language in Society, 18*(1), 1–21.

Freire, P. (1997). *Pedagogy of the oppressed* (new revised 20th anniversary ed.). New York: Continuum.

Garcia, E. (1999). *Student cultural diversity: Understanding and meeting the challenge* (2nd ed.). Boston: Houghton Mifflin.

Garcia, J. (1993). The changing image of ethnic groups in textbooks. *Phi Delta Kappan, 75*(1), 29–35.

Gay, G. (1973). Racism in America: Imperatives for teaching ethnic studies. In J. A. Banks (Ed.), *Teaching ethnic studies: Concepts and strategies* (pp. 27–49). Washington, DC: National Council for the Social Studies.

Gay, G. (1983). Multicultural education: Historical developments and future prospects. *Phi Delta Kappan, 64,* 560–563.

Gay, G. (1985). Implications of selected models of ethnic identity development for educators, *Journal of Negro Education, 54*(1), 43–55.

Gay, G. (1988). Designing relevant curricula for diverse learners. *Education and Urban Society, 20,* 327–340.

Gay, G. (1994). *At the essence of learning: Multicultural education,* West Lafayette, IN: Kappa Delta Pi.

Gay, G. (1995). A synthesis of scholarship in multicultural education. Oak Brook, IL: North Central Regional Educational Laboratory.

Gay, G. (2000). *Culturally responsive teaching: Theory, research, and practice,* New York: Teachers College Press.

Gibson, M. (1976/1984). Approaches to multicultural education in the United States: Some concepts and assumptions. *Anthropology & Education Quarterly, 1*(1), 94–119.

Gill, D., & Levidow, L. (1987). *Anti-racist science teaching.* London: Free Association Books.

Giroux, H. A. (1997a). *Channel surfing: Race talk and the destruction of today's youth*. New York: St. Martin's Press.

Giroux, H. A. (1997b). Rewriting the discourse of racial identity: Towards a pedagogy and politics of Whiteness. *Harvard Educational Review, 67*(2), 285–319.

Gollnick, D. (1995). National and state initiatives for multicultural education. In J. A. Banks & C. M. Banks (Eds.), *Handbook of Research on Multicultural Education* (pp. 44–64). New York: Macmillan.

Gomez, M. L. (1996). Prospective teachers' perspectives on teaching "other people's children." In Zeichner, K., Mulnick, S., & Gomez, M. L. (Eds.), *Currents in teacher education reform* (pp. 109–132). New York: Teachers College Press.

Gonzalez, N. (1995). Processual Approaches to multicultural education, *Journal of Applied Behavioral Science, 31*(2), 234–244.

Grant, C. A. (Ed.). (1978). *Multicultural education: Commitments, issues, and applications*. Washington, DC: Association for Supervision and Curriculum Development.

Grant, C. A., & Tate, W. F. (1995). Multicultural education through the lens of multicultural education research literature. In J. A. Banks (Ed.), *Handbook of Research on Multicultural Education* (pp. 145–166). New York: Macmillan.

Greenberg, E. (1972). Black children, self-esteem, and the liberation movement. *Politics and Society, 2*, 293–302.

Greenstein, F. (1960). The benevolent leader, *American Political Science Review, 65*, 353–371.

Gudykunst, W. B., & Hammer, M. R. (1983). Basic training design: Approaches to intercultural training. In D. Landis & R. W. Brislin (Eds.), *Handbook of intercultural training* (Vol. 1, pp. 118–154). New York: Pergamon.

Hale-Benson, J. (1986). *Black children: Their roots, cultures, and learning styles.* (revised ed.). Baltimore: The Johns Hopkins University Press.

Hall, E. T. (1959). *The silent language*. New York: Doubleday.

Hall, E. T. (1966). *The hidden dimension*. New York: Doubleday.

Hall, E. T. (1976). *Beyond culture*. New York: Doubleday.

Hall, E. T. (1983). *The dance of life*. New York: Doubleday.

Harada, V. H. (1994). An analysis of stereotypes and biases in recent Asian American fiction for adolescents. *Ethnic Forum, 14*(2), 43–48.

Hess, R. (1968). Political socialization in the schools. *Harvard Educational Review, 38*, 528–536.

Hilliard, A. G. (1992). Behavioral style, culture, and teaching and learning. *Journal of Negro Education, 61*, 370–377.

Hoffman, D. M. (1996). Culture and self in multicultural education: Reflections on discourse, text, and practice. *American Educational Research Journal, 33*(3), 545–569.

Irvine, J. J. (1990). *Black students and school failure: Policies, practices, and prescriptions*. New York: Greenwood.

Irvine, J. J. (2000, May). *Seeing with the cultural eye: Different perspectives of African American teachers and researchers*. Invited address presented at the annual meeting of the American Educational Research Association, New Orleans.

Johnson, D. W., & Johnson, R. T. (1992a). Positive interdependence: Key to effective cooperation. In R. Hertz-Lazarowitz & N. Miller (Eds.), *Interaction in cooperative groups* (pp. 174–199). New York: Cambridge University Press.

Johnson, D. W., & Johnson, R. T. (1992b). Social interdependence and cross-ethnic relationships. interdependence: Key to effective cooperation. In J. Lynch, C. Modil, & S. Modil (Eds.), *Cultural diversity in the schools* (Vol. II, pp. 179–190). London: Falmer Press.

Kallen, H. M. (1924). *Culture and democracy in the United States*. New York: Boni and Liveright.

Katz, M., Noddings, N., & Strike, K. (Eds.). (1999). *Justice and caring: The search for common ground in education*. New York: Teachers College Press.

Katz, S. R. (1999). Teaching in tensions: Latino immigrant youth, their teachers, and the structures of schooling, *Teachers College Record, 100*(4), 809–840.

King, J. E. (1992). Diaspora literacy and consciousness in the struggle against miseducation in the Black community. *Journal of Negro Education, 61*(3), 317–340.

Kochman, T. (Ed.). (1972). *Rappin' and stylin' out: Communication in urban Black America.* Urbana: University of Illinois Press.

Konvitz, M. R. (1974). Horace Meyer Kallen (1882–1974): Philosopher of the Hebraic American idea. In M. Find & M. Himmelfarb (Eds.), *American Jewish yearbook, 1974–1975* (pp. 65–67). Philadelphia: Jewish Publication Society of America.

Kozol, J. (1991). *Savage inequalities: Children in America's schools.* New York: Crown.

Ladson-Billings, G. (1994). *The dreamkeepers: Successful teachers of African American children.* San Francisco: Jossey-Bass.

Ladson-Billings, G. (1995a). Toward a theory of culturally relevant pedagogy. *American Educational Research Journal, 32*(3), 465–491.

Ladson-Billings, G. (1995b). But that's just good teaching! The case for culturally relevant pedagogy. *Theory Into Practice, 34*(3), 159–165.

Lee, C. D. (1991). Big picture talkers/words walking without masters: The instructional implications of ethnic voices for an expanded literacy. *Journal of Negro Education, 60*(3), 291–304.

Lee, C. D. (1995). A culturally based cognitive apprenticeship: Teaching African American high school students' skills in literary interpretation. *Reading Research Quarterly, 30*(4), 608–630.

Lee, S. (1996). *Unraveling the model minority stereotype: Listening to Asian American youth.* New York: Teachers College Press.

Levine, L. (1977). *Black culture and Black consciousness: Afro-American folk thought from slavery to freedom.* New York: Oxford University Press.

Levine, A., & Cureton, J. (1992). The quest revolution: Eleven facts about multiculturalism and the curriculum. *Change, 24*(1), 25–29.

Locust, C. (1988). Wounding the spirit: Discrimination and traditional American Indian belief systems. *Harvard Educational Review, 58*(3), 315–330.

Mahan, J. (1982). Native Americans as teacher educators: Anatomy and outcomes of a cultural immersion project. *Journal of Educational Equity & Leadership, 2*(2), 100–109.

Mahan, J. (1993). Teacher education in American Indian communities: Learnings from reservation sources. *Journal of Navajo Education, 11*(1), 13–21.

Miller, R. M. (Ed.). (1978). *The Kaleidoscopic lens: How Hollywood views ethnic groups.* Englewood, NJ: Jerome S. Ozer.

Moll, L., Amanti, C., Neff, D., & Gonzalez, N. (1992). Funds of knowledge for teaching: Using a qualitative approach to connect homes and classrooms. *Theory Into Practice, 31*(2), 132–140.

Morris, V. G., & Morris, C. L. (2000). *Creating caring and nurturing educational environments for African American children.* Westport, CT: Bergin and Garvey.

Nieto, S. (1998, Summer). Fact and fiction: Stories of Puerto Ricans in U.S. schools. *The Harvard Educational Review, 68*(2), 133–163.

Oakes, J. (1985). *Keeping Track: How schools structure inequality.* New Haven: Yale University Press.

O'Connor, C. (1997). Dispositions toward (collective) struggle and educational resilience in the inner city: A case analysis of six African-American high school students. *American Educational Research Journal, 34*(4), 593–629.

Orfield, G. (1988). Exclusion of the majority: Shrinking college access and public policy in metropolitan Los Angeles. *Urban Review, 20*(3), 147–163.

Orfield, G. (1999). Politics matters: Educational policy and Chicano students. In J. Moreno (Ed.), The elusive quest for equality [Special issue]. *Harvard Educational Review,* pp. 111–119.

Padilla, A. M., & Lindholm, K. J. (1995). Quantitative educational research with minorities. In J. A. Banks (Ed.), *Handbook of research on multicultural education* (pp. 97–113). New York: Macmillan.

Pai, Y. (1990). *Cultural foundations of education.* New York: Merrill/Macmillan.

Pang, V. O. (1995), Asian Pacific American students: A diverse and complex population. In J. A. Banks & C. M. Banks (Eds.), *The handbook on research in multicultural education* (pp. 412–424). New York: Macmillan.

Pang, V. O., & Sablan, V. (1995, April). *Teacher efficacy: Do teachers believe they can be effective with African American students?* Paper presented at the annual meeting of the American Educational Research Association, San Francisco.

Pewewardy, C. (1998). Fluff and feathers: Treatment of American Indians in the literature and the classroom. *Equity & Excellence in Education, 31* (1), 69–76.

Phelan, P., & Davidson, A. L. (1993). *Renegotiating cultural diversity in American schools.* New York: Teachers College Press.

Pohan, C. A., & Aguilar, T. E. (2001). Measuring educators' beliefs about diversity in personal and professional contexts. *American Educational Research Journal, 38*(1), 159–182.

Ponterotto, J. G., & Pedersen, P. B. (1993). *Preventing prejudice: A guide for counselors and educators.* Newbury Park, CA: Sage.

Price, J. N. (2000). *Against the odds: The meaning of school and relationships in the lives of six young African-American men.* Stamford, CT: Ablex Publishing Corporation.

Ramírez, M., III, & Castañeda, A. (1974). *Cultural democracy, bicognitive development and education.* New York: Academic Press.

Ramos-Zayas, A. Y. (1998). Nationalist ideologies, neighborhood activism, and educational spaces in Puerto Rican Chicago. *Harvard Educational Review, 68*(2), 164–192.

Reyes, P., Scribner, J. D., & Paredes Scribner, A. (Eds.). (1999). *Lessons from high-performing Hispanic schools.* New York: Teachers College Press.

Rist, R. (1970). Student social class and teacher expectations: The self-fulfilling prophecy in ghetto education. *Harvard Education Review, 40*(3), 411–451.

Ruiz, R. (1991). The empowerment of language-minority students. In C. Sleeter (Ed.), *Empowerment through multicultural education* (pp. 217–227). Albany, NY: SUNY Press.

Sagar, H. A., & Schofield, J. W. (1984). Integrating the desegregated school: Problems and possibilities. In D. E. Bartz & M. L. Maehr (Eds.), *Advances in motivation and achievement* (pp. 204–242). Greenwich, CT: JAI Press.

Schofield, J. W. (1995). Improving intergroup relations. In W. Hawley & A. Jackson (Eds.), *Realizing our common destiny: Improving race and ethnic relations in America.* San Francisco: Jossey Bass.

Shade, B. J. (1982). African-American cognitive style: A variable in school success? *Review of Educational Research, 52*(2), 219–244.

Shade, B. J. (Ed.). (1989). *Culture, style, and the educative process.* Springfield, IL: Thomas.

Shade, B. J. (1994). Understanding the African American learner. In E. R. Hollins, J. E. King, & W. C. Hayman (Eds.), *Teaching diverse populations* (pp. 175–189). Albany, NY: SUNY Press.

Shinn, R. (1972). *Culture and school: Socio-cultural influences.* San Francisco: Intext Educational Publishers.

Sills, D. L. (1968). Assimilation. In *International encyclopedia of the social sciences* (Vol. 1, pp. 438–444). New York: Macmillan/Free Press.

Slavin, R. (1990). *Cooperative learning: Theory, research, and practice.* Englewood Cliffs, NJ: Prentice Hall.

Slavin, R. (1995). Cooperative learning and intergroup relations. In J. A. Banks & C. M. Banks (Eds.), *Handbook of research on multicultural education* (pp. 628–633). New York: Macmillan.

Sleeter, C. (1989). Multicultural education as a form of resistance to oppression. *Journal of Education, 17*(3), 51–71.

Sleeter, C. (Ed.). (1991). *Empowerment through multicultural education.* Albany, NY: SUNY Press.

Sleeter, C. (1996). *Multicultural education as social activism.* Albany, NY: SUNY Press.

Sleeter, C. & Grant, C. (1987). An analysis of multicultural education in the United States. *Harvard Educational Review, 57*(4), 421–444.

Smitherman, G. (1977). *Talkin' and testifyin': The language of Black America.* Boston: Houghton Mifflin.

Smitherman, G. (1998). Black English/Ebonics: What it be like? In T. Perry & L. Delpit (Eds.), *The real Ebonics debate: Power, language, and the education of African-American children* (pp. 29–37). Boston: Beacon.

Spindler, G., & Spindler, L. (1994). *Pathways to cultural awareness: Cultural therapy with teachers and students.* Thousand Oaks, CA: Sage Publications.

Spindler, G., & Spindler, L. (1993). The processes of culture and person: Cultural therapy and culturally diverse schools. In P. Phelan & A. Davidson (Eds.), *Renegotiating cultural diversity in American schools* (pp. 27–51). New York: Teachers College Press.

Spring, J. (1992). *Images of American life: A history of ideological management in schools, movies, radio, and television.* Albany, NY: SUNY Press.

Steele, C. M. (1997). A threat in the air: How stereotypes shape intellectual identity and performance. *American Psychologist, 52*(6), 613–629.

Suzuki, B. H. (1979). Multicultural education: What's it all about? *Integratededucation, 17,* 43–50.

Suzuki, B. H. (1984). Curriculum transformation for multicultural education. *Education and Urban Society, 16,* 294–322.

Takaki, R. (1989). *Strangers from a different shore: A history of Asian Americans.* New York: Little, Brown.

Takaki, R. (1993). *A different mirror: A history of multicultural America.* New York: Little, Brown.

Tatum, B. (1992). Talking about race, learning about racism: The application of racial identity development theory in the classroom. *Harvard Educational Review, 62*(1), 1–24.

Tharp, R. (1989). Psychocultural variables and constants: Effects on teaching and learning in school. *American Psychologist, 44,* 349–359.

Tharp, R., Jordan, C., Speidel, G., Au, K., Klein, T., Calkins, R., Sloat, K., & Gillmore, R. (1984). Product and process in applied developmental research: Education and children of a minority. In A. Brown & B. Rogoff (Eds.), *Advances in developmental psychology* (Vol. 3, pp. 91–141). Hillsdale, NJ: Erlbaum.

Titus, C. (in press). *Secondary social studies teachers and multicultural education: A case study of attitudes, actions, and constraints.* Unpublished doctoral dissertation, Indiana University, Bloomington.

Triandis, H. (1972). *The analysis of subjective culture.* New York: Wiley.

Valdés, G. (1996). *Con respeto: Bridging the distance between culturally diverse families and schools: An ethnographic portrait.* New York: Teachers College Press.

Valenzuela, A. (1999). *Subtractive schooling: U.S.-Mexican youth and the politics of caring.* Albany, NY: SUNY Press.

Vogt, L. A., Jordan, C., & Tharp, R. G. (1987). Explaining school failure, producing school success: Two cases. *Anthropology & Education Quarterly, 18,* 276–286.

Weatherford, J. (1988). *Indian givers: How the Indians of the Americas transformed the world.* New York: Crown Publishers, Inc.

Weatherford, J. (1991). *Native roots: How the Indians of the Americas enriched America.* New York: Crown Publishers, Inc.

Woodson, C. G. (1933/1969). *Mis-education of the Negro.* Washington, DC: Associated Publishers.

Zavlasky, C. (1993). *Multicultural mathematics.* Portland, OR: J. Weston Walch.

Zeichner, K. (1996). Educating teachers for cultural diversity. In K. Zeichner, S. Melnick, & M. L. Gomez (Eds.), *Currents of reform in preservice teacher education* (pp. 133–175). New York: Teachers College Press.

Zeichner, K., & Melnick, S. (1996). The role of community field experiences in preparing teachers for cultural diversity. In K. Zeichner, S. Melnick, & M. L. Gomez (Eds.), *Currents of reform in preservice teacher education* (pp. 176–196). New York: Teachers College Press.

Zinn, H. (1995). *A people's history of the United States, 1492–present* (revised and updated ed.). New York: Harper Perennial.

CHAPTER 8

CREATING AN EMPOWERING MULTICULTURAL CURRICULUM (2000)

Christine E. Sleeter

Recently, a preservice teacher education student who had been in one of my courses the previous semester, was working on a curriculum project for another course. She emailed me asking how I thought "other cultures" should be incorporated into the classroom. She asked specifically about adding in "other cultures" holidays and traditions. Her question illustrates a tremendous problem in creating multicultural curriculum in a way that examines race, social class, and gender issues. Embedded in her question were common assumptions that she seemed unaware of until I pointed them out. She assumed a division between "our culture" and "other cultures"—an "us" and a "them." She also assumed culture to be equivalent to ethnic group: artifacts and "Old World" traditions. Ethnic groups are discrete entities that have culture, which is something like a bag of folk traditions a teacher can dip into, to bring pieces into the classroom. Further, she assumed holidays to be a key construct to multicultural curriculum.

But holidays are a superfacial way of framing multicultural curriculum, and she should have known that. We had certainly spent time in my course on substantive issues related to race, gender, class, and curriculum. The course was an introduction to elementary education; a primary focus was on how we decide what is most worth teaching in a pluralistic society. As we talked, she remembered course discussions. And I realized how salient were assumptions that had remained deeply embedded in her thinking.

Creating and teaching a multicultural curriculum takes places within a long history of oppressive and colonial relations. How issues are framed within that curriculum can simply reproduce those relations. This is a very deep concern, and one reflected in my student's question about including "other cultures" holidays. Incorporating "others" into the curriculum does not necessarily change anything. The issue is not only whether to add attention to those who have been excluded, but also how to address exclusion itself. I open this article with the example of holidays because it is a common, and simplistic, approach to adding "difference" to the curriculum. Later I will note growth this particular student made; one's conception of a multicultural curriculum can certainly deepen, and this student's did. At the same time, simplistic holiday approaches are all too common. The substance of this article will examine central ideas that should undergird a multicultural curriculum that empowers.

Willinsky (1998) examined the history of education in the context of European colonialism. He showed how education historically helped to rationalize colonialism by dividing the world into distinct "cultures," and portraying European culture as superior. "Learning provided another way for the West to take the rest of the world in hand, whether by conducting geological surveys, preserving ancient texts, or setting up schools. . . . The globalization of Western understanding was always about a relative positioning of the West by a set of coordinates defined by race, culture, and nation" (p. 253). It wasn't so much the case that Europeans did not learn and teach anything about the rest of the world. Rather, the issue was what sense Europeans made of the world and of their own relationship to it, and how they taught their children to view the world.

Whether one is speaking about multicultural curricula that add in American "others" or Third World "others," the result is still colonizing if the underlying worldview structuring knowledge and action is not transformed. As Perez-Torres (1993/94) argued

> Multiculturalism does not simply involve the recuperation of "lost" traditions in order to prove the richness and diversity of "America," . . . Rather, multiculturalism interrogates which traditions are valorized and by whom, which are devalued and by whom, which serve to empower marginalized peoples, which serve even further to disempower, which traditions provide strength, how traditions provide agency, when traditions provide knowledge. (p. 171)

The curriculum we teach is as good as our own understanding of what we are teaching (Howard, 1999). The beliefs we bring about what is worth teaching, and about diverse people, the society in which we live, the students we are teaching, and the various academic disciplines have a good deal to do with the substance of the curriculum we create and teach.

Narratives for citizenship

Dewey (1944) argued that a democratic society needs citizens who can grapple intelligently with the most pressing issues they encounter and share. Education in a democratic society must enable young people to think about and act responsibly and ethically on social issues, and help young people learn to see others' points of view. In a stratified society, it must help young people learn to empathize, and to cultivate "rebellion at whatever unnecessarily divides them" (p. 121).

Many young people show great interest when issues they recognize as real, challenging, and ethical are opened up in the classroom. Two university students, one white and the other Black, collaborated on a unit on racism, for example, to teach in writing classes in a multiracial junior high. One of them, whom I had taught in class, invited me to come watch. The topic of the day was racism in the peer culture. This student was a young white woman from northern Wisconsin, and her life experience and previous education had not provided her with tools to analyze racism in urban youth peer culture. She did, however, have a wonderful capacity to raise questions in class and encourage students to talk. She also had a curriculum unit full of conceptual tools and background information about racism, around which she wove student discussions. I had spent many hours in that particular school, observing in classrooms, and this was the first time I saw students come alive to the curriculum. They participated, they probed each other, they raised questions, they delved into the topic. For them, the topic itself was real. It connected with their everyday experiences, and with public life. It engaged them.

These university students had learned to go beyond superficialities in conceptualizing a multicultural curriculum, to address issues of racism. They were not yet able to consider how racism intersects with class and gender, or with global relations of power, but they had a substantive beginning. Connecting multiple forms of difference and oppression is complicated, and teachers too often are not sure how to do that well.

Cornbleth (1998) studied eleven classrooms, both urban and suburban, at grade levels ranging from fifth through eleventh, to find out how multicultural curriculum is being constructed in social studies classrooms today. A couple of decades ago, the predominant narrative would have been one of bounty and progress, with the U.S. portrayed as leading the world in democracy, fairness, and justice. White men would have thoroughly dominated. Cornbleth found that today, social studies curricula include a wider diversity of people, but have yet to re-work content into a comprehensible new narrative that analyzes racism, poverty, and sexism, and does so in a way that suggests citizen action.

Most of the teachers in her study presented the U.S. as imperfect, but still the best in the world. According to that narrative, historic unjust treatment has been largely a matter of prejudice, and as people become more enlightened, prejudice is diminishing; the U.S. has always absorbed newcomers with some difficulty, but over time things work out. Lessons about "cultural contributions" and inventions of diverse people support this view. Some teachers presented the U.S. as a prism of multiple viewpoints and experiences. They tried to emphasize divergent viewpoints and experiences through materials, although oddly, they excluded students' viewpoints. Cornbleth noted that teachers who tried to present multiple viewpoints, however, still tended to divide society into an "us"—white middle class people—and a "them"—everyone else. One teacher, for example, teaching to a class in which at least half of the students were of African descent, described how "we" Americans used to think of "brown-skinned people."

For the most part, the teachers did not give students a sense that there are problems and issues that people can address through collective work. In fact, there was almost an absence of attention to social and political processes that might join people in addressing problems. Instead, teachers tried to present a largely positive image of the U.S., even when acknowledging historic problems. Cornbleth also found social studies curricula to be fragmented and disjointed. In the classrooms she studied, the curriculum was more like a montage of M-TV images than a coherent set of ideas.

Scholarship in the various critical studies (such as ethnic studies, women's studies, disability studies) continues to transform how it is possible to think about humanity, the various disciplines, and social issues. Most teachers have little or no awareness of this scholarship, and as a result, frame multicultural curriculum in terms of cultural superficialities. Even a cursory glance at this scholarship would lead toward much deeper issues. At the same time, it is possible to read that scholarship in a way that highlights difference without interrogating power relations and social structures. The teachers in Cornbleth's study either used a traditional meta-narrative as an organizing theme, or no meta-narrative at all. Their curriculum presented difference in the form of different people with different stories, but did not have a way of connecting the diverse stories.

We are living in a time of rapid global consolidation of power into the hands of a very wealthy, predominantly white elite. As McLaren and Torres (1999) point out, while poor communities nationally and globally are being gutted of resources, a non-elected elite is consolidating power in the form of huge transnational corporations. I will argue that multicultural curricula must focus on key issues surrounding exclusion and power, and tie diverse experiences to those key issues in order to create citizen coalitions who are able to identify common concerns, common sources of marginalization, and common strategies for action.

What counts as knowledge in a multicultural and unequal society

What counts as knowledge is a political issue. Who decides which books and articles get published? Which research gets funded? Which courses are offered in schools and universities, and which texts are used? Which intellectual perspectives count as legitimate? Intellectual work consists of knowledge or theory that is produced for some definable public, according to standards for knowledge production that are acceptable to that public (Danziger, 1990). Intellectual work consists of not simply information, but also interpretation. As Fraser (1989) argues, how human needs are understood depends on who articulates and frames them, using a discourse that appeals to perspectives of which public.

Creating multicultural curriculum entails synthesizing intellectual work around some set of ideas. In the context of a conference on "The Nature and Context of Minority Discourse," JanMohamed and Lloyd (1987) argued that,

> on the one hand, premature integration of discourse is exactly what is to be avoided at present. Those who argue for the creation of canons of various ethnic and feminist writings do so with the full awareness that formations of different canons permit the self-definition, and, eventually, self-validation that must be completed before there is any talk of integration. For, to date, integration and assimilation have never taken place on equal terms, but always as assimilation by the dominant culture. (p. 9)

But on the other hand, they argued, oppressed groups do share minority positioning relative to the dominant society. This positioning is a political rather than cultural issue. As a result, oppressed groups share "the effects of economic exploitation, political disenfranchisement, social manipulation, and ideological domination on the cultural formation of minority subjects and discourses" (p. 11). It is possible, therefore, to identify themes that run through much of the intellectual work produced by groups that share minority positioning.

What follows is my interpretation of five themes that cut across such intellectual work. These themes are consistent with JanMohamed and Lloyd's observation that conditions of oppression give rise to similar concerns and ways of interpreting experience. My argument is that multicultural curriculum that is informed by these themes provides the tools for coalition-building and empowerment.

Centering whose experience frames what we know?

A history student in one of my classes was trying to explain why Mexican Americans do not appear in the U.S. history curriculum prior to the Mexican War. He argued that studying what happened in Mexico before the U.S. colonized half of it is not U.S. history. U.S. history covers what happened within the political borders of the United States and, prior to its founding, what happened in Europe that shaped its founding. I countered that, from a Mexican American (and Indian) perspective, history goes back to the ancient Mayas and Aztecs. The U.S.

colonization is a relatively recent event in a long history. Since we centered U.S. history differently, our views about what counts as U.S. history differed. He centered his understanding within the political boundaries of the United States at any given time; I centered mine in the land of North America, including the beginning of civilization in Mexico.

History is somebody's story about what happened. Renditions of U.S. history in most textbooks start in Europe and move west, which structures and supports a story line that is based on experiences of people of European descent, defines the U.S. as essentially European, and excludes analysis of racial oppression. But if one starts in Mexico, as does a colleague who teaches U.S. history from the vantage point of Aztlan, the whole narrative is different, even when it involves many of the same places and people as history centered around Europeans. Political boundaries are viewed differently, allowing into the narrative people of Mexico before U.S. conquest, and interrogating the conquest itself. If one adds African Americans onto the history of Europeans and Euro-Americans, one begins African American history with slavery and disconnects African Americans from African civilizations. An Afrocentric perspective, on the other hand, redefines the starting place of African American history from slavery to ancient Africa, framing the American experience as part of a diaspora of highly cultured African peoples, preceded by strong precolonial African civilizations. A historical trajectory envisions the future of people of African descent as reclaiming the self-determination, prosperity, and intellectual creativity of Africa's past.

Questions about what it means to "center" can be answered differently, depending on whose experience one is considering. For example, American Indians center time differently than do Europeans or Euro-Americans. Allen (1986) pointed out that, "the tendency of the American Indian [is] to view space as spherical and time as cyclical, whereas the non-Indian tends to view space as linear and time as sequential" (p. 59). The story of the Americas cast within an Indian framework is a multilayered, cyclical story of endurance and connection in the face of sustained genocide.

The dominant society framed individuals with disabilities as having certain characteristics without any particular community or history. Padden and Humphries (1988) critiqued this perspective with respect to Deaf people (using lowercase "d" to designate a physical condition of the individual and capital "D" to designate affiliation with the Deaf community):

> Ways of living proposed for Deaf people that ignore their past, that attempt to remove, either directly or indirectly, their historically created solutions, are not possible lives. . . . When deaf children are denied connections with Deaf people, . . . they lose access to a history of solutions created for them by other people like themselves. (p. 120)

When one centers knowledge around the Deaf community, the story is not one of individuals with certain characteristics, but rather one of communities claiming voice and power against a hostile society.

At first, asking whose experience defines how a narrative is centered may lead to fragmentation, as a multiplicity of narratives come forth. However, centering narratives from the margins has the potential to open up an examination of marginalization itself. For teachers building multicultural curriculum, this is critically important. The examples above illustrate the construction of oppressed groups in terms of strengths, and also in terms of connected global diasporas that are divided by political boundaries (such as national boundaries) and social arrangements (such as who lives where, and with whom). The remaining four themes flow from this first theme of shifting the center.

Social construction of theory

The dominant society, having historically excluded marginalized groups from education, has maintained that if one is well-educated, scientifically trained, and gathers information properly, one can come to valid and objective conclusions about anybody or anything. Educated people have difficulty, therefore, thinking of other educated people, and the knowledge produced by trained researchers, as biased.

At the same time, professionals and researchers from dominant social groups have a long history of producing "knowledge" about oppressed groups, that oppressed communities view as very biased and damaging. White professionals theorize about communities of color; professional-class people theorize about children from poor communities; men theorize about women, people without disabilities theorize about people with disabilities. (Much special education research can be thought of in this way.) IQ research, for example, has been published in very scholarly places, such as the Harvard Educational Review, asserting objectivity and rigor in its claims that Blacks are, on the average, intellectually inferior to whites, and that this is based in genetics. Similarly, many years ago, male scholars asserted that the study of math made women infertile. "Science" and "objectivity" were used to make knowledge claims that described one group as less capable than another, and that legitimated policies of exclusion.

In school, students usually encounter knowledge as a set of fixed facts, which presumably are true and correspond to something "real" and "out there."

For example, a social studies teacher says, "On May 29, 1985, Ronald Reagan was president." The truth value of this statement is highly certain and is determined by the condition that on May 29, 1985, Ronald Reagan was president. When a social studies teacher says, "The Reagan administration made a complete commitment to supply-side economics," we are less certain about its truth value, because it is not clear what conditions would make the statement true. Textbooks are filled with cases like this (Cherryholmes, 1988:53).

Schools reinforce the assumption that knowledge can be discovered in an objective manner by those who are trained formally to discover it. As those who benefit most from the status quo theorize about various dimensions of human life, theories get created that explain "how things are" in a manner that renders the existing social order as inevitable and legitimate.

Scholars from marginalized groups challenge and re-think much of what passes for "truth" and "fact" in the dominant society by establishing how "accepted" ideas are actually the creations of people with particular points of view. Imagine two different theoreticians. Theorist A creates a narrative by selecting data that seem most important, and putting them into a coherent theory. When this theory is told and re-told as "truth," the data that theorist A decided not to use are left out, and eventually disappear from view. Theorist B looks at the same broad set of data, but from a different perspective. Theorist B may or may not select the same data as Theorist A did. She may decide to say explicitly why she chose the data she did, and why she put them together differently from Theorist A. But to the extent Theorist A's work is taken for granted as "truth," Theorist B's work will be perceived as biased. What biases informed Theory A? This is a very important question that marginalized groups raise about knowledge. If knowledge produced by Theorist A makes up most of the canonized curriculum, how was it constructed, around whose vested interests? From the perspectives of marginalized communities, knowledge should serve the purpose of empowering the community and enabling people to solve problems of concern to the community. To do that, knowledge must be created with sensitivity to what the community sees as its problems and concerns, build on the strengths and resources of the community, and take account of the actual lived experiences of people in the community.

Take the example of disability. Most of the literature on disability has been generated by people without disabilities. It generally rests on a medical model of disability, locating disability within the individual and framing the individual as defective in some way. This theorizing, then draws attention to processes designed to fix defective people, or, if they are not fixable, contain them (such as in special classrooms or institutions). In schools, disability becomes institutionalized in the form of special education; the main way students encounter any curricular discourse about disability is in the form of a character in a story in which the story is partly about the disability, or in the form of lessons designed to reduce name-calling and stereotyping. These various forms of institutionalization support the commonly-held idea that disability is a characteristic of individuals.

Charleton (1998) retheorizes disability, locating the status of people with disabilities within the world political economy (other disability-studies scholars have located disability within social structures, but generally have not situated these structures within global power structures). He argues that, since most people with disabilities live in poverty, disability needs to be connected with class exploitation. The larger political economy limits how people in various locations and social positions can live. For example, what kind of education or health care does one have access to, or does one even have access to education or health care at all? The resources one has access to, and the ways of living that are possible within those resources, interact with the person, producing disability. Disability, in this view, is not a characteristic of individuals so much as it is a set of structural relationships that benefit some people and disable others.

Theories from the margins are based on the lives of oppressed peoples, and arise from communities that historically have been silenced and framed as "underdeveloped," "culturally deprived or disadvantaged" or "uneducated." Delgado Bernal (1998), for example, in a discussion of Chicana feminist epistemology, develops the idea of "cultural intuition," which rests on four sources. 1) Personal experience includes one's own lived experience, in addition to the group's lived experience as transmitted through stories passed down from generation to generation. (Years ago, when an African American sociologist was asked by a white historian about his qualifications for teaching African American history, he replied: "I've been Black all my life, and taking notes.") 2) Existing literature written by the group provides insight and interpretive frameworks for examining one's own experience as well as one's research data. 3) Professional experience yields insights into the actual workings of a school (or other institution), especially as those workings affect the lives of children (or clients) who are members of one's own group. 4) Analytical research processes that explicitly invite research "subjects" and other members of the community (Chicana, in Delgado Bernal's case) to help make sense of the data calls on insiders to validate knowledge claims about their own community. A tenet of transformative theory generated by oppressed communities is that the theory be constructed and validated by the community itself (see also Collins, 1990; Ladson-Billings, 1995).

If we regard every socio-cultural group's knowledge to be human created, we can then ask: who created it, for what purposes, and who benefits by its creation? The knowledge that members of oppressed groups construct is very likely to question rationales for oppression, and to seek means of making change. Students in schools need to learn to question and critique knowledge, asking how it was constructed, by whom, for what purpose, and what biases informed the knowledge construction process. A high school teacher I know designs her history curriculum specifically around such questions. One of her greatest challenges is that her students have spent ten years learning not to ask them, and regard textbook knowledge as unbiased truth.

Critique and redefinition of social collectives

Intellectuals from many marginalized groups question categories that are imposed and naturalized in the dominant discourse—race, ethnicity, nation, sex and gender, and disability—in order to construct alternative identities and social arrangements. The "obvious" and assumed fixed nature of such categories as conceptualized by the dominant society has worked against oppressed groups, who reexamine how categories are socially created and reinforced. We might define this as a process of dismantling naturalized categories and reconstructing politically strategic categories and identities.

Many naturalized categories are popularly presumed to have a biological basis. Race, for example, was created to legitimize colonialism and slavery. Euro-Americans created the categories of "white" and "Negro" to consolidate slavery (Omi & Winant, 1986). To dismantle racism, the presumed biological underpinnings of racial groups must be dismantled, including the category of whiteness. Gender and sexuality are also popularly conceived as being rooted primarily in biology and, thus, natural. Patriarchy is supported by reinforcing a clear distinction between the sexes; people who do not conform to traditional gender identities threaten "ideological beliefs and cultural values [that] prop up existing relations of power and control within society" (Sears, 1992:145). Disability, the study of which has been dominated by a medical perspective, can also be dismantled. Social arrangements that benefit socially constructed ideas of "normalcy" are buttressed by arguments that locate disability within individuals. Disability studies challenge the social context that disables people.

National borders are also social constructions, that are increasingly being blurred by transnational capital. La Raza de Aztlan, for example, designates the "race" of Mexican people, which the U.S. border bifurcates. More and more, diasporas of people who have cultural and ethnic tics, but have been scattered across modern nation-states (such as Jewish people, people of African descent, or people of Middle Eastern descent) are being conceptualized around an idea of "peoplehood" that transcends national borders. With the increasing globalization of the capitalist economy, interrogating systems of oppression that cross national borders is essential. When nation-states are viewed as autonomous units, "issues of domination and exploitation within a global system of nation states is ... often elided" (Yadav, 1993/94:210). For example, in order to ask why the U.S. has committed acts of military aggression against several non-white nations in the past three decades, why it has sent disproportionate numbers of soldiers of color to the front lines, or why Third World workers, especially women and children, have been conscripted as "cheap labor" to maximize corporate profits, we must link concerns of oppressed peoples in the U.S. with those outside the U.S.

Naming and consolidating emancipatory collective identities is the other side of the process of dismantling social categories. Successful liberation movements happen when a group has pressed collectively for change, and constituents have forged a sufficiently shared identity to stand together. Identities are emancipatory when they inscribe power and strength on people and point toward social arrangements that are free of subjugation. Political categories speak to problems members of a collective face in everyday life and point toward solutions to those problems. Obstacles to group mobilization include emotional bonds that cut across groups and acceptance of the dominant ideology of difference (i.e., race, sex, disability) as rooted in biology.

For example, women of European descent, living in the context of family relationships with men, are trained very often to view a subordinate position as "natural." It is often difficult to get such women to question gender issues, since identifying with other women can conflict with family loyalties, and revisioning one's life disrupts existing domestic arrangements. People with disabilities experience isolation from each other, since individuals living in families with nondisabled members are taught dominant definitions of normalcy and difference and may lack contact with other disabled people and alternative identities (Checkoway & Norsman, 1986). Developing collectives requires networking individuals, politicizing their interpretation of their lives, and creating identities in which people can see themselves. The redefinitions focus on strengths and capabilities of people, and social arrangements that can be changed.

Debates over group identity are important in articulating and affirming a sense of self and a connection with an empowering history and empowering politics. Such debates often, however, become detached from political endeavors, and work against productive coalition-building. For example, on my own campus most Latino students divide themselves into three groups: Mexicans, Mexican Americans, and Chicana/os. The African American students find themselves feeling like they are competing for attention on a stage divided into white-Latino. White students, unsure how to identify ethnically in this context, either argue that we are all just people, or put forth European ethnic identities (such as Dutch). Gay/lesbian identities are articulated mainly by white gay/lesbian students and faculty; feminist identities are articulated mainly by white faculty. The faculty and administration identify the students mainly as working class, but I hear very few students frame identities in terms of class. One can analyze the construction of identities and collectivities in terms of huge array of fragmentation, and often proactive responses to campus events are quite fragmented. The question becomes: how can identities be connected around common political concerns? As Stuart Hall puts it: "I think of politics as the mobilization of social identities for particular purposes, rather in terms of political identities as things in their own right" (Osborn & Segal, 1999:404).

People who are unfamiliar with these issues often wonder why so much intellectual effort goes into debating terms for groups. The reason is that many terms were invented by the dominant society, and acquire baggage that is consistent with the dominant society's worldview. It matters whether one chooses to adopt a particular name, and to identify with others who have adopted that name. In the long run, it matters greatly in terms of the group's ability to press successfully for social changes that benefit the group. But since groups are not discrete, walled-off entities (for example, I am both a woman and white; Alicia is Mexican, Black, a woman, and from a working class family), reconstruction of collectives needs to be tied with social and political issues, so that common grounds for action can be forged.

In school curricula, young people need to begin to understand the politics of identity formation. It isn't enough to simply tell young people that this or that group is called "X". Rather, young people should learn to question how groups come to be called groups in the first place, who defined them that way, who benefits from particular conceptions of social groups, who is questioning them and why, and why this matters in the first place. This is an issue young people can readily engage with, since their own peer groups are usually rich in struggles for identity formation. What youth generally do not have is a very rich conceptualization of how identify formation is connected with power and historical events in the wider society. This is where teaching is important.

Subjugation and liberation

Knowledge created by the dominant society valorizes the existing social order and the traditions upholding it. It explains why things are the way they are, in a manner that usually makes the status quo seem inevitable. The dominant society will not necessarily pass on a history of struggle to members of subordinated groups, because such historical memory can fuel and strengthen movements for change today. Flores (1997), for example, points out that young people today were not born yet when the civil rights struggles of the 1960s were occurring, and do not necessarily know what was being struggled for, how, or why. Arising from real life conditions of struggle, liberatory knowledge speaks directly to "basic questions of power and oppression in America" (Omatsu, 1994:26).

Different groups define subjugation and liberation somewhat differently, but share a desire for liberation that contrasts markedly with the dominant society's desire to justify existing social arrangements. Labor studies, for example, envisions a world in which the organization of work does not place large segments of society under the control of a wealthy elite. If people generally believe that corporate leaders act in the best interest of everyone, and have little or no sense of the history of labor, they tend to acquiesce to the "needs" of business and the corporate world. Labor history, however, chronicles activism of the working class— battles both won and lost—to generate a vision of a possible future in which "common" people and poor people exercise more control over their lives (Bigelow & Diamond, 1988).

The dominant society has defined Asian Americans as the "model minority," not needing liberation but rather flourishing within existing social arrangements. Many Asian American intellectuals challenge that definition. Takaki (1989), for example, has argued, Asian Americans historically were defined as strangers and silenced in order to legitimate their status as low-wage workers. But Asians have increasingly demanded liberation from exclusion, racism, imposed identities, and institutionalized marginalization. "To confront the current problems of racism, Asian Americans know they must remember the past and break its silence" (Takaki, 1989:484).

Many heterosexual people view gay and lesbian people as not normal, perhaps even immoral. But the editors of The Gay and Lesbian Studies Reader argue differently:

Like women's studies, lesbian/gay studies has an oppositional design. It is informed by the social struggle for the sexual liberation, the personal freedom, dignity, equality, and human rights of lesbians, bisexuals, and gay men; it is also informed by resistance to homophobia and heterosexism—by political and cultural opposition to the ideological and institutional practices of heterosexual privilege, Lesbian/gay studies necessarily straddles scholarship and politics, but it is more than a means of breaking down divisions between the two. It is also a field of scholarly inquiry and critical exploration whose intellectual distinction has been repeatedly demonstrated and whose influence is changing the shape of every branch of learning in the humanities and social sciences. (Alelove, Barale & Halperin, 1993, p. xvi)

Liberation is a goal to strive for, rather than a reality that has been achieved.

Striving for it requires understanding how oppressions work, how a given group has adapted to and coped with oppression, and what kinds of strategies actually challenge roots of oppression. Within scholarship in the critical tradition, debates rage about how oppression works, and what are the main structures or constructs that should be challenged. Most such scholars go beyond prejudice as the main source of oppression; teachers from the dominant society tend to reduce issues of oppression to prejudice, not seeing more fundamental political relations as problematic. For example, local migrant laborers experience racism, but are also situated within global agribusiness. The exploitation of migrant labor cannot be reduced to prejudice against Mexican and other dark-skinned people, or only to class conflict, or only to U.S.–Mexico colonial relations. Rather, it needs to be understood as a combination of these factors, situated within global capitalism which eases the ability of business owners to bid globally for the cheapest labor. Women migrant laborers experience sexism within their workplaces and families, but are also working in an economy that is increasingly not supportive of Third World women and children.

This kind of analysis is plentiful in intellectual work of marginalized communities, and needs to inform the school curriculum. Specifically, young people need to learn to employ structural analyses of subjugation, and explore connections among various forms of subjugation, such as race and class. For students who are members of dominant groups, a structural analysis of oppression offers an alternative to framing oneself as "prejudiced" or "not prejudiced," a framing that places the onus of oppression on one's sense of being a good person. Structural analyses of oppression re-define members of the dominant society from good or bad, prejudiced or not, to people who benefit from the social location in which they were born, and who may choose to act in ways that change social structures. Young people can embrace investigations into actions we choose to make, much more so than discussions about attitudes and inner dispositions.

Oppressed groups are durable, strong, and active

If we live in a free and open society, why do some groups fare better economically, educationally, and politically than others? The dominant society generally answers this question in terms of presumed characteristics of groups: strengths and abilities of Euro-American male leaders and thinkers, and deficiencies of "have not" groups, such as in culture, morals, will, language, or family. These assumed virtues and deficiencies become the stuff of stereotypes.

Minority intellectual work, conversely, develops depictions of strength, wisdom, and the ability of a group to get things done. For example, what role did African Americans play in the abolition of slavery, and what difference does this make? Conventional wisdom suggest that slaves were passive and powerless and that a few great people, particularly Lincoln, ended slavery. If this were true (which it was not), it would suggest that the masses should wait for a few great men, particularly the President, to solve things. However, African American history highlights the active role of many African Americans, both slave and free, in ending slavery. Bennett (1982) described this work as the "expressions of the tenacity of spirit of a people who never stopped testing the wall, sending line after line into the breach, losing many and paying a frightfully high price for the handful who managed to slip through" (p. 177).

Minority discourses develop strengths, wisdom, creativity, and durability of groups—present as well as past. Allen (1986), for example, pointed out that Indian history, properly understood, shows that Indian people endure: after 500 years of systematic policies of genocide (by disease, murder, forced sterilization, severe impoverization), Indian people are still here, and still creating.

Women, when they have access to athletic opportunities, are now breaking Olympic records that men set years ago (Linn & Hyde, 1989). Women have the capability to do whatever we want, but the institutional context we inhabit tries to limit us. Asians are neither quiet nor passive. In their introduction to the anthology Making Waves, the editors explained that, "we are not afraid to rock the boat. Making waves. This is what Asian American women have done and will continue to do" (Asian Women United of California, 1989, p. xi).

It is impossible to depict oppressed groups as strong and active without situating them within oppressive contexts. (If we are so strong and capable, why are so many of us still poor?) This does not mean that a group's entire portrayal revolves around oppression. But it does mean that a curriculum that denies oppression ends up either trivializing the strengths of an oppressed group or highlighting only that segment that has experienced success. This observation brings us full circle back to the first theme: whose story is one actually telling?

Constructing a multicultural curriculum

Learning to construct a good multicultural curriculum is an on-going process. One is never finished learning to do this, because in the process of grappling with the questions about what is most worth teaching in a pluralistic society, one is constantly learning. And, curriculum is something a teacher never does quite "right." Every time I teach, the students are different, the context is different, and I bring to the enterprise a deeper understanding of the central issues than I had last time I taught similar concepts. Since a multicultural curriculum delves into issues that touch the core of our own personal and community-based identities, doing it well brings a personal, as well as an intellectual response.

The student with whom I opened this article presented her senior project, several months after emailing me. Her project turned out to be a critique of the "heroes and holidays" approach to multicultural curriculum design, and reported on a multicultural unit that she designed and taught in a racially-mixed elementary school, that centered around ideas of justice. While at this university, she had been steeped in a strong multicultural curriculum; my prodding of her in the context of learning disciplinary knowledge from multicultural perspectives helped her shift paradigms related to what it means to know from the standpoints of diverse, historically excluded groups. Her curriculum did not yet interrogate systems of power at a deep level, but it had moved away from a "heroes and holidays" approach, and toward one examining public life in a diverse society.

In the late 1990s, I increasingly heard multiculturalism described as passe—or simply not discussed at all. The most recent school reform efforts, for example, involve standardizing the curriculum (again!) in ways that mention diversity, but incorporate it into dominant ways of thinking. Elsewhere, for example, I use the themes in this article to critique a state's social studies curriculum framework, which purports to be multicultural (Sleeter, 1999; see also Cornbleth and Waugh, 1995). Many educators and citizens have grown tired of struggling over issues related to diversity, and prefer to think about more "pressing" concerns, such as increasing students' test scores. And, many believe that multicultural discourses create dissention, and that unity will come about only by teaching some form of consensus.

At the same time, the population of schools and the wider society continues to diversify, and gaps among racial and social class groups widen. The dominant society's perspectives—like any group's perspectives—will not provide solutions to problems and challenges in a multicultural society. Multicultural curricula for tomorrow's citizens must work with insights of minority position intellectual work. Young people need access to the intellectual tools that will enable them to address issues of race, class, and gender, and to connect these within current global systems of power.

Bibliography

Abelove, H., Barale, M.A., Halperin, D.M. Eds. (1993). *The Lesbian and Gay Studies Reader*. New York: Routledge.

Allen, P.G. (1986). *The Sacred Hoop*. Boston: Beacon Press.

Asian Women United of California. (1989). *Making Waves: An Anthology of Writings by and About Asian American Women*. Boston: Beacon Press.

Bennett, L., Jr. (1982). *Before the Mayflower: A History of Black America*. 5(th) ed. New York: Penguin Books.

Bigelow, W., Diamond, N. (1988). *The Power in our Hands*. New York: Monthly Review Press.

Charleton, J.I. (1998). *Nothing About Us Without Us*. Berkeley: University of California Press.

Checkoway, B., Norsman, A. (1986). Empowering Citizens with Disabilities. *Community Development Journal*, 21: 270–277.

Cherryholmes, C.H. (1988). *Power and Criticisms: Poststructural Investigations in Education*. New York: Teachers College Press.

Collins, P.H. (1990). *Black Feminist Thought*. New York: Routledge.

Cornbleth, C. (1998). An American Curriculum? *Teachers College Record*, 99(4): 622, 25p.

Cornbleth C., Waugh, D. (1995). The Great Speckled Bird: Multicultural Politics and Education Decision-Making. New York: St. Martin's Press.

Danziger, K. (1990). *Constructing the Subject: Historical Origins of Psychological Research*. New York: Cambridge University Press.

Dewey, J. (1944). *Democracy and Education*. New York: The Free Press.

Delgado Bernal, D. (1998). Using a Chicana Feminist Epistemology in Educational Research. *Harvard Educational Review*, 68(4).

Flores, J. (1997). Latino Studies: New Contexts, New Concepts. *Harvard Educational Review*, 67(2): 208–221.

Fraser, N. (1989). *Unruly Practices: Power, Discourse and Gender in Contemporary Social Theory*. Minneapolis, MN: University of Minnesota Press.

Howard, G. (1999). *You Can't Teach What You Don't Know*. New York: Teachers College Press.

JanMohamed, A., Lloyd, D. (1987). Minority Discourse: What Is to Be Done? *Cultural Critique*, 7: 5–17.

Ladson-Billings, G. (1995). Toward a Theory of Culturally Relevant Pedagogy. *American Educational Research Journal*, 32(3): 465–492.

Linn, M., Hyde, J. (1989). Gender, Mathematics and Science. *Educational Researcher*, 18(8): 17–27.

McLaren, P., Torres, R. (1999). Racism and Multicultural Education: Rethinking "Race" and "Whiteness" in Late Capitalism. In S. May (ed), *Critical Multiculturalism*, London: Falmer Press, 42–75.

Omatsu, G. (1994). The Four "Prisons" and the Movements of Liberation: Asian American Activism from the 1960s to the 1990s. In K. Aguilar-San Juan (ed), *The State of Asian America*, Boston: South End Press, 19–70.

Omi, M., Winant, H. (1986). *Racial Formation in the United States*. New York: Routledge & Kegan Paul.

Osborn, P., Segal, L. (1999). An Interview with Stuart Hall: Culture & power. In R. Torres, L. Miron & J.X. Inda (eds), *Race, Identity and Citizenship*, Malden, MA: Blackwell, 389–412.

Padden, C., Humphries, T. (1988). *Deaf in America: Voices from a Culture*. Cambridge, MA: Harvard University Press.

Perez-Torres (1993/94) R. 1994. Nomads and Migrants: Negotiating a Multicultural Post-modernism. *Cultural Critique*, 26: 161–190.

Willinsky, J. (1998). *Learning to Divide the World: Education at Empire's End*. Minneapolis: University of Minnesota Press.

Sears, J.T. (1992). The Impact of Culture and Ideology on the Construction of Gender and Sexual Identities. In J.T. Sears (ed), *Sexuality and the Curriculum*, New York: Teachers College Press, 139–156.

Sleeter, C.E. (1999). Keeping the Lid on: Multicultural Curriculum and the Organization of Consciousness. Unpublished manuscript.

Takaki, R. (1989). The Fourth Iron Cage: Race and Political Economy in the 1990s. Paper presented at the Green Bay Colloquium on Ethnicity in Public Policy, Green Bay, Wisconsin.

Yadav, A. (1993/94). Nationalism and Contemporaneity: Political Economy of a Discourse. *Cultural Critique*, 26: 191–229.

CHAPTER 9

EDUCATION THAT IS MULTICULTURAL—ISN'T THAT WHAT WE MEAN? (1978)

Carl Grant

Education today must prepare individuals to live in a racially and culturally pluralistic society. This fact has been recognized by Congress, the courts, and many educational organizations. In 1972, Congress passed legislation enacting the Ethnic Heritage Studies Program. This legislation, which has been called the first official recognition by Congress of the heterogeneous population of this country, proposes that people living in a multiethnic society need to have a greater understanding of their own history and the history of others. It is believed that this knowledge will contribute to a more "harmonious, patriotic and committed populace, [and] in recognition of the principle that all persons in the educational institutions of the nation should have an opportunity to learn about the differing and unique contributions to the national heritage made by each ethnic group." (Title IX, 1965.)

The case of *Hernandez v. Texas*, argued before the Supreme Court in 1954, exemplifies the court's recognition of our racially and culturally pluralistic society. The litigation involved the exclusion of persons of Mexican descent from jury service. In delivering the court's opinion, Chief Justice Warren (1954) stated:

> The State of Texas would have us hold that there are only two classes—White and Negro—within the contemplation of the 14th Amendment. The decisions of this court do not support that view. . . . The 14th Amendment is *not* directed solely against discrimination due to a "two-class theory"—that is based upon differences between White and Negro.

The acknowledgement of the importance of cultural diversity in education by a major educational organization was reflected in AACTE's 1973 statement, *No One Model American*. In the introduction, the drafting commission noted, "The Statement . . . is presented . . . in the interest of improving the quality of society through an increased social awareness on the part of teachers and teacher educators." The statement declares, "To endorse cultural pluralism is to endorse the principle that there is no one model American [and] to understand and appreciate the differences that exist among the nation's citizens."

Since Congress, the courts, and educational organizations have begun to recognize both society's pluralistic nature and the importance of educational programs that prepare individuals to live in it, it is important that the terminology applied to this educational concept and process be descriptive and assertive.

Importance of definitions

There has been frequent discussion among educators and interested laypersons of the relative importance of the definitions of the terms used in education. In a discussion of the definition and philosophy of education, Broudy (1963) notes:

> One cannot be sure whether people line up their practice to fit their definitions or vice versa. They may fashion their definitions to give what they do a respectable air of theoretical consistency. Yet, granting this possibility, *once the definition is framed, it does tend to crystallize and congeal the practice which it justifies, so that further deviation from it is discouraged as not being quite respectable.* ... Definitions of education not only can make a difference, but what is even more important, they do.

Terms serve as ground rules for perceiving and understanding educational concepts. Terms may have more than one meaning and thus may convey varying perceptions to different people. This type of variation frequently results in educational programs that are weakly conceptualized, poorly designed, and misinterpreted. For instance, a number of teacher training programs have used instructional modules which some erroneously thought were competency-based.

The history of 20th century American education also records a number of programmatic failures for educational endeavors whose terminology has, in practice, promoted a different conceptual interpretation than was originally intended. For example, the activities Dewey advocated through the "Learning by Doing" premise were misunderstood by many of his contemporaries as preparation for future vocations rather than as reflections of fundamental human activities.

Although these misconceptions were not the sole reasons for failures in the competency-based teacher education and progressive education movements, they are characteristic of one major source of program failure which can be attributed to lack of clearly defined and appropriately directed terminology.

If educational needs in a pluralistic society really are to be met, it is imperative that the applied terminology be clearly defined and truly represent the nature of multicultural programs.

Term's implicit weakness

Multicultural is defined in Webster's *19th Collegiate Dictionary* as an adjective meaning: "of, relating to, or designed for a combination of several distinct cultures." As an adjective, *multicultural* modifies education. Webster defines *modify* as: "1. to make less extreme; and 2. to limit or restrict the meaning."

Discussing modifiers, Lamberts (1972) states, "Modification may be regarded as a change of some sort which involves the external aspects of anything, but which leaves the basic pattern or structure unaffected."

Used as an adjective, *multicultural implicitly suggests an education that has a limiting and supplementary purpose and focus.* It suggests a restrictive, a special, a narrow as opposed to broader, concept of education. In contrast, terms such as *special education, secondary education, and higher education,* are appropriately named because they are restricted areas concerned with the special needs of exceptional children or directed towards specific levels of instruction.

Education that promotes respect for the racial and cultural differences of individuals, however, must pervade all aspects of educational programs. Thus, the concepts and purposes related to such education must be comprehensive, pene-trating, and integrating—not narrow, restrictive, or supplementary. By definition, *multicultural education** suggests an educational concept concerned only with changing the external aspects without altering the basic patterns of education in a pluralistic society.

Rationale

In a society which has always been pluralistic, one of the basic philosophical tenets underlying American democracy has been the belief that every person has the right to and potential for self-actualization.

Kluger (1977) notes:

> Of the ideals that animated the American nation at its beginning, none was more radiant or honored than the inherent equality of [hu]mankind. There was dignity in all human flesh, Americans proclaimed, and all must have its chance to strive and to excel.

Translated into daily life, perhaps nowhere was this belief more obviously professed than in the right to public education. In his first annual report to the Massachusetts State School Board in 1837, Horace Mann eloquently stated the goals of schooling for every child:

> The object of the common school systems is to give every child a free, straight, solid pathway by which he [she] can walk directly up from the ignorance of an infant to a knowledge of the primary duties of a man [woman], and can acquire a power and an invincible will to discharge them.

However, it appears that there has been a gap between the philosophical intent and the actual conditions of schooling in American society. More than a century after Mann's report, the Supreme Court's historic 1954 decision in *Brown v. Board of Education of Topeka* clearly demonstrated the need to reaffirm the belief in the dignity of all humans. Chief Justice Warren stated:

> Today it [education] is a principal instrument in awakening the child to cul-tural values, in preparing him [her] for later professional training, and in helping him [her] to adjust normally to his [her] environment. In these days, it is doubtful that any child may reasonably be expected to succeed in life if he [she] is denied the opportunity of an education. Such an opportunity, where the state has undertaken to provide it, is a right which must be made available to all on equal terms.

> . . . To separate them [Black students] from others of similar age and qualifi-cations solely because of their race generates a feeling of inferiority as to their status in the community that may affect their hearts and minds in a way unlikely ever to be undone.

---

* Author's Note: I have made the focus of my argument the term multicultural education because it is receiving the greatest usage in the educational community. However, the argument is also applicable to terms such as multiracial education, ethnic studies, etc.

The court concluded that "separate educational facilities are inherently unequal," thus unconstitutional, and urged that such schooling conditions be remedied "with deliberate speed."

Yet more than two decades later, we were faced with massive resistance in Boston, Chicago, Milwaukee and other cities. Despite the reality of American racial and cultural pluralism and more than three centuries of ostensibly professing respect for the equality of all, our educational system fails to foster respect for racial and cultural diversity.

The belief that all people must be accorded respect regardless of their racial, social, ethnic, cultural, or religious backgrounds; age; sex; or physical differences is undergirded by a fundamental acceptance of the premise that all people have intrinsic worth. If true, it seems reasonable to conclude that all people should be accorded equal respect. Consequently, it should be the goal of society's socializing institutions—particularly the schools—to instill and maintain such respect. Education that respects and affirms racial and cultural diversity and individual differences is needed for achieving this goal.

Education that is multicultural must be manifested in an educational process that neither advocates nor tolerates heating up the old "melting pot" nor creating multi "monocultural" educational programs.

Instead, *education that is multicultural* should include such features as:

1   staffing composition and patterns throughout the organizational hierarchy that reflect American society's pluralistic nature;
2   curricula that are appropriate, flexible, unbiased, and incorporate the contributions of all cultural groups;
3   affirmation of the languages, belief systems, values, and lifestyles of cultural groups *as different rather than deficient*;
4   instructional materials that are free of bias, omissions, and stereotypes; that are inclusive rather than supplementary; and that show individuals from different groups fulfilling different occupational and social roles.

The demand for educational program evaluation, including curricula, instructional materials, and their success in helping achieve more respect for humankind, is implicit.

Education that is multicultural values the concepts implied by cultural pluralism, multilingualism, crosscultural studies, intercultural studies, and intergroup and human relations. The concept may be described in terms of the manifest, implied, and latent components (Grant, 1975). (See Figure 9.1.)

An education that is multicultural is comprehensive and fundamental to all educational endeavors. Given an understanding of the nature of human differences and the realization that individuals approach concepts from their own perspectives, advocates of education that is multicultural are consistent in their belief that respect for diversity and individual difference is the concept's central ingredient. Defined this way, the concept suggests descriptions, prescriptions, and directions for encouraging apposite discussion and programmatic implementation. Regardless of the specific form each program takes, education that is multicultural must be pervasive and everlasting. It must take place throughout life; and the school, as society's education agent, needs to manifest and articulate it in every aspect of its program, especially in staff personnel, curricula, and instructional materials.

MANIFEST COMPONENTS (ESSENTIAL)	IMPLIED COMPONENTS	LATENT (BUT NONETHELESS DESIRABLE) COMPONENTS
Respect for all people, regardless of sex; racial, cultural, ethnic, and religious backgrounds; age; physical handicaps; or physical size.	Acknowledgment by all individuals within society of the variability and diversity of humankind. Opportunities for contact with people of different backgrounds. Freedom from coercion by any special interest group. Tangible forms (properly trained teachers, unbiased materials, etc.) Social and political institutions whose leadership and membership reflect diverse constituencies. Mass media messages that reflect the racial, cultural, and individual diversity within U.S. society.	Culturally diverse staff; pluralistic focus, configurations, and approaches in teaching/learning environments. Active community involvement.

Figure 9.1 Description of education that is multicultural concept

Possibilities for change

There are two distinct concepts of education in a racially and culturally pluralistic society. One concept views education as comprehensive and assertive; the other as supplementary and restrictive. The implications of this distinction are crucial to the fundamental concept of U.S. education.

I recommend that the term education that is multicultural be used, although I realize that multicultural education is the term that we have become accustomed to and say with great facility. I also realize that most people are hesitant about change. Nevertheless, this change is needed.

I am encouraged that this change can take place, because I have witnessed recently the exclusion of such sexual stereotypic terms as chairman and mankind and the subsequent inclusion of such terms as chairperson and humankind in everyday speech. The exclusion/inclusion of these words in our vocabulary may have caused us awkward moments initially, but now the awkward moments are caused when we use stereotypic terms.

Language is a tool that we use to give shapes and forms to our world (Rank, 1974). It is the medium by which individuals communicate their thoughts and feelings to other individuals; it is the tool with which we conduct our business, the vehicle by which we have transmitted the philosophy, science, and literary arts of the world. It helps communicate specific ideas, plans, and goals. It allows us to be descriptive and prescriptive, as well as casual and flexible. Words, the basic building blocks of verbal language, either intensify or diminish our ideas and ideals.

To use the words multicultural education is to diminish unwittingly and make narrow and supplementary a critically important educational concept. To use the words education that is multicultural provides depth, completeness, sustaining strength, and virility to this important concept and process.

References

Broudy, H.S. Definitions and philosophy of education. In W. Lucio (Ed.) *Readings in American education*. Glenview, Ill.: Scott, Foresman, 1963.

Brown v. Board of Education of Topeka, Supreme Court of the United States, 347 US. 483 (1954).

Ethnic Heritage Studies Program, *Title IX, Elementary and Secondary Education Act of 1965*.

Grant, C.A. (Ed.). *Sifting and winnowing: An exploration of the relationship between multicultural education and CBTE*. Madison, Wis.: Teacher Corps Associates, 1975.

Hernandez v. Texas, certiorari to the court of criminal appeals of Texas, No. 406, 1954.

Kluger, R. *Simple justice*. New York: Random House, 1977.

Lamberts, J.J. *A short introduction to English usage*. Hightstown, N.J.: McGraw-Hill, 1972.

No one model American. *Journal of Teacher Education*, Winter 1973, 24(4).

Discussion based on views expressed by Rank, H. The teacher heal-thyself myth. In H. Rank (Ed.), *Language and public policy*. Urbana, Ill.: National Council of Teachers of English, 1974.

Cited by Wimpey, J.A. Horace Mann's influence in today's schools. In A. and L.D. Crow (Eds.), *Vital issues in American education*. New York: Bantam Books, 1964.

CHAPTER 10

THE RELATIONSHIP BETWEEN MULTICULTURAL AND DEMOCRATIC EDUCATION (1997)

Geneva Gay

Citizenship education and multicultural education at a crossroads

In the traditions, beliefs, and language of the progressives of an earlier generation and the critical or post-modern theorists of today, multicultural education can be perceived as a pedagogy of the oppressed, resistance, hope, possibility, equity, emancipation, and reconstruction. It is both an advocacy and agency of peoples, perspectives, and issues marginalized in U.S. society because of race, ethnicity, and class. The visions, missions, and agendas of multicultural education can be described, simultaneously, as "borderland" and "transformative." They are borderland because they speak from within, about, and for the margins (borderlands) of mainstream social and educational policies, procedures, and practices. Their leading spokespersons are individuals who themselves are inhabitants of societal borderlands (either literally or symbolically) because of their ideological and political affiliations, and frequently their ethnic, cultural, and racial identities.

The representative constituents of multicultural education are individuals, groups whose experiences and perspectives have relegated to the margins of educational programs and societal priorities. However, its critical concerns are at the core of the sociopolitical promises and rights of democracy, and its consumers are all citizens. Multicultural education is intended for all students and deals with issues that affect everyone. In other words, its benefactors are both the privileged and the oppressed; the European American majority as well as the many minority groups of color; the valiant and the vanquished; men and women.

Embedded within the major concerns of multicultural education are two essential concepts of democracy—equality and interdependence; that is, the lives of the citizens of the United States, individually and collectively, are inextricably interrelated and what happens to one invariably affects the other. Put simply, the creation of U.S. history, life, and culture resulted from the contributions of a wide variety of individuals and groups with different ethnic and racial backgrounds. Its future development is as dependent on the resourcefulness of diversity as its past has been. The collective well-being and genius of society correlate directly with the health, happiness, and vitality of its individual members. Consequently, knowledge of, respect for, and promotion of cultural diversity are essential to the effective preparation of education for democratic citizenship.

U.S. society and its schools cannot meet the terms of the social contract they make with citizens if diversity is ignored. In order for a government of, by, and for the people to be representative and responsive, its fundamental structures and processes must incorporate cultural diversity because the people themselves are diverse. Schools cannot maximally serve the needs of the greatest number of students without dealing with ethnic, racial, and cultural diversity. This is necessary because students, like the populous of society in general, are highly pluralistic, and the educational process is, by nature, a sociocultural process (Pai 1990). Multicultural education recognizes both of these essential facts in its visions and strategies. It thereby conjoins principles of democratic education and high quality pedagogy in its efforts simultaneously to teach skills for effective citizenship in a pluralistic society, to ensure the rights of democracy to marginalized and oppressed groups, and to improve the academic performance of all students in all subjects. These general relationships between multicultural and citizenship education for a democratic society are developed in greater detail in the remainder of this discussion.

Similar missions

In the United States, democracy as an institution, ethic, and political system was conceived in struggle and born out of change. It is a social contract of the people, by the people, and for the people, and education is instrumental to its creation, survival, and vitality. Both the social contract and the agencies it generates are supposed to represent the interests and serve the needs of their creators. These ideas are well established in such formative documents as the Mayflower Compact, the Declaration of Independence, and the Constitution of the United States. They are ideological, political, moral, ethical, and legal mandates. These social contracts also grant permission for renegotiation and revision when their provisions are violated or fail to continue to serve the needs of the people. If a revision amenable to the greater number of the co-signers to the contracts cannot be accomplished, then entirely new social contracts can be created.

Multicultural education is both a symbol and an evocation of the right of the social contract of democracy. It says, in effect, that neither students in school nor society at large are best served by the way schooling (the social contract of education) is traditionally conceived and practiced. Therefore, the structure and processes of education need to be renegotiated to make them more inclusive of the cultures, experiences, perspectives, and contributions of all ethnic groups that comprise the United States. Consequently, in purpose, nature, and function, multicultural education is situated well within the fundamental core of the democratic tradition. For disenfranchised groups, it evokes their *right of citizenship* to protest, resist, and change actions that violate the democratic imperatives of political, cultural, and social representation and relevance.

Democracy in its fullest meanings and manifestations is still in the process of being constructed, and some degree of conflict is inherent to its continuing development. The same is true for multicultural education. As Bickmore (1993) explained, "[P]luralistic democracy in particular relies on conflict as a mechanism of change" (341), and "No other concept captures so well the difficulty (and beauty) of democracy in a pluralistic and rapidly changing society" (343). To these benefits of dissent and conflict can be added social enrichment, genius, and progress. Without some conflict and the changes it generates, society is stagnant, unproductive, unimaginative, uncreative! This is most certainly true, as the United States confronts the challenge of creating a genuine democratic society out of its increasingly ethnically, culturally, and socially diverse populations, impulses, and experiences.

Multicultural education is challenging and problematic to many existing mainstream societal and conventional school practices. Although its tenets and intentions neither contradict nor compromise those of democracy, they do represent a serious critique of how high-status knowledge, academic achievement, and versions of the American story are usually taught and how sociopolitical power and privilege are distributed among ethnic, racial, and social groups. Multicultural education demands the elimination of inequities in these various forms of the cultural capital of the United States. This can be accomplished by applying the principles of social and political democracy to the educational enterprise so that students of color, non-European origins, and poverty are academically enfranchised to the same extent as their White, male, European American, and middle-class counterparts.

Multicultural education is challenging in another fundamental way. It requires the revision of some long-held beliefs and assumptions about what constitutes quality curriculum content and pedagogical processes, and the most desirable sociocivic order. Inclusion of more knowledge, respect, and promotion of ethnic, cultural, and social diversity is an essential part of this revision. These demands pose serious dilemmas—even threats—to many school leaders because they feel unprepared to respond adequately to them. They, in effect, place society and schools in tension with themselves, torn between needs for continuity, stability, and change. These tensions between change and stability are consistent with the character of the democratic spirit and experiment.

Psychologists from Piaget to Maslow, Erickson to Kohlberg, Skinner to Vygotsky have long recognized the inevitability of conflict in the cognitive, social, emotional, moral, and identity development of healthy, competent, empowered, fully functioning individuals and groups. In a similar vein, the struggles, questions, discomforts, perspectives, and possibilities that multicultural education represents—and even provokes—should be seen as a natural part of U.S. society's efforts to align its practical realities more closely with its philosophical ideals for its diverse citizenry and maximize the human potential of all individuals.

In 1849, Frederick Douglass (Bobo, Kendall, and Max 1991) spoke eloquently about the necessity of struggle in the pursuit of personal liberation and social change. He said that all progress made in the quest for human liberty had been born of earnest struggle. Moreover,

> The conflict has been exciting, agitating, and all absorbing. . . . It must do this or it does nothing. If there is no struggle there is no progress. Those who profess to favor freedom, and yet depreciate agitation, are men who want crops without plowing up the ground. They want rain without thunder and lightning. They want the ocean without the awful roar of its many waters. This struggle may be a moral one; or it may be a physical one; or it may be both moral and physical; but it must be a struggle. Power concedes nothing without demand. It never did and it never will. (vii)

Bickmore (1993) has contended that social conflict and dissent are particularly relevant to education for and about democracy and diversity. They are equally important in the process of teaching and the selection of the content to be taught. This is so because conflict and dissent in living and learning (*a*) recognize the importance of public discourse and the potential for action beyond the realm of private disagreement; (*b*) facilitate the construction of more inclusive, comprehensive, and accurate portrayals of who makes history and culture, (*c*) bring multiple viewpoints to bear upon the analysis of social issues; and their resolution, (d) require pedagogical strategies that allow students to have face-to-face encounters with opportunities to practice skills of conflict resolution.

Effective multicultural education has all of these traits. It teaches students how to be critical thinkers and sociopolitical analysts, to challenge all presumptions of absolute truths, and to be moral agents and socially conscious activists committed to making society model the principles of democracy for diverse people. It confronts and deconstructs some of the deeply-held assumptions and practices about the values, rights, and responsibilities of powerful and powerless, marginal and mainstream, majority and minority groups and individuals in society. These goals cannot be accomplished without personal and social struggle. This is a definitive attribute of multicultural and democratic education agendas.

Multicultural education, like the quest for democracy, leads ultimately to the reconstruction and transformation of society. It endeavors to create a new sociocivic center—a new social order—that is inclusive of the perspectives, experiences, and contributions of all segments of the United States population, especially those people who have been previously marginalized because of their race, ethnicity, language, social class, and gender. Nowhere in this goal is there any hint of ignoring, by-passing, or violating the overarching cultural ethos of the United States as embodied in its democratic ethic. Instead, this educational reform movement is designed to extend the principles and boundaries of democracy to all citizens. Thus, multicultural education promotes an inclusive conception of the people of, by, and for whom the United States and its attendant institutions were created to reflect, serve, promote, protect, and celebrate.

Democracy and multiculturalism are noble, but unfinished, enterprises. The struggle to achieve them is a dialectic and complementary one. Efforts to accomplish the one will, of necessity, facilitate the achievement of the other. Thomas Jefferson argued that a democracy requires an educated citizenry for its creation and perpetuation. The U.S. Supreme Court reaffirmed this principle in the 1954 Brown v. Board of Education of Topeka. In rendering its decision, the Court declared that education is the very foundation of democracy, and a major instrument for awakening the child to democratic cultural values (Morris 1980). In reminding the nation of the original conceptions of democracy, Abraham Lincoln pointed out that the U.S. government began by affirming equal rights and equal chances for all. These principles were not based on the assumption that all individuals who entered into the social contract were already maximally competent and fulfilled in the ways of democracy. Rather, society was expected to help the weak grow stronger, the ignorant wiser, and the marginal and underprivileged as fully enfranchised as the majority and privileged (Cuomo and Holzer 1990).

More recently, Jesse Goodman (1992) has argued that developing values, feelings, ethics, and skills of "community" is the centerpiece of education for critical and actively engaged democracy. To accomplish these ends, schools should foster perspectives that place "one's connection to the lives of all human beings and other living things on our planet at the center of the educational process" (28). Instead of overemphasizing individualism and competition (as has often been the case in the past), schools should create classrooms that are societies of intimates in which collective identities, shared responsibilities, and interrelated destinies among ethnically, racially, socially, and culturally individuals and groups are normalized, honored, and advocated (Goodman 1992). These kinds of preparatory experiences are essential to quality education for citizenship and personal development in a pluralistic democratic society. With a citizenry and society as ethnically and culturally pluralistic as that which now exists in the United States (and will become even more so in the future), multicultural education has become an imperative. To the extent that it is a part of the educational experiences of all children, school will be better able to fulfill its mission of preparing new generations of citizens to ensure the survival and growth of democracy.

Key assertions about diversity, democracy, and education

Education for citizenship in an ethnically and culturally pluralistic society is based upon several major assertions. Embedded within them are the central ideas and spirit of democracy as a bill of sociopolitical rights, and an ethic of community living. Some of these assertions are briefly discussed here to illuminate further the relationship between education for diversity and democracy.

To begin with, there is nothing un-American about multicultural education and cultural pluralism. Nor are they contradictory to or incompatible with citizenship education for a democratic society. As Roberta Sigel (1991, 3) explains, "There is, of course, nothing intrinsically incompatible between democratic practices and multi-ethnic living." In fact, it is impossible to achieve a genuine representative democracy in the United States without developing multicultural competence.

Multiculturalism represents an inescapable truth about U.S. society and the human family. Personal, ethnic, cultural, and gender diversity is an inherent feature of both. It is a major source of individual and group strength, vitality, creativity, and worth. Thus, it should be a central feature of any and all efforts to improve the quality of our individual and collective lives through the educational process. Given the pluralistic nature of U.S. society and the dependency of democracy on an educated citizenry, teaching students skills in multicultural education promotes democracy.

Education for democracy involves more than merely transmitting past experiences, heritages, and contributions to students. An even more important element is teaching students to recognize the skills and the need for mastering them in order to transform society. These competencies are especially needed to prevent past violations of democratic principles, such as racial discriminations and oppressions, from reoccurring in the future. James Banks (1990, 211) explains further that:

> Citizenship education in a multicultural society must have as an important goal helping all students, including mainstream students, to develop the knowledge, attitudes, and skills needed not only to participate in, but also to transform and reconstruct, society. . . . To educate future citizens merely to fit into and not to transform society will result in the perpetuation and escalation of [existing social] problems, including the widening gap between the rich and the poor, racial conflict and tension, and the growing number of people who are victims of poverty and homelessness.

Because democracy is still a developing enterprise, it "has to be recreated in the understanding and behavior of each new generation of citizens or it is jeopardized" (Mosher, Kenny, and Garrod, 1994, 23). Schools play a crucial role in this re-creation through their obligation to educate all students (not just the racially, intellectually, or socially privileged) to be informed, rational, and responsible participants in and contributors to society. The fullest possible development of individuals' human competencies is every child's birthright and the best guarantee of the promotion of the common good. This means that all children should have an "equal opportunity to benefit from programs that demostrably enhance their cognitive and sociomoral competencies" (Mosher, Kenny, and Garrod, 1994, 27). Multicultural education is a pedagogical tool for achieving these goals.

Multicultural education is a creation and outgrowth of the Western cultural tradition. It began in the heyday of the larger Civil Rights Movement of the 1960s (Banks 1991/92; Gay 1994). Both movements are committed to closing "the gap between Western democratic ideals of equality and justice and societal practices that contradict those ideals, such as discrimination based on race, gender, and social class" (Banks 1991/92, 32). Included within the missions of multicultural education is a desire to strengthen the nation by teaching understanding and respect for ethnic and cultural diversity. As Banks (1993, 23) has explained, "Multicultural education is designed to help unify a deeply divided nation rather than to divide a highly cohesive one."

Many of the ideas on democracy and education espoused by John Dewey are endorsed by multicultural education. Among them are:

- The environments in which children live are constantly influencing what and who they are as well as what and who they will become. These influences can be educative (constructive) or mis-educative (destructive) to both societal and individual possibilities.
- Democracy is more a moral imperative and way of living than a form of government.
- A democratic community is characterized by consciously shared interests and free social interactions among its varied and numerous membership.
- A fundamental objective of education is the development of individual dignity and self-realization within the context of community. Although personal dignity and fulfillment may be defined in many different ways, the nature of the society in which they are nurtured is crucial to their realization.
- The growth of the individual and society is inextricably related, and democracy is the ideal form of socialization and education for both of their maximal development.
- Because psychological, intellectual, sociological, and moral competencies are equally importance in individual and societal development, cognitive skills alone are not sufficient preparation for effective citizenship in a democratic society. Instead, the democratic imperative demands teaching the whole child (Dewey 1916).

The personal enfranchisement, sociopolitical competence, and self-determination multicultural education promotes for marginalized groups are empowering processes that have individual and collective benefits. These are expressed behaviorally in the form of increased social consciousness and active participation in collaborative efforts to achieve common causes. Paulo Freire (Ball, Gaventa, and Peters 1990, 145) recognized these relationships and their sociocivic effects in his observation that "[t]he more the people participate in the process of their own education . . . the more . . . [they] participate in the development of their own selves. The more the people become themselves, the better the democracy." Mosher, Kenny, and Garrod (1994) added that all children, regardless of their ethnic, racial, social, and cultural identities, should be given equal access to whatever cultural capital exists in society for the enhancement of their individual human resources. It is "[o]nly when schools are committed to a comprehensive and inclusive vision of education for all children can they be genuine examples of and advocates for democracy" (169).

Schools can fulfill these functions by providing an education that places greater emphasis on teaching critical, liberatory, and transformative knowledge and skills than adaptive and conformative ones. Multicultural education does this. It is an emancipatory approach to citizenship education for a culturally pluralistic society. It addresses issues of power, privilege, perspective, hegemony, personal consciousness, and social action at multiple levels (local, regional, national), and in varied domains of human activities (social, cultural, moral, environmental, political, economic). Learning how to deal with these issues is a dynamic process of awareness, critique, competence, action, and actualization (Lynch 1992).

To be most effective, multicultural and democratic education must permeate all dimensions of the educational enterprise. In making this case for education for democratic citizenship, Sigel (1991, 7) declared that it "cannot be restricted to, let alone equated with, a course or two on civics or citizenship, or studies in democracy. Such courses . . . [are] but one part of the educational equation. . . . [H]ow [the instructional process] comports itself in the classroom, how it deals with controversies and authority relationships, the treatment it accords students, etc., make an equally important and perhaps more lasting contribution to the student's democratic orientation." The same can be said about multicultural education. Regardless of how comprehensive and qualitative the factual content taught about cultural diversity is, it alone is not sufficient to prepare students adequately to be effective and responsive citizens in a pluralistic society. Developing attitudes, values, thinking, ethics, and actions congruent with respect and promotion of cultural diversity are of equal importance.

Intersecting principles

All of the major principles of political democracy are embedded in the tenets of multicultural education. These intersections have ideological, ethical, and action dimensions, and they comprise natural bridges between education for diversity and democracy. Space limitations do not permit a detailed explication all of these relationships. Instead, only ten of the leading tenets of multicultural education can be discussed briefly. The related democratic principles are identified in parenthesis following the discussions.

- Education should embody the cultural heritages and experiences of all the peoples who comprise the United States; should respond directly to needs and interests of all segments of the population; and its policy and operational decisions should reflect the perspectives, presence, and influence of diverse ethnic, cultural, and social groups (*Enfranchisement; Representation; Participation*).
- All students should have access to a free and public education. Access has several critical dimensions, including availability of resources; quality and relevance of instructional content and learning activities to the lives of diverse students; the absence of intrusive obstacles in the form of negative teacher attitudes and expectations; equity of educational opportunities for ethnically and culturally diverse student populations; and more accurate exposures to the multitude of voices that were and

continue to be actively involved in the creation of the United States and its human stories. As principle, voice is analogous to the democratic ideals of freedom of speech and the right to be actively involved in determining one's own destiny. As content, it is accepting the experiences and contributions of different ethnic, cultural, racial, and gender groups as legitimate and worthy knowledge in be included in the school curricula of all students (*Enfranchisement: "Equal Protection Under the Law"; Participation; Representation*).

- All students have the right to have accurate knowledge about the history, life, and culture of their country. An essential feature of this truth is that the creation and development, as well as the problems and potentials, of the United States are shaped by the ever-present influences and contributions of individuals and groups of different ethnicity, race, gender, and culture. (*Entitlement; Participation; Representation*)

- The racist, oppressive, and hegemonic practices often imposed upon different marginalized minority racial, ethnic, and social groups by the European American majority are violations of the letter and spirit of democracy, as well as of those terms of the social contract having to do with protecting the rights of the minority. Therefore, students should be taught skills to combat racism, sexism, and all other forms of oppression and to reconstruct all dimensions of society to achieve a more equitable distribution of social, political, economic, and educational resources and opportunities (*Equality; Justice; Enfranchisement*).

- The commonly held belief that mainstream culture is a creation of only the dominant European American ethnic group is a fallacy. In fact, the majority culture of the United States is a composite, a synergy, a conglomeration of pluralistic contributions from many different ethnic, gender, and racial groups. Consequently, when the principle of majority rule is applied to teaching about the national culture, the resulting "story" must be multiethnic, multiracial, and multicultural (*E pluribus unum; Interdependence; Community*).

- All students in all grade levels, subject areas, and school settings should learn about ethnic, cultural, and racial diversity. Therefore, multicultural education is both about and for everyone, not just the groups marginalized because of race, class, ethnicity, gender, language, or national origins (*Inclusion; Community; Participation; Enfranchisement*).

- Education in the United States is a *public creation*, a *public mandate*, and a *public service*. The public is increasingly racially, ethnically, socially, and culturally pluralistic. For schools to fulfill their most fundamental functions, their instructional programs must be multiculturalized. To the extent that this is not done, some segments of the public are systematically denied their entitlement to basic education for citizenship rights and responsibilities (*Entitlement; Enfranchisement; Citizenship*).

- Multicultural education can better prepare all students to reach higher levels of personal development, academic excellence, and social competence than some of the pedagogical practices previously employed. Educational excellence in the form of content relevance, personal confidence, and academic achievement is facilitated through the affirmation and celebration of diversity. Social responsiveness is enhanced by students learning about the contributions and problems of various groups, understanding how the lives and destinies of groups and individuals are interrelated, developing an egalitarian ethnic and a moral intolerance for all forms of injustice and inequality, and acquiring sociopolitical action skills and value commitments for working toward the betterment of society for everyone's benefit (*E pluribus unum; Community; Interdependence; Equality; Justice; Morality*).

- Multicultural education provides a critical voice, a civic conscience, a reality filter, a reflective screen for assessing the appropriateness of conventional approaches to citizenship and general education for ethnically diverse students in a culturally pluralistic society. The critique it provides is a springboard for the initiation of social and educational reform. This reform requires cross-racial and interethnic group collaboration and collective action (*Truth/Honesty/Integrity; Empowerment; Community; Participation*).

- Multicultural education builds on the diversity that is inherent to the human and social conditions. It assumes that diversity is an inalienable right and a source of regeneration that deserves honor, respect, understanding, and promotion. The potential of diversity for human enrichment should not be neglected or compromised in educational and sociopolitical processes. To do so places undue limitations on the potentialities of diverse individuals. Furthermore, ignoring, demeaning, or rejecting the cultural experiences of diverse students constitutes an act of psychological and moral violence. These actions also restrict the creative horizons of society. Conversely, cultural diversity in individuals and societies is a source of vitality, strength, renewal, and development (*Empowerment; Enfranchisement*).

Conclusion

From the preceding discussion, it is evident that the relationship between multicultural education and democratic education is a natural, healthy, and complementary one. In fact, neither genuine educational excellence nor social and political democracy can be achieved without dealing conscientiously with ethnic and cultural diversity. Multicultural education facilitates the translation of principles of democratic living into practice for a society populated by people from many different ethnic, racial, cultural, and social backgrounds.

Multicultural education and democratic education can be advanced simultaneously if several reform techniques are pursued rigorously. These include (*a*) making all dimensions of the educational enterprise (curriculum, instruction, climate, assessment, personnel, policy, etc.) culturally pluralistic; (*b*) creating and disseminating multicultural prototypes of effective citizenship in a pluralistic democratic society; (*c*) adopting and enforcing standards of citizenship that include knowledge, values, and skills for functioning in a culturally pluralistic society; (*d*) teaching a multicultural code of ethics; (*e*) holding students and teachers accountable for knowing, respecting, and promoting cultural diversity; and (*f*) developing exemplary models of multicultural curriculum and instruction appropriate for the subjects taught at different levels of schooling. If the complementary relationship between multicultural and democratic education is clearly understood and taught, students will be better prepared to assume their citizenship rights, roles, and responsibilities in a culturally pluralistic society. The resulting skills will ensure that the promises of democracy will be realized for all the diverse peoples of the United States.

References

Banks, J. A. 1990. Citizenship education for a pluralistic democratic society. *THE SOCIAL STUDIES* 81 (5): 210–214.

——. 1991/92. Multicultural education: For freedom's sake. *Educational Leadership*: 32–36.

——. 1993. Multicultural education: Developments, dimensions, and challenges, *Phi Delta Kappan* 75: 22–28.

Bell, B., J. Gaventa, and J. Peters (Eds.). 1990. *We make the road by walking: Conversations on education and social changes/Myles Horton and Paulo Freire*. Philadelphia: Temple University Press.

Bickmore, K. 1993. Learning inclusion/inclusion in learning: Citizenship education for a pluralistic society. *Theory and Research in Social Education* XXI (4): 341–384.

Cuomo, M., and H. Holzer. (Eds.). 1990. *Lincoln on democracy*. New York: Harper Collins.

Dewey, J. 1916. *Democracy and education*. New York: Macmillan.

Douglass, F. [1849]. 1991. Letter to an abolitionist associate. In *Organizing for social change: A mandate for activity in the 1990s*, edited by K. Bobo, J. Kendall, and S. Max. Washington, D.C.: Seven Locks Press.

Goodman, J. (1992). *Elementary schooling for critical democracy*. Albany: State University of New York Press.

Lynch, J. 1992. *Education for citizenship in a multicultural society*. New York: Cassell.

Morris, A. A. 1980. *The constitution and American education*. St. Paul, MN: West Publishing.

Mosher, R., R. A. Kenny, Jr., and A. Garrod. 1994. *Preparing for citizenship: Teaching youth to live democratically*. Westport, Conn.: Praeger.

Pai, Y. 1990. *Cultural foundations of education*. New York: Merrill/Macmillan.

Sigel, R. S. 1991. Democracy in the multi-ethnic society. In *Education for democratic citizenship: A challenge for multi-ethnic societies*, edited by R. A. Sigel and M. Hoskin. Hillsdale, N.J.: Lawrence Erlbaum.

PART 2

CURRICULUM CONTENT

MULTICULTURAL IMPERATIVES FOR CURRICULUM DEVELOPMENT IN TEACHER EDUCATION (1977)

Gwendolyn C. Baker

Teacher education programs in the United States have not changed as much as they should have in order to accommodate the rapid growth and development of our society and world. Political thought, economic pressures, and social climates have had little impact on the manner in which teachers are trained and on the curricula of most teacher training institutions. Some programs have reflected attempts at change by extending the length of professional training. This extension of training appears to be the result of the recognition that teachers in training need longer contact with students and more experience in educational settings. Other training institutions have established field-based-oriented programs and have begun to develop competency-based-teacher approaches. But for the most part, even these changes have not deviated significantly from traditional approaches to teacher education. Curricula appear to be heavily laden with outdated instructional content; methodology remains the same.

Educational history, philosophy, and psychology are still taught with strong emphasis upon the early needs of rurally-oriented communities.

> Public schools were originally designed for a rural society and have persisted largely unchanged. As a society we should be able to construct an educational system that is capable of meeting the needs of our changing society. (Howsman, et al., 1976)

Students in training continue to learn and develop instructional techniques and strategies appropriate only for a rurally homogeneous society.

Although teacher education remains unchanged, it has the potential for developing the kind of training that will prepare teachers for teaching in a society and world characterized by diversity and change. Society is complex; teacher education must incorporate responses to this complexity in its training programs.

Characterized by complex social organizations, today's world is complicated by inflexible bureaucracies which have depersonalized the decision-making process. Influenced by technology in all aspects of our lives, we have become technology dependent. Our shrinking world has given us access to each other through various forms of communication. We are now forced to depend upon each other; this demands a degree of cooperation.

The world is becoming increasingly non-white. Of the six billion people who will inhabit the earth by the year 2000, five billion will be nonwhite. Political power is growing, especially in countries where population growth and economic development are inevitable. The United States is being forced to accommodate its nonwhite population in different ways than it has in the past.

Urban life is becoming more popular as the rural areas rapidly decrease in size and population. By the turn of the century, it is expected that ninety percent of the more than 300 million persons living in this country will live on one percent of the land.

The complexity of a highly developed social system produces a situation where even its most productive citizens question their usefulness. For the first time in the history of our nation, we are not dependent upon unskilled labor for survival. The poor perceived their uselessness in this type of social structure and are unable to function in this monolithic bureaucracy.

Communication between groups is blocked by the practice of segregation and bureaucratic organizations. Because of the lack of opportunity to meet face to face, Blacks and Whites and other racial groups find it difficult to resolve their differences. Their separation increases their hostility. Segregation can and will destroy our society.

The problem of racial and minority group separation must be dealt with through teacher training; therefore, many questions must be answered by teacher training institutions. How can the crucial attitudes of the emerging world be reflected in the preparation of teachers? How relevant must education be? Can the school, its curricula and teachers resound with today's crucial issues? (Smith, Cohen, and Pearl, 1969)

Teacher education can respond to the many issues and realities of social complexity. The changing and developing of our nation and world have implications for the education and training of our youth. As we instruct and prepare our youth for a world growing in concern for political freedom for all people, the need for political freedom of oppressed people throughout the world cannot go unnoticed. The very fact that our nation and others have become more urban oriented makes our traditional rural approaches to education obsolete. The needs of economically and socially disadvantaged populations must influence how we prepare teachers to work with these groups. Issues of racially segregated and integrated education must be explored by those preparing to teach. All aspects of racism must be confronted so that teachers in training can understand the price of racial superiority in the United States.

> The teacher who is not alerted to the devastations of enforced uselessness, segregation, and bureaucratic management is not adequately educated. The teacher who is not prepared to alter through the schools the devastating conditions of enforced uselessness, segregation, and bureaucratic management is not adequately trained. (Smith, Cohen, and Pearl, p. 3, 1969)

Teacher education and cultural diversity

If schools and teachers assume the responsibility for educating our youth, then they are compelled to equip our children to live in a culturally diverse nation and world. According to Taylor (1969), education is:

> ... the process by which each person becomes aware of himself (herself) and his (her) place in the world at large and learns how best to conduct himself (herself) in it and to contribute to it. To achieve such awareness, he (she)

needs the opportunity to explore the world's geography, its people, including those of his (her) *own society* . . .

The process of helping each person to understand and to be aware of one's own culture is one of the basic goals of multicultural instruction. Helping children to understand their own cultures is paramount in developing an understanding and appreciation of larger societies and of the world.

In 1971 at the National Conference on Education and Teacher Education for Cultural Pluralism, the concept of cultural diversity and its ramifications for teacher education were explored.

The implications of cultural pluralism for education and teacher education are monumental. For schools and universities to accept cultural pluralism as both fact and concept would revolutionize what passes now for schooling and teacher training. The basic assumptions underlying school governance, curriculum, academic and nonacademic standards, and educational reward systems would be dramatically reformed. The school mission, now focused on conformity to monolithic social and intellectual expectations, necessarily would broaden and, paradoxically, would narrow on a new focus. At the present time schools (and teacher-producing institutions for that matter) struggle to build defensible rationales for failure. Elaborate justifications emerge to explain why substantial numbers of children do not learn and substantial numbers of teachers cannot teach. (Stent, Hazard, and Rivlin, 1973)

Most teachers are from middle or lower middle-class homes and communities. Having had no contact with lower socio-economic groups, many possess traditional bias toward minorities. Few teachers look forward to inner-city school assignments; fewer know how to go about redressing both instructionally and socially the injustices committed upon ethnic and racial minorities. All teachers need professional preparation for this role. Multicultural education is an official response to equal access to educational opportunity. As defined by the government, multicultural education includes the following:

(a) knowledge of cultures and of subcultures, with special emphasis on those minority groups which are pervasively represented in American communities;
(b) awareness of how specific cultures influence learners' responses to school and learning situations, and skill in sensitizing professional behaviors to learners;
(c) transformation of personal prejudices so that negative biases are minimized, and positive appreciation of minority children increased; and
(d) adjustments in curricula to implement the transition from the concept of "melting pot" to "cultural pluralism." (Howsman, et al., 1972)

Training teachers to teach multicultural instruction involves several considerations. The first is a concern for helping teachers in training to acquire knowledge of their own culture or cultures as well as cultures of other ethnic/racial minority and religious groups in the United States. Understanding how culture influences the way in which students behave and learn best is important. Teachers need to have a commitment to the philosophical basis for multicultural instruction.

Hopefully, knowledge of other cultures and the importance of cultural influences on the learning behavior of students will help teachers acknowledge and support the need for multicultural education. Minimizing negative and biased attitudes of teachers through an effective multicultural teacher training program should produce individuals who will be able to successfully implement multicultural instruction in the classroom. Hilliard defines multicultural teacher education as:

> . . . the focus in teacher education which is designed to help teacher to function effectively with pupils in a culturally diverse society. The focus here is upon teaching behavior that facilitates or retards pupil growth. This does not refer to teacher education exclusively for working with a single cultural group, either by a member of the single group or by a person external to the group. The fundamental assumption here is that teachers can improve their teaching of school subjects to their own or other cultural groups if the appropriate attitudes, cultural experiences, and self-understanding are present. (Hunter, 1974)

Multicultural education is a process through which individuals are exposed to the diversity that exists in the United States and to the relationship of this diversity to the world. This diversity includes ethnic, racial minority populations as well as religious groups and sex differences. The exposure to diversity should be based on the foundation that every person in our society has the opportunity and option to support and maintain one or more cultures, i.e., value systems, life styles, sets of symbols; however, the individual, as a citizen of the United States has a responsibility for contributing to and maintaining the culture which is common to all who live in this country. An objective of multicultural education is to provide freedom for individuals to be whatever it is they so desire to be but at the same time recognizing that they are also a part of a national culture.

If education of the teacher is viewed in the context of the great variation among the people of the United States, the enormous dimensions of the teacher's task are obvious. The educational system in the United States is devoted to the idea of a common school. The school is the only institution through which all children of all cultures can share the heritage and life of this nation. The teacher who can work only with children from one socioeconomic or cultural group is inadequately prepared to teach in the common school. If children are to receive effective and appropriate education, the interests and cultural backgrounds of these children must be understood. The skills and techniques effective with children of diverse backgrounds must be built into the competency of every teacher (Smith).

Teacher education's responsibility

In restructuring teacher education programs to meet the needs of multicultural education, several dimensions will need considerable attention. It is almost impossible to plan multicultural education training for students without first giving some thought to what implications this may have for faculty and curriculum as well as for the students.

The instruction in schools and colleges of education throughout the country is primarily being done by faculty who received their training and education during a period when cultural differences were not accepted as differences but as deficits to be ignored or handled as a disadvantage. This climate produced, for the most part, individuals who are not particularly sensitive to multicultural education. Many have little knowledge of ethnic/racial cultures other than their own. Experiences with those who may differ from them have also been limited. Segregated schools and lack of knowledge have contributed to limiting the degree to which multicultural instructional techniques and strategies were implemented and developed. Culturally integrated instructional materials have only recently been available and this too has posed a handicap. In general, there appears to be a need to provide multicultural in-service education for the trainers of teachers.

The present curricula of most of the teacher training institutions remain unchanged. As was noted earlier, curricula that was originally designed to prepare teachers to teach in a homogeneous type society has never been relevant and certainly is not appropriate for today's complex and diverse society and world. All aspects of curricula that effect the student in preservice training should be examined for multicultural relevancy. It is not enough to require a course or two in multicultural education in hopes that this approach will suffice. Suggestions for designing teacher training programs will be discussed after a review of some existing programs has been presented.

Students in training reflect our heterogeneous population. To provide the same type of training for all would be disastrous. The ethnic/racial and cultural backgrounds of the students need to be considered in every classroom whether it is on the college level or in the elementary school. However, there are some basic foundations and concerns of multicultural education that should be shared with all students. The section Imperatives for a Teacher Training Model with offer more discussion in the area of student needs.

Selected existing teacher training programs: an analysis

Four teacher training programs designed to achieve multicultural teacher training education have been selected for review and analysis in this section. These four programs were among those included for review at the AACTE Multiethnic Leadership Training Institute held in April, 1976, in Washington, D. C. The Institute review of programs included a variety of training programs but only those programs housed in teacher training institutions and whose programs were described in detail were selected for further analysis here. Programs that resulted from general assistance centers supported through Title IV of the 1964 Civil Rights Act are therefore not included. Much of the effort and work of the general assistance centers has certainly enhanced and promoted multicultural education training but are not presently incorporated in total into the structure of most colleges and schools of education. The programs that will be analyzed include the Institute for Cultural Pluralism, School of Education, San Diego State University, San Diego, California; the Multicultural Program Area, University of Houston, Houston, Texas; The Human Relations Program, University of Wisconsin, Milwaukee, Wisconsin; and The Multicultural Program, University of Michigan, Ann Arbor, Michigan.[1]

Each program will be described briefly and analyzed for the following: impetus for the establishment of the program, content, target populations, extent of program which will include student participation, financial support, and faculty participation. Elements of the programs that appear to be basic and essential considerations for the development of multicultural teacher training programs will appear in the discussion on imperatives for teacher training programs.

San Diego State University

The Institute for Cultural Pluralism developed a teacher training process which is known as "Community, Home, Cultural Awareness and Language Training (CHCALT). This process was developed for Teacher Corps in 1970. In 1973–74 the institute developed the Bilingual/Cross-Cultural Specialist Credential Program which was approved by the State of California Commission for Teacher Preparation and Licensing.

Impetus for establishment of program

The CHCALT program appears to be a response to a variety of recent federal and state legislative enactments. The following California legislative acts and codes are cited as a means of identifying specific state involvement. These acts and codes are as follows:

- In 1973 California Commission for Teacher Preparation and Licensing established guidelines for the issuing of a Bilingual/Cross-Cultural Specialist Credential under the authority of California Assembly Bill No. 122 (Ryan Act, 1970).
- California Senate Bill No. 1135 (1973) provides for the implementation of programs for training Bilingual/Cross-Cultural Teacher Aides and Specialists; and provides funds for program and professional development purposes.
- California Education Code, Article 3.3, Section 13344, requires that schools with substantial proportions (25%) of minority students provide in-service training for teachers in the history, culture, and current problems of students with diverse ethnic backgrounds.
- California Assembly Bill 2817 enacts the state Bilingual Teacher Corp Program, which seeks to provide teachers and school administrators that are qualified to meet the needs of the limited English-speaking and non English-speaking children in the state. The program provides stipends and tuition to teaching aides pursuing approved teaching creditial programs.

Content of program

The CHCALT process is organized into four basic components. They are:

I   Philosophy of Education for the Culturally and Linguistically distinct
II Sociocultural Awareness—Home and Community Based
III Oral Language and Assessment Techniques
IV Diagnostic and Prescriptive Strategies

Figure 11.1 illustrates the four components and presents the manner by which each component is expanded and viewed.

Component I provides for the philosophical basis of the program. It allows students in training an opportunity to examine their own and other cultures from the perspective of anthropology, sociology, psychology, aesthetics, linguistics, and history.

The second component emphasizes field experiences that involve a particular culture selected by the student. This opportunity provides experiences with the home and family environment of the selected cultural group. This experience is

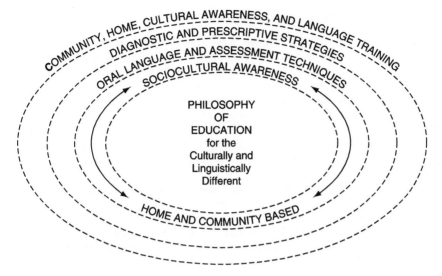

Figure 11.1 The CHCALT model

then expanded to include the community culture with exposure to the cultural heritage and contemporary life style of that group.

The purpose of the third component is to provide knowledge of the linguistic characteristics of the cultural group selected by the student. This component includes: (a) communications, (b) social function, (c) characteristics, (d) comprehension, differences, and dominance as they pertain to the brand area of oral language and assessment techniques.

The final component helps students translate the knowledge and skills gained in the first three components into specific techniques and strategies for classroom instruction. Experience at this point involves developing skill in (a) individual instruction, (b) small group and peer teaching, (c) performance criteria, (d) relevant diagnosis, (e) teaching techniques and relevant materials and (f) planning and program strategies as they relate to the general area of Diagnostic and Prescriptive Strategies.

Target populations

The first component appears to be designed for all students enrolled but as one moves through the process, work with a specific ethnic/cultural group is necessary. The masters degree and specialist credential programs in the bilingual/ cross-cultural education programs are offered with specialization in Afro-American, American-Indian or Pan Asian-American culture.

Extent of program

At present it appears that this program is primarily for graduate students. However, interest and efforts to develop multicultural training for undergraduate students is underway. Because this program is not open to undergraduates, the program is not an integral part of the total teacher training program in the school of education. However, the university did allocate faculty and budget to implement the pilot phase of the credential program Fall term, 1974.

The University of Wisconsin-Milwaukee

The School of Education's Human Relations Program at the University of Wisconsin-Milwaukee was designed in 1973. The program title in no way indicates the extent to which the program is multicultural. However a closer examination of this Program will reveal its relevancy to this discussion.

Impetus for establishment of the program

The Human Relations Program at the University of Wisconsin-Milwaukee is one of the state teacher training institution's responses to specific legislation requiring preparation in intergroup relations for initial teacher certification in the state of Wisconsin.

The Wisconsin Administration Code was amended, in 1973, to include a requirement that preparation in human relations including intergroup relations, be a part of all programs leading to initial certification in education. Because of the effect this code requirement has had for teacher training institutions in the State of Wisconsin and its implications on National multicultural training, the code is included as follows:

Wisconsin Department of Public Instruction

Administrative Code Requirement in Human Relations

Pl 3.03(1) is created to read:

(1) Human Relations
 (a) Preparation in human relations, including intergroup relations, shall be included in programs leading to initial certification in education. Institutions of higher education shall provide evidence that preparation in human relations, including intergroup relations, is an integral part of programs leading to initial certification in education and that members of various racial, cultural, and economic groups have participated in the development of such programs.
 (b) Such preparation shall include the following experiences:

   1   development of attitudes, skills, and techniques so that knowledge of human relations, including intergroup relations, can be translated into learning experiences for students.
   2   a study of the values, life styles, and contributions of racial, cultural, and economic groups in American society.
   3   an analysis of the forces of racism, prejudice, and discrimination in American life and the impact of these forces on the experience of the majority and minority groups.
   4   structured experiences in which teacher candidates have opportunities to examine their own attitudes and feelings about issues of racism, prejudice, and discrimination.
   5   direct involvement with members of racial, cultural, and economic groups and/or with organizations working to improve human relations, including intergroup relations.
   6   experiences in evaluating the ways in which racism, prejudice, and discrimination can be reflected in instructional materials.

(c) This code requirement shall apply only to teachers prepared in Wisconsin. Programs of implementation and evaluation shall be submitted by Wisconsin teacher training institutions to the department of public instruction for approval.

In addition to stipulating specific experiences for teacher education candidates in an approved program construct, the Code statement makes it clear that certain other programmatic conditions must be met:

1 human relations preparation cannot be "tack-on" courses or experiences;
2 members of target groups must have participated in program development;
3 an evaluation program must be developed and implemented.

Content of the program

The School of Education's Human Relations Program was designed to meet the objectives of the Wisconsin Administrative Code. It was designed around the following four tasks:

I To involve all students in an examination of their ethnic background.
II To encourage students to study the meaning of racism.
III To provide an examination of society's heritage of racist beliefs, attitudes, and myths.
IV To teach skills for combating racism.

Student participation in the program begins with the freshman year and extends through the balance of the professional training. Each student is required to complete a minimum of 12 semester credits as follows:

(a) 6 credits—study of racial, cultural, and economic diversity and of the impact of racism within our society.
(b) 4 units—field experiences focusing on the application of the above study.
(c) 2 units—structured group experiences designed to increase self-identity and to value differences in ethnicity.

This Human Relations Program for undergraduate students has the following program components:

(a) Students are allowed to satisfy part of their six-hour requirements from *new courses* offered in Urban Society, Sociology of Minorities, and Cultural Pluralism.
(b) *Existing courses* are expanding so as to include human relations content and therefore are an additional means by which students may partially fulfill the requirement.
(c) *Organizers* are thematic packages of materials that may be used as instructional guides on an individual basis and in a variety of ways.
(d) *Colloquia* are required during the freshman or sophomore year and coordinated with related organizers and field experiences.
(e) *Field experiences* are required at each level including classroom involvement.

(f) A *Structural Group Experience* is required either in the freshman or sophomore year that involves contact with others who differ racially, culturally, and economically from each student.

(g) *Mini-courses* are offered to students after admission to the School of Education. These courses vary in content and provide a variety of experiences.

Participation in these components is distributed throughout the undergraduate years.

Target population
This program is comprehensive concerning target population and students may choose to study a variety of ethnic, minority, religions and/or socio-economic groups. Specific groups include: Blacks, Latinos, Native Americans, Asian-Americans, Jewish Americans and the culture of poverty as well as that of ageism.

Extent of program
The program is integrated throughout the four years of training and is required of all students seeking certification. Because it is an integral part of the overall teacher training program, the financial support appears to be a part of the total economic structure. Faculty and staff participate in the preservice activity as well as in the in-service training provided by the institution.

University of Houston

The Multicultural Program at the University of Houston is an established program area in the College of Education. The program area was originally supported by a HEW grant for developing institutions.

Impetus for establishment of the program
Original interest in the development of a multicultural program at the University of Houston stemmed from the initiative of some faculty members and was supported by a HEW grant. In 1972, the Texas Education Agency mandated multicultural emphasis in the training of teachers. This was translated into a three-hour course requirement for both undergraduates and graduates.

The Texas Education Agency in 1972 in its Revised Standards for Teacher Education and Certification included the following:

E. Multicultural Emphasis
The institution seeking approval for undergraduate level teacher preparation shall design its program of general education so that each student recommended for certification shall have a knowledge and understanding of the multicultural society of which he is a part. To verify this standard, the institution shall present evidence that:
1 its program of general education is designed to give emphasis to the multicultural aspects of society.
2 each student recommended for certification has a knowledge and understanding of our multicultural society.

The bilingual component of the existing program was encouraged by legislation adopted by the Texas senate.

Content of the program

The undergraduate program has been organized around four sequential phases. Phase I and II contain competencies that are basic to the teaching process. These competencies include cross-cultural communication, bilingualism, intercultural conflict, community involvement, power, racism, and prejudice. Students are required to demonstrate (1) knowledge of content, (2) application of knowledge, and (3) consequence oriented activities. The program involves a field-based component.

Phases III and IV provide experiences for students that prepare them for implementation of a multicultural curriculum. Methodology and field centered activities provide the basis for these two phases.

The master degree program includes a multicultural component that has been developed to satisfy the Texas Education Association Standards. This requirement is also centered around a competency based approach. However, candidates at this level may satisfy the requirements in other departments other than through the multicultural program area.

The doctoral program requires candidates to complete approximately one-third of the course work in the area of multicultural education. The courses offered include: (1) development, implementation, and evaluation of multi-cultural teaching techniques and strategies, (2) bilingual education, and (3) research opportunities applicable to multicultural education.

Bilingual specialization is provided to students at the undergraduate level. This program is interdisciplinary and involves the English and Spanish departments as well as the Department of Mexican-American Studies. The bilingual training is also organized around a competency based approach. The following four categories serve to provide the foundation for bilingual specialization: (1) language, (2) culture, (3) preferred mode of learning, and (4) parental involvement.

Target population

The multicultural program at this university appears to be operating in a broad based approach to multicultural education. In other words, the purpose appears to be to expose students to diversity in general and provide training that will produce students who can function in many capacities utilizing a multicultural philosophy. There is a bilingual program aimed at preparing teachers to teach in Spanish-speaking communities. These communities appear to be the only population receiving emphasis.

Extent of the program

This program is integrated into the total undergraduate program to a limited degree. Students must satisfy the Texas Education Agency requirement and at the University of Houston this means a three-hour course. The same requirement holds for graduates at the masters level.

The overall approach is an integrated one where courses are offered within the teaching training institution but through a separate multicultural program area. This program like others faces problems with financial and faculty support but is now operating on existing funds rather than on special or separate funding.

The University of Michigan

The multicultural program at The University of Michigan began in the Fall of 1972 and has evolved from a workshop approach to training to a specific course requirement for all students seeking teacher certification.

Impetus for establishment of program

The multicultural requirement for preservice teachers was instituted as a result of legislation included in the 1972–73 Master Agreement between the local teacher association, the Ann Arbor Education Association, and the Ann Arbor Board of Education. The legislation read as follows:

> Beginning in the 1972–73 school year, no student teacher shall be accepted by the Ann Arbor Schools unless he can demonstrate attitudes necessary to support and create the multiethnic curriculum. Each such student teacher must provide a document or transcript which reflects training in or evidence of substantive understanding of the multiethnic or minority experience.

The School of Education was made aware of this provision in the Spring of 1972. Although there had been previous attempts to include multiethnic training in the curriculum of the school, nothing had been accepted or planned. There was no evidence of multiethnic/cultural education in the formal curriculum of the teacher training program, except for the Urban Program in Education and the Program for Educational Opportunity, a Title IV sponsored project.

Content of the program

This program was organized around multicultural objectives by the faculty of the School of Education in 1973. These objectives included three areas which are as follows:

KNOWLEDGE
1   to expand the participants' knowledge of their own and other cultures.
2   to deepen and to increase the participants' awareness of their own cultural identity.
3   to help participants develop a better understanding of various ways to expand their contact with other cultural groups, and to become better acquainted with their own cultural roles.

PHILOSOPHY
1   to develop the participants' capacities for humane, sensitive, and critical inquiry into the nature of cultural issues, particularly as these may relate to education.
2   to study the aesthetic, epistomological, and ethical interrelationships of cultural life in the United States and elsewhere through their psychological, social, economic, and political dimensions.
3   to increase the participants' capacity for examining their own cultural attitudes and values in the light of history and the current situation.
4   to augment to participants' abilities for envisaging future developments and engaging in planning for cultural interchange within an emerging world society.

METHODOLOGY
To help participants develop the ability to develop and plan multicultural learning experiences by:

1   investigating, developing, and testing suitable teaching strategies for a multicultural curriculum.

2   increasing skills in locating, developing, and using instructional resources for multicultural education.
3   learning to assess the effectiveness of a multicultural curriculum.

In an effort to satisfy the objectives of the knowledge component, students are required to elect three multicultural courses from an interdisciplinary list of course offerings that are relevant to multicultural concepts. These courses may be taken at any time but must be completed prior to the directed teaching experience.

The philosophical component was to be achieved: (1) through non-education courses that were considered multicultural in focus and/or content and (2) through the incorporation of multicultural concepts in education courses, particularly those offered in the department of social foundations. The methodological aspects were to be offered and available in all of the courses in methodology.

Target population
In The University of Michigan program, there is no emphasis upon specific ethnic/minority cultures. The focus is left entirely up to students, but they are encouraged to select courses from a variety of areas so as to provide them with a broad exposure to diversity. There is a bilingual program for master degree students, but it is serving a limited number of students.

Extent of the program
Involvement in this program is required of all students, undergraduate or graduate, seeking teacher certification. Although students are encouraged to satisfy the three course requirement through an interdisciplinary approach, many courses are offered in the School of Education that may be elected to fulfill the requirement. Primarily the multicultural training is confined to undergraduate students but graduate students may plan programs on both the masters and Ph.D. level to obtain a degree of competency in the area of multicultural education. Because the program is an integral part of the School of Education, all financial support is provided through general funds. Participants from administration and faculty has been supportive.

Imperatives for a multicultural teacher training model

The four programs reviewed in the preceding section possess common characteristics that may be considered as essential to the organization and development of teacher training models for multicultural education.

All four programs presented included at one stage or another an opportunity for students to have some exposure to the philosophy that supports multiculturalism. This component in most of the programs included experiences and opportunities for students to examine their own ethnic/cultural backgrounds as a prerequisite for understanding and developing supportive rational-philosophy for multicultural education. Therefore, the following imperatives are offered as initial areas for concern in developing multicultural training models:

1   There is a need for students to be involved in experiences that will allow them to examine their own cultures and to have an understanding of the importance of cultures including ethnic/minority backgrounds in the development of the individual.
2   Students need opportunities that will expose them to the diversity of the

United States with emphasis on those groups which are prevasively represented in this country.

3 Students need experiences that will encourage the development of positive and supportive attitudes about ethnic/cultural diversity thereby establishing a philosophy consistent with the objectives of multicultural education.

4 Students need to be involved in situations that will provide opportunities for them to have direct contact with individuals who differ from them.

The San Diego program and the University of Houston program appeared to have extensive bilingual education offerings. Although emphasis in the area was to a lesser degree at the other two institutions, some attention was given to bilingualism. Therefore, imperative (5) and (6) must be included if a program is to be inclusive.

5 Students need to understand the importance of language to culture and the implications bilingualism has for both learner and teacher.

6 Students should be familiar with a second language and the culture from which the language eminates.

Two of the programs presented allowed for concentration in the study of a particular ethnic/minority culture. The other two programs provided for a broad based approach. It is suggested that a multicultural training program consider imperative (7).

7 Students should have an opportunity to specialize in one or more ethnic/minority cultures of their choice after the overall and underlying principles of multiculturalism have been grasped.

The ability to transform knowledge, philosophy, and experience into methodology can be achieved if the following imperatives are integrated into a training model:

8 Students need to be instructed as to how to design, implement, and evaluate instructional materials appropriate for multicultural instruction.

9 Students must acquire the ability to analyze, evaluate, and select for use, existing and commercial instructional materials for their relevancy to achieve multicultural objectives.

10 Emphasis must be placed on guiding students to develop teaching strategies and techniques that will allow for cultural individualized teaching/learning environments.

In order to adequately integrate the above imperatives into a multicultural training program, these additional considerations must be adhered to:

11 Total commitment to the need for and to the goals of multicultural education must be achieved at every level of the training institution and, where appropriate, the entire institution of higher education.

12 The composition of faculty must be representative of the ethnic/cultural diversity of the United States including representation from both sexes.

13 Financial support for multicultural training in teacher education should not be separate from the total financial support structure.
14 A multicultural training program must be an integral part of the entire training process and integrated into every aspect of the total curriculum of an institution.

Considering all of the stated imperatives and the various components included in the four existing teacher training programs that were evaluated, the model in Figure 11.2 is presented as a suggested way to proceed in establishing a multi-cultural teacher training program.

STAGE I   STAGE II   STAGE III   STAGE IV

Knowledge
(1, 2, 3) ——————————————————————

Experiences
(4) ——————————————————————

Language (5) ———————————————

Proficiency Language (6) ————————————

Specific Cultural
Exposure Involvement (7)

Methodology
(8, 9, 10)

Philosophy

Total institutional-faculty
commitment
(curriculum integration including finance)
(11, 12, 13, 14)

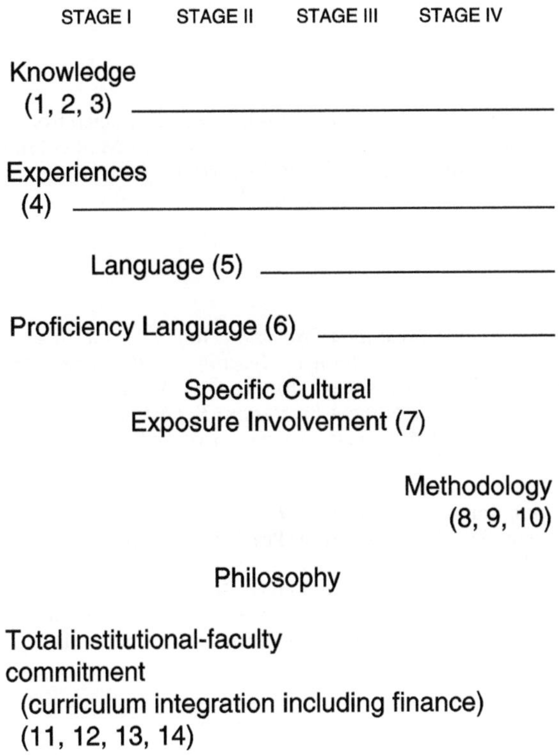

Figure 11.2 Suggested model for developing a multicultural teacher training program

Summary

This discussion has attempted to establish the need for multicultural education and to make clear the responsibility teacher training institutions have for providing effective training in this area.

The four programs presented are examples of what presently exists. No one program has completely satisfied all of the desired elements that the Imperatives tend to suggest. It is hoped that by examining existing programs, certain aspects of each will serve as guides in developing new programs.

The Imperatives are important. If they are adhered to as guidelines in developing multicultural teacher training programs, more thorough and effective programs may result.

Note

1   Material for a review of these four programs has been abstracted from papers prepared for presentation at the Leadership Training Institute on Multicultural Education in Teacher Education, sponsored by the American Association of Colleges for Teacher Education and the United States Office of Education (Grant #G007501382 Washington, D. C. April 28–30, 1976.

References

Howsman, Robert B., et al. *Educating a Profession: Report of the Bicentennial Commission on Education for the Profession of Teaching of the American Association of Colleges for Teacher Education.* Washington, D. C.: AACTE, 1976, 20.

Howsman, Robert B., et al. *Educating a Profession: Report of the Bicentennial Commission on Education for the American Association of Colleges for Teacher Education.* Washington, D. C.: AACTE, 1972.

Hunter, William A. (Ed.). *Multicultural Education Through Competency-Based Teacher Education.* Washington, D. C.: AACTE, 1974, 41.

Smith, B. Othanel, Saul B. Cohen, and Arthur Pearl. *Teachers for the Real World.* Washington, D. C.: AACTE, 1969, 1–3.

Stent, Madelon D., William R. Hazard, and Harry N. Rivlin. *Cultural pluralism in education: A mandate for change.* New York: Appleton-Century-Crofts, 1973, 20.

Taylor, Harold. *The World and the American Teacher.* Washington, D. C.: AACTE, 1969, 18.

CHAPTER 12

A CONTENT ANALYSIS OF THE BLACK AMERICAN IN TEXTBOOKS (1969)

James A. Banks

Introduction

The urgent racial crisis in our nation has evoked considerable concern among educators about the roles of the school and teaching materials in intergroup education. Research indicates that teaching materials *do* affect youngsters' racial attitudes. Trager and Yarrow found that a curriculum which emphasized cultural diversity had a positive influence on children's racial attitudes.[1] Research by Johnson indicated that courses in black history could help black children feel better about themselves and their race.[2] Litcher and Johnson investigated the effects of multiethnic readers on the racial attitudes of second-grade white pupils and concluded that ". . . use of multiethnic readers resulted in marked positive change in the subjects' attitudes toward Negroes."[3] Since textbooks, which comprise the core of the social studies curriculum, can influence racial attitudes, it becomes imperative to evaluate carefully the content of textbooks with a view toward ascertaining the contributions which they might be making toward helping youngsters clarify their racial attitudes, self-perceptions, and value orientations. The careful study of textbooks is especially urgent in this time of high racial tension and polarization.

The problem

The purpose of this study was to analyze the content of a selected sample of elementary American history textbooks in terms of major themes used to discuss the Negro and race relations. A review of the literature revealed the need for a current, scientific, and comprehensive study of the black American in textbooks.

In recent years, a number of researchers have studied the image of the black American and other minority groups in textbooks. While these studies are significant contributions to the literature on race relations,[4] none utilized a content analysis technique which met the criteria of scientific content analysis as promulgated by researchers such as Berelson, Budd, Thorp and Donohew, Kerlinger, and Borg. These writers maintain that a scientific content analysis must be *objective, systematic,* and *quantitative.*[5] To satisfy these criteria, a study must have well delineated categories, a measure of reliability, clearly formulated data gathering procedures, and research hypotheses which can be tested by analyzing the data gathered during the investigation.

The study reported here was designed to utilize a scientific content analysis technique to illuminate the dominant themes (major ideas) used to discuss the Negro and race relations in a sample of 36 American history books for use in grades 4, 5, 6, 7, and 8. A sub-sample of six books was used to compare the frequency of selected theme units in books published in 1964 and in 1968.[6]

Procedures

Unit of analysis

A technique called *thematic analysis* was used in this study. According to Budd, Thorp, and Donohew, a theme is a major idea or single thought unit. A sentence may contain one or more theme units. The sentence, "John is handsome and intelligent," contains *two* themes or ideas. They are, "John is handsome," and "John is intelligent."[7] The total number of themes in *each* sentence analyzed were ascertained and reported in this study.

Formulation of categories and coding sheet

Theme units were classified under one of eleven categories (described below). Initially, theme units were selected from a sample of elementary American history textbooks, and the categories developed on the basis of the content of these theme units, recommendations made by social scientists and educators (studies on minority groups in textbooks were analyzed for the major ideas which were recommended for inclusion in textbooks by these researchers), and reading in black history by the investigator. Sample theme units were added and some minor modifications made in category definitions during the analysis, since as Budd, Thorp, and Donohew noted ". . . because it is virtually impossible to anticipate every situation that will arise during the coding, each category definition should allow for expansion . . ."[8]

Validity of the coding sheet

The "jury method" was used to ascertain the validity of the procedures in this study. In this method, ". . . experts are asked to judge relevant parts of the methodology . . . or measuring instruments."[9] Four experts in the teaching of black history, one historian and three social studies educators, were identified and asked to serve on the panel of jurors to validate the instrument.[10] These individuals were selected because of their publications and reputations in the area of race relations and black history. Each juror was asked to judge whether the theme units from the initial sample of books were *appropriately* or *inappropriately* categorized. All four jurors judged 89% of the theme units to be *appropriately* categorized. *All* theme units were judged appropriately categorized by at least two jurors.

Reliability of the procedures

The reliability of the coding procedure was established by having two coders independently code the theme units in five books randomly selected from the total sample.[11] The coder proportion of agreement was .64.

Formulation of hypotheses

Each hypothesis stated a predicted relationship between the frequencies of two theme categories. *The investigator assumed that the categories selected for comparison had a high degree of comparability, importance, and the greatest potential for yielding meaningful information.* For example, the theme unit frequencies in the categories "Racial Harmony" and "Racial Violence and Conflict" were compared because they had contrasting definitions and because previous researchers had reported that authors frequently employ units in the former category and rarely in the latter. "Racial Harmony" and "Principal Discrimination" theme unit frequencies were compared for similar reasons. The purpose and scope of this study did not warrant that all possible comparisons between categories be made.

All hypotheses were stated in the null form. The hypotheses stated that there was no difference in the frequencies of theme units in the categories compared. The .05 level of significance was selected as sufficient to reject the null hypothesis. Chi-square was used in the analysis.

Categories and examples

Explained discrimination. Theme units which state reasons for differential treatment based on race but make no attempt to distinguish moral issues and causal issues. Such theme units are susceptible to being interpreted as *justifications* for discrimination.

> Example: Negroes could withstand the hot Southern climate much better than whites.

Principal Discrimination. Theme units which describe deliberate differential treatment based on race in which no attempt is made by the writer to explain the discriminatory practices depicted.

> Example: The Plessy vs. Ferguson Decision upheld segregation.

Non-Violent Resistance to Discrimination. Theme units which describe acts or words which *did not* involve violence but were designed primarily to resist discriminatory practices based on race.

> Example: The NAACP worked to end discrimination.

Deliberate Desegregation. Theme units which describe deliberate behavior on the part of majority groups or established institutions which ended or intended to end racial discrimination or segregation.

> Example: The Brown Decision of 1954 prohibited segregation in the public schools.

Expedient Desegregation. Theme units which describe behavior by majority groups or established institutions which resulted in ending segregation or discrimination but had other dominant objectives, such as political or social advancement of individuals, groups or a nation.

> Example: Lincoln freed the slaves to weaken the Confederacy.

Racial Violence and Conflict. Theme units which describe acts of violence which were caused in part or whole by factors involving racial confrontation and racial antagonism.

Example: The Ku Klux Klan committed violent acts against Negroes.

Deprivation. Theme units which describe the physical and psychological poverty of black Americans.

Example: Slaves were poorly fed.

Stereotypes. Theme units which describe conventional, fixed, and unverified characteristics of Negroes.

Example: Slaves were happy.

Prejudice. Theme units which describe unfavorable racial attitudes which are held or were held in disregard of facts.

Example: Southern whites felt that the Negro was innately inferior.

Racial Harmony. Theme units which describe peaceful and friendly relations between Negroes and whites, or events or acts which contributed to good race relations.

Example: Some masters freed their slaves.

Achievements. Theme units which describe the accomplishments of Negroes in literature, music, art, science, industry, sports, entertainment, education and in other fields.

Example: Booker T. Washington was a famous scientist.

Summary of major findings

Theme units to be classified in the eleven categories were selected from the 36 American history textbooks used in the main analysis by checking the table of contents and index of each book and reading those parts of the book which discussed the Negro or race relations. The following comparisons of the resulting frequencies of theme units are of particular interest:

"Principal Discrimination" theme units had a higher frequency than "Racial Violence and Conflict" theme units.

"Explained Discrimination" theme units had a higher frequency than "Racial Violence and Conflict" theme units.

"Principal Discrimination" theme units had a higher frequency than "Racial Harmony" theme units.

"Racial Harmony" theme units and "Racial Violence and Conflict" theme units had equal frequencies.

"Achievement" theme units had a higher frequency than "Deprivation" theme units.

"Non-Violent Resistance to Discrimination" theme units and "Racial Violence and Conflict" theme units had equal frequencies.

"Principal Discrimination" and "Deliberate Desegregation" theme units had equal frequencies.

"Deliberate Desegregation" theme units had a higher frequency than "Expedient Desegregation" theme units.

Table 12.1 Total Unit Frequencies by Category

Theme Category	Total Unit Frequency
Achievements	367
Principal Discrimination	279
Deliberate Desegregation	261
Explained Discrimination	206
Non-Violent Resistance to Discrimination	165
Racial Harmony	164
Racial Violence and Conflict	140
Deprivation	82
Prejudice	25
Stereotypes	19
Expedient Desegregation	14

Table 12.2 Minimum and Maximum Frequencies of Theme Units

Theme Category	Minimum units in any book	Maximum units in any book
Achievements	4	80
Principal Discrimination	14	40
Deliberate Desegregation	3	28
Explained Discrimination	8	12
Non-Violent Resistance to Discrimination	3	16
Racial Harmony	10	24
Racial Violence and Conflict	5	18
Deprivation	3	12
Prejudice	0	5
Stereotypes	0	3
Expedient Desegregation	0	4

"Racial Harmony" theme units had a higher frequency than "Prejudice" theme units.

"Stereotypes" and "Prejudice" theme units had equal frequencies.

Theme units which referred to achievements, racial violence and conflict, peaceful resistance to discrimination, and deliberate acts of discrimination occurred more frequently in books published in 1968 than in 1964.

Discussion of findings

While textbook authors often attempt to explain or rationalize racial discrimination, they more frequently discuss discrimination without either explaining or condemning it. This finding supports that of other researchers who have suggested that textbook writers "avoid taking a moral stand."[12]

The authors of elementary history textbooks do not frequently depict racial violence. They seek to explain discrimination more frequently than they mention incidents of racial violence and conflict. However, authors refer to racial violence as often as they relate peaceful and friendly relations between blacks and whites. This finding conflicts with those of Stampp[13] and other writers who suggest that authors emphasize harmonious race relations and neglect discussion of racial conflict. The authors in this study also mentioned racial violence as frequently as they referred to peaceful resistance to discrimination.

Other findings in this study suggest that authors do not emphasize harmonious race relations. The authors referred to deliberate acts of discrimination much more often than they related incidents of racial harmony. However, they mentioned racial harmony more frequently than they did racial prejudice.

The textbook writers mentioned deliberate acts of discrimination as often as they related deliberate acts of desegregation. However, they referred to deliberate acts of desegregation more frequently than they mentioned acts which lead to desegregation but were expedient gestures.

The authors depicted the achievements of black Americans in literature, music, art, science, industry, sports, entertainment, education and in other fields much more frequently than they referred to any other events which relate to the black man and race relations. For example, the physical and psychological deprivations of black Americans were rarely discussed. Thus, the achievements of individual black heroes were emphasized rather than the plight of the majority of black people in this country.

The authors of textbooks rarely used theme units which could be characterized as "stereotypes." This finding does not support the often heard contention that textbooks frequently describe Negroes in a stereotypic fashion.

A comparison of books published in 1964 and in 1968 revealed that significant changes had occurred in the frequency of several types of theme units used to discuss the Negro and race relations. Theme units which referred to achievements, violence and conflict, peaceful resistance to discrimination, and deliberate acts of discrimination occurred more frequently in books published in 1968 than in 1964. This finding indicates that textbook authors have responded, to some degree, to the demand for more comprehensive coverage of the black American in textbooks, and to the black American's increasingly active role in American life.

Conclusions and recommendations

1. This study indicates that authors rarely take a moral stand when discussing such issues as racial discrimination and racial prejudice. Those who maintain that one of the major goals of the social studies is to inculcate democratic racial attitudes will find reason here to ask for a reevaluation of the textbook author's role in intergroup education.

2. Theme units which refer to racial violence and conflict have low frequencies in elementary American history textbooks. Since racial violence and conflict are currently pervasive in our nation, a greater frequency of these units in textbooks appears necessary if that part of the curriculum is to reflect reality accurately.

3. Racial prejudice theme units appear infrequently in elementary American history textbooks. A greater number of these units might provide a context for helping children to deal with racial prejudice and conflict more intelligently.

4. This study indicates that most textbooks have "integrated" by extolling the virtues of "selected" black heroes. While both black and white youngsters need

black heroes with whom they can identify, they need to know the plight of the masses of black people even more. Children cannot be expected to grasp the full significance of the black experience in America unless they are keenly aware of the social and historical factors which have kept the black man at the lower rungs of the social ladder.[14]

5. While the findings of this study support some of those of other researchers, they conflict with others. This suggests that more extensive and careful research is needed before we can derive conclusive statements regarding the treatment of the black American in teaching materials.

Notes

1 Helen G. Trager and Marian R. Yarrow, *They Learn What They Live*. New York: Harper and Brothers, 1952.
2 David W. Johnson, "Freedom School Effectiveness: Changes in Attitudes of Negro Children," *The Journal of Applied Behavioral Science*, 2:325–330, 1966.
3 John H. Litcher and David W. Johnson, "Changes in Attitudes of White Elementary School Students After Use of Multiethnic Readers," *Journal of Educational Psychology*, 60:148–152, 1969.
4 A partial list of these studies includes: Committee on the Study of Teaching Materials in Intergroup Education, *Inter-group Relations in Teaching Materials*. Washington, D.C. American Council on Education, 1949; Lloyd Marcus, *The Treatment of Minorities in American History Textbooks*. New York: Anti-Defamation League, 1961; Kenneth M. Stampp, W. D. Jordan, L. W. Levine, R. L. Middlekeuff, C. G. Sellers and G. W. Stocking, "The Negro in American History Textbooks," *Integrated Education*, 2:9–24: October-November 1964; Department of Public Instruction, *A Report on the Treatment of Minorities in American History Textbooks*. Lansing, Michigan: Michigan Department of Education, 1968.
5 See Bernard Berelson, *Content Analysis in Communication Research*. Glencoe: The Free Press Publishers, 1952; Richard W. Budd, Robert K. Thorp, and Lewis Donohew, *Content Analysis of Communications*. New York: The Macmillan Company, 1967; Fred N. Kerlinger, *Foundations of Behavioral Research: Educational and Psychological Inquiry*. New York: Holt, Rinehart & Winston, Inc., 1966; and, Walter R. Borg, *Educational Research: An Introduction*. New York: David McKay Company, Inc., 1963.
6 The six books were: Orrel T. Baldwin, *The Story of Our America*. New York: Noble & Noble Publishers, Inc., 1964; Richard C. Brown, Arlan C. Helgeson, and George H. Lobdell, *The United States of America: A History for Young Citizens*. Atlanta: Silver Burdett Company, 1964; Mabel B. Casner and Ralph H. Gabriel, *Story of the American Nation*. New York: Harcourt, Brace and World, Inc., 1964; Stephen H. Bronz, Glenn W. Moon, and Don C. Cline, *The Challenge of America*. New York: Holt, Rinehart & Winston, 1968; Harold H. Eibling, Fred M. King, and James Harlow, *History of Our United States*. River Forest, Illinois: Laidlaw Brothers, 1968; Jerome R. Reich and Edward L. Biller, *Building the American Nation*. New York: Harcourt, Brace and World Inc., 1968.
7 Richard W. Budd, Robert K. Thorp, and Lewis Donohew, *op. cit.*, pp. 44–46.
8 *Ibid.*, p. 28.
9 *Ibid.*, p. 69.
10 The jurors were: Dr. Nancy Arnez, Professor of Education, Northeastern Illinois State College; Dr. Dewitt Dykes, Professor of American History, Michigan State University; Miss Astrid C. Anderson, Research Associate, the Lincoln Filene Center for Citizenship and Public Affairs, Tufts University; and Mr. Irving J. Sloan, author of books on the black American and Social Studies Teacher, Scarsdale (New York) Junior High School.
11 The five books were: Orrel T. Baldwin, *The Story of Our America*. New York: Noble and Noble Publishers, Inc., 1964; Herbert H. Gross, Dwight W. Follett, Robert E. Gabler, William L. Burton, and Ben F. Ahlscwede, *Exploring Regions of the United States*. Chicago: Follett Publishing Company, 1966; Rembert W. Patrick, John K.

Bettersworth, and Ralph W. Steen, *This Country of Ours*. Austin: The Steck Company, 1965; John A. Rickard and Rolor E. Ray, *Discovering American History*. Boston: Allyn and Bacon, Inc., 1965; and, Clarence L. Ver Steeg, *The Story of Our Country*. New York: Harper and Row Publishers, 1965.

12 Department of Public Instruction, *A Report on the Treatment of Minorities in American History Textbooks*. Lansing: Michigan Department of Education, 1968.

13 Kenneth M. Stampp, *et al., op. cit.*, pp. 9–24.

14 James A. Banks. "The Need for Positive Racial Attitudes in Textbooks" in Robert L. Green (editor), *Racial Crisis in American Education*. Chicago: Follett Publishing Company, 1969.

CHAPTER 13

SEX ROLE STEREOTYPING IN THE PUBLIC SCHOOLS (1973)

Terry N. Saario, Carol Nagy Jacklin, and Carol Kehr Tittle

> If the children and youth of a nation are afforded opportunity to develop their capacities to the fullest, if they are given the knowledge to understand the world and the wisdom to change it, then the prospects for the future are bright. In contrast, a society which neglects its children, however well it may function in other respects, risks eventual disorganization and demise.
>
> (Bronfenbrenner, 1970, p. 3)

The concern of one generation in a society for the next has been variously described and labeled by historians, psychologists, sociologists, and anthropologists. Such concern is a constant in all societies, and is frequently called socialization. Socialization is the process of preparing children to assume adult statuses and roles. The family, the school, the church, peer groups, economic institutions, political institutions, and the media would be identified by most thoughtful people as the principal socializing institutions in our society. Of these institutions only the school has the socialization of youth as a principal function. Schools, whether formal or informal, whether inner city or rural, function as transmitters of certain societal norms and mores from one generation to the next.

It is our argument that schools not only socialize children in a general way but also exert a powerful and limiting influence on the development of sex roles. Instead of encouraging diversity within broad limits of conduct, they define specific attitudes, modes of acting, and opportunities which are appropriate for boys and girls. This serves to limit the choices open to each sex and contributes to a sense of inadequacy when individuals do not live up to the stringently defined norm or average. We acknowledge that a child's gender awareness and self-identification is critical to her or his development. However, it is reasonable to question the utility of inculcating within our children "fixed patterns of behaviors defined along traditional sex-role lines" (Emmerich, 1972, p. 7). Traditional sex role categories are simply conventions which hold significance in the social order of the day.

Educational reformers and critics in the last decade have heightened our awareness of the symbolism and hidden messages inherent in the structure of the school. They have shown us how schools function as sorting and classifying mechanisms and how schools foster and amplify such questionable personality traits as passivity, conformity, and dependency. Schools usually function in these ways *sub rosa*. Obviously, most students learn much more than reading, writing, and arithmetic. The content of the school or classroom may include curriculum materials, testing materials, and programmatically prescribed curricular patterns—which are the focus of this article—as well as teacher behavior, counseling practices, peer group influences, and many other instructional factors. All these factors convey multiple messages to children.

It is in these many ways that schools and their content carry hidden messages to the young about sex role mythologies in our society. The very structure of the school portrays males and females in somewhat idealized, rigid, and nonoverlapping roles. As many developmental psychologists have noted, role models do contribute to the definition of the limits or boundaries of a child's self-expectations (Mischel, 1970). These limits may be set very early in life (Mead, 1971; Kagan, 1969; Levy, 1972). And yet, as Betty Levy (1972, p. 5) and others have noted, "as children grow older their awareness of 'appropriate' sex role behavior increases and becomes more restricted and stereotyped." Looft (1971), for example, asked a sample of six to eight-year-old children what they wanted to be when they grew up. He found a striking contrast between the variability of the boys' responses and the unanimity of the girls'. Seventy-five per cent of all the girls' responses in this age group were in two categories—teacher and nurse. The two most popular categories for boys—football player and fireman—were selected by less than ten per cent of the boys. In all, eighteen potential occupational categories were elicited from the males in the sample, eight from the girls. Differential socialization could account for these results.

There is increasing reason to believe that agents outside the home are important as differential socializers. Developmental theory, for example, points to the influence of the environment, including the family, in the rate and mode of children's development. Evidence of differential treatment of the sexes has not been well documented before the age of six (see Maccoby, 1972, for a review); but the research literature in this area is not ample. Perhaps acts of parents subtler than the looks, smiles, touches, and amount-talked-to counted by developmental psychologists are the important variables. Subtle expectations or punishments and sanctions against inappropriate sex-stereotyped behaviors may be the real differential socializers that parents are consciously or unconsciously using.

Although home influences certainly contribute to the sex role modeling which is prevalent in our society, we feel other influences such as schooling are important determinants to be considered. Research to date into the nature and origins of sex role stereotyping in schools has been limited and scattered at best. In undertaking the present studies, we sought to focus our research on some concrete aspects of schooling where stereotyping was blatantly fostered, and where changes in policy could be effected in relatively short order. Certainly hidden curriculum aspects of classroom interactions contribute to the images children have of themselves; and yet this area is so vague and undefined that mere documentation of the effects would not serve to change educational policy. The hidden curriculum exerts influence despite policy. Sex role stereotyping pervades every aspect of education and gradually it must be documented and rooted out of each area. For the moment, however, we have chosen to investigate its presence in elementary basal readers, to describe the sex bias in educational achievement tests, and to discuss some of the curricular requirements which are differentially imposed on male and female students throughout primary and secondary education.

We focus on elementary readers because a child's first contact with school is likely to leave a lasting impact. Since learning to read is the principal task of the early years at school, the content of the books with which children spend so much time merits investigation. Similarly, the study of sex bias in the content of achievement tests is important because the child so frequently encounters them during the school years. Finally, differential curriculum requirements for girls and boys automatically limit the choices each can make while they are in school and in later life.

We outline the research and findings in each of these three areas, and conclude with some recommendations for policy and research which begin to point the way to a less restricted system of education.

Sex role stereotyping in early readers

Much of the content of the school day in the first few grades is focused upon learning to read and write. Whether the child is taught in an open classroom or a traditional one, at some point the child encounters reading textbooks. These readers sustain an image of authority merely by being textbooks (California Advisory Commission, 1971; Child, Potter, and Levine, 1946). Unlike the substance of the textbooks a student encounters in later grades, the substance of early readers is not usually assumed to be central to the teaching and learning activity. The child is being taught to read, not to remember the intricacies of the story of Jack and Jill falling down the hill. Hence, we usually assume the content of the stories in the early readers is innocuous. But is it really? Do children learn something beyond how to read when they encounter these basal readers?

One of the first studies which examined this question of stereotyping in reading textbooks was the Child, Potter, and Levine (1946) content analysis of portions of third grade readers. They assumed, as have many researchers since, that principles of reinforcement and avoidance learning are operative as a child reads. "It is assumed that in reading a story a child goes through symbolically, or rehearses to himself, the episode that is described. The same principles, then, are expected to govern the effect of the reading on him as would govern the effect of actually going through such an incident in real life" (p. 3). Given these assumptions, they examined the role third grade readers would play in determining what motives children develop, how they learn to satisfy these motives, and what expectations they develop about the consequences of trying to satisfy these motives in various ways.

Their unit of analysis was the major theme of the reader. A theme was defined as a recurrent pattern of events including the situation confronting a person, the behaviors with which the person responded, and the consequences of that behavior to that person. They found striking differentiation of roles by sex in their sample of readers. Female characters more often showed affiliation, nurturance, and harm-avoidance, and were the ones nurtured. Males more often provided information, showed activity, aggression, achievement, construction, and behavior directed at gaining recognition. The general absence of females in these readers was as prominent as any differences in behavior: seventy-three per cent of all central characters were male, only twenty-seven per cent female.

Zimet (1970) studied primers spanning the period from 1600 to 1966 to determine whether boys and girls had always been portrayed as engaging in the undifferentiated activities found in modern readers. She found that diffusion or ambiguity of sex role models had increased over the period studied. However, "diffusion" was not clearly defined or quantified. A N.O.W. task force, Women on Words and Images (1972), reviewed 134 readers from fourteen publishers.

Each story was categorized in terms of its hero or heroine by sex (male or female), age (adult or child), and whether it was a biography or fantasy story.

In 1972, Blom, Waite, Zimet, and Edge examined the activities portrayed in the first grade readers in twelve frequently used textbook series. They classified the activities according to: a) age of the child to which the activity would appeal (six, older, or younger); b) sex of the child to which the activity would appeal (as determined by agreement of the researchers); and c) the outcome of the activity in terms of success or failure. They found that masculine activities in these stories ended in failure more often than did feminine activities. (A caveat should be inserted here. These stories seem to have contained some ambiguity about the relationship between sex roles and activities, since forty-six per cent of all activities were performed by both boys and girls while only twenty-six per cent were performed by boys alone and only twenty-eight per cent by girls alone.)

When U'Ren (1971) studied textbooks recommended by the California State Board of Education she found seventy-five per cent of the main characters in these stories were male with less than twenty per cent of story space devoted to females. Many stories with male main characters presented no females at all, but female centered stories usually included males. Stories about girls were usually shorter than stories about boys. In another recent study, Graebner (1972) tried to determine whether the role of women has changed in elementary texts over the last decade. Five hundred and fifty-four stories were analyzed using texts from Scott, Foresman, 1962–63 and 1971, and Ginn, 1961 and 1969. She concluded that almost no change in the portrayal of the role of women has occurred and that texts "have not kept pace with a changing society" (p. 52).

In an analysis of a series of social studies books and readers produced by ten publishing houses, De Crow (1972) found no women portrayed as working outside the home except as a teacher or nurse. Those who were teachers and nurses were all labeled "Miss," perhaps implying that no married women work. Men were more often depicted as making decisions, including household decisions. Boys showed initiative, were creative, and did things while girls were fearful, dependent, and watched other people doing things. Friendships between boys, and between girls and boys, were frequently displayed, but friendships between girls were quite rare.

Potter (1972) has described the effect of books as symbolic models much as Child, Potter, and Levine did in justifying their content analysis. She argues that sequences of behavior which are punished or rewarded in stories should be vicariously rewarding and punishing to the reader. This effect is expected to vary with the ease the child has in identifying with a specific character, a phenomenon which may be partially dependent on such variables as age and sex.

These studies strongly suggest pervasive sex role stereotyping in early readers. But all are generally limited in that they seldom provide reliability data on categories used in content analysis, and they provide only descriptive statistics. While most of the studies agree that textbooks do portray stereotypic sex role models for children, few specify the types of stereotyping that occur.

Carol Jacklin and her associates (1972) undertook the present study to provide some information on the magnitude, direction, and type of stereotyping present in early basal readers.[1] If stereotyping does exist in these readers, they also wanted to find out whether it changed from one grade level to the next, from kindergarten to third grade, and whether publishers differ very much in the amount or kind of sex role stereotyping which occurs in their texts. Answers to these questions would be a basis for estimating the role early readers play in constricting and reinforcing the behavior patterns and psychological characteristics a child associates with particular sex roles.

Four elementary reading textbook series were chosen for analysis. Those published by Ginn, Harper and Row (the California state approved series), and Scott, Foresman were chosen because of their widespread use. The Bank Street series was included because of its reputation for innovation. A complete list of specific texts analyzed can be obtained from the authors.

A systematic sample of every third story in the selected books was examined.[2] The total number of stories analyzed, by publisher, were: Bank Street, sixty-one; Ginn, sixty-nine: Harper & Row, sixty-three; and Scott, Foresman, seventy-seven.

Publisher, grade level, book and story title were recorded. Each character in each story, classified by age and sex, was coded on five additional categories: a) occurrence as main character; b) occurrence in specific environments; c) occurrence as exhibiting specific behaviors; d) occurrence as beaters of specific consequences; e) occurrence as recipients of specific behaviors and consequences. Stories were analyzed person by person, i.e., the environments, behaviors, and consequences related to a given character were scored for the entire story before the next character was begun. The actual taxonomy of attributes and categories employed in the procedure is presented below, with selected examples.

1 Main and secondary characters
2 Type of environment:
   Home
   Outdoors
   Place of business
   School
3 Behavior exhibited:
   Nurturant (helping, praising, serving)
   Aggressive (hitting, kicking, verbal put-downs)
   Self-care (dressing, washing)
   Routine-repetitive (eating, going to school)
   Constructive-productive (building, writing story, planning party)
   Physically exertive (sports, lifting heavy objects)
   Social-recreational (visiting someone, card games)
   Fantasy activity (doll play, cowboys and Indians)
   Directive (initiating, directing, demonstrating)
   Avoidance (stop trying, run away, shut eyes)
   Statement about self—positive, negative, neutral ("I have blue eyes," "I'm too stupid.")
   Problem-solving (producing idea, unusual combinations)
   Statements of information ("I know . . ."; non-evaluative observations about other people)
   Expression of emotion (crying, laughing)
   Conformity (express concern for rules, social norms, others' expectations, do as told)
   General verbal (trivial motor behavior such as dropping something, looking for something, listening)
4 Types of consequences:
   Positive consequences—
   From others—directed toward subject (praise, recognition, support, signs of affection)

From self—self-praise, satisfaction
From situation—reaching goal, unintended positive results
Chance
Author's statement, text
Negative consequences—
From others—directed toward subject (criticism, correction, rejection of ideas)
From self
From situation—inability to reach goal, unintended negative results
Chance
Author's statement, text
Neutral consequences—not clearly positive or negative

In addition to the above, the agent and recipient of all consequences was noted. Changes in environment were recorded as they occurred. Data from individual stories at each grade level were collected separately for each publisher.

All scoring was performed by trained graduate students. Four potential sources of error in scoring existed: a) classification of the person-type; b) classification of the behavior; c) classification of the consequences; and d) classification of the environment. In order to assess inter-rater scoring reliability, eight stories were selected and each of the scorers was asked to score each of the stories, according to the taxonomy presented above. The total number of behaviors, consequences, and environments was recorded for each person-type in each of the eight stories. Pearson product moment correlation coefficients were computed among scorers on the total number of counts in each of these categories. Correlation coefficients for behaviors and consequences ranged from .953 to 1.00 with seventy-five per cent of the correlations greater than .98. There was perfect agreement between scorers for the environment categories.

Results

Combining data across all publishers and grade levels (first through third), fewer female than male characters appeared in these stories. A breakdown of the total number of characters by person-type in the sampled stories is presented in Table 13.1.

Because female characters occurred less frequently than males, comparisons of total frequencies within each category would reflect this difference. To avoid such a misrepresentation, proportional comparisons were made within each category (i.e., behaviors, environments, and consequences), and chi-square tests of significance for differences in proportions were computed. Thus, taking into account

Table 13.1 Total Number of Characters in the Sampled Stories Displayed by Person Type

	Child	Adult	TOTAL
Female	241	124	365
Male	324	256	580
	565	480	945

Table 13.2 Number of Main Characters by Age and Sex

	Female	Male
Adults		
Number main characters	7	33
Total number in stories	124	256
Chi square = 3.95; df = 1, p. 05		
Children		
Number main characters	61	110
Total number in stories	241	324
Chi square = 3.49; df = 1, p. 05		

the smaller total number of adult female characters, female adults are still significantly under-represented as main characters (see Table 13.2).

The behaviors, environments, and consequences associated with each person-type are presented in Tables 13.3, 13.4, and 13.5. Although only significant findings are discussed in the text, the results for all categories of behaviors, environments, and consequences are presented. In this way, each reader can examine the results from her or his own point of view.

The data are organized according to the frequency of each category by person-type, and the percentage of each category of the total counts for that attribute for each person-type. Two chi-square statistics were computed for each category. The first compared child female vs. child male proportions for each category. The second comparison was adult female vs. adult male proportions for each category.

As shown in Table 13.3, boys were portrayed as demonstrating signficantly higher amounts of aggression, physical exertion, and problem-solving. Girls were significantly more often displayed as characters enveloped in fantasy, carrying out directive behaviors, and making (positive and negative) self-statements.

Adult males were shown in significantly higher proportions of constructive-productive behavior, physically exertive behavior, and problem-solving behavior. Adult females were shown in significantly higher proportions of conformity behavior and verbal behavior other than statements about themselves.

In examining the data of Table 13.4, we find no significant sex differences in the environment categories in which children appear. However, there are significant sex differences for *every* environment category for adults. Adult males were found significantly more frequently outdoors or in business. Women were portrayed significantly more frequently in the home and in the school.

Table 13.5 presents the consequences experienced by each person-type. Young females were significantly more often shown as the recipients of positive consequences coming from a situation, and young males were significantly more often the recipients of positive consequences from their own action. Adult males were more frequently shown as the recipients of positive consequences coming from others and were shown as experiencing significantly more self-delivered negative consequences. In contrast, women more frequently experienced neutral consequences of acts.

In examining differences across grades, the total number of female characters declined sharply from the primers through the third grade readers. An analysis of

Table 13.3 Types of Behaviors Performed by Children (C) and Adults (A) of each Sex (M/F) Given in Frequencies and in Percentages of Total Behaviors by each Age and Sex

	Frequencies and Percentages			
Behaviors	CF $n = 241$	CM $n = 324$	AF $n = 124$	AM $n = 256$
Nurturant	101	169	109	156
	6.3%	6.1%	14.3%	11.3%
Aggressive	19	90	14	26
	1.2%***	3.3%	1.8%	1.9%
Routine-Repetitive	131	261	94	153
	8.2%	9.5%	12.3%	11.1%
Constructive-Productive	21	56	2	60
	1.3%	2.0%	0.3%***	4.4%
Physically Exertive	60	195	5	68
	3.7%***	7.1%	0.7%***	4.9%
Fantasy	39	30	5	14
	2.4%***	1.1%	0.7%	1.0%
Directive	221	282	156	212
	13.8%	10.2%	20.5%	15.4%
Statements about self – positive	53***	46	11	12
	3.3%	1.7%	1.4%	0.9%
Statements about self – negative	8	2	2	5
	0.5%*	0.1%	0.3%	0.4%
Statements about self – neutral	50	64	15	23
	3.1%	2.3%	2.0%	1.7%
Problem solving	39	118	12	65
	2.4%***	4.3%	1.6%***	4.7%
Statements of information	203	372	99	73
	12.7%	13.5%	13.0%	12.5%
Expression of Emotion	94	15.3	36	85
	5.9%	5.6%	4.7%	6.2%
Conformity	121	170	21	17
	7.5%	6.2%	2.8%*	1.2%
Watching	61	111	15	37
	3.8%	4.0%	2.0%	2.7%
Other Verbal	224	389	131	186
	14.0%	14.1%	17.2%*	13.5%
Totals: Frequency	1,604	2,763	763	1,830
Percentage	90.1%	91.1%	95.6%	93.8%

*   = p < .05
**   = p < .01
*** = p < .001

NOTE: The percentages do not add to 100% because of the three omitted behaviors. Self-care, avoidance, social-recreational activities, expression of emotion, and the miscellaneous categories mentioned in the taxonomy were omitted due to their infrequent occurrence.

Table 13.4 Types of Environments in Which Children (C) and Adults (A) of Each Sex (M/F), are Shown Given in Frequencies and in Percentages of Total Environments Shown by Each Age and Sex

	Frequencies and Percentages			
Environment	CF *n* = 241	CM *n* = 324	AF *n* = 124	AM *n* = 256
Home	97 34.2%	111 29.0%	83*** 54.6%	59 23.6%
Outdoors	157 55.2%	234 61.1%	47*** 30.9%	144 57.6%
Business	15 5.3%	16 4.2%	8*** 5.3%	40 16.0%
School	15 5.3%	22 5.7%	14*** 9.2%	7 2.8%
Totals: Frequency	284	383	152	250
Percentage	100%	100%	100%	100%

*   = p < .05
** = p < .01
*** = p < .001

the stories revealed two factors which contributed to this decline: a decrease of child females and an increase of adult males. One also finds an increase (with each grade level) in the number of significant sex differences between males and females for both child and adult behaviors, consequences, and environments. The stereotypic portrayal of male and female roles (both child and adult) increased with grade level.

There were also significant differences in the way the sexes were portrayed in each publisher's series. Not one of the series was egalitarian in its presentation of the sexes, that is, not one presented either adult males or females or male and female children as more *alike* than different in behavior characteristics, personality traits, and expected behaviors. Harper and Row, among the texts examined, presented the fewest number of total sex differences among children and adults. Scott, Foresman and Bank Street had the greatest differentiation in the presentation of adult characters. Conversely, Ginn portrayed children more stereotypically in their series. The pattern of each publisher is similar to the general pattern across grades. In each case, incidence of child females in the stories declines from grades K through three and incidence of adult males in the stories increases from grades K through three. Also, number of adult females stays uniformly low, and number of child males stays uniformly high.

It may be argued that the authors and publishers of these books are simply mirroring the real world and that they should not be expected to provide a false picture of equality. But reality belies such an assertion. Children encounter women far more frequently than the average reading textbook would suggest. Even more to the point, children encounter women in many occupational roles and activities. As the 1973 *Economic Report of the President* noted, "One of the most important changes in the American economy in this century has been the increase in the proportion of women who work outside the home" (p. 89).

Table 13.5 Types of Consequences for Children (C) and Adults (A) of Each Sex (M/F) Given in Frequencies and in Percentages of Total Consequences for Each Age and Sex

	Frequency and Percentages			
Consequences	*CF* *n* = 241	*CM* *n* = 324	*AF* *n* = 124	*AM* *n* = 256
Positive-other	115 16%	230 17.1%	27 8.3%*	94 14.1%
Positive-self	17 2.4%*	57 4.2%	6 1.8%	14 2.1%
Positive-situation	336 46.6%***	488 36.3%	173 53.1%	328 49.3%
Positive-author	4 0.6%	14 1.0%	1 0.3%	7 1.1%
Neutral	87 12%	197 14.6%	57 12.5%	70 10.5%
Negative-other	73 10.1%	153 11.4%	30 9.2%	39 5.9%
Negative-self	4 0.6%	16 1.2%	0 0.0%*	12 1.8%
Negative-situation	84 11.7%	180 13.4%	32 9.8%	95 14.3%
Totals: Frequency Percentage	721 98.7%	1,346 98.3%	326 98.5%	666 99.1%

*   = p < .05
**   = p < .01
*** = p < .001

Women constitute approximately thirty-eight per cent of the labor force and are distributed across a wide variety of occupational statuses. What is presented in the texts reviewed is an *idealized* view of society with the breadth and diversity of human endeavors eliminated.

Thus, it appears that these texts do not mirror the reality experienced by large groups of children: urban children, ghetto children, children with working mothers, children of divorced parents. Since we cannot depict for children what their lives will be, especially as we witness the rapid changes our society and culture are undergoing, the critical question becomes: What are we doing to children's aspirations when a sterile and unrealistic world is portrayed in the books that they read?

Although it is true that women today have fewer roles and opportunities than men and engage in more limited behaviors in more restricted settings, what are the consequences of portraying this state of affairs in elementary texts? Since textbooks reach a child at an early and impressionable age, children may attempt to perpetuate the stereotypes which the textbooks portray. The pervasiveness of sex role stereotyping in basal readers has been documented in this article. Future research efforts should explore in greater depth the relationship between such literary stereotypes and the development of sex roles.

In passing, it should be noted that many other stereotypes exist in these texts. The real world is more varied than the one depicted in elementary readers. Boys and girls, and men and women, are fat and skinny, short and tall. Boys and men are sometimes gentle, sometimes dreamers. Artists, doctors, lawyers, and college professors are sometimes mothers as well. Rather than limiting possibilities, elementary texts should seek to maximize individual development and self-esteem by displaying a wide range of models and activities. If the average is the only model presented to a child and therefore assumed to be the child's goal, most children—and most adults—would probably be unable to match the model.

Sex bias in educational testing

Soon after children enter school they encounter a barrage of testing which is likely to continue throughout their school careers. Educators use tests for diagnosis and prescription in classrooms and for assessment and normative placement purposes as they sort, select, and classify students. Test data and comparative performance information are recorded on permanent cards which are transferred to each school a child attends. The child's placement on a variety of instruments is then noted by counselors as they advise the child about her or his future potential. Teachers also view the scores and often sort students into learning groups accordingly.

The wide usage of test data has been documented by a number of sources (Holmen & Docter, 1972; College Entrance Examination Board, 1970; Educational Testing Service, 1968). Holmen and Docter noted, for example, that approximately two hundred million achievement test forms and answer sheets are used annually in the United States alone. Moreover, there is evidence that students, teachers, and parents believe in the accuracy of intelligence test results (Brim *et al.*, 1969; Kirkland, 1971) and in the results of standardized achievement tests, and act upon them (Goslin, 1967). Tests are most widely used to assess educational achievement in the schools; Holmen and Docter point out that sixty-five per cent of all educational tests are achievement tests, while five per cent are used for counseling and guidance, and thirty per cent are used for selection and placement purposes. No one until now has systematically reviewed educational achievement tests to determine whether these tests contribute to the stereotyping of male and female roles. Are tests structured so as to reinforce existing stereotypic notions of male and female academic performance? Are the items selected to favor individuals who have encountered specific academic subjects (i.e., mathematics, science, home economics)? And do the items connote preference for males or females in their content or in the pronouns which dominate the content?

Carol Tittle and her associates (1973) noted this absence in the field and undertook a study[3] to examine two aspects of potential sex discrimination in achievement tests: sex bias in language usage (see Gunderson, 1972) and sex role stereotyping in item content. The goal of their study was to examine aspects of test content for potential sex bias; their study did not deal with bias in the uses of test results.

Several writers have recently noted the general male orientation of the English language, and what appears to be sex-typed usage of language. Strainchamps (1971) and Key (1971) have discussed the stereotyped characterization of English as masculine. Key outlined some of the preliminary work in language research which reported differing male and female usage of language, and several studies have examined classroom transcripts of four female and four male social studies teachers (Barron, 1971; Barron & Marlin, 1972; and Barron, Loflin, & Biddle, 1972). These latter studies begin to suggest the type of linguistic analysis which may be required to understand more fully the relationship between attributes of language, language usage, and the continuation of prejudice against women. Thus, bias in testing could arise in selecting item content (i.e., items drawn from chemistry or home economics), bias could be mainly a function of language use (i.e., word choice such as generic pronouns) and not subject to change by the test publisher, or bias could result from a combination of selection and usage. A large ratio of male to female references, for example, could result primarily from the use of generic nouns and pronouns, and would be less susceptible to change than if bias had resulted from content selection.

While a series of studies which have examined stereotyping in children's books and textbooks are available (Key, 1971; Frasher & Walker, 1972; and Grambs, 1972; as well as Jacklin's study described in the previous section), not one study has systematically reviewed the educational measurement literature and analyzed educational and occupational achievement tests for sex role stereotyping. Tittle's study included an exploratory survey of several aspects of educational testing, with a view toward identifying stereotypic presentations of women. It provides an important sequel to Jacklin's work.

The data examined in this study consist of test batteries from each of the major test publishing companies.[4] The procedures and recording forms for data collection were developed and pretested by two graduate students specializing in educational measurement.[5] The recorders first tabulated language usage defined as the ratio of male nouns and pronouns to female nouns and pronouns. A ratio close to 1.00 would indicate an equal use of male and female nouns and pronouns. A ratio above 1.00 would indicate that males were referred to more frequently than females, and in this sense would be indicative of biased content.

Two sets of analyses were performed to determine whether bias resulted from content selection or from the nature of the English language. The first analysis was designed to examine each subtest in each test battery. Generic nouns and pronouns were tallied. Ratios of male to female nouns and pronouns were then compared to determine whether language usage or content was sexually biased. One set which is based on all nouns and pronouns, including generic ones, is labeled *All*. A second set, labeled *Regular*, excludes the generic nouns and pronouns and counts only those nouns and pronouns which refer specifically to males and females. If the ratio of males to females is greater than 1.00 for the *Regular* ratios as well as for the *All* ratios, then it can be concluded that the bias is largely a function of content selection and is therefore readily subject to change. Additionally, there are nouns which are not sex-designated in and of themselves, but are designated by a pronoun following them. Here, the test publisher can provide a balance in designating the sex as female in such contexts as "the doctor" or "the lawyer."

In the second analysis, recorders were asked to identify stereotypic content and list such instances on the same form used to record nouns and pronouns. General guidelines were given the recorders to suggest types of sex role stereotypes which might occur in test content. Do females appear in other than traditional jobs such as teachers and nurses? Are girls shown as active and independent? The question was whether educational achievement tests contain the same sex role stereotyping of women that is present in other educational materials. Stereotyped activities for women were identified: Mary helped her mother set the table. Women mentioned in a stereotyped profession were also listed: the teacher ... Mrs. Jones; the secretary . . . Miss Ward. Items or descriptions which assign women to a secondary or helpless status were included as stereotypic: Bob was elected class president and Susan was elected secretary.

Two other categories listed as identifying stereotypic content were those which limited female occupational pursuits and references to activities which were distinctly male or female. It should be noted that the purpose of this aspect of the study was to produce examples of sex stereotypes and was not considered a formal content analysis.

Results

Table 13.6 shows the ratio of male noun and pronoun referents to female noun and pronoun referents for the educational achievement test batteries analyzed. These total battery data were obtained by summing the male-female references for all the tests in the battery and computing the ratios for the total counts.

There are few differences between the conclusions which would be drawn by using the ratios based on *All* nouns and pronouns and those based only on *Regular* nouns and pronouns. As can be seen in the table, deleting the generic pronouns reduces only a few of the ratios. Thus, any bias which exists is primarily a function of the content of educational achievement tests rather than the nature of the language, and should be amenable to change by test developers and publishers.

Each test battery, with one exception, showed a higher frequency of male nouns and pronouns. In Table 13.6 the distribution of *All* noun and pronoun ratios indicates that in all but eight of the twenty-seven batteries analyzed, the ratios of male to female are greater than 2.00. In one case, the ratio is as high as 14.00. There is a tendency for the test batteries developed for the early grade levels, kindergarten through grade three or four, to have lower ratios than the test batteries for the higher grades. This is largely because the tests at the early grades have fewer extended reading passages. Another reason for the low ratio may be the home orientation of primary education. Examples and discussion may revolve more around the home and mother. These findings are analogous to those in the previously discussed Jacklin *et al.* report; the pattern of stereotypic portrayal of males and females heightens and intensifies as grade level is raised.

Our analysis of language usage suggests that educational achievement tests reflect the general bias in school instructional materials, referring much more frequently to males and their world, seldom balancing references and drawing on content equally for the two sexes. Nevertheless, since this bias results from the use of regular rather *than* generic nouns and pronouns, it is susceptible to change.

Sex role stereotypes evident in item content were also recorded for each test analyzed. Women were portrayed almost exclusively as homemakers or in the pursuit of hobbies (e.g., "Mrs. Jones, the President of the Garden Club . . .").[6] Young girls carry out "female chores" (e.g., Father helps Betty and Tom build a playhouse; when it's completed, "Betty sets out dishes on the table, while Tom carries in the chairs . . .").[7]

In numerous activity-centered items, boys were shown playing, climbing, camping, hiking, taking on roles of responsibility and leadership. Girls help with the cooking, buy ribbon and vegetables, and, when participating in any active pursuit, take the back seat to the stronger, more qualified boys (e.g., Buddy says to Clara, "Oh, I guess it's all right for us boys to help girls. I've done some good turns for girls myself, because I'm a Scout.")[8]

In addition, some items implied that the majority of professions are closed to

Table 13.6 Ratios of Male Noun and Pronoun (nM) Referents to Female Noun and Pronoun (nF) Referents—Educational Achievement Test Batteries

Test	Total No. of Test Items	Nouns and Pronouns			
	Items	All nM/nF = Ratio		Regular nM/nF = Ratio	
Test A					
Grade level 4–6	343	190/47	4.04	190/47	4.04
Grade level 6–9	337	84/46	1.83	84/46	1.83
Grade level 9–12	349	93/36	2.58	93/36	2.58
Test B					
Grade level 3–8	1,232	1221/368	3.31	1211/368	3.29
Test C					
Grade level 9–12	330	262/195	1.34	219/195	1.12
Test D					
Grade level 1.5–2.4	174	51/59	.86	48/54	.89
Grade level 2.5–3.4	257	137/86	1.59	137/86	1.59
Grade level 3.5–4.9	300	124/42	2.95	121/42	2.88
Grade level 5.0–6.9	534	181/44	4.11	178/44	4.05
Grade level 7.0–9.5	524	198/51	3.88	195/51	3.82
Test E					
Grade level 3–5	420	366/103	3.55	322/98	3.29
Grade level 6–9	420	443/150	2.95	408/149	2.74
Grade level 9–12	470	468/134	3.49	360/120	3.00
Grade level 13–14	320	448/32	14.00	390/32	12.19
Test F					
Grade level 1–2	320	179/88	2.03	179/88	2.03
Grade level 2–4	276	333/241	1.38	330/234	1.41
Grade level 4–9	1,070	1513/231	6.55	1462/229	6.38
Test G					
Grade level K – 1	126	217/93	2.33	217/93	2.33
Grade level 1	259	192/168	1.14	190/168	1.13
Grade level 1.5–2: Form 1	251	134/53	2.52	123/51	2.41
Grade level 1.5–2: Form 2	251	119/78	1.53	115/78	1.47
Grade level 2–3: Form 1	409	209/89	2.34	192/87	2.20
Grade level 2–3: Form 2	409	143/87	1.64	143/87	1.64
Grade level 4–5	540	221/83	2.66	198/71	2.78
Grade level 5–6	544	171/58	2.95	166/58	2.96
Grade level 7–9	532	181/46	3.93	157/46	3.41
Grade level 9–12	478	245/40	6.13	242/39	6.21

women. A reading comprehension passage about the characteristics and qualifications required for the Presidency began with the statement: "In the United States, voters do not directly choose the man they wish to be President." It repeatedly says "he must be," "he must have . . ."[9] Most short biographies were written about men. Practically all teachers were listed as female, while professors, doctors, and presidents of companies were listed as male. If a team was mentioned, it usually had all male members. Thus an examination of the content of these tests for sex role stereotypes suggests that achievement tests do not differ from other instructional materials in education: their content contains numerous sex role stereotypes.

Tittle's analysis of educational achievement tests demonstrates both substantial bias in the number of male and female noun and pronoun references, and frequent stereotypic portrayals in the content. These aspects of testing could easily be altered to present a more equitable and less prejudiced view of women, for example, by showing women in a variety of occupations and activities. Test publishers can easily address these criticisms by initiating a review procedure very early in the test development process. Specifications to item writers can encourage a less stereotypic presentation. Examples can be drawn from history, literature, science, and other areas where women have made contributions. Test editors can review the content before specific items are tried out. Review procedures to ensure balanced presentation of males and females can be instituted when a test is assembled.[10]

One last point should be stressed. Tests have been used extensively in school settings with little thought given to the socializing aspects of their content. The last decade has heightened awareness of potential cultural bias in the content of testing. Perhaps now is the time to stress that testing instruments not only *assess* but also convey and *teach* much about the latent aspects of our culture—our prejudices, our mores, and our way of life.

Curricular requirements

The small amount of evidence available on school curriculum suggests it too may promote sex role stereotyping and sex discrimination. Acceptable avenues for the expression of a variety of interests are prescribed differently for males and females. Girls are told at an early age that boys are mechanically and scientifically inclined while girls excel at reading and language. To some extent this is reinforced by a division of males and females into seventh grade shop and home economics. Later vocational education tracks usually vary by sex; boys acquire a series of shop and mechanical skills while girls prepare for a life as a wife and mother, sometimes with secretarial skills on the side in case there is need to supplement a husband's income. Physical education classes for the most part are segregated by sex and as such often establish different physical expectations for individual performance by sex. All males are expected to be athletic superstars, while girls are not expected to aspire to anything beyond a good intramural fray. These expectations are often vigorously reinforced with substantially different financial allocations to boys' and girls' physical education programs.

Sex bias in vocational and physical education curricula is relatively easy to document and shall be the focus of this discussion. The deliberate segregation of the sexes according to preconceived notions of appropriate curricular activities is open to question in terms of the limitations it imposes on both sexes. Whose decision has led to sex-segregated classes? How pervasive is such segregation? Are such decisions made by students and their families or tacitly made *a priori*?

Education is not specifically mentioned in the United States Constitution, and hence its control constitutionally becomes the prerogative of each state. All fifty states have explicit constitutional provisions and numerous statutes and regulations which establish specific state responsibilities for the education of their citizenry. The National Education Association is one of the few existing sources of information about states' curricular and graduation requirements (Thompson, 1972). Most state requirements address only a limited number of academic subjects and a few non-academic ones like physical education, health, and practical arts. According to the NEA Educational Research Service (1972), no states patently discriminate by sex in the specification of their curricular requirements although variations by state do occur in those curricular items specified as mandatory and those considered to be the option of local school boards and administrators. Decisions about curricula and sexual composition of classes largely become the prerogative of local authorities.

Perhaps the most extreme form of discrimination in the exercise of local options occurs in metropolitan areas where a high concentration of students allows specialized high schools to appear. By design or default they usually become unisexual institutions and often male institutions. Given that public funds support these public schools, simple equity would require that male and female students have equal access to the programs offered. Females frequently are not admitted, and, when they are, often face more stringent entrance requirements, i.e., higher academic performance is demanded (Bryan, 1972; New York N.O.W., 1972). For example, of those courses listed in *Public High Schools, New York City* (New York City Board of Education, 1970), seventy-seven are designated as technical courses restricted to males and thirty-six are designated for females. Discrimination does not stop at the door to the classroom; as the New York City Board of Education (1972) notes, the system of vocational education in New York City discriminates against girls in three significant ways. First, more class slots are open to boys than to girls. Second, a "greater variety of more useful courses" are offered to boys than to girls, and, finally, even within a vocational program, such as fashion or dentistry, courses are labeled as being appropriate for one sex or the other. Such sex distinctions in vocational courses limit potential occupational roles for both males and females.

In the case of the vast majority of secondary schools in the United States local educational options are translated into some variation on the comprehensive high school theme James Conant advocated (1959). These options often result in a curriculum which is discriminatory in terms of specified vocational tracks and physical education courses. Frequently such discrimination occurs with the implicit consent of school boards. Data available from the USOE's Bureau of Adult, Vocational and Technical Education (1972) substantially reflect this skewed sorting of students into "sex-appropriate" vocational tracks. Ninety-five per cent of all students registered in vocational agriculture courses are male. These figures represent the beginning of a new trend, for in 1970 no females were enrolled in agriculture. The field of health has also recently experienced a shift of minimal magnitude. In 1965, males constituted 4.9 per cent of those registered in health courses, as compared to 12.3 per cent of the health student population in 1971. Male and female distributions in other categories for which the Bureau aggregates data conform to the same stereotypic pattern: ninety-three per cent of all students registered in consumer and homemaking courses are female;

eighty-five per cent of those enrolled in home economics courses which lead to gainful employment are female; ninety-two per cent of those registered in technical courses—metallurgy, engineering, oceanography, police science—are male; seventy-five per cent in office occupations are female; and eighty-nine per cent of all registered in trade and industrial courses are male.

These issues take on particular urgency when it is realized that recently there has been renewed interest in questions of career education and choice. The year 1971 saw the largest investment ever in vocational education by federal, state, and local governments, a combined increase of twenty-two per cent over 1970 ($1,952,000,000 by state and local governments and $396,000,000 by the federal government). In addition, career education has become a banner program of the current Secretary of Health, Education, and Welfare. Renewed interest in vocational and career education is thus reflected in financial and political support, and yet the distribution of the sexes into fields over the last decade has continued to follow traditional sex role patterns.

Perhaps such simple injustices could be accepted if labor market statistics revealed a different reality. In 1971, however, according to the Women's Bureau of the United States Department of Labor (1972), one-third of the thirty-two million women who were in the labor force were clerical workers. These figures included 3.6 million stenographers, typists, and secretaries. Seventeen per cent of the thirty-two million were service workers, fifteen per cent were professional or technical workers, of whom 1.9 million were teachers, and thirteen per cent were operatives, chiefly in factories. Women who were employed full-time in 1970 earned as a median income $5,323, or 59.4 per cent of the $8,966 median income earned by fully employed men. Surely no one would argue that women deliberately prefer such narrow, low paying, and low status sectors of the labor market. In fact, once given the opportunity, a noticeable insurgence of women is found in those fields which traditionally had been masculine domains. Soon these fields aggressively recruit female participation (Hedges, 1970; Zellner, 1972; Levitin, Quinn, and Staines, 1973).

As Crowley, Levitin, and Quinn (1973) point out:

> The 'average woman' is a statistical creation, a fiction. She has been used to defend the status quo of the labor market, on the assumption that knowing the sex of an employee reliably predicts his or her job attitudes. This assumption is false. Knowing that a worker is female allows us to predict that she will hold a job in a 'woman's field,' and that she will be substantially underpaid for a person of her qualifications. But knowing that a worker is female does not help us much to predict what she wants from her job. (p. 96)

While half of all women employed in 1969 were concentrated in 21 of the 250 distinct occupations listed by the Census Bureau (Hedges, 1970), an increasing proportion of these women assumed responsibility for some portion of their own or their household's income during their lifetime (Levitin, Quinn, and Staines, 1973). Thus to argue that women prefer low incomes and less secure positions in the labor market is fallacious. Unfortunately, the onus of such occupational distributions must lie at the feet of industries seeking unskilled cheap labor, and on the shoulders of schools which counsel and prepare women for limited future occupational roles.

Allocation of money to support sports and physical education programs represents another very clear instance in which resources are allocated differentially on the basis of sex. The tendency to support a major sports program for boys but not for girls starts early, often at the initiative of the local community. While there have been a few recent outstanding exceptions, communities typically organize Little League baseball and football teams, leaving young girls to their dolls. Eight-year-old girls quickly learn that only males "are proficient enough to form leagues, play regulation length games with paid umpires, uniforms, full schedules, and championship playoffs" (Dunning, 1972, pp. 28–29). Such activities are usually neither sponsored nor organized by the elementary school, but do set the precedent for sex-segregated physical education after the fourth or fifth grade. Little rationale other than tradition exists for such segregation when students are being taught the same sport and are of approximately the same height, strength, weight, and skill level. Of course, young males are encouraged by their family, the media, and their peers to spend many hours a week on athletic activities outside of school, and by the time they are ten or eleven their athletic skills have been finely honed.

Real discrimination in the allocation of time, financial resources, and physical facilities is most evident in junior and senior high school. The largest swimming pool, the best playing fields, the finest tennis courts are usually reserved for male sporting events. Most schools offer male students a sports program composed of varsity competition in football, basketball, baseball, track, swimming, and other sports. These activities are considered to be an essential element in the comprehensive educational package offered by the school. Coaches are hired, uniforms purchased, and facilities built. Such expenditures are considered to be legitimate line-items in a school's budget. Seldom does a school's budget reflect comparable line-item expenditures for a girls' athletic program. Girls Athletic Associations (GAA) are usually voluntary, "out-of-school" programs. At a high school in California, for example, "the GAA must sell hot dogs at football games, bake cupcakes and other such things to support their limited program which . . . includes field hockey, basketball, volleyball, tennis and softball. In other words, there is no pre-existing program at the high school for female athletes or those girls who wish to become athletes. If the GAA cannot sell enough hot dogs and popcorn, there will be no field hockey team. If enough cupcakes aren't sold or bottles collected, basketball may have to go. The boys' programs do not face similar problems" (Dunning, p. 26).

Even the salary supplements that coaches receive highlight the school's discrimination in physical education. According to the N.E.A. (1972), in 1971–72 the extra-curricular salary supplements for head coaches ranged from a low of $1,226 to a high of $5,500. Intramural sports coaches received supplements which ranged from $554 to $1,920 and the cheerleader advisor received from a low of $347 to a high of $2,240. These salary supplements were not reported by sex but it is highly likely that the head coach is a male and the cheerleader advisor and possibly some of the intramural coaches are females. Schools do communicate in many ways that boys' athletic programs are of greater significance to the school's educational programs than are those for girls; the best physical facilities are reserved for male use, financial support of girls' programs is minimal, and an elaborate system of athletic options for girls and boys of varying abilities is nonexistent.

It is not our intent in this article to substitute one curricular prescription for another, nor do we suggest that any arbitrary concept of equal curricular opportunity is either desirable or feasible. We do assert that girls and boys should be treated by the school as individuals each with her or his own individual curricular interests and needs. Schools should make available to girls as well as boys a full range of options in physical education and interscholastic athletics. Shorthand and typing skills are at least as useful to boys as woodworking. The school curriculum has clearly functioned to reinforce rigid, educationally discriminatory, and sexually stereotypic attitudes in both students and school staff. Schools seeking to free the next generation of youth from the dysfunctional constraints of the past will have to change curricular requirements and redress inequities in the options open to boys and girls. But in order to accomplish these structural reforms schools must face the serious problem of changing the attitudes of administrators, counselors, and teachers.

Conclusions

Until quite recently, no one had challenged the long-standing tendency of school boards, state boards of education, and other authoritative educational bodies to mandate curricular requirements and other educational practices which differ by sex. Now a substantial number of local groups have begun to do just that. Organizations have begun to analyze the textbooks being used in districts around the country, to challenge physical educational policies, to press for class action suits on vocational educational issues, and to review employment advancement practices.[11]

Many of these activities have been spurred by recent federal legislation, specifically, Title IX of the Education Amendments Act of 1972, Executive Order #11246, Title VII of the Civil Rights Act of 1964, and the Equal Pay Act, all of which prohibit discrimination on the basis of sex in federally assisted programs. Unfortunately, to date no substantial federal effort has been launched to notify states and local school systems of the content of this legislation. Guidelines for enforcement of Title IX are in the process of being designed by H.E.W.'s Office of Civil Rights. Once these guidelines are adopted, legal action against school districts in violation of the intent of the legislation becomes an imminent possibility. Until such guidelines are issued, complaints are processed under the aegis of Executive Order #11246 and Title VII of the Civil Rights Act of 1964, both of which prohibit discrimination in employment on the basis of sex, and the Equal Pay Act, which prohibits discrimination in salaries on the basis of sex. Once issued, the guidelines will indicate the extent to which federal leverage will be applied to reduce sex discrimination in public educational agencies. Evidence regarding H.E.W.'s record to date, however, does not support an optimistic outlook (Knox & Kelly, 1972).

There are, of course, many actions which local school districts, school boards, state educational agencies, and textbook and test publishers can take which need not wait for the prod of federal legislation (see Lyon & Saario, 1973). Much of the structure and content of the American school system has evolved rather haphazardly over time and without grand design; there is very little that ought to be sacrosanct about the system. Local administrators and educational policy makers need to identify and eradicate all those elements of sex discrimination in their schools which prohibit and constrain the options of every adult and student in the system. Textbook and test publishers need to marshall their products in the same way. The issue ultimately becomes a matter of conscience and simple justice.

This article has presented a few examples of the way in which existing elements of the school contribute to sex role stereotyping and discriminate against both male and female students. Textbooks and other curricular materials, testing and counseling procedures, and mandated curriculum and sports requirements sort and classify students in alignment with society's reified notions regarding appropriate sex role behaviors.

We have not addressed a series of far knottier questions. To what extent are children already socialized by the time that they reach the school so that changing school policy will make little or no difference in shaping attitudes? Even if it is assumed that schools have an impact on children's attitudes, how can aspects of the schooling process which contribute most strongly to sex role stereotyping be isolated? And once relevant schooling factors have been identified, what is the best way to study their impact upon children? Questions about the ways in which teachers react to, reward, and reinforce the behaviors of male and female students have not been addressed in this article. Some researchers argue that girls more than boys tend to imitate and respond positively to teacher reinforcements (see Smith, 1972, for a review). If that is the case, then girls are responding to strong pressures to be compliant, passive, tractable, and dependent. The same researchers suggest that an opposite trend may be operating for boys. Getting less approval from teachers and needing less from their peers, boys may become more self-motivated and more confident. There is a school of thought which argues the converse, i.e., that schools reinforce femininity in boys (Sexton, 1969). Obviously, more empirical research on the impact of teachers' behaviors upon sex role development is needed.

Little longitudinal research has been conducted in the field of sex role development, and its absence has contributed to confusion regarding the relative impact of hormones and socialization upon the development of sex role differences. At Standford University, Maccoby and Jacklin recently initiated an eight-year study of two cohorts of children from birth to the age of first school attendance to examine the interaction of hormones and parental socialization practices. This study and similar or related research, such as John Money's at Johns Hopkins, should illuminate to some extent the "nature-nurture" argument as it is related to the development of sex differences. Parallel and longitudinal studies which simultaneously test the multiplicity of theories in the field of sex role development could clarify the significance of some of these models and could move the field toward greater theoretical sophistication (see Emmerich, 1972).

A new concept has been introduced into the common parlance of the field of sex role development by Sandra Bem (1972). Many individuals, according to Bem, do not fall at the extremes in the distribution of such sex-related characteristics as aggression, dependence, and sociability. Rather, most people evidence behaviors which are truly androgynous, i.e., neither representative of maleness nor femaleness. Bem is now attempting to develop instruments which could establish the degree to which such traits are present in an individual's behavior. Studies like Bem's have begun to question the stereotypic perception of male and female behavior which is implicit in many research designs. Too frequently variations between the sexes have been reported and magnified while the variation which exists within each sex category has been overlooked or masked.

Once research has documented the impact of all school factors upon sex role development (i.e., guidance counselors, peer group influences, the media used in school settings, the intervention of the home, in addition to those variables already discussed), then the task becomes one of developing and testing new behavioral models for school settings. As yet, little is known about how effective androgynous materials and behaviors will be upon future generations of students. Most studies simply scratch the surface. Present understanding of the socialization and maturation processes which lead toward mature sex role identities is rather limited.

The examples of sex discrimination addressed in this article are merely symptomatic of a far greater and more pervasive phenomenon in our society. All social institutions promote stereotypic conceptions of male and female roles; all societies contain their own peculiar sex role mythologies. Some permit far greater latitude in the definition of boundaries between male and female roles than others. The definition of these boundaries, as Ruth Benedict (1961) so eloquently argued, is nothing more than a cultural artifact. Some societies rigidly adhere to a bimodel distribution of behavioral traits, aptitudes, and emotional expression; others acknowledge the necessity of having a community of adults whose characteristics overlap considerably on a number of dimensions.

We argue for such diversity, and for more flexible and more tolerant definitions of sex roles, because the livelihood and health of the American nation depends upon the talents of all its members, because the absence of restrictive stereotypes enhances the liberty and human potential of all persons, and because simple fairness and equity demand it.

Notes

1 The Jacklin research was sponsored by the Ford Foundation.
2 Individual stories were analyzed as titled and listed in the table of contents of each book. To limit the number of stories examined, every third story listed was analyzed. Poems were omitted, as were animal or fantasy stories without people. Stories with historical settings were included. In cases where a single plot was continuous throughout an entire book, the procedure of analyzing every third unit listed in the table of contents was maintained.
3 This research was sponsored by the Ford Foundation. In addition to discussing the research described here in more detail, Tittle *et al.* review literature on test bias and the use of vocational and occupational tests, and present an extensive annotated bibliography on women and testing.
4 The tests analyzed include the California Achievement Tests, Iowa Test of Basic Skills, the Iowa Test of Educational Development, Metropolitan Achievement Tests, Sequential Tests of Educational Progress, SRA Achievement Series, Stanford Early School Achievement Test, and the Stanford Achievement Test.
5 The graduate students were Karen McCarthy and Jane Stekler of the City University of New York.
6 *California Achievement Tests*—Language Usage, Level 5, Form A, 1970, item no. 43, p. 43.
7 SRA Achievement Series—Reading 1–2, Form D, 1963, p. 17.
8 SRA Achievement Series—Grammatical Usage, Multilevel Edition, Form D, 1963, p. 45.
9 *SRA Achievement Series*—Reading, Multilevel Edition, Form D, 1963, p. 76. See also *Sequential Tests of Educational Progress*, Series II Reading Form 1A, 1969, p. 18.
10 Women on Words and Images (1972) describe a form for evaluating sexism in readers. A similar form could be developed for test content, considering the illustrations, main characters and characteristics of children and adults. The categories developed by Jacklin *et al.* could also be valuable in a review procedure.
11 Best known among these groups are Women on Words and Images in New Jersey; the Emma Willard Task Force in Minneapolis; Know, Inc, in Pennsylvania; and numerous local chapters of the National Organization for Women. An excellent source for information regarding these groups and the grounds upon which they intend to test these issues is the Resource Center on Sex Roles in Education which has been established under the auspices of the National Foundation for the Improvement of Education, in Washington, D.C. The Resource Center was established to offer technical assistance to state departments of education and local school districts as they begin to understand

and adjust to recent federal landmark legislation which bears on the issue of sex discrimination in public education.

References

Barron, N. M. Sex-typed language: The production of grammatical cases. *Acta Sociologica*, 14, No. 1 & 2 (1971), 24–42.

Barron, N. M., Lofflin, M. D., & Biddle, B. J. *Sex role and the production of case frames.* Columbia, Mo.: University of Missouri, 1972.

Barron, N. M., & Marlin, M. J. Sex of the speaker and the grammatical case and gender of referenced persons. Technical Report C153. Columbia, Mo.: Center for Research in Social Behavior, University of Missouri, 1972.

Bem, S. L. The measurement of psychological androgny. Unpublished paper, Stanford University, 1972.

Benedict, R. *Patterns of culture.* New York: Houghton-Mifflin, 1961.

Blom, G. E., Waite, R. R., Zimet, S. G., & Edge, S. What the story world is like. In Zimet (Ed.), *What children read in school.* New York: Grune & Stratton, 1972, 1–18.

Boserup, E. *Women's role in economic development.* New York: St. Martin's Press, 1970.

Brim, O. G., Jr., Glass, D. C., Neulinger, J., & Firestone, I. J. *American beliefs and attitudes about intelligence.* New York: Russell Sage Foundation, 1969.

Bronfenbrenner, U. *Two worlds of childhood.* New York: Russell Sage Foundation, 1970.

Bryan, G. Discrimination on the basis of sex in occupational education in the Boston public schools. Paper prepared for the Boston Commission to Improve the Status of Women, Eastern Massachusetts Chapter of N.O.W., 1972.

California Advisory Commission on the Status of Women. *California women.* Sacramento, Calif.: Author, 1971.

Child, I. L., Potter, E. H., & Levine, E. L. Children's textbooks and personality development: An explanation in the social psychology of education. *Psychological Monographs*, 60, No. 3 (1946), 1–54.

Civil Liberties in New York, Vol. XX, No. 8, May 1973.

College Entrance Examination Board. *Report of the commission on tests: I. Righting the balance.* New York: 1970.

Collins, R. A conflict theory of sexual stratification. In H. P. Dreitzel (Ed.), *Family, marriage and the struggle of the sexes: Recent sociology.* No. 4. New York: Macmillan, 1972.

Conant, J. B. *The American high school today.* New York: Macmillan, 1959.

Crowley, J. E., Levitin, T. E., & Quinn, R. P. Seven deadly half-truths about women. *Psychology Today*, 6 (March 1973), 94–96.

De Crow, K. Look, Jane, look! See Dick run and jump! Admire him! In S. Anderson (Ed.), *Sex differences and discrimination in education.* Worthington, Ohio: Charles A. Jones, 1972.

Dunning, R. Discrimination: Women in sports. Unpublished manuscript, F35 No. Campus Way, Davis, California, 1972.

Economic report of the President. Washington, D.C.: U. S. Government Printing Office, 1973.

Educational Testing Service, Evaluation and Advisory Service. *State testing programs: A survey of functions, tests, materials and services.* Princeton, N. J.: Author, 1968.

Emmerich, W. Continuity and change in sex role development. Paper presented at a Symposium in Sex Role Learning in Childhood and Adolescence, American Association for the Advancement of Science, Washington, D.C., December, 1972.

Emmerich, W. Socialization and sex-role development. In P. B. Baltes & K. W. Schaie (Ed.), *Life-span developmental psychology: Personality and socialization.* New York: Academic Press, in press.

Frasher, R., & Walker, A. Sex roles in early reading textbooks. *The Reading Teacher*, 25 (May 1972), 741–9.

Goslin, D. A. *Teachers and testing.* New York: Russell Sage Foundation, 1967.

Graebner, D. B. A decade of sexism in readers. *The Reading Teacher*, 26 (October 1972).

Grambs, J. D. Sex-stereotypes in instructional materials, literature, and language: A survey of research. *Women Studies Abstracts*, 1 (Fall 1972), 1–4, 91–94.

Gunderson, D. V. Sex roles in reading and literature. Paper presented at the meeting of the American Educational Research Association, Chicago, April, 1972.

Hedges, J. N. Women at work: Women workers and manpower demands in the 1970's. *Monthly Labor Review*, 93 (June 1970), 19–29.

Holmen, M. G., & Docter, R. F. *Educational and psychological testing: A study of industry and its practices.* New York: Russell Sage Foundation, 1972.

Jacklin, C., Heuners, M., Mischell, H. N., & Jacobs, C. As the twig is bent: Sex role stereotyping in early readers. Unpublished manuscript, Department of Psychology, Stanford University, 1972.

Kagan, J. The three faces of continuity in human development. In D. A. Goslin (Ed.), *Handbook of socialization theory and research.* Chicago: Rand McNally, 1969.

Key, M. R. The role of male and female in children's books—dispelling all doubt. *Wilson Library Bulletin*, 46 (October 1971), 167–76.

Kirkland, M. C. The effects of tests on students and schools. *Review of Educational Research*, 41 (October 1971), 303–350.

Knox, H., & Kelly, F. A look at women in education: Issues and answers for HEW. Report of the Commissioner's Task Force on the Impact of Office of Education Programs on Women. Unpublished report, Washington, D.C., November, 1972.

Levitin, T. E., Quinn, R. P., & Staines, G. L. A women is fifty-eight per cent of a man. *Psychology Today*, 6 (March 1973), 89–91.

Levy, B. Sexism, sex role, and the school in the sex role stereotyping of girls: A feminist review of the literature. Unpublished manuscript, Columbia University, 1972.

Looft, W. R. Sex differences in the expression of vocational aspirations by elementary school children. *Developmental Psychology*, 5 (November 1971), 366.

Lyon, C., & Saario, T. Women in public education: Sexual discrimination in promotions. *Phi Delta Kappan*, 54 (October 1973), in press.

Maccoby, E. Differential socialization of boys and girls. Paper presented at the meeting of the American Psychological Association, Honolulu, September, 1972. In E. E. Maccoby and C. N. Jacklin, *Psychology of sex differences.* Palo Alto, Calif.: Standford University Press, in press.

Malcolm, A. H. Most common verb in schools, study finds, is . . . is. *New York Times*, September 4, 1971, p. 22.

Mead, M. Early childhood experience and later education in complex cultures. In M. L. Wax, S. Diamond, & F. O. Gearing (Ed.), *Anthropological perspectives on education.* New York: Basic Books, 1971.

Mischel, W. Sex-typing and socialization. In P. H. Mussen (Ed.), *Carmichael's manual of child psychology.* Vol. 2. New York: John Wiley & Sons, 1970.

Money, J., & Ehrhardt, A. A. *Man and women, boy and girl.* Baltimore: Johns Hopkins University Press, 1972.

National Education Association Educational Research Service. *State graduation requirements.* Washington, D.C.: Author, May, 1972.

National Education Association. *Salary schedule supplements for extra duties, 1971–72.* Research Memo, Washington, D.C.: April, 1972.

New York Chapter, N.O.W., Education Committee. *Report on sex bias in the public schools.* New York: Author, 1972.

New York City Board of Education. *Public high schools, New York City 1970–71.* New York: Bureau of Educational and Vocational Guidance, 1970.

New York State Commission on the Quality, Cost and Financing of Elementary and Secondary Education Report. Vol. 2. New York: Viking Press, 1972.

Potter, B. A. *The shaping of woman.* Unpublished manuscript, Stanford University, 1972.

Sexton, P. *The feminized male.* New York: Random House, 1969.

Smith, M. He only does it to annoy. . . . In S. Anderson (Ed.), *Sex differences and discrimination in education.* Worthington, Ohio: Charles A. Jones, 1972.

Strainchamps, E. Our sexist language. In V. Gornick & B. K. Moran (Ed.), *Women in sexist society: Studies in power and powerlessness.* New York: Basic Books, 1971.

Thompson, M. Sex discrimination in the schools. Unpublished manuscript, 3400 Dent Place, N.W., Washington, D.C., 1972.

Tittle, C. K., McCarthy, K., & Steckler, J. F. *Women and educational testing: A selective review of the research literature and testing practices.* Unpublished manuscript, Office of Teacher Education, City University of New York, 1973.

U. S. Department of HEW, Office of Education, Bureau of Adult, Vocational, and Technical Education. *Trends in vocational education.* Washington, D.C.: General Services Administration, 1972.

U'Ren, M. B. The image of woman in textbooks. In V. Gornick & B. K. Moran (Ed.), *Woman in sexist society: Studies in power and powerlessness.* New York: Basic Books, 1971.

Women on Words and Images. *Dick and Jane as victims: Sex stereotyping in children's readers.* Princeton, N.J.: Central New Jersey N.O.W., 1972.

Women's Bureau, Employment Standards Administration, United States Department of Labor. *Highlights of Women's Employment and Education.* Women's Bureau WB72–191, Washington, D.C.: U. S. Government Printing Office, March 1972.

Zellner, H. Discrimination against women, occupational segregation, and the relative wage. *American Economic Review,* 62 (May 1972), 157–160.

Zimet, S. G. Little boy lost. *Teachers College Record,* 72 (September 1970), 31–40.

CHAPTER 14

SEXISM IN TEACHER-EDUCATION TEXTS (1980)

Myra Pollack Sadker and David Miller Sadker

Awareness of sex bias in education is increasing, but the extent to which this awareness has influenced the curricula of teacher preparation programs is for the most part unknown. A 1974 survey of schools and departments of education revealed that most preservice teacher-education faculty are not adequately informed about sex-equity provisions, and few courses are offered in that area (McCune & Matthews, 1975). The implication of the survey is that as late as the mid-1970s sex equity remained a marginal issue in teacher-preparation programs. To provide an up-to-date analysis of the treatment of sex equity in these programs, a comprehensive study was conducted of teacher-education textbooks used in core courses. Supported by funding from the Women's Educational Equity Act, the contents of twenty-four of the most widely adopted teacher-education textbooks were analyzed to determine how issues of sex equity in education are now being treated.

Discussion of sex bias in education has existed since the late 1960s. This discussion led to the enactment of Title IX of the Higher Education Amendments of 1972 and it seemed reasonable to expect that the texts published between 1973 and 1978 would reflect that legislation by including information on sexism in education. Therefore, only texts published during that period were examined. Since the majority of today's educators are women, it would seem especially important that professional education texts would emphasize that issue.

The content of books is likely to affect the attitudes and perhaps even the behaviors of their readers. Although research on the influence of books on their readers is not entirely consistent, at least a few investigators have identified some significant influence among both adult and child readers (Zimet, 1976; Britton & Lumpkin, 1977). One assumption of this essay is that professional textbooks have an important role in most education courses, and that those most widely adopted are likely to reflect the nature and scope of teacher-education course content on a national scale. In fact, these books are often based on marketing research efforts that indicate what professors across the country are currently teaching and are thus deliberately formulated and designed to reflect existing course content. The topics found in these texts are also the topics most often discussed, analyzed, and emphasized in courses; topics omitted are unlikely to be noted in course syllabi or in class lectures and discussions. Textbooks, then, both reflect and influence the nature and scope of teacher-education courses.

It seems likely that if teacher-education texts included the material on sexism in schools and its possible impact on children, future teachers might be more likely to alleviate sex bias in the classroom. If their texts included information on legal remedies to problems of sexism in education, such as Title IX, as well as curricular and instructional remedies and resources, they would also be equipped to take concrete steps.

Research methodology

Two factors were given high priority in designing our research methodology. First, effort was made to identify the most influential textbooks currently in use rather than simply to investigate a few "typical" texts. The education editors of thirteen major publishing companies were asked to specify what they considered to be the most widely used texts on the market today. Their selections included texts used in the following areas: foundations or introduction to education; psychology of education; and teaching methods in the five content areas of reading, language arts, social studies, mathematics, and science. Based on the responses of these companies, the twenty-four texts listed in the Appendix were selected for analysis. Several of them were mentioned by all the editors and appear to dominate the market in their respective fields. In other fields, however, the market is shared by a number of texts.

A second methodological priority was a comprehensive content analysis. Although content-analysis procedures and instrumentation have been developed and used effectively with elementary and secondary school textbooks, few studies have used college level texts. Instrumentation specifically designed for teacher-education texts was developed and the completed instrument consisted of seventy-two items for analysis in four areas: content, research framework, language, and illustration. A detailed raters' manual was also developed. Twelve raters were trained to use the instrument and manual. Every page of text was analyzed by at least two raters working independently. Interrater reliability was set at 85 percent agreement; if this was not attained, a third rating was made.

The content section of the instrument provided for a line-by-line examination of the entire text as well as its index to determine space allocation in five categories: sexism: experiences and contributions of females; sex differences; total content concerning males; and total content concerning females. It is important to distinguish the category "total content concerning females" from the one entitled "experiences and contributions of females." To qualify for the latter category the topic had to contain information specifically pertinent to women. No such requirement applied to the category, "total content concerning females," which included the above category, plus references to any female name, even if the entry offered no information specifically related to females. For example, the sentence, "A test was being given in Ms. Washington's class," was counted only in the category "total content concerning females"; discussion of the contributions of, say, Emma Willard was tabulated in both categories.

The research-framework section of the instrument provided a tabulation of males and females cited in the index, footnotes, and bibliography. In the illustration section, the ratio of females to males was tabulated to assess sexual balance. Finally, the language section counted the number of times male pronouns and nouns such as "he," "mankind," "forefathers," or "policeman" were used generically.

The second part of the instrument used qualitative measures of material on sex equity. Judgments of the content were made according to the following criteria: accuracy, balance and comprehensiveness, nonstereotypic presentation, and integration of information throughout the entire text. Such qualitative assessments allowed the raters to go beyond the counting of pictures and pronouns to make interpretations of the textbook material. Raters were instructed to use direct quotations and cite text pagination to support and document all qualitative assessments.

The major finding of the research, however, was quantitative rather than qualitative: teacher-education texts were characterized by an overwhelming lack of information on sex equity in education. Of these twenty-four widely used texts, twenty-three allocated less than one percent of narrative space to the issue of sexism, and one third of the books failed to mention the topic. Most of the texts characterized by these omissions were in methods of teaching mathematics and science—the very areas in which girls are most likely to experience difficulties.

Foundations of education texts

Four foundation or introduction-to-education texts were analyzed. These texts typically attempt to orient prospective teachers to the profession, provide an overview of outstanding past and present contributors to the field and of contemporary issues, discuss innovations in education, and suggest directions for the future. Our study indicated that issues relating to sex equity in education appear to be omitted entirely or at best given minor and incomplete treatment. An average of five times more space is allocated to males than to females in their pages. The most space any text allocates to the topic of sexism is one-half of 1 percent.

Ryan and Cooper's *Those Who Can, Teach* (1975) is unusual in its focus on sexism in education. A two-page section entitled "Sexism and Sex-Role Stereotyping" discusses bias in books, counseling, and educational administration. There is no mention of Title IX, however, or of strategies that teachers can use to counteract sexism in schools. The section concludes as follows:

> The elimination of sexism and sex-role stereotyping in schools will be a complex procedure that will require the cooperation of teachers, administrators, school boards, counselors, educational publishers, and parents. Your role as a teacher will be especially important. As you interact with your pupils and as you select and use instructional materials, your sensitivity to this problem will help determine the attitudes of our future generations. Hopefully, educators will lead in efforts to evaluate school policies, curriculum and practices with regard to sex bias and will eliminate sexist discrimination (along with racial and ethnic discrimination) in our schools. Remember, if you're not a part of the solution, you're part of the problem. (p. 348)

This vague call to action includes no detailed explanation and leaves prospective teachers with no clear direction or strategy.

In a field that has always relied on the efforts of women, one would expect that the contributions of outstanding women would be represented. When Richey's text devotes a chapter to leaders in education, only white males are mentioned—from Socrates, Plato, and Aristotle, to James, Dewey, Piaget, and Bloom. Although lesser-known figures like Pestalozzi and Vergerius are included, women who have made outstanding contributions, for example, Emma Willard, Catherine Beecher, Elizabeth Peabody, Sylvia Ashton Warner, and Maria Montessori, are not mentioned. Not only are the contributions of individual females slighted, but the collective efforts of women are ignored as well. One gets little sense from any of these books that the majority of educators is female. A true history of education should note not only the contributions of women but also the discriminatory experiences they have suffered. These data indicate that future teachers are given an inaccurate and imbalanced introduction to the profession.

Educational psychology texts

In the three educational psychology texts analyzed, more attention is devoted to males than to females: the ratio of male to female names in the Gage and Berliner index is 18 to 1. In both this text and in Biehler, four times as many footnotes and bibliographic citations refer to works by males as by females. The implications of this ratio are difficult to interpret. The greater number of male authors cited may reflect an imbalance not so much in the choice of citation of the texts as in the field of educational psychology itself; however, a ratio of six to one overall reflects an imbalance in the information selected for inclusion and emphasis.

Gage and Berliner's *Educational Psychology* is the only book of all twenty-four analyzed that attributes more than 1 percent of its content space to women. Even this text, however, quotes guidelines for nonsexist language which it fails to implement in its own text.

All three educational psychology texts discuss sex differences. Gage and Berliner present the most comprehensive treatment, noting at the outset that the range of individual differences within each sex is in fact greater than the range of differences between them. Despite their introduction, some of their later conclusions are puzzling and their analysis counters Maccoby and Jacklin's exhaustive review of the literature in *The Psychology of Sex Differences* (1974).

A topic that receives particularly imbalanced treatment in educational psychology texts is achievement motivation. Typically, the texts offer extended discussion of studies conducted by male researchers with all-male subjects. Gage and Berliner discuss the role of mothers in developing achievement motivation in their sons but fail to mention the role mothers may play in developing achievement motivation in their daughters. The role of fathers in the process is omitted entirely.

Methods texts
Social studies

Both of the social studies texts analyzed display a sensitivity to, and moral support for, educational equity. But in practice both texts devote less than 1 percent of their content to the topics of sexism and the experiences and contributions of females, although a major purpose of social studies is to direct attention to contemporary social issues and problems. Elementary and secondary school social studies texts tell children about a nation created, maintained, and led by men. Both future and experienced teachers need resources if they are to provide students with a more accurate assessment of past and present. Many such supplementary resources are now available, but while these social-studies-methods books offer extensive and specific discussion on making bulletin boards, developing units, and using color in maps, far less attention is accorded the issue of sex equity.

Reading and language arts

No single text dominates the textbook market in reading and language arts. In the five reading texts analyzed, over twice as much attention is allocated to males as to females. The language arts texts, on the other hand, are relatively equitable in terms of overall attention to both sexes, authors cited in references, and figures in illustrations, although in all categories slightly more emphasis is accorded males than to females.

Several widely publicized content-analysis studies have demonstrated patterns of omission and stereotyping in basal readers and children's literature. In fact, this research has helped convince several major publishing companies to issue guidelines to ensure that children's reading material will treat both sexes more equitably and realistically in the future. Reading and language-arts-methods texts rarely mention these efforts, however. The resource lists, lessons, units, and instructional approaches that have been developed to counteract sexism in language and literature are not adequately covered.

Several of these methods texts discuss sex differences in reading achievement. Data from the National Assessment of Educational Progress indicate that male students are more likely to have difficulty in the area of reading, particularly in the elementary grades. Some of the reasons given for these differences are fascinating. Zintz (1975), for example, attributes the superior reading performance of girls to the following factors:

(1) greater ability to sit still and do "sitting still" activities and (2) greater facility with language. Add to this the bland pre-primer reading one can do with eighteen or twenty basic sight words and a woman teacher who may emphsize female values and the girls *do* have an advantage.

Durkin has suggested that if first grade teachers could liven up beginning reading with stories about jet planes, and how they work, or rockets and the boosters they need to get into space, boys would probably fare much better. (p. 214)

While it is important that these texts discuss problems boys may experience in reading, these discussions are characterized by stereotypic and patronizingly offensive portrayals of female students and teachers. Surely one must question the implication that dull reading materials and boring activities are more acceptable for female than for male students. Incidentally, research indicates that the reading performance of boys is not affected much by the gender of their teachers (Asher & Gottman, Note 1).

Six of the nine texts discuss sex differences in reading preferences. A clear division is made between what boys and girls like to read. Petty, Petty, and Becking note, for example, that "boys scoff at love and avoid books in which the principal character is feminine" (p. 376). Burns and Broman comment: "Boys prefer studies of science, invention, and vigorous action. . . . Girls will read a book considered to be of interest to boys, but the reverse is seldom true" (p. 216). The research cited to support these recommendations is dated, and the discussion is presented without regard for individual differences and in a manner that condones stereotypic reading interests. Such statements serve to perpetuate sex-role stereotyping rather than to eradicate it.

Mathematics and science

The three mathematics-methods texts and three science-methods texts analyzed reflect a severe imbalance in the treatement of males and females. Current research on the disparity in math achievement between males and females, math as a "male domain," and the development of innovative curricula to help reduce math anxiety and avoidance receive no mention. It is unlikely that such comments as those made by Rowe (1978, p. 69) that girls "know less, do less, explore less, and are prone to be more superstitious than boys" will give future teachers an adequate perspective on the nature of sex differences. Although the treatment of this issue in the Rowe text is both superficial and possibly even misleading, it must be noted that this text is the only one of the six that recognizes the existence of a problem.

The texts in science and math reflect the least sensitivity to issues of sex equity of all the areas studied. The greater number of male authors cited in footnotes and bibliographies may, in fact, indicate the lack of female access to and representation in these fields. But precisely in these areas where females are most likely to have achievement difficulties, there is an almost total absence of sex-equity discussion. In areas where males are more likely to have achievement difficulties, such as reading, sex differences in achievement and methods for addressing the problem are discussed.

Language and illustrations

Only four texts allocate more than one-half of 1 percent of their content to sexism, and even this miniscule figure may be inflated. We determined that it would be more useful to allow overlap in categories and a process of occasional double or triple counting than to assign the content arbitrarily to a single category. However, even with such occasional inflation, it is clear that sex bias in the textbooks of this study most often took the form of pervasive omission.

Bias in language usage was also found. Twenty texts used supposedly generic pronouns or nouns such as he, man, and mankind to refer to all people; few inserted disclaimers for this usage. Sociolinguistic theory suggests that language usage goes far beyond mere ease of reading to the way language shapes the direction and content of text narrative. The Houghton Mifflin guidelines, *Avoiding Stereotypes* (1975), quote the linguist Benjamin Whorf: "Language is more than a reflection of the structural arrangements in society; it is intimately linked to the creation and perception of reality itself. Eliminating biased terminology is one concrete way to change and to correct the way we view ourselves and others" (p. 5).

Pictorial representation was the one area studied that did not show any particular imbalance. The number of males in illustrations was equal to or only slightly greater than the number of females. Publishers attempt to follow the nonsexist guidelines they have issued when it comes to illustration and, therefore, may show more sensitivity to sex equity than their authors. It is also clearly easier for authors and publishers to include an equitable illustration program than it is to represent sex equity in content and language. Illustrations in most of the books analyzed took the form of photographs of actual school life in which both girls and boys are usually present in more or less equal numbers. When illustrations took the form of line drawings, they were far less equitable in their depiction of females and males.

Racial and ethnic bias

Although this study focused on sex equity in teacher-education texts, the raters also made a line-by-line analysis of attention to racial and ethnic minorities. The data revealed that slightly greater emphasis is given to racial and ethnic minorities than to women. But even those groups represented receive only a small proportion of the books' focus. In half the texts analyzed, the proportion of textbook content concerned with the issue of racial or ethnic discrimination was still less than 1 percent. When information on this topic is included, it is sometimes based on dated references, and the conclusions drawn have stereotypic and demeaning implications. The textbooks lack precision and clarity and instead deal in broad generalizations when referring to minority groups. Umbrella terms such as "culturally different," "disadvantaged," and "low socioeconomic" made sorting out which information refers to which group a constant challenge. If they depend on these texts, then, prospective teachers will get little or no preparation for understanding and instructing children from diverse racial and ethnic backgrounds.

Recommendations

Any discussion of contemporary concerns in education will not be complete without attention to sex bias in instructional materials, teacher expectations, counseling materials and testing procedures, physical education, athletics, special education, vocational education, and educational employment. The potential impact of sexism on students, males as well as females, must be noted. Since it is often difficult for classroom teachers to gain access to educational research, it is crucial that this information be included in teacher-education texts.

Texts in the methods areas could offer curricular and instructional approaches and resources that would enable prospective teachers to operate classrooms free of sex bias. Clear and specific resources are necessary for beginning teachers. These would include nonsexist bibliographies, instructional guides, and instruments for assessing sex bias in curricular materials, classroom organization, and institutional policies. Text layout, design, illustrative material, and language usage also convey messages to prospective teachers about the meaning and importance of sex equity. As texts begin to include this information, they should avoid segregating the material. If it is not incorporated as part of the main discussion, it will appear to be a diversion and not an integral and important part of training. To provide an adequate balance and perspective, textbooks must include analyses of factors that create, reinforce, and intensify sex differences.

The first enunciation of specific criteria for nonsexist materials came in 1972 with the Scott, Foresman *Guidelines for Improving the Image of Women in Textbooks*, and several other publishing companies have since followed this lead. These guidelines urge that females and males be equitably represented in content and illustrations and that both sexes of all racial and ethnic groups exhibit a full range of human emotions and behaviors. While disparity between the publishers' guidelines and the publishers' texts remains, they represent an important initial effort in textbook reform. In terms of attention and responsiveness to sex equity issues, however, elementary- and secondary-textbook publishers are still ahead of their teacher-education counterparts. We hope that our findings and recommendations will encourage the development of teacher-education texts that treat issues of sex, racial, and ethnic equity with greater balance and scope. The policies of elementary- and secondary-textbook publishers are probably more conducive to widescale textbook reform than are those of their teacher-education counterparts. Elementary- and secondary-school publishing is sensitive to organized pressure from the textbook market, particularly through the vehicle of state, city, and local text-adoption committees which often formulate their own guidelines. Publishers then exert editorial influence to ensure that their texts conform to those guidelines.

At the teacher-education level, the publishing process is more idiosyncratic; control over authors is far less stringent, and market pressures are far less organized. Individual professors select texts for their classes and adoption committees do not influence this process. Reform may, however, be achieved through the influence of acquisition editors who select textbook authors as well as textbook topics. They can inform authors of nonsexist and multi-ethnic guidelines, of the need to include issues of sex and race equity in education, and to consider the available research on these topics. Similarly, production editors can influence textbook illustration, layout, and design. Those involved in textbook production must realize that the development of equitable texts is not simply a matter of counting male-oriented pictures and pronouns. Their attention must be directed to the selection and integration of content that reflects significant developments, contributions, and experiences of females as well as males in the educational process.

Further investigation of the politics and procedures that characterize textbook publishing is needed to determine the obstacles to change as well as the mechanisms to encourage it. Most of our recommendations have their most immediate implications for textbook publishers and authors; however, the 200,000 teachers who graduate each year from our colleges and universities cannot wait for newer and fairer texts to become available. It is the vital role of teacher educators to move sex equity from the periphery of teacher preparation to its mainstream. As one response to the current state of teacher-education texts, the authors with funding from the Women's Educational Act are co-directing a project to develop a nonsexist teacher-education curriculum. Their materials will be designed to supplement teacher-education texts and will be available during the academic year 1980–1981. Meanwhile, teacher educators can develop course objectives related to sex equity by making use of available supplementary resources. But whatever actions they choose to take it is clear that to accept current teacher-education textbooks is to perpetuate sex bias and stereotyping and to limit the potential of tomorrow's teachers and the next generation of students.

Appendix: teacher education texts selected for content analysis

Foundations or introduction to education

Johnson, J., Collins, H., Dupuis, V., & Johansen, J. *Introduction to the foundations of American education* (3rd ed.). Boston: Allyn & Bacon, 1976.

Richey, R. *Planning for teaching* (5th ed.). New York: McGraw-Hill, 1973.

Ryan, R., & Cooper, J. *Those who can, teach* (2nd ed.). Boston: Houghton Mifflin, 1975.

Van Til, W. *Education: A beginning* (2nd ed.). Boston: Houghton Mifflin, 1974.

Psychology of education

Biehler, R. *Psychology applied to teaching* (3rd ed.). Boston: Houghton Mifflin, 1978.

Gage, N.L., & Berliner, D. *Educational psychology*. Chicago: Rand McNally, 1975.

Good, T., & Brophy, J. *Educational psychology: A realistic approach*. New York: Holt, Rinehart & Winston, 1977.

Methods of teaching reading

Dallmann, M., Rouch, R., Chang, L., & Deboer, J. *The teaching of reading* (4th ed.). New York: Holt, Rinehart & Winston, 1977.

Durkin, D. *Teaching them to read* (2nd ed.). Boston: Allyn & Bacon, 1974.

Karlin, R. *Teaching elementary reading* (2nd ed.). New York: Harcourt, Brace, Jovanovich, 1975.

Spache, G., & Spache, E. *Reading in the elementary school* (4th ed.). Boston: Allyn & Bacon, 1977.

Zintz, M. *The reading process* (2nd ed.). Dubuque, Iowa: Wm. C. Brown, 1975.

Methods of teaching language arts

Burns, P., & Broman, B. *The language arts in childhood education* (3rd ed.). Chicago: Rand McNally, 1975.

Lundsteen, S. *Children learn to communicate.* Englewood Cliffs, N.J.: Prentice Hall, 1976.

Petty, W., Petty, D., & Becking, M. *Experiences in language* (2nd ed.). Boston: Allyn & Bacon, 1976.

Rubin, D. *Teaching elementary language arts.* New York: Holt, Rinehart & Winston, 1975.

Methods of teaching science

Blough, G., & Schwartz, J. *Elementary school science* (5th ed.). New York: Holt, Rinehart & Winston, 1974.

Gega, P. *Science in elementary education* (3rd ed.). New York: John Wiley, 1977.

Rowe, M.B. *Teaching science as continuous inquiry* (2nd ed.). New York: McGraw-Hill, 1978.

Methods of teaching mathematics

Grossnickle, F.L., & Reckzeh, J. *Discovering meanings in elementary school mathematics* (6th ed.). New York: Holt, Rinehart & Winston, 1973.

Heddens, J. *Today's mathematics* (3rd ed.). Chicago: Science Research Associates, 1974.

Marks, J., Purdy, C.R., Kinney, L., & Hiatt, A. *Teaching elementary school mathematics for understanding.* New York: McGraw-Hill, 1975.

Methods of teaching social studies

Jarolimek, J. *Social studies in elementary education* (5th ed.). New York: Macmillan, 1977.

Michaelis, J. *Social studies for children in a democracy* (6th ed.). Englewood Cliffs, N.J.: Prentice Hall, 1976.

Note

1 Asher, S., & Gottman, J. *Sex of teacher and student reading achievement.* Paper presented at the meeting of the American Educational Research Association, Chicago, April 1972.

References

Avoiding stereotypes. Boston: Houghton Mifflin, 1975.

Biehler, R. *Psychology applied to teaching* (3rd ed.). Boston: Houghton Mifflin, 1978.

Britton, G., & Lumpkin, N. For sale: Subliminal bias in textbooks. *The Reading Teacher*, 1977, 31, 40–45.

Burns, P., & Broman, B. *The language arts in childhood education* (3rd ed.). Chicago: Rand McNally, 1975.

Dallmann, M., Rouch, R., Chang, L., & Deboer, J. *The teaching of reading* (4th ed.). New York: Holt, Rinehart & Winston, 1974.

Durkin, D. *Teaching them to read* (2nd ed.). Boston: Allyn & Bacon, 1974.

Gage, N.L., & Berliner, D. *Educational psychology.* Chicago: Rand McNally, 1975.

Guidelines for Improving the Image of Women in Textbooks. Glenview, Ill.: Scott, Foresman, 1972.

Jarolimek, J. *Social studies in elementary education* (5th ed.). New York: Macmillan, 1977.

Johnson, J., Collins, H., Dupuis, V., & Johansen, J. *Introduction to the foundations of American education* (3rd ed.). Boston: Allyn & Bacon, 1976.

Karlin, R. *Teaching elementary reading* (2nd ed.). New York: Harcourt, Brace, Jovanovich, 1975.

Lunsteen, S. *Children learn to communicate.* Englewood Cliffs, N.J.: Prentice Hall, 1976.

Maccoby, E., & Jacklin, G. *The psychology of sex differences.* Stanford, Calif.: Stanford University Press, 1974.

Marks, J., Purdy, R., Kinney, L., & Hiah, A. *Teaching elementary school mathematics for understanding.* New York: McGraw-Hill, 1975.

McCune, S., & Matthews, M. Eliminating sexism: Teacher education and change. *Journal of Teacher Education,* 1975, 26, 294–300.

Michaelis, J. *Social studies for children in a democracy* (6th ed.). Englewood Cliffs, N.J.: Prentice Hall, 1976.

Petty, W., Petty, D., & Backing, M. *Experiences in language* (2nd ed.). Boston: Allyn & Bacon, 1976.

Richey, R. *Planning for teaching* (5th ed.). New York: McGraw-Hill, 1973.

Rowe, M.B. *Teaching science as continuous inquiry* (2nd ed.). New York: McGraw-Hill, 1978.

Rubin, D. *Teaching elementary language arts.* New York: Holt, Rinehart & Winston, 1975.

Ryan, K., & Cooper, J. *Those who can, teach* (2nd ed.). Boston: Houghton Mifflin, 1975.

Spache, G., & Spache, E. *Reading in the elementary school* (4th ed.). Boston: Allyn & Bacon, 1977.

Van Til, W. *Education: A beginning* (2nd ed.). Boston: Houghton Mifflin, 1974.

Zimet, S. G. *Print and prejudice.* London: Hodder & Stoughton, in association with the United Kingdom Reading Association, 1976.

Zintz, M. *The reading process* (2nd ed.). Dubuque, Iowa: Brown, 1975.

CHAPTER 15

JUSTICE AND CULTURAL CONFLICT (1978)
Racism, sexism, and instructional materials
Joel Taxel

The heated and often bitter debates surrounding the selection and use of various curricular materials have been a source of alarm to those concerned with the future well-being of public education in America. The contentiousness and violence which accompanied the adoption of a series of Language Arts and English textbooks in Kanawha County, West Virginia, in the fall of 1974, is perhaps the most widely publicized example of a phenomenon which has affected virtually every state in the nation—a fact easily verified by examination of any recent issue of the *Newsletter on Intellectual Freedom*, which regularly lists books and curricular materials "now troublesome." The controversy over the elementary social studies program "Man: A Course of Study" (widely known as "Macos") even reached the floor of Congress, where in April 1975 it was attacked by Congressman John B. Conlan (R-California) as a dangerous intrusion on children's values which threatens to "mold children's social attitudes and beliefs along lines that set them apart and alienate them from the beliefs and moral values of their parents and local communities."[1]

Most of the writers discussing the increasingly numerous efforts to limit or proscribe the use of various controversial curricular materials have tended to conceive of these efforts almost exclusively in terms of attempts at censorship: "the withholding of a communication from one person by another" (Ahrens, 1965, p.3). While in most cases there is more than ample justification for such a designation, it is also a fact that the invocation of such hallowed concepts as intellectual or academic freedom[2] and First Amendment rights has the additional effect of deflecting attention from the other exceedingly complex, often emotional issues involved in selection-censorship controversies.[3] These include one's conception of the very purposes of schooling; a delineation and specification of the responsibilities and authority to be delegated to the various faculty, administrative, and lay groups in the selection and review procedures; and the decision as to whether classroom materials are to be reflective of the values and attitudes of the local community or of the more pluralistic nation at large. Also needed is a determination of the role, if any, to be given to the federal government in setting up curricular guidelines and standards.[4] Finally there is the question, rarely addressed in the literature, of whether in selection-censorship controversies there is a difference and a consequent need to distinguish between trade books – works by individual authors, especially fiction – and textbooks. Regardless of the merits of the distinction, there does exist an axiom regarding the connection between attacks on curricular materials and those housed in school libraries (generally trade books): "The axiom states that an attack on curricular materials will soon be extended to include school library materials" (Krug, 1976, p.53).

A further consequence of an exclusive reliance on the language of censorship to discuss these complex matters was alluded to by John Egerton (1975), who indicated that such language tends to conjure up images of clashes between book burners and defenders of academic freedom, fundamentalists and atheists, or intellectuals and know-nothings (p.13). Such unidimensional explanations, though often accurate, do obscure two additional critical points. The first is that the selection of books for use in the curriculum itself amounts to a form of censorship—certain books being preferred and selected over others for very specific reasons (Luebke, 1976, p.1).[5] Second is the rarely mentioned fact that few, if any, would suggest that public school children (those in elementary, junior, and senior high schools) be granted the absolute, unlimited freedoms supposedly afforded adults in our public libraries. Indeed, Jack Welch (1977), in an insightful and revealing look at the "Appalachian folk class" who led the battle against the books in Kanawha County, reports that "no one in the textbook dispute was interested in absolute freedom in the schools" (p.21). Even the supporters of the textbooks "did not say that a teacher should have no guidelines in choosing books. Freedom versus censorship was not the issue" (p.22). The critical issue, at least from the perspective of those challenging the texts, was "the right of one group to dictate to another group what all children must read." The protest against this situation, according to Welch, was less an invocation of censorship in the community than a "protest against a form of authoritarianism, albeit benign and unconscious" (p.22). Egerton (1975), Humphreys (1976), and Trillin (1974), who have all discussed events in West Virginia, support Welch's contention that the conflict was reflective of class and cultural as well as religious differences amongst the contending groups.

My point here is not to become engaged in a semantic debate over what constitutes censorship, or to belittle the danger our schools face when confronted by self-righteous individuals and groups who would prescribe and proscribe all that we read, watch, think, and feel. Rather, my purpose is to offer some perspectives which will, hopefully, enable us to begin better to comprehend the extreme complexity of the issues which have so enflamed emotions in recent years. Nowhere are the difficulties more discernible than in the exceedingly bitter debate over the disposition of materials, both trade and text, which are allegedly racist or sexist in content. Jack Kean, writing in the February 1975 issue of *Arizona English Bulletin* (which is devoted entirely to "Censorship and the Teaching of English"), underlined the basic dilemma when he stated that:

> It is my contention that the principles of intellectual freedom and the principle of promoting non-discriminatory materials for children are on a collision course. They are on this course because both positions are valuable to most of us; we find ourselves caught with internal conflicts because there is value in both positions. They are on this course because the major advocates and promoters of each fail to deal with the major positions of the other side. The advocates of intellectual freedom don't respond to those who claim that the material is biased. Those who claim material currently available is discriminatory don't seem to be at all concerned about principles of intellectual freedom. Hence the advocates of intellectual freedom find themselves using tortuous logic to support intellectual freedom. And those who are worried about discrimination seem to be ready to sacrifice all that has been gained in

intellectual freedom to get rid of materials that they find inappropriate to their own beliefs. (p.59)

Kean goes on to point out that this conflict is further exacerbated by the adoption of legislative statutes and administrative codes "that call on us to do things that now seem almost contradictory" (p.59). Stein (1976), for example, reports the case of a California teacher who sought to apply new sections of that state's education code, which requires that the content of materials cannot reflect adversely upon persons because of their race, color, creed, national origin, ancestry, sex, or occupation, to approximately 65 sets of Language Arts materials. After listening to the publishers of these materials present their case, she determined that not a single one qualified under the new statutory requirements (pp.41–42).

Thus, we find ourselves confronted with a situation in which two compelling values or causes – intellectual freedom and the elimination of racism, sexism, and other forms of prejudice – are in seeming contradiction. The difficulties posed by this dilemma are especially urgent in that the decisions we reach are of such vital importance to the education and future of our children. Jack Kean (1975) again points to what is perhaps the essential predicament:

> I support the freedom to read and to view; yet, I recognize that what one reads or views affects how one views the world, that children's perceptions of their own identity, their futures, can and are in some senses controlled, in fact warped, by what they have read. Thus for students under my control am I justified in censoring what they have access to? (p.61)[6]

It is my belief that the conflict between the principles of intellectual freedom and the goal of having instructional materials respect the humanity and worth of all children represents what might be termed a case of competing claims to justice. Another widely publicized example of such competing claims to justice occurs in those cases involving so-called "reverse discrimination" which have generally grown out of situations where "affirmative action" has been taken to compensate for past discrimination. Here, to put it simply, the right of those victimized by past discrimination (e.g., a woman, or member of a minority group) is seen as conflicting with the right of persons who are themselves not responsible for that discrimination (e.g., a white male student applying to medical or law school).[7] Another example involves attempts to deny public forums to Arthur Jensen and William Schockley to air their racist and thoroughly discredited[8] views on the relationship between heredity and intelligence. This case is noteworthy in that it also involves First Amendment issues in conflict with the basic human rights of minorities. The immediate and compelling presence of children does, I believe, make for a very important difference between this example and the case under discussion.

This paper proposes to take cognizance of the profound moral and ethical, as well as legal, issues at stake when our belief in the value of intellectual freedom comes in conflict with the rights of all children to utilize materials which respect those very qualities which define them as distinctive human beings. It is my hope that in my presenting some new perspectives on this issue, as well as laying out the more widely known forms of argumentation on the subject, we can begin to conceptualize this case of competing claims to justice in a manner enabling us to begin the serious debate demanded by such a question.

It is imperative that any attempt to grapple with as complex a problem as the one under discussion be grounded in an understanding of the history of the issues in question.[9] Therefore, my first task will be to outline, in an admittedly cursory fashion, the history of some of the major selection-censorship controversies of the last quarter century. This discussion will hopefully make clear the connection between such challenges and the socio-historical context in which they occur. We shall see noticeable shifts in the targets of protesters as we move from the Cold War era to that of Vietnam and the Civil Rights movement, although certain concerns, such as "vulgar" language and the realistic treatment of sex, seem to remain rather constant despite changing historical circumstances. As we move closer to the present, I shall give special attention to studies which have scrutinized trade and text materials for racial and sexual stereotyping, as these bear directly on the primary focus of this paper. I shall then turn to developments within the library establishment, particularly the Children's Services Division of the American Library Association, where much of the controversy over the disposition of alleged racist and sexist materials has raged. Within these circles, the fight to have these materials "reevaluated" has, to a great extent, been led by the Council on Interracial Books for Children (CIBC). A discussion of this group and an outline of its positions will therefore be presented. Finally, I will attempt to demonstrate how the perspectives offered by the "sociology of school knowledge" afford the means by which important light can be shed on the racism/sexism censorship question. Michael Apple has described this approach to curricular questions as an attempt to merge curriculum scholarship, sociological understanding, and the study of political and economic ideologies into a unified perspective "that enables us to delve into the place of schools in the cultural reproduction of class relations in advanced industrial society" (Apple, 1977, p.6). A primary focus of such scholarship would be, in the words of Michael F. D. Young (1971), the need to relate the "principles of selection and organization that underlie curricula to their institutional and interactional setting in schools and to the wider social structure" (p.24). Such an approach would, in part, have us desist from viewing curricular materials as being somehow value neutral and instead attempt to conceive of them as ideology-laden cultural artifacts representing, almost invariably, the dominant interests in society. Central to this approach is Young's dictum that "those in positions of power will attempt to define what is taken as knowledge [and] how accessible to different groups any knowledge is" (p.32). It is my belief that application of the perspectives of the sociology of school knowledge can provide us with needed insight into aspects of the question under examination which are too often ignored. It is hoped that this insight will facilitate an end to the deadlock which has characterized this debate—a debate marked by the persistent tendency of the disputants to talk past, instead of to, each other.

Historical background: the Cold War era

In 1953, the National Council of Teachers of English, in response to a wave of challenges to classroom materials, issued its initial published pronouncement on censorship. Entitled *Censorship & Controversy*, it indicated that, despite few actual bannings, there was "sufficient cause for concern" (p.51). Two years later, Paul Blanshard (1955) provided a more elaborate and detailed treatment of the problem. By placing censorship controversies in a historical perspective, Blanshard made it possible to comprehend the phenomenon as a product of evolving forces and changing social concerns.[10] States Blanshard:

In one generation it is the slavocracy of the South that insists on indoctrinating Southern children with a flattering representation of slavery and "Southern values"; in the next it is the orthodox leaders of Christian fundamentalism who would eliminate the "heresy" of evolution. Then it is the turn of the anti-British segments to have their day. In the '20's, socialism was a subject to be omitted from history textbooks altogether. At the same time, however, public utility corporations ... initiated a drive to rewrite the textbooks in such a way that children would appreciate the philosophy of American private enterprise. (p. 88)

Blanshard concluded that struggles over school texts are "inevitable." Although the actors may change from generation to generation, "the motives for suppression and control are essentially the same"—a segment of society is seeking to have the schools reflect its own prejudices and convictions (p. 86).

The picture of censorship which emerges from these works is one in which highly organized, predominantly ultra-conservative groups sought to exert control over classroom materials by purging them of alleged "pro-New Deal," "pro-U.N.," "soft on communism" influences. This extremism is illustrated by Blanshard's report of the somewhat ludicrous efforts of a parent who sought to have the story of Robin Hood removed from a text on the grounds that his "rob from the rich, give to the poor" dictum was communistic (p.83).

While Blanshard and others (Nelson & Roberts, 1962) give primary attention to censorship incidents involving texts, librarian Harry Bach (1965), in a review of censorship activities between 1953 and 1963, expands the scope of the discussion to include troublesome library (trade) books. Among the titles and authors he reported as having aroused the censors' wrath are Steinbeck's *East of Eden* (described as "vulgar trash") and the works of Pearl Buck (because she allegedly appealed for help, in 1941, on behalf of the war-devastated Russian people), Eugene O'Neill, William Faulkner, Sinclair Lewis, Ernest Hemingway, and Theodore Dreiser (pp.3–4). Bach shares the view of the previously mentioned authors that the preponderant majority of would-be censors are of a superpatriotic, reactionary political persuasion. He sees the likelihood of increased censorship as being greatest in times of heightened uneasiness, tension, and frustration, when people reach out for easy solutions to complex problems and are willing to "flail the handiest strawman and burn in effigy the most visible or vulnerable enemy" (p.7). Despite his understanding that many decent, conscientious, and honest parents are up in arms about the content of school materials (p.9), Bach unhesitatingly condemns their actions and points to his perception of the danger they pose:

Censorship, therefore, has been held out as a convenient and simple weapon readily available to people who feel deprived of an effective voice through democratic means, a club with which to defend and enforce their own views on public issues, a means of destroying liberty in the name of liberty. (p.7)

Marjorie Fiske's (1959) landmark study of censorship in California schools and public libraries was the first of a series which sought objective evidence of the existence of censorship on either a local or a national scale.[11] Studies conducted by Burress (1963), Ahrens (1965), Donelson (1969, 1975), Douma (1973), and Woodworth (1976) all sought to illuminate censorship controversies by describing them in terms of such variables as the teachers and administrators involved, the school and community contexts, the would-be censors, the books in question, and the episodes themselves. The most recent of these studies, that of librarian Mary Woodworth, indicates that the pervasive fears brought on by the Cold War are no longer preeminent in the minds of the protesters, as was the case in Fiske's study. "Foul," "pornographic," "suggestive," "too realistic," "immoral," and "ghetto" language remains the primary focus of complaints (Woodworth, 1976, p.41). Indeed, a full 25 years after its initial publication, J. D. Salinger's *Catcher in the Rye* retains the distinction of being the most-frequently-objected-to book (Ahrens, p.68; Woodworth, p.43; Donelson, 1975, p.4).

Although in the past these controversies were, for the most part, restricted to high schools (because the books were written for adults and thus were of relatively difficult reading levels), an entirely new class of works and an expanded set of concerns came to the fore by the mid-1960s. As we shall see, materials read by junior high school and even elementary school children have become the subject of heated, often bitter controversy.

The era of the Vietnam War and the Civil Rights movement

The analyses of Blanshard and of Nelson and Roberts both made clear the need to situate censorship activity in the 1950s and early 1960s within the context of a pervasive Cold War mentality. Likewise, it may be useful to view the protests lodged against various curricular materials beginning in the mid-1960s from a perspective mindful of the profound impact of the Vietnam War and the Civil Rights movement. As a result of the latter, organizations representing women, blacks, Native Americans, and other minority groups became increasingly vocal and insistent that they be given equal treatment and justice. The movement also had an especially important impact on questions relating to children's reading materials, both trade and text.

Kenneth Donelson, who has written often and persuasively about matters pertaining to censorship, in a 1972 article delineated the areas which "have come more and more under the eagle eye of the censor" (p.1192). The first area includes the "usual books" mentioned above, cited by Bach, Burress, and Ahrens.[12] The second area concerns the growing body of literature written specifically for adolescents.[13] Donelson pointed out that as long as adolescent literature stayed at a low and unrealistic level "censors could hardly object to the morality of the books, though teachers and students could object to their lack of reality and literary value" (p.1193). Indeed, the absence of realism in works for adolescents, and even younger children, became a persistent theme of writers who around 1965 began to demand that the literature offered to children be more reflective of the troublesome, rapidly changing world in which they lived. In a series of articles, librarian Dorothy Broderick (1965a, 1965b, 1966) urged that librarians and educators desist from arguing over whether the presence of "hell" or "damn" will corrupt young people and realize the profound changes being wrought in society and the consequent need of young people for books which depict people grappling with these changes. Subsequent articles by Helfand (1967), Killifer (1969), Broderick (1970), and Larrick (1972) expanded on these themes and demanded that children's writers take cognizance of the profound metamorphosis in national consciousness, due in large part to dissension over the Vietnam War, recurring violence in our inner cities, and changing sexual and cultural mores. Given the preeminent role played by electronic media in our society, these authors maintained that it was folly to insist that children's books continue to present a cloistered view of reality. Norma Klein (1974), herself an author of children's books, even went so far as to call for books for the youngest readers, aged 4 to 6, which deal with sexuality. Klein also wondered why it was not possible to have a book about a teen-aged girl's love affair in which she and the boy were "nice kids" and in which "no one got pregnant, no one had to undergo an abortion and no one ended up getting married" (p.132).

While these writers did not directly address the censorship question, the realistic literature which they were demanding, and which began to appear with increased frequency, brought it to the fore. Titles such as Bonham's *Durango St.* (1965), Hinton's *The Outsiders* (1967), Mead's *Mr. & Mrs. BoJo Jones* (1967), Donovan's *I'll Get There. It Better Be Worth the Trip* (1969), and the anonymously written *Go Ask Alice* (1972) dealt in realistic, often harsh language with such topics as street gangs and violence, the issues of war and peace, premarital sex and pregnancy, homosexuality, and the so-called drug culture. These books and others have evoked the wrath of parents who would prefer to shield their children's impressionable minds from subjects they deem suitable for adults only. It is within the context of the furore touched off by protests against this new literature for children that one must view the decision, on June 27, 1967, of the American Library Association to repudiate separate library access standards for adults and children. By inserting the term "age" into provision 5 of the *Library Bill of Rights*, the ALA took the position that access to library materials should "not be denied or abridged because of . . . age, race, religion, national origins or social or political views" (Merritt, 1970, p.82). Although this decision evoked little controversy in 1967 (Krug, 1972, p.811), it was vital in that it put the ALA, the enormously influential bastion of the library establishment, squarely on record as opposing denial of access to materials to persons on account of their age. This apparent consensus in the library community would, however, be shattered within a few short years by the "reevaluation" movement, a drive which has sought to reexamine books for their allegedly racist and/or sexist content. The debates which raged within library circles, and especially within the Children's Services Division of the ALA, will be presented after a glimpse at the increasingly vocal argumentation precipitated by minority groups who, during the late 1950s and 1960s, were demanding more equitable treatment at the hands of textbook writers. These controversies over textbook content did, in fact, foreshadow the reevaluation controversy just referred to and provide yet another example of the axiom presented earlier: that protests against textbooks are invariably followed by complaints about library (trade) books.

Racial minorities and women in textbooks

To a remarkable degree, the status of minorities such as blacks or native Americans has been reflected in the treatment they have received from writers of textbooks (and, I might add, trade books). Even after the Civil War and Emancipation, textbook authors did not see fit to deal with blacks in history, "whether they eliminated them as insignificant to the historical account or eliminated them prejudicially" (Thompson, 1968, p.1). While it is certain that both factors were of vital importance in writing the history of blacks *out* of the textbooks, it is also the case that black people themselves had little opportunity to protest the state of affairs, being preoccupied, as they were, in obtaining civil and economic rights. It was not until 1954 that blacks began to push strongly for the "integrated textbook" (ibid.). Thereafter, blacks, both individually and collectively, began to protest their "invisibility" in textbooks. They claimed that virtually all educational material "wrongly implied an inferiority on the part of Negroes . . . and made it difficult for Negro children trying to learn to read . . . in stories about white children remote from their experience" (ibid.). The National Association for the Advancement of Colored People went even further, urging its local branches to scrutinize "material used in schools and seek to eliminate material therefrom which is racially derogatory" (ibid.).

While blacks did enjoy some success in having works they regarded as offensive removed from required reading lists,[14] more concerted effort was directed at lobbying various state departments of education to end what distinguished historian Kenneth Stampp called "the virtual omission of the Negro" from history texts (Thompson, p.3). Stampp himself headed a committee of historians who read and critiqued seven widely used American history texts.[15] In a report to the California State Department of Education, the committee stated that the treatment of blacks in the texts "reinforces notions among whites of their superiority and among Negroes of their inferiority. When treatment is casual and perfunctory the implication to children may be that Negroes are not part of America" (ibid.). Stampp's committee went on to state:

> The tone of a textbook is almost as important as anything it has to say. In their blandness and amoral optimism, these books implicitly deny the obvious deprivations suffered by Negroes. In several places they go further, implying approval for the repression of Negroes or patronizing them as being unqualified for life in a free society.
>
> The textbooks fall short of revealing either the extent of Negro contributions to American history or the harsher aspects of the truth—the fact that Negroes entered American society as slaves, the brutalities of slavery, the racism of the Reconstruction and post-Reconstruction eras and the continuing depth and harshness of the problem of segregation and discrimination.
>
> Most of the textbooks we have examined reflect views on racial and sectional themes that have been rejected or drastically modified by the best of current historical scholarship. The deference of the textbook publishers to the special sensitivities of the Southern market has caused the "Southern view," by and large, to prevail in textbooks until this day.

The impact of committees such as the one quoted above had several dimensions. They succeeded in creating an atmosphere which made possible the publication of textbooks which reflected a greater appreciation of the role of blacks in American history (Thompson, p.9). They also led to charges of censorship (Thompson, pp.5–6; Nelson & Roberts, pp.167–177) and a willingness of other minority groups to insist on a more accurate depiction of their own history and culture in textbooks. In August of 1965, for example, a group representing the American Indian Historical Society presented the following report to the California State Curriculum Commission:

> We have studied many textbooks now in use . . . [and] our examination discloses that not one book is free from error as to the role of the Indian in state and national history. We Indians believe that everyone has the right to his opinion. A person also has the right to be wrong. But a textbook has no right to be wrong, or to lie, hide the truth, or falsify history, or insult and malign a whole race of people. That is what these textbooks do. At best, these books are extremely superficial in their treatment of the American Indian,

oversimplifying and generalizing the explanation of our culture and history, to the extent where the physical outlines of the Indian as a human being are lost. Misinformation, misinterpretation, and misconception—all are found in most of the books. A true picture of the American Indian is entirely lacking . . . instead, the Indian is made to appear as a subhuman being whose lands were taken in the name of progress. This, most clearly, is a falsification of history. (American Indian Historical Society, 1970, p.7)

Other, more recent studies have sought to measure the impact of these earlier studies on the textbook industry by subjecting newer texts to similar analysis. While most of these studies indicate some improvement over the earlier texts, especially in the depiction of the black experience, the newer texts are still chided as being woefully inadequate and are taken to task for their continued distortion of minority history. Katz (1973) reports the "chilling" results of a study conducted by the Michigan Department of Education on 25 texts used in its secondary schools.[16] Well over half of the books were rated negatively. The authors of the report admitted to "a sense of disappointment" in that

> after a good many years of admonishing textbook publishers to improve their materials in terms of the extent to which they reflect the pluralistic, multi-racial, and multi-ethnic elements of our society, both past and present, they still, on the whole, do not seem to be doing well, at least in the opinion of these 46 reviewers. (p.1)

While the Michigan study did not focus on the treatment given to women in the texts, Katz does note that "women receive scant attention in most texts" and cites the remarks of a reviewer who stated that "one is left with the feeling that women played no role in the making of the American experience." This reviewer was prompted to make this statement after reading a text in which women receive "three paragraphs out of 832 pages" (Katz, p.4).

There are, however, studies which have analyzed the manner in which women are depicted in both history texts and children's readers. Janet Law Trecker (1971), for example, examined the treatment afforded women in American history texts written between 1957 and 1966. The picture that she described is hardly encouraging.

> Texts omit many women of importance, while simultaneously minimizing the legal, social and cultural disabilities they faced. The authors tend to depict women in a passive role and to stress that their lives are determined by economic and political trends. Women are rarely shown fighting for anything; their rights have been "given" to them. (p.271)

A study of recent textbooks by the Council on Interracial Books for Children (1977) indicates that newer texts have shown little improvement in this regard.

An analysis of 2760 stories found in 134 children's reading texts by a group called "Women on Words and Images" (1972) documented the overwhelmingly pervasive existence of sex-role stereotyping in these texts. Female characters, adult as well as child, are consistently depicted in limited, stereotyped sets of roles and are shown as being passive rather than active, unadventurous, often dull-witted, and having limited aspirations. These findings are confirmed in a later study by Oliver (1974).

The Michigan study referred to above was particularly harsh in its condemnation of the treatment given to Native Americans by textbooks writers.

> ... few texts consider Indian culture, or show Indians achieving anything on their own. Native Americans are depicted as problems for whites to solve rather than a proud and unique culture almost annihilated by whites. (Katz, p.3)

Supporting this contention is Arlene Hirschfelder's (1975) review of the treatment given to the complex life style and political organization of the Iroquois Indians in 27 American history textbooks published in the late 1950s and 1960s. Hirschfelder concluded that the textbook information was "inaccurate, ethnocentric, misleading, insufficient, or altogether missing from the narrative" (p.38). Similarly, Swanson (1977) compared 21 high school textbooks published between 1961 and 1964 with 20 published between 1969 and 1972, and found that

> there has been painfully little change in the presentation of Indian–White history although, given the social concerns of the 1960s, we should have every reason to expect that there would be. Simply put, the majority of textbooks examined, regardless of the period of time, refused to deal with and critically examine what might be construed as controversial issues. (p.35)

As one might expect, those seeking to uncover biased treatment of minorities and women in materials read by children did not limit their analyses to text materials. Such studies were extended to trade materials, and the results, not surprisingly, paralleled those of the text analyses. Perhaps the most noticeable of these is Dorothy Broderick's study which elucidated "the portrait of the Black which emerges from children's books published between 1827 and 1967" (p.vii). Broderick's book, *Image of the Black in Children's Fiction*, based on her dissertation, offers much data documenting the slander and debasement to which black people and their culture have been subjected by children's authors.[17] Similar studies by Byler (1974), Troy (1975), and Herbst (1975) point to the pervasive stereotyping of Native Americans in children's books, while Weitzman et al. (1972), Higgs and Stewig (1973), Feminists on Children's Literature (1973), Stewig and Knipfel (1975), and Lieberman (1972) offer similar evidence on the sex-role stereotyping of women. A recent study by the Council on Interracial Books for Children (1976b) indicates that Asian Americans have likewise been subjected to stereotyping.

The accumulation of this substantial body of evidence pointing to the omission and/or distortion of the culture and experience of minorities and women in curricular materials has, of course, been accompanied by demands that these images be either clarified, rectified, or removed altogether. This, in turn, has led to charges of censorship. Judith Krug (1976), for example, recently spoke of "a relatively new source of censorship attempts" which generally focus on how minority groups and women are portrayed. White (1974) had previously noted that controversies over stereotyping which had "originated as literary criticism" had grown into emotional issues "that surpassed the boundaries of literature itself" (p.6)—the inference being that such protests constituted attempted censorship. As early as 1973 James Harvey of the ALA's Office of Intellectual Freedom described "reevaluation" as a "most dangerous threat to intellectual freedom in libraries." Finally, Barbara Luebke (1976), in her review of the "new aspects" of textbook censorship, talks of "the textbook censorship movement" as having taken on new dimensions. "While the traditional 'isms' continue to come under attack, there is also firing from the other side," which Leubke has designated as being "on the left." This side is reported to be seeking "to have textbooks thrown out not for what is in them but for what is not in them" (p.1). Thus, there seems to be a considerable body of opinion which perceives those protesting "the social views presented in creative endeavors" (trade books) or historical distortion and omission to be censors as surely as their ideological opposites in West Virginia.

Historically, those protesting against curricular materials have almost invariably sought to justify their actions as being essential protection for the impressionable minds of children against dangerous and alien social viewpoints or ideas. While those challenging trade and textbooks guilty of the sins of racist and/or sexist commission and omission have been no exception in purporting to be protecting the best interest of children, it is also the case that their arguments in support of their position contain much that is new in the debate over censorship and selection. Many of those issues and concerns have been the subject of heated debates within library circles, and it is to these discussions that I now turn.

The Statement on the Reevaluation of Children's Materials

On January 23, 1973, the Board of Directors of the American Library Association's Children's Service Division, in response to demands that some action be taken against the blatant racism and sexism of many children's books, adopted the *Statement on the Reevaluation of Children's Materials* (reprinted in *Council on Interracial Books for Children Bulletin*, 1976a, p.8). This document spoke of the need for librarians "to espouse critical standards in selection and evaluation of library materials" and urged those librarians working with children "to be aware that the child lacks the breadth of experience of the adult." Because the "social climate and man's state of knowledge are constantly changing," librarians must "continually reevaluate their old materials in the light of growing knowledge and broadening perspectives." The *Statement* declared that the decision as to whether given books "no longer serve a useful role in the collection" and "may have been superseded by better books" must be made only after careful deliberation by those delegated that responsibility. In discharging this duty the librarian is obliged to:

> set aside personal likes and dislikes, to avoid labeling materials, to consider the strengths and weakness of each title, and to consider the material taken as a whole with objectivity and respect for all opinions. (CIBC, 1976a, p.8)

The *Statement* concludes with a reaffirmation, by the Children's Services Division, of their support of the Library Bill of Rights and of free access to libraries for minors. Reevaluation is seen as "a positive approach to sound collection building" and "not to be equated with censorship."

To many, this statement was perceived as the rationale by which librarians would be able to justify the removal of books which they deemed undesirable. It was also seen as a radical departure from traditional ALA advocacy of total opposition to censorship, this despite the CSD disclaimer of that intent.

In a blistering piece directed squarely at Sarah Innes Fenwick (1972) and Dorothy Broderick (1971), two of reevaluation's chief proponents, James Harvey (1973) challenged them for having forsaken traditional evaluation criteria (such as accuracy, up-to-dateness, style, theme, and content) and having replaced them with obscure concepts of "right and wrong" (Broderick) and "quality of experience" (Fenwick)—both being "highly subjective value judgements" (Harvey, p.69). Harvey rejected totally the claim of those advocating reevaluation that it constitutes "collection building." Rather, he insisted, "it is more likely synonymous with censorship: the exclusion of library materials because of the *views* of the author" (ibid., emphasis Harvey). A bit further on Harvey arrived at his central thesis (p.69):

> These contemporary efforts to rid libraries of objectionable children's materials, under the guise of reevaluation, are much different in substance from traditional efforts. In some instances, the identity of the censors and the means they use have changed, but the motivation remains the same. The *superficial* motivation involved in such efforts has always been one of moral values, whether the subject matter was sex, politics, religion, race, or drugs. As Ms. Broderick so succinctly illustrates, rare is the censor who does not believe he is acting in a socially responsible manner, and "some things are right and some things are wrong and it is that simple" has been the credo of all censors since before the invention of the eraser. (p.69)[18]

The ALA's Intellectual Freedom Committee (IFC) also responded to this break in the Association's ranks by urging that the ALA, as a whole, adopt its advisory statement on this increasingly contentious problem (Farrell, 1976). The ALA Council did, in fact, follow the advice of the IFC and on February 2, 1973, adopted a statement entitled "Sexism, Racism and Other 'Isms' in Library Materials, An Interpretation of the Library Bill of Rights" (American Library Association, 1973). This document reiterated the Association's commitment to the Library Bill of Rights and came out strongly against the restriction of any materials from minors, its censoring because of a racist/sexist viewpoint, or the labeling of such objectionable material. The statement did, however, acknowledge the difficulty of "dealing with ideas, such as racism and sexism, which many find abhorrent, repugnant and inhumane," but concluded that "toleration is meaningless without toleration of the detestable" (pp.227–228).

The debate over the reevaluation of racially and sexually biased trade books for children and the disposition of historically inaccurate and distorted textbooks has continued unabated despite the rescinding of the *Statement on the Reevaluation of Children's Materials* in December of 1975. It seems apparent that many conceive of those opposing and protesting the use of such materials as persons who, because of the frustration of the slow pace of the civil rights movement, have resorted to what Bach (1965) called the "flailing of the handiest strawman"—children's reading materials. Such persons are also seen as being insufficiently sensitive to the paramount importance of the First Amendment, which guarantees the free and unrestricted access to all ideas, opinions, and points of view. However, this very claim, that racism and sexism are ideas which can be equated with other diverse or unpopular political or religious viewpoints, is one which the opponents of the biased materials have increasingly rejected. Since, as I have noted, the Council on Interracial Books for Children has been among the most forceful and vocal groups articulating this rejection, it is appropriate that we examine in some detail the group and its position.

The Council on Interracial Books for Children

The Council on Interracial Books for Children is a non-profit organization, founded in 1965, dedicated "to promoting anti-racist and anti-sexist literature and instructional materials."[19] In addition to publishing the *Interracial Books for Children Bulletin* and running a yearly contest for unpublished minority writers of children's literature, the CIBC seeks to advance its aims by conducting clinics and workshops on racism and sexism and providing resource specialists and consultants in awareness training to educational institutions. The CIBC has also established the "Racism and Sexism Resource Center for Educators," which issues a wide variety of publications "designed to help teachers eliminate racism and sexism and to develop pluralism in education." Jean Carey Bond, a member of the CIBC staff, discussed the critical question of whether racism and sexism are merely unpopular ideas at a recent convention of the National Council of Teachers of English, held in Chicago. Bond, apparently well aware of controversy which the work conducted by the CIBC has engendered, declared:

> Some people are confused, others are angered by our strong condemnation of books that contain elements of racism or sexism. They feel that racism and sexism are ideas which, however invalid or repugnant, should have free expression. One position is that to put a person down because he or she has an opinion one doesn't approve of is one thing, but to put someone down, overtly and subtly, because he or she is a certain color or a certain sex . . . is another thing entirely. The latter constitutes an assault on a person's very condition of being—a condition which is involuntary and irrevocable. Children who are black cannot turn white because someone has told them black is inferior, nor can a girl change her sex. Therefore, we say the "right" of an author to depict characters in children's books in a racist, sexist . . . manner is superseded by the birthright of all children to encounter images of themselves that are unbiased and non-stereotypical.

An earlier statement by the CIBC (1976a, p.4) clarifies this important point still further:

> One can choose whether or not to be in sympathy with books that express particular ideologies. If a book extols or derides communism, for example, readers can choose to change their persuasion on that topic. If a book extols or derides theism (or pornography, or narcotics use, etc.) readers can agree or disagree with the author. By contrast, books which insult or demean one group's color or sex while exalting another group's color or sex are attacking inalterable physical realities. One cannot choose whether to be affected by such books because one cannot choose one's color or sex. These are attributes one is born with.
>   To circulate to young children books which abuse their racial or sexual identities, thus undermining their self images—and further to defend such books in the name of "intellectual freedom"—is cruel in the extreme.

The second major component of the CIBC's challenge to racist and/or sexist materials is the notion of "covert" or "racist" censorship. Albert Schwartz (1975), a member of the CIBC's Editorial Advisory Board, conceives of "racist" censorship as being effectuated through "two frameworks":

One, the Invisible Man syndrome . . . eliminated historical truth and actual real-life facts of Third World people and hence incapacitated whites' perception and second, substituted stereotypes and myths about Third World people which controlled whites' perception. The usual direction of these frameworks was to enforce the concept that white existence was superior and should rule Third World people who were too inferior to be anywhere but in a demeaning place. (pp.120–121)[20]

In an article "Censorship and Racism: A Dilemma For Librarians" (CIBC, 1975), the concept of "covert" censorship and its fundamental relationship to challenges to racist and sexist literature was further advanced. After equating the act of "overt" censorship with a "clear and deliberate process, set in motion . . . to eliminate or label materials that are felt to offend prevailing public attitudes," the CIBC proceeds to posit its notion of "covert" censorship:

> Censorship also has a covert aspect. When a book, for example, presents one set of facts or one viewpoint about a given subject and excludes other facts or viewpoints—and when the inclusion of some facts and the ommission of others results in a picture of reality that is different from the one that would have emerged had all the facts been presented—then covert censorship has taken place. Only parts of the truth have been presented, other parts of the truth have been censored. (p.1)

When this is repeated thousands of times, it results "in the perpetuation of distorted pictures of reality" (p.1). "Covert" censorship is thus seen as being instrumental to the perpetuation of sexism and racism in literature and the means by which "racist and sexist stereotypes have passed from generation to generation" (p.10).

Thus, the CIBC's approach to the evaluation of curricular materials can be seen to rest on two fundamental premises. The first is that race and sex, which are unalterable conditions of being, are not to be equated with political ideologies or religious philosophies, which are mutable ideas. The second is that educational materials have traditionally reflected the perspectives and concerns of the upper-class white males who control this society, and that through the process of covert censorship these materials "have failed to represent the perspectives and concerns of racial minorities and women" (Moore, 1977, p.4). Beginning with these premises, Robert Moore of the CIBC argued, at a recent conference of the National Coalition Against Censorship, that educational institutions must share a large part of the responsibility for the extent to which racism and sexism exploit and oppress millions of people in this society and that "instructional materials have played a significant role in public education's reinforcement of racism and sexism" (ibid.). He then proceeds to advance an intriguing relationship between the First and Fourteenth Amendments, which he conceives as being applicable to the selection of classroom materials. Noting that social studies materials have been consistently found to perpetuate "white chauvinism and male chauvinism," Moore states:

> The First Amendment grants authors and publishers the right to produce such materials and grants individuals the right whether to purchase and read these materials.
> However, within the public school environment, the First Amendment

rights of textbook authors and publishers are superseded by the students' Fourteenth Amendment rights. Compulsory education laws compel young people to attend public schools and within these schools students are frequently required to take certain courses. The Fourteenth Amendment requires the state to assure all students "equal protection" under these laws. Since instructional materials are purchased with *public* funds and students are *compelled* to study from them, it is the responsibility of the state to assure that those texts do not infringe on the human rights and freedom of any student.

Moore reasons that human dignity is critical to freedom and that it is the right of all children to grow up with positive self-esteem and an accurate image of the humanity of others. Given the claim that materials which perpetuate racist or sexist attitudes inhibit the development of a positive self-image and human dignity, the continued use of such materials is, in consequence, seen as a denial to equal access to life, liberty, and the pursuit of happiness. In light of these premises Moore and the CIBC

> strongly support the regulation of instructional materials selection to insure that educational materials reflect the reality of this pluralistic society *as perceived by all groups*, not simply the self-serving perceptions of reality of the upper-class white, male-dominated establishment which controls the publication and communication industry.[21]

The CIBC responds to the charges that the establishment of regulations or selection guidelines and criteria constitutes censorship: it first denies that they are demanding that books be censored,[22] and then calls for recognition of the fact that "a selection process exists and has always existed." In addition, selection is viewed as a process which "has and does involve some degree of covert censorship" (CIBC, 1976, p.4). Granting the existence of selection processes and procedures, the CIBC calls for the participation in that selection process by racial-minority and feminist representatives and the introduction of criteria referring to racism and sexism. The CIBC also asks for the "relocation of a few blatantly offensive young children's books on reference shelves to be used by adults to teach constructively about racism/sexism and their manifestations" (ibid.).

The foregoing discussion has, hopefully, made it possible to comprehend the extent of the disagreement which exists between such writers as James Harvey (1973) and Judith Krug (1972, 1976), both of whom have long records of service in the Intellectual Freedom Committee of the ALA and in groups like the CIBC. In addition, I trust that my presentation of the views of the disputants in this controversy make apparent the nature of the difficulties which arise when two cherished ideals—in this case opposition to overt censorship and the compelling need to take positive action against the evils of racism and sexism—come into seeming conflict. One is, however, left with the rather imposing task of sorting out these claims and attempting to arrive at some means in which to begin to resolve them.

The competing claims in perspective

Whether one completely accepts the CIBC's assertion that it is possible to distinguish between religious and political ideas and states of being such as race and sex,[23] it is difficult to conceive of an argument to counter their claims of the existence of covert censorship on a massive scale or the pervasive slander, distortion, and omission that the images of women and minorities have been subject to at the hands of writers of both trade and textbooks. The evidence supporting these claims (and what has been cited in this paper is but a fraction of what could have been included) seems beyond challenge or refute. While the damage which has resulted from exposure to such materials can never be fully ascertained,[24] there are in existence several tragically poignant accounts which document the painful humiliation endured by children as a result of such exposure.[25] Surely some protection must be afforded to children within our schools to ensure that such traumatic experiences do not recur. Whether this will entail a rethinking of our notion of intellectual freedom and censorship as it relates to schools or, as was suggested by Moore, the superseding of the First Amendment by the equal protection clause of the Fourteenth Amendment, are issues which demand both serious debate by all parties concerned with our schools and clarification by the courts. What does seem clear is that to continue to conceive of protests against such materials *exclusively* in terms of attempts at censorship serves only to postpone the serious debate which is needed.

One can readily anticipate the charges that such an interpretation would prove fatal to our system of education, a system in which the school is purported to exist as an open and free marketplace for ideas where students have supposedly unlimited opportunity to pick and choose "the truth" from among competing philosophies and points of view. Such a perspective, while perhaps a worthwhile goal and possibly a valid description of some of our institutions of higher education, belies the reality of our public school system. This point was directly addressed in an exhaustive 1968 study of academic freedom conducted by the *Harvard Law Review*, in which the purposes of elementary and secondary education were contrasted with those of higher education.

> The assumptions of the "free marketplace of ideas" in which free speech rests do not apply to school aged children, especially in the classroom where the word of the teacher may carry great authority. It seems unwise to assume as a matter of constitutional doctrine that school children possess sufficient sophistication or experience to distinguish "truth" from "falsity." Furthermore, since one function of elementary and even secondary education is indoctrinative—to transmit to succeeding generations the body of knowledge and set of values shared by members of the community—some measure of public regulation of classroom speech is inherent in the very provision of public education. (quoted by Schauer, 1976, pp.299–300)

Schauer's (1976) review of litigation concerning the rights of teachers, administrators, parents, and students in relation to decisions about curricular content and speech supports the above-quoted contention. Schauer states that "classroom academic freedom exists mainly within the parameters set by the appropriate governing body." Furthermore, "the school administration has ultimate control over subject matter, the materials which will be used, and the manner in which the subject will be taught (pp.305–306). While a recent court decision has placed limits on the rights of school administrations to place and remove books in school libraries,[26] such authority is nonetheless generally accepted by the courts. Schauer concludes his review of judicial opinion by declaring that:

> The schoolroom is not yet so universally accepted as an open marketplace of

ideas that this concept rises to the level of a Constitutional right, either for the teacher or for the student. And in the absence of such a right, there is nothing to preclude the school administration or the school board from making binding decisions as to teaching methods, subjects to be covered, and materials to be used. (p.306)

The sociology of school knowledge

Given Schauer's assertion that public schools are not, and never really have been, "open marketplaces" for ideas, the manner in which particular kinds of knowledge are selected and incorporated into the school curriculum becomes increasingly important. It is here that the sociology of school knowledge is helpful. As indicated earlier, we must view curricular materials (and organization) not as a mere collection of neutral artifacts but rather as "value-governed selections from a much wider universe of possible knowledge and collection principles" (Apple & King, 1977, p.343). A central assumption which underpins this approach to curricular questions is the belief that "social action, cultural artifacts, educational events, even everyday items in use in our homes and offices, are 'defined' not by their obvious qualities that we get at with our senses" but instead are "given meaning *relationally*, by their concrete ties and connections, to the ways other aspects of a complex social reality are organized" (Apple, 1977, p.40). Such a "relational" approach to curricular materials and concerns stands in direct contrast to the dominant tendency in British and American literary criticism, which has been to conceive of literary works[27] as objects or artifacts best understood in relative isolation from a writer's personal biography and undistorted by associations brought to the work from the readers' daily life (Greene, 1975, p.300). The "relational" approach challenges the notion that literary or curricular works can be dealt with in a manner which divorces them from the experience and history of either their producers or their consumers and in absence of a discussion of the ideology and values they carry as part of their message.[28] Dale et al. (1976), the editors of a sociology reader which is used as a required text in Britain's government-financed "Open University," speak to this very point when they state:

> By alienating cultural goods and their producers from both the social condition of their existence and the patterns of cultural production and consumption, we are presented with a view of their impeccable neutrality. Similarly we find the ideology of political neutrality applied to education, the agency for both cultural creation and dissemination. Seen as objective, apolitical and internally governed, the selection, modification and transmission of a cultural heritage, through the curriculum and pedagogical practice of education, is assigned more often than not a total autonomy from the society of which it is part. *Academic freedom, teacher autonomy, the denial of censorship and bias are all called in to support the view of a world in which the free flow of ideas is beyond ideological control.* (p.5; emphasis added)

A basic thrust, therefore, of the sociology of school knowledge lies in an attempt to illuminate the interconnections between ideology and the curriculum:

> We need to examine critically not just "how a student acquires more knowledge" (the dominant question in our efficiency minded field) but "why and how particular aspects of the collective culture are presented in school as

objective, factual knowledge. How, concretely, may official knowledge represent ideological configurations of the dominant interests in society? How do schools legitimate these limited and partial standards of knowing as unquestioned truths? (Apple, 1975, pp. 354–355)

A fundamental starting point in these investigations has been perhaps most cogently articulated in an observation by Young (1971) that there exists a "dialectical relationship between access to power and the opportunity to legitimize certain dominant categories, and the process by which the availability of such categories enables them to assert power and control over others" (p.8). Seen from this perspective, the absence or distortion of the history of minorities and women from our textbooks is not only a reflection of their historical and current status but an important means by which their powerlessness is perpetuated. Apple and Franklin (forthcoming) speak to this point in greater detail when they state:

Schools . . . help control meaning. They preserve and distribute what is perceived to be "legitimate knowledge"—the knowledge that "we all must have." Thus schools confer cultural legitimacy on the knowledge of specific groups. The very fact that certain groups' knowledge becomes school knowledge is prima facie evidence of its perceived legitimacy. . . . But this is not all, for the ability of a group to make its knowledge into "knowledge for all" is related to that group's power in the larger political and economic arena. Power and culture, then, need to be seen not as static entities with no connection to each other but as attributes of existing economic relations in a society. They are dialectically interwoven so that economic power and control is interconnected with cultural power and control.

Seen in this light, the sociology of school knowledge conceives of the knowledge schools distribute as being a "form of the larger distribution of goods and services in society" (Apple & King, p.31). Thus schools, and the "cultural capital" they distribute, must not be viewed in social isolation but be seen "relationally" as playing an integral role in advancing, legitimating, and preserving the existing distribution of wealth and power in society.[29] Thus, protests against curricular materials which either omit reference to or slander women and minority-group members must not be narrowly construed as the efforts of yet another misguided interest group to interfere with affairs which are best left to professional educators and administrators. Instead they need to be viewed as being part of a wider struggle to understand the vital role which schools, and the knowledge they distribute, play in the active reproduction of a stratified society.

To argue, as have groups such as the CIBC,[30] that women and minority peoples be given a role in the selection and shaping of curricular materials is not to ignore the questions which such a policy would raise about matters such as intellectual freedom, censorship, etc. Protection of such rights is especially critical today as ever-increasing aspects of our lives become controlled and rationalized by bureaucratic forms of organization. Such recognition must also, however, bear in mind the fact that such rights (e.g., the Bill of Rights) are, and have been, biased in favor of very particular classes and against others (Friedenberg, 1976). It is hardly an accident of history that those very groups which have been less than fully protected by such rights are now demanding that action be taken to redress past injustices—action which others feel threatens the sanctity of these same rights. This, then, is the essential predicament posed by our competing claims to justice.

It must be stressed, however, that to be in favor of textbooks which accurately present the history of *all people* who are citizens of this nation, or to insist that trade book selection, review, and criticism be more conscious and critical of the ideology and values put forward by writers of children's literature, is not to favor wholesale or even limited removal of books already in libraries. The dangers of advocating a policy which actively promotes the removal of a particular class of books already on library shelves are known to groups such as the CIBC[31] as well as to civil libertarians. A far better policy would seem to be one which actively seeks to utilize both blatantly and subtly racist and/or sexist materials as teaching devices. Such a policy would have the critical advantage of being positive; it assumes that, given adequate guidance and instruction, children can, and in fact need to, understand all of our history, the ugly as well as the beautiful. It also takes cognizance of the irony that the notoriety conferred on books which become the subject of heated controversy invariably results in their increased circulation and readership.[32] A policy which actively seeks to incorporate racist and sexist materials into a teaching program will also avoid endless rounds of debate as to what makes a book sufficiently objectionable to warrant removal. Must it be blatantly racist, as in the case of Lofting's *The Story of Dr. Doolitle* (1920) or Bannerman's *Little Black Sambo* (1918)? What of more subtly racist, though well-intentioned, books such as de Angelis's *Bright April* (1946), Carlson's *The Empty School House* (1965), Armstrong's *Sounder* (1969), or Taylor's *The Cay* (1970)? seen and understood as products of very specific historical periods, such books can be utilized as one kind of evidence in a study of the history of racism and sexism in this nation. Such an examination would, in essence, be an analysis of the content of these books and therefore be similar to many of the studies cited earlier in this paper. By having children became aware of the relationship between societal attitudes and the content of literary and other curricular materials, we can hopefully begin to disrupt the circular situation described by Dorothy Broderick (1973) in which "society dictates the content and attitudes within the books and the books serve to perpetuate the societal attitudes from one generation to the next" (p.177).

Ideology and form

It is critical that I reiterate the fact that the sociology of school knowledge does not restrict itself to analyses of the content of curricular materials but places equal, if not greater, emphasis on seeking to explicate the ideology embodied in their form. Thus, as Eagleton points out, studies of the novel form, regardless of content, reveal changing sets of ideological interests which need to be seen in relation to the historical evolution of the form if they are to be fully comprehended (1976, p.25).[33] Similarly Apple's (forthcoming) examination of several curricular innovations demonstrates that these materials are the bearers of very specific ideological messages to which most of us remain relatively unconscious. Analysis of this sort will hopefully make evident the fact that literary and other curricular works

> are not mysteriously inspired, or explicable simply in terms of the author's psychology. They are forms of perception, particular ways of seeing the world; and as such they have a relation to that dominant way of seeing the world which is the "social mentality" or ideology of an age. That ideology, in turn, is the product of the concrete social relations into which men enter at a particular time and place. . . . (Eagleton, p.6)

The notion of establishing the linkages between the ideology which lies behind the form and the content of various curricular materials and the society and culture from which they are generated thus becomes a central task of the sociology of school knowledge. As Michael Apple and Nancy King (1977) have recently stated:

> the study of educational knowledge is a study in ideology, the investigation of what is considered legitimate knowledge ... by specific social groups and classes, in specific institutions, at specific historical moments. It is, further, a critically oriented form of investigation, in that it chooses to focus on how this knowledge, as distributed in schools, may contribute to cognitive and dispositional development that strengthens and reinforces existing (and often problematic) institutional arrangements in society. (p.342)

Thus, a thesis which must be seriously entertained is that the well-documented and pervasive stereotyping of women and minorities in the various curricular materials discussed in this paper not only reflects but actively contributes to the perpetuation of the often second-class and oppressed status of these groups.

Conclusions

This paper has sought to raise questions about the limits we have imposed on ourselves as we discuss the relationship between racism, sexism, and instructional materials. In addition to attempting to outline the historical evolution of concerns about the content of curricular materials, and the manner in which this issue is currently being debated, I have tried to demonstrate that the ground rules and definitions we have accepted have limited our ability to apprehend the real complexity of the issue (e.g., a definition of censorship which omits the notion of covert censorship). Perhaps the most important belief which I have sought to question is that the content of literary and curricular materials can be discussed in isolation from the ideologies which they consciously or unconsciously manifest. There is a relationship between these ideologies and the wider distribution of power and resources in society. To discuss challenges to racially or sexually biased instructional materials exclusively in terms of a perceived threat to intellectual freedom and in absence of a discussion of the role such materials play in the continuation and re-creation of racial and sexual discrimination in society is, as has been stated, to ignore matters which demand consideration. It is my conviction that the debate surrounding this question has, for too long, been abstracted from the concrete historical concerns of those directly involved, and has ignored the appeals to justice and fairness which adhere to the claims of those demanding redress of past grievances.

Furthermore, the debate has been too often guided by assumptions (e.g., the existence of schools as an open and free marketplace for the exchange of all ideas) which simply cannot withstand close scrutiny. It is clear to me that the perspectives offered by the sociology of school knowledge offer the means to make possible a fuller disclosure of the serious issues raised by this controversy.

Notes

I wish to express my thanks to Professor Michael Apple for his helpful suggestions and comments on the various drafts of this paper.

1 Congressional Record, April 9, 1975 (H2585). A debate on the merits of "Macos" by Conlan and Peter Dow, one of the program's developers, is available in the October 1975 issue of *Social Education* (pp.388–396). Further discussion between Dow and George Weber, of the Council for Basic Education, is available in the October 1975 issue of *Phi Delta Kappan* (pp. 79–82).

2 Intellectual freedom has been defined as "the right of any person to believe whatever he wants on any subject, and to express his beliefs or ideas in whatever way he thinks appropriate. The freedom to express one's beliefs on ideas, through any mode of communication, becomes virtually meaningless when accessibility to such expression is denied to other persons" (ALA, Office of Intellectual Freedom, *Intellectual Freedom Manual*, Chicago: ALA, 1974, p. viii). The act of censorship, "the with-holding of communication," is thus a direct violation of one's intellectual freedom.

3 The question of selection vs. censorship is a perennial source of contention amongst librarians, if not those concerned with the content of the curriculum. In a classic and much quoted article written in 1953, Lester Asheim, in describing the positive nature of selection and the essential negativity of censorship, stated: "Selection seeks to protect the right of the reader to read; censorship seeks to protect not the right but the reader himself from the fancied effects of his reading. The selector has faith in the intelligence of the reader; the censor has faith only in his own" (Asheim, 1953, p.67).

4 Conlan (1975) suggests that the active involvement of agencies of the federal government in the production and promotion of "Macos" was a primary reason for protests against these materials. The government's involvement with "Macos" was seen as "an ominous move toward a uniform federal standard in education" (p.389). In a similar vein, Parker (1976) states that "eruptions—from textbook censorship to anti-busing riots—indicate(s) the presence of current explosive school pressures stemming, in large part, from federal influences producing curriculum change" (p.114). On the other hand, Moore (1977), writing for the Council on Interracial Books for Children, states that his group "strongly supports the regulation of instructional materials selection to ensure that educational material reflects the reality of this pluralistic society as it is perceived by all groups" (p.4).

5 Luebke (p.2) reports an excellent example of precisely this kind of censorship occurring in Mississippi, where a revisionist history textbook entitled *Conflict & Change* was denied approval by a subcommittee of the state Textbook Purchasing Board. While this committee can approve as many as five books (with local districts then selecting from the approved list), it chose to endorse only John Bettersworth's *Your Mississippi*, a book which is said to "treat Blacks of old as complacent darkies or a problem to whites." For a revealing comparison of these texts, see Robert B. Moore, *Two History Texts: A Study in Contrast* (New York: The Racism and Sexism Resource Center for Educators). Moore's analysis provides considerable support for the above-quoted allegation. Paredes (1975), discussing the invisibility of Chicano literature from anthologies of American literature, states that such exclusion . . . "may be construed as censorship, insofar as the term implies a deliberate and systematic omission of Chicano literature from the national consciousness" (p.213).

6 Beach (1976), after a review of empirical research on effects and response to reading, concludes that readers' responses are highly unique and vary considerably from book to book, thus making predictions of readers' responses highly suspect. Further, the research indicates that differences in age, sex, values, personality, literary training result in "highly unique meanings for different readers" (p.18). These conclusions seem to cast doubt on Kean's rather forceful assertion that reading and viewing can have a negative impact on the reader. However, given the seriousness of the methodological problems inherent in the attempt to quantify and measure something as complex, personal, and situational as response to reading (issues discussed briefly by Beach, pp.5–6), the hope for conclusive, empirical evidence may well be illusory. The ethical questions involved (e.g., let us take a 7-year-old child and measure his/her response to a blatantly racist or pornographic book) hopefully need no further discussion. This paper will, therefore, take the position put forth by Kelly (1973, p.91) that books created for children "are simply one among several agencies contributing to the socialization of children." Since books (and I would include here both trade and textbooks as well as television and movies created expressly for children) "do constitute a kind of linguistic

behavior addressed to children by adults ... they are of crucial importance for what they may suggest about those things that children were expected to know and believe ... and about the structure of values and the basis of the social order considered central if a particular way of life was to be maintained."

7 Cf. Ronald Dworkin, "The Defunis Case: The Right to Go to Law School," *New York Review of Books*, February 5, 1976, and J. W. Foster, "Race and Truth at Harvard," *The New Republic*, July 17, 1976.

8 Cf. Jerry Hirsch, "Jensenism: The Bankruptcy of Science Without Scholarship," *Educational Theory*, Winter, 1975; P. B. Medawar, "Unnatural Science," *The New York Review of Books*, February 3, 1977; Philip Green, "The Pseudoscience of Arthur Jensen," *Dissent*, Summer 1976.

9 Curriculum historian Herbert Kliebard (1975) makes note of the fact that workers in the curriculum field have traditionally shown little awareness of their historical antecedents. This "ahistorical posture" has often resulted in an ignorance of the fact that issues under discussion have their counterparts in an earlier period (p.41).

10 Boyer's (1968) *Purity in Print*, traces the history of the so-called "vice societies" from their origins in the late 19th century through the 1930s. Boyer quite effectively relates this phenomenon to the pressures and tension resulting from such factors as rampant industrialism, the influx of great numbers of uneducated immigrants, and the decline of such institutions as the family, church, and neighborhood community.

11 Fiske's data indicated that 73% of the objections to books came from within the schools themselves: librarians, 42%; administrators, 23%; and teachers, 8% (p.123).

12 Other titles mentioned by Donelson are *The Grapes of Wrath, To Kill a Mockingbird, Brave New World, The Scarlet Letter,* and *The Oxbow Incident* (p. 1192).

13 Other troublesome areas mentioned by Donelson include literature by and about ethnic and racial minorities (e.g. Cleaver's *Soul on Ice*; Brown's *Manchild in the Promised Land*; Deloria's *Custer Died for Your Sins*, etc.), magazines, films, and student-made films. Interestingly, except for his mention of challenges to Sterling's *Mary Jane*, attacked for stereotyping black people, which he discusses along with those works mentioned above, Donelson does not at all discuss the racism/sexism censorship controversy.

14 Thompson (p.2) reports that, as a result of NAACP pressure, the New York City Board of Education dropped Twain's *The Adventures of Huckleberry Finn* from the approved textbook list for elementary and junior high schools, because of "passages derogatory to Negroes." Harvey (1973; p.70) reports the unsuccessful attempts in 1950 of some New York City taxpayers to suppress Dickens's *Oliver Twist* and Shakespeare's *Merchant of Venice* on the grounds that the works were "antisemitic." See also Nelson and Roberts (pp.167–177). Technically, a work like *Huck Finn* is a trade book, at least under the definitions I have been using. Thompson seems to define it as a textbook in that it is a specific work required by the curriculum, rather than being merely one of myriad library books.

15 Stampp, being the author of one of the seminal works in the historiography of slavery, *The Peculiar Institution* (New York: Knopf, 1956), was eminently qualified for the task. The books reviewed were *Trailblazers of American History* (Ginn & Co., 1961); *The Story of American Freedom* (Macmillan, 1961); *America is My Country* (Houghton Mifflin, 1961); *The Growth of America* (Prentice-Hall, 1959); *Story of the American Nation* (Harcourt, Brace & World, 1962); *The Story of American Democracy* (Harcourt, Brace & Co., 1955); and *Story of America* (Henry Holt & Co., 1957).

16 Simms (1975, p.201) reports the results of a study conducted in Texas whose findings are similar to those of the Michigan study under discussion. This study "reveals that the slant towards racism is still part of social studies textbooks today, even though these books are better now than before."

17 In her final chapter, Broderick states: "Whether one likes or dislikes, approves or disapproves, the image of the black that emerges from the sample of children's books analyzed, the fact is that the image does reflect a high degree of reality in terms of how a great part of White America viewed Black America" (p.177).

There is little doubt that books written since 1967 have improved markedly in their depiction of black characters (Baker, 1975). Despite this improvement, and the relative absence of the blatant racism which pervaded the books in Broderick's sample, many of the newer books, several of them award-winners, have been subject to rather heated criticism for a more subtle, covert stereotyping. See, for example, critiques by Tate (1974) of Paula Fox's Newbery-Award-winning book *The Slave Dance*; Schwartz (1970) on Armstrong's *Sounder* (Newbery Award, 1970); and Schwartz (1971) on Taylor's *The Cay* (winner of the Jane Addams and Lewis Carroll Shelf awards).

18 This was particularly in response to an article by Dorothy Broderick (1971), which declared: "For me, racist materials are simply another form of pornography. They are anti-human . . . so I object to the stocking of materials that say bigotry is just another point of view. I fail to understand how the people who are concerned with social responsibilities can also be gung-ho for the current stance being offered by the Office of Intellectual Freedom. The whole concept of social responsibilities implies value judge-ments—some things are right and some things are wrong and it's that simple" (p.3818). It seems rather likely that the research which led to Ms. Broderick's dissertation and book (*Image of the Black in Children's Fiction*, Bowker, 1973) had much to do with her decision to take this rather forthright stand.

19 This statement and the descriptive information about CIBC which follows has been taken from the statement entitled "What Is the Council," which is included in each issue of *Interracial Books for Children Bulletin*, CIBC's publication, issued eight times a year.

20 Schwartz later ties the fight against sexist materials to that against racist materials because sexism is "a form of oppression paralleling racism" (p.122). To the best of my knowledge neither Schwartz nor the CIBC currently utilizes the term "racist" censorship, preferring the term "covert."

21 Note that Moore speaks of the selection of materials, not the reevaluation of old. Later in his address he urges that systems using biased materials seek to undertake efforts to overcome these biases. (p.5)

22 In the previously discussed statement entitled "Censorship and Racism: A Dilemma for Librarians," the CIBC (1975) spoke to this point: "Appreciating the opposition of civil libertarians to overt censorship (and realizing that such censorship has usually been imposed for undemocratic purposes) we are not inclined to advocate overt censorship as the way to deal with racism and sexism in books" (p.10).

23 While, in many respects, I find this argument to be quite persuasive, I am at a loss as to how one would convince, say, President Carter, not to mention a West Virginia funda-mentalist that their religion is any less an integral part of their being than their race or sex. Of course, one could counter that the President always has the option to change his religion. Such a claim does, however, belittle the deepness with which many people hold their religious convictions. Jack Kean, in a personal correspondence, has expressed the opinion that such distinctions "do not hold semantic water in the real world." Despite all this, I find it impossible to equate a challenge to a book because it teaches evolution (and goes against someone's religious beliefs) and one which questions continued use of a book which is an insult and a slander to one's race (e.g. Bannerman's *Little Black Sambo*).

24 Harvard psychiatrist Alvin Poussaint (1976) has stated that "for minority children, books are often an assault which injures them and interferes with their development" (p.2). Poussaint also indicated that: "Cultural racism as expressed in educational materials limits the development of white children and engenders in them the neurotic tendency towards scapegoatism instead of helping them to perceive real courses of action. It also provides them with a false sense of their own self esteem" (p.3).

25 Phyllis Yuill (1976) in an account of the continuing controversy surrounding *Little Black Sambo* recounts the bitter experiences of two black adults who, as school chil-dren, were disgraced and mortified as a result of this book being read in their classes (p.74). Similar evidence was offered by the American Indian Historical Society (1970) before the Senate Committee on Indian Education held in San Francisco on January 4, 1969. The Society stated: "There is not one Indian in this country who does not cringe in anguish and frustration because of . . . textbooks. There is not one Indian child who has not come home in shame and tears after one of those sessions in which he is taught that his people were dirty, animal-like, something less than human."

26 See Minarcini vs. Strongville City School District, Nos. 75–1467–69, 6th cir. This

decision is excerpted in the November 1976 issue of *The Newsletter on Intellectual Freedom* (pp.140, 155–156).

27 See Mann (1975) for an important discussion of the notion that curricula can be fruitfully looked at as literary objects. Further discussion of this point is offered by Willis (1975).

28 This is, of course, the basis of the CIBC's approach to children's literature and other curriculum materials. Writers such as Kelly (1970), MacLeod (1975), and Saul (1976) have also all examined large samples of literature written for children and analyzed the values, norms, predispositions, and beliefs which these works reflect. Elsewhere, Kelly (1974) has spoken of the tendency of literary critics to examine and define literature solely in terms of its inherent power to generate emotional and intellectual responses. Such definition, claims Kelly, "reduce[s] the need to examine the social forces which might otherwise be presumed to shape both the creation and the effect of literature" (p.144). An additional advantage of this presumed autonomy of literary works (e.g. the critic need only consider a work's "literary" values) is its ability to allow the study of literature to "appear to be free from political and ideological influences and of permitting the claim that aesthetic judgements are largely independent of the critic's cultural context." Marxist literary criticism, despite an often ignominious history, seeks a more relational approach to literature, one which tries to grasp literary "forms, styles and meanings as the products of a particular history" (Eagleton, 1976, p.3). Eagleton's brief and lucid account provides an excellent introduction to this tradition.

29 The need to see the content of instructional materials in the context of the larger social structure has been a persistent theme in the work of the CIBC. See for example the chapter entitled "The Mirror and the Matrix" in the CIBC's (1976c) *Human and Anti-Human Values in Children's Books*. Elsewhere CIBC (1976b) has stated: "We want people to view and evaluate racism and sexism, not as isolated phenomena, but as part of and caused by [an] inequitable social and economic system" (p.5).

30 I have, throughout this paper, presented the views of the CIBC in a most favorable light. To a great extent I share and support both their perception of the problems discussed in this paper, and their belief in the need for forthright action. I must, however, admit to a certain discomfort, difficult to define, which I feel towards their approach to literature. I share with Dorothy Broderick (1976) an uneasiness and concern in regards to the CIBC reviewers' insistence that an author must "batter the reader over the head with a message approved by the Council [or] the book is no good" (p.124). This tendency of Council reviewers probably stems from their belief that children's writers should *actively* seek to convey anti-racist, anti-sexist messages in their works.

31 I have already noted the CIBC's reluctance to advocate a policy of overt censorship. Furthermore, given the fact the censorship has historically been a weapon of the dominant groups in society (Gaines, 1970; p.39), advocacy of such a policy would, more than likely, result in the removal of books which depict minorities and women in a more realistic light. The perusal of virtually any issue of the *Newsletter on Intellectual Freedom* will indicate that books by black authors (Malcolm X, Claude Brown, Eldrige Cleaver) are among the titles most frequently listed as "troublesome" and thus subject to challenge.

32 The December 1973 issue of *School Library Journal*, for example, reported that the banning by the Fairfax California School District of the book *Go Ask Alice* resulted in its being sold out in local bookstores.

33 The work of Lucien Goldman (1976) and especially Raymond Williams (1961) are exemplars of work of this sort. A similar approach to cultural analysis is taken in a series of articles, edited by Lazere (1977), in the April 1977 issue of *College English*.

References

Ahrens, N. *Censorship and the teacher of English: A questionnaire survey of a selected sample of secondary school teachers of English*. Ann Arbor: Univ. Microfilms, Inc., 1965.

American Indian Historical Society. *Textbooks and the American Indian*, Rupert Castro (ed.), Indian Historian Press, 1970.

American Library Association. Sexism, racism and other 'isms' in library materials, an interpretation of the Library Bill of Rights. *American Libraries*, April 1973.

American Library Association, Office of Intellectual Freedom. *Intellectual freedom manual*. Chicago: ALA, 1974.

Apple, M. W. Ivan Illich and deschooling society: The politics of slogan systems. In *Social forces and schooling*, Nobuo Shimahara and Adam Scrupski (eds.). New York: David McKay, 1975.

Apple, M. W. Curriculum as ideological selection. *Comparative Education Review*, 1976, 2(2).

Apple, M. W. Power and school knowledge. *The Review of Education*, 1977, 3(1).

Apple, M. W. Ideology and form in curriculum evaluation. In *Qualitative education*. Berkeley: McCutchan, forthcoming.

Apple, M. W., & King, N. What do schools teach? *Curriculum Inquiry*, 1977, 6(4).

Apple, M., & Franklin, B. Curricular history and social control. In *Community participation in education*, Carl Grant (ed.). Boston: Allyn & Bacon, forthcoming.

Asheim, L. E. Not censorship, but selection. *Wilson Library Bulletin*, Sept. 1953, 63–67.

Bach, H. Censorship of library books and textbooks in American schools. *Journal of Secondary Education*, Jan. 1965, 3–12.

Baker, A. The changing image of the black in children's literature. *The Horn Book Magazine*, Feb. 1975.

Beach, R. Issues of censorship & research on effects and response to reading. *Journal of Research and Development in Education*, 1976, 9(3).

Blanshard, P. *The right to read: The battle against censorship*. Boston: Beacon Press, 1955.

Boyer, P. S. *Purity in print: The vice-society movement and book censorship in America*. New York, Scribner, 1968.

Broderick, D. The twelve year old adult reader. *School Library Journal*, May 15, 1965. (a)

Broderick, D. Carping critics, instant experts. *School Library Journal*, Sept. 15, 1965. (b)

Broderick, D. A study in conflicting values. *School Library Journal*, May 15, 1966.

Broderick, D. The conspiracy against youth. *School Library Journal*, January 1970, 30–31.

Broderick, D. Censorship—reevaluated. *School Library Journal*, Nov. 15, 1971, 3816–3818. Also reprinted in *Issues in children's book selection*. New York & London: Bowker, 1973.

Broderick, D. *Image of the black in children's fiction*. New York: Bowker, 1973.

Broderick, D. Racism, sexism, intellectual freedom and youth librarians. *PLA Bulletin*, Nov. 1976.

Burress, L. A., Jr. How censorship affects the schools. *Wisconsin English Journal*, October 1963, 6–28.

Byler, M. G. The image of American Indians projected by non-Indian writers. *School Library Journal*, Feb. 1974.

Conlan, J. B. MACOS: The push for a uniform national curriculum. *Social Education*, Oct. 1975.

CIBC (Council on Interracial Books for Children). Censorship & racism: A dilemma for librarians. *Interracial Books for Children Bulletin*, 1975, 6(3/4).

CIBC. A centennial challenge for A.L.A.: Human or anti-human values in children's books? *Interracial Books for Children Bulletin*, 1976, 7(4). (a)

CIBC. "Asian Americans in Children's Books," *Interracial Books for Children Bulletin*, 1976, 7(243). (b)

CIBC. *Human and anti-human values in children's books*. New York: Racism and Sexism Resource Center for Educators, 1976. (c)

CIBC. *Stereotypes, distortions and omissions in U.S. history textbooks*. New York: Racism and Sexism Resource Center for Educators, 1977.

Dale, R., et al. *Schooling and capitalism, a sociological reader*. London: Routledge & Kegan Paul, 1976.

Darling, R. Censorship—an old story. *Elementary English*, May 1974.

Donelson, K. L. Censorship & Arizona schools: 1966–68. *Arizona English Bulletin*, Feb. 1969, 29–44.

Donelson, K. L. White walls and high windows: Some contemporary censorship problems. *English Journal*, Nov. 1972, 1191–1198.

Donelson, K. L. Censorship and Arizona English teaching: 1971–74. *Arizona English Bulletin*, Feb. 1975, 1–38.

Douma, R. *Book selection policies, book complaint policies and censorship in selected Michigan public schools.* Ann Arbor: University Microfilms, 1973.

Eagleton, T. *Marxism and literary criticism.* Berkeley: University of California Press, 1976.

Egerton, J. The battle of the books. *The Progressive*, June 1975.

Farrell, D. CSD Intellectual Freedom Committee statement to the CSD Board, January 21, 1976, *Top of the News*, April 1976.

Feminists on Children's Literature. A feminist look at children's books. In *Issues in Children's Book Selection.* N.Y. & London: Bowker, 1973. First published in *School Library Journal*, Jan. 1971.

Fenwick, S. I. Re-evaluation 1971, 1972 . . . *The Calendar*, Jan.–April, 1972.

Fiske, M. *Book selection & censorship: A study of school & public libraries in California.* Berkeley & Los Angeles: University of California Press, 1959.

Friedenberg, E. Z. Our class-biased Bill of Rights. *Civil Liberties Review*, Oct./Nov. 1976, 10.

Gaines, E. J. Libraries and the climate of opinion. *Library Trends*, July 1970, 39–46.

Goldman, L. *Cultural creation in modern society.* St. Louis: Telos Press, 1976.

Greene, M. Curriculum & consciousness. In *Curriculum theorizing: The reconceptualists*, William Pinar (ed.). Berkeley, Calif.: McCutchan, 1975.

Harvey, J. Acting for children. In *Issues in children's book selection.* New York & London: Bowker, 1973. First published in *School Library Journal*, Feb. 1973.

Helfand, E. Love and humanity—not intellectual freedom. *Top of the News*, June 1967.

Herbst, L. That's one Good Indian: Unacceptable images in children's novels. *Top of the News*, Jan. 1975, 192–198.

Higgs, M., & Stewig, J. Girls grow up to be mommies: A study of sexism in children's literature. *School Library Journal*, Jan. 1973.

Hirschfelder, A. B. The treatment of Iroquois Indians in selected American history textbooks. *The Indian Historian*, 8(2), Fall 1975.

Humphreys, J. Textbook war in West Virginia. *Dissent*, Spring 1976.

Katz, W. A. Minorities in American history textbooks. *Equal Opportunity Review*, June 1973 (ERICED 085431).

Kean, J. M. Censorship, sexism and racism. *Arizona English Bulletin*, Feb. 1975, 59–63.

Kelly, R. G. Mother was a lady: Strategy & order in selected American children's periodicals, 1865–1890. Dissertation, University of Iowa, 1970. Ann Arbor: University Microfilms.

Kelly, R. G. American children's literature: An historiographical overview. *American Literary Realism*, 1870–1890, Spring 1973, 89–107.

Kelly, R. G. Literature and the historian. *American Quarterly*, May 1974, 141–159.

Killefer, C. Double standard: Intellectual freedom & the post-modern generation. *Top of the News*, June 1969, 392–399.

Klein, N. More realism for children. *Newsletter on Intellectual Freedom*, Sept. 1974, 131–134.

Kliebard, H. Persistent curriculum issues in historical perspective. In *Curriculum theorizing: The reconceptualists*, William Pinar (ed.). Berkeley, Calif.: McCutchan, 1975.

Krug, J. F. Growing pains: Intellectual freedom and the child. *English Journal*, Sept. 1972.

Krug, J. Censorship in school libraries: National overview. *Journal of Research & Development in Education*, 1976, 9(36).

Larrick, N. Divorce, drugs, desertion, the draft: Facing up to the realities in children's literature. *Publishers Weekly*, Feb. 21, 1972, 90–91.

Lazere, D. (ed.). Mass culture, political consciousness & English studies. *College English*, 1977, 38(8).

Lieberman, M. Some day my prince will come: Female acculturation through the fairy tale. *College English*, Dec. 1972.

Luebke, B. F. Textbook censorship: New aspects. *Freedom of Information Center Report*, No. 349, Feb. 1976.

MacLeod, A. S. *A moral tale: Children's fiction and American culture, 1820–1860.* Hamden, Conn: Archon Books, 1975.

Mann, J. S. Curriculum criticism. In *Curriculum theorizing: The reconceptualists*, William Pinar (ed.). Berkeley, Calif.: McCutchan, 1975.

Merritt, L. C. *Book selection and intellectual freedom*. H. W. Wilson Co., 1970.

Moore, R. Toward unbiased textbooks. *Interracial Books for Children Bulletin*, 1977, 8(2).

National Council of Teachers of English. *Censorship & controversy*, Urbana, Ill.: NCTE, 1953.

Nelson, J., & Roberts, G. *The censors and the schools*. Boston: Little, Brown, 1963.

Oliver, L. Women in aprons: The female stereotype in children's readers. *The Elementary School Journal*, Feb. 1974.

Paredes, R. Exclusion and invisibility: Chicano literature not in textbooks. *Arizona English Bulletin*, 1975, 17(2).

Parker, F. National policy & curriculum controversy. *Educational Leadership*, Nov. 1976, 34, 112–117.

Poussaint, A. Responding to racism and sexism: New challenge to old assumptions. *Interracial Books for Children Bulletin*, 1976, 7(1).

Saul, W. The making of a hero: Ideology in the school sports stories of Ralph Henry Barbour. Unpublished paper, University of Wisconsin, Madison, 1976.

Schauer, F. School books, lesson plans, and the constitution. *West Virginia Law Review*, 1976, 78(3).

Schwartz, A. "Sounder": A black or a white tale. *Interracial Books for Children Bulletin*, 1970, 3(1).

Schwartz, A. "The Cay": Racism rewarded. *Interracial Books for Children Bulletin*, 1971, 3(4).

Schwartz, A. Censorship and racism: In pursuit of a relationship. *Arizona English Bulletin*, Feb. 1975, 120–124.

Simms, R. L. Bias in textbooks: Not yet corrected. *Phi Delta Kappan*, Nov. 1975.

Stein, R. Confronting censorship in the elementary school. *Journal of Research and Development in Education*, 1976, 9(3).

Stewig, J. W., & Knipfel, M. L. Sexism in picture books: What progress? *The Elementary School Journal*, Dec. 1975.

Swanson, C. The treatment of the American Indian in high school history texts. *The Indian Historian*, Spring 1977.

Tate, B. Racism & distortions pervade *The Slave Dance*. *Interracial Books for Children Bulletin*, Fall 1974.

Thompson, F. Textbooks and racial pressure groups. *Freedom of Information Center Report No. 195*, Feb. 1968.

Trecker, J. L. Women in U.S. history high school textbooks. *Social Education*, March 1971.

Trillin, C. U.S. journal: Kanawha County, West Virginia. *The New Yorker*, Sept. 30, 1974.

Troy, A. The Indians in adolescent novels. *The Indian Historian*, 1975, 8(4).

Weitzman, L., Eifler, D., Hokada, E., & Ross, C. Sex-role socialization in picture books for preschool children. *American Journal of Sociology*, May 1972, 125–150.

Welch, J. Cultural revolution in Appalachia. *The Educational Forum*, Feb. 1977.

White, M. L. Censorship—threat over children's books. *The Elementary School Journal*, Oct. 1974.

Williams, R. *The long revolution*. London: Chatto and Windus, 1961.

Willis, G. H. Curriculum criticism and literary criticism. *Journal of Curriculum Studies*, May 1975.

Women on Words and Images. *Dick & Jane as victims: Sex stereotyping in children's readers*. Princeton, N.J., 1972.

Woodworth, M. L. *Intellectual freedom, the young adult, & schools: A Wisconsin study*. Madison: University of Wisconsin–Extension, 1976.

Young, M. F. D. (ed.). *Knowledge & control: New directions for the sociology of education*. London: Collier-Macmillan, 1971.

Yuill, P. Little Black Sambo: The continuing controversy. *School Library Journal*, 1976, 22(7).

CHAPTER 16

THE MULTICULTURAL EVALUATION OF SOME SECOND AND THIRD GRADE TEXTBOOK READERS—A SURVEY ANALYSIS (1981)

Carl A. Grant and Gloria W. Grant

Introduction

Concern over the limited and biased portrayal of minorities in textbooks was documented as early as 1935 by the Conference on Education and Race Relations. Members of this Conference believed that these portrayals of minorities in textbooks were contributing to racial antagonism in the United States.[1] Over the years other individuals and organizations took up the banner of protest. However, it was not until the Civil Rights protests of the 1960s that publishers seriously heeded requests to improve the portrayal of minorities in textbooks.

By the mid-sixties, minorities began to appear more frequently in textbooks; however, the books were still biased and minority group members were still stereotyped. We can best understand these biased and stereotyped portrayals by examining the areas in which they occur. Three such areas are the *diversity* (i.e., ethnic group representation) of characters, the *settings* (i.e., time, location, socio-economic class) in which characters appear, and their *involvement* (i.e., roles and the extent of their roles) in the stories.

The *diversity* of minority groups in the illustrations and content of textbooks prior to the early sixties could be best described as limited or non-existent. White characters dominated both the content and illustrations.[2] By the mid-sixties, publishers began to integrate their books with more minority characters. In other words, while the earlier textbooks, especially reading textbooks, had never shown minority children running with Spot, playing with Dick and Jane, or petting pretty Puff, by the mid-sixties textbooks began to feature minority children in similar roles.

The *setting* of stories in which minority group members were featured also had similar limitations. For example, Fisher[3] noted that most American Indians are "treated only in the past," and Kane[4] stated that the historical references to Indians have improved, but a portrayal of American Indians in contemporary society is still either missing or inaccurate. O'Donnell[5] reported that too many of the integrated books are still being dominated by stories of middle socioeconomic class children.

Similarly, analyses of textbooks printed between 1964 and 1975[6] revealed that the *involvement* of minorities in textbooks was also severely limited. In integrated stories, minorities were rarely portrayed as decision makers or in positions of authority, but instead were often shown in stereotyped occupations or activities (e.g., Chinese as workers in laundries; Blacks as athletes or musicians). Minorities appeared frequently in illustrations but were given very few, if any, lines of dialogue in the story content. Furthermore, these textbooks sometimes contained inaccurate or incomplete information about minorities.

While more recent research has revealed some change in the portrayal of minorities in textbooks, the change has not been that extensive, particularly as it relates to the proportions of characters and perspectives that are presented. In other words, the greater visibility of minorities in today's texts does not, in any way, approach the proportion of minorities present in our pluralistic society. Likewise, the perspectives of minorities in today's texts are severely limited.[7]

Although the blatant racism which appeared in the textbooks of the sixties and early seventies no longer exists, the changes which have occurred have not been consistent across all minority groups. For example, Blacks appear more frequently and have more significant roles in stories than other minority groups.[8] In addition, the portrayal of Native Americans in textbooks, according to Kirkness,[9] is still prejudiced, "but in a more subtle manner." In an attempt to produce textbooks that are more integrated, some publishers are adding minority characters in the illustrations; however, they are still giving these characters few if any lines of dialogue in the content. Thus, although books have greater diversity in the illustrations, the roles of minority group characters and the extent of their roles in the content are still minimal or non-existent. Token efforts of this kind really emphasize the need for teachers to analyze their books carefully and systemically. Too often, teachers assume that a book is not biased because minority faces are in the illustrations. Teachers need to look beyond these illustrations to investigate the extent and way in which minorities are portrayed in stories. For example, teachers need to note whether minorities have something to say in the content of the story. Also, it is important that teachers check their evaluations of textbooks with other colleagues, especially minority group members. Frequently, bias will not be recognized by a teacher because he/she does not have the appropriate background or knowledge necessary for making such determinations. Because all individuals have their own perceptions stemming from their own racial background and experiences, these perceptions should always be checked with others for bias.

Purpose of the study

The purpose of this study was to analyze three aspects of minority representation—diversity, settings, and involvement—in selected textbooks. More specifically, the study was to determine from each of the texts the following information: (1) the proportion of Multicultural, All-Majority and All-Minority stories (Diversity scores); (2) the proportion of Contemporary, Historical and Fantasy stories (Setting/time scores); (3) the proportion of Urban Rural and Suburban stories (Setting/location scores); (4) the proportion of Lower, Middle and Upper socioeconomic status content stories (Setting/socioeconomic status scores); (5) the proportion of ethnic characters participating directly or indirectly in the stories (Involvement scores); (6) the correlation of Involvement scores among the different ethnic characters and across all groups. The hypotheses for this study were as follows:

1   No significant differences in Diversity scores exist: 1.1 across all groups, between All-Majority and Multicultural and between All-Majority and All-Minority stories; 1.2 between groups (Urban Majority and Urban

Minority, Rural Majority and Rural Minority, Urban and Rural) in each of the Multicultural, All-Majority and All-Minority stories.

2 No significant differences exist between the means of Urban Majority and Urban Minority, Rural Majority and Rural Minority, and between Urban and Rural in *Setting/time* scores.

3 No significant differences exist between the means of Urban Majority and Urban Minority, Rural Majority and Rural Minority, and between Urban and Rural in *Setting/location* scores.

4 No significant differences exist between the means of Urban Majority and Urban Minority, Rural Majority and Rural Minority, and between Urban and Rural in *Setting/socioeconomic status* scores.

5 No significant differences exist between the means of Urban Majority and Urban Minority, Rural Majority and Rural Minority, and between Urban and Rural in *Involvement* scores (across all nine categories) among the different racial characters.

6 No significant differences exist between the means of the Majority group and Blacks and between the Majority group and Asians, Hispanics and Native Americans in *Involvement* scores (across the nine categories) among the four sample groups.

7 No significant correlations of *Involvement* scores (all categories) exist among the racial characters found in the books across all groups.

Method
Textbook sample

From a list of ten of the most widely used reading textbooks in the country, three were selected at random for the purposes of this study. This list was obtained by telephone interviews with State departments of education that had state textbook adoption and selection procedures.

Subject sample

From the population of the Wisconsin Education Association membership (excluding the cities of Madison and Milwaukee), a total of 57 elementary school educators (42 women, 15 men) were randomly selected to serve as textbook evaluators and thus constituted the subject sample. The sample was composed of the following groups: 15 white teachers (9 female and 6 male) and 15 minority teachers (11 female and 4 male from Asian American, Black American, Hispanic American, and Native American racial groups) *who worked in cities* with populations of around 45,000 people. It also included 15 white teachers (12 female and 3 male) and 12 minority teachers (10 female and 2 male from Asian American, Black American, Hispanic American, and Native American groups) *who worked in rural areas* with a population of around 3,000 people. The average number of years of teaching experience of the subjects was six (6). The average age was 32 years. For the purpose of this study, the racial backgrounds of the majority group and the minority group teachers as well as teaching location (Urban/Rural) were considered as the relevant independent variables.

Instrument

The Multicultural Textbook Survey Evaluation Instrument (MCTSEI) was developed by the authors to evaluate the multicultural content of elementary reading textbooks currently used in the public schools. The MCTSEI is composed of a total of 21 items, divided into 3 scales: diversity (3 items), setting (9 items), and involvement (9 items). Each scale provides separate scores on different aspects of the illustrations and content of stories found in the reading books sampled. *Diversity* scores give information about the range and variety of the different types of characters included in the stories. *Setting* scores provide information about time and location of the stories as well as the socioeconomic status of the characters. *Involvement* scores indicate the types of roles played by and the degree of participation of the characters in the stories. Scores in the three scales were computed by obtaining relative frequencies (proportions) for each of the instrument items.

Utilization of the Survey Instrument: The instrument, accompanied by a set of instructions and a copy of the book to be evaluated, was sent by mail to each of the teacher evaluators. The teacher evaluators were asked to evaluate the book by following the directions on the instrument. Although books were randomly assigned to teacher evaluators, approximately the same proportion of teachers within each of the four sample groups for each of the three books was maintained. Upon completion of the evaluation, the teachers were to mail the finished instrument and book back to the researchers.

Results

Most of the stories, (57.32 percent) in the readers were all-majority stories, 29.69 percent of the stories were multicultural, and 11.61 percent were all-minority stories.

Hypothesis 1.1: To test the hypothesis of no significant mean differences between All-Majority and Multicultural and between All-Majority and All-Minority categories, across all teacher evaluators, t tests with corrected a were performed on the log transformed data.[10] Two comparisons were significant: t $(56) = 4.4894$, p < $a/k = .05/2 \simeq .025$ between All-Majority and Multicultural stories, and t $(56) = 5.2239$, p < $a/k = .05/2 \simeq .025$ between All-Majority and All-Minority stories. These significant results show that most of the stories found in the books are related only to Majority group characters.

Hypothesis 1.2: Planned comparisons were performed using ONEWAY[11] for each of the three categories to test the hypothesis of nonsignificant mean differences of Diversity scores between the teacher evaluators (Urban Majority and Urban Minority, Rural Majority and Rural Minority, Urban and Rural), using again the log transformed data. None of the comparisons among the teacher evaluators was significant at the .05 level. This indicates that the teacher evaluators have a general consensus in terms of the proportion of stories found in the books under those categories.

Results on setting

The mean and standard deviations of raw scores on Setting are provided in Table 16.1. Contemporary stories appear to have the highest frequency, while Upper-Socioeconomic status stories have the lowest.

Table 16.1 Means and standard deviations for Setting scores (percentages)

Categories	Teacher Evaluators[a]				
	UMA	UMI	RMA	RMI	ALL
TIME					
Contemporary	68.15	62.15	65.10	69.22	66.17
	(16.56)[b]	(25.95)	(18.51)	(12.24)	(18.50)
Historical	15.99	14.68	8.83	7.78	11.94
	(13.84)	(12.14)	(4.83)	(3.95)	(10.19)
Fantasy	19.13	29.09	27.46	21.07	24.53
	(9.11)	(23.36)	(19.57)	(6.61)	(16.89)
LOCATION					
Urban	22.96	28.72	26.18	32.75	27.50
	(11.92)	(24.53)	(7.89)	(18.96)	(16.57)
Rural	33.75	30.48	37.89	35.96	34.87
	(13.94)	(13.76)	(8.04)	(14.73)	(12.59)
Suburban	23.83	41.57	26.98	16.70	28.89
	(7.53)	(22.28)	(21.65)	(7.13)	(19.54)
SOCIOECONOMIC STATUS					
Lower SES	19.08	11.81	16.47	21.20	16.83
	(12.09)	(7.56)	(10.07)	(15.89)	(11.58)
Middle SES	48.09	43.85	59.77	55.58	52.05
	(24.88)	(20.49)	(21.51)	(22.67)	(22.67)
Upper SES	7.65	21.50	11.41	4.75	14.03
	(2.41)	(13.77)	(10.76)	(1.06)	(12.03)

[a] = UMA—urban majority (14 subjects)
  UMI—urban majority (15 subjects)
  RMA—rural majority (15 subjects)
  RMI—rural minority (12 subjects)
  ALL—all groups (56 subjects)
[b] = standard deviations (unbiased)

Hypotheses 2, 3, and 4: The hypotheses of no significant mean differences in Time, Location and Socioeconomic Status of the stories among groups of teacher evaluators—specifically the contrasts between Urban Majority and Urban Minority, Rural Majority and Rural Minority, and between Urban and Rural—were tested using planned mean comparisons on the log transformed data for each of the categories utilizing ONEWAY. Among all nine categories, the contrasts between Urban Majority and Urban Minority for both the Suburban setting and the Upper-Socioeconomic Status were significant: $F(1,50) = 4.97$, $p < .05$ and $F(1,50) = 3.57$, $p < .05$.[12] These significant F tests suggest that the Urban Majority and Urban Minority teacher evaluators disagreed when determining whether the stories found in the books depicted a Suburban background or whether the stories denoted Upper-Socioeconomic Status.

Results on involvement

For each group of teacher evaluators, a 6×9 matrix (6 ethnic character types, 9 categories) of Involvement scores was constructed. Table 16.2 shows the matrix for all groups of teacher evaluators (pooled). From the data, it can be observed that for almost all nine categories (the exception being group scene characters) Majority group characters showed the highest proportions, followed in order by the Black-Americans, Hispanic-Americans, Asian-Americans, Native-Americans, and other minority characters. Whenever a White-American was the principal character, the proportion of dialogue in lines was much higher (67.19%) than when a Black-American was the principal character (27.61%).

Across all categories, it is clear that the Involvement percentage scores of the White-American characters were the highest (54.07%), followed by the Black-American characters (36.22%), while the other minority group characters showed very low percentage scores (a combined total of about 8.12%).

Hypothesis 5: To test the hypothesis of no significant mean difference in involvement scores among the four groups of teacher evaluators, planned comparison tests were performed using the log transformed data for each of the types of racial group characters.[13] Among the six racial group characters and across all six categories, only the Hispanic-American showed some significant mean differences for the contrast between Urban Majority and Urban Minority, $F (1,53) = 4.53$, $p < .05$ (means of 1.71% and 6.59%, respectively), and the contrast between Urban and Rural, $F (1,53) = 4.91$, $p < .05$ (means of 4.15% and 2.63%, respectively). This suggests that there are differences in the number of Hispanic-American characters found in the books between the Urban Majority and the Urban Minority teacher evaluators, as well as between the pooled Urban and pooled Rural groups.

Hypothesis 6: To test the hypothesis of no significant mean differences within and across the groups of teacher evaluators, between Majority group and Blacks, and between Blacks and other minority group characters, including Asians, Hispanics and Native Americans, t tests were computed using a corrected alpha for non-independence of the two comparisons on the log transformed data. The two comparisons were significant within each of the sample groups of teacher evaluators as well as in the pooled total.

These results clearly indicate that within sample groups of teacher evaluators, as well as in the total sample, majority group characters always show the highest frequency or proportion of Involvement in the books used for this survey; Black American characters show the second highest frequency but significantly lower involvement than that of the majority group characters. When all the other minority characters (Asian, Hispanic, Native-American) are pooled together and compared with the Black characters, the involvement frequency of Black characters is significantly higher.

Hypothesis 7: To test the hypothesis of no significant correlation of involvement scores (all categories) among the racial characters, across all teacher evaluators, a correlation matrix was computed utilizing DSTAT2[14] groups.

The moderately high positive and significantly different from zero correlations found are those between Asians and Native Americans (.54), between Majority and Blacks (.41), and between Hispanics and Native Americans (.30)—indicating the tendency for characters of these ethnic groups to appear simultaneously in the same story. Moderately negative and significantly different from zero correlations were found between Hispanics and Blacks (−.40) and between majority group and

Table 16.2 Means and standard deviations for Involvement scores (all teacher evaluators, N-57)

Categories	Ethnic Characters[a]					
	AS	BL	NA	HI	OM	WH
Total Characters	3.68	42.33	1.72	3.96	.57	47.55
	(4.97)[b]	(7.34)	(2.83)	(6.30)	(2.35)	(3.42)
Group Scene Characters	4.32	60.44	5.40	3.73	.80	19.63
	(8.18)	(27.09)	(8.78)	(9.09)	(3.81)	(18.19)
Adult Characters	1.12	35.50	1.69	2.41	.71	57.14
	(3.22)	(13.41)	(2.92)	(4.86)	(2.65)	(9.55)
Principal Character	1.20	29.76	.55	3.53	.19	62.89
	(3.50)	(8.32)	(2.36)	(7.83)	(1.47)	(10.51)
Decision Making Character	2.18	28.04	.69	4.36	.00	62.30
	(5.68)	(14.40)	(2.96)	(9.37)	(.00)	(15.96)
Principal Character Dialogue	1.37	27.61	.27	4.13	.05	67.19
	(6.66)	(11.54)	(1.46)	(10.12)	(.39)	(13.09)
Other Character Dialogue	4.70	34.17	.43	2.82	.46	56.22
	(5.83)	(8.07)	(2.41)	(5.84)	(2.11)	(7.84)
Non-Principal Character Decision Maker	3.02	25.76	.68	2.53	.18	65.30
	(6.13)	(15.75)	(3.99)	(7.99)	(.93)	(19.52)
Total Characters Dialogue	2.92	42.34	1.58	4.74	.00	48.42
	(4.01)	(6.12)	(2.34)	(7.03)	(.00)	(2.35)
GRAND MEAN	2.72	36.22	1.45	3.58	.37	54.07
MEAN OF STANDARD DEVIATIONS	(5.35)	(12.45)	(3.33)	(7.60)	(1.52)	(11.16)

[a] = AS—Asian
BL—Black
NA—Native American
HI—Hispanic
OM—Other Minorities
WH—White
[b] = standard deviations

Hispanics (–.31), suggesting a reverse trend to that of the previously discussed ethnic group. In general, the same pattern of correlations was observed within each of the groups of teacher evaluators.

Summary of results

After analyzing the data obtained through the Multicultural Survey Evaluation Instrument, we found that across all teacher evaluator groups more than half the stories in the books were about All-Majority group characters (57.32%), while only about one-third (29.69%) had characters from more than one cultural group, and just 11.63 percent were about All-Minority characters. Statistical comparisons of these differences were significant. The null hypothesis of no significant differences among the teacher evaluators in the obtained proportions of Multicultural, All-Majority and All-Minority stories was not rejected, thus indicating considerable agreement.

For story settings, the analysis revealed three trends. First, across all teacher evaluator groups, the Time setting of most stories was Contemporary (66.17%), while Historical and Fantasy stories were relatively less frequent (11.99% and 24.53%, respectively). Second, across all teacher evaluator groups, the Location of the stories was fairly evenly distributed among urban (27.50%), rural (34.87%), and suburban (28.89%) settings. Third, across all teacher evaluator groups, the socioeconomic status of the stories was in many cases Middle SES (52.05%), while the Lower and the Upper SES were evident in smaller proportions (16.83% and 14.03%, respectively). The hypotheses of no significant mean differences in the proportion of Time and Socioeconomic Status stories among the four groups were not rejected. However, the hypothesis of no significant mean differences in the proportion of Location of the stories among the groups was rejected, revealing disagreement in identifying Suburban Setting stories between the Urban Majority (23.83%) and the Urban Minority (41.57%).

An examination of the data about the involvement of characters showed that the majority group characters had the highest proportion of involvement in the stories across all groups of teacher evaluators (an overall average of 54.07%). This group was followed by Blacks (36.22%), Hispanics (3.58%), Asians (2.72%), Native Americans (1.45%), and other minorities (.37%). The hypothesis of no significant mean differences among the groups in the proportion of racial characters found in the stories was rejected for the Hispanics only, where discrepancies were found between the Urban Majority and the Urban Minority and between the pooled Urban and Rural. The null hypothesis of no significant mean differences within and across groups, between Majority group and Blacks, and between Blacks and other minority group characters, including Asians, Hispanics, Native Americans, was rejected—indicating that the Majority group characters appear with the highest proportion of Involvement, in the stories and that the combined proportion of Asian, Hispanic, Native American, and other minority character Involvement does not reach the same proportion as that of the Black characters. The hypothesis of no significant correlations of Involvement scores (all categories) among the ethnic characters, across all groups, was rejected for the relationship between Asians and Native Americans, between Majority group and Blacks, and between Hispanics and Native Americans. Instead, the correlation was found to be positive. However, Hispanics and Blacks, the Majority groups and Hispanics, were found to be negatively related.

Conclusions and implications

This study demonstrated that more than one-half of the stories in the three most widely used second grade reading texts were all-majority. Most of these stories depicted the middle class and were set in a contemporary timeframe. The location of the stories was evenly distributed among urban, rural and suburban settings. In the stories white characters most often had the major role, with Black characters taking a distant second. None of the other minority group characters (Asian, Hispanic, and Native American) were as involved in the stories as were the Black characters.

This study has implications for both textbook editors and teachers. Before developing textbooks, editors must devise guidelines that will enable them to produce materials that are racially balanced. They must also have their texts examined using a procedure that will evaluate them carefully for racial biases in illustrations and in story content.

Teachers must look beyond the illustrations into the story content to see if their texts are really racially balanced or just appear to be so. If they are biased, it is imperative that other non-biased materials be used in addition to or in place of those that stereotype certain groups. It is also important that biases found in the materials be discussed with the students in order to help them to learn how to identify and eliminate bias. Finally, since some of the teacher evaluators in the study were not in agreement, this indicates that teachers, when evaluating for bias, should seek the help of individuals who represent different backgrounds from their own.

Notes

1 R. B. Eleazer, "School Books and Racial Antagonism: A Study of Omissions and Inclusions That Make for Misunderstanding," *The High School Journal*, 18 (October 1935), 197–199.
2 See: Committee on the Study of Teaching Materials in Intergroup Relations, *Intergroup Relations in Teaching Materials* (Washington, D. C.: American Council on Education, 1949); L. Marcus, *The Treatment of Minorities in Secondary School Textbooks* (New York: Anti-Defamation League of B'nai B'rith, 1961); O. Klineberg, "Life is Fun in a Smiling, Fair-Skinned World," *The Saturday Review*, February 16, 1963, pp. 75–77; and, Michigan Department of Public Instruction. *The Treatment of Minority Groups in Textbooks* (Lansing: Michigan Department of Public Instruction, 1963).
3 L. Fisher, "All Chiefs, No Indians: What Children's Books Say About American Indians," *Elementary English*, 51 (February 1974), 285.
4 Michael B. Kane, *Minorities in Textbooks: A Study of Their Treatment in Social Studies Texts* (Chicago: Quadrangle Books, 1970).
5 H. O'Donnell, "Cultural Bias: A Many Headed Monster," *Elementary English*, 51 (February 1974), 182.
6 See: American Indian Historical Society, Presentation before the California State Curriculum Commission. August 19, 1965; Kane, *op. cit.*; J. H. Wong, *Chinese-American Identity and Children's Picture Books* (Bethesda, Md.: ERIC Document Reproduction Service, ED067663, 1971); Kay Gurule, "Truthful Textbooks and Mexican Americans," *Integrated Education*, 11 (March 1973), 35–42; O'Donnell, *op. cit.*; and, G. Britton, "Primers for Prejudice," in *The Reading Letter* (Waterford, Ct.: Croft-Nei, June 1975).
7 "School Textbooks: A Social Responsibility," *Interracial Books for Children Bulletin*, 10 (1979), 3–5.
8 Robin A. Butterfield *et al.*, "Multicultural Analysis of a Popular Basal Reading Series in the International Year of the Child," *Journal of Negro Education*, 48 (Summer 1979), 382–389.

9 Verna J. Kirkness, "Prejudice About Indians in Textbooks," *Journal of Reading*, 20 (April 1977), 595–600 (600).

10 A log plus one transformation was performed on the raw data (percentages) to meet the assumptions for the Analysis of Variance, as suggested by William L. Hays, *Statistics* (New York: Holt, Rinehart and Winston, 1973).

11 ONEWAY2: One-way analysis of variance. Stat. Job Series 1712. Madison Area Academic Computer Center (hereafter referred to as MAAC). University of Wisconsin, 1975.

12 There were nine subjects instead of 12 from the Rural Minority group responding to this category.

13 MAAC, 1975.

14 *Descriptive Statistics and Correlations* (1st rev.). Stat. Job Series 1708. MAAC, 1973.

CHAPTER 17

THE BATTLE TO IMPRINT CITIZENS FOR THE 21ST CENTURY (1984)

Gwyneth Britton, Margaret Lumpkin, and Esther Britton

Race and sex bias in basal reading textbooks have been scrutinized by both liberals and conservatives for 15 years. The reason for concern is evident; 85 to 90% of U.S. public school classrooms use reading series as the basis for reading instruction in the first eight grades.

Textbooks are a major influence in shaping attitudes. Subliminally and overtly, they teach attitudes about self, career options, ethnic group, the elderly and society's sex role expectations. Repetitious exposure to reading texts can influence children at an impressionable age. Therefore, it is of utmost importance to be alert to the values being imprinted on today's school children, the citizens of the 21st century. We must not leave this important molding of tomorrow's adults to pressure groups, unexamined assumptions, or publishers whose primary concern may be profits.

While societal forces such as television and parent bias are often cited as sources of prejudices, textbooks' impact has been universally acknowledged. An unpublished manuscript from one publisher states: "Although textbooks compete with the mediating forces of culture and mass media, books still remain the authoritative vehicle for prescribing the knowledge and roles which students are expected to assimilate" (Scott, Foresman, 1972). Black claims that 75% of a student's classwork and 90% of the homework focuses on textbooks (cited in Campbell and Wirtenberg, 1981). Goodlad (1974) observed, "With each advance in grade level, dependence on the textbook increases."

The central role of texts in perpetuating bias is enhanced by inflation and the back-to-basics trend. To economize, publishers purchase older, less expensive stories. Many were copyrighted prior to the civil rights advances of the 1970s and reflect practices that are today unacceptable or illegal. When reductions are made in school budgets, textbooks are used longer. Resources for current supplementary materials are invariably reduced.

Budgetary decreases also result in larger classes. When teacher-pupil ratios increase, the overburdened teacher will rely even more heavily on the textbooks and workbooks. Finally, the back-to-basics trend encourages greater use of textbooks and workbooks.

These three factors—budget constraints for supplementary materials, increasing class size, and the back-to-basics trend—further emphasize the central role of textbooks in the early 1980s. The enlarged role of textbooks has not gone unnoticed by those outside publishing and education.

Textbook control is a goal for the New Right. "The New Right's educational policies promote white supremacy, male domination, religious ethnocentrism, and knee-jerk patriotism" (Pincus, 1983). It seems that the Moral Majority and New Right textbook analysts such as Mel and Norma Gabler propose to censor texts and narrow their focus to promote only Christian and "American" concepts. A recent Proclamation of the Texas State Board of Education is an example: "Textbook content shall promote citizenship and the understanding of the free enterprise system, emphasize patriotism and respect for recognized authority. Textbook content shall not encourage life styles deviating from generally accepted standards of society" ("Showdown in Texas," 1982).

Schlafly (1983) claims that the role of the fulltime stay-at-home mother has been removed from texts. Other New Right critics are creating their own censorship group: Censors of the Left. According to Pincus (1983), critics such as Edward P. Jenkinson, Chair of the National Council of Teachers of English, spend considerable time criticizing feminist and antiracist groups such as the Council on Interracial Books for Children, the National Organization for Women, and the National Association for the Advancement of Colored People. On the other hand, the goal of feminist and antiracist groups is to expand the treatment of women and minorities in texts, not to preserve the status quo or narrow life choices to fit the ideals of any one group.

The concerns of diverse groups about the content of textbooks lead one to an inescapable conclusion: There is a widespread belief that texts are capable of influencing the attitudes that children develop.

Let's look at basals

We chose to analyze those textbooks that we feel are most central to the educational process: the reading series used in grades one to nine. More than 11 years have been spent analyzing reading texts published between 1958 and 1982 in an attempt to determine which attitudes are being promoted by these texts.

Much of the reported textbook research has been cross-sectional, analyzing only the current editions, rather than longitudinal, which traces the evolution of a reading series through several editions. Although publishers have published no systematic procedure and reporting format for comparing editions, they have still claimed improvements, improvements that remain unverified.

In a 1980 article, Campbell and Wirtenberg outline the myriad studies in this area and conclude that:

> The need for books to be both non-sexist and non-racist has been ignored by researchers. It is a rare book and an even rarer study that deals with both racism and sexism, and the books and research suffer as a consequence.
>
> Research to date indicates that books can make a difference—and that they can be an effective tool in reducing racism and sexism in society. However, existing research is not enough. Educators must update, expand, and most important, disseminate the work that has been done.

Are the acknowledged stereotypes still with us? What about the problems of omission or clustering of certain groups in a single grade level textbook? Does the percentage profile of these series show any change in bias factors? What gains have been made in achieving sex and culture-fair texts, and at what expense? What new directions are evident in reading materials for the 1980s?

We attempt to chronicle the changes in certain key factors in reading textbooks that have been in evidence over a 24-year period. Questions have arisen as to the changes shown in these materials relating to the frequency and quality of major character assignments and career roles (Rupley, Garcia, and Longnion, 1981). Our purpose is to examine objectively the major reading series published from 1958 to 1982, to trace changes in certain bias factors and to report these changes and directions.

The study

A longitudinal study investigating gender and ethnic bias in reading series was begun in 1972 (Britton, 1973). Reading texts were selected on the basis of availability and common use in the U.S. public schools. This analysis included 17,694 stories or chapters taken from 57 reading and literature textbooks published 1958–82.

The bias factors that were quantified included major character and career role assignements by gender and ethnicity. In addition, the 1980–82 reading texts were analyzed for bias about the aged, handicapped persons, and the single parent family.

The reading series were divided into five time zones by publication date so that changes could be compared over time (see Table 17.1).

The standard analysis procedures formulated in 1972 held constant throughout the study. Recording forms were designed and later refined to facilitate the collection of additional data about the elderly, the handicapped, and one-parent families (Britton, 1975a; 1975b).

All of the analyses were completed by one researcher and an assistant who was trained in the procedure and who has participated since 1972. The consistency of the evaluative procedures has been verified periodically, showing uniformity of evaluation between the evaluators.

Data collection procedures included identifying the major characters from each story, defined as either the person(s) around whom the action or plot centered, or the character whose activity was essential to the plot. The major character had the primary dialogue and was usually the decision maker. The major character was assigned to one of the following categories: Male, Female, Male/Female Shown Equally, Other.

If the major character was male, the story was categorized as male. If two or several characters, male and female, were shown equally, the story was placed in the Male/Female Shown Equally category. If an entire race, inanimate object, or abstract concept was featured, the story was placed in the category of Other—for example, when the concept of democracy was the focus of a story without any identifiable major characters. When a particular race of people was featured

Table 17.1 Number of series and stories analyzed

Time period	Number of stories	Number of series
1958–1970	4,102	15
1971–1973	3,793	14
1974–1976	3,926	13
1977–1979	2,901	8
1980–1982	2,972	7*

* Includes Ginn Reading Program, Rainbow 1980 (7–8).

detailing their culture, geographic locale, of important contributions, without identifying specific major characters, the story was placed in the category of Other for ethnic groups. Plays, skill concept chapters, and fact sheet stories were counted as stories. Poetry was not analyzed.

Ethnic evaluations of the textbook stories were reported in categories similar to those identified by the 1970 and 1980 U.S. Bureau of the Census (U.S. Department of Commerce, 1981). The major classifications were Anglo, Black, American Indian, Asian, and Hispanic. "Ethnic origin" was determined on the basis of the researchers' perceptions of the major character's origin. Occasionally, it was difficult to determine the race of an ethnic major character due to the dialogue and the artistic treatment of the illustrations, and the story was listed in Nonidentifiable Ethnic Minority.

Career assignments were recorded by gender and ethnicity for adult men and women. Careers not identified by gender or race were recorded as Neutral. A career was defined as work providing an assumed means of financial support for a person or family. A career was recorded each time it was shown in an illustration or mentioned in the narrative. Titles of each occupation came from the story author. The careers were assigned to the following categories: Anglo Male, Anglo Female, Ethnic Male, Ethnic Female, Neutral. An alphabetical listing was generated for the careers shown in illustrations or mentioned in the story. Each was followed by the frequency count for that occupation.

The research procedures stipulated that whenever possible a career was recorded for major characters and all others mentioned in the narrative or shown by illustration. If the same bus driver or scientist was shown several times, the career role count was recorded as "one." However, if there were seven different bus drivers or scientists in the story, the career of bus driver or scientist was recorded seven times.

When one illustration showed more than 10 people assigned to a career role, a maximum frequency of 10 was recorded. For example, 18 warriors shown in a single illustration would be recorded as "warriors 10." This limit prevented the disproportionate representation of one career by a mention of, for example, "hundreds of soldiers." The procedure was an elective delimiter used infrequently.

When an indefinite group of people was referred to in this story, such as "the guards who were watching the tower," or "the waitresses who were serving breakfast," a count of two was assigned so as to record a plural number for the career assignment. At times the career of an adult could not be identified—for example, a man walking along a street—so none was recorded. Primary level stories included some animals as major characters; they were assigned to gender categories but not to any career roles.

The neutral career category is a new designation appearing in the mid-1970s textbooks and showing an increasing frequency in the 1980s. The neutral career could not be assigned to a gender or ethnic group. For instance, the text might read, "The engineer studied the difficult problem."

We looked at the number of times the adult characters were shown or mentioned in some identifiable, fulltime, income-producing career role. The most frequent career roles were then ranked by gender and race. The quality of career roles (doctor vs. general worker) was compared.

Analyzing 17,694 stories, we accumulated a massive data bank. Since a book had been published on the 1958–77 series, only the major trends and the career roles of 1980–82 will be reported here (Britton and Lumpkin, 1977a; 1977b).

The findings

Table 17.2 summarizes the changes in major character assignments by gender and race from 1958 to 1982. The proportion of major character roles for females of all races has risen from 14% to 20%. The representation of minority women has risen from 2% to 6%.

In the category of Males/Females Shown Equally for all races, the percentage has risen from 9% to 20%. Interestingly, many stories remained essentially the same as in earlier editions with the addition of a female in a male story, or a male changed to a female character. For example, two brothers become brother and sister.

The Other category, which included entire races, inanimate objects such as microscopes, and abstract concepts such as truth or evil, increased from 19% to 25%. The category of Male Major Characters for all races decreased from 58% to 35%. The percentage of stories about ethnic males dropped from 10% to 9%.

An examination of the data reveals interesting changes. The proportion of all women as major characters, including minority women, shows a small but steady percentage increase from 1977–79, with the largest increase (4%) occurring during 1980–82. The percentage ranged from 14% to 20% over 24 years. The Ethnic Female Major Character roles tripled, from 2% to 6%, with the greatest change in the most recent series.

The representation of males, however, shows a different pattern. The percentage of males increased from 58% in 1958–70 to 60% in 1974–76. Industry giants published most of the "culture and gender-fair" guidelines for authors during 1972–75. The proportion of male major characters decreased to 44% in 1977–79, a precipitous decrease of 73%. This was followed by an additional decrease from 44% to 35% in 1980–82, a decrease of 79%. From 1974 to 1982, the

Table 17.2 Major character assignments by gender and race in 57 basal reading series grades 1–9*

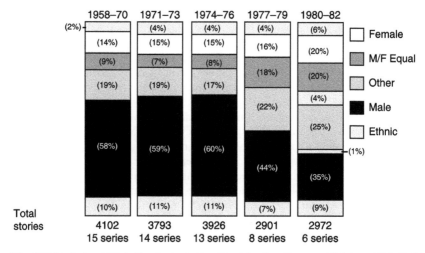

*N = 17,694 stories, 681 textbooks; including Ginn Reading Program, Rainbow 1980 (7–8)

number of male major characters for all races decreased from 60% to 35%. In perspective, however, the ratio of male to female character roles has decreased from 4:1 to 1.75:1.

The major character roles of the ethnic minority males has shown an irregular pattern over the years, moving from 10% to 11% to 7% and finally in 1980–82 to 9%. Ethnic minority females shown as major characters have a pattern of increasing representation: 2%, 4%, 4%, 4%, and in 1980–82, 6%. This 6% figure is a significant increase for ethnic minority. Also, the overall ratio of minority males to minority females has changed from 5:1 in 1958–70 to 1.5:1 in 1980–82.

One of the most provocative findings deals with the role assignments of adult male and female characters in the newest reading series. Future career options for children are represented by the adult characters shown in the several hundred stories read during a student's elementary and middle school years. Children may be absorbing what they are expected to become from these symbolic textbook career models. What models are publishing houses providing as appropriate, well balanced, wide-ranging careers for children?

When looking at the number or frequency of career roles assigned to males and females in six 1980–82 basal reading series, a pattern of vast differences between the sexes and races emerges. The gender and ethnic differences are quite apparent. Table 17.3 shows that of a total of 5,501 careers depicted, 64% or 3,538 careers was assigned to Anglo males, while 14% or 746 were assigned to Anglo females. The Anglo female category excluded the fulltime stay-at-home mother role because the U.S. Census Bureau does not recognize that category. Ethnic males were assigned to 17% or 926 career roles, while ethnic females were assigned to 5% or 291 career roles, again excluding the fulltime stay-at-home mother role.

The Anglo male is shown in 64% of the textbook careers, while the 1981 U.S. Bureau of the Census indicates they are only 51% of the labor force. This 13% overrepresentation is significant. Anglo females, however, are grossly underrepresented in textbook story careers. While the Census states that 36% of the labor force is Anglo women (and growing), reading textbooks show 14% of the women in the labor force. The difference is strikingly unrealistic. Thus, textbooks disregard a major percentage of U.S. working women.

The representation of ethnic minorities in the labor force shows a pattern similar to the Anglos. The Census Bureau shows an ethnic minority male labor force of 6%, while the textbooks show 17%, so ethnic males in careers are overrepresented in the basal stories. The Census Bureau shows ethnic females make up 6% of the labor force, while the textbooks show only 5%, so ethnic minority women are underrepresented by 20% (U.S. Department of Commerce, 1981).

Neutral career roles were about 493 or approximately 8% of the total textbook careers represented; no stay-at-home mothers were included in the textbook labor force comparison table. Since the U.S. Census Bureau does not have either neutral or stay-at-home categories, they were not included in *some* of the comparison tables. If neutral career roles had been assigned equally to both male and female career role categories, it would still not substantially change the relationship between the textbook labor force and the Census data. However, the addition of the stay-at-home mother would change the relationship significantly and cannot be used to compare with the Census data.

The quality of the top five career assignments in the 1980–82 textbooks, by rank order, shows some interesting trends. The decision-making, authoritarian models of soldier, farmer, doctor, police officer, and scientist are

Table 17.3 10 years comparison of the top six ranked careers by frequency of occurrence from 1972–73 and 1980–82 basal readers according to gender and race

From five 1972–73 basal reading series[1] *(1,864 stories)*							
Anglo male		*Ethnic male*		*Anglo female*		*Ethnic female*	
Soldier	75	Warrior	97	Mother	435	Mother	84
Farmer	66	Laborer	21	Teacher	80	Librarian	13
Police officer	62	Hunter	20	Librarian	23	Singer	5
Sailor	61	Fisher	15	Queen	14	Teacher	3
King	54	Pearl diver	13	Nurse	11	Weaver	2
Scientist	40	Musician	13	Maid	11	Chemist	2
						Diver	2
From six 1980–82 basal reading series[2] *(2,843 stories)*							
Anglo male		*Ethnic male*		*Anglo female*		*Ethnic female*	
Soldier	155	Worker	56	Mother	367	Mother	187
Farmer	102	Farmer	39	(full time)		Teacher	23
Doctor	89	Warrior	21	Teacher	78	Slave	19
Police officer	77	Doctor	19	Queen	37	Worker	16
King	76	Indian chief	18	Author	25	Potter	9
Scientist	72	Hunter	15	Princess	17	Artist	9
				Factory	16		
				worker			

[1] Allyn and Bacon Sheldon Reading Series Pacing Edition 1973 (1–6)
Economy Keys to Reading 1972 (1–8)
Ginn Reading 360 1973 (1–8)
Harper and Row Design for Reading 1972 (1–8)
Holt Basic Reading System 1972 (1–6)
[2] Addison-Wesley Reading Program 1982 (1–6)
Ginn Reading Program 1982 (1–6)
Houghton Mifflin Reading Program 1981 (1–8)
Lippincott Basic Reading Series 1981 (1–6)
Macmillan Series r 1980 (1–8)
Scott, Foresman Reading 1981 (1–8)

assigned to Anglo males. Three of the five most frequent career roles for ethnic males are historic: warrior, Indian chief, and hunter. General worker and farmer are the major current career roles for ethnic males in basals.

Anglo females were shown as fulltime stay-at-home mothers about 33% of the time, with teacher and author as two additional high-ranking roles. The number three and five career roles were queen and princess—for American girls, definitely unrealistic, a part of the continuing "Cinderella syndrome."

Ethnic females were assigned to the fulltime stay-at-home mother role 187 times, or 39%. The careers of teacher, slave, general worker, and potter followed in rank order. The career role of slave is a historic, unrealistic role not balanced by futuristic stories. The neutral career roles in the textbook labor force showed a rank order of scientist, teacher, author, reporter and doctor (Table 17.4).

The representation of three special groups was monitored for the 1980–82 reading series: the handicapped, the aged, and the one-parent families (Table 17.4). Of the six widely used reading series containing 2,972 stories, handicapped individuals were shown in 70 stories or 2% of the total. When comparing this

Table 17.4 Representation of handicapped, aged, and one-parent families in six 1980–82 basal reading series (2,843 stories)

	1980–82 Basal reading series	*1980 U.S. Census Bureau*
Handicapped	2% (N = 70)	11%
Aged 55 or older	2% (N = 67)	21%
One-parent families	1% (N = 22)	20%

representation with the 10.5% of handicapped children ages 3–21 reported in the Fifth Annual Report to Congress on the Implementation of U.S. Public Law 94–142, or the 17.2% of the labor force aged 18–44 that are disabled workers as reported in the 1980 Census, handicapped individuals are greatly under-represented (U.S. Department of Education, 1983).

The elderly were shown in 2% (67) of the stories, while they number 21% of the population (9.6% of age 55–64, and 11.3% of age 65 and above).

The most striking underrepresentation is that of the one-parent family. In the textbooks, the one parent family is shown in only 22 out of 2,972 stories, or less than 1%, yet the 1981 Census reported that 20% or one of five children under 18 years live in one-parent households. Moreover, it is predicted that nearly half (48%) of the children born in 1980 will live in a one-parent family at some time before they are 18 years old (Talbott, 1982).

Conclusion

Social agencies, such as government, schools, and media whose functions include the production or distribution of information, are the major sources of socially approved knowledge. If the views embedded in the information distributed by these agencies influence people to accept some values and not others or to express some attitudes and not others, the agencies possess a significant controlling force.

In this case, publishers and editors owe children a complete and realistic view of today's society. They owe all children the right to see themselves at least once every year as a fully functioning person with an array of career choices. They owe every child a positive and realistic picture of the world of work today and tomorrow, not just yesterday. With regard to these minimal demands, how do publishers of basal reading texts measure up?

In the texts studied there is clear evidence that women are being programmed to remain at home fulfilling the fulltime mother role, although economic conditions and personal choice now lead a large percentage of women to work outside the home. In addition, publishers show women and minorities primarily in historic career roles, effectively excluding them both from current realistic career choices.

The handicapped are difficult to locate in the 1980–82 textbook grouping. Given their underrepresentation, how will children who are free from handicaps reconcile this textbook representation to the reality of having 10% of their peers in grades 1–12 in special education programs? More important, how do these children who are handicapped relate to texts, to each other, and to themselves?

In schools today, approximately 20% of the children under 18 years are from one-parent families, yet less than 1% of the stories studied are about one-parent families. Does this place a stigma on that 20%? How will children who cannot find their own family situation reflected in their textbooks respond to these books, to their education, and to their families? Indeed, their self-concept may be diminished as they perceive their omission from the world created by textbooks.

The 1980 U.S. Census Bureau figures show that 21% of U.S. population is over 55 years of age. In the textbooks studied, these older persons appear in only 2% of the stories, shown walking in parks, rocking in chairs, being cranky and scolding young children. They are not achievers, and their contributions (if any are shown) are not respected. How can children have respect for older people and a clear understanding that the process of aging is universal and normal, if that respect and understanding is consistently missing from their textbooks? With a steadily aging population, is it wise to instruct children that the aging process is a misfortune?

There have been some changes in major reading series. The ratio between the sexes has dropped to 1.75 Anglo males to 1 female Anglo major character. The ratio of ethnic males to ethnic female major characters is 1.5:1. The ratio of minority representation as major characters is improving. The figures are almost congruent with the Census data. However, there are still problems with the clustering of stories about a particular ethnic group at one reading grade level. Ideally, the stories should be distributed evenly across all grade levels.

It is clear from these figures that current textbooks do not yet meet the demand that they reflect their society realistically. What can be done? We have asked publishers to expand the roles of the underrepresented Americans, to update the career choices for today, and to use accurate information to project realistic career choices, families, and individuals of the future. The results of the demands of groups such as the National Organization of Women, the Council on Interracial Books for Children, the American Association of University Women, the National Education Association, the American Federation of Teachers, and the American School Boards Association have yet to be met.

Publishers, educators, and parents owe children the right to be taught from textbooks with a full array of career options. Mothers should be portrayed as important, caring people. The elderly should be portrayed as capable and caring citizens. The handicapped should be depicted as successful people who deal with their limitations and whose numbers make up a significant portion of the population. Ethnic groups should be seen as significant contributors to American society, and the one-parent family should be viewed as worthy of a place in texts that show happy cohesive social and family groups.

Maintaining the textbook status quo and ignoring reality leaves the not-so-fair texts to continue their teaching of yesterday's values and careers—and to ignore whole segments of the U.S. The imprinting and shaping of children's minds by textbooks continue. The battle over who will control what is imprinted continues. Tomorrow's attitudes are formed today—from textbooks.

References

Britton, Gwyneth E. "Danger: State Adopted Texts May be Hazardous to Our Future." *The Reading Teacher*, vol. 29 (October 1975a), pp. 52–58.

Britton, Gwyneth E. "Primers for Prejudice." *The Reading Letter*, June 15, 1975b.

Britton, Gwyneth E. "Sex Stereotyping and Career Roles." *Journal of Reading*, vol. 17 (November 1973), pp. 140–48.

Britton, Gwyneth E., and Margaret C. Lumpkin. *Consumers' Guide to Sex, Race, and Career Bias in Public Schools Textbooks*. Corvallis, Ore.: Britton and Associates. 1977a.

Britton, Gwyneth E., and Margaret C. Lumpkin. "For Sale. Subliminal Bias in Textbooks." *The Reading Teacher*, vol. 31 (October 1977b), pp. 40–45.

Campbell, Patricia, and Jeana Wirtenberg. "How Books Influence Children: What the Research Shows." *Bulletin of Interracial Books for Children*, vol. 2 (1980), p. 3.

Campbell, Patricia, and Jeana Wirtenberg. "The Influence of Textbooks." In *Guidelines for Selecting Bias Free Textbooks and Storybooks*. New York, N.Y.: Council on Interracial Books for Children, 1981.

Goodlad, John I. *Looking Behind the Classroom Door*. Worthington, Ohio: Charles A. Jones, 1974.

Pincus, Fred. "Censorship in the Name of Civil Rights: A View from the Left." *Education Week*, vol. 2 (January 1983), p. 20.

Rupley, William H., Jesus Garcia, and Bonnie Longnion. "Sex Roles Portrayed in Reading Materials: Implications for the 1980s." *The Reading Teacher*, vol. 34 (April 1981), pp. 786–91.

Schlafly, Phyllis. "Censorship—Real and Phony." *The Phyllis Schlafly Report*, vol. 16 (February 1983), p. 1.

Scott, Foresman and Co. "Guidelines for Improving the Image of Women in Textbooks." Gienview, Ill.: Scott Foresman, 1972.

"Showdown in Texas, Proclamation of the Texas State Board of Education, 1982." *Time*, August 23, 1982. p. 47.

Talbott, John E. "Dick and Jane Grow Up." *Education Week*. December 8, 1982, p. 181.

U.S. Department of Commerce, Bureau of the Census. "Statistical Abstract of the United States." In *National Data Book and Guide to Sources*. 102nd ed. Washington, D.C.: U.S. Department of Commerce, 1981, p. 3.

U.S. Department of Education. *To Assure the Free Appropriate Public Education of All Handicapped Children*. Fifth Annual Report to Congress on the Implementation of Public Law 94–142. Washington, D.C.: U.S. Department of Education, 1983, pp. 1–4.

PART 3

RE-ENVISIONING THE CURRICULUM

CHAPTER 18

TOWARD A CRITICAL RACE THEORY OF EDUCATION (1995)

Gloria Ladson-Billings and William F. Tate IV

> The presentation of truth in new forms provokes resistance, confounding those committed to accepted measures for determining the quality and validity of statements made and conclusions reached, and making it difficult for them to respond and adjudge what is acceptable.
> —Derrick Bell, *Faces at the Bottom of the Well*

> I am not included within the pale of this glorious anniversary! Your high independence only reveals the immeasurable distance between us. The blessings in which you this day, rejoice, are not enjoyed in common. The rich inheritance of justice, liberty, prosperity and independence bequeathed by your fathers, not by me . . .
> —Frederick Douglass, *My Bondage and My Freedom*

In 1991 social activist and education critic Jonathan Kozol delineated the great inequities that exist between the schooling experiences of white middle-class students and those of poor African-American and Latino students. And, while Kozol's graphic descriptions may prompt some to question how it is possible that we allow these "savage inequalities," this article suggests that these inequalities are a logical and predictable result of a racialized society in which discussions of race and racism continue to be muted and marginalized.[1]

In this article we attempt to theorize race and use it as an analytic tool for understanding school inequity.[2] We begin with a set of propositions about race and property and their intersections. We situate our discussion in an explication of critical race theory and attempt to move beyond the boundaries of the educational research literature to include arguments and new perspectives from law and the social sciences. In doing so, we acknowledge and are indebted to a number of scholars whose work crosses disciplinary boundaries.[3] We conclude by exploring the tensions between our conceptualization of a critical race theory in education and the educational reform movement identified as multicultural education.

Understanding race and property

Our discussion of social inequity in general, and school inequity in particular, is based on three central propositions:[4]

1   Race continues to be a significant factor in determining inequity in the United States.
2   U.S. society is based on property rights.
3   The intersection of race and property creates an analytic tool through which we can understand social (and, consequently, school) inequity.

In this section we expand on these propositions and provide supporting "meta-propositions" to make clear our line of reasoning and relevant application to educational or school settings.

Race as factor in inequity

The first proposition—that race continues to be a significant factor in determining inequity in the United States—is easily documented in the statistical and demographic data. Hacker's look at educational and life chances such as high school dropout rates, suspension rates, and incarceration rates echoes earlier statistics of the Children's Defense Fund.[5] However, in what we now call the postmodern era, some scholars question the usefulness of race as a category.

Omi and Winant argue that popular notions of race as either an ideological construct or an objective condition have epistemological limitations.[6] Thinking of race strictly as an ideological construct denies the reality of a racialized society and its impact on "raced" people in their everyday lives. On the other hand, thinking of race solely as an objective condition denies the problematic aspects of race—how do we decide who fits into which racial classifications? How do we categorize racial mixtures? Indeed, the world of biology has found the concept of race virtually useless. Geneticist Cavalli-Sforza asserts that "human populations are sometimes known as ethnic groups, or 'races.'... They are hard to define in a way that is both rigorous and useful because human beings group themselves in a bewildering array of sets, some of them overlapping, all of them in a state of flux."[7]

Nonetheless, even when the concept of race fails to "make sense," we continue to employ it. According to Nobel Laureate Toni Morrison:

> Race has become metaphorical—a way of referring to and disguising forces, events, classes, and expressions of social decay and economic division far more threatening to the body politic than biological "race" ever was.
>
> Expensively kept, economically unsound, a spurious and useless political asset in election campaigns, racism is as healthy today as it was during the Enlightenment. It seems that is has a utility far beyond economy, beyond the sequestering of classes from one another, and has assumed a metaphorical life so completely embedded in daily discourse that it is perhaps more necessary and more on display than ever before.[8]

Despite the problematic nature of race, we offer as a first meta-proposition that race, unlike gender and class, remains untheorized.[9] Over the past few decades theoretical and epistemological considerations of gender have proliferated.[10] Though the field continues to struggle for legitimacy in academe, interest in and publications about feminist theories abound. At the same time, Marxist and Neo-Marxist formulations about class continue to merit consideration as theoretical models for understanding social inequity.[11] We recognize the importance of both gender- and class-based analyses while at the same time pointing to their short-comings vis-à-vis race. Roediger points out that "the main body of writing by White Marxists in the United States has both 'naturalized' whiteness and oversimplified race."[12]

Omi and Winant have done significant work in providing a sociological explanation of race in the United States. They argue that the paradigms of race have been conflated with notions of ethnicity, class, and nation because

> theories of race—of its meaning, its transformations, the significance of racial events—have never been a top priority in social science. In the U.S., although the "founding fathers" of American sociology . . . were explicitly concerned with the state of domestic race relations, racial theory remained one of the least developed fields of sociological inquiry.[13]

To mount a viable challenge to the dominant paradigm of ethnicity (i.e., we are all ethnic and, consequently, must assimilate and rise socially the same way European Americans have), Omi and Winant offer a racial formation theory that they define as "the sociohistorical process by which racial categories are created, inhabited, transformed and destroyed. . . . [It] is a process of historically situated *projects* in which human bodies and social structures are represented and organized." Further, they link "racial formation to the evolution of hegemony, the way in which society is organized and ruled." Their analysis suggests that "race is a matter of both social structure and cultural representation."[14]

By arguing that race remains untheorized, we are not suggesting that other scholars have not looked carefully at race as a powerful tool for explaining social inequity, but that the intellectual salience of this theorizing has not been systematically employed in the analysis of educational inequality. Thus, like Omi and Winant, we are attempting to uncover or decipher the social-structural and cultural significance of race in education. Our work owes an intellectual debt to both Carter G. Woodson and W. E. B. Du Bois, who, although marginalized by the mainstream academic community, used race as a theoretical lens for assessing social inequity.[15]

Both Woodson and Du Bois presented cogent arguments for considering race as *the* central construct for understanding inequality. In many ways our work is an attempt to build on the foundation laid by these scholars.[16] Briefly, Woodson, as far back as 1916, began to establish the legitimacy of race (and, in particular, African Americans) as a subject of scholarly inquiry.[17] As founder of the Association for the Study of Negro Life and History and editor of its *Journal of Negro History*, Woodson revolutionized the thinking about African Americans from that of pathology and inferiority to a multitextured analysis of the uniqueness of African Americans and their situation in the United States. His most notable publication, *The Miseducation of the Negro*, identified the school's role in structuring inequality and demotivating African-American students:

> The same educational process which inspires and stimulates the oppressor with the thought that he is everything and has accomplished everything worthwhile, depresses and crushes at the same time the spark of genius in the Negro by making him feel that his race does not amount to much and never will measure up to the standards of other peoples.[18]

Du Bois, perhaps better known among mainstream scholars, profoundly impacted the thinking of many identified as "other" by naming a "double consciousness" felt by African Americans. According to Du Bois, the African American "ever feels his two-ness—an American, a Negro; two souls, two thoughts, two unreconciled strivings."[19] In a current biography of Du Bois, Lewis details the intellectual impact of this concept:

> It was a revolutionary concept. It was not just revolutionary; the concept of the divided self was profoundly mystical, for Du Bois invested this double consciousness with a capacity to see incomparably further and deeper. The African-American—seventh son after the Egyptian and Indian, the Greek and Roman, the Teuton and Mongolian—possessed the gift of "second sight in this American world," an intuitive faculty (prelogical, in a sense) enabling him/her to see and say things about American society that possessed a heightened moral validity. Because he dwelt equally in the mind and heart of his oppressor as in his own beset psyche, the African American embraced a vision of the commonweal at its best.[20]

As a prophetic foreshadowing of the centrality of race in U.S. society, Du Bois reminded us that "the problem of the twentieth century is the problem of the color line."[21]

The second meta-proposition that we use to support the proposition that race continues to be significant in explaining inequity in the United States is that class- and gender-based explanations are not powerful enough to explain all of the difference (or variance) in school experience and performance. Although both class and gender can and do intersect race, as stand-alone variables they do not explain all of the educational achievement differences apparent between whites and students of color. Indeed, there is some evidence to suggest that even when we hold constant for class, middle-class African-American students do not achieve at the same level as their white counterparts.[22] Although Oakes reports that "in academic tracking, . . . poor and minority students are most likely to be placed at the lowest levels of the school's sorting system,"[23] we are less clear as to which factor—race or class—is causal. Perhaps the larger question of the impact of race on social class is the more relevant one. Space limitations do not permit us to examine that question.

Issues of gender bias also figure in inequitable schooling.[24] Females receive less attention from teachers, are counseled away from or out of advanced mathematics and science courses, and although they receive better grades than their male counterparts, their grades do not translate into advantages in college admission and/or the work place.[25]

But examination of class and gender, taken alone or together, do not account for the extraordinarily high rates of school dropout, suspension, expulsion, and failure among African-American and Latino males.[26] In the case of suspension, Majors and Billson argue that many African-American males are suspended or expelled from school for what they termed "non-contact violations"—wearing banned items of clothing such as hats and jackets, or wearing these items in an "unauthorized" manner, such as backwards or inside out.[27]

The point we strive to make with this meta-proposition is not that class and gender are insignificant, but rather, as West suggests, that "race matters," and, as Smith insists, "blackness matters in more detailed ways."[28]

The property issue

Our second proposition, that U.S. society is based on property rights, is best explicated by examining legal scholarship and interpretations of rights. To develop this proposition it is important to situate it in the context of critical race theory. Monaghan reports that "critical race legal scholarship developed in the 1970s, in part because minority scholars thought they were being overlooked in critical legal studies, a better-known movement that examines the way law encodes cultural norms."[29] However, Delgado argues that despite the diversity contained within the critical race movement, there are some shared features:

> an assumption that racism is not a series of isolated acts, but is endemic in American life, deeply ingrained legally, culturally, and even psychologically;
>
> a call for a reinterpretation of civil-rights law "in light of its ineffectuality, showing that laws to remedy racial injustices are often undermined before they can fulfill their promise";
>
> a challenge to the "traditional claims of legal neutrality, objectivity, color-blindness, and meritocracy as camouflages for the self-interest of dominant groups in American society";
>
> an insistence on subjectivity and the reformulation of legal doctrine to reflect the perspectives of those who have experienced and been victimized by racism firsthand;
>
> the use of stories or first-person accounts.[30]

In our analysis we add another aspect to this critical paradigm that disentangles democracy and capitalism. Many discussions of democracy conflate it with capitalism despite the fact that it is possible to have a democratic government with an economic system other than capitalism. Discussing the two ideologies as if they were one masks the pernicious effects of capitalism on those who are relegated to its lowest ranks. Traditional civil rights approaches to solving inequality have depended on the "rightness" of democracy while ignoring the structural inequality of capitalism.[31] However, democracy in the U.S. context was built on capitalism.

In the early years of the republic *only* capitalists enjoyed the franchise. Two hundred years later when civil rights leaders of the 1950s and 1960s built their pleas for social justice on an appeal to the civil and human rights, they were ignoring the fact that the society was based on *property rights*.[32] An example from the 1600s underscores the centrality of property in the Americas from the beginning of European settlement:

> When the Pilgrims came to New England they too were coming not to vacant land but to territory inhabited by tribes of Indians. The governor of the Massachusetts Bay Colony, John Winthrop, created the excuse to take Indian land by declaring the area legally a "vacuum." The Indians, he said, had not "subdued" the land, and therefore had only a "natural" right to it, but not a "civil right." A "natural right" did not have legal standing.[33]

Bell examined the events leading up to the Constitution's development and concluded that there exists a tension between property rights and human rights.[34]

This tension was greatly exacerbated by the presence of African peoples as slaves in America. The purpose of the government was to protect the main object of society—property. The slave status of most African Americans (as well as women and children) resulted in their being objectified as property. And, a government constructed to protect the rights of property owners lacked the incentive to secure human rights for the African American.[35]

According to Bell "the concept of individual rights, unconnected to property rights, was totally foreign to these men of property; and thus, despite two decades of civil rights gains, most Blacks remain disadvantaged and deprived because of their race."[36]

The grand narrative of U.S. history is replete with tensions and struggles over property—in its various forms. From the removal of Indians (and later Japanese Americans) from the land, to military conquest of the Mexicans,[37] to the construction of Africans as property,[38] the ability to define, possess, and own property has been a central feature of power in America. We do not suggest that other nations have not fought over and defined themselves by property and landownership.[39] However, the contradiction of a reified symbolic individual juxtaposed to the reality of "real estate" means that emphasis on the centrality of property can be disguised. Thus, we talk about the importance of the individual, individual rights, and civil rights while social benefits accrue largely to property owners.[40]

Property relates to education in explicit and implicit ways. Recurring discussions about property tax relief indicate that more affluent communities (which have higher property values, hence higher tax assessments) resent paying for a public school system whose clientele is largely non-white and poor.[41] In the simplest of equations, those with "better" property are entitled to "better" schools. Kozol illustrates the disparities: "Average expenditures per pupil in the city of New York in 1987 were some $5,500. In the highest spending suburbs of New York (Great Neck or Manhasset, for example, on Long Island) funding levels rose above $11,000, with the highest districts in the state at $15,000."[42]

But the property differences manifest themselves in other ways. For example, curriculum represents a form of "intellectual property."[43] The quality and quantity of the curriculum varies with the "property values" of the school. The use of a critical race story[44] appropriately represents this notion:

The teenage son of one of the authors of this article was preparing to attend high school. A friend had a youngster of similar age who also was preparing to enter high school. The boys excitedly poured over course offerings in their respective schools' catalogues. One boy was planning on attending school in an upper-middle-class white community. The other would be attending school in an urban, largely African-American district. The difference between the course offerings as specified in the catalogues was striking. The boy attending the white, middle-class school had his choice of many foreign languages—Spanish, French, German, Latin, Greek, Italian, Chinese, and Japanese. His mathematics offerings included algebra, geometry, trigonometry, calculus, statistics, general math, and business math. The science department at this school offered biology, chemistry, physics, geology, science in society, biochemistry, and general science. The other boy's curriculum choices were not nearly as broad. His foreign language choices were Spanish and French. His mathematics choices were general math, business math, and algebra (there were no geometry or trig classes offered). His science choices were general science, life science, biology, and physical science. The differences in electives were even more pronounced, with the affluent school offering courses such as Film as Literature, Asian Studies, computer programming, and journalism. Very few elective courses were offered at the African-American school, which had no band, orchestra, or school newspaper.

The availability of "rich" (or enriched) intellectual property delimits what is now called "opportunity to learn"[45]—the presumption that along with providing educational "standards"[46] that detail what students should know and be able to do, they must have the material resources that support their learning. Thus, intellectual property must be undergirded by "real" property, that is, science labs, computers and other state-of-the-art technologies, appropriately certified and prepared teachers. Of course, Kozol demonstrated that schools that serve poor students of color are unlikely to have access to these resources and, consequently, students will have little or no opportunity to learn despite the attempt to mandate educational standards.[47]

Critical race theory and education

With this notion of property rights as a defining feature of the society, we proceed to describe the ways that the features of critical race theory mentioned in the previous section can be applied to our understanding of educational inequity.

Racism as endemic and deeply ingrained in American life

If racism were merely isolated, unrelated, individual acts, we would expect to see at least a few examples of educational excellence and equity together in the nation's public schools. Instead, those places where African Americans do experience educational success tend to be outside of the public schools.[48] While some might argue that poor children, regardless of race, do worse in school, and that the high proportion of African-American poor contributes to their dismal school performance, we argue that the cause of their poverty in conjunction with the condition of their schools and schooling is institutional and structural racism. Thus, when we speak of racism we refer to Wellman's definition of "culturally sanctioned beliefs which, regardless of the intentions involved, defend the advantages Whites have because of the subordinated positions of racial minorities." We must therefore contend with the "problem facing White people [of coming] to grips with the demands made by Blacks and Whites while at the same time *avoiding* the possibility of institutional change and reorganization that might affect them."[49]

A reinterpretation of ineffective civil rights law

In the case of education, the civil rights decision that best exemplifies our position is the landmark *Brown* v. *Board of Education of Topeka, Kansas.* While having the utmost respect for the work of Thurgood Marshall and the National Association for the Advancement of Colored People (NAACP) legal defense team in arguing the *Brown* decision, with forty years of hindsight we recognize some serious shortcomings in that strategy. Today, students of color are more segregated than ever before.[50] Although African Americans represent 12 percent of the national population, they are the majority in twenty-one of the twenty-two largest (urban) school districts.[51] Instead of providing more and better educational opportunities, school desegregation has meant increased white flight along with a loss of African-American teaching and administrative positions.[52] In explaining the double-edge sword of civil rights legislation, Crenshaw argued that

> the civil rights community . . . must come to terms with the fact that antidiscrimination discourse is fundamentally ambiguous and can accommodate conservative as well as liberal views of race and equality. This dilemma suggests that the civil rights constituency cannot afford to view antidiscrimination doctrine as a permanent pronouncement of society's commitment to ending racial subordination. Rather, antidiscrimination law represents an ongoing ideological struggle in which occasional winners harness the moral, coercive, consensual power of law. Nonetheless, the victories it offers can be ephemeral and the risks of engagement substantial.[53]

An example of Crenshaw's point about the ambiguity of civil rights legislation was demonstrated in a high school district in Northern California.[54] Of the five high schools in the district, one was located in a predominantly African-American community. To entice white students to attend that school, the district funded a number of inducements including free camping and skiing trips. While the trips were available to all of the students, they were attended largely by the white students, who already owned the expensive camping and skiing equipment. However, these inducements were not enough to continuously attract white students. As enrollment began to fall, the district decided to close a school. Not surprisingly, the school in the African-American community was closed and all of its students had to be (and continue to be) bused to the four white schools in the district.

Lomotey and Staley's examination of Buffalo's "model" desegregation program revealed that African-American and Latino students continued to be poorly served by the school system. The academic achievement of African-American and Latino students failed to improve while their suspension, expulsion, and dropout rates continued to rise. On the other hand, the desegregation plan provided special magnet programs and extended day care of which whites were able to take advantage. What, then, made Buffalo a model school desegregation program? In short, the benefits that whites derived from school desegregation and their seeming support of the district's desegregation program.[55] Thus, a model desegregation program becomes defined as one that ensures that whites are happy (and do not leave the system altogether) regardless of whether African-American and other students of color achieve or remain.

Challenging claims of neutrality, objectivity, color-blindness, and meritocracy

A theme of "naming one's own reality" or "voice" is entrenched in the work of critical race theorists. Many critical race theorists argue that the form and substance of scholarship are closely connected.[56] These scholars use parables, chronicles, stories, counterstories, poetry, fiction, and revisionist histories to illustrate the false necessity and irony of much of current civil rights doctrine. Delgado suggests that there are at least three reasons for naming one's own reality in legal discourse:

1   Much of reality is socially constructed.
2   Stories provide members of outgroups a vehicle for psychic self-preservation.

3 The exchange of stories from teller to listener can help overcome ethno-centrism and the dysconscious conviction of viewing the world in one way.[57]

The first reason for naming one's own reality is to demonstrate how political and moral analysis is conducted in legal scholarship. Many mainstream legal scholars embrace universalism over particularity.[58] According to Williams, "theoretical legal understanding" is characterized, in Anglo-American jurisprudence, by the acceptance of transcendent, acontextual, universal legal truths or procedures.[59] For instance, some legal scholars might contend that the tort of fraud has always existed and that it is a component belonging to the universal system of right and wrong. This view tends to discount anything that is nontranscendent (historical), or contextual (socially constructed), or nonuniversal (specific) with the unscholarly labels of "emotional," "literary," "personal," or "false."

In contrast, critical race theorists argue that political and moral analysis is situational—"truths only exist for this person in this predicament at this time in history."[60] For the critical race theorist, social reality is constructed by the formulation and the exchange of stories about individual situations.[61] These stories serve as interpretive structures by which we impose order on experience and it on us.[62]

A second reason for the naming-one's-own-reality theme of critical race theory is the psychic preservation of marginalized groups. A factor contributing to the demoralization of marginalized groups is self-condemnation.[63] Members of minority groups internalize the stereotypic images that certain elements of society have constructed in order to maintain their power.[64] Historically, storytelling has been a kind of medicine to heal the wounds of pain caused by racial oppression.[65] The story of one's condition leads to the realization of how one came to be oppressed and subjugated and allows one to stop inflicting mental violence on oneself.

Finally, naming one's own reality with stories can affect the oppressor. Most oppression does not seem like oppression to the perpetrator.[66] Delgado argues that the dominant group justifies its power with stories—stock explanations—that construct reality in ways to maintain their privilege.[67] Thus, oppression is rationalized, causing little self-examination by the oppressor. Stories by people of color can catalyze the necessary cognitive conflict to jar dysconscious racism.

The "voice" component of critical race theory provides a way to communicate the experience and realities of the oppressed, a first step on the road to justice. As we attempt to make linkages between critical race theory and education, we contend that the voice of people of color is required for a complete analysis of the educational system. Delpit argues that one of the tragedies of education is the way in which the dialogue of people of color has been silenced. An example from her conversation with an African-American graduate student illustrates this point:

There comes a moment in every class when we have to discuss "The Black Issue" and what's appropriate education for Black children. I tell you, I'm tired of arguing with those White people, because they won't listen. Well, I don't know if they really don't listen or if they just don't believe you. It seems like if you can't quote Vygotsky or something, then you don't have any validity to speak about your own kids. Anyway, I'm not bothering with it anymore, now I'm just in it for a grade.[68]

A growing number of education scholars of color are raising critical questions about the way that research is being conducted in communities of color.[69] Thus, without authentic voices of people of color (as teachers, parents, administrators, students, and community members) it is doubtful that we can say or know anything useful about education in their communities.

The intersection of race and property

In the previous sections of this article we argued that race is still a significant factor in determining inequity in the United States and that the society is based on property rights rather than on human rights. In this section we discuss the intersection of race and property as a central construct in understanding a critical race theoretical approach to education.

Harris argues that "slavery linked the privilege of Whites to the subordination of Blacks through a legal regime that attempted the conversion of Blacks into objects of property. Similarly, the settlement and seizure of Native American land supported White privilege through a system of property rights in land in which the 'race' of the Native Americans rendered their first possession right invisible and justified conquest." But, more pernicious and long lasting then the victimization of people of color is the construction of whiteness as the ultimate property. "Possession—the act necessary to lay the basis for rights in property—was defined to include only the cultural practices of Whites. This definition laid the foundation for the idea that whiteness—that which Whites alone possess—is valuable and is property."[70]

Because of space constraints, it is not possible to fully explicate Harris's thorough analysis of whiteness as property. However, it is important to delineate what she terms the "property functions of whiteness," which include: (1) rights of disposition; (2) rights to use and enjoyment; (3) reputation and status property; and (4) the absolute right to exclude. How these rights apply to education is germane to our discussion.

Rights of disposition.   Because property rights are described as fully alienable, that is, transferable, it is difficult to see how whiteness can be construed as property.[71] However, alienability of certain property is limited (e.g., entitlements, government licenses, professional degrees or licenses held by one party and financed by the labor of the other in the context of divorce). Thus, whiteness when conferred on certain student performances is alienable.[72] When students are rewarded only for conformity to perceived "white norms" or sanctioned for cultural practices (e.g., dress, speech patterns, unauthorized conceptions of knowledge), white property is being rendered alienable.

Rights to use and enjoyment.   Legally, whites can use and enjoy the privileges of whiteness. As McIntosh has explicitly demonstrated, whiteness allows for specific social, cultural, and economic privileges.[73] Fuller further asserts that whiteness is both performative and pleasurable.[74] In the school setting, whiteness allows for extensive use of school property. Kozol's description of the material differences in two New York City schools can be interpreted as the difference between those who possess the right to use and enjoy what schools can offer and those who do not:

The [white] school serves 825 children in the kindergarten through sixth grade. This is approximately half the student population crowded into [black] P.S. 79, where 1,550 children fill a space intended for 1,000, and a great deal smaller than the 1,300 children packed into the former skating rink.[75]

This right of use and enjoyment is also reflected in the structure of the curriculum, also described by Kozol:

The curriculum [the white school] follows "emphasizes critical thinking, reasoning and logic." The planetarium, for instance, is employed not simply for the study of the universe as it exists. "Children also are designing their own galaxies," the teacher says. . . .

In my [Kozol's] notes: "Six girls, four boys. Nine White, one Chinese. I am glad they have this class. But what about the others? Aren't there ten Black children in the school who could *enjoy* this also?"[76]

Reputation and status property. The concept of reputation as property is regularly demonstrated in legal cases of libel and slander. Thus, to damage someone's reputation is to damage some aspect of his or her personal property. In the case of race, to call a white person "black" is to defame him or her.[77] In the case of schooling, to identify a school or program as nonwhite in any way is to diminish its reputation or status. For example, despite the prestige of foreign language learning, bilingual education as practiced in the United States as a nonwhite form of second language learning has lower status.[78] The term *urban*, the root word of *urbane*, has come to mean black. Thus, urban schools (located in the urbane, sophisticated cities) lack the status and reputation of suburban (white) schools and when urban students move to or are bused to suburban schools, these schools lose their reputation.[79]

The absolute right to exclude. Whiteness is constructed in this society as the absence of the "contaminating" influence of blackness. Thus, "one drop of black blood" constructs one as black, regardless of phenotypic markers.[80] In schooling, the absolute right to exclude was demonstrated initially by denying blacks access to schooling altogether. Later, it was demonstrated by the creation and maintenance of separate schools. More recently it has been demonstrated by white flight and the growing insistence on vouchers, public funding of private schools, and schools of choice.[81] Within schools, absolute right to exclude is demonstrated by resegregation via tracking,[82] the institution of "gifted" programs, honors programs, and advanced placement classes. So complete is this exclusion that black students often come to the university in the role of intruders—who have been granted special permission to be there.

In this section we have attempted to draw parallels between the critical race legal theory notion of whiteness as property and educational inequity. In the final section we relate some of the intellectual/theoretical tensions that exist between critical race theory and multicultural education.

The limits of the multicultural paradigm

Throughout this article we have argued the need for a critical race theoretical perspective to cast a new gaze on the persistent problems of racism in schooling.

We have argued the need for this perspective because of the failure of scholars to theorize race. We have drawn parallels between the way critical race legal scholars understand their position vis-à-vis traditional legal scholarship and the ways critical race theory applied to education offers a way to rethink traditional educational scholarship. We also have referred to the tensions that exist between traditional civil rights legislation and critical race legal theory. In this section we identify a necessary tension between critical race theory in education and what we term the multicultural paradigm.

Multicultural education has been conceptualized as a reform movement designed to effect change in the "school and other educational institutions so that students from diverse racial, ethnic, and other social-class groups will experience educational equality."[83] In more recent years, multicultural education has expanded to include issues of gender, ability, and sexual orientation. Although one could argue for an early history of the "multicultural education movement" as far back as the 1880s when George Washington Williams wrote his history of African Americans, much of the current multicultural education practice seems more appropriately rooted in the intergroup education movement of the 1950s, which was designed to help African Americans and other "unmeltable" ethnics become a part of America's melting pot.[84] Their goals were primarily assimilationist through the reduction of prejudice. However, after the civil rights unrest and growing self-awareness of African Americans in the 1960s, the desire to assimilate was supplanted by the reclamation of an "authentic black personality" that did not rely on the acceptance by or standards of white America. This new vision was evidenced in the academy in the form of first, black studies and later, when other groups made similar liberating moves, ethnic studies.[85]

Current practical demonstrations of multicultural education in schools often reduce it to trivial examples and artifacts of cultures such as eating ethnic or cultural foods, singing songs or dancing, reading folktales, and other less than scholarly pursuits of the fundamentally different conceptions of knowledge or quests for social justice.[86] At the university level, much of the concern over multicultural education has been over curriculum inclusion.[87] However, another level of debate emerged over what became known as "multiculturalism."

Somewhat different from multicultural education in that it does not represent a particular educational reform or scholarly tradition, multiculturalism came to be viewed as a political philosophy of "many cultures" existing together in an atmosphere of respect and tolerance.[88] Thus, outside of the classroom multiculturalism represented the attempt to bring both students and faculty from a variety of cultures into the school (or academy) environment. Today, the term is used interchangeably with the ever-expanding "diversity," a term used to explain all types of "difference"—racial, ethnic, cultural, linguistic, ability, gender, sexual orientation. Thus, popular music, clothes, media, books, and so forth, reflect a growing awareness of diversity and/or multiculturalism. Less often discussed are the growing tensions that exist between and among various groups that gather under the umbrella of multiculturalism—that is, the interests of groups can be competing or their perspectives can be at odds.[89] We assert that the ever-expanding multicultural paradigm follows the traditions of liberalism—allowing a proliferation of difference. Unfortunately, the tensions between and among these differences is rarely interrogated, presuming a "unity of difference"—that is, that all difference is both analogous and equivalent.[90]

To make parallel the analogy between critical race legal theory and traditional civil rights law with that of critical race theory in education and multicultural education we need to restate the point that critical race legal theorists have "doubts about the foundation of moderate/incremental civil rights law."[91] The foundation of civil rights law has been in human rights rather than in property rights. Thus, without disrespect to the pioneers of civil rights law, critical race legal scholars document the ways in which civil rights law is regularly subverted to benefit whites.[92]

We argue that the current multicultural paradigm functions in a manner similar to civil rights law. Instead of creating radically new paradigms that ensure justice, multicultural reforms are routinely "sucked back into the system" and just as traditional civil rights law is based on a foundation of human rights, the current multicultural paradigm is mired in liberal ideology that offers no radical change in the current order.[93] Thus, critical race theory in education, like its antecedent in legal scholarship, is a radical critique of both the status quo and the purported reforms.

We make this observation of the limits of the current multicultural paradigm not to disparage the scholarly efforts and sacrifices of many of its proponents, but to underscore the difficulty (indeed, impossibility) of maintaining the spirit and intent of justice for the oppressed while simultaneously permitting the hegemonic rule of the oppressor.[94] Thus, as critical race theory scholars we unabashedly reject a paradigm that attempts to be everything to everyone and consequently becomes nothing for anyone, allowing the status quo to prevail. Instead, we align our scholarship and activism with the philosophy of Marcus Garvey, who believed that the black man was universally oppressed on racial grounds, and that any program of emancipation would have to be built around the question of race first.[95] In his own words, Garvey speaks to us clearly and unequivocally:

> In a world of wolves one should go armed, and one of the most powerful defensive weapons within the reach of Negroes is the practice of race first in all parts of the world.[96]

Notes

1 Jonathan Kozol, *Savage Inequalities* (New York: Crown Publishers, 1991). For further discussion of our inability to articulate issues of race and racism see Toni Morrison, *Playing in the Dark: Whiteness and the Literary Imagination* (Cambridge: Harvard University Press, 1992); Cornel West, "Learning to Talk of Race," *New York Times Magazine*, August 2, 1992, pp. 24, 26; and Beverly Daniel Tatum, "Talking about Race, Learning about Racism: The Application of Racial Identity Development Theory in the Classroom," *Harvard Educational Review* 62 (1992): 1–24.

2 Throughout this article the term *race* is used to define the polar opposites of "conceptual whiteness" and "conceptual blackness" (Joyce King, "Perceiving Reality in a New Way: Rethinking the Black/white Duality of our Time [Paper presented at the annual meeting of the American Educational Research Association, New Orleans, April 1994]). We do not mean to reserve the sense of "otherness" for African Americans; rather, our discussion attempts to illuminate how discussions of race in the United States positions *everyone* as either "white" or "nonwhite." Thus, despite the use of African-American legal and educational exemplars, we include other groups who have been constructed at various time in their history as nonwhite or black. Readers should note that some of the leading legal scholars in the critical race legal theory movement are of Latino and Asian-American as well as African-American heritage.

3 See, for example, Patricia Hill Collins, *Black Feminist Thought* (New York: Routledge, 1991); Joyce King and Carolyn Mitchell, *Black Mothers to Sons: Juxtaposing African American Literature and Social Practice* (New York: Peter Lang, 1990); and Patricia

Williams, *The Alchemy of Race and Rights: Diary of a Law Professor* (Cambridge: Harvard University Press, 1991).

4 These propositions are not hierarchical. Rather, they can be envisioned as sides of an equilateral triangle, each equal and each central to the construction of the overall theory.

5 Andrew Hacker, *Two Nations: Black and White, Separate, Hostile, Unequal* (New York: Ballantine Books, 1992); and Marian Wright Edelman, *Families in Peril: An Agenda for Social Change* (Cambridge: Harvard University Press, 1987).

6 Michael Omi and Howard Winant, "On the Theoretical Concept of Race," in *Race, Identity and Representation in Education*, ed. C. McCarthy and W. Crichlow (New York: Routledge, 1993), pp. 3–10.

7 Luigi Luca Cavalli-Sforza, "Genes, People and Languages," *Scientific American*, November 1991, p. 104.

8 Morrison, *Playing in the Dark*, p. 63.

9 This assertion was made forcefully by the participants of the Institute NHI (No Humans Involved) at a symposium entitled "The Two Reservations: Western Thought, the Color Line, and the Crisis of the Negro Intellectual Revisited," sponsored by the Department of African and Afro-American Studies at Stanford University, Stanford, Calif., March 3–5, 1994.

10 See, for example, Nancy Chodorow, *The Reproduction of Mothering* (Berkeley: University of California Press, 1978); Simone DeBeauvoir, *The Second Sex* (New York: Bantam Books, 1961); Vivian Gornick, "Women as Outsiders," in *Women in Sexist Society*, ed. V. Gornick and B. Moran (New York: Basic Books, 1971), pp. 70–84; Nancy Hartsock, "Feminist Theory and the Development of Revolutionary Strategy," *Capitalist Patriarch and the Case for Socialist Feminism*, ed. Z. Eisenstein (London and New York: Monthly Review Press, 1979); and Alison Jagger, *Feminist Theory and Human Nature* (Sussex, England: Harvester Press, 1983).

11 See, for example, Samuel Bowles and Herbert Gintis, *Schooling in Capitalist America* (New York: Basic Books, 1976); Martin Carnoy, *Education and Cultural Imperialism* (New York: McKay, 1974); Michael W. Apple, "Redefining Inequality: Authoritarian Populism and the Conservative Restoration," *Teachers College Record* 90 (1988): 167–84; and Philip Wexler, *Social Analysis and Education: After the New Sociology* (New York: Routledge & Kegan Paul, 1987).

12 David Roediger, *The Wages of Whiteness* (London: Verso, 1991), p. 6.

13 Michael Omi and Howard Winant, *Racial Formation in the United States from the 1960s to the 1990s*, 2nd ed. (New York: Routledge, 1994), p. 9.

14 Ibid., p. 56.

15 Carter G. Woodson, *The Miseducation of the Negro* (Washington, D.C.: Association Press, 1933); and W. E. B. Du Bois, *The Souls of Black Folks* (New York: Penguin Books, 1989; first published in 1903).

16 Our decision to focus on Woodson and Du Bois is not intended to diminish the import of the scores of African-American scholars who also emerged during their time such as George E. Haynes, Charles S. Johnson, E. Franklin Frazier, Abram Harris, Sadie T. Alexander, Robert C. Weaver, Rayford Logan, Allison Davis, Dorothy Porter, and Benjamin Quarles. We highlight Woodson and Du Bois as early seminal thinkers about issues of race and racism.

17 See John Hope Franklin, *From Slavery to Freedom*, 6th ed. (New York: Alfred A. Knopf, 1988).

18 Woodson, *The Miseducation of the Negro*, p. xiii.

19 Du Bois, *The Souls of Black Folks*, p. 5. Other people of color, feminists, and gay and lesbian theorists all have appropriated Du Bois's notion of double consciousness to explain their estrangement from mainstream patriarchal, masculinist U.S. culture.

20 David Levering Lewis, *W. E. B. Du Bois: Biography of a Race, 1868–1919* (New York: Henry Holt, 1993), p. 281.

21 Du Bois, *The Souls of Black Folks*, p. 1.

22 See, for example, Lorene Cary, *Black Ice* (New York: Alfred A. Knopf, 1991); and Jeannie Oakes, *Keeping Track: How Schools Structure Inequality* (New Haven: Yale University Press, 1985).

23 Oakes, *Keeping Track*, p. 67.

24 American Association of University Women, *How Schools Shortchange Girls: A Study of Major Findings on Gender and Education* (Washington, D.C.: Author and National Education Association, 1992).

25 Myra Sadker, David Sadker, and Susan Klein, "The Issue of Gender in Elementary and Secondary Education," in *Review of Educational Research in Education, vol. 19*, ed. G. Cerant (Washington, D.C.: American Educational Research Association, 1991), pp. 269–334.

26 Hacker, *Two Nations*, puts the dropout rate for African-American males in some large cities at close to 50 percent.

27 Robert Majors and Janet Billson, *Cool Pose: The Dilemmas of Black Manhood in America* (New York: Lexington Books, 1992).

28 Cornel West, *Race Matters* (Boston: Beacon Press, 1993); and David Lionel Smith, "Let Our People Go," *Black Scholar* 23 (1993): 75–76.

29 Peter Monaghan, " 'Critical Race Theory' Questions the Role of Legal Doctrine in Racial Inequity," *Chronicle of Higher Education*, June 23, 1993, pp. A7, A9.

30 Delgado, cited in Monaghan, "Critical Race Theory." Quotations are from p. A7. For a more detailed explication of the first item in the list, see Bell, *Faces at the Bottom of the Well*.

31 Manning Marable, *How Capitalism Underdeveloped Black America* (Boston: South End Press, 1983).

32 Derrick Bell, *And We Are Not Saved: The Elusive Quest for Racial Justice* (New York: Basic Books, 1987).

33 Howard Zinn, *A Peoples History of the United States* (New York: Harper & Row, 1980), p. 13.

34 Bell, *And We Are Not Saved*.

35 William Tate, Gloria Ladson-Billings, and Carl Grant, "The *Brown* Decision Revisited: Mathematizing Social Problems," *Educational Policy* 7 (1993): 255–75.

36 Bell, *And We Are Not Saved*, p. 239.

37 Ronald Takaki, *A Different Mirror: A History of Multicultural America* (Boston: Little Brown, 1993).

38 Franklin, *From Slavery to Freedom*.

39 Clearly, an analysis of worldwide tensions reinforces the importance of land to a people—Israel and the Palestinians, Iraq and Kuwait, the former Soviet bloc, Hitler and the Third Reich, all represent some of the struggles over land.

40 Even at a time when there is increased public sentiment for reducing the federal deficit, the one source of tax relief that no president or member of Congress would ever consider is that of denying home (property) owners their tax benefits.

41 See, for example, Howard Wainer, "Does Spending Money on Education Help?" *Educational Researcher* 22 (1993): 22–24; or Paul Houston, "School Vouchers: The Latest California Joke," *Phi Delta Kappan* 75 (1993): 61–66.

42 Kozol, *Savage Inequalities*, pp. 83–84.

43 This notion of "intellectual property" came into popular use when television talk show host David Letterman moved from NBC to CBS. NBC claimed that certain routines and jokes used by Letterman were the intellectual property of the network and, as such, could not be used by Letterman without permission.

44 Richard Delgado, "When a Story Is Just a Story: Does Voice Really Matter?" *Virginia Law Review* 76 (1990): 95–111.

45 See, for example, Floraline Stevens, *Opportunity to Learn: Issues of Equity for Poor and Minority Students* (Washington, D.C.: National Center for Education Statistics, 1993); idem, "Applying an Opportunity-to-learn Conceptual Framework to the Investigation of the Effects of Teaching Practices via Secondary Analyses of Multiple-case-study Summary Data," *The Journal of Negro Education* 62 (1993): 232–48; and Linda Winfield and Michael D. Woodard, "Assessment, Equity, Diversity in Reforming America's Schools," *Educational Policy* 8 (1994): 3–27.

46 The standards debate is too long and detailed to be discussed here. For a more detailed discussion of standards see, for example, Michael W. Apple, "Do the Standards Go Far Enough? Power, Policy, and Practices in Mathematics Education," *Journal for Research in Mathematics Education* 23 (1992): 412–31; and National Council of Education Standards and Testing, *Raising Standards for American Education: A Report to*

Congress, the Secretary of Education, the National Goals Panel, and the American People (Washington, D.C.: Government Printing Office, 1992).

47 Kozol, *Savage Inequalities.*

48 Some urban Catholic schools, black independent schools, and historically black colleges and universities have demonstrated the educability of African-American students. As of this writing we have no data on the success of urban districts such as Detroit or Milwaukee that are attempting what is termed "African Centered" or Africentric education. See also Mwalimu J. Shujaa, Ed., *Too Much Schooling. Too Little Education: A Paradox of Black Life in White Societies* (Trenton, N.J.: Africa World Press, 1994).

49 David Wellman, *Portraits of White Racism* (Cambridge, England: Cambridge University Press, 1977). Quotations are from pp. xviii and 42.

50 See, for example, Gary Orfield, "School Desegregation in the 1980s," *Equity and Choice*, February 1988, p. 25; Derrick Bell, "Learning from Our Losses: Is School Desegregation Still Feasible in the 1980s?" *Phi Delta Kappan* 64 (April 1983): 575; Willis D. Hawley, "Why It Is Hard to Believe in Desegregation," *Equity and Choice*, February 1988, pp. 9–15; and Janet Ward Schofield, *Black and White in School: Trust, Tension, or Tolerance?* (New York: Teachers College Press, 1989).

51 James Banks, "Teaching Multicultural Literacy to Teachers," *Teaching Education* 4 (1991): 135–44.

52 See Karl Taeuber, "Desegregation of Public School Districts: Persistence and Change," *Phi Delta Kappan* 72 (1990): 18–24; and H. L. Bisinger, "When Whites Flee," *New York Times Magazine*, May 29, 1994, pp. 26–33, 43, 50, 53–54, 56. On loss of professional positions, see Sabrina King, "The Limited Presence of African American Teachers," *Review of Educational Research* 63 (1993): 115–49; and Jacqueline Irvine, "An Analysis of the Problem of Disappearing Black Educators," *Elementary School Journal* 88 (1988): 503–13.

53 Kimberle Williams Crenshaw, "Race Reform, and Retrenchment: Transformation and Legitimation in Antidiscrimination Law," *Harvard Law Review* 101 (1988): 1331–87.

54 Ibid., p. 1335.

55 Kofi Lomotey and John Statley, "The Education of African Americans in Buffalo Public Schools" (Paper presented at the annual meeting of the American Educational Research Association, Boston, 1990).

56 Richard Delgado, "Storytelling for Oppositionists and Others: A Plea for Narrative," *Michigan Law Review* 87 (1989): 2411–41.

57 See Richard Delgado et al., "Symposium: Legal Storytelling," *Michigan Law Review* 87 (1989): 2073. On dysconsciousness, see Joyce E. King, "Dysconscious Racism: Ideology, Identity and the Miseducation of Teachers," *Journal of Negro Education* 60 (1991): 135. King defines dysconsciousness as "an uncritical habit of mind (including perceptions, attitudes, assumptions, and beliefs) that justifies inequity and exploitation by accepting the existing order of things as given. . . . Dysconscious racism is a form of racism that tacitly accepts dominant White norms and privileges. It is not the *absence* of consciousness (that is, not unconsciousness) but an *impaired* consciousness or distorted way of thinking about race as compared to, for example, critical consciousness."

58 These notions of universalism prevail in much of social science research, including educational research.

59 Williams, *Alchemy of Race and Rights.*

60 Richard Delgado, "Brewer's Plea: Critical Thoughts on Common Cause," *Vanderbilt Law Review* 44 (1991): 11.

61 For example, see Williams, *Alchemy of Race and Rights*; Bell, *Faces at the Bottom of the Well*; and Mari Matsuda, "Public Response to Racist Speech: Considering the Victim's Story," *Michigan Law Review* 87 (1989): 2320–81.

62 Delgado, "Storytelling."

63 Ibid.

64 For example, see Crenshaw, "Race, Reform, and Retrenchment."

65 Delgado, "Storytelling."

66 Charles Lawrence, "The Id, the Ego, and Equal Protection: Reckoning with Unconscious Racism," *Stanford Law Review* 39 (1987): 317–88.

67 Delgado et al., "Symposium."

68 Lisa Delpit, "The Silenced Dialogue: Power and Pedagogy in Educating Other People's Children," *Harvard Educational Review* 58 (1988): 280.

69 At the 1994 annual meeting of the American Educational Research Association in New Orleans, two sessions entitled "Private Lives, Public Voices: Ethics of Research in Communities of Color" were convened to discuss the continued exploitation of people of color. According to one scholar of color, our communities have become "data plantations."

70 Cheryl I. Harris, "Whiteness as Property," *Harvard Law Review* 106 (1993): 1721.

71 See Margaret Radin, "Market-Inalienability," *Harvard Law Review* 100 (1987): 1849–906.

72 See Signithia Fordham and John Ogbu, "Black Student School Success: Coping with the Burden of 'Acting White,' " *The Urban Review* 18 (1986): 1–31.

73 Peggy McIntosh, "White Privilege: Unpacking the Invisible Knapsack," *Independent School*, Winter, 1990, pp. 31–36.

74 Laurie Fuller, "Whiteness as Performance" (Unpublished preliminary examination paper, University of Wisconsin–Madison, 1994).

75 Kozol, *Savage Inequalities*, p. 93.

76 Ibid., p. 96; emphasis added.

77 Harris, "Whiteness as Property," p. 1735.

78 David Spener, "Transitional Bilingual Education and the Socialization of Immigrants," *Harvard Educational Review* 58 (1988): 133–53.

79 H. G. Bissinger, "When Whites Flee," *New York Times Magazine*, May 29, 1994, pp. 26–33, 43, 50, 53–54, 56.

80 Derrick Bell, *Race, Racism, and American Law* (Boston: Little, Brown, 1980).

81 We assert that the current movement toward African-centered (or Africentric) schools is not equivalent to the racial exclusion of vouchers, or choice programs. Indeed, African-centeredness has become a logical response of a community to schools that have been abandoned by whites, have been stripped of material resources, and have demonstrated a lack of commitment to African-American academic achievement.

82 Oakes, *Keeping Track*.

83 James A. Banks, "Multicultural Education: Historical Development, Dimensions, and Practice," in *Review of Research in Education*, vol. 19, ed. L. Darling-Hammond (Washington, D.C.: American Educational Research Association, 1993), p. 3.

84 George Washington Williams, *History of the Negro Race in America from 1619–1880: Negroes as Slaves, as Soldiers, and as Citizens* (2 vols.) (New York: G. P. Putnam & Sons, 1882–1883). On the intergroup education movement, see, for example, L. A. Cook and E. Cook, *Intergroup Education* (New York: McGraw-Hill, 1954); and H. G. Traeger and M. R. Yarrow, *They Learn What They Live: Prejudice in Young Children* (New York: Harper and Brothers, 1952).

85 See, for example, Vincent Harding, *Beyond Chaos: Black History and the Search for a New Land* (Black Paper No. 2) (Atlanta: Institute of the Black World, August 1970): J. Blassingame, ed., *New Perspectives in Black Studies* (Urbana: University of Illinois Press, 1971); James A. Banks, ed., *Teaching Ethnic Studies* (Washington, D.C.: National Council for the Social Studies, 1973); and Geneva Gay, "Ethnic Minority Studies: How Widespread? How Successful?" *Educational Leadership* 29 (1971): 108–12.

86 Banks, "Multicultural Education."

87 In 1988 at Stanford University the inclusion of literature from women and people of color in the Western Civilization core course resulted in a heated debate. The university's faculty senate approved this inclusion in a course called Cultures, Ideas, and Values. The controversy was further heightened when then Secretary of Education William Bennett came to the campus to denounce this decision.

88 In the "Book Notes" section of the *Harvard Educational Review* 64 (1994): 345–47, Jane Davagian Tchaicha reviews Donaldo Macedo's *Literacies of Power* (Boulder: Westview Press, 1994) and includes two quotes, one from noted conservative Patrick Buchanan and another from Macedo on multiculturalism. According to Buchanan, "Our Judeo-Christian values are going to be preserved, and our Western heritage is going to be handed down to future generations, not dumped into some landfill called multiculturalism" (quoted in Tchaicha, p. 345). Macedo asserts that "the real issue

isn't Western culture versus multiculturalism, the fundamental issue is the recognition of humanity in us and in others" (quoted in Tchaicha, p. 347).

89　In New York City, controversy over the inclusion of gay and lesbian issues in the curriculum caused vitriolic debate among racial and ethnic groups who opposed their issues being linked to or compared with homosexuals. Some ethnic group members asserted that homosexuals were not a "culture" while gay and lesbian spokespeople argued that these group members were homophobic.

90　Shirley Torres-Medina, "Issues of Power: Constructing the Meaning of Linguistic Difference in First Grade Classrooms" (Ph.D. diss., University of Wisconsin–Madison, 1994).

91　Richard Delgado, "Enormous Anomaly? Left-Right Parallels in Recent Writing about Race," *Columbia Law Review* 91 (1991): 1547–60.

92　See Bell, *And We Are Not Saved.*

93　See Cameron McCarthy, "After the Canon: Knowledge and Ideological Representation in the Multicultural Discourse on Curriculum Reform," in *Race, Identity and Representation*, ed. C. McCarthy and W. Crichlow (New York: Routledge, 1994), p. 290; and Michael Olneck, "Terms of Inclusion: Has Multiculturalism Redefined Equality in American Education," *American Journal of Education* 101 (1993): 234–60.

94　We are particularly cognizant of the hard-fought battles in the academy waged and won by scholars such as James Banks, Carlos Cortez, Geneva Gay, Carl Grant, and others.

95　Tony Martin, *Race First: The Ideological and Organizational Struggles of Marcus Garvey and the Universal Negro Improvement Association* (Dover, Mass.: The Majority Press, 1976).

96　Marcus Garvey, cited in ibid., p. 22.

CHAPTER 19

HELPING STUDENTS UNDERSTAND AND ACCEPT SEXUAL DIVERSITY (1991)

James T. Sears

Back from summer vacation, Phillip ambled up the red brick steps of Strom Thurmond Junior High School. At the top of the steps stood Edith, a big-boned 9th grader. A group of "redneck brats" stood behind her. Phillip had feared something like this would happen. "The night before I started 7th grade, Edith called me up. She said, 'I hope you know I have a lot of friends. I told them *all* about you. We're going to make your junior high days pure hell.' "

Mary sat in study hall staring out into the unknown. "Are we deciding too fast? Maybe we should just not label ourselves and just experiment. But Connie says 'I don't think we should knock being with a boy until we've tried it.' I like boys—I just don't think about them so much sexually or emotionally. I like Connie. Am I the only one who feels this way?" Mary lays her head down on her unopened math book.

Though Phillip and Mary may feel alone, they are not. There are many Phillips and Marys who experience intimidation and suffer in fearful silence within our nation's schools. In response to their plight, the NEA, the AFT, and ASCD recently passed resolutions calling upon their members and school districts to acknowledge the special needs of students like Phillip and Mary, to provide supportive services to these students, and to adopt anti-harassment guidelines. The in-school counseling program for homosexual-identified youth established by the Los Angeles Unified School District, the Harvey Milk School supported by the New York public school system, and the anti-slur/anti-discrimination policies adopted by school districts in cities such as Cambridge, Des Moines, and Cincinnati exemplify such efforts (Grayson 1989, Rofes 1989, Sears 1987).

Educators, school board members, and parents who have spearheaded these efforts acknowledge the simple social fact that being sexually different in a society of sexual sameness exacts a heavy psychological toll. Struggling to cope with their sexual identity, gay and bisexual students are more likely than other youth to attempt suicide, to abuse drugs or alcohol, and to experience academic problems (Brown 1987, Gibson 1989, Martin and Hetrick 1988; Remafedi 1987, Sears 1989). Of course, gay and bisexual students do not always display these symptoms—in fact, they may excel in schoolwork, extracurricular activities, or sports as a means of hiding their sexual feelings from themselves or others (Sears 1991). When they hide their feelings, however, their emotional and sexual development languishes (Martin 1982).

The diversity of sexuality

Tagging these young people "at risk," providing supportive services, establishing policies and guidelines, and integrating homosexuality into sex education acknowledges sexual differences among people. Splitting the school and society into unequal heterosexual and homosexual categories, however, does not enhance an understanding of sexual diversity within each person.

Being gay or lesbian is a modern-day phenomenon. Just as "homosexual" is a 19th century, enlightened, medical construction, "gay" and "lesbian" are social artifacts popularized in contemporary America (Altman 1982, Greenberg 1988). However, the basic emotional and erotic attraction to members of one's own sex is not a social artifact. As Freud (1964), Bullough (1976), and Kinsey and Associates (1948, 1953) have shown, *human beings are diverse sexual creatures*: Our capacity to relate emotionally and physically to other human beings is not limited to the other gender.

More than 40 years ago, Alfred Kinsey and his associates found that nearly half of the adult population engaged in both heterosexual and homosexual activities—a finding that still troubles many Americans. Kinsey concluded that the world is not divided into sheep and goats; he contended that "patterns of heterosexuality and patterns of homosexuality represent learned behavior which depends, to a considerable degree, upon the mores of the particular culture in which the individual is raised" (Kinsey et al. 1948, p. 660). The construction of sexual identities does not take place within a social vacuum.

On the contrary, scholars such as Kenneth Plummer (1981), Carol Kitzinger (1987), and Michael Foucault (1978) have illustrated that *sexual biographies are integrally related to society*. Society provides the collective cultural history, social scripts, and language that form the foundation for these constructed identities. The personal meanings of our regional, social class, racial, gender, and sexual identities are inextricably woven into a culture in which being upper class or working class, black or white, male or female, homosexual or heterosexual, from the North or the South, have social significance. While the intersections of social class, race, gender, sexuality, and region vary for each person, their existence and importance within our culture are, for those who do not share membership in the dominant groups, social facts with social consequences.

Shaping heterosexual destinies

The culture of the school mirrors the larger society. Schools socialize boys and girls into their presumed heterosexual destiny. From every vantage point, there are couples: couples holding hands as they enter school; couples dissolving into endless wet kisses between school bells; couples exchanging rings with ephemeral vows of devotion and love. Sex, as many a high school student will freely admit, is an integral part of school life. And while educators may be reluctant to integrate this topic into the curriculum, covert sexual instruction comprises a large part of the hidden curriculum at any junior or senior high school: the exchange of lustful looks in the hallway or romantic notes in the classroom, the homoerotic comradery of sports teams, and the sexual energy pulsating in even the most boring of classes.

At any given day in any particular school these feelings span the sexual continuum, yet only those at the heterosexual end are publicly acknowledged and peer approved. When sexuality is formally discussed in health or biology class, heterosexual mechanics are most often presented (leave it to schools to make even the most interesting subject emotionally dry, moralistically rigid, and intellectually sterile). Homosexuality, safer sex practices, abortion ethics, and sources of birth control are the topics least discussed by sex educators (Forrest and Silverman 1989, Sears in press).

In many school districts, developing critical thinking skills is a stated priority, yet few districts extend these skills across the curriculum. Sexuality education is a case in point: sexual values are taught, not explored; sexual danger is stressed while sexual pleasure is minimized; heterosexual intercourse is presented as the apex of the pyramid of sexual desire. Questions such as how being male or female defines one's sexual options, how sexual options and values vary across time and culture, why masturbation is considered less desirable than sexual intercourse, and how one distinguishes the "gays" from the "straights" are never asked, never encouraged, never addressed.

Breaking through the conspiracy of silence

There is a great need for a healthy, frank, and honest depiction of the fluidity of sexual behavior and sexual identities. Yet too many educators are partners in a conspiracy of silence in which sexual knowledge is what is salvaged after the scissors-and-paste philosophy of religious zealots or anti-homosexual activists are applied.

The capacity of people to create and recreate their sexual identities is an integral component of the new holistic sexuality curriculum, which must redefine the meaning of "teaching for diversity." Then, we will not only recognize and support the development of the Phillips and Marys among us, but we will help all students realize their full human potential.

References

Altman, D. (1982). *The Homosexualization of America, The Americanization of the Homosexual*. New York: St. Martin's Press.

Brown, L. (1987). "Lesbians, Weight, and Eating: New Analyses and Perspectives." In *Lesbian Psychologies: Exploration and Challenges*, edited by the Boston Lesbian Psychologies Collective. Urbana: University of Illinois Press.

Bullough, V. (1976). *Sex, Society, and History*. New York: Science History.

Foucault, M. (1978). *The History of Sexuality*, Vol. I. New York: Pantheon.

Freud, S. (1964). *Leonardo da Vinci and a Memory of Childhood*, translated by A. Tyson. New York: Norton.

Forrest, J., and J. Silverman. (1989). "What Public School Teachers Teach About Preventing Pregnancy, AIDS, and Sexually Transmitted Diseases." *Family Planning Perspectives* 21,2: 65–72.

Gibson, P. (1989). "Gay Male and Lesbian Youth Suicide." In *Report of the Secretary's Task Force on Youth Suicide, Vol. 3: Prevention and Interventions in Youth Suicide*. Washington, D.C.: U.S. Department of Health and Human Services.

Grayson, D. (1989). "Emerging Equity Issues Related to Homosexuality in Education." *Peabody Journal of Education* 64,4: 132–145.

Greenberg, D. (1988). *The Construction of Homosexuality*. Chicago: University of Chicago Press.

Kinsey, A., W. Pomeroy, and C. Martin. (1948). *Sexual Behavior in the Human Male*. Philadelphia: Saunders.

Kinsey, A., W. Pomeroy, C. Martin, and P. Gebhard. (1953). *Sexual Behavior in the Human Female*. Philadelphia: Saunders.

Kitzinger, C. (1987). *The Social Construction of Lesbianism*. London: Sage.

Martin, A. (1932). "Learning to Hide: The Socialization of the Gay Adolescent." In *Adolescent Psychiatry: Developmental and Clinical Studies*, edited by S. Feinstein and J. Looney, pp. 52–65. Chicago: University of Chicago Press.

Martin, A., and E. Hetrick. (1988). "The Stigmatization of Gay and Lesbian Adolescents." *Journal of Homosexuality* 15,1–2: 163–185.

Plummer, K. (1981). *The Making of the Modern Homosexual.* London: Hutchinson.

Remafedi, G. (1987). "Adolescent Homosexuality: Psychosocial and Medical Implications." *Pediatrics* 79,3: 331–337.

Rofes, E. (1989). "Opening Up the Classroom Closet: Responding to the Educational Needs of Gay and Lesbian Youth." *Harvard Educational Review*, 59,4: 444–453.

Sears, J. (1987). "Peering Into the Well of Loneliness: The Responsibility of Educators to Gay and Lesbian Youth." In *Social Issues and Education: Challenge and Responsibility*, edited by A. Molnar. Alexandria, Va.: Association for Supervision and Curriculum Development.

Sears, J. (1989). "The Impact of Gender and Race on Growing Up Lesbian and Gay in the South." *NWSA Journal* 1,3: 422–457.

Sears, J. (1991). *Growing Up Gay in the South: Race, Gender, and Journeys of the Spirit.* New York: Haworth Press.

Sears, J. (in press). "Reproducing the Body Politic: Dilemmas and Possibilities in Sexuality Education." In *Sexuality and the Curriculum*, edited by J. Sears. New York: Teachers College Press.

CHAPTER 20

WHY WE MUST PLURALIZE THE CURRICULUM (1991)

Asa G. Hilliard III

Within the past two to three years, the number of scholars who assert the exclusive political and cultural correctness of "Western culture" has greatly increased. These voices have viciously attacked the very thought associated with cultural pluralism in American society, especially as it applies to school curriculums. Attempts to pluralize the curriculum such as Stanford University's Western Civilizations program, New York State's Curriculum of Inclusion, and Portland, Oregon's Multicultural Curriculum effort have been met with bitter opposition by conservative scholars throughout the nation, who have taken this position without benefit of a constructive dialogue with a broad base of minority group representatives.

What accounts for this standardized formula response? It is becoming increasingly clear that some private groups have decided, unilaterally, on a course of action for the general public. They are beginning to express xenophobia at the national level. For example, a recent news article in *The Atlanta Constitution* (Auster 1991), cited the fact that the United States is undergoing major shifts in its ethnic population and that Europeans are rapidly becoming the minority. "Minorities" are becoming the "majority." The great cultural diversity among minority cultural populations, the author feared, will lead to a "disuniting" of the United States.

This fear is reminiscent of a similar type of thinking present in the 1920s. White supremacists Madison Grant and Lothrup Stoddard, among many others, were fearful of new immigrants from Europe, especially those from Eastern and Southern Europe. They visualized the advent of these new groups in the United States as a "Rising Tide of Color Against White World Supremacy" (Stoddard 1971) and "The Passing of the Great Race" (Grant 1924).

Restoring the true human record

But the demands made by diverse ethnic groups for inclusion in the curriculum will not go away. In fact, African Americans' demands for pluralistic curriculum changes were initiated long before the terms *Eurocentric, Afrocentric,* and *multicultural* were introduced (Woodson 1933, Dubois 1969). Attempts to include black history in the curriculum go almost as far back as four centuries, when the first struggles for liberation began. One need only read Carter G. Woodson's classic work *The Miseducation of the Negro* (1933) in order to understand this. W. E. B. DuBois' *The Souls of Black Folk* (1969) and his other essays in *The*

Education of Black People: Ten Critiques (Aptheker 1973), are also required reading.

Those who have studied worldwide liberation struggles know that the manipulation of information, including propaganda and disinformation, are primary tactics employed in the domination process. Oppressive populations defame, stigmatize, stereotype, and distort the reality of dominated populations. Oppressive populations change the true human record through denial of the very reality of the total human experience, including their own (Barzun 1965, Benedict 1959, Biddis 1970, Carlson 1972, Gossett 1973, Montague 1968, Stanton 1960, Kamin 1974, Chase 1977, Gould 1981, Serfontein 1978, Schwartz and Disch 1970, Jones 1972).

The mass media, entertainment, and schools are an integral part of the information process and, in oppressive societies, are a part of the domination process as well. Schools in apartheid, segregated, or racist societies are not neutral, nor is their information base.

A valid curriculum

Centuries of falsehood and defamation cannot be corrected simply by ceasing to present overt expressions of false and defamatory data. The old record must be purged! The primary goal of a pluralistic curriculum process is to present a truthful and meaningful rendition of the whole human experience. This is not a matter of ethnic quotas in the curriculum for "balance"; it is purely and simply a question of validity. Ultimately, if the curriculum is centered in truth, it will be pluralistic, for the simple fact is that human culture is the product of the struggles of all humanity, not the possession of a single racial or ethnic group.

We must consider curriculum equity in the schools from two angles. On the one hand, the academic level of the content can be pitched much higher and yet be well within reach of the masses of our children, provided that we equitably distribute high-quality instruction. On the other hand, we must awaken to the fact that no academic content is neutral nor is the specific cultural content of any ethnic group universal in and of itself. Under the old white supremacy system, the white European culture was considered both "universal" and "superior" to all other cultures. Some contemporary scholars in the multicultural curriculum dialogue still hold this view.

We say that the search for truth is our highest goal for students. To foster it, we must facilitate in students the assumption of a critical orientation. Of course, criticism implies an awareness of all cultural alternatives and a thoughtful and honest examination of those alternatives. No cultural tradition can be regarded as immune to criticism.

Preserving diversity

I agree with E. D. Hirsch (1987) and others who say that there are many interests to be served by the development and presentation of certain common cultural content for all our children. However, I do not believe that it is necessary to choose between uniqueness and commonality. This is a false dichotomy. Human minds and systems are powerful and flexible enough to handle both. Nevertheless, in a democratic society it makes all the difference how we arrive at a common core.

We must not commit cultural genocide by crushing cultural uniqueness. A politically correct curriculum "canon" is more appropriate for sectarian religion than it is for a scientific and democratic school and society. Curriculum catechism and cultural totalitarianism are more associated with propaganda than with truth. It's hard to see how some conservative ideologues can argue for "school choice" and for a curriculum "canon" at the same time, for intellectual freedom and cultural indoctrination at the same time, for multiculturalism on the one hand and for coerced conformity on the other.

Respect for diversity is the hallmark of democracy. This nation was founded by those who fled the cultural totalitarianism of Europe to seek religious and political freedom. Do the critics of pluralistic curriculums wish to require "universalism" in religion and politics?

Beyond self-esteem

Pluralism in the curriculum is not a matter of "trivial pursuit." Many of the justifications the media give for a multicultural curriculum are minor and irrelevant to the central issue: editorial arguments about "self-esteem" and the role of multicultural curriculum in "producing academic achievement" miss the mark. Valid scholarship must be the source of curriculum content.

Children can handle the truth, warts and all. Scholars can produce it, provided that they create the appropriate multidisciplinary, multiracial, multinational, non-sexist forums for research, development, and dissemination (UNESCO 1978). The United Nations Educational and Cultural Organization provides us with a model approach for the correction of defamation and distortion: In 1981, UNESCO published an eight-volume *General History of Africa*. The organization brought together scholars of all races, nationalities, and many academic disciplines to create a more valid rendering of African history than the defamatory and false records that were extant as late as the early part of this century. Much more of this work must be done.

Our book. *The Infusion of African and African American Content in the School Curriculum* (Hilliard et al. 1990), includes an extensive outline and bibliography in the chapter "African People in World History" by John H. Clarke. One look at this work will reveal the huge gap between what is known and what is taught about people of African descent in the mainstream curriculum. This bibliography provides a model of what must be done for Hispanics, American Indians, Asians, and other under- or misrepresented groups. It also challenges the antiminority and antipluralism rhetoric that implies that trivial changes in existing curriculum are sufficient. By trivial changes, I refer to the common practice of adding a sprinkling of minority individuals to "color" a manuscript rather than incorporating data on the influence of all human groups on major human events.

The whole story

Curriculum change must proceed first and foremost from the assumption that there is truth in the whole of human experience. Schools must also accept the fact that some racial and ethnic groups have endured hundreds of years of systematic defamation that has distorted, denied, and deformed the truth of their cultural and historical reality.

A wealth of old, multidisciplinary, international, and multiracial literature exists that would allow us to find the true stories of the roles of all groups in human history so that we could include them in the school curriculums. Nothing less than the full truth of the human experience is worthy of our schools and our children.

References

Aptheker, H. (1973). *The Education of Black People: Ten Critiques, 1906–1960* by W. E. B. DuBois. New York: Monthly Review Press.

Auster, L. (May 15, 1991). "Immigration Gives Birth to Unfree America." *The Atlanta Journal/The Atlanta Constitution*: A13.

Barzun, J. (1965). *Race: A Study in Superstition*. New York: Harper.

Benedict, R. (1959). *Race: Science and Politics*. New York: Viking.

Biddis, M. D. (1970). *Father of Racist Ideology: The Social and Political Thought of Count Gobineau*. New York: Weinright and Talley.

Carlson, L. H. and Colburn, G. A. (1972). *In Their Place: White America Defines Her Minorities, 1850–1950*. New York: John Wiley and Sons.

Chase, A. (1977). *The Legacy of Malthus: The Social Costs of the New Scientific Racism*. New York: Alfred A. Knopf.

DuBois, W.E.B. (1969). *The Souls of Black Folk*. New York: Signet. (First published 1903).

Gossett, T.F. (1973). *Race: The History of an Idea in America*. New York: Schoken.

Gould, S.J. (1981). *The Mismeasure of Man*. New York: W. W. Norton.

Grant, M. (1924). *The Passing of the Great Race: Or, The Racial Basis of European History*. New York: Charles Scribner's Sons.

Hilliard, A. G. III, L. Patyon-Stewart, and L. Obadele. (1990). *The Infusion of African and African American Content in the School Curriculum*. Morristown, N.J.: Aaron Press.

Hirsch, E.D. (1987). *Cultural Literacy: What Every American Needs to Know*. Boston: Houghton Mifflin.

Jones, S.M. (1972). "The Schlesingers on Black History," *PHYLON: The Atlanta University Review of Race and Culture* 33, 2: 104–111.

Kamin, K. (1974). *The Science and Politics of I.Q.* Potomac, Md.: Lawrence Erlbaum Associates.

Montague, A. (1968). *The Concept of the Primitive*. New York: Collier-Macmillan.

Schwartz, B. N. and R. Disch. (1970). *White Racism: Its History, Pathology, Practice*. New York: Dell.

Serfontein, J.H.P. (1978). *Brotherhood of Power: An Expose of the Secret Afrikaner Broederbond*. Bloomington, Indiana: Indiana University Press.

Stanton, W. (1960). *The Leopard's Spots: Scientific Attitudes Toward Race in America 1915–1959*. Chicago: University of Chicago Press.

Stoddard, L. (1971). *The Rising Tide of Color Against White World Supremacy*. Westport, Conn.: Negro University Press. (First Published 1920).

UNESCO. (1978). "The Peopling of Ancient Egypt and the Deciphering of the Mereotic Script." Proceedings of the Symposium held in Cairo from 28 January to 3 February 1974. Paris: United National Educational, Scientific and Cultural Organization.

UNESCO. (1981). *General History of Africa*. Berkeley: University of California Press.

Woodson, C. G. (1933). *The Miseducation of the Negro*. Washington, D.C.: Associated Publishers.

PART 4

CRITIQUE

CHAPTER 21

MULTICULTURALISM (1990)
E pluribus plures
Diane Ravitch

Questions of race, ethnicity, and religion have been a perennial source of conflict in American education. The schools have often attracted the zealous attention of those who wish to influence the future, as well as those who wish to change the way we view the past. In our history, the schools have been not only an institution in which to teach young people skills and knowledge, but an arena where interest groups fight to preserve their values, or to revise the judgments of history, or to bring about fundamental social change. In the nineteenth century, Protestants and Catholics battled over which version of the Bible should be used in school, or whether the Bible should be used at all. In recent decades, bitter racial disputes—provoked by policies of racial segregation and discrimination—have generated turmoil in the streets and in the schools. The secularization of the schools during the past century has prompted attacks on the curricula and textbooks and library books by fundamentalist Christians, who object to whatever challenges their faith-based views of history, literature, and science.

Given the diversity of American society, it has been impossible to insulate the schools from pressures that result from differences and tensions among groups. When people differ about basic values, sooner or later those disagreements turn up in battles about how schools are organized or what the schools should teach. Sometimes these battles remove a terrible injustice, like racial segregation. Sometimes, however, interest groups politicize the curriculum and attempt to impose their views on teachers, school officials, and textbook publishers. Across the country, even now, interest groups are pressuring local school boards to remove myths and fables and other imaginative literature from children's readers and to inject the teaching of creationism in biology. When groups cross the line into extremism, advancing their own agenda without regard to reason or to others, they threaten public education itself, making it difficult to teach any issues honestly and making the entire curriculum vulnerable to political campaigns.

For many years, the public schools attempted to neutralize controversies over race, religion, and ethnicity by ignoring them. Educators believed, or hoped, that the schools could remain outside politics; this was, of course, a vain hope since the schools were pursuing policies based on race, religion, and ethnicity. Nonetheless, such divisive questions were usually excluded from the curriculum. The textbooks minimized problems among groups and taught a sanitized version of history. Race, religion, and ethnicity were presented as minor elements in the American saga; slavery was treated as an episode, immigration as a sidebar, and women were largely absent. The textbooks concentrated on presidents, wars, national politics, and issues of state. An occasional "great black" or "great woman" received mention, but the main narrative paid little attention to minority groups and women.

With the ethnic revival of the 1960s, this approach to the teaching of history came under fire, because the history of national leaders—virtually all of whom were white, Anglo-Saxon, and male—ignored the place in American history of those who were none of the above. The traditional history of elites had been complemented by an assimilationist view of American society, which presumed that everyone in the American melting pot would eventually lose or abandon those ethnic characteristics that distinguished them from mainstream Americans. The ethnic revival demonstrated that many groups did not want to be assimilated or melted. Ethnic studies programs popped up on campuses to teach not only that "black is beautiful," but also that every other variety of ethnicity is "beautiful" as well; everyone who had "roots" began to look for them so that they too could recover that ancestral part of themselves that had not been homogenized.

As ethnicity became an accepted subject for study in the late 1960s, textbooks were assailed for their failure to portray blacks accurately; within a few years, the textbooks in wide use were carefully screened to eliminate bias against minority groups and women. At the same time, new scholarship about the history of women, blacks, and various ethnic minorities found its way into the textbooks. At first, the multicultural content was awkwardly incorporated as little boxes on the side of the main narrative. Then some of the new social historians (like Stephan Thernstrom, Mary Beth Norton, Gary Nash, Winthrop Jordan, and Leon Litwack) themselves wrote textbooks, and the main narrative itself began to reflect a broadened historical understanding of race, ethnicity, and class in the American past. Consequently, today's history textbooks routinely incorporate the experiences of women, blacks, American Indians, and various immigrant groups.

Although most high school textbooks are deeply unsatisfactory (they still largely neglect religion, they are too long, too encyclopedic, too superficial, and lacking in narrative flow), they are far more sensitive to pluralism than their predecessors. For example, the latest edition of Todd and Curti's *Triumph of the American Nation*, the most popular high school history text, has significantly increased its coverage of blacks in America, including profiles of Phillis Wheatley, the poet; James Armistead, a revolutionary war spy for Lafayette; Benjamin Banneker, a self-taught scientist and mathematician; Hiram Revels, the first black to serve in the Congress; and Ida B. Wells-Barnett, a tireless crusader against lynching and racism. Even better as a textbook treatment is Jordan and Litwack's *The United States*, which skillfully synthesizes the historical experiences of blacks, Indians, immigrants, women, and other groups into the mainstream of American social and political history. The latest generation of textbooks bluntly acknowledges the racism of the past, describing the struggle for equality by racial minorities while identifying individuals who achieved success as political leaders, doctors, lawyers, scholars, entrepreneurs, teachers, and scientists.

As a result of the political and social changes of recent decades, cultural pluralism is now generally recognized as an organizing principle of this society. In contrast to the idea of the melting pot, which promised to erase ethnic and group differences, children now learn that variety is the spice of life. They learn that America has provided a haven for many different groups and has allowed them to maintain their cultural heritage or to assimilate, or—as is often the case—to do both; the choice is theirs, not the state's. They learn that cultural pluralism is one of the norms of a free society; that differences among groups are a national resource rather than a problem to be solved. Indeed, the unique feature of the United States is that its common culture has been formed by the interaction of its subsidiary cultures. It is a culture that has been influenced over time by immigrants, American Indians, Africans (slave and free) and by their descendants. American music, art, literature, language, food, clothing, sports, holidays, and customs all show the effects of the commingling of diverse cultures in one nation. Paradoxical though it may seem, the United States has a common culture that is multicultural.

Our schools and our institutions of higher learning have in recent years begun to embrace what Catherine R. Stimpson of Rutgers University has called "cultural democracy," a recognition that we must listen to a "diversity of voices" in order to understand our culture, past and present. This understanding of the pluralistic nature of American culture has taken a long time to forge. It is based on sound scholarship and has led to major revisions in what children are taught and what they read in school. The new history is—indeed, must be—a warts-and-all history; it demands an unflinching examination of racism and discrimination in our history. Making these changes is difficult, raises tempers, and ignites controversies, but gives a more interesting and accurate account of American history. Accomplishing these changes is valuable, because there is also a useful lesson for the rest of the world in America's relatively successful experience as a pluralistic society. Throughout human history, the clash of different cultures, races, ethnic groups, and religions has often been the cause of bitter hatred, civil conflict, and international war. The ethnic tensions that now are tearing apart Lebanon, Sri Lanka, Kashmir, and various republics of the Soviet Union remind us of the costs of unfettered group rivalry. Thus, it is a matter of more than domestic importance that we closely examine and try to understand that part of our national history in which different groups competed, fought, suffered, but ultimately learned to live together in relative peace and even achieved a sense of common nationhood.

Alas, these painstaking efforts to expand the understanding of American culture into a richer and more varied tapestry have taken a new turn, and not for the better. Almost any idea, carried to its extreme, can be made pernicious, and this is what is happening now to multiculturalism. Today, pluralistic multiculturalism must contend with a new, particularistic multiculturalism. The pluralists seek a richer common culture; the particularists insist that no common culture is possible or desirable. The new particularism is entering the curriculum in a number of school systems across the country. Advocates of particularism propose an ethnocentric curriculum to raise the self-esteem and academic achievement of children from racial and ethnic minority backgrounds. Without any evidence, they claim that children from minority backgrounds will do well in school *only* if they are immersed in a positive, prideful version of their ancestral culture. If children are of, for example, Fredonian ancestry, they must hear that Fredonians were important in mathematics, science, history, and literature. If they learn about great Fredonians and if their studies use Fredonian examples and Fredonian concepts, they will do well in school. If they do not, they will have low self-esteem and will do badly.

At first glance, this appears akin to the celebratory activities associated with Black History Month or Women's History Month, when schoolchildren learn about the achievements of blacks and women. But the point of those celebrations is to demonstrate that neither race nor gender is an obstacle to high achievement. They teach all children that everyone, regardless of their race, religion, gender, ethnicity, or family origin, can achieve self-fulfillment, honor, and dignity in society if they aim high and work hard.

By contrast, the particularistic version of multiculturalism is unabashedly filiopietistic and deterministic. It teaches children that their identity is determined by their "cultural genes." That something in their blood or their race memory or their cultural DNA defines who they are and what they may achieve. That the culture in which they live is not their own culture, even though they were born here. That American culture is "Eurocentric," and therefore hostile to anyone whose ancestors are not European. Perhaps the most invidious implication of particularism is that racial and ethnic minorities are not and should not try to be part of American culture; it implies that American culture belongs only to those who are white and European; it implies that those who are neither white nor European are alienated from American culture by virtue of their race or ethnicity; it implies that the only culture they do belong to or can ever belong to is the culture of their ancestors, even if their families have lived in this country for generations.

The war on so-called Eurocentrism is intended to foster self-esteem among those who are not of European descent. But how, in fact, is self-esteem developed? How is the sense of one's own possibilities, one's potential choices, developed? Certainly, the school curriculum plays a relatively small role as compared to the influence of family, community, mass media, and society. But to the extent that curriculum influences what children think of themselves, it should encourage children of all racial and ethnic groups to believe that they are part of this society and that they should develop their talents and minds to the fullest. It is enormously inspiring, for example, to learn about men and women from diverse backgrounds who overcame poverty, discrimination, physical handicaps, and other obstacles to achieve success in a variety of fields. Behind every such biography of accomplishment is a story of heroism, perseverance, and self-discipline. Learning these stories will encourage a healthy spirit of pluralism, of mutual respect, and of self-respect among children of different backgrounds. The children of American society today will live their lives in a racially and culturally diverse nation, and their education should prepare them to do so.

The pluralist approach to multiculturalism promotes a broader interpretation of the common American culture and seeks due recognition for the ways that the nation's many racial, ethnic, and cultural groups have transformed the national culture. The pluralists say, in effect, "American culture belongs to us, all of us; the U.S. is us, and we remake it in every generation." But particularists have no interest in extending or revising American culture; indeed, they deny that a common culture exists. Particularists reject any accommodation among groups, any interactions that blur the distinct lines between them. The brand of history that they espouse is one in which everyone is either a descendant of victims or oppressors. By doing so, ancient hatreds are fanned and recreated in each new generation. Particularism has its intellectual roots in the ideology of ethnic separatism and in the black nationalist movement. In the particularist analysis, the nation has five cultures: African American, Asian American, European American, Latino/Hispanic, and Native American. The huge cultural, historical, religious, and linguistic differences within these categories are ignored, as is the considerable intermarriage among these groups, as are the linkages (like gender, class, sexual orientation, and religion) that cut across these five groups. No serious scholar would claim that all Europeans and white Americans are part of the same culture, or that all Asians are part of the same culture, or that all people of Latin-American descent are of the same culture, or that all people of African descent are of the same culture. Any categorization this broad is essentially meaningless and useless.

Several districts—including Detroit, Atlanta, and Washington, D.C.—are developing an Afrocentric curriculum. *Afrocentricity* has been described in a book of the same name by Molefi Kete Asante of Temple University. The Afrocentric curriculum puts Africa at the center of the student's universe. African Americans must "move away from an [*sic*] Eurocentric framework" because "it is difficult to create freely when you use someone else's motifs, styles, images, and perspectives." Because they are not Africans, "white teachers cannot inspire in our children the visions necessary for them to overcome limitations." Asante recommends that African Americans choose an African name (as he did), reject European dress, embrace African religion (not Islam or Christianity) and love "their own" culture. He scorns the idea of universality as a form of Eurocentric arrogance. The Eurocentrist, he says, thinks of Beethoven or Bach as classical, but the Afrocentrist thinks of Ellington or Coltrane as classical; the Eurocentrist lauds Shakespeare or Twain, while the Afrocentrist prefers Baraka, Shange, or Abiola. Asante is critical of black artists like Arthur Mitchell and Alvin Ailey who ignore Afrocentricity. Likewise, he speaks contemptuously of a group of black university students who spurned the Afrocentrism of the local Black Student Union and formed an organization called Inter-race: "Such madness is the direct consequence of self-hatred, obligatory attitudes, false assumptions about society, and stupidity."

The conflict between pluralism and particularism turns on the issue of universalism. Professor Asante warns his readers against the lure of universalism: "Do not be captured by a sense of universality given to you by the Eurocentric viewpoint; such a viewpoint is contradictory to your own ultimate reality." He insists that there is no alternative to Eurocentrism, Afrocentrism, and other ethnocentrisms. In contrast, the pluralist says, with the Roman playwright Terence, "I am a man: nothing human is alien to me." A contemporary Terence would say "I am a person" or might be a woman, but the point remains the same: You don't have to be black to love Zora Neale Hurston's fiction or Langston Hughes's poetry or Duke Ellington's music. In a pluralist curriculum, we expect children to learn a broad and humane culture, to learn about the ideas and art and animating spirit of many cultures. We expect that children, whatever their color, will be inspired by the courage of people like Helen Keller, Vaclav Havel, Harriet Tubman, and Feng Lizhe. We expect that their response to literature will be determined by the ideas and images it evokes, not by the skin color of the writer. But particularists insist that children can learn only from the experiences of people from the same race.

Particularism is a bad idea whose time has come. It is also a fashion spreading like wildfire through the education system, actively promoted by organizations and individuals with a political and professional interest in strengthening ethnic power bases in the university, in the education profession, and in society itself. One can scarcely pick up an educational journal without learning about a school district that is converting to an ethnocentric curriculum in an attempt to give "self-esteem" to children from racial minorities. A state-funded project in a Sacramento high school is teaching young black males to think like Africans and to develop the "African Mind Model Technique," in order to free themselves of the racism of American culture. A popular black rap singer, KRS-One, complained in an op-ed article in the *New York Times* that the schools should be teaching blacks about their cultural heritage, instead of trying to make everyone

Americans. "It's like trying to teach a dog to be a cat," he wrote. KRS-One railed about having to learn about Thomas Jefferson and the Civil War, which had nothing to do (he said) with black history.

Pluralism can easily be transformed into particularism, as may be seen in the potential uses in the classroom of the Mayan contribution to mathematics. The Mayan example was popularized in a movie called *Stand and Deliver*, about a charismatic Bolivian-born mathematics teacher in Los Angeles who inspired his students (who are Hispanic) to learn calculus. He told them that their ancestors invented the concept of zero; but that wasn't all he did. He used imagination to put across mathematical concepts. He required them to do homework and to go to school on Saturdays and during the Christmas holidays, so that they might pass the Advanced Placement mathematics examination for college entry. The teacher's reference to the Mayans' mathematical genius was a valid instructional device: It was an attention-getter and would have interested even students who were not Hispanic. But the Mayan example would have had little effect without the teacher's insistence that the class study hard for a difficult examination.

Ethnic educators have seized upon the Mayan contribution to mathematics as the key to simultaneously boosting the ethnic pride of Hispanic children and attacking Eurocentrism. One proposal claims that Mexican-American children will be attracted to science and mathematics if they study Mayan mathematics, the Mayan calendar, and Mayan astronomy. Children in primary grades are to be taught that the Mayans were first to discover the zero and that Europeans learned it long afterwards from the Arabs, who had learned it in India. This will help them see that Europeans were latecomers in the discovery of great ideas. Botany is to be learned by study of the agricultural techniques of the Aztecs, a subject of somewhat limited relevance to children in urban areas. Furthermore, "ethnobotanical" classifications of plants are to be substituted for the Eurocentric Linnaean system. At first glance, it may seem curious that Hispanic children are deemed to have no cultural affinity with Spain; but to acknowledge the cultural tie would confuse the ideological assault on Eurocentrism.

This proposal suggests some questions: Is there any evidence that the teaching of "culturally relevant" science and mathematics will draw Mexican-American children to the study of these subjects? Will Mexican-American children lose interest or self-esteem if they discover that their ancestors were Aztecs or Spaniards, rather than Mayans? Are children who learn in this way prepared to study the science and mathematics that are taught in American colleges and universities and that are needed for advanced study in these fields? Are they even prepared to study the science and mathematics taught in *Mexican* universities? If the class is half Mexican-American and half something else, will only the Mexican-American children study in a Mayan and Aztec mode or will all the children? But shouldn't all children study what is culturally relevant for them? How will we train teachers who have command of so many different systems of mathematics and science?

The efficacy of particularist proposals seems to be less important to their sponsors than their value as ideological weapons with which to criticize existing disciplines for their alleged Eurocentric bias. In a recent article titled "The Ethnocentric Basis of Social Science Knowledge Production" in the *Review of Research in Education*, John Stanfield of Yale University argues that neither social science nor science are objective studies, that both instead are "Euro-American" knowledge systems which reproduce "hegemonic racial domination." The claim that science and reason are somehow superior to magic and witchcraft, he writes, is the product of Euro-American ethnocentrism. According to Stanfield, current fears about the misuse of science (for instance, "the nuclear arms race, global pollution") and "the power-plays of Third World nations (the Arab oil boycott and the American-Iranian hostage crisis) have made Western people more aware of nonscientific cognitive styles. These last events are beginning to demonstrate politically that which has begun to be understood in intellectual circles: namely, that modes of social knowledge such as theology, science, and magic are different, not inferior or superior. They represent different ways of perceiving, defining, and organizing knowledge of life experiences." One wonders: If Professor Stanfield broke his leg, would he go to a theologian, a doctor, or a magician?

Every field of study, it seems, has been tainted by Eurocentrism, which was defined by a professor at Manchester University, George Ghevarughese Joseph, in *Race and Class* in 1987, as "intellectual racism." Professor Joseph argues that the history of science and technology—and in particular, of mathematics—in non-European societies was distorted by racist Europeans who wanted to establish the dominance of European forms of knowledge. The racists, he writes, traditionally traced mathematics to the Greeks, then claimed that it reached its full development in Europe. These are simply Eurocentric myths to sustain an "imperialist/racist ideology," says Professor Joseph, since mathematics was found in Egypt, Babylonia, Mesopotamia, and India long before the Greeks were supposed to have developed it. Professor Joseph points out too that Arab scientists should be credited with major discoveries traditionally attributed to William Harvey, Isaac Newton, Charles Darwin, and Sir Francis Bacon. But he is not concerned only to argue historical issues; his purpose is to bring all of these different mathematical traditions into the school classroom so that children might study, for example, "traditional African designs, Indian *rangoli* patterns and Islamic art" and "the language and counting systems found across the world."

This interesting proposal to teach ethnomathematics comes at a time when American mathematics educators are trying to overhaul present practices, because of the poor performance of American children on national and international assessments. Mathematics educators are attempting to change the teaching of their subject so that children can see its uses in everyday life. There would seem to be an incipient conflict between those who want to introduce real-life applications of mathematics and those who want to teach the mathematical systems used by ancient cultures. I suspect that most mathematics teachers would enjoy doing a bit of both, if there were time or student interest. But any widespread movement to replace modern mathematics with ancient ethnic mathematics runs the risk of disaster in a field that is struggling to update existing curricula. If, as seems likely, ancient mathematics is taught mainly to minority children, the gap between them and middle-class white children is apt to grow. It is worth noting that children in Korea, who score highest in mathematics on international assessments, do not study ancient Korean mathematics.

Particularism is akin to cultural Lysenkoism, for it takes as its premise the spurious notion that cultural traits are inherited. It implies a dubious, dangerous form of cultural predestination. Children are taught that if their ancestors could do it, so could they. But what happens if a child is from a cultural group that made no significant contribution to science or mathematics? Does this mean that children from that background must find a culturally appropriate field in which to strive? How does a teacher find the right cultural buttons for children of mixed heritage? And how in the world will teachers use this technique when the children in their classes are drawn from many different cultures, as is usually the case? By the time that every culture gets its due, there may be no time left to teach the subject itself. This explosion of filiopietism (which, we should remember, comes from adults, not from students) is reminiscent of the period some years ago when the Russians claimed that they had invented everything first; as we now know, this nationalistic braggadocio did little for their self-esteem and nothing for their economic development. We might reflect, too, on how little social prestige has been accorded in this country to immigrants from Greece and Italy, even though the achievements of their ancestors were at the heart of the classical curriculum.

Filiopietism and ethnic boosterism lead to all sorts of odd practices. In New York State, for example, the curriculum guide for eleventh grade American history lists three "foundations" for the United States Constitution, as follows:

A   Foundations
   1   17th and 18th century Enlightenment thought
   2   Haudenosaunee political system

     (a) Influence upon colonial leadership and European intellectuals (Locke, Montesquieu, Voltaire, Rousseau)
     (b) Impact on Albany Plan of Union, Articles of Confederation, and U.S. Constitution

   3   Colonial experience

Those who are unfamiliar with the Haudenosaunee political system might wonder what it is, particularly since educational authorities in New York State rank it as equal in importance to the European Enlightenment and suggest that it strongly influenced not only colonial leaders but the leading intellectuals of Europe. The Haudenosaunee political system was the Iroquois confederation of five (later six) Indian tribes in upper New York State, which conducted war and civil affairs through a council of chiefs, each with one vote. In 1754, Benjamin Franklin proposed a colonial union at a conference in Albany; his plan, said to be inspired by the Iroquois Confederation, was rejected by the other colonies. Today, Indian activists believe that the Iroquois Confederation was the model for the American Constitution, and the New York State Department of Education has decided that they are right. That no other state sees fit to give the American Indians equal billing with the European Enlightenment may be owing to the fact that the Indians in New York State (numbering less than forty thousand) have been more politically effective than elsewhere or that other states have not yet learned about this method of reducing "Eurocentrism" in their American history classes.

Particularism can easily be carried to extremes. Students of Fredonian descent must hear that their ancestors were seminal in the development of all human civilization and that without the Fredonian contribution, we would all be living in caves or trees, bereft of art, technology, and culture. To explain why Fredonians today are in modest circumstances, given their historic eminence, children are taught that somewhere, long ago, another culture stole the Fredonians' achievements, palmed them off as their own, and then oppressed the Fredonians.

I first encountered this argument almost twenty years ago, when I was a graduate student. I shared a small office with a young professor, and I listened as she patiently explained to a student why she had given him a D on a term paper. In his paper, he argued that the Arabs had stolen mathematics from the Nubians in the desert long ago (I forget in which century this theft allegedly occurred). She tried to explain to him about the necessity of historical evidence. He was unconvinced, since he believed that he had uncovered a great truth that was beyond proof. The part I couldn't understand was how anyone could lose knowledge by sharing it. After all, cultures are constantly influencing one another, exchanging ideas and art and technology, and the exchange usually is enriching, not depleting.

Today, there are a number of books and articles advancing controversial theories about the origins of civilization. An important work, *The African Origin of Civilization: Myth or Reality*, by Senegalese scholar Cheikh Anta Diop, argues that ancient Egypt was a black civilization, that all races are descended from the black race, and that the achievements of "western" civilization originated in Egypt. The views of Diop and other Africanists have been condensed into an everyman's paperback titled *What They Never Told You in History Class* by Indus Khamit Kush. This latter book claims that Moses, Jesus, Buddha, Mohammed, and Vishnu were Africans; that the first Indians, Chinese, Hebrews, Greeks, Romans, Britains, and Americans were Africans; and that the first mathematicians, scientists, astronomers, and physicians were Africans. A debate currently raging among some classicists is whether the Greeks "stole" the philosophy, art, and religion of the ancient Egyptians and whether the ancient Egyptians were black Africans. George G. M. James's *Stolen Legacy* insists that the Greeks "stole the Legacy of the African Continent and called it their own." James argues that the civilization of Greece, the vaunted foundation of European culture, owed everything it knew and did to its African predecessors. Thus, the roots of western civilization lie not in Greece and Rome, but in Egypt and, ultimately, in black Africa.

Similar speculation was fueled by the publication in 1987 of Martin Bernal's *Black Athena: The Afroasiatic Roots of Classical Civilization*, Volume 1, *The Fabrication of Ancient Greece, 1785–1985*, although the controversy predates Bernal's book. In a fascinating foray into the politics of knowledge, Bernal attributes the preference of Western European scholars for Greece over Egypt as the fount of knowledge to nearly two centuries of racism and "Europocentrism," but he is uncertain about the color of the ancient Egyptians. However, a review of Bernal's book last year in the *Village Voice* began, "What color were the ancient Egyptians? Blacker than Mubarak, baby." The same article claimed that white racist archeologists chiseled the noses off ancient Egyptian statues so that future generations would not see the typically African facial characteristics. The debate reached the pages of the *Biblical Archeology Review* last year in an article titled "Were the Ancient Egyptians Black or White?" The author, classicist Frank J. Yurco, argues that some Egyptian rulers were black, others were not, and that "the ancient Egyptians did not think in these terms." The issue, wrote Yurco, "is a chimera, cultural baggage from our own society that can only be imposed artificially on ancient Egyptian society."

Most educationists are not even aware of the debate about whether the ancient Egyptians were black or white, but they are very sensitive to charges that the schools' curricula are Eurocentric, and they are eager to rid the schools of the taint of Eurocentrism. It is hardly surprising that America's schools would recognize strong cultural ties with Europe since our nation's political, religious, educational, and economic institutions were created chiefly by people of European descent, our government was shaped by European ideas, and nearly 80 percent of the people who live here are of European descent. The particularists treat all of this history as a racist bias toward Europe, rather than as the matter-of-fact consequences of European immigration. Even so, American education is not centered on Europe. American education, if it is centered on anything, is centered on itself. It is "Americentric." Most American students today have never studied any world history; they know very little about Europe, and even less about the rest of the world. Their minds are rooted solidly in the here and now. When the Berlin Wall was opened in the fall of 1989, journalists discovered that most American teenagers had no idea what it was, nor why its opening was such a big deal. Nonetheless, Eurocentrism provides a better target than Americentrism.

In school districts where most children are black and Hispanic, there has been a growing tendency to embrace particularism rather than pluralism. Many of the children in these districts perform poorly in academic classes and leave school without graduating. They would fare better in school if they had well-educated and well-paid teachers, small classes, good materials, encouragement at home and school, summer academic programs, protection from the drugs and crime that ravage their neighborhoods, and higher expectations of satisfying careers upon graduation. These are expensive and time-consuming remedies that must also engage the larger society beyond the school. The lure of particularism is that it offers a less complicated anodyne, one in which the children's academic deficiencies may be addressed—or set aside—by inflating their racial pride. The danger of this remedy is that it will detract attention from the real needs of schools and the real interests of children, while simultaneously arousing distorted race pride in children of all races, increasing racial antagonism and producing fresh recruits for white and black racist groups.

The particularist critique gained a major forum in New York in 1989, with the release of a report called "A Curriculum of Inclusion," produced by a task force created by the State Commissioner of Education, Thomas Sobol. In 1987, soon after his appointment, Sobol appointed a Task Force on Minorities to review the state's curriculum for instances of bias. He did this not because there had been complaints about bias in the curriculum, but because—as a newly appointed state commissioner whose previous job had been to superintend the public schools of a wealthy suburb, Scarsdale—he wanted to demonstrate his sensitivity to minority concerns. The Sobol task force was composed of representatives of African American, Hispanic, Asian American, and American Indian groups.

The task force engaged four consultants, one from each of the aforementioned racial or ethnic minorities, to review nearly one hundred teachers' guides prepared by the state. These guides define the state's curriculum, usually as a list of facts and concepts to be taught, along with model activities. The primary focus of the consultants, not surprisingly, was the history and social studies curriculum. As it happened, the history curriculum had been extensively revised in 1987 to make it multicultural, in both American and world history. In the 1987 revision the time given to Western Europe was reduced to one-quarter of one year, as part of a two-year global studies sequence in which equal time was allotted to seven major world regions, including Africa and Latin America.

As a result of the 1987 revisions in American and world history, New York State had one of the most advanced multicultural history-social studies curricula in the country. Dozens of social studies teachers and consultants had participated, and the final draft was reviewed by such historians as Eric Foner of Columbia University, the late Hazel Hertzberg of Teachers College, Columbia University, and Christopher Lasch of the University of Rochester. The curriculum was overloaded with facts, almost to the point of numbing students with details and trivia, but it was not insensitive to ethnicity in American history or unduly devoted to European history.

But the Sobol task force decided that this curriculum was biased and Eurocentric. The first sentence of the task force report summarizes its major thesis: "African Americans, Asian Americans, Puerto Ricans/Latinos, and Native Americans have all been the victims of an intellectual and educational oppression that has characterized the culture and institutions of the United States and the European American world for centuries."

The task force report was remarkable in that it vigorously denounced bias without identifying a single instance of bias in the curricular guides under review. Instead, the consultants employed harsh, sometimes inflammatory, rhetoric to treat every difference of opinion or interpretation as an example of racial bias. The African-American consultant, for example, excoriates the curriculum for its "White Anglo-Saxon (WASP) value system and norms," its "deep-seated pathologies of racial hatred" and its "white nationalism"; he decries as bias the fact that children study Egypt as part of the Middle East instead of as part of Africa. Perhaps Egypt should be studied as part of the African unit (geographically, it is located on the African continent); but placing it in one region rather than the other is not what most people think of as racism or bias. The "Latino" consultant criticizes the use of the term "Spanish-American War" instead of "Spanish-Cuban-American War." The Native American consultant complains that tribal languages are classified as "foreign languages."

The report is consistently Europhobic. It repeatedly expresses negative judgments on "European Americans" and on everything Western and European. All people with a white skin are referred to as "Anglo-Saxons" and "WASPs." Europe, says the report, is uniquely responsible for producing aggressive individuals who "were ready to 'discover, invade and conquer' foreign land because of greed, racism and national egoism." All white people are held collectively guilty for the historical crimes of slavery and racism. There is no mention of the "Anglo-Saxons" who opposed slavery and racism. Nor does the report acknowledge that some whites have been victims of discrimination and oppression. The African American consultant writes of the Constitution, "There is something vulgar and revolting in glorifying a process that heaped undeserved rewards on a segment of the population while oppressing the majority."

The New York task force proposal is not merely about the reconstruction of what is taught. It goes a step further to suggest that the history curriculum may be used to ensure that "children from Native American, Puerto Rican/Latino, Asian American, and African American cultures will have higher self-esteem and self-respect, while children from European cultures will have a less arrogant perspective of being part of the group that has 'done it all.' "

In February 1990, Commissioner Sobol asked the New York Board of Regents to endorse a sweeping revision of the history curriculum to make it more multicultural. His recommendations were couched in measured tones, not in the angry rhetoric of his task force. The board supported his request unanimously. It remains to be seen whether New York pursues the particularist path marked out by the Commissioner's advisory group or finds its way to the concept of pluralism within a democratic tradition.

The rising tide of particularism encourages the politicization of all curricula in the schools. If education bureaucrats bend to the political and ideological winds, as is their wont, we can anticipate a generation of struggle over the content of the curriculum in mathematics, science, literature, and history. Demands for "culturally relevant" studies, for ethnostudies of all kinds, will open the classroom to unending battles over whose version is taught, who gets credit for what, and which ethno-interpretation is appropriate. Only recently have districts begun to resist the demands of fundamentalist groups to censor textbooks and library books (and some have not yet begun to do so).

The spread of particularism throws into question the very idea of American public education. Public schools exist to teach children the general skills and knowledge that they need to succeed in American society, and the specific skills and knowledge that they need in order to function as American citizens. They receive public support because they have a public function. Historically, the public schools were known as "common schools" because they were schools for all, even if the children of all the people did not attend them. Over the years, the courts have found that it was unconstitutional to teach religion in the common schools, or to separate children on the basis of their race in the common schools. In their curriculum, their hiring practices, and their general philosophy, the public schools must not discriminate against or give preference to any racial or ethnic group. Yet they are permitted to accommodate cultural diversity by, for example, serving food that is culturally appropriate or providing library collections that emphasize the interests of the local community. However, they should not be expected to teach children to view the world through an ethnocentric perspective that rejects or ignores the common culture. For generations, those groups that wanted to inculcate their religion or their ethnic heritage have instituted private schools—after school, on weekends, or on a full-time basis. There, children learn with others of the same group—Greeks, Poles, Germans, Japanese, Chinese, Jews, Lutherans, Catholics, and so on—and are taught by people from the same group. Valuable as this exclusive experience has been for those who choose it, this has not been the role of public education. One of the primary purposes of public education has been to create a national community, a definition of citizenship and culture that is both expansive and *inclusive*.

The curriculum in public schools must be based on whatever knowledge and practices have been determined to be best by professionals—experienced teachers and scholars—who are competent to make these judgments. Professional societies must be prepared to defend the integrity of their disciplines. When called upon, they should establish review committees to examine disputes over curriculum and to render judgment, in order to help school officials fend off improper political pressure. Where genuine controversies exist, they should be taught and debated in the classroom. Was Egypt a black civilization? Why not raise the question, read the arguments of the different sides in the debate, show slides of Egyptian pharoahs and queens, read books about life in ancient Egypt, invite guest scholars from the local university, and visit museums with Egyptian collections? If scholars disagree, students should know it. One great advantage of this approach is that students will see that history is a lively study, that textbooks are fallible, that historians disagree, that the writing of history is influenced by the historian's politics and ideology, that history is written by people who make choices among alternative facts and interpretations, and that history changes as new facts are uncovered and new interpretations win adherents. They will also learn that cultures and civilizations constantly interact, exchange ideas, and influence one another, and that the idea of racial or ethnic purity is a myth. Another advantage is that students might once again study ancient history, which has all but disappeared from the curricula of American schools. (California recently introduced a required sixth grade course in ancient civilizations, but ancient history is otherwise *terra incognita* in American education.)

The multicultural controversy may do wonders for the study of history, which has been neglected for years in American schools. At this time, only half of our high school graduates ever study any world history. Any serious attempt to broaden students' knowledge of Africa, Europe, Asia, and Latin America will require at least two, and possibly three years of world history (a requirement thus far only in California). American history, too, will need more time than the one-year high-school survey course. Those of us who have insisted for years on the importance of history in the curriculum may not be ready to assent to its redemptive power, but hope that our new allies will ultimately join a constructive dialogue that strengthens the place of history in the schools.

As cultural controversies arise, educators must adhere to the principle of "E Pluribus Unum." That is, they must maintain a balance between the demands of the one—the nation of which we are common citizens—and the many—the varied histories of the American people. It is not necessary to denigrate either the one or the many. Pluralism is a positive value, but it is also important that we preserve a sense of an American community—a society and a culture to which we all belong. If there is no overall community with an agreed-upon vision of liberty and justice, if all we have is a collection of racial and ethnic cultures, lacking any common bonds, then we have no means to mobilize public opinion on behalf of people who are not members of our particular group. We have, for example, no reason to support public education. If there is no larger community, then each group will want to teach its own children in its own way, and public education ceases to exist.

History should not be confused with filiopietism. History gives no grounds for race pride. No race has a monopoly on virtue. If anything, a study of history should inspire humility, rather than pride. People of every racial group have committed terrible crimes, often against others of the same group. Whether one looks at the history of Europe or Africa or Latin America or Asia, every continent offers examples of inhumanity. Slavery has existed in civilizations around the world for centuries. Examples of genocide can be found around the world, throughout history, from ancient times right through to our own day. Governments and cultures, sometimes by edict, sometimes simply following tradition, have practiced not only slavery, but human sacrifice, infanticide, cliterodectomy, and mass murder. If we teach children this, they might recognize how absurd both racial hatred and racial chauvinism are.

What must be preserved in the study of history is the spirit of inquiry, the readiness to open new questions and to pursue new understandings. History, at its best, is a search for truth. The best way to portray this search is through debate and controversy, rather than through imposition of fixed beliefs and immutable facts. Perhaps the most dangerous aspect of school history is its tendency to become Official History, a sanctified version of the Truth taught by the state to captive audiences and embedded in beautiful mass-market textbooks as holy writ. When Official History is written by committees responding to political pressures, rather than by scholars synthesizing the best available research, then the errors of the past are replaced by the politically fashionable errors of the present. It may be difficult to teach children that history is both important and uncertain, and that even the best historians never have all the pieces of the jigsaw puzzle, but it is necessary to do so. If state education departments permit the revision of their history courses and textbooks to become an exercise in power politics, then the entire process of state-level curriculum-making becomes suspect, as does public education itself.

The question of self-esteem is extraordinarily complex, and it goes well beyond the content of the curriculum. Most of what we call self-esteem is formed in the home and in a variety of life experiences, not only in school. Nonetheless, it has been important for blacks—and for other racial groups—to learn about the history of slavery and of the civil rights movement; it has been important for blacks to know that their ancestors actively resisted enslavement and actively pursued equality; and it has been important for blacks and others to learn about black men and women who fought courageously against racism and who provide models of courage, persistence, and intellect. These are instances where the content of the curriculum reflects sound scholarship, and at the same time probably lessens racial prejudice and provides inspiration for those who are descendants of slaves. But knowing about the travails and triumphs of one's forebears does not necessarily translate into either self-esteem or personal accomplishment. For most children, self-esteem—the self-confidence that grows out of having reached a goal—comes not from hearing about the monuments of their ancestors but as a consequence of what they are able to do and accomplish through their own efforts.

As I reflected on these issues, I recalled reading an interview a few years ago with a talented black runner. She said that her model is Mikhail Baryshnikov. She admires him because he is a magnificent athlete. He is not black; he is not female; he is not American-born; he is not even a runner. But he inspires her because of the way he trained and used his body. When I read this, I thought how narrow-minded it is to believe that people can be inspired *only* by those who are exactly like them in race and ethnicity.

CHAPTER 22

MULTICULTURAL EDUCATION (1984)
A valued but problematic ideal
Charles A. Tesconi

The analysis of multicultural education which follows has been shaped by several assumptions. Among the most noteworthy are:

- The term *multiculturalism*, as typically used in educational literature, speaks to the reality of group diversity, cultural and otherwise;
- advocates for multicultural education are in pursuit of a generally valued, but ambiguous ideal;
- the theoretical/social philosophical foundations of multicultural education are derived from the ideology of cultural pluralism;
- any assessment of the multicultural education movement and proposed educational policies and practices favoring multiculturalism must begin with an analysis of cultural pluralism ideology;
- cultural pluralism ideology emphasizes ethnic group diversity, while multicultural education addresses diversity in virtually all its forms, ethnic and otherwise;
- multicultural education is more broadly based than education for cultural pluralism;
- cultural diversity and equal opportunity could be eroded, given the rush to practice multicultural education in the face of ambiguities and unknowns.

We all know or should know by now that homogeneity has not and does not characterize American society. We know how great a myth the "melting pot" turned out to be. But we should also be aware of how much did actually melt—being Irish-American or Italian-American is very different from being Irish or Italian. Moreover, in addition to American inter-ethnic and intra-ethnic group diversity, there are myriad differences associated with age, gender, economic status, regionalism, and human exceptionality of all sorts, to cite only a few. American society, then, is best characterized as a mosaic of an extensive, highly diverse array of cultural elements.

This diversity has not gone unnoticed, especially in education. Congress, the courts, educational organizations, and numerous professional and citizen groups have recognized that public schools must prepare individuals to appreciate, value, and function effectively in this diverse society. This recognition has been translated into educational policies and practices which reflect the conviction that individuals must have a deeper understanding of their cultural heritages and those of others, that prejudices must be minimized, and the appreciation of all differences maximized. These and other related efforts, it is claimed, will create a more "harmonious, patriotic, and committed populace" (Title IX, Ethnic Heritages Act, 1974).

Multicultural education and multiculturalism

Multicultural education is the currently favored term which is employed to label these efforts. As set forth by the National Council for the Accreditation of Teacher Education, multicultural education is:

> ... preparation for the social, political, and economic realities individuals experience in culturally diverse and complex human encounters. These realities have both national and international dimensions. This preparation provides a process by which an individual develops competencies for perceiving, believing, evaluating, and behaving in differential cultural settings. Thus, multicultural education is viewed as an intervention and an ongoing assessment process to help institutions and individuals become more responsive to the human condition, individual cultural integrity, and cultural pluralism in society. (NCATE, 1979)

Educational policies and practices derived from this broad concept vary widely, as would be expected. But all tend to subsume the following:

- knowledge of cultures and subcultures with emphasis on significant minority groups
- awareness of how specific cultures shape student responses to schooling
- minimizing prejudice and maximizing tolerance for different others
- adjustments in curricula aimed at promoting non-assimilationist strategies and values

Multicultural education is derived, in turn, from the term multiculturalism. It is important to recognize that the latter possesses a *descriptive meaning*, which portrays an empirical state of affairs, and a *prescriptive meaning*, carrying ideological connotations, and suggesting a particular forging of social and educational policy. Multicultural education is one derivative of the prescriptive meaning.

In these ways, the term multiculturalism is not unlike others employed in American social and philosophical discourse regarding the state of diversity in American society. Specifically, multiculturalism, like cultural pluralism and the melting pot, is, at once, offered as an empirical descriptor regarding the state of cultural and other differences in American society and as a value prescriptor in terms of what should be done relative to such differences.

As a descriptor, multiculturalism points to a condition of numerous life styles, values, and belief systems. It labels, in short, the empirical fact of cultural diversity. It should be noted that the inclusion of *culture* or *cultural* in multiculturalism serves to ascribe cultural status to the extensive phenomena the term is purported to address. The same holds for multicultural education. This raises problems, some of which will be addressed later in this paper.

As prescriptors, weighted with ideological values, multiculturalism and multicultural education have been heavily imbued with the tenets and assumptions of the ideology of cultural pluralism. They are typically employed in ways which hold that any human society is best served by maximizing (or at least maintaining) the distinctiveness of different tastes and values in just about every conceivable realm of human experience—political, religious, social, linguistic, and so on.

Several premises are presumed to provide the foundation for translating the descriptive and prescriptive meanings of multiculturalism into education policy and practice. These include the following:

- Multiculturalism is a fact of American society (the descriptive meaning of the term).
- Multiculturalism is a resource that should be preserved, if not extended, in American society (the prescriptive and ideological meaning of the term).
- By treating diverse cultural groups and ways of life as equally legitimate, and by teaching about them in positive ways, legitimizing differences through various education policies and practices, self-understanding, self-esteem, intergroup understanding and harmony, and equal opportunity are promoted.
- The school is society's major socialization agency and it is the logical, if not natural, place to preserve and extend this resource.

It is interesting to note that these premises are virtually the same as those embedded in cultural pluralism ideology and in efforts to ensure such pluralism is accommodated in educational policy and practice. In short, proponents of multicultural education have wittingly or unwittingly embroidered their advocacy with the tenets of cultural pluralism ideology.

The heavy reliance on cultural pluralism reflects the failure of multicultural education proponents to carve out a unique theoretical foundation. As a consequence, multicultural education advocates are vulnerable to the limitations which inhere in cultural pluralism ideology; that is, questions and challenges which can be directed at cultural pluralism ideology are also appropriately raised relative to multiculturalism and multicultural education. It is to these we now turn.

Cultural pluralism ideology

It should come as no surprise that multiculturalism (in its prescriptive sense) and multicultural education are attracting controversy and confusion. After all, the term cultural pluralism and its ideology, upon which the former are founded, are as controversial and illusive today as they were in the 1950s when Horace Kallen (1956) sought to clarify their meaning some five decades after he had introduced them (p. 46). Kallen recognized that the wide-ranging sociopolitical implications of cultural pluralism would attract much attention and criticism. Cultural pluralism ideology speaks primarily to the way in which a society *should* be organized and the manner in which oncoming generations should be socialized. Most significant, the term and ideology were introduced during a time when assimilationist ideology fueled public and education policy.

Despite a relatively long history as an ideology prescribing how a democratic society should work—including a growing body of literature calling for the incorporation of cultural pluralism in all institutional sectors—there is no comprehensive, systematic analysis of this ideology, and little direct testing of its assumptions and promises. Indeed, the effects of living in a culturally pluralistic society upon the developing as well as the adult human are for the most part unknown. Gordon pointed out in 1961 what remains essentially accurate today: "No close analytical attention has been given either by social scientists or practitioners of intergroup relations to the meaning of cultural pluralism, its nature and relevance for a modern industrialized society, and its implications for problems of prejudice and discrimination" (p. 275). The same and more must be said about multiculturalism and multicultural education for, as suggested earlier, their advocates use the phrase cultural pluralism to suggest meanings not implied by the originators and advocates of cultural pluralism ideology.

Nevertheless, demands for promoting a greater cultural pluralism, heard today largely in terms of multicultural education, grow louder every day. And the promises of cultural pluralism ideology, in spite of their reliance on untested assumptions, are used to legitimize these demands.

Several interrelated assumptions underlie cultural pluralism ideology and hence its step-child, multiculturalism. We shall look at five of these which relate directly or indirectly to socialization processes and goals and to group diversity.[1]

Five assumptions in search of evidence

The first assumption of cultural pluralism ideology, and hence multiculturalism, is that an individual's membership in and attachment to primary ethnic or cultural group life, and the socially encouraged involvement in it, promote those characteristics in a person usually associated with a healthy personality type—self-esteem, sense of belonging, respect for others, purposefulness, and critical thinking (Kallen, 1956, p. 25).

This assumption must be counted among the least controversial of cultural pluralism ideology; yet, some major questions present themselves. Although few of us would take issue with the claim that strong primary group ties lead to a sense of security and "rooted" identity, is it true that respect for others follows from such ties? What happens to individuality in organic community? Under what conditions do such ties lead to respect for others?

This latter question suggests another assumption, namely, that a personality characterized by tolerance and openness to different others—necessary to a truly democratic society—is dependent upon the opportunity of individuals to encounter and interact with a variety of culturally different others. As Kallen (1956) argued, the more groups an individual can encounter, join, or leave, the more varied their characters and functions, the more civilized is likely to be the individual and society as a whole.

This second assumption serves to answer the question raised previously regarding respect for others following primary group attachment. Specifically, intergroup fluidity protects against what otherwise could be negative consequences following socially encouraged group membership, especially if that membership means parochialism, is not open to change, and/or does not allow contact with other groups.

However, consideration should be given to the possibility that intergroup fluidity in the context of potent assimilative pressures or in the absence of strong reinforcements for ethnic group identification could lead to, indeed often does lead to, acculturation or assimilation. This poses a serious question for cultural pluralism advocates: What does freedom of association and intergroup fluidity do to the culture which binds one to a primary group? What does it do, ultimately, to the cultural differences so highly valued?

Before these assumptions can pass an adequate test, several additional questions present themselves. What characterizes "fluidity" in group membership? How is it achieved? What happens to membership in a primary group when a member moves into and out of the primary group, into and out of other groups? Could it mean, for example, as Green (1966) suggested regarding a related phenomenon, that "the Jew has less identity as a Jew, the Catholic less as a Catholic, and even the Episcopalian less as Episcopalian" (p. 11)?

It should also be noted in these regards that cultural pluralists are not always explicit in their discussion of the notion of freedom of association as it applies to what might be considered political groupings (or functional as opposed to organic groups). Research findings relating to such matters as tolerance and ethnic group attachment, and tolerance as a function of intergroup mobility, ethnic group membership, and political interest group membership, must be identified and related to cultural pluralism ideology and multiculturalism. As Merton pointed out (Merton & Rossi, 1950), there is need for a close study of the processes in group life which sustain or inhibit orientations to non-membership groups, thus perhaps leading to a linking of reference group theory and current theories of social organization, including cultural pluralism ideology.

Related to the freedom of association principle is a third assumption which, as pointed out by Green (1966, p. 11), holds that no one way of life can be said to be better than any other and that to be humane a society must afford room for many competing and oftentimes conflicting ways of life. If no one way of life can without question claim superiority over any other, how does one go about resolving competing and conflicting values? What are the criteria for such judgments? If we are to live by the ideology of cultural pluralism (and multiculturalism), it is necessary to identify or create some effective principles and means for resolving conflicts in values and goals.

These questions raise fundamental problems for cultural pluralism ideology and, thus, for multiculturalism. They suggest a need for a process to identify those aspects of a particular group's culture which should be maintained and perpetuated in a society which claims to operate on the basis of cultural pluralism ideology. Surely we can conceive of aspects of particular cultures that could be considered unworthy of perpetuation. For example, I know that my daughter is not interested in seeing the perpetuation of the kinds of male dominance and the roles for women associated with some cultural groups. How will we decide what is and what is not to be sustained? Who will make these decisions? Should they be made? If they are made, what happens to the maintenance of the society whose very existence gives a basis of the celebration of cultural diversity?

In this light, then, we must ask what elements are referred to by *culture* in cultural pluralism and multiculturalism. Moreover, since multicultural education, at least in terms of usage, points to valued differences that some would not label as cultural, it is necessary to analyze the way these differences interact with and impact upon those that are clearly accepted as cultural phenomena. Indeed, the interaction between cultural phenomena and other valued differences is crucial to helping decide policies and strategies for education.

A fourth assumption and attendant claim of cultural pluralism ideology and multiculturalism is that it is valuable to have many ways of life in competition and that such competition leads to a balance or equilibrium in the social order. Yet, equilibrium in a democratic society is a question of power, specifically, a question of a fair and equal distribution of power. Thus, friendly contact and open competition among and between groups can only take place when equilibrium is present and when one or more culture(s) or cultural group(s) does not seek to destroy others. How does one reach this point if reaching it demands intergroup contact on a fair and equal basis and if, in turn, "a fair and equal basis" is, *a priori*, dependent upon equilibrium?

A final assumption, at least for the purposes of this analysis, bears directly on the processes and goals of socialization. This is the assumption that loyalty to a larger society—a nation—is a function of, and dependent on, socially sanctioned loyalties rooted in a multiplicity of diverse ethnic and cultural groups. It is this assumption which leads cultural pluralists and multiculturalists to the notion that a society will be rich, unified, healthy, and nourished to a fuller life to the extent that it is fashioned out of genuine human groupings.

Kallen (1956) points out in these regards that a nation can be unified "only as a union on equal terms of sovereign and independent diversities alone whose agreement could make and keep it thus one . . . The oneness they turn to must . . . start from plurality and can live only as the associative pattern which this plurality consent to" (p. 47). In short, a healthy society must be based on a mosaic of autonomous groupings reflecting the underlying differences in the population. Grodzins (cited in Wolff, 1968), in *The Loyal and Disloyal*, presented this assumption thus:

> Groups, large and small, play a crucial, independent role in the transference of allegiance to the nation. For one thing, they are the means through which citizens are brought to participate in civic affairs and national ceremony . . . Individuals, in short, act for the nation in response to the smaller groups with which they identify themselves . . . Their loyalty to smaller groups ensures their doing it. . . . So it is that loyalties to smaller groups supply the guts of national endeavor even when that endeavor has no meaning to the individual concerned. (pp. 135–136)

From these and other assumptions, cultural pluralists are led to claim that, as an operational set of social beliefs, cultural pluralism would prevent dangerous social and personal disorganization which follow when culturally diverse individuals are pressured to reject their primary group ties. It is these assumptions, furthermore, which lead cultural pluralists to assert that a fusion of primary group loyalty with loyalty to a larger cultural entity—society at large or the nation—can only come about when the primary group is able to enjoy all those social freedoms which come to those who express basic loyalty to the larger society. In short, democracy for the whole, and attachment to the whole, comes only with democracy for, and socially encouraged attachment to, the constituent parts.

We must ask, however, if loyalty to the nation does indeed follow from group loyalty? If so, how does it come about? Alternatively, could it be that in a time of mass society the assumed human need for a sense of community is so great that it gradually dissolves the bonds of some from national territory or from the common culture that unites diverse groups into a national state? In short, the bonds-that-tie at the nation level may dissolve in a mass society with the help of intensified primary group consciousness and membership need.

Further considerations

Finally, a few other criticisms, of a different sort, are in order. When we link multicultural with education and come up with the phrase multicultural education, we need to be clear about what we mean. An essay by Grant (1978) is enlightening in these regards. He reminds us that the word multicultural is an adjective, meaning "of," "relating to," or "designed for a combination of distinct cultures." As an adjective, multicultural modifies education. More specifically, as Grant suggests, when we use the phrase multicultural education we are limiting or restricting the meaning of education. In this sense, multicultural education takes on a meaning function not unlike terms such as health education, special education, physical education, and the like. However, this does not appear to be what multiculturalists have in mind or intend when they use this phrase. Moreover, it may account, at least in part, for the fact that multicultural education has become something that is tacked on to the curriculum at some point—added to it along the way here and there—rather than being infused throughout.

Another issue relates to the need for a distinction between cultural pluralism or multiculturalism and structural pluralism or social stratification. Structural pluralism refers to the fact that American society is socially stratified and structured to give various groups different access to its socioeconomic resources. Theoretically, cultural pluralism or multiculturalism could exist without structural pluralism or social stratification. But, given social reality and our history, the former tend to coincide to some degree with the latter. In other words, some cultural groups wind up on top of the heap, others in the middle, and others on the bottom.

The past two decades have produced some rather important changes in the correlations between cultural group membership and group standing in the social stratification system, but the changes have not been as dramatic or as great as rhetoric might lead us to believe or as great as many think they should be. The question is this: What characterizes educational efforts that are designed to at once sustain or extend multiculturalism or cultural pluralism and at the same time promote greater opportunity or access for all?

Consider that efforts to date fall into at least two categories. The first is what we might call *transitory or compensatory* efforts that tend to get at the social stratification problems. The second might be called *enlightenment or enrichment* efforts that have been inclined toward fostering cultural pluralism, but have not dealt directly with the issue of social stratification (Harrington, 1978). There is some literature which suggests that the elimination of structural pluralism would lead to the elimination of cultural pluralism or multiculturalism (see, for example, Gordon, 1961, and Harrington, 1978). Conversely, such literature also suggests that the maintenance of the latter ensures the former. These possibilities must be examined before we rush to practice whatever it is we mean by multicultural education.

Conclusion

Multiculturalism is too precious a societal resource to put at risk through ill-conceived public policies and practices based on limited understandings and fuzzy concepts. In turn, the laudable goals of cultural pluralists and multiculturalists are also too important to be put at risk. The educational "rush to practice" in the face of questionable and untested assumptions and concepts which fuel this movement must be balanced by a large-scale, systematic effort to clarify and search out means for testing these matters.

In sum, educators should be mindful of the significance of group affiliation, but at the same time recognize that group togetherness may be unthinking and unimaginative, its only purpose to maintain separateness and divisiveness.

One wonders about American society's dilemma of finding a balance between the two ideals of "groupism" and "the nation." Today this problem defines the next stage in the evolution of the American people. But it is important for us as educators to remember that the American nationality is still forming. Its processes are not in the final form, if there is ever to be a final form.

Notes

1   The identification and analysis of these assumptions have been influenced by Thomas Green (1966).

I wish to note that I use the term assumption in its fundamental sense; it refers to matters taken for granted. Horace Kallen's insights, and many of those coming from latter-day advocates of cultural pluralism and multiculturalism, emerged from an examination of personal ethnic experiences. Kallen tested these insights as hypotheses with his own and other ethnic conferees, with people who prized and acted on their own ethnicity. Long before the so-called radical or third-force historians and social scientists, he acted on the principle that the only reality was that which emerged from phenomenologically tested experience.

References

Gordon, M. (1961, Spring). Assimilation in America: Theory and reality. *Daedalus*, 90.

Grant, C. (1978, September-October). Education that is multicultural: Isn't that what we mean? *Journal of Teacher Education, 29*, p. 46.

Green, T. (1966). Education and pluralism: Ideal and reality. *Twenty-Sixth Annual J. Richard Street Lecture*, Syracuse University.

Harrington, C. (1978, Summer). Bilingual education, social stratification, and cultural pluralism. *Equal Opportunity Review*.

Kallen, H. (1956). *Cultural pluralism and the American idea.* Philadelphia: University of Pennsylvania Press.

Merton, R.K., & Rossi, A.K. (1950). Reference group theory and social mobility. In R.K. Merton & P.L. Lazasfeld (Eds.), *Continuities in sociological research.* New York: The Free Press.

National Council for Accreditation of Teacher Education. (1979). *Standards for the accreditation of teacher education.* Washington, DC: Author.

Wolff, R.P. (1968). *The poverty of liberalism.* Boston: Beacon Press.

CHAPTER 23

A NEW WORD FOR AN OLD PROBLEM (1994)
Multicultural "school wars" date to the 1840s
Nathan Glazer

Recent proposals that schools and colleges in the United States give greater emphasis to the history and accomplishments of America's racial and ethnic minorities—become more "multicultural"—have generated an intense public debate.

None of the leading critics of a multicultural curriculum—neither Arthur Schlesinger, Jr., author of *The Disuniting of America*, nor Diane Ravitch, the educational historian and former assistant secretary of education, nor Albert Shanker, president of the American Federation of Teachers—argues against a healthy diversity that acknowledges the varied sources of the American people and our culture. Still, all see a multicultural curriculum as a threat to the way we live together in a common nation.

Specifically, the critics envisage the possibility that large sections of the American population, particularly poor racial and ethnic groups that have been subjected to discrimination, will receive an education that attributes blame for their condition to the white or European majority and thereby worsen political and social splits along racial and ethnic lines. The gravest fear is that "oppression studies," as opponents label multiculturalism, will cultivate an active hostility among some minorities to the key institutions of state and society, making effective government, as well as the economic progress of such groups, more difficult.

To its critics, multiculturalism looks like a very new thing in American education. In many respects, it is. However, viewed in the long stretch of the history of American public schooling, we can recognize it as a new word for an old problem: how public schools are to respond to and take account of the diversity of backgrounds of their students—religious, ethnic, racial. American public education, at least that part of it in our major cities, has rarely been free of this issue. For some decades, between the decline of European immigration in the 1920s and the rise of black nationalism in the 1960s, we were free of it. Undoubtedly, this halcyon period, during which many of the chief participants in the debate were themselves educated, colors their view of the current dispute.

With the origins of urban public education in the 1840s, the first of the "great school wars," as Diane Ravitch calls them in her history of New York City public education, broke out. That first war centered on the demands of Catholic leaders for something like equal treatment for Catholic students in public schools whose principal aim was to socialize children into the Protestant moral and religious world of the mid-19th century. Catholic religious leaders objected in particular to readings from the Protestant King James Bible. Why not the Catholic Douay translation? (No one dreamed, in those distant days, that the First Amendment to the Constitution, with its prohibition of an "establishment of religion," would in time be used to ban all Bible reading in schools.) The outcome of the conflict was that Catholics decided to establish their own schools, to the degree their capacities allowed, and created a separate, Catholic system of education in the major cities of the country.

In the 1880s, bitter public disputes broke out about the rights of the children of German immigrants to receive instruction in German. Teaching in German was widely established in Cincinnati, St. Louis, and elsewhere, to the discomfort of nativists and those concerned with the assimiliation of immigrants. In 1889, the historian David Tyack tells us, Illinois and Wisconsin "tried to regulate immigrant private and parochial schools by requiring that most instruction be conducted in English. As in the case of Protestant rituals in the schools, the contest over instruction in language other than English became a symbolic battle between whose who wanted to impose one standard of belief and those who welcomed pluralistic forms of education."

World War I, with its encouragement of a fierce national (or was it ethnic?) chauvinism, finished off the acceptance of German as a language of instruction in public schools. Nevertheless, it was during the build-up to entry into the war that the first major arguments for multiculturalism in American education were set forth.

"Cultural pluralism" was the term Horace Kallen, a student and follower of John Dewey, used to describe a new kind of public education, in which a variety of cultures besides that of England would receive a significant place in American public education.

John Dewey himself, in 1916, speaking to the National Education Association, took up the cudgels for cultural pluralism:

> Such terms as Irish-American or Hebrew-American or German-American are false terms, because they seem to assume something that is already in existence in America, to which the other factors may be hitched on. The fact is, the genuine American, the typical American, is himself a hyphenated character. It does not mean that he is part American and that some foreign ingredient is in his make-up. He is not American plus Pole or German. But the American is himself Pole-German-English-French-Spanish-Italian-Greek-Irish-Scandinavian-Bohemian-Jew—and so on. The point is to see to it that the hyphen connects instead of separates. And this means at least that our public schools shall teach each factor to respect every other, and shall take pains to enlighten us all as to the great past contributions of every strain in our composite make-up.

But the wave of postwar chauvinism that led Americans to deport East Europeans to Bolshevik Russia, to ban mass immigration, and to revive the Ku Klux Klan was too strong. In 1919, Nebraska forbade the teaching of any foreign language before the eighth grade (the Nebraska courts exempted Greek, Latin, and Hebrew, all presumed safely dead). In the 1920s, Oregon tried to ban any private schools at all. (Both laws were overturned by the Supreme Court.) In the public schools, Americanization was the order of the day, and prevailed without a check through the 1940s, while the children of the last great wave of European immigration were being educated.

I attended the schools of New York City from 1929 to 1944 (I include the public City College of New York in that stretch), and not a whiff of cultural pluralism was to be found. Americanization was strong, unself-conscious, and self-confident. Although probably two-thirds of the students in New York's public schools were Jewish or Italian, no Jewish or Italian figure was to be found in our texts for literature, for social studies, for history. All cultures but that of the founding English and its American variant were ignored, and students were left to assume, if they thought about the matter at all, that the cultures of their homes and parental homelands were irrelevant or inferior.

And that singularly unicultural educational background is having an important effect on the current debates over multiculturalism. For many protagonists in this debate, the conflicts over educating Catholic and later, German-speaking students, as well as the arguments for multiculturalism in the age of mass immigration, are all a kind of murky prehistory, wiped out in a flood that deposited a uniform silt over our past, leaving only fossil remains of that earlier diversity and those earlier conflicts. Advocates of multiculturalism today often do not know that they had forebears; nor do opponents of multiculturalism today know that the education they experienced was the expression of an age singularly free of conflict over issues of cultural pluralism.

The arguments for cultural pluralism began to emerge again during World War II, and the motivating force was Hitler. If he argued that one race and one people was superior and should be dominant, then it was in the interest of the war effort to teach equality and tolerance. In the 1940s, a small movement for "intercultural education" sprouted. Its aim was to teach something about the various ethnic and racial groups that made up America, and to teach tolerance. Just how extensive it actually was in the schools is not clear, but it did not survive the 1950s and 1960s, when cultural pluralism was pushed aside by the shock of Sputnik and the issue of desegregation.

Something of a contradiction existed between desegregation, as then envisaged, and cultural pluralism. The aim of black and liberal civil rights leaders was for blacks to get the same education that whites received. If whites' education had precious little of cultural pluralism or multiculturalism in it, why should that be changed for blacks? The black objective, through the entire course of the struggle in the courts in the 1940s and 1950s for equality, was assimilation. Blacks should not be treated differently because they were black.

But that was transmuted rapidly into the demand of many militants that blacks must get something different because they were black. By the late 1960s, a "black power" movement, black Muslims, and other manifestations of black nationalism were already challenging the assimilationist civil-rights leadership. Black schools were started in black communities, and some were even established under the aegis of liberal public school systems (as in Berkeley, California).

Soon Mexican Americans and Puerto Ricans raised their own grievances against the public school system, and political activists demanded the recognition of Spanish. Civil rights laws that guaranteed equality were interpreted by the Supreme Court to mean that equality for those speaking a foreign language could require instruction in that language; liberal states passed laws giving a limited right to instruction in one's native language, and federal laws and regulations and court decisions made that a requirement in many school systems.

Bilingualism is, of course, not the same thing as multiculturalism, but it was generally taken for granted that instruction in one's native language for those speaking Spanish also meant to some degree instruction in Puerto Rican or Mexican culture and history. Through the 1970s, bilingualism and the acknowledgement of distinctive group cultures and histories in social studies and history classes spread and established themselves in the public schools.

One might well ask why multiculturalism has become such an important issue today. It has been at least 20 years since public schools started adapting themselves to the presumed cultural distinctiveness and interests of blacks and Hispanics, by modifying textbooks, introducing new reading materials, changing examinations, and instructing non-English-speaking students in Spanish for a few years. What has put the issue on the agenda today, not only in the public schools, but in colleges and universities, public and private?

I believe the basic explanation is a build-up of frustration in the black population in recent years over the failure of civil rights reforms to deliver what was expected from them. In the colleges, affirmative action—well established as it is—has not increased markedly the number of black instructors or the number of black students who can qualify for the more selective institutions without special consideration. In the public schools, black achievement as measured by NAEP scores, SAT scores, and high school completion rates has improved somewhat, but the gaps between black and white achievement remain large. Blacks on the whole do worse than Hispanic groups despite the very large numbers of new, non-English-speaking immigrants, and far worse than the Asian groups.

One can record substantial black achievement in politics, in the armed forces, in the civil service, and in some high positions in the private economy, but alongside these successes a host of social problems afflicting a large part of the black population has, by some key measures, grown, not declined, in the past 20 years.

One might have expected that the multicultural debate would be fueled by the large new immigration of the past 20 years. But that is really not the moving force. The Asian immigrants, almost half the number, seem quite content with the education they get. Nor are Hispanic immigrants making demands on the public school system that necessitate radical change. Mexican Americans would like to see their children do better in school, to have more of them graduate. But they have no strong commitment to the idea that this objective will be enhanced by more teaching in Spanish, or more Mexican cultural and historical content.

For the critics of multiculturalism, the issue that ultimately determines its acceptability is a judgment as to the underlying purpose of the curriculum reform. Is it to promote harmony and an acceptance of our society? Or to portray our society as so fatally flawed by racism, so irredeemably unfair and unequal that it must be rejected as evil?

The critics fear that the second vision underlies the strong multicultural position. On one level, they are right. But if we look more deeply into the objectives of those who promote a strong multicultural thrust, and who in doing so present a somewhat lopsided view of our history, we will find that they promote multiculturalism not because they aim at divisiveness and separation as a good, not because they—to put it in the strongest terms possible—want to break up the union, but because they aim at a fuller inclusiveness of deprived groups.

In the short term, their vision may well mean more conflict and divisiveness, but they see this as a stage on the way to a greater inclusiveness. They are no Quebec separatists, Croatian nationalists, Sikh or Tamil separatists. They seek inclusion and equality in a common society.

Critics of the new multiculturalism will see my judgement as far too benign. Undoubtedly one can point to some leading advocates of multiculturalism whose intentions are not benign. But I would emphasize that we deal with a spectrum of views, some mild enough to gain the endorsement of Ravitch, Schlesinger, and Shanker. In the middle there is much to argue about.

What sort of students do multicultural schools turn out? The Catholic schools of the mid-19th century, so fearful to many as a threat to national unity, produced Americans as patriotic or more patriotic than the norm. Nor did the German-language schools do badly in molding upstanding Americans, though equally upstanding Americans were doing their best to stamp out those schools. Even Amish, Hasidic, and Black Muslim schools, while I do not know whether they produced patriots, turn out, I think, citizens as good by many measures as the public schools.

Our diversity has one major binding force in the Constitution under which we live and which still, through the procedures that it first laid down and that have been further developed in our history, governs at the margin what we can and cannot do in our public schools. The Constitution guarantees that Amish children need not attend schools after the age when their parents feel they will be corrupted, and that Mormons and Black Muslims can teach their own version of the truth, which is as fantastic to many of us as the further reaches of Afrocentrism. Even the most dissident call on the Constitution for protection, yet few people are ready to tear it up as a compact with the devil. This common political bond keeps us together—nationalists and anti-nationalists, Eurocentrists and Afrocentrists— and may continue to through the storms of multiculturalism.

America has changed. It is not God's country, anymore. We can lose wars—real ones—and we can be beaten in economic competition by the Japanese. We have become only one of a number of economically powerful, democratic countries, and not in every respect the best. And America exists in the larger reality of the non-Western world. A good deal of that world is sunk in poverty and political disorder, but some of it is teaching lessons in economic effectiveness to the West. Western hubris can never again be what it was in the late 19th and early 20th centuries.

Finally, America's population is changing in its racial and ethnic composition. Its values are changing. Its notions of the proper relation of groups and individuals to the national society are changing. As hard as it may be for veterans of the educational system of earlier decades to wrench free of their own schooling, it is even harder to see how such a system can be defended in the face of these changes.

CHAPTER 24

RETHINKING THE NATURE OF MULTICULTURAL EDUCATION (1992)

Has it lost its focus or is it being misused?

P. Rudy Mattai

Introduction

The ethnic revitalization movements of the 1960s were more than optimistic with respect to the future of communal rivalry in the United States of America. The renaissance of ethnic vitality that manifested itself in the late sixties and early seventies could very well be seen as contradicting the contentions of social scientists who, in the preceding three decades, had predicted the demise of ethnic prominence (Omni & Winant, 1986; Rex, 1983). One of the most central concerns of that ethnic renaissance was the pivotal role accorded to education (Banks, 1978, 1986, 1988; Berlowitz, 1984; Bullivant, 1981). As Banks (1986), a noted scholar in multicultural education, contends, the schools were accorded that status primarily because they were seen as instrumental in contributing to the disillusioned situation in which ethnic minorities found themselves:

> The school is usually viewed by the victimized ethnic group not only as an important vehicle that can help it to attain equality, but also as an institution that contributes to the group's exclusion because it reinforces the dominant anti-egalitarian ideologies and valued of the nation-states. Since the school is viewed by ethnic reformers as an important institution in their oppression, they attempt to reform it because they believe that it can be a pivotal vehicle in their liberation. (pp. 221, 222)

Those who were actively involved in agitating to make the schools respond to ethnic issues were not oblivious to the discriminatory fashion in which the schools selectively addressed particular bodies of knowledge and the reproduction of subcultures among their students. Numerous scholars focus on the discriminatory relationships the schools chose to foster (Anyon, 1979, 1983; Apple, 1979, 1982, 1983, 1986, 1988; Apple & Weis, 1983; Bowles & Gintis, 1976; Carnoy, 1972, 1974, 1982; Carnoy & Levin, 1985; Everhart, 1983). Despite these analyses the schools felt compelled to respond to the demands that were being placed upon them, and thus the sixties witnessed the emergence of a curricular shift. At the precollegiate level the curriculum was altered to reflect "studies of separate racial and other minority groups" (Ramsey, Vold, & Williams, 1989, pp. 7, 8). At the collegiate level whole programs in social and ethnic studies—particularly African American, Latino, and Native American studies—were added to the curriculum. Understandably, these attempts were not comprehensive, but they significantly influenced the curriculum as a whole by catalyzing the escalation of appreciation for and awareness of the contributions of heretofore excluded racial and ethnic groups (Boyer, 1985; Foerster, 1982; Vold, 1979). At best, however, such efforts were but manifestations of paternalistic attitudes and the products of decisions made by hesitant administrators. In much the same way the ethnic studies movement was catapulted to the forefront in the sixties, subsequent societal happenings led to its undermining in the seventies, and they became mere appendages to a larger, extant organism.

Notwithstanding, the agitation of ethnic minorities in the sixties gave impetus to the escalating momentum in demands for genuine incorporation of ethnic minorities (particularly African Americans, Latinos, and Native Americans) into the mainstream of American society. These ethnic populations vehemently resisted the ideological tenets of assimilation and challenged the notion that meaningful participation in American society demanded the abandonment of their cultural distinctiveness and affirmation of the ideological tenets of the dominant culture. Their intensified struggle led to the development and introduction of multicultural education into the educational curriculum at the elementary and secondary levels. Ostensibly, the purpose of the multicultural approach, according to Ramsey et al. (1989), was:

> . . . to sensitize all individuals toward ethnic and racial differences, and to increase individual awareness of cultural traditions and sociological experiences. It was also to help all individuals understand their race and culture, including language and socialization experiences, had value, and could and should exist on a coequal basis with mainstream American values and experiences. (pp. 8, 9)

In most cases, however, attempts to introduce multiculturalism into the curriculum appear to be mere political responses, and efforts to infuse the American educational curriculum with multiculturalism largely partisan activities engaging only those few who are committed to effecting significant educational and societal changes. Thus, after almost two decades of curricular engineering, a great deal of suspicion regarding the multicultural education movement exists among African Americans, Latinos, and Native Americans, many of whom presently raise serious questions about what the movement has done and/or failed to do for them.

Has multicultural education forged a situation in which African Americans, Latinos, and Native Americans can, as Ramsey et al. contend, "exist on a coequal basis with mainstream American values and experiences"; or do these groups still exist on the fringe of society? Are they able to pursue the existing educational curriculum in such a way that helps them to "understand [that] their race and culture, including language and socialization experiences, have value"? Moreover, has multicultural education subtly circumvented its original intentions? Is it now being strategically used—by those who engineer the "hidden" curriculum—to reinterpret the assimilationist perspective, albeit in disguise, and subsequently move historically disenfranchised ethnic minority groups further toward this pursuit?

The present article focuses on the seeming inability of multicultural education to address the issue of race despite the contention that race is an important variable in the consideration of the continuing disenfranchisement, largely attributable to the educational system, that minorities experience. This article argues that multicultural education curricula do not directly address eliminating racism and its vestiges nor do they provide strategies for empowering minorities to effectively counteract such phenomena. It further argues that the present manifestations of multicultural education in higher education lack institutional commitment and are thus largely palliative in nature. Consequently, attempts to introduce multiculturalism to the curricula are suspect in most cases and seem to be political responses to relatively powerful interest groups. They thereby manifest a "subtly different inflection on the question of what is to [be achieved]" (McCarthy, 1990, p. 55).

The nature of multicultural education

The official "stamp of approval" for the entrenchment of multicultural education programs in mainstream American education can be traced back to the definitive statement adopted in 1972 by the American Association of Colleges for Teacher Education (AACTE) (1973) in its publication, *No One Model American*:

> Multicultural education is education which values cultural pluralism. Multicultural education rejects the view that schools should seek to melt away cultural differences or the view that schools should merely tolerate cultural pluralism. ... It affirms that major education institutions should strive to preserve and enhance cultural pluralism. To endorse cultural pluralism is to endorse the principle that there is no one model American. (p. 264)

The AACTE statement provides more than just an operational definition of multicultural education. It goes on to demand strongly that multicultural education "must become an integral part of the education process at every level" (p. 264):

> Education for cultural pluralism includes four major thrusts: (1) the teaching of values which support cultural diversity and individual uniqueness; (2) the encouragement of the qualitative expansion of existing ethnic cultures and their incorporation into the mainstream of American socioeconomic and political life; (3) the support of explorations in alternative and emerging life styles; and (4) the encouragement of multiculturalism, multilingualism, and multidialectism . . . (p. 264)

However, what appears to be a rather pellucid statement and comprehensive position on the nature of multicultural education raises some problematic concerns. First, there is the question of definition, which goes beyond the issue of clarity. Second, there is the question of the potency or efficacy of multicultural education to change the situation of disenfranchised persons (particularly African Americans, Latinos, and Native Americans) in the educational system. Third, there is the question of whether multicultural education addresses the issue of racism in American society or circumvents this issue altogether.

The place of definitions

The definitional aspects of any discussion of multicultural education should not be dismissed as being merely semantical. Rather, because definitions may serve to justify a particular kind of practice, or vice-versa (Broudy, 1975), the importance of definitions as they relate to practice is of primary concern. Modgil, Verma, Mallick, and Modgil (1986) treat definitional clarity extensively in their discussion of multicultural education. Indeed, Verma's (1984) early position was that primarily because early definitions of multicultural education lacked clarity, they provided fertile ground for both the possibility of conceptual confusion and subsequent distraction from the objective moral and social conditions affecting minority populations. Banks (1986) therefore defines multicultural education as "an *inclusive* concept used to describe *a wide variety* of school practices, programs and materials designed to help children from diverse groups to experience educational equality [italics added]" (p. 222). Despite Banks' definition, Grant (1978) insists that "by definition, multicultural education suggests an educational concept concerned only with changing the external aspects [of education] without altering the basic patterns of education in a pluralistic society" (p. 45). He further suggests that so long as educators and activists continue to speak about multicultural education—and not education that is multicultural—no substantive change in curricula or society will occur. Grant's contention is a rather valid one that has been posited by several others. Summarizing such positions, Parekh (1986) writes:

> For the conservative critics, [multicultural education] represents an attempt to politicize education in order to pander to minority demands, whereas for some radicals it is the familiar ideological device of perpetuating the reality of racist exploitation of ethnic minorities by pampering their cultural sensitivities. (p. 19)

In the absence of clear definition, and therefore direction, McCarthy (1990) identifies three distinct models of multicultural education: the (1) cultural understanding, (2) cultural competence, and (3) cultural emancipation or social reconstruction models. According to McCarthy, the cultural understanding models were established in institutions of higher education. Their intent was to achieve a climate in which the curriculum provided opportunities for cultural understanding, the net effect being the reduction and gradual elimination of prejudice. In his view, "[t]he strong version of these programs directly target white students and teachers . . . [while] the weak version . . . emphasized the promotion of racial harmony and tolerance of social and ethnic differences" (p. 45). The cultural competence models are seen as having a more established tradition and as drawing upon the work of Reisman, Glazer, and Denney (1969) and Glazer and Moynihan (1963), who espouse an environment in which greater appreciation and understanding are shown for the plurality of ethnic configurations. These models also incorporate the AACTE's officially promulgated notion that education for cultural pluralism includes four major thrusts:

> (1) the teaching of values which support cultural diversity and individual uniqueness; (2) the encouragement of the qualitative expansion of existing ethnic cultures and their incorporation into the mainstream of American socioeconomic and political life; (3) the support of explorations in alternative and emerging life styles; and (4) the encouragement of multiculturalism, multilingualism, and multidialectism. (p. 264)

McCarthy contends that this is the background against which Banks (1987, 1988), Cortes (1986), Pettigrew (1974), Gollnick (1980), Gollnick and Chin (1990), Hernandez (1989), and Trueba and Barnett-Mizrahi (1979) approached multicultural education. Banks (1983), writing as guest editor of a special edition of *Phi Delta Kappan* on multicultural education, sums up rather pungently the general rubric under which scholars espousing the cultural competence model write:

> Education programs that spring from the idea of cultural deprivation show disrespect for student's home cultures. Educational programs that spring from the genetic hypothesis violate human dignity, and other values set forth in the American creed, because they deny the possibility of a dignified existence for minority youths, such as the cultural difference or multicultural hypothesis which provides the greatest possibility for an education that engenders justice and equity and thus improves the human condition. (p. 585)

Sleeter and Grant (1987, 1989), Suzuki (1979, 1984), Bullivant (1981), Rushton (1981), and Swartz (1989) are foremost among those who espouse cultural emancipation/social reconstruction models of multicultural education. While they eschew much of that posited by theorists of the cultural competence models, they embellish that approach by including analyses of the factors that mitigate against minority students' classroom achievement. According to McCarthy:

> They link the issue of minority underachievement in the classroom to the attitudinal prejudice of teachers and the suppression of minority culture in the school curriculum. . . . The second conceptual strand of this emancipatory agenda is related to the first, but more directly links race relations in the classroom to the economy. They suggest that curriculum and social changes in minority fortunes are possible if the school curriculum is redefined in response to the needs of minority youth . . . (pp. 51–52)

Multicultural education and the educationally disenfranchised

Stone (1981), Dhondy (1978), Carby (1980, 1982), and Mullard (1982, 1983, 1985) are equivocal in their contention that multicultural education circumvents central societal issues or that it perpetuates the conditions of the disenfranchised in the educational system. McCarthy notes that the cultural understanding approach to multicultural education received an overwhelming degree of negative criticism from a wide range of scholars (Baker, 1973, 1977; Buckingham, 1984; Garcia, 1974; Gibson, 1984; Troyna & Williams, 1986), who generally conclude that it fails for two reasons: First, it tends to generalize about the distinctiveness of racial and ethnic groups, thereby creating conditions ripe for stereotyping. Second, it naively presumes that teachers will eagerly embrace the programs, become *au fait* with the material to be covered, and faithfully "deliver the goods." McCarthy also expresses doubt regarding whether multicultural education applying the cultural competence approach can influence or call into being an educational system that achieves Banks's stated goals. He views this second approach as fraught with contradictions:

> On the one hand, the affirmation of minority culture in various bilingual, bicultural and ethnic studies programs represents a direct challenge to the centrality of Anglo values in the school curriculum and the notion that minority culture and language are "naturally" deficient. . . . On the other hand, the closely related objective of "building bridges" . . . from minority groups to

mainstream society privileges individual mobility over a collective-identity politics oriented toward change in the current structure of race relations in schools and society. (pp. 49, 50)

Concerned that participation in the American mainstream may imply conformity to the process of "normalization" Focault (1970, 1972, 1977) describes, McCarthy further questions Banks's contention that the educational system should prepare minority students to participate in the American mainstream. He doubts whether minority students educated via cultural competence-modeled multicultural curricula would be predisposed to perceiving their role as articulating both sets of cultural norms (their own and that of the dominant group) but responding appropriately only to the requisites of the latter in order to achieve gains in the American mainstream. Indeed, if the educational system merely provides minority students with the perception that they must respond appropriately to the normative practices of the dominant group to get ahead, then that perception will drive them to abandon their own cultural norms. That situation then becomes problematic for their social and psychological well-being because one's perceptions have a tendency to become one's world of reality. As the social psychologist W. I. Thomas concludes: "If men perceive their situations to be real, then they are real in their consequences" (Coser, 1977, p. 521). It is precisely this dilemma, whereupon racist practices in the society devalue minority groups' cultural reference points, that faces minority students and that multicultural education has not addressed, let alone provided strategies for empowering such students to counteract effectively.

McCarthy sees the cultural emancipation approach as offering some hope for educationally disenfranchised minority students, but he asserts that it makes two presumptions, both of which are rather simplistic. First, it assumes that both the racial and ethnic prejudices of teachers and the forces that suppress minority cultures can be easily obliterated, and that curriculum can be made apolitical. Second, as Bullivant (1981) and Rushton (1981) agree, this approach assumes that the meritocratic system will open up to ensure the wider participation of minorities in the labor market. Regarding the difficulty of achieving the first condition, Banks (1989) writes:

The struggle over the inclusion of ethnic content and the content about women in the university mainstream curriculum can best be understood as a battle over who will participate in or control the formulation of the canon or standard used to determine what constitutes a liberal education. The guardians and defenders of the established canon believe that it best serves their interests and consequently the interests of the society and nation-state. They also view it as consistent with their experience, perspectives, and visions of the future. (p. 2)

Regarding the latter, even more evidence exists that networking in employment practices tends largely to discriminate against minorities (Carmichael & Hamilton, 1967; Farley & Allen, 1987; Marable, 1983; Mullard, 1985). Of even greater concern is the tendency among members of the majority population to stymie the advancement of minorities in the work force. As Farley and Allen note:

History shows that when opportunities for [African-American] advancement become available, [African Americans] moved swiftly to take advantage, often at great personal risk and sacrifice. The historical record also reveals this society's discomfort with sustained [African American] progress, particularly when this progress results in any diminution in the economic status of Whites. (p. 419)

Race and the curriculum

The overarching criticism of multicultural education is that it fails to address the most formidable problem confronting the American educational system: racism. Helms (1990) contends that attempts to improve the racial climate in the United States have been characterized as "theoretical, sparse and superficial at best" (p. 205). Indeed, when the issue of race is broached in the curriculum, invariably it is treated only with reference to people of color. Of even more significance is the way in which the concepts "race" and "ethnicity" are used; the tendency exists to treat persons from the African diaspora as a homogeneous racial group and to treat persons of Caucasian descent as heterogeneous ethnic groups. The end result is that, in curricular and educational treatments of people of color, "one's ostensible 'Africanness' [accounts] for one's development regardless of ethnicity, [while] one rarely finds scholarly considerations of how the condition of being White influences Whites' development" (Helms, p. 4).

Although McCarthy maintains that each of the three approaches to multicultural education represents a "subtly different inflection on the question of what is to be done about racial inequality in schooling" (p. 55), he notes that they all seem to deflect attention away from confronting the issue of racism in American society. According to Yeakey (1988):

> Education marginality parallels the economic marginality of any racial and ethnic group in America. To understand the current educational and economic marginality of [African Americans] today, it is necessary to examine the historical conditions which gave rise to the present statues of millions of [African Americans] . . . The root exploitation of [African Americans] lies in a system of economic power and privilege in which ascriptive variables such as race (skin color), sex, age, and family background have a stratifying and mutually reinforcing effect. The lower school performance of [African Americans] is not the central problem, but an expression of a more fundamental one, namely racial barriers and the ideology that support and legitimize inequality. (p. 285)

A rich body of literature treats the issues surrounding race and the curriculum (Anyon, 1979; Apple & Weis, 1983; Bourdieu & Passeron, 1977; Carnoy, 1974; Giroux, 1981; JanMohamed, 1987; JanMohamed & Lloyd, 1987; Mullard, 1985; Ogbu, 1978; Wexler, 1982); and both neoliberals and neoconservatives have made contributions to the debate. The neoliberals contend that the body of literature is too critical of the role of the school and the nature of prejudice among teachers and administrators in the school. They have reacted somewhat sharply to the work of Dale (1982), Carnoy (1982, 1984), Carnoy and Levin (1985), Apple (1982, 1988), Popkewitz (1984, 1987), Sarup (1986), Wexler (1976), Carew (1984), and others. Like Banks (1981, 1987), they argue that revising the curriculum and obliterating teachers' prejudice will ensure minorities' success in schooling and the marketplace. They further contend that to some extent the state (in albeit a hegemonic role) has "bought into" the demands of minorities and neoliberals, and has made some concessions by providing an array of reforms aimed (in the minds of the "guardians and defenders of the canon") at ameliorating ethnic and racial disparities in the educational system. According to McCarthy (1990), such programs include:

(a) federal and state legislative and monetary incentives with respect to such programs as compensatory education (Head Start, Upward Bound), desegregation, and so on;
(b) community and school-based efforts to extend equality of opportunity to minorities by increasing minority representation on school faculty and in educational administration;
(c) curricular reform emphasizing multicultural and bilingual education and the wider inclusion of minority history, language and achievement in textbooks and other curricular materials. (p. 102)

While such initiatives may appear rather bold moves to eradicate prejudice and discrimination in the curriculum, they have led to the present bombardment of the state by the neoconservative upsurge. Consequently, in its role as mediator, the state is faced with the constant task of reinterpretation and redirection of its efforts.

Conclusion

The frustrations related to creating an educational environment that is supportive of the presence and contributions of ethnic and racial minorities are manifestations of the magnitude of the problems facing multiculturalists in education. Although it has not provided the proverbial "light at the end of the tunnel," the multicultural education movement has undoubtedly brought some gains and it may yet offer some hope. However, as the interminable debate continues to focus on the issue of race, multiculturalists must rethink their cause and revise their agenda and strategies. It may be that multicultural education must return to its original thrust of ensuring that "diverse groups experience educational equality" (Banks, 1986, p. 222). Those in the multicultural education movement may have to throw the weight of their support toward reinforcing the work of ethnic and gender studies programs in higher education. The task ahead would thus be to initiate and sustain scholarly efforts challenging present and historical notions of race and racism and expanding the parameters of discussion. Whatever the shift, the multicultural education movement can no longer postpone articulating a more functional mandate, and it can no longer attribute the disparate nature of its programs and practices as its "search of its *raison d'etre*" (Banks, 1986, p. 222), for the fears Gay articulated in 1983 may have come to pass:

Another potential threat to [multicultural] education comes from within. Although any educational idea must grow and change if it is to stand the test of time, such growth must remain within reasonable boundaries and retain a certain degree of continuity. If many dimensions are added to an idea too rapidly, the original idea may be distorted beyond recognition. This may be beginning to happen to [multicultural] education. (p.563)

Multicultural education must transcend the walls of education, if not to tear them down and become "linked to larger movements and political projects aimed at securing social change," as McCarthy (1990, p. 98) attests; then to engage in addressing the myopia, if not schizophrenia, of the Blooms, Hirsches, Steeles, Pattersons, and Lourys. Lastly, multiculturalists must reassess the cynicism of Parekh (1986), who writes:

> . . . the school can hope to undercut the intellectual and moral roots of racism and weaken it. It cannot, of course hope to eliminate it altogether, for education has its limits and the social and political roots of racism lie beyond the control of the school. However, it can make its distinctive contribution by tackling the intellectual and moral basis of racism that is amenable to an indeed falls within its purview. To ask it to do more is perhaps the surest way to ensure that it will not be able to do even this much. (p. 31)

References

American Association of Colleges for Teacher Education (AACTE) Commission on Multicultural Education. (1973). No one model American. *Journal of Teacher Education, 24*(4), 264–265.

Anyon, J. (1979). Ideology and the United States history textbooks. *Harvard Educational Review, 49*(3), 361–386.

Anyon, J. (1983). Workers, labor and economic history, and textbook content. In M. W. Apple & L. Weis (Eds.), *Ideology and practice in schooling* (pp. 37–60). Philadelphia: Temple University Press.

Apple, M. W. (1979). *Ideology and curriculum.* Boston: Routledge & Kegan Paul.

Apple, M. W. (1982). *Education and power.* Boston: Routledge & Kegan Paul.

Apple, M. W. (1983). Curricular form and the logic of technical control. In M. W. Apple & L. Weis (Eds.), *Ideology and practice in schooling* (pp. 143–165). Philadelphia: Temple University Press.

Apple, M. W. (1986). *Teachers and texts: A political economy of class and gender relations in education.* New York: Routledge & Kegan Paul.

Apple, M. W. (1988). Redefining inequality: Authoritarian populism and the conservative restoration. *Teachers College Record, 90*(2), 167–184.

Apple, M. W., & Weis, L. (Eds.). (1983). *Ideology and practice in schooling.* Philadelphia: Temple University Press.

Baker, G. (1973). Multicultural training for student teachers. *The Journal of Teacher Education, 24,* 306–307.

Baker, G. (1977). Development of the multicultural program: School of Education, University of Michigan. In F. H. Klassen & D. M. Gollnick (Eds.), *Pluralism and the American teacher: Issues and case studies* (pp. 163–169). Washington, DC: Ethnic Heritage Center for Teacher Education (AACTE).

Banks, J. A. (1978, March). Multiethnic education across cultures: United States, Mexico, Puerto Rico, France, and Great Britain. *Social Education, 42,* 177–185.

Banks, J. A. (1981). *Multiethnic education: Theory and practice.* Boston: Allyn & Bacon.

Banks, J. A. (1983). Multiethnic education at the crossroads. *Phi Delta Kappan, 64*(8), 559–569.

Banks, J. A. (1986). Multiethnic education and its critics: Britain and the United States. In S. Modgil, G. K. Verma, K. Mallick, & C. Modgil (Eds.), *Multicultural education: The interminable debate* (pp. 221–232). London: Falmer Press.

Banks, J. A. (1987). *Teaching strategies for ethnic studies.* Boston: Allyn & Bacon.

Banks, J. A. (1988). *A multicultural education: Theory and practice* (2nd ed.). Boston: Allyn & Bacon.

Banks, J. A. (1989). The battle over the canon: Cultural diversity and curriculum reform. *Allyn and Bacon Educators' Forum, 1,* 11–13.

Banks, J. A., & Banks, C. A. M. (1989). *Multicultural education: Issues and perspectives.* Boston: Allyn & Bacon.

Berlowitz, M. (1984). Multicultural education: Fallacies and alternative. In M. Berlowitz & R. Edari (Eds.), *Racism and the denial of human rights: Beyond ethnicity* (pp. 37–52). Minneapolis, MN: Marxism Educational Press.

Bloom, A. (1987). *The closing of the American mind.* New York: Simon & Schuster.

Bourdieu, P., & Passeron, J. (1977). *Reproduction in education, society and culture.* London: Sage.

Bowles, S., & Gintis, H. (1976). *Schooling in capitalist America.* New York: Basic Books.

Boyer, J. B. (1985). *Multicultural education: Product or process?* Kansas City, KS: Kansas Urban Education Center.

Broudy, H. S. (1975). Cultural pluralism: New wine in old bottles. *Educational Leadership, 33,* 173–175.

Buckingham, D. (1984). The Whites of their eyes: A case study in responses to educational television. In M. Straker-Welds (Ed.), *Education for a multicultural society* (pp. 137–143). London: Bell & Hyman.

Bullivant, B. (1981). *The pluralist dilemma in education.* Sydney, Australia: Allen & Unwin.

Carby, H. (1980, Spring). Multi-culture. *Screen Education,* p. 64.

Carby, H. (1982). Schooling in Babylon. In Centre for Contemporary Cultural Studies (Eds.), *The empire strikes back: Race and racism in the '70's* (pp. 183–211). London: Hutchinson.

Carew, J. (1984). Fulcrums of change. *Race and Class, 26,* 1–14.

Carmichael, S., & Hamilton, C. (1967). *Black power.* New York: Vintage.

Carnoy, M. (Ed.). (1972). *Schooling in corporate society.* New York: David McKay.

Carnoy, M. (1974). *Education and cultural imperialism.* New York: Longmans.

Carnoy, M. (1982). Education, economy, and the state. In M. W. Apple (Ed.), *Cultural and economic reproduction in education* (pp. 79–126). New York: Routledge & Kegan Paul.

Carnoy, M. (1984). *The state and political theory.* Princeton, NJ: Princeton University Press.

Carnoy, M., & Levin, H. (1985). *Schooling and work in the democratic state.* Stanford, CA: Stanford University Press.

Cortes, C. (1986). The education of language minority students: A contextual interaction model. In California State Department of Education, *Beyond language: Social and cultural factors in schooling language-minority students* (pp. 3–33). Los Angeles: Evaluation, Dissemination and Assessment Center, California State University.

Coser, L. A. (1977). *Masters of sociological thought: Ideas in historical and social context.* New York: Harcourt Brace Jovanovich.

Dale, R. (1982). Education and the capitalist state: Contributions and contradictions. In M. W. Apple (Ed.), *Cultural and economic reproduction in education* (pp. 127–161). Boston: Routledge & Kegan Paul.

Dhondy, F. (1978, May). The Black explosion in schools. *Race Today,* pp. 80–85.

Elkins, S. M. (1968). *Slavery: A problem in American institutional and intellectual life.* Chicago: University of Chicago Press.

Everhart, R. (1983). *Reading, writing and resistance.* London: Routledge & Kegan Paul.

Farley, R., & Allen, W. R. (1987). *The color line and the quality of life in America.* New York: Oxford University Press.

Focault, M. (1970). *The order of things: An archaeology of human sciences.* New York: Pantheon.

Focault, M. (1972). *The archaeology of knowledge.* New York: Harper Colophon.

Focault, M. (1977). *Discipline and punish.* London: Allen Lane.

Foerster, L. (1982). Moving from ethnic studies to multicultural education. *The Urban Review, 14,* 121–126.

Garcia, E. (1974). Chicano cultural diversity: Implications for competency-based teacher education. In W. Hunter (Ed.), *Multicultural education through competency-based teacher education.* Washington, DC: American Association of Colleges for Teacher Education.

Gibson, M. (1984). Approaches to multicultural education in the United States: Some concepts and assumptions. *Anthropology and Education Quarterly, 15,* 94–119.

Giroux, H. (1981). *Ideology, culture and the process of schooling.* New York: Falmer Press.

Glazer, N., & Moynihan, D. (1963). *Beyond the melting pot.* Cambridge, MA: Harvard University Press.

Gollnick, D. M. (1980). Multicultural education. *Viewpoints in Teaching and Learning, 56,* 1–17.

Gollnick, D. M., & Chin, P. C. (1990). *Multicultural education in a pluralistic society.* Columbus, OH: Merrill.

Grant, C. (1978). Education that is multicultural—Isn't that what we mean? *Journal of Teacher Education, 29,* 45–48.

Helms, J. (Ed.). (1990). *Black and White racial identity: Theory, research, and practice.* New York: Greenwood Press.

Hernandez, H. (1989). *Multicultural education: A teacher's guide to content and process.* Columbus, OH: Merrill.

Hirsch, E. D. (1987). *Cultural literacy: What every American needs to know.* Boston: Houghton Miflin.

JanMohamed, A. (1987). Introduction: Toward a theory of minority discourse. *Cultural Critique, 6,* 5–11.

JanMohamed, A. & Lloyd, D. (1987). Introduction: Minority discourse—What is to be done? *Cultural Critique, 7,* 5–17.

Loury, G. (1985). The moral quandary of the Black community. *In The Public Interests, 75,* 19.

Marable, M. (1983). *How capitalism underdeveloped Black America: Problems in race, political economy and society.* Boston: South End Press.

McCarthy, C. (1990). *Race and curriculum: Social inequality and the theories and politics of difference in contemporary research on schooling.* New York: Falmer Press.

Modgil, S., Verma, G. K., Mallick, K., & Modgil, C. (1986). *Multicultural education: The interminable debate.* London: Falmer Press.

Mullard, C. (1981). Black kids in White schools: Multiracial education in Britain. *Plural Societies, 12,* 1–12.

Mullard, C. (1982). Multicultural education in Britain: From assimilation to cultural pluralism. In J. Tierney (Ed.), *Race, migration and schooling* (pp. 15–27). London: Holt, Rinehart & Winston.

Mullard, C. (1983). The racial code: Its features, rules and change. In L. Barton & S. Walker (Eds.), *Race, class and education* (pp. 25–32). London: Croom Helm.

Mullard, C. (1985). Racism in society and school: History, policy, and practice. In F. Rizvi (Ed.), *Multiculturalism as educational policy* (pp. 64–81). Geelong, Victoria, Australia: Deakin University Press.

Ogbu, J. (1978). *Minority education and caste.* New York: Academic Press.

Omni, M., & Winant, H. (1986). *Racial formation in the United States.* New York: Routledge & Kegan Paul.

Parekh, B. (1986). The concept of multi-cultural education. In S. Modgil, G. K. Verma, K. Mallick, & C. Modgil (Eds.), *Multicultural education: The interminable debate.* London: Falmer Press.

Patterson, O. (1967). *The sociology of slavery.* London, Granada.

Patterson, O. (1977). *Ethnic chauvinism: The reactionary impulse.* New York: Stein & Day.

Pettigrew, L. W. (1974). Competency-based teacher education: Teacher training for multicultural education. In W. Hunger (Ed.), *Multicultural education through competency-based teacher education* (pp. 53–65). Washington, DC: American Association of Colleges for Teacher Education.

Popkewitz, T. (1984). *Paradigm and ideology in educational research.* Lewes: Falmer Press.

Popkewitz, T. (1987). *The formation of school subjects.* Lewes: Falmer Press.

Ramsey, P. G., Vold, E. B., & Williams, L. R. (1989). *Multicultural education; A source book.* New York: Garland.

Reisman, D., Glazer, N., & Denney, R. (1969). *The lonely crowd.* New Haven: Yale University Press.

Rex, J. (1983). *Race relations in sociological theory.* London: Routledge & Kegan Paul.

Rushton, J. (1981). Careers and the multicultural curriculum. In J. Lynch (Ed.), *Teaching in the multicultural school* (pp. 163–170). London: Ward Lock.

Sarup, M. (1986). *The politics of multiracial education.* London: Routledge & Kegan Paul.

Swartz, E. (1989). *Multicultural curriculum development.* Rochester, NY: Rochester City School District.

Sleeter, C. E., & Grant, C. (1987). An analysis of multicultural education in the United States. *Harvard Educational Review, 57,* 421–444.

Sleeter, C. E., & Grant, C. (1989). *Making choices for multicultural education: Five approaches to race, class, and gender.* Columbus, OH: Merrill.

Steele, S. (1989, February). The recoloring of campus life: Student racism, academic pluralism, and the end of a dream. *Harper's,* pp. 47–55.

Steele, S. (1990). *The content of our character.* New York: St. Martin's Press.

Stone, M. (1981). *The education of the Black child in Britain: The myth of multicultural education.* Glasgow, Scotland: Fontana.

Suzuki, B. H. (1984). Multicultural education: What's it all about? *Integrated Education, 97,* 43–50.

Swartz, E. (1989). *Multicultural curriculum development.* Rochester, NY: Rochester City School District.

Troyna, B., & Williams, J. (1986). *Racism, education, and the state.* London: Croom Helm.

Trueba, H. (1980–1981). On ethnographic studies and multicultural education. *Journal of the National Association of Bilingual Education, 5*(2), 29–56.

Trueba, H. T., & Barnett-Mizrahi, C. (Eds.). (1979). *Bilingual multicultural education and the professional.* Cambridge, MA: Newbury House Publishers.

Verma, G. K. (1984). Multiculturalism and education: Prelude to practice. In G. K. Verma & C. Bagley (Eds.), *Race relations and cultural differences.* London: Croom Helm.

Vold, E. B. (1979). Multicultural perspectives. In T. Hunt & T. Whitehurst (Eds.), *Society, culture and schools: The American approach* (pp. 11–17). Garrett Park, MD: Garrett Park Press.

Vold, E. B., Williams, L. R., & Ramsey, P. G. (1989). Future directions in multicultural education. In P. G. Ramsey, E. B. Vold, & L. R. Williams (Eds.), *Multicultural education: A source book.* New York: Garland.

Wexler, P. (1976). *The sociology of education: Beyond equality.* Indianapolis, IN: Bobbs–Merrill.

Wexler, P. (1982). Structure, text, and subject: A critical sociology of school knowledge. In M. W. Apple (Ed.), *Cultural and economic reproduction in education* (pp. 275–303). Boston: Routledge & Kegan Paul.

Yeakey, C. C. (1988). The public school monopoly: Confronting major national policy issues. In D. Slaughter and D. J. Johnson (Eds.), *Visible now: Blacks in private schools* (pp. 284–307). Westport, CT: Greenwood Press.

CHAPTER 25

CULTURAL LITERACY (1990)

E. D. Hirsch, Jr.

For the past twelve years I have been pursuing technical research in the teaching of reading and writing. I now wish to emerge from my closet to declare that technical research is not going to remedy the national decline in our literacy that is documented in the decline of verbal SAT scores. We already know enough about methodology to do a good job of teaching reading and writing. Of course we would profit from knowing still more about teaching methods, but better teaching techniques alone would produce only a marginal improvement in the literacy of our students. Raising their reading and writing levels will depend far less on our methods of instruction (there are many acceptable methods) than on the specific contents of our school curricula. Commonsensical as this proposition might seem to the man in the street, it is regarded as heresy by many (I hope by ever fewer) professional educators. The received and dominant view of educational specialists is that the specific materials of reading and writing instruction are interchangeable so long as they are "appropriate," and of "high quality."

But consider this historical fact. The national decline in our literacy has accompanied a decline in our use of common, nationwide materials in the subject most closely connected with literacy, "English." From the 1890s to 1900 we taught in English courses what amounted to a national core curriculum. As Arthur Applebee observes in his excellent book *Tradition and Reform in the Teaching of English*, the following texts were used in those days in more than 25 percent of our schools: *The Merchant of Venice, Julius Caesar*, "First Bunker Hill Oration," *The Sketch Book, Evangeline*, "The Vision of Sir Launfal," "Snow-Bound," *Macbeth*, "The Lady of the Lake," *Hamlet*, "The Deserted Village," Gray's "Elegy," "Thanatopsis," *As You Like It*. Other widely used works will strike a resonance in those who are over fifty: "The Courtship of Miles Standish," "Il Penseroso," *Paradise Lost*, "L'Allegro," "Lycidas," *Ivanhoe, David Copperfield, Silas Marner*, etc., etc. Then in 1901 the College Entrance Examination Board issued its first "uniform lists" of texts required to be known by students in applying to colleges. This core curriculum, though narrower, became even more widespread than the earlier canon. Lest anyone assume that I shall urge a return to those particular texts, let me at once deny it. By way of introducing my subject, I simply want to claim that the decline in our literacy and the decline in the commonly shared knowledge that we acquire in school are causally related facts. Why this should be so and what we might do about it are my twin subjects.

That a decline in our national level of literacy has occurred few will seriously doubt. The chief and decisive piece of evidence for it is the decline in verbal SAT scores among the white middle class. (This takes into account the still greater lowering of scores caused by an increased proportion of poor and minority students taking the tests.) Now scores on the verbal SAT show a high correlation with reading and writing skills that have been tested independently by other means. So, as a rough index to the literacy levels of our students, the verbal SAT is a reliable guide. That is unsurprising if we accept the point made by John Carroll and others that the verbal SAT is chiefly a vocabulary test, for no one is surprised by a correlation between a rich vocabulary and a high level of literacy. A rich vocabulary is not a purely technical or rote-learnable skill. Knowledge of words is an adjunct to knowledge of cultural realities signified by words, and to whole domains of experience to which words refer. Specific words go with specific knowledge. And when we begin to contemplate how to teach specific knowledge, we are led back inexorably to the contents of the school curriculum, whether or not those contents are linked, as they used to be, to specific texts.

From the start of our national life, the school curriculum has been an especially important formative element of our national culture. In the schools we not only tried to harmonize the various traditions of our parent cultures, we also wanted to strike out on our own within the dominant British heritage. Being rebellious children, we produced our own dictionary, and were destined, according to Melville, to produce our own Shakespeare. In this self-conscious job of culture making, the schools played a necessary role. That was especially true in the teaching of history and English, the two subjects central to culture making. In the nineteenth century we held national conferences on school curricula. We formed the College Board, which created the "uniform lists" already referred to. The dominant symbol for the role of the school was the symbol of the melting pot.

But from early times we have also resisted this narrow uniformity in our culture. The symbol of the melting pot was opposed by the symbol of the stew pot, where our national ingredients kept their individual characteristics and contributed to the flavor and vitality of the whole. That is the doctrine of pluralism. It has now become the dominant doctrine in our schools, especially in those subjects, English and history, that are closest to culture making. In math and science, by contrast, there is wide agreement about the contents of a common curriculum. But in English courses, diversity and pluralism now reign without challenge. I am persuaded that if we want to achieve a more literate culture than we now have, we shall need to restore the balance between these two equally American traditions of unity and diversity. We shall need to restore certain common contents to the humanistic side of the school curriculum. But before we can make much headway in that direction, we shall also need to modify the now-dominant educational principle that holds that any suitable materials of instruction can be used to teach the skills of reading and writing. I call this the doctrine of educational formalism.

The current curriculum guide to the study of English in the state of California is a remarkable document. In its several pages of advice to teachers I do not find the title of a single recommended work. Such "curricular guides" are produced on the theory that the actual contents of English courses are simply vehicles for inculcating formal skills, and that contents can be left to local choice. But wouldn't even a dyed-in-the-wool formalist concede that teachers might be saved time if some merely illustrative, non-compulsory titles were listed? Of course; but another doctrine, in alliance with formalism, conspires against even that concession to content—the doctrine of pluralism. An illustrative list put out by the state would imply official sanction of the cultural and ideological values expressed by the works on the list. The California Education Department is not in the business of imposing cultures and ideologies. Its business is to inculcate "skills" and "positive self-concepts," regardless of the students' cultural backgrounds. The contents of English should be left to local communities.

This is an attractive theory to educators in those places where spokesmen for minority cultures are especially vocal in their attack on the melting-pot idea. That concept, they say, is nothing but cultural imperialism (true), which submerges cultural identities (true) and gives minority children a sense of inferiority (often true). In recent years such attitudes have led to attacks on teaching school courses exclusively in standard English; in the bilingual movement (really a monolingual movement) it has led to attacks on an exclusive use of the English language for instruction. This kind of political pressure has encouraged a retreat to the extreme and untenable educational formalism reflected in the California curriculum guide.

What the current controversies have really demonstrated is a truth that is quite contrary to the spirit of neutrality implied by educational formalism. Literacy is not just a formal skill; it is also a political decision. The decision to *want* a literate society is a value-laden one that carries costs as well as advantages. English teachers by profession are committed to the ideology of literacy. They cannot successfully avoid the political implications of that ideology by hiding behind the skirts of methodology and research. Literacy implies specific contents as well as formal skills. Extreme formalism is misleading and evasive. But allow me to illustrate that point with some specific examples.

During most of the time that I was pursuing research in literacy I was, like others in the field, a confirmed formalist. In 1977 I came out with a book on the subject, *The Philosophy of Composition*, that was entirely formalistic in outlook. One of my arguments, for instance, was that the effectiveness of English prose as an instrument of communication gradually increased, after the invention of printing, through a trial-and-error process that slowly uncovered some of the psycho-linguistic principles of efficient communication in prose. I suggested that freshmen could learn in a semester what earlier writers had taken centuries to achieve, if they were directly taught those underlying psycholinguistic principles. (With respect to certain formal structures of clauses, this idea still seems valid.) I pre-dicted further that we could learn how to teach those formal principles still more effectively if we pursued appropriately controlled pedagogical research.

So intent was I upon this idea that I undertook some arduous research into one of the most important aspects of writing pedagogy—evaluation. After all, in order to decide upon the best methods of inculcating the skills of writing, it was essen-tial to evaluate the results of using the different teaching methods. For that we needed non-arbitrary, reliable techniques for evaluating student writing. In my book I had made some suggestions about how we might do this, and those ideas seemed cogent enough to a National Endowment for the Humanities panel to get me a grant to go forward with the research. For about two years I was deeply engaged in this work. It was this detailed engagement with the realities of reading and writing under controlled conditions that caused me finally to abandon my formalistic assumptions. (Later I discovered that experimentation on a much bigger scale had brought Richard C. Anderson, the premier scholar in reading research, to similar conclusions.)

The experiments that changed my mind were, briefly, these: To get a non-arbitrary evaluation of writing, we decided to base our evaluations on actual audience effects. We devised a way of comparing the effects of well-written and badly written versions of the same paper. Our method was to pair off two large groups of readers (about a hundred in each group), each of which, when given the *same* piece of writing, would read it collectively with the same speed and comprehension. In other words, we matched the reading skills of these two large groups. Then, when one group was given a good version and the other given a degraded version, we measured the overall effect of these stylistic differences on speed and accuracy of comprehension. To our delight, we discovered that good style did make an appreciable difference, and that the degree of difference was replicable and predictable. So far so good. But what became very disconcerting about these results was that they came out properly only when the subjects of the papers were highly familiar to our audiences. When, later in the experiments, we introduced unfamiliar materials, the results were not only messy, they were "counterintuitive," the term of art for results that go against one's expectations. (Real scientists generally like to get counterintuitive results, but we were not altogether disinterested onlookers and were dismayed.) For what we discovered was that good writing makes very little difference when the subject is unfamiliar. We English teachers tend to believe that a good style is all the more helpful when the content is difficult, but it turns out that we are wrong. The reasons for this unexpected result are complex, and I will not pause to discuss them at length, since the important issues lie elsewhere.

Briefly, good style contributes little to our reading of unfamiliar material because we must continually backtrack to test our different hypotheses about what is being meant or referred to. Thus, a reader of a text about Grant and Lee who is unsure just who Grant and Lee are would have to get clues from later parts of the text, and then go back to re-read earlier parts in the light of surer conjectures. This trial-and-error backtracking with unfamiliar material is so much more time-consuming than the delays caused by a bad style alone that style begins to lose its importance as a factor in reading unfamiliar material. The contribution of style in such cases can no longer be measured with statistical confidence.

The significance of this result is, first of all, that one cannot, even in principle, base writing evaluations on audience effects—the only non-arbitrary principle that makes any sense. The reading skill of an audience is not a constant against which prose can be reliably measured. Audience reading skills vary unpredictably with the subject matter of the text. Although we were trying to measure our prose samples with the yardstick of paired audiences, the contrary had, in effect, occurred; our carefully contrived prose samples were measuring the background knowledge of our audiences. For instance, if the subject of a text was "Friendship," all audiences pairs, everywhere we gave the trials, exhibited the same differentials. Also, for all audiences, if the subject was "Hegel's Metaphysics," the differential between good and bad writing tended to disappear. Also, so long as we used university audiences, a text on Grant and Lee gave the same sort of appropriate results as did a text on friendship. But for one community college audience (in, no less, Richmond, Virginia) "Grant and Lee" turned out to be as unfamiliar as "Hegel's Metaphysics"—a complacency-shattering result.

While the variability of reading skills within the same person was making itself disconcertingly known to me, I learned that similar variability was showing up in formal writing skills—and for the same reasons. Researchers at the City University of New York were finding that when a topic is unfamiliar, writing skill declines in all of its dimensions—including grammar and spelling—not to mention sentence structure, parallelism, unity, focus, and other skills taught in writing courses. One part of the explanation for such results is that we all have limited attention space, and cannot pay much heed to form when we are devoting a lot of our attention to unfamiliar content. But another part of the explanation is more interesting. Part of our skill in reading and in writing is skill not just with linguistic structures but with words. Words are not purely formal counters of language; they represent large underlying domains of content. Part of language skill is content skill. As Apeneck Sweeney profoundly observed: "I gotta use words when I talk to you."

When I therefore assert that reading and writing skills are content-bound, I mean also to make the corollary assertion that important aspects of reading and writing skills are *not* transferable. Of course some skills *are* carried over from task to task; we know that broad strategies of reading and writing can become second nature, and thereby facilitate literary skills at all levels. But the content-indifferent, how-to approach to literacy skills is enormously oversimplified. As my final example of this, I shall mention an ingenious experiment conducted by Richard C. Anderson and his colleagues at the University of Illinois. It, too, was an experiment with paired audiences and paired texts. The texts were two letters, each describing a wedding, each of similar length, word-familiarity, sentence complexity, and number of idea units. Each audience group was similarly paired according to age, educational level, marital status, sex, professional specialty, etc. Structurally speaking, the texts were similar and the audiences were similar. The crucial variables were these: one letter described a wedding in America, the other a wedding in India. One audience was American, the other Indian. Both audiences read both letters. The results were that the reading skills of the two groups—their speed and accuracy of comprehension—were very different in reading the two linguistically similar letters. The Americans read about an American wedding skillfully, accurately, and with good recall. They did poorly with the letter about the Indian wedding. The reverse was the case with the group of Indian readers. Anderson and his colleagues concluded that reading is not just a linguistic skill, but involves translinguistic knowledge beyond the abstract sense of words. They suggested that reading involves both "linguistic-schemata" (systems of expectation) and "content-schemata" as well. In short, the assumptions of educational formalism are incorrect.

Every writer is aware that the subtlety and complexity of what can be conveyed in writing depends on the amount of relevant tacit knowledge that can be assumed in readers. As psycholinguists have shown, the explicitly stated words on the page often represent the smaller part of the literary transaction. Some of this assumed knowledge involves such matters as generic conventions, that is, what to expect in a business letter, a technical report, a detective story, etc. An equally significant part of the assumed knowledge—often a more significant part—concerns tacit knowledge of the experiential realities embraced by the discourse. Not only have I gotta use words to talk to you, I gotta assume you know *something* about what I am saying. If I had to start from scratch, I couldn't start at all.

We adjust for this in the most casual talk. It has been shown that we always explain ourselves more fully to strangers than to intimates. But, when the strangers being addressed are some unknown collectivity to whom we are writing, how much shall we then need to explain? This was one of the most difficult authorial problems that arose with the advent of printing and mass literacy. Later on, in the eighteenth century, Dr. Johnson confidently assumed he could predict the knowledge possessed by a personage whom he called "the common reader." Some such construct is a necessary fiction for every writer in every literate culture and subculture. Even a writer for an astrophysics journal must assume a "common reader" for the subculture being addressed. A newspaper writer must also assume a "common reader" but for a much bigger part of the culture, perhaps for the literate culture as a whole. In our own culture, Jefferson wanted to create a highly informed "common reader," and he must have assumed the real existence of such a personage when he said he would prefer newspapers without government to government without newspapers. But, without appropriate, tacitly shared background knowledge, people cannot understand newspapers. A certain extent of shared, canonical knowledge is inherently necessary to a literate democracy.

For this canonical information I have proposed the term "cultural literacy." It is the translinguistic knowledge on which linguistic literacy depends. You cannot have the one without the other. Teachers of foreign languages are aware of this interdependency between linguistic proficiency and translinguistic, cultural knowledge. To get very far in reading or writing French, a student must come to know facets of French culture quite different from his own. By the same token, American children learning to read and write English get instruction in aspects of their own national culture that are as foreign to them as French. National culture always has this "foreignness" with respect to family culture alone. School materials contain unfamiliar materials that promote the "acculturation" that is a universal part of growing up in any tribe or nation. Acculturation into a national literate culture might be defined as learning what the "common reader" of a newspaper in a literate culture could be expected to know. That would include knowledge of certain values (whether or not one accepted them), and knowledge of such things as (for example) the First Amendment, Grant and Lee, and DNA. In our own culture, what should these contents be? Surely our answer to that should partly define our school curriculum. Acculturation into a literate culture (the minimal aim of schooling; we should aim still higher) could be defined as the gaining of cultural literacy.

Such canonical knowledge could not be fixed once and for all. "Grant and Lee" could not have been part of it in 1840, or "DNA" in 1940. The canon changeth. And in our media-paced era, it might change from month to month— faster at the edges, more slowly at the center, and some of its contents would be connected to events beyond our control. But much of it is within our control and is part of our traditional task of culture making. One reassuring feature of our responsibilities as makers of culture is the implicit and automatic character of most canonical cultural knowledge; we get it through the pores. Another reassuring aspect is its vagueness. How much do I *really* have to know about DNA in order to comprehend a newspaper text directed to the common reader? Not much. Such vagueness in our background knowledge is a feature of cultural literacy that Hilary Putnam has analyzed brilliantly as "the division of linguistic labor." An immensely literate person, Putnam claims that he does not know the difference between a beech tree and an elm. Still, when reading those words he gets along acceptably well because he knows that under the division of linguistic labor somebody in the culture could supply more precise knowledge if it should be needed. Putnam's observation suggests that the school curriculum can be vague enough to leave plenty of room for local choice regarding what things shall be studied in detail, and what things shall be touched on just far enough to get us by. This vagueness in cultural literacy permits a reasonable compromise between lockstep, Napoleonic prescription of texts on the one side, and extreme laissez-faire pluralism on the other. Between these two extremes we have a national responsibility to take stock of the contents of schooling.

Although I have argued that a literate society depends upon shared information, I have said little about what that information should be. That is chiefly a political question. Estimable cultures exist that are ignorant of Shakespeare and the First Amendment. Indeed, estimable cultures exist that are entirely ignorant of reading and writing. On the other hand, no culture exists that is ignorant of its own traditions. In a literate society, culture and cultural literacy are nearly synonymous terms. American culture, always large and heterogeneous, and increasingly lacking a common acculturative curriculum, is perhaps getting fragmented enough to lose its coherence as a culture. Television is perhaps our only national curriculum, despite the justified complaints against it as a partial cause of the literacy decline. My hunch is that this complaint is overstated. The decline in literacy skills, I have suggested, is mainly a result of cultural fragmentation. Within black culture, for instance, blacks are more literate than whites, a point that was demonstrated by Robert L. Williams, as I learned from a recent article on the SAT by Jay Amberg (THE AMERICAN SCHOLAR, Autumn 1982). The big political question that has to be decided first of all is whether we *want* a broadly literate culture that unites our cultural fragments enough to allow us to write to one another and read what our fellow citizens have written. Our traditional, Jeffersonian answer has been yes. But even if that political decision remains the dominant one, as I very much hope, we still face the much more difficult political decision of choosing the contents of cultural literacy.

The answer to this question is not going to be supplied by theoretical speculation and educational research. It will be worked out, if at all, by discussion, argument, and compromise. Professional educators have understandably avoided this political arena. Indeed, educators should *not* be left to decide so momentous an issue as the canonical contents of our culture. Within a democracy, educational technicians do not want and should not be awarded the function that Plato reserved for philosopher kings. But who is making such decisions at a national level? Nobody, I fear, because we are transfixed by the twin doctrines of pluralism and formalism.

Having made this technical point where I have some expertise, I must now leave any pretense of authority, except as a parent and citizen. The question of guidance for our national school curriculum is a political question on which I have only a citizen's opinion. For my own part, I wish we could have a National Board of Education on the pattern of the New York State Board of Regents—our most successful and admirable body for educational leadership. This imposing body of practical idealists is insulated by law from short-term demagogic pressures. It is a pluralistic group, too, with representation for minority as well as majority cultures. Its influence for good may be gauged by comparing the patterns of SAT scores in New York with those in California, two otherwise comparable states. To give just one example of the Regents' leadership in the field of writing, they have instituted a requirement that no New Yorker can receive a high school diploma before passing a statewide writing test that requires three types of prose composition.

Of course I am aware that the New York Regents have powers that no National Board in this country could possibly gain. But what a National Board could hope to achieve would be the respect of the country, a respect that could give it genuine influence over our schools. Such influence, based on leadership rather than compulsion, would be quite consistent with our federalist and pluralist principles. The Board, for instance, could present broad lists of suggested literary works for the different grades, lists broad enough to yield local freedom but also to yield a measure of commonality in our literary heritage. The teachers whom I know, while valuing their independence, are eager for intelligent guidance in such matters.

But I doubt that such a Curriculum Board would ever be established in this country. So strong is our suspicion of anything like a central "ministry of culture," that the Board is probably not a politically feasible idea. But perhaps a consortium of universities, or of national associations, or of foundations could make ongoing recommendations that arise from broadly based discussions of the national curriculum. In any case, we need leadership at the national level, and we need specific guidance.

It would be useful, for instance, to have guidance about the *words* that high school graduates ought to know—a lexicon of cultural literacy. I am thinking of a special sort of lexicon that would include not just ordinary dictionary words, but would also include proper names, important phrases, and conventions. Nobody likes word lists as objects of instruction; for one thing, they don't work. But I am not thinking of such a lexicon as an object of instruction. I am thinking of it rather as a guide to objects of instruction. Take the phrase "First Amendment," for instance. That is a lexical item that can hardly be used without bringing in a lot of associated information. Just what *are* the words and phrases that our school graduates should know? Right now, this seems to be decided by the makers of the SAT, which is, as I have mentioned, chiefly a vocabulary test. The educational technicians who choose the words that appear on the SAT are already the implicit makers of our national curriculum. Is then the Educational Testing Service our hidden National Board of Education? Does it sponsor our hidden national curriculum? If so, the ETS is rather to be praised than blamed. For if we wish to raise our national level of literacy, a hidden national curriculum is far better than no curriculum at all.

Where does this leave us? What issues are raised? If I am right in my interpretation of the evidence—and I have seen no alternative interpretation in the literature—then we can only raise our reading and writing skills significantly by consciously redefining and extending our cultural literacy. And yet our current national effort in the schools is largely run on the premise that the best way to proceed is through a culturally neutral, skills-approach to reading and writing. But if skill in writing and in reading comes about chiefly through what I have termed cultural literacy, then radical consequences follow. These consequences are not merely educational but social and political in their scope—and that scope is vast. I shall not attempt to set out these consequences here, but it will be obvious that acting upon them would involve our dismantling and casting aside the leading educational assumptions of the past half century.

APPENDIX 1: OTHER SUGGESTED READINGS

Anaya, R. A. (1984). The light green perspective: An essay concerning multi-cultural American literature. *MELUS, 2*(1), 27–32.

Bacchus, M. K. (1969). Education, social change, and cultural pluralism. *Sociology of Education, 42*(4), 368–385.

Banks, J. A. (1983). Multiethnic education and the quest for equality. *Phi Delta Kappan, 64*(8), 582–585.

Baptiste, H. P., & Baptiste, M. L. (1977). Multicultural education: Knowing me and you. *Educational Perspectives, 16*, 23–25.

Barnes, W. J. (1979). Developing a culturally pluralistic perspective: A community involvement task. *Journal of Negro Education, 48*(3), 419–430.

Bernstein, G. (1984). Ethnicity: The search for characteristics and contexts. *Theory into Practice, 23*, 98–103.

Bigelow, W. (1989). Discovering Columbus: Rereading the past. *Language Arts, 66*(6), 635–643.

Carter, D. A. (1983). Selecting resources for the multicultural classroom. *Momentum, 14*(1), 46–48.

Cervantes, R. A. (1984). Ethnocentric pedagogy and minority student growth: Implications for the common school. *Education and Urban Society, 16*(3), 274–293.

Christian, C. C. (1977). The role of language in multicultural education. *Educational Horizons, 55*(4), 184–188.

Cox, G. R., & Fundis, R. J. (1982). Multicultural education: Issues, a model and recommendations. *Action in Teacher Education, 4*(2), 33–39.

Deyoe, R. M. (1977). Theory as practice in multicultural education. *Educational Horizons, 55*(4), 181–183.

Dolce, C. J. (1973). Multicultural education: Some issues. *Journal of Teacher Education, 24*(4), 282–284.

Ellison, R. (1988). Who were the pilgrims? *New England Monthly,* 69–70, 119.

Gay, G. (1977). Changing conceptions of multicultural education. *Educational Perspectives, 16,* 4–9.

Hernandez, N. G. (1977). Another look at multicultural education. *Journal of Research and Development in Education, 11*(1), 4–9.

Hernandez-Chavez, E. (1977). Meaningful bilingual/bicultural education: A fairytale. *NABE Journal, 1*(3), 49–54.

Katz, J. H. (1980). Multicultural education: Games educators play. *Integrateducation, 18*(1–4), 101–104.

Levy, J. (1980). Multicultural education and intercultural education: A family affair. *Viewpoints in Teaching and Learning, 56*(1), 64–76.

McIntosh, P. (1989). White privilege: Unpacking the invisible knapsack. *Peace and Freedom, July/August,* 10–12.

McLaren, P. (1997). Decentering whiteness. *Multicultural Education, 4,* 4–9.

Payne, C. R. (1977). A rationale for including multicultural education and its implementation in the daily lesson plan. *Journal of Research and Development in Education, 11*(2), 31–45.

Stewart, W. J. (1978). Infusing multiculturalism into the curriculum through broad themes. *Education, 98*(3), 334–336.

Suzuki, B. H. (1984). Curriculum transformation for multicultural education. *Education and Urban Society, 16*(3), 294–322.

Thomas, L. (1989). Multiculturalism and school libraries. *International Federation of Library Associations, 15*(3), 203–209.

APPENDIX 2: JOURNAL PUBLISHERS AND CONTACT INFORMATION

Action in Teacher Education
Association of Teacher Educators
1900 Association Drive, Suite ATE
Reston, VA 20191–1502
(703)620–2110; (703)620–9530
http://www.ate1.org

American Association of Colleges for Teacher Education
1307 New York Avenue, NW Suite 300
Washington, DC 20005–4701
(202)293–2450; (202)457–8096 (Fax)
www.aacte.org

American Educational Research Association
1230—17th Street NW
Washington, DC 20036
(202)223–9485, × 100; (202)775–1824
http://aera.net

American Journal of Education
University of Chicago Press
Permissions Department
1427 East 60th Street
Chicago, IL
(773)702–6096; (773)702–9756

American Sociological Association
1307 New York Avenue, NW Suite 700
Washington, DC 20005–4701
Jill Campbell
Publications Manager
(202)383–9005, × 303; (202)638–0882
www.asanet.org

Anthropology and Education
Anthropology and Education Quarterly
University of California Press
Journals and Digital Publishing Division
2000 Center Street, Suite 303
Berkeley, CA 94704

Association for Supervision and Curriculum Development
1703 N. Beauregard Street
Alexandria, VA 22311–1714
(703)578–9600; (703)575–5400 (Fax)
www.ascd.org

Banks, Cherry A. McGee
Professor, Education
University of Washington, Bothell
18115 Campus Way NE Room UW1 244
Bothell, WA 98011–8246

Banks, James A.
University of Washington
Box 353600, 110 Miller Hall
Seattle, WA 98195–3600
(206)543–3386; (206)542–4218 Fax
http://faculty.washington.edu/jbanks

Comparitive Education Review
University of Chicago Press
Permissions Department
1427 East 60th Street
Chicago, IL
(773)702–6096; (773)702–9756

Curriculum and Teaching
James Nicholas Publishers
PO Box 244
Albert Park, Australia, 3206

Education
Dr. George E. Uhlig
PO Box 8826
Spring Hill Station
Mobile, AL 36689

Education and Urban Society
Corwin Press, Inc.
2455 Teller Road
Thousand Oaks, CA 91320–2218
(805)499–9734; (805)499–0871 (Fax)
http://www.sagepub.com

Educational Horizons
National Association for Ethnic Studies, Inc. &
American Cultural Studies Department
Western Washington University
516 High Street—MS 9113
Bellingham, WA 98225–9113
(360)650–2349; (360)650–2690 (Fax)

Educational Leadership
Association for Supervision and Curriculum Development
PO Box 79760
Baltimore, MD 21279–0760
(703)578–9600; 1–800–933–2723; (703)575–5400 Fax
www.ascd.org

Educational Research Quarterly
113 Greenbriar Drive
West Monroe, LA 71291
(318)274–2355
hashway@alphagram.edu

Educators for Urban Minorities
Long Island University Press (No longer in operation)
Eugene E. Garcia, Ph.D.
Vice President Education Partnerships
Professor of Education
Arizona State University
Eugene.Garcia@asum.edu

English Journal
1111 W. Kenyon Road
Urbana, IL 61801–1096
(217)328–3870; (217)328–9645 (Fax)
http://www.ncte.org

Exceptional Children
Council for Exceptional Children
Permissions Department
1110 North Glebe Road Suite 300
Arlington, VA 22201–5704
(703)264–1637

FOCUS
Joint Center for Political Studies
1301 Pennsylvania Avenue, NW
Washington, DC 20004
(202)626–3500

Ford Foundation
320 East 43rd Street
New York, NY 10017

Gibson, Margaret A.
Professor of Education and Anthropology
Department of Education
University of California, Santa Cruz
1156 High Street
Santa Cruz, CA 95064
(831)459–4740; (831)459–4618 (Fax)

Harvard Educational Review
Harvard Graduate School of Education
8 Story Street, 1st Floor
Cambridge, MA 02138
(617)495–3432; (617)496–3584 (fax)
www.hepg.org
+
HarperCollins Publishers
10 East 53rd Street
New York, NY 10022
(212)207–7000

Interchange
Nel van der Werf
Assistant Rights and Permissions/Springer
Van Godewijckstraat 30
PO Box 17
3300 AA Dordrecht
The Netherlands
31 (0) 78 6576 298; 31 (0) 78 6576 323 (Fax)
Nel.vanderwerf@springer.com
www.springeronline.com

Journal of Curriculum Studies
Routledge (Taylor & Francis, Inc.)
4 Park Square, Milton Park
Abingdon, Oxon OX14 4RN United Kingdom
44–1235–828600; 44–1235–829000 (Fax)
http://www.routledge.co.uk

Journal of Curriculum and Supervision
Association for Supervision and Curriculum Development
1703 North Beauregard Street
Alexandria, VA 22311–1714
(703)578–9600/(800)933–2723; (703)575–3926 (Fax)
http://www.ascd.org

Journal of Teacher Education
American Association of Colleges for Teacher Education
1307 New York Avenue NW Suite 300
Washington, DC 20017–4701
(202)293–2450; (202)457–8095 (Fax)
www.aacte.org

Journal of Research and Development in Education
Julie P. Sartor, Editor
Office of the Associate Dean for Research,
Technology, & External Affairs
UGA College of Education
(706)542–4693; (706)542–8125 (Fax)
jsartor@uga.edu

Journal of Negro Education
Howard University Press
Marketing Department
2600 Sixth Street, NW
Washington, DC 20059
(202)806–8120; (202)806–8434 (Fax)

Journal of Literacy Research (formerly *Journal of Reading Behavior*)
Lawrence Erlbaum Associates, Inc.
10 Industrial Avenue
Mahwah, NJ 07430–2262
(201)258–2200; (201)236–0072 (Fax)

Journal of Educational Thought
University of Calgary
Faculty of Education – Publications Office
2500 University Drive N.W.
Education Tower, Room 1310
Calgary, Alberta, Canada T2N 1N4
(403)220–7499/5629; (403)284–4162 (Fax)
www.ucalgary.ca

Journal of Teacher Education
American Association of Colleges for Teacher Education
1307 New York Avenue NW 300
Washington, DC 20005–4701
(202)293–2450; (202)457–8095 (Fax)
www.aacte.org

Language Arts
The National Council of Teachers of English
1111 W. Kenyon Road
Urbana, IL 61801–1096
(217)278–3621
permissions@ncte.org

Momentum
National Catholic Educational Association
1077—30 Street, NW Suite 100
Washington, DC 2007
(202)337–6232; (202)333–6706 (Fax)
nceaadmin@ncea.org

Multicultural Education
Gaddo Gap Press
3145 Geary Boulevard PMB 275
San Francisco, CA 94118
(414)666–3012; (414)666–3552
http://www.caddogap.com

National Catholic Educational Association
1077—30 Street, NW Suite 100
Washington, DC 20007
(202)337–6232; (202)333–6706 (Fax)
nceaadmin@ncea.org

National Council for the Social Studies
8555 Sixteenth Street, Suite 500
Center for Multicultural Education
Silver Spring, MD 20910
(301)588–1800 × 122;
(301)588–2049 Fax

National Educational Service
1252 Loesch Road
PO Box 8 Department V2
Bloomington, IN 47402

Negro Educational Review
NER Editorial Offices
School of Education
1601 East Market Street
Greensboro, NC 27411
Alice M. Scales (scales@pitt.edu)
Shirley A. Biggs (biggs@pitt.edu)

Peabody Journal of Education
Lawrence Erlbaum Associates
10 Industrial Avenue
Mahwah, NJ 07430–2262

Phi Delta Kappan
Phi Delta Kappa International
408 N. Union Street
PO Box 789
(812)339–1156; 800–766–1156; (812)339–0018 fax

Race, Class, and Gender
Southern University at New Orleans (No Response)
Carl contact Jean Belkhir (jbelkhir@uno.edu)

Radical Teacher
Center for Critical Education
PO Box 382616
Cambridge, MA 02238
Saul Slapikoff, Permissions Editor
slap2@comcast.net

Researching Today's Youth: The Community Circle of Caring Journal
Dr. Carlos E. Cortes
Professor Emeritus
Department of History
University of California,
Riverside, CA 92521–0204
(951)827–1487
(951)827–5299 fax
carlos.cortes@ucr.edu

Review of Educational Research
American Educational Research Association
1230—17th Street NW
Washington, DC 20036–3078

Sage Publications, Inc.
Corwin Press, Inc
2455 Teller Road
Thousand Oaks, CA 91320
(805)410–7713; (805)376–9562 (Fax)
permissions@sagepub.com

Southeastern Association of Educational Opportunity Program Personnel (SAEOPP)
75 Piedmont Avenue NE
Suite 408
Atlanta, GA 30303–2518
(404)522–4642

Teachers College Record
Blackwell Publishing
PO Box 805
9600 Garsington Road
Oxford OX4 2ZG United Kingdom
44 (0) 1865 776868; 44 (0) 1865 714591 Fax
www.blackwellpublishing.com

Teacher Education and Special Education
Dr. Fred Spooner, Editor
Teacher Education and Special Education
SPCD/College of Education
University of North Carolina at Charlotte
Charlotte, NC 28223

(704)687–8851; (704)687–2916 Fax
fhspoone@email.uncc.edu

The American Scholar
1606 New Hampshire Avenue NW
Washington, DC 20009
(202)265–3808; (202)265–0083

The Educational Forum
Kappa Delta Pi
3707 Woodview Trace
Indianapolis, IN 46268–1158

The High School Journal
The University of North Carolina Press
PO Box 2288
Chapel Hill, NC 27515–2288
(919)966–3561; (919)966–3829
www.uncpress.unc.edu

The Journal of Educational Research
Heldref Publications
1319 Eighteenth Street, NW
Washington, DC 20036–1802
(202)296–6267; (202)296–5146 (Fax)
www.heldref.org

The New Advocate
Christopher-Gordon Publishers, Inc.
1502 Providence Hwy, Suite 12
Norwood, MA 02062–4643
(781)762–5577; (781)762–7261
http://www.christopher-gordon.com

The Social Studies
Heldref Publications
1319 Eighteenth Street, NW
Washington, DC 20038–1802
(202)296–6267; (202)296–5149 (Fax)
permissions@heldref.org

The Teacher Educator
Ball State University
Teachers College
TC 1008
Muncie, IN 47306
(765)285–5453; (765)285–5455

The Urban Review
Nel van der Werf
Assistant Rights and Permissions/Springer
Van Godewijckstraat 30
PO Box 17
3300 AA Dordrecht
The Netherlands
31 (0) 78 6576 298; 31 (0) 78 6576 323 (Fax)
Nel.vanderwerf@springer.com
www.springeronline.com

Theory into Practice
Lawrence Erlbaum Associates, Inc.
10 Industrial Avenue
Mahwah, NJ 07430–2262

Viewpoints in Teaching and Learning
Indiana University
School of Education
Education Building 109
Bloomington, IN 47405

Young Children
National Association for the Education of Young Children
1313 L Street, NW, Suite 500
Washington, DC 20036–1426
(202)232–8777; (202)328–1846 (Fax)
http://www.naeyc.org

PERMISSION CREDITS

Part 1: Conceptual Frameworks

Margaret A. Gibson, "Approaches to Multi-Cultural Education in the United States: Some Concepts and Assumptions." *Anthropology and Education Quarterly*, 7:4 (1976), 7–18. Copyright © 1976 by the University of California Press. Reprinted by permission of Margaret Gibson and University of California Press.

Donna M. Gollnick, "Multicultural Education." *Viewpoints in Teaching and Learning*, 56:1 (1980), 1–17. Copyright © 1980 by Indiana University. Reprinted with permission.

Cameron McCarthy, "Multicultural Approaches to Racial Inequality in the United States." *Curriculum and Teaching*, 5:1/2 (1990), 25–34. Copyright © 1990 by James Nicholas Publishers. Reprinted with permission.

Etta Ruth Hollins, "Beyond Multicultural Education." *Negro Educational Review*, 33:3–4 (July–October 1982), 140–145. Copyright © 1982 by the *Negro Educational Review*. Reprinted with permission.

Violet J. Harris, "Continuing Dilemmas, Debates, and Delights in Multicultural Literature." *The New Advocate*, 9:2 (1996), 7–122. Copyright © 1996 by Christopher-Gordon Publishers. Reprinted with permission.

Leona Foerster, "Moving from Ethnic Studies to Multicultural Education." *The Urban Review*, 14:2 (1982), 121–126. Copyright © 1982 by Springer. Reprinted with permission.

Christine Bennett, "Genres of Research in Multicultural Education." *Review of Educational Research*, 71:2 (2001), 171–217. Copyright © 2001 by the American Educational Research Association. Reprinted with permission.

Christine Sleeter, "Creating an Empowering Multicultural Curriculum." *Race, Class, and Gender*, 7:3 (2000), 178–196. Copyright © 2000 by Southern University at New Orleans. Reprinted with permission.

Carl Grant, "Education That Is Multicultural—Isn't That What We Mean?" *Journal of Teacher Education*, 29:5 (September–October 1978), 45–48. Copyright © 1978 by Caddo Gap Press. Reprinted with permission.

Geneva Gay, "The Relationship Between Multicultural and Democratic Education." *The Social Studies* (1997), 5–11. Copyright © 1997 by Heldref

Part 2: Curriculum Content

G. Baker, "Multicultural Imperatives for Curriculum Development in Teacher Education." *Journal of Research and Development in Education,* 11:1 (1977). Copyright © 1977 by the University of Georgia. Reprinted with permission.

James A. Banks, "A Content Analysis of the Black American in Textbooks." *Social Education,* 33:8 (1969), 954–958. Copyright © 1969 by the National Council for the Social Studies. Reprinted by permission of J. A. Banks and National Council for the Social Studies.

Terry N. Saario, Carol Nagy Jacklin, and Carol Kehr Tittle, "Sex Role Stereotyping in the Public Schools." *Harvard Educational Review,* 43:3 (1973), 386–416. Copyright © 1973 by the President and Fellows of Harvard College. All rights reserved. Reprinted with permission.

Myra Pollack Sadker and David Miller Sadker, "Sexism in Teacher Education Texts." *Harvard Educational Review,* 50:1 (1980), 36–46. Copyright © 1980 by the President and Fellows of Harvard College. Reprinted with permission.

Joel Taxel, "Justice and Cultural Conflict: Racism, Sexism, and Instructional Materials." *Interchange,* 9:1 (1978), 56–83. Copyright © 1978 by Springer. Reprinted with permission.

Carl A. Grant and Gloria W. Grant, "The Multicultural Evaluation of Some Second and Third Grade Textbook Readers: A Survey Analysis." *Journal of Negro Education,* 50:1 (Winter 1981), 63–74. Copyright © 1981 by the President and Fellows of Harvard College. Reprinted with permission.

Gwyneth Britton, Margaret Lumpkin, and Esther Britton, "The Battle to Imprint Citizens for the 21st Century," *The Reading Teacher,* 37:8 (1984), 724–732. Copyright © 1984 by International Reading Association. Reprinted by permission of Gwyneth Britton and International Reading Association.

Part 3: Re-envisioning the Curriculum

Gloria Ladson-Billings and William F. Tate, "Toward a Critical Race Theory of Education," *Teachers College Record,* 97:1 (Fall 1995), 47–68. Copyright © 1995 by Blackwell Publishing. Reprinted with permission.

James T. Sears, "Helping Students Understand and Accept Sexual Diversity." *Educational Leadership,* 49:1 (September 1991), 54–56. Copyright © 1991 by the Association for Supervision & Curriculum Development. Reprinted with permission.

Asa G. Hilliard III, "Why we must pluralize the curriculum," *Educational Leadership,* 49:4 (December 1991), 12–14. Copyright © 1991 by the Association for Supervision & Curriculum Development. Reprinted with permission.

Part 4: Critique

AUTHOR INDEX

SUBJECT INDEX